D0617095

ROBERT BOSCH

ROBERT BOSCH

HIS LIFE AND ACHIEVEMENTS

———

THEODOR HEUSS

*Translated by Susan Gillespie
and Jennifer Kapczynski*

HENRY HOLT AND COMPANY

NEW YORK

HD
9710.3
.G42
B67415
1994

Henry Holt and Company, Inc.
Publishers since 1866
115 West 18th Street
New York, New York 10011

Henry Holt® is a registered
trademark of Henry Holt and Company, Inc.

Copyright © 1994 by Susan Gillespie
All rights reserved.
Published in Canada by Fitzhenry & Whiteside Ltd.,
195 Allstate Parkway, Markham, Ontario L3R 4T8.

Originally published in 1946 by
Rainer Wunderlich Verlag Hermann Leins
(Tübingen, Germany) under the title
Robert Bosch: Leben und Leistung.

Library of Congress Cataloging-in-Publication Data
Heuss, Theodor, 1884–1963.
[Robert Bosch, Leben und Leistung. English]
Robert Bosch, his life and achievements/Theodor Heuss;
translated by Susan Gillespie and Jennifer Kapczynski.—1st ed.
p.   cm.
Translation of Robert Bosch, Leben und Leistung.
Includes index.
1. Bosch, Robert, 1861–1942. 2. Industrialists—Germany—
Biography. 3. Robert Bosch GmbH—History. I. Title.
HD9710.3.G42B67415   1994
338.7'629254'092—dc20
[B]   93-39242
                                                      CIP

ISBN 0-8050-3067-0

Henry Holt books are available for special promotions and
premiums. For details contact: Director, Special Markets.

First Edition—1994

Designed by Paula R. Szafranski

Printed in the United States of America
All first editions are printed on acid-free paper. ∞

1   3   5   7   9   10   8   6   4   2

Fairleigh Dickinson
University Library

Teaneck, New Jersey

CONTENTS

This new edition appears for the first time under the imprint of the Deutsche Verlags-Anstalt (DVA), a publisher whose majority ownership Robert Bosch had assumed in the early 1920s in order to ward off influences from north Germany. Theodor Heuss describes this on page 439. In 1936, when Robert Bosch was forced to divest himself of the publishing house, he owned 54.6 percent of the stock. The shares of DVA, which had been transformed from a joint-stock company to a limited liability company in 1941, were not returned to the Bosch family until 1950, and then only after lengthy legal proceedings. Thirty years later, the issue of the publishing house was resolved by creating a foundation; since then the Frankfurter Allgemeine Zeitung G.m.b.H., the majority of whose shares are owned by a charitable foundation, and the DVA-Foundation, which was created with the help of Robert Bosch G.m.b.H., are co-owners.

The idea of the foundation fell on particularly fertile ground in Swabia. Today, approximately 90 percent of the capital of Robert Bosch G.m.b.H. is held by a charitable foundation, the Robert Bosch Foundation G.m.b.H. The main focus of its responsibilities is the Robert Bosch Hospital in Stuttgart, for which a new facility was built in 1973. Along with the hospital, the foundation has always supported projects in the areas of natural science and the humanities, art and culture, education, and understanding among the world's peoples—true to the will of Robert Bosch, whose spirit was acknowledged by his heirs in the early 1960s when they transferred the greatest part of the firm's capital to the foundation.

In the hundredth year after the founding of the firm (and forty years after the first edition of this biography, which was published by Rainer Wunderlich Verlag Herman Leins, Tübingen), the Bosch group of companies had more than 145,000 employees in Germany and abroad. After 1948, the company lived for four years under the threat of antitrust action, which could only be prevented by the renunciation of several investment opportunities and the willingness of the firm to give up all its patents and technical manuals. In the meantime, the gross international sales of the Bosch Group rose to more than 21 billion German marks in 1985.

Theodor Heuss's faith in the lasting value of intellectual and moral achievements, his trust in the "indestructible substance" of the Swabian population have been validated. Many things in his description of the life and achievements of Robert Bosch could be described differently today based on documents that were not available to Heuss in the midst of the war; some things that do appear were not confirmed by later developments. Thus, to name but one example, the raising of cattle on the Boschhof has been discontinued; large areas of cultivated land were planted with trees. Nevertheless, we are offering the biography in the original text out of respect for Theodor Heuss. It is a complete work composed in a single draft.

Hans L. Merkle
Stuttgart, August 1986

Translators' Note

Few liberties have been taken in rendering Theodor Heuss's *Robert Bosch: His Life and Achievements* in English. Heuss's German prose can be daunting; in general, the translators have chosen to err on the side of simplicity, while striving to achieve factual accuracy and preserve the full range of semantic possibilities of the German original.

From time to time, to bring the book closer to English-language readers, we have added a few explanatory words identifying individuals or events that may not be common knowledge. More could have been done to place the book in its historical and political context; we have refrained from doing so. A few prefatory remarks may, however, help readers to negotiate the distance in time and space that separates them from Theodor Heuss's 1945 narrative.

Above all, it is important to note the author's own role in German history. As the first president of the Bundestag after the Hitler era, and as one of the leading figures in formulating the Basic Law of the Federal Republic, Theodor Heuss is a figure of considerable renown. Before World War II, Heuss was a supporter of Friedrich Naumann, the Protestant theologian and politician. He served as director of the Alliance of

German Craftsmen. In 1930, he was elected to parliament, where he represented the German Democratic Party until Hitler's seizure of power in 1933. After the war, Heuss was one of the founders of the Free Democratic Party, and he taught modern history at the Technical University in Stuttgart before being elected president.

Because of this record, Heuss has considerable credibility as a writer on the Third Reich. The case for this credibility must be made in light of certain substantive limitations of the present biography of Robert Bosch. Written during World War II under circumstances of dictatorship, it lacks, for example, a clear description of Robert Bosch's views on Hitler's race laws or their effects on the Bosch firm or on Germany and its people. There are also a number of telling details that, had they been more fully explicated, would have shed important light on Bosch's political alliances. As an example, Bosch's employment of Karl Goerdeler assumes heightened significance in light of the leading role Goerdeler would later play in organizing the group that attempted to assassinate Hitler on July 20, 1945—an act for which Goerdeler was executed.

In his introduction, Heuss himself notes the difficulties that lie in wait for nontechnical writers when it comes to science and engineering. The translators would like to thank Max Lands and Margret Nordquist of the Robert Bosch Corporation in Chicago for their assistance with technical terms pertaining to electrical engineering and the development of the German automobile industry. Professor Burt Brody helped us to avoid a number of scientific errors; Professor David Kettler kindly advised on historical questions.

Any remaining infelicities or errors are the responsibility of the translators alone.

Susan Gillespie and Jennifer Kapczynski
January 1994

Letter from Margarete Bosch
to Theodor Heuss

About two years before he died, my father said to me, "The things that have been written about me until now make me think that some day I should arrange for someone to write my biography who comes from a background that enables him to understand me as I really am. I would not be pleased if one day a celebratory biography of me were to be published."

Since my father did not live to see the completion of his biography, I am privileged to say to you today, as his eldest daughter, that you have fulfilled his hope completely. You have grasped Robert Bosch in his innate being with fine and loving psychological sensitivity, and you have drawn him in a living way. You have described him as he really was. Along with his great goodness and desire to help, you have also shown his abrupt and harsh sides. You have made clear—and this is what mattered to my father—that his character traits are rooted in the peasant milieu from which he came. You have painted his portrait with great love, but you have avoided doing what he wanted to avoid; you have not idealized it. For this truthfulness I thank you, as his daughter, most warmly.

Stuttgart, April 4, 1947

PREFACE

On March 4, 1942, Robert Bosch wrote to me asking if I could get used to the idea, at some point, of writing a description of his life; if so, it would probably be necessary for me to go to Stuttgart to have a conversation with him and get a preliminary idea of the type and extent of the written materials that were available. I responded that although the idea held great appeal for me, its realization would depend upon what I found when I reviewed the documents that were available or would still need to be gathered. In a few weeks, it would probably be possible for me to make the visit he had suggested. A few lines dated March 9 confirmed the receipt of my response and interpreted it, in principle, in the affirmative. This letter had scarcely reached my hands when a messenger arrived bearing the news of Robert Bosch's death.

The close proximity of these two dates gave the letter and its suggestion the character of a last wish or testamentary obligation. Over the next few days, part of which I spent in Stuttgart attending the funeral, my conversations with members of Bosch's family and his closest colleagues revealed that the question of his biography had arisen repeatedly during the last weeks of his life. It is true, as the following portrayal will show, that he had a certain hesitancy about becoming the object of too much public attention. But the many written assessments, both accurate and inaccurate, that had appeared six months earlier on the occasion of his eightieth birthday had shown him pointedly enough that his persona had long since crossed over into the public domain and was already taking on somewhat legendary traits. Since it was now clear to him that his name and work were going to outlast his earthly existence, he had to have some interest in seeing that the elements of his nature and the motives of his actions were recorded and interpreted for posterity.

A word about my personal relationship with Robert Bosch seems in order. When I returned home to Württemberg in 1912 for six years, for professional reasons, the first contact with the Bosch circle was not long in coming and soon developed into a friendship.

I probably met Robert Bosch for the first time in 1917 or 1918; then, during the 1920s, I met with him often in Berlin, mainly at the home of Ernst Jäckh, a publisher and a promoter of the German crafts movement. Later, during my frequent stays in Stuttgart, I visited him on a fairly regular basis. I could sense a friendly concern for me and my work and felt that he approached me, despite my youth, with a generous human trust. He did not always agree with everything I did, said, or wrote, and if he didn't fire off a critical letter, he would store the matter away in his memory, for discussion at the next opportunity. That was always an intellectual pleasure.

It would have been natural to give the suggestion of writing the biography to a technical writer. This possibility was weighed and considered. As chance and various requests would have it, I had published several works in recent years whose subjects were somewhat removed from my real field of historical and political expertise. These included a slim volume on the historical and intellectual significance of chemist Justus Liebig, and a comprehensive biography of the zoologist Anton Dohrn of Naples. To my delight, these two works earned Bosch's particular approbation. Friends reported to him that the scientists were quite pleased by the fact that it was not a scholarly colleague of Dohrn's who had undertaken to describe his scientific and organizational work, but someone who came to it without preconceptions, indeed in a state of sheer ignorance, and thus was not susceptible to the temptation or the danger of falling into a discussion of scientific-historical details.

Bosch knew that specialized questions of technology were foreign to me. But what I myself could not help viewing as a serious disability, after I had examined the wide-ranging materials, was in his eyes perhaps not exactly an advantage, but an insignificant disadvantage if the portrayal was to emphasize the other aspects of his life's work.

For Bosch, as conversations with his closest colleagues revealed, had in mind a biography in which the industrial factory and the history of the firm would recede into the background. Whether such an attempt was feasible or objectively justified was something I could no longer toss back and forth in discussions with him. For myself, I found it quite clear, after I had begun to grapple with the material, that a description of his life without continuous reference to the history of the firm would be quite incomplete, and would be omitting very essential things about him as well. He may have been motivated by his sense that the full development and expansion of the firm, especially in the previous decade and a half, had been accomplished, above all, by his colleagues. But their quality and behavior were inconceivable without Bosch's prior achievement. At the same time, this achievement, as no one appreciated more warmly than Bosch himself, also reflected the participation of several individuals who would have to be described, along with him, as part of a broad historical portrayal.

The technical specialists will probably look in vain in this book for a number of answers and revealing, detailed descriptions. They will have to be satisfied with the commemorative publication *Fifty Years of Bosch 1886–1936*—as imposing as it is detailed—in which the process of achieving technical perfection of the various products, over the course of years and in response to changing needs, is described. A number of monographs written by employees of the firm about the electrical equipment of motor vehicles have also appeared. Naturally, I have benefited from this literature, but I have quite consciously made only sparing use of it, for this is an area in which I feel unsure of myself, as the reader would very soon have noticed. From time to time, when the issues themselves were unclear to me, I could have drawn directly on the writings of the technicians, but the result would have been to introduce an alien tone. So I have contented myself, for the most part, with pointing out the technical task and the basis for its solution. This is justified because this is, after all, not the life history of an inventor, a machine builder or scientific researcher who added new knowledge to our understanding of processes (how often Bosch said and wrote that he had never "invented" anything!). His extraordinary significance for the history of technology does not lie in any specific technical or scientific achievements that bear his personal mark, as was the case, for example, with Werner von Siemens, the German founder of electrotechnology and of the firm that bears his name. Therefore, technology in the narrower sense did not have to be accorded such a central place as some might have hoped or others feared.

In a file from the office of Bosch's private secretary, I found an exchange of letters from the fall of 1924. A few years earlier, the Württemberg genealogist Dr. Georg Thierer had published a large-scale genealogical study of the Bosch clan, with its divisions into many family lines throughout the Swabian highlands. He had been assisted by the writer C. A. Schnerring, who had worked on the Albeck Boschs. In a letter to Robert Bosch, Schnerring regretted the fact that Thierer had not drawn on his manuscript for the publication. He himself was planning to write a novel in which the Albeck Boschs would assume their rightful place, and he asked Robert Bosch not to object. In his answer of November 10, 1924, Bosch remarked that he did not have the right to hinder Schnerring in any way. But he was apprehensive, given the manner in which it had been announced, that the work might give the impression that it was being written at his request. Avoiding this was of serious concern to him. "As far as I myself am concerned," he wrote, "what I would most like would be if nothing at all were to be written about me during my lifetime; in any case it should not be done in a laudatory fashion. The description that the deceased Herr Thierer was planning to give of me in his genealogical essay, although well meant, went much too far in the direction of individual glorification for my taste, and therefore I could not give my assent to its publication."

The whereabouts of this Thierer-Schnerring manuscript could no longer be ascertained after twenty years. From the point of view of content, this has probably not resulted in any significant loss. But it would have been interesting to see what already went "much too far" for Bosch in the treatment of his person. These words may be taken as a kind of directive. But basically, for anyone who thought he knew and understood Bosch, no such directive was needed. I developed a simple method: whenever there were difficult passages in the book, I placed a picture of Bosch on my desk and worked under the critical scrutiny of his interrogating eyes, so to speak, always mindful of the way I might have launched into a high-spirited or thoughtful debate with him. I knew that he suffered contradiction well, especially when he sensed the presence of love. What mattered was the truth.

That in the writing of the book there would be difficult passages of both a substantive and a personal nature was fully clear to me from the beginning. There is a simple reason for this: the close proximity in time and the closeness of individual people about whom I would have to write. Some events and decisions, whether of a business or a more general nature, may not yet be judged from the simplifying perspective of greater distance. It is perfectly clear that a company—although I was allowed generous access to confidential decisions and contracts—cannot permit every detail to be made public. For this reason, particularly in describing the more recent history of the firm, I have generally based my conclusions on the published business reports, in an attempt to show not the gaps but the flow of events. In the personal sphere, the situation is as follows: Most of the people who participated with Bosch in his professional and personal career, whether they acted in concert or in conflict with him, are still alive. For the author, this was naturally a great advantage, enabling me, during the course of many conversations, to sound out the psychological core of documented conclusions and to augment my own knowledge of the man by many a fascinating detail. The writer who approached this material thirty or forty years hence would be the poorer for not having had access to this atmosphere. But he would also be able to speak more freely about many issues, where today a certain restraint is self-evidently called for. In spite of this, I do not believe that any distortions have crept into the overall scheme, with perhaps the single exception that, given this state of affairs, the supporting achievement of Bosch's colleagues during more recent periods may not have been adequately acknowledged, compared with the unquestionably strong influ-

ence that Gustav Klein and Gottlob Honold, for example, are acknowledged to have had during the period of the firm's great expansion. They
will, I think, not take this amiss, but will understand the state of affairs.

Bosch's wish that nothing at all should be written about him during his
lifetime was not respected. In the year 1931, on the occasion of his sev-
entieth birthday, several books about him appeared. The Association of
German Engineers published a volume whose text was written by Conrad
Matschoss and Eugen Diesel. His friends Paul Reusch and Hermann
Bücher produced a private edition that contained many intimate details.
I myself, at that time, was responsible for a collection of essays about
Bosch, to which Theodor Bäuerle, Peter Bruckmann, Johannes Fischer,
Hans Kneher, and Otto Mezger also contributed. The collection brought
out a number of points that were quite welcome. But, of course, the
important thing was to have access to the original sources. These were of
an uneven quality. Bosch himself wrote *Life Recollections*, fragments of
which were occasionally published. He never envisioned that they
should be published in their entirety; they are unsystematic and sometimes exaggerated in their subjectivity. In addition, there are quite a
number of notes, longer or shorter essays, biographical stories, anecdotes, and character sketches, as well as sociopolitical, pedagogical, and
medical reflections. Especially during his last years, Theodor Bäuerle
often succeeded in encouraging Bosch to put down on paper some of the
stories he liked to tell. There are some interesting and revealing pieces
among these writings. Most important, however, was the examination of
the hundreds of Leitz binders in which was stored the correspondence of
several decades. The material was available from about 1908 or 1909 on.
For the period before that, I mainly had family letters at my disposal. The
gaps in the business and personal correspondence had been filled in by
Dr. Otto Fischer's analysis of the first fifteen to twenty years of the firm's
internal policies. From then on, the material was more than abundant.
For months I sat over the collections of letters, work that was occasionally stimulating but was often boring and difficult—anyone who has done
this kind of work knows the alternation of pleasure and weariness. But
only this kind of work could enable me to accomplish what I desired—to

express Bosch's manifold drive and activities, as well as his position on the issues of the day and on personal matters in the form that was natural to him.

The important sources naturally included the factory newspaper *The Bosch Spark Plug*, whose issues I went through thoroughly. Many, many conversations with friends and coworkers helped fill out the picture. Paul Reusch also gave me access to his complete correspondence, spanning many years, with the friend of both his youth and his old age. I cannot thank all the individuals who assisted me in the compilation of the material, but I would like to mention the support that I received from the Bosch family; the director of the museum and archive, Dr. Fritz Schildberger; and all the members of the private secretary's office, above all, its director Willy Schlosstein.

In June 1942, after completing an initial overview of the as yet unevaluated material, I had a conversation with the firm's manager Hans Walz. We were in agreement concerning the stance that the book would take. I would be responsible for the interpretation of the man as I am now presenting it, in complete and unquestioned freedom. Even in the treatment of political questions—and, given Bosch's active participation and emotional involvement in the world around him, these would have to be emphasized at times—the aim would not be to write with an eye to the present. Bosch knew me and my position in public matters well enough to know that he would be protected from the danger of being recast according to the dictates of current fashion. At the time, Walz asked me how long I thought I would need to do the work. I responded, mentioning the existence of certain firm commitments of a journalistic nature, "About two to three years." He was horrified. "That is too long. The book should be finished when the war is over." I responded, "That is approximately how long it will take." This rather lightly tossed off remark was to prove uncannily accurate. It is true that after the demise of the German press I was able to concentrate on the Bosch book during working hours, but these working hours, as a consequence of the war, the constant alarms, and air raids, were seriously limited. There were repeated changes of place and constant worry about the stacks of notes—difficulties encountered by anyone who attempted to do this kind of work in these years and did not happen to be sitting in a far-off corner. There were other problems, as well. Libraries transferred their holdings; sending books became more and more risky, indeed impossible, over long periods of time. This made the implementation of certain plans impossible. For example, the developments at the Bosch firm were meant to be embedded in a descriptive overview of motorization in both Germany and the world. I was now forced to abandon this, along with a number of bibliographical references and comparisons. For who could hazard a guess as to when it would be possible, once again, to conduct halfway normal scholarly research of this type?

While this book was being brought to its conclusion, the mortal threat to Germany was becoming greater with every passing week, then with every passing day. The catastrophe whose occurrence had always been painfully clear to this writer could be clearly foreseen. In my consciousness, the events of the day, with their unbelievable vehemence, pushed all those things that had been part recent past, part present, back into history, into a declining epoch that may now perhaps be irretrievably lost. Now is not the time, nor is this the place, to speak about what comes after, to deal with guilt and cause. But it may be that in a temporal environment like the one that awaits us as a people, a phenomenon of creative power like Robert Bosch—educating, warning, pointing the way forward in all his historically conditioned particularity and individual uniqueness—can assume a more than passing significance as a model and a possibility of German existence and as an expression of peculiarly Swabian genius.

Theodor Heuss
Heidelberg, Spring 1945

PART I

YOUTH

1

BIRTHPLACE AND
FAMILY ORIGINS

The stately, sprawling inn Zur Krone in the upper village of Albeck exudes an atmosphere that is countrified without betraying its peasant origins. The inn is a reconstruction from the year 1834. The original building had been located farther to one side, near the path that ascends the hill in a steep S curve. In 1833, the government built a new road that headed straight for the top of the mountain in a more gradual, less taxing ascent, no longer passing through the lower village at all. This meant that the Krone was left on one side. But since one of the innkeeper's main sources of income had always been the transient business of the considerable number of travelers who passed over the old trade route connecting Nuremberg, Nordlingen, and Ulm, bearing their goods from the Frankish part of Württemberg to the Danube, it was necessary to relocate the property's main building closer to the new front. A few years later, in 1836, large horse barns were added; the owners could look forward confidently to a growing stream of customers. That in a few areas of Germany tracks were being laid and railroads were beginning to run was something that might be reported in the new newspaper in Ulm, but who would think such newfangled things would ever effect Albeck, much less the innkeeper of the Krone? A couple of decades later, however, railroads did arrive in the region, and since there would evidently never again be much of a future for long-distance travel via covered wagon, with its wagon teams, roadhouses, and stables, Servatius Bosch sold the inn in 1869, along with the beer brewery, the fields, and the grazing meadows, and moved to Ulm. He kept only a piece of woods with hunting rights; he did not want to give up his occasional hunting altogether. His youngest son, Robert, had recently begun to attend the village school. Later, Robert's memories of childhood would dwell on anecdotes that harked back to the peasant world, but real peasant life, in the solid and limiting sense of the word, was no longer really at home in the Krone. Something resembling a worldly wind blew through the rooms when the wagoners exchanged their stories and news. The carrier from Aalen had his regular spot in the Aalen Room, where he did his accounts. It was not the wide world, but it was restless and stirring and quite free of the well-regulated smugness that—despite the hard work—prevailed on large peasant farms in the Swabian highlands. And in the innkeeper's living room there were things on the bookshelf that one would probably have looked for in vain in the parsonage—for example, the poems of the elegant Count August von Platen.

Albeck had been home to the Boschs for several generations. It is a settlement with a long and eventful history, a history that has left its mark on the area surrounding the Krone. The place was fortified, and there are the remains of a castle. The printmaker Matthäus Merian considered it important enough to make an engraving of it for his *Topografia Suaviae,* which appeared in 1643. By then, the castle had long since ceased to be an independent center of power; for some 250 years the imperial office of *landvogt* had been held by patricians from Ulm. In 1383, the free imperial city of Ulm had bought everything—fortress, city, and land—from the deeply indebted Count Werdenberg, who came from the upper Rhine Valley. That spelled the end of the town's independence, but something may have survived of the distant knowledge that it had once been a city, or that during the Frankish period the count had had his seat there, as some people claimed. Later, the name was linked with a wealthy family of knights who had been prominent under the reign of the Staufen dynasty, but who had disappeared from view before the mid-thirteenth century. Still, today, in the little city that has now become a parish town, one can hear comments like: "If nowadays we call it 'Albeck near Ulm,' there was once a time when they said 'Ulm near Albeck,' you can be sure of that!"

A gifted teacher who wanted to weave the great events of the German nation into local history would have an easy time of it. The fortress was occupied with regularity. During military campaigns, this safe haven acted as a magnet for armies. In struggles between local forces, as well as in the European conflicts of the Thirty Years' War and the War of the Spanish Succession, battles for possession of the fortress left many victims and many a heroic legend behind. On several occasions, the castle was able to fend off attack after the city had already fallen, but in 1704 it, too, succumbed and was leveled. Since then, the main tract of the property has remained a ruin, but some of the buildings were temporarily rebuilt to house the administration. There is an old tower that has preserved the castle's romantic essence down through the ages, and the view from the village is still quite charming. The fact that the siting of the settlement, whose name Albeck means "hill corner," was based on considerations of military defense is something that today requires a certain mental effort to recall.

The first member of the extended Bosch family, Johann Georg Bosch (1713–1789), was raised in Albeck in the first half of the eighteenth century. The family tree, which has been researched, reaches back two centuries earlier to the peasant Matthias Bosch, who had a hereditary fiefdom in Heldenfingen (born in Heidenheim, no date given; his year of birth is thought to be circa 1522). The secure dates begin with Matthias's great-grandson, who also served as mayor of his home town. The sons of Hans Bosch (1617–1680) founded the five lines of the Heldenfingen branch of the family, which are described by Georg Thierer in his *Chronicle and Family Tree of the Bosch Families on the Swabian Highlands* (1921). The eldest, Jacob (1648–1727), farmed the Ugenhof near Bolheim. Georg (1675–1743), a beer brewer and attorney in Gussentritt, was the father of the Johann Georg who took over the Krone in Albeck. Of all these men and their wives, tradition has preserved only the dates. The second innkeeper of the Krone, Servatius Bosch (1742–1827), outlived his son, another Johann Georg (1785–1816). When Johann died at the age of thirty-one, he left behind an only child who was barely seven months old and who bore the name of his grandfather. The widow, Marie Elisabeth Bühler (1784–1864), remarried the peasant Jakob Friedrich Vöhringer, and one may assume that it was the stepfather who took care of young Servatius's education. The grandfather was already an old man; he had probably transferred the farm and business in 1808, when his son married.

We have no detailed information about Servatius Bosch, who was born on March 19, 1816, in Albeck. What educational influences shaped the boy who would one day be the sole heir to a considerable property? By the time his father came into his inheritance there had only been one sister to be taken care of, for of the thirteen children the grandmother had brought into the world, no fewer than eleven died young. The property would have to be preserved and altered—the laying of the new road and the decision to construct the large new building for the Krone (1834) occurred as Servatius Bosch was just coming into his own. His stepfather and mother may have had a word or two of cautious advice about these changes, but the will of the young farmer and beer brewer was essential. On August 1, 1837, then barely twenty-one years old, he married Maria Margareta Dölle, whose father ran the inn in nearby Jungingen, the Adler. The bride, who was born on December 1, 1818, was not yet nineteen on her wedding day; she, too, was her parents' only child.

From this marriage twelve children ensued, of whom three died young. The difference in age among the siblings seems rather significant when one considers that the oldest son, Jacob, was born in 1838 and the youngest daughter, Maria, in 1865. Robert Bosch remarked in his memoirs that he had two nephews, the first two sons of his brother Jacob, who were older than he. The family tree, which runs almost without gaps through six generations with 126 ancestors, reveals that the paternal and maternal families both had the same social and geographical origins. They were peasants, innkeepers, and beer brewers, and came from the region of the Swabian highlands near Ulm that today belongs to Bavaria. Next to some of the names, their honorific public positions are also listed; this one is a mayor, that one a deacon or solicitor or judge. The number of craftsmen is small: there are a couple of blacksmiths, butchers, weavers, and brush makers. In the fifth generation there is a lone representative of the educated professions, the pastor Plättlin. The son of a craftsman from Ulm, Plättlin married the daughter of an official from a free imperial city, through whose mother, Katharina Fingerlin, the bloodlines lead to the bourgeoisie of the city of Ulm, indeed to one of its leading families. The Fingerlins, who belonged to the wool-weavers' guild, were given their coat of arms in 1490 by the Emperor Maximilian, and intermarried extensively with the city's patrician families, including the Baldingers, the Bessers, and others. They played a significant role in the textile trade of the free imperial city, as well as in its officialdom. One can imagine in the wide-ranging organizational ability of Robert Bosch and his nephew Carl, creative captain of the German chemical industry, the distant influence of those merchants from Renaissance Ulm, whose peculiar force was not diminished when it was mingled with the peasant lineage from the countryside.

Robert Bosch was quite conscious of his peasant origins, and later on, when he himself began to turn his tenacious will to the practice of agriculture, he occasionally referred to the fact that as a young man he had become familiar with the world of planting and animal husbandry. But he was never sentimental about it. Servatius Bosch certainly does not fit neatly into any cliché of a peasant, even if he did work his considerable farm, which encompassed 375 acres of agricultural and pasture land and 75 acres of woodland. There were 25 head of cattle and 6 to 8 horses in his stalls. Tradition has it that he was the first person in Albeck to try artificial fertilizer, which was developed and recommended by Justus Liebig during the years when Servatius was first setting out on his own. That is not improbable. For Servatius Bosch was progressive in all things, and an eager reader of the newspapers. The management of the brewery and the wagon teams required active involvement. This was not a product that, as is often the case with country breweries, merely served to satisfy the needs of the local population; Bosch traveled and sold his product as Ulm beer as far away as Stuttgart. In the big barn there were six strong horses held in reserve and used only as an extra team for climbing the hill; there was room for two dozen more. For wagoners coming from the north, Albeck was the last station before Ulm, the place where they spent the night in order to reach the old trading center early the next morning. Something was always happening, and the workday had no clear-cut conclusion. One

of Bosch's early memories was of his mother having to make one more dinner for the wagon drivers in the late evening; his father, meanwhile, might
have been having the newcomers regale him with stories.

When the last-born son of the family began to form memories of his
mother, she was no longer young. Servatius had had a portrait painted of
himself and his wife; there are also two group portraits of the first five
children, in a quaint imitation of Biedermeier style. For a peasant in
those days to have had the interest and the money for such a thing is
unusual and suggests a kind of gentlemanly awareness. The young
woman in the portrait, which seems a bit prosaic but characteristic, has
a quiet grace. She must have been not only a capable worker in her own
world, so alive with children's sounds and household cares, but a woman
of compassion and goodness. Robert Bosch once wrote that it was his
mother, above all, to whom he owed his social awareness. The Krone was
an especially lively place during holiday celebrations. The cupboards
contained enough pewter ware for an entire peasant wedding, and when
it was set out, it was first polished with horsetail until it was burnished
like silver. The boy held his mother's image fast as she busied herself
with preparations like these or pulled candles from tallow (petroleum was
just beginning its conquest of the market).

Childhood memories of his father, to the extent that they have to do
with Albeck, were few. During the harvest, perhaps to let him feel he was
being useful, young Robert was allowed to sit on a horse that moved up a
few yards every time the sheaves of grain were loaded. From time to time
he was taken along as a companion on a hunt and was taught to observe
wild animals. He may also have begun to sense from the conversations in
the inn that the grown-ups talked a lot about politics and political parties
and about the Prussians; the latter did not inspire friendly comments. "I
can still remember," Bosch wrote in October 1941, to the descendant of
a family from Langenau, "how my father and others from Albeck went to
the election in Langenau, and the flag-bearer, a long tall tailor, had a
beer mug hung on his cap—the candidate they were voting for was
named Becher, or 'mug.' " That was in the spring of 1869, when the vot-
ers of Ulm elected August Becher to replace Albert Schäffle, who had
followed a call to Vienna. Becher was elected to the customs parliament,
one of the Reich Regents of the Stuttgart Rump Parliament of 1849.

Servatius Bosch must have done his part to assure that the citizens of Albeck made the "right" decision in this special election, which at the time attracted a good deal of attention as a test of the public mood. He was the village leader of the opposition to the mayor, with whom he lived in continuing hostility. According to Württemberg law, the head of the town was elected for life, and this lifelong office endowed him with extraordinary power. Divisions that tore a community into opposing groups were a feature of the times; in Albeck the Krone was the headquarters of the opposition party, and the innkeeper of the Krone once allowed things to come to a head in a battle that had unfortunate consequences for him, but also gave him something of a martyr's legendary glow. It is a wonderful story from the world of village politics, one that characterizes not only the jousting for power of two opposing forces, but also the angry and touchy sense of justice of the man himself. A man comes to Servatius Bosch of the Krone and tells him that the local beadle has gone around after curfew the day before and written up everyone who was sitting there—peasants, craftsmen, and so one—but had arrested only one, the poor brush maker, who was put in jail. Bosch is incensed; he runs straight to the beadle to see whether the story is true. The policeman is not home, but his wife gives the protesting man the key to the village jail and Bosch sets the brush maker free. Justice is restored, but there is no doubt that the law has been broken, and the mayor presses charges. Servatius Bosch is saddled with a lawsuit. The criminal court in Ulm that has jurisdiction over the Danube district reaches its decision on December 13, 1853. The judges have been lenient. As they recognize the honorable motives of the accused, they have given him a two-month sentence, which he serves from April 18 to June 17, 1854, in Hohenasperg. Requests for his early release, submitted on behalf of the municipal council, are to no avail. This incident was by no means detrimental to Bosch's reputation—the Asperg jail had already been consecrated, first by Schubart and List, and then again after the revolutionary uprisings of 1848. In Swabian democratic circles it is almost a matter of pride to have had a member of the family incarcerated there. Servatius Bosch may have thought along these lines, for he did not fail to have an engraving of the impressive hilltop site, set in the Württemberg plain, framed and hung on the wall as a memento.

This active public instinct was the most important psychological legacy Servatius Bosch passed on to his children. He was evidently a man of more than ordinary intellectual interests. Religious matters played no role in the family, or at the most only a very conventional one. The minister responsible for Albeck lived in the neighboring village of Göttingen. There is no evidence of any ties with him. "As far as religion was concerned, we were brought up very free-thinking," wrote Robert Bosch in an 1885 letter. "But we were not influenced in any particular direction; we were left to form our own opinions. My father, who never went to church and whose religion was 'Be a human being and respect human dignity,' died with courage and stoicism, without calling for a priest." Servatius Bosch—in a move that was quite surprising if one measures him against traditional standards—found his inner connection with the lodge of the Freemasons in Ulm, to which he maintained a loyal and enthusiastic attachment. In the style of the times, he may have been dubbed a freethinker. His son praised him as well read; the books arrayed in his living room were not mere wall decorations, but were very much used. Some of them have been preserved. Count Platen may be considered a curiosity in a Swabian farmhouse, but it is not insignificant that among the classics was the forty-volume edition of Goethe published by Cotta in the year 1857.

The elder Bosch's political awareness seems to have been devoid of personal ambition. Here was a man who was not at all interested in public appearances; the standoffishness toward all kinds of public meetings that was later so evident in the son was already apparent in the father. Again and again, as his obituary in the *Observer* (October 14, 1880) mentioned, he turned down offers of candidacy for district office, and later for the municipal council of Ulm. But his unselfishness and reliable character earned him more than local recognition. When some of the leaders of the 1848 movement, who had fled abroad, were granted amnesty and returned in 1863, and when it came time to reestablish the democratic organization (called the German People's Party), the innkeeper of the Albeck Krone was already well enough known to be immediately drafted for membership on the provincial committee. He would remain a member until his death. The members in Ulm elected him honorary chairman of their group. If the political role played by Servatius Bosch was small in terms of the larger picture, it was still important enough to make its mark on the atmosphere at home.

Robert Bosch once called his father sparing of words. That is the judgment of an old man looking back. In an early letter from December 1885, he characterized him to his fiancée Anna Kayser in this way: "My father was very soft-hearted and wanted above everything in the world to avoid letting this be seen; instead, he avoided every occasion at which he might have been moved; this explains the fact that I cannot remember my father ever kissing me. And as for my mother, I can only remember two times . . ." This is in a letter from England that expresses his feelings about American and English customs. In a late reminiscence about the spirit that prevailed in the household, the son pens a sentence of simple gratitude: "We children hung on our parents, who approached us with understanding, even if tenderness was never put on display in our house." The relationships among the siblings were good. The great difference in age could not help but have an effect; the eldest brother, Jakob, was already married and had taken over the maternal property in Jungingen by the time Robert was born. The second son, Johann Georg, died in 1864 at the age of twenty-four. The solemnness of his burial remained one of the earliest fearful experiences in the memory of young Robert, who was not yet three.

This death had a very decisive impact on the fate of the family, for Johann Georg had been destined to take over the property in Albeck, and had already become active in the parental business as a beer brewer and farmer. Who should take his place? Karl, who was born in 1843, had studied to be a merchant and was just making a trip abroad prior to settling down in Cologne. From Marseille he would not find his way home again to the village on the highlands. The ten-year-old Albert might be viewed as the next candidate, but he had other things on his mind; he was already beginning to attend classes at the *Realanstalt* in Ulm, and his father was quite satisfied with his desire to have a career in the building trades. For the father to intervene at this early stage in his son's independent life, because of the property, would have been contrary to his style; he preferred to leave a broad latitude for individual ambitions and wishes. The inheritance from the generations in Albeck waited for the youngest, August Robert, born on September 23, 1861—especially since the sisters had all married city dwellers. When his chosen successor predeceased him, Servatius Bosch was still strong enough and healthy enough to take care of the property, his tireless wife at his side, until such time as he would be able to give it over into the hands of his youngest.

But this was not to be, after all. The impetus to part with the property came from the outside. The railroad that headed north from Ulm, where it passed through Heidenheim and Aalen to make the connections to Nördlingen and Nuremberg, had been decided on in 1868. It left Albeck in the lurch. But even if it had passed through the town, the heart of the Bosch family business—the roadhouse with its wagon teams serving the cross-country transport of messengers and express wagons—had been damaged. The steep incline that was once so feared by drivers and was so profitable for those who lived on its edge had lost its interest as a technical problem for overland traffic. The defender of progress could not really object, rationally speaking, and so he joined the railroad committee. But he also came to a quick conclusion where he himself was concerned. He did not want to be the master of empty stalls and vacant rooms at the inn, and even if the agricultural property itself was large enough to occupy a man's energy and strength, Servatius was no longer enough of a peasant in his instincts to find satisfaction in it. He sold his property and retired somewhat prematurely to Ulm to live on his income when he was fifty-three years old. No one was interested in taking over the whole property, including real estate and livestock, and the auction lasted a week. It reigned in the memory of the local inhabitants as a kind of popular festival, due to the comings and goings of so many curious or interested buyers. The son's opinion about his father's decision is recorded in a letter to his boyhood friend Burkhardt (January 5, 1899): "My father retired with 250,000 to 300,000 marks. That is not something I wish to emulate. In the end, one could wind up running around like a poor sausage-eating pensioner."

In his later years, Robert Bosch cultivated the ties of friendship and concern which bound him to the community that had been the family's home for one and a half centuries and remained the place of his childhood memories. He participated, with hefty contributions, in the construction of a schoolhouse, a gymnasium and athletic field, and other similar projects. But he was careful that this relationship never took on a sentimental coloring. The house of his birth changed hands and fates many times, and it was suggested to Bosch more than once that he should buy it for one reason or another. Whether this made sense to him or not, it would have been entirely contrary to his way of thinking to attach particular dignity to a house just because he had been born in it. Equally unbearable was the thought of spending money that might generate rumors of even the slightest interest in the appearance of wealth and social prominence, or the idea that other people, speculating on his sentimentality, should try and actually succeed in making a profit from it!

2

———◆———

SCHOOL YEARS AND APPRENTICESHIP IN ULM

Bosch occasionally speaks of the people of Ulm as his closest compatriots. In a letter from his later years, he described them this way: "The citizen of Ulm has a great love for his hometown. This sometimes makes him a bit intolerant of everything that is not from Ulm. I have learned to appreciate the people of Ulm and the surrounding area more and more, by the way. With all their love of life's pleasures, they are hard-working and reliable, and as long as they have the right circle of coworkers, it is possible to accomplish something with them." Similarly appreciative remarks turn up on more than one occasion; they fit in well with the good-natured irony of his comment that people in cities "like to live comfortably and well."

He may well have had the image of Servatius Bosch, the private gentleman, in mind. Servatius was wealthy enough to lead a life of leisure. He had put his professional obligations behind him, and along with his participation in the public affairs of city and state, he allowed himself the time for a couple of hobbies. He rented a garden and tended apiaries; he had already kept bees in Albeck, and urged his son to observe him. Robert also accompanied him on visits to the piece of wooded property near Göttingen. Servatius had not sold it, and he looked forward to the day when the stand of young trees that he had planted himself would be a proper forest. Good-natured Jakob was sitting at the Adler in nearby Jungingen, and whenever Robert thought back to his youthful adventures, his thoughts always seemed to lead back to the village.

Ulm was a midsized city at the time, with approximately 25,000 inhabitants, many of them soldiers, and a large class of civil servants along with the long-established bourgeoisie. Industry had not grown very much yet; the few companies that would later achieve great fame had not been developed. The healthy, rich farm life that surrounded the town on all sides exuded an air of crude tranquillity that seeped in over the town's walls and ramparts. Since the 1840s, urban life had begun to find a center for its activities. Under a late-Romantic influence, people were imitating Cologne and its policy of cathedral building. The cathedral was to be given towers, and a decade later young Albert Bosch, who was just entering the upper classes of the *Realanstalt,* following his parents' move to the city, would be one of the cathedral architects under August von Beyer.

Karl and Albert Bosch appeared to their youngest brother to be the most gifted of the siblings. "Albert represents the aristocratic side of our family, and in doing so he comes into conflict with the rest of us now and again," says the "familiography" that Bosch sent to his bride in a letter dated April 1885. Certainly, the two eldest boys, who were generally at the head of their classes, had raised the teaching staff's notions of the academic ability to be expected from a Bosch to a level higher than anything the younger brother was inclined to attain. Later, Robert had no great regard for what he had meant to the school or the school to him. The village schoolteacher in Albeck made no particular impression, since Robert was there only a year, and the transition to new surroundings was successful if less than brilliant. He was also lacking in perseverance and ambition; the old and old-fashioned teachers did not quite know how to elicit his cooperation. He had "managed to muddle through as best I could," although as he remembered it he was generally in the first third of his class. He did reasonably well in languages and physics, as long as study consisted solely of experimentation. However, he did not acquire a foundation in mathematics and geometry.

Very late in his life, in a correspondence with his childhood friend Karl Hausmann—a professor of geodesy and the only member of Bosch's circle to embark on a scientific career—he wrote (February 2, 1938): "I was always very weak in mathematics. At the time it forced me out of school. Since I am not actually so bad at logic, the school, or more likely the teachers, must have been at fault. I am thinking of Rauss and Nagel, whom you never got to know, and of Ziegler. In any case, at the examination for the Middle School Certificate, which marked the end of my school career, I was unable to prove the Pythagorean theorem. I seem to have been too lazy to make up for this deficiency later, and thus have I journeyed through life and even had success that by all rights should not be mine. It was only my good technical instinct that got me through."

The older man's perspective may be a bit more skeptical than the truth of the matter warrants. In the memory of his classmates, Robert Bosch, although he did not stand out by virtue of his academic accomplishments, was considered talented—a boy with definite opinions who bravely argued his ideas in the face of contradiction. His classmates, in their sarcasm, had dubbed him "the all-knowing," but he seems to have been well-liked. Until the end, Bosch loyally cultivated his close association with his school friends—for example, with the salesman Eduard Gebhardt—but as he noted, "We grew apart from one another over the years, especially those schoolmates who stayed home and never saw a foreign country." He was not comfortable with the kind of conformity and stodginess that tend to cast a veil of youthful sentimentality over contradictions. He could be quite abrupt in response to a brand of familiarity that claimed to trace itself back to his old school crowd. His school report cards, organized with the detailed orderliness that characterized old Württemberg, paint a fairly confusing picture. The evaluations of his aptitude range from average (3) to good (6); his hard work and good conduct are consistently noted and praised. His final evaluation contains a "good" in the subjects of English and religion, and a "fair to good" in German, French, history, and geometric drawing, while geography, mathematics, physics, and drawing are judged "fair." The fact that gymnastics received the same modest grade makes one wonder, for gymnastics was an early and ardently pursued passion of Bosch's. He remarked about his graduation, "If they had not put mercy before justice, a great number of us, myself included, would have failed."

The memories Bosch retained into his old age were linked to vague musings about whether they were reflected in his later self. Some go as far back as the years in Albeck. Among these memories is a lesson about the dangers of lying that would remain with him. As a child, while playing, he had fallen into the basin of the trough in his father's courtyard, and on being fished out had explained that he had been pushed in. The intentional lie was immediately revealed, and young Bosch was sent to bed in the middle of the day. It was a successful punishment; he learned not to lie. He also recalled the amazement caused by his childlike questioning of whether people were also animals; perhaps he was feeling the early stirrings of a thoughtful scientific spirit. Did he like to make things? Although he may have had the patience for this kind of work, he used to tell a story about how he was supposed to make tiny feeding troughs for his father's apiary, for which he was to receive ten pfennigs each in return. Robert was almost too fast and clever for Servatius, who quickly withdrew the order.

The most detailed of his youthful memories "were those connected with shooting: spears, bows and arrows, slingshots, blow pipes with mud pellets." Life with his young comrades was undoubtedly peppered with various and sundry tales of boyish mischief, although without any extraordinary incidents: "I always tended toward foolhardy pranks, but I was aware of my limits, and nothing ever happened to me. I never looked for fights, but I didn't dodge them either, especially if it might have seemed like cowardice."

In the files of the *Realanstalt* in Ulm, the students' future professions were entered well before their graduation. Under Robert Bosch, "business" was entered for both reports in 1874. From Easter 1875 on, and in his final report, is written "precision-instrument maker." It is quite apparent that he had no clearly expressed preference as to his impending career goal. Bosch had very matter-of-fact thoughts on his choice of a career: "When it was time for me to decide on a career, my father asked me once whether I wanted to become a precision-instrument maker, and I said yes. My interests actually lay more in zoology and botany, but I took no pleasure in school, where I would only be made to feel constantly uncomfortable by the gaping holes in my knowledge, and so I became an instrument maker." One can hear an underlying tone of resignation in his statement. His father, we may assume, would hardly have objected if his youngest child had also finished school and devoted himself to the investigation of biological questions; as it was, the fifteen-year-old became an instrument maker almost out of petulance.

What would someday evolve from this, he himself could not yet conceive, especially since his apprenticeship turned out to be not at all encouraging. Servatius Bosch apparently did not take the necessary care in selecting a master for his son. Even in his later years, Robert Bosch spoke with abrupt anger of the man who had been entrusted with giving him his basic career training. His disparaging judgment was shared by other apprentices to the man, who, with his fairly prosperous background, was more often seen tippling in the taverns at breakfast than at the workplace. Bosch told of an instance in which he had to file iron base plates for a rather large job and requested a new file, as the one he had was in very poor condition. The master's reply impressed itself upon Bosch's memory: "I have had that file for twelve years and now all of a sudden it is supposedly no good!" Bosch's quick and critical mind protected him from the stupidity of the remark. Here and there, when the master did not know how to proceed, his apprentice was able to help him with good suggestions for which he got no thanks but which increased his self-esteem. The technical disciplines of craftsmanship were not as specialized as they would later become. The master was a watchmaker and an optician, and he also began taking orders for home telegraphs and telephones, which were just beginning to come into fashion. The apprentice soon figured out that the man didn't know anything about such things and always had to seek outside advice, thus losing his authority. The boy rebelled when the master tried to use him to carry out personal errands, and had to be calmed down at home. In retrospect, the apprenticeship was not a happy one; he actually felt it was a waste of his time. In those years, his active participation in the gymnastic club became the center of his life outside of work.

The fact that Robert Bosch was forced to complete an apprenticeship that was so personally and professionally unsatisfying was not without consequences, but not in the sense that his professional progress suffered from it. His traveling years served as his real apprenticeship. But the memory of the shortcomings of his own youthful education sharpened his determination to avoid making similar mistakes after he came into his own. The great care that he devoted to his apprentices, right from the beginning of the development of his business, did not grow out of a rational decision or a humanitarian inclination to educate, although both played a role, but out of the unhappy experience to which he had been subjected in his own youth.

3

———•———

JOURNEYMAN YEARS,
TRAVEL, AND MILITARY SERVICE

In the fall of 1879, Robert Bosch's school days were over. The eighteen-year-old had his mind set on faraway places; he wanted to stand on his own two feet. This was not to be accomplished as quickly and easily as self-confidence and romanticism might imagine; in neither Pforzheim nor Karlsruhe was there work to be found where he sought it. He seemed to have lost the courage to visit more masters in search of a position, and on the second day he put an abrupt end to his time as an apprentice craftsman and left for Cologne to visit his brother Karl. Since he did not find anything that suited him in Cologne or in Bonn, his older brother at first kept him on at his business. Karl had opened a business that sold elements for gas and water pipe installation, and the world traveler felt a sense of safety when his brother took him on and gave him a job as a belt maker. Karl Bosch would continue to take an interest in the development of his youngest brother. The object of his stout pedagogical concern responded with occasionally ironic resistance—the arrangement of September 1879 was a matter of blatant expediency and lasted only a few weeks. The young journeyman discovered that the common practice among trained fine-instrument makers was not to ask for work at the workshop door but rather to inquire by letter.

The voyage to faraway places, which had landed him in the second family home, came to an abrupt end. Robert Bosch returned to Swabia and entered the firm of C. & E. Fein as a journeyman. Here, for the first time, he was face-to-face with a master who really was a master, and in proximity to tasks that a decade later would influence his own independent research and experiments. Wilhelm Emil Fein, who had founded his precision engineering workshop in 1867 and had moved it to Stuttgart in 1870, conducted his business with great resourcefulness; as a young man in the 1860s, he had worked for Siemens & Halske in Berlin and then for Wheatstone in London. Now he became a pioneer of early electrical engineering in his own country. It was an impressive, somewhat confusing program with which the young businessman tried, successfully, to establish a place for himself. Along with physical and therapeutic devices, he developed the Bell telephone to a new and current standard by using the horseshoe magnet, created portable electric lighting systems and later the mobile telephone for military purposes, and was tremendously imaginative as a designer, with a talent for the practical improvement and simplification of existing inventions. Fein's influence on the development of the electronics industry in all of southern Germany must be considered very significant, in part due to his involvement with activities of a literary and propagandistic nature. A tireless worker, Fein became the inventor of the electric motor for machine tools, and one of the fathers of the electric tools of the future; it was this specialization that garnered his firm its nationwide fame. But in those early days, there was as yet no hint of all this. The firm, with a workforce of fifty or sixty men, was just in the process of expanding from a local workshop into a factory with far-flung connections.

It is difficult to determine which particular tasks in the ever-changing fabrication process were assigned to Bosch during his six months with Fein. At the time, a large contract for fire alarms was of foremost importance, business that gave Bosch an idea of the diversity of the burgeoning field of electrical engineering, although he felt no certainty that his own path would one day follow a similar course. When the journey to faraway places was undertaken for the second time, in the spring of 1880, he went into a new branch of industry, chain manufacture, in Hanau am Main. There Bosch was employed for a year with a small group of workers engaged in the production of specialized machines for chain manufacture. Little is known about this interlude, and Bosch's own observations are scanty. Nonetheless, any task that demanded a new way of thinking was not useless. Each task brought Bosch closer to the building of machine tools—the very thing with which he would occupy himself so intensely. Once again, gymnastics brought him social contact with others. In the volatile city of Hanau, gymnastics had taken on an aspect of political radicalism in 1848–49. The Hanauer Gymnasts had become competitors of the old conservative "father of gymnastics" Friedrich Ludwig Jahn and had joined the Palatine revolt, thus creating a legend that fit in quite well with the Bosch family legacy.

In an act that would become important for Robert Bosch's professional future, his brother Karl called him back to Cologne. This time, it was no forced landing but more of a purposeful beginning. Robert would surely want to make himself independent in a few years. In that case it would be good if he understood something about bookkeeping and the like, and Karl intended to train him in business. This was done at the firm of Bosch & Haag, which the founder ran with his brother-in-law Gustav Haag. Cologne had become a kind of family branch office, second only to the one in Ulm. Gustav Haag of Stuttgart had married Karolina Bosch, and in 1877 Franz Decker, from Söflingen, had married Barbara Bosch and relocated to the city on the Rhine. Karl Bosch, who was born in 1843, had made his home in Cologne since the 1870s. Through circumspection and hard work, he had led the joint business, of which he served as the chief manager, to quick success, and had gained a respected and influential position. His active participation in public life—a legacy from his father—helped win him the trust of his new neighbors, and he was elected a member of the Chamber of Commerce. His most important accomplishment, toward the end of the century, was his active involvement in the founding of the business school in Cologne, on whose board of trustees he became the most willing and stimulating participant. He felt a share of responsibility for the brother who was eighteen years his junior, especially following the death of their father. For Robert Bosch, then and for a long time afterward, Karl represented the standard of bourgeois ambition and personal behavior. Robert liked to proclaim how important the harmony of their political beliefs and view of the world had been to him. Now this brother had become his immediate supervisor.

Karl Bosch did not turn his almost twenty-year-old trainee into a perfect accountant, for when Robert Bosch was once again confronted with such duties a decade later, they caused him more trouble and annoyance than gratification. Although he never became a real businessman, the return on this six-month introduction to the commercial aspects of business was his confidence with the details of transactions and balance sheets and a sense of the importance of solid accounting.

The twenty-one-year-old returned to Ulm in the fall of 1881 to fulfill his military service. The year before, while Robert had been in Hanau, his father had rapidly succumbed to a raging lung infection. He died on September 11, 1880. In retrospect, the son thought his father's early retirement had had an adverse effect on his health.

For a few years now, his brother Albert—"the aristocrat"—had been back in Ulm after having completed his study of architecture in Munich and Stuttgart. In May of 1878, Albert joined the cathedral construction crew under the architect August von Beyer as the foreman responsible for overseeing the finishing of the northern side tower. He also assisted in the completion of blueprints and calculations for the main tower. Little is known about his individual role in the great project; a few surviving plans with detail sketches and architectural forms indicate the sure hand of a professional. Albert's obviously fresh and self-confident air impressed Robert. It is apparent that Albert represented the only artistic element in the Bosch family, with a nature that stood out in contrast to the correct bourgeois habits of the others. He was considered to be someone who loved the pleasures of the table, a hearty round of drinks, and merry company, and this brought him into contact with a circle of officers from the garrison. And yet a shadow seems to have darkened his outwardly unproblematic life—the feeling that in his dependence on Beyer he could not fully realize his own potential. At one point he voiced a lament over how wrong it had been for him to devote the years of his youth so exclusively to the building of the cathedral. In May 1886, he left the cathedral construction project. But he had already become so specialized in the field of neo-Gothic architecture that he took on a similar, if more intimate, assignment: the restoration of the monastery church in Frankish Öhringen, a fine work that would be completed by others. At the young age of thirty-one, his strength suddenly broken, Albert Bosch passed away after a long-neglected lung illness.

In 1881, when his brother Robert joined the army, Albert was a husky, robust fellow; his premature and sad departure was surely not without its influence on Robert Bosch's strict, even cautious, lifestyle in later years. Robert, who was a volunteer serving for one year, chose engineering battalion number thirteen as the unit to which he would be assigned. The combination of military and technological elements made it a logical choice. Actually, there is little to report about his year of service. In his *Life Recollections*, Robert Bosch confined himself to a few short sentences to the effect that, in retrospect, he found little of importance in the experience: "Although I really took no pleasure in the soldier's life, I found the work occasionally entertaining. Physically fit and daring to the point of foolhardiness, I nonetheless did not overestimate my strength, but understood how to find my way out of sometimes dangerous situations." In his occasional journal entries, a few incidents of such foolhardiness are noted—swimming races during maneuvers near Coblenz; the leap across a moat four or five meters wide, which made lieutenants and sergeants hesitate. It was the sense of gymnastic sureness, the knowledge that he correctly judged the strength of his muscles and the agility of his body, that made him a technically proficient soldier.

His military career proceeded without a hitch. After the usual intervals, Bosch became a private first class and then a corporal. His superiors were evidently pleased with his performance, perhaps particularly with his ability to draw maps. At the end of his service, the battalion commander suggested to him that he become a career officer. "But I didn't want to hear anything about the life of a soldier," he said in retrospect. At the time, instinct must have told him that a career in military service went against his fundamental nature. Yet he may well not have been fully aware of his inherent yearning for freedom or of the militant individualism of his character, which was opposed to all merely conventional ties. He was not an early bloomer; rather, his individuality emerged in ways that were rather uncertain and he was mistrustful of his own natural ability. Bosch would have been a good, supportive, accomplished, and just superior, but an uncomfortable and difficult subordinate.

Evidently the question of a possible career change had occupied the family as well, which, in keeping with the tendency among members of the German People's Party at the time, did not exactly lean toward the military. Perhaps Albert thought differently on the subject. In the previously cited letter from the spring of 1885, in which Robert introduced the family history to his future bride, he mentioned the matter good-humoredly within the context of a characterization of his eldest brother, the innkeeper from Jungingen: "Jakob is a chief democrat and tribune of the people, whose particular good will I earned by virtue of not becoming an officer, although Major Ziegler had told him that it would be good for me."

Bosch had been discharged as an officer candidate, and he now took a leave from the army reserve, since he did not want to interrupt the furthering of his career. During an examination while he was in America in 1885 by a doctor from the German consulate, Bosch was proclaimed unfit for field and garrison duty. A defect in his eardrum that stemmed from his youthful fondness for shooting, and that had proved bothersome more than once during his military service, had worsened. This hearing problem in his left ear was never eliminated, but it remained at a tolerable level so that Bosch was only occasionally annoyed by it.

The year in the military brought about a meeting that would be of lifelong significance. He must generally have been a good comrade, although he later refused to participate in clubs or groups organized to perpetuate the memory of a time that had been so indifferent for him. Among the first-year members of the battalion was a young engineer about three years older than Bosch, well-trained and of a somewhat soft disposition, who was in need of companionship and friendly exchange and whose name was Eugen Kayser. Kayser came from a merchant's family in Obertürkheim. It was in his house that Bosch made the acquaintance of his friend's sister, Anna, the woman who would later become his wife. After a somewhat indecisive beginning, Eugen Kayser confidently made his way through various large industrial firms in Berlin, and then, in the last decade of his life, played an important and independent role in the expansion and establishment of the firm of Robert Bosch.

At the time, Bosch sensed in his newfound older friend the very things he lacked in the way of theoretical knowledge and a command of the connections among various technical matters. His failed apprenticeship could not have provided him with anything of the sort, and his present work was a kind of continuous empirical experiment from which useful ideas would occasionally emerge.

Bosch's development, seen from afar, easily gives the impression that from the start he was consciously striving toward a goal. This is by no means the case, however, the more so because he was vividly aware of the gaps in his education. Textbooks would have to serve as his teachers. Once, in Hanau, when he opened a book he had brought from home he found a note inside that his mother had written for him:

A ship with no rudder must trust to the sea—
Not long before dashed on the rocks it will be.
Life is the sea, the small vessel is you,
And wisdom, my friend, is the rudder thereto.

This well-intentioned bit of rhyming pedagogy from afar may have touched him at the time; at any rate, the anecdote remained with him, as well as the place where he had found it—Pisko's book *Light and Color*. The memory is incidental, but it reveals something of his tentative autodidactic attempts.

The sea of life onto which the young engineer had ventured in 1880 was then in a state of the most violent motion, stirred up by favorable winds; he needed to understand how to steer the rudder skillfully and choose the course wisely.

When Robert's military service was over, his brother Karl took him on a trip to Nuremberg and Munich. The trip was not the result of some sudden, unsuspected enthusiasm for art or medieval beauty—a citizen of Ulm hardly needed to take the train to see that—nor did they intend to visit famous old art collections. This trip was about new, useful things. On the Pegnitz there was a Bavarian State Fair, in Munich an International Electricity Exposition, and at both there were astounding things to be seen, things that really could make a trip worthwhile, such as electric arc lamps, incandescent bulbs, and the first attempts at electrical power transmission.

The Munich Exposition was particularly important for the popularization of electricity in Germany. Young Oskar von Miller—a go-getter of a hydraulic engineer whose energy was infectious—had initiated it, and had completed his journeyman's labor as a tireless and inventive organizer. To some, the whole thing may have seemed a bit forced, for only a year earlier a great spectacle had been arranged in Paris with the same intention of successfully reaching an international audience. Werner von Siemens did not think much of creating more ballyhoo of this kind; the leading German firm stayed home. But the show turned into a triumph for Sigmund Schuckert, a twenty-seven-year-old man who only a few years before, in 1873, had established a small, two-window mechanic's workshop in Nuremberg.

Schuckert's beginnings, with only a single assistant, are reminiscent of Bosch's own early independent years. Schuckert took in repairs, began to fabricate precision instruments, and made scientific devices for various institutes in Erlangen. But he soon reached for greater challenges, and applied himself to the construction of a dynamo. In 1867, only a few years earlier, Werner von Siemens had discovered and described the dynamoelectric principle that formed the basis of the electric generator. W. E. Fein had taken up the same task, but his production program, still in its early phases, reflected its inventor's imaginative skills and remained multifaceted, with the emphasis on low voltage. Schuckert's practical concentration commenced earlier. It was focused on lighting, which, together with the generation of electricity and the transmission of electrical power, had fascinated the world since the recent invention of the arc lamp. Schuckert represented a new type of man. It was not for nothing that he had spent five years living in America, had worked with Thomas Alva Edison, and had brought home with him a lively impression not only of the technological and scientific possibilities of the new field of electricity, but also of its economic and capitalist potential.

With his starting capital—$1,000 in savings—he was enterprising in the daring sense, an experienced practitioner who sensed what was necessary and had a feel for the forces that make a thing marketable. He was not actually an inventor by nature (as Fein was, to a certain extent), nor did he have the mind of a scientist. It would have seemed very inappropriate to him to think of himself in terms comparable with Werner von Siemens, in whom the rise of the lively competitor from Franconia inspired considerable discomfort. Schuckert produced good, reliable work, recognized his own limits, and recruited the scientific or organizational coworkers he needed. One cannot wholly overlook the fact that he achieved his great success by applying the patents of others (arc lamps and headlights), but he knew what was good and could be made better, and he insisted on good, clean work.

Robert Bosch was too young to experience the problem of the capitalist expansion that would give the entire undertaking a different look, with the establishment of electric power stations a few years later. Later Bosch, too, often faced the question that Schuckert had to confront, namely, whether he would allow himself to be supported by outside investors. Yet one gets the impression that the Nuremberg business was Bosch's first and most experientially crucial contact with a growing industrial firm. "In those days everyone flocked to Schuckert. His employees were well paid, and it was a mighty business," he noted in 1921. By comparison to today, the mighty business operated within modest limits. In 1882, a boom led to the firm's first purposefully constructed and systematically organized industrial plants, but when the firm moved in, in 1883, the workforce comprised only about 100 men.

In Bosch's recollections, the particular work he did during this period was not very important to him. He was employed in the section that made voltage and ampere meters, which the chief designer of the firm, Uppenborn, had designed and which Bosch referred to as "instruments of a rather primitive nature." Bosch remembered the social atmosphere. The technicians, who were highly paid and came from many different places—for the city could not meet the rapidly growing demand for new workers—were "not very used to order," led "easy lives," and grumbled when a medical fund was set up, when the entrance and the exit to the factory were guarded, and when working hours were controlled. "I, too, had to accustom myself to this order, for better or for worse, but I was not very happy about it." The individualist in him reacted instinctively against the strict regulations, but had to recognize the rationale behind them. It is telling that in his old age, after he had long since learned to function within such exacting rules, Bosch could write this sentence about his earlier sentiments. But he also quoted from a speech that the Schuckert factory manager of the time, Franz Decker, from Esslingen, had given at an office party to the effect that "in a factory there has to be one leadership, like the army, to make the factory productive and quick on the trigger." This man had clearly made an impression on his listener.

One of the benefits of his employment at Schuckert was his friendly relationship with an old Swiss technician who worked in the experimental workshop, August Utzinger, from Zurich, a man with a solid education and a helpful manner; Bosch felt that he could learn a lot from him, and Utzinger liked to teach. His occasional shop talks found an attentive listener in Bosch.

Robert Bosch's stay in Nuremberg continued until the summer of 1883; it was followed by a brief stint at a factory in Göppingen where Bosch worked on the manufacture of arc lamps. This period left no impression on him, and the experiences of his early working life suggested to him that he should further his school education.

4

———

AT THE
TECHNICAL UNIVERSITY
IN STUTTGART

Bosch planned to take the fall semester of 1883–84 for the continuation of his theoretical education at the Stuttgart Technical University. In 1921, he wrote a bit summarily of the events and results of that half year. "It is true," he wrote, "that I did not have the necessary prerequisites for such a course of study, nor did I have the energy required to bring my inadequate knowledge of mathematics at least up to a level of acceptability. What I learned at school in Stuttgart was to lose my fear of technical terms. Afterward, I knew what voltage and amperage and horsepower were. On the other hand, I also discovered that I had many more fellow sufferers in the field of electrical engineering, who did not have much more knowledge, but who also lacked the capacity to think coherently, observe, and draw conclusions. At the time, my electrical engineering professor thought quite well of me, because of my observations, although my actual gain in scientific understanding during that half year was obviously negligible."

The teacher, Professor Wilhelm Dietrich, had just been awarded a newly created full professorship for electrical engineering; in the previous semesters he had still been an assistant teacher. Naturally, electricity had already been taught for several decades as a division of general physics. The research of Galvani and Volta, of Davy, Faraday, and Maxwell, of Ohm, Gauss, and Siemens had revealed new phenomena, principles, and measurable quantities in this realm of mysteries. Nor had there been any lack of early attempts to make what was already known serve a useful purpose. Yet for a long time it would be only work in the laboratory, experimental models that history would carefully preserve and to which it would attach various nations' claims to priority, but which would have no widespread practical impact. This would change around the middle of the century, with Werner von Siemens's achievement and its impact on the construction of a reliable telegraph, and, in another area, the manifold experiments with electrolytes. After that, the new inventions would follow in rapid succession: the arc lamp, the incandescent bulb, the telephone. With Werner von Siemens's dynamo, many technological and industrial possibilities opened up. In 1882, the first German professorship in electrical engineering was created in Darmstadt for Erasmus Kittler.

Small wonder that the boundless new territory attracted people of talent, no matter what school had signed their regular diploma, if indeed they had one at all. The most active and successful of these men, Thomas Alva Edison, certainly did not. It is important to recognize the strong, effective impact of men in the early period of development who had no schooling or were at best semieducated. Sigmund Schuckert and Sigmund Bergmann are among those who, as boys of fourteen, were sent from primary school straight into apprenticeships; physicist Johann Philipp Reis also belonged to this group. This would remain true even after what we now know as electrical engineering had become, as a consequence of the practical needs of society, a recognized university discipline.

Wilhelm Dietrich was one of the pioneers. He himself left behind no great achievements in research or design to make his name well known. His commitment outside his career was to city politics; for many years he played an important role in the Stuttgart town hall as a stimulating and opinionated city councillor. Above all, he was an excellent and attentive teacher, who, although he came from a background in theoretical physics and did not deny this, provided his disciples with solid assistance by simplifying and clarifying ideas and phenomena.

The special student Bosch, if he wanted to be admitted to the individual subjects he requested, was required to demonstrate previous knowledge "without which the students could not usefully attend the various subject lectures." The requirements were modest. Professor von Zech, with whom Bosch studied experimental physics, required only elementary mathematics. Professor Dietrich, with three hours of lectures and two half-days of training per week for electricians, focused entirely on practice. That fall he was discussing the generation of electrical current, electric lighting, the transmission of electrical power, electrolysis, and the fundamentals of the measurement of electricity. Bosch had already worked in some of these areas. Above all, the exercises centered on measuring the strength of electrical currents and on methods for their measurement. One of Dietrich's specialized lecture courses, which Bosch was able to hear, dealt with telegraphy and railroad signal systems. Bosch also enrolled in an English language course.

The few companions from that time who are still living report that Bosch was a very conscientious and hard-working student. He knew that this sort of apprenticeship was of limited duration and that it should be used well. Hence his seriousness in putting his newly acquired knowledge to work. Here, in addition to the technical instinct with which he credited himself, he gained that sureness in the fundamentals that would remain within his firm possession. He found companionship at the Hut Club, including a number of friendships that would carry over into his later life. But by nature he was not inclined to student camaraderie of any lasting kind. His encounter with one of his peers, Richard Stribeck, would later become important; in Stribeck he sensed the academic determination that he himself lacked and that he had come to appreciate. Stribeck's career led by way of professorships in Darmstadt and Dresden to the Neubabelsberg Center for Scientific Analysis and from there to the board of directors of Krupp. He became an authority in the scientific study of materials for engine construction. In 1918, he returned home, and the youthful friendship was renewed as a mutually rewarding collaboration in their old age.

Bosch's career was clearly foremost in his mind. But in those days at the Technical University in Stuttgart there were a few men in the general education department who were able to make a strong impression on young people who were open-minded and curious about life. Friedrich Theodor Vischer was still lecturing on the history of German literature, and even for a student who was not devoted to the muses, part of the university experience was to subject oneself to the old man's graphic and spirited eloquence. For Bosch, the encounter with this teacher remained a passing incident; he would refer to him only now and again. But Gustav Jäger's teachings struck at the heart of Bosch's being. They were a decisive factor in how he would lead his life, and laid the groundwork for the far-reaching and serious interest that Bosch, in his later years, would take in matters of medical science and public health.

Gustav Jäger held three professorships, at the Hohenheim Academy of Agriculture, the School of Veterinary Medicine, and the Technical University. In 1884, he took a leave from his academic duties in order to dedicate himself completely to his work on the reform of everyday life and medical policy, into which he had ventured a few years earlier, belligerent and controversial. Like a number of other odd, significant figures with strong Swabian characteristics, his somewhat grotesque tendencies were more readily recalled by legend than the important stimulus provided by his work, which would finally become so widely accepted as to be almost banal. Trained as a physician, he had become a zoologist and had established an aquarium and a zoological garden in Vienna, when his encounter with Darwin's *Origin of Species* made him into one of the most determined public champions of evolutionary theory. His own original achievement came about when, based on his observations of animals, he began to examine the question of human clothing. What Max von Pettenkofer did for residential hygiene, Jäger undertook to do for human clothing. The result is well-known. He radically rejected textiles produced from plant substances and preached the "wool regime": conditioning of the skin, greater permeability for perspiration, and so forth. His aim was to toughen the body—a concept to which Jäger, in conjunction with his studies of human work capacity and the "specific weight" of human beings, gave a specialized meaning. Obviously, with this thesis he came into conflict with powerful economic and industrial interests, but this did not disturb him. The further development of his teachings had to do with scent. Here, too, his point of departure had been his observation of animal life. He examined and measured reactions to particular scents and to sexual emanations; this path led him to the "discovery of the soul." It was daring enough that he began operating with this term as a sort of biological essence; one could speak of a sublimated materialism. "Wool Jäger" became "soul Jäger," or in German, "soul hunter."

This man, who was fifty-one years old at the time, stocky, robust, healthy, and full of occasionally coarse humor, must have made a strong impression on the young Robert Bosch. Jäger was a tireless, if somewhat careless and formless, writer possessed of a gripping clarity. He offered a dual reward. Professionally, Bosch appreciated his rational scientific method—the fact that he made a point of distinguishing his research from physiological and anatomical school medicine did not mean that he relinquished the claim to rational knowledge, but only that the end goal of natural observation was reached by different means. Morally, he was the image and model of an uninhibited nature that did not conform to conventions, and, while he did not exactly seek out controversy, he certainly did nothing to avoid it. His laughing resistance to the sneering of his professional colleagues made an impression.

Later, Jäger would also profess adherence to the principles of Samuel Hahnemann's homeopathy, and would build its doctrine of the effectiveness of small doses into his own overall views. For Bosch, in whose paternal family homeopathy was already the house rule, this must have sounded like a confirmation. The influence that Jäger had on the youthful Bosch was strong enough to be life-altering. It was not simply that he became a strict and thorough Jägerian who believed in wool and put up with all the discomforts of rigid adherence to the rules. The impulse to reform life, in the broad sense, originated here, and it became a part, in all its strict seriousness and oddness, of his nature.

5

———◆———

WORK IN AMERICA

On May 24, 1884, the Dutch steamer *Caland* set sail for America. Among the passengers on the second deck was twenty-three-year-old Robert Bosch, a bit excited by the commotion created by the several hundred emigrants all crammed together below the decks. They were enjoying themselves and soon began dancing to the melody of a harmonica. The waterway was full of small fishing boats and steamers, even after the noisy harbor had been left behind. Bosch eagerly looked forward to being on the ocean for the first time in his life. There was so much to see—the gulls that accompanied the ship, land swallows, sea swallows, the way the water's color changed with the changes in the weather. He watched the sailors work; there was much to learn and take note of, for example, the way one could determine the ship's driving speed with log and log line.

In fact, the young traveler had begun to make proper written notes on his impressions and experiences, and when one of his fellow travelers asked him whether he was composing his memoirs, he answered yes, inwardly amused that the curious passenger could not know that his alcoholic swaggering had just been the subject of an ironic character study.

In short, Bosch kept a travel diary. The modest little black oilcloth book with the red-rimmed pages, from the year 1884, survived over the years in some corner where it had been tossed, and thus became the earliest firsthand document that we possess for Robert Bosch. This lends it its anecdotal and also psychological importance. Naturally, during his early separations from his parents he had reported to his mother in letters, but this must not have been too frequent, for the family was thrifty with displays of emotion. And in the peasant or urban households of Swabia with their many children, it would not have occurred to anyone to keep such letters, as they would see each other again soon.

The personal testimony from the year 1884 has the charm of fresh and unselfconscious vividness. Here the reader encounters things that are quite different from Bosch's other observations about his childhood and youth, written from the distance of age, experience, and success, and with the aim of clarifying or explaining his actions. Here, rather, his comments are stylistic exercises born of good humor. Bosch is lighthearted, sometimes surprised, very open to all impressions, and ready to see himself ironically. He is sometimes quite banal and pedantic in his registering of the ship's course and speed, of mealtimes and the stages of seasickness, but his writings are also permeated with reflections pertaining to the national peculiarities of his fellow travelers or to his own future. The carefree leisure that is a feature of ocean voyages evidently stimulated Bosch to put down small experiences, take note of things to reflect upon, and conjure up images from memory. A similar little oilcloth book has been preserved from his return trip from America, in the summer of 1885, along with the comprehensive if somewhat unsystematic summary of his *Life Recollections*, written in 1921 on a trip to South America.

"It is a good thing I was a soldier and learned to call my thoughts up for review," he wrote. "This way I am never bored, and there is something pleasant about lying on one's back hour after hour and gazing at the stars. My Dutch and English acquaintances think I am homesick if I don't chat with them about silly things." He was not homesick, but it would have been nice if Eugen Kayser and "Nottele," his university friend Maurer, had been there. He imagined how they might be sitting together with some other journeyman friends in a little inn in Gaisburg. And if he was homesick, he found enough Swabians below the decks who wanted to try life in America and who were now mostly singing songs of parting. He enjoyed the singing; his companions could only sing crass popular ballads with familiar melodies. All in all, he found the others, particularly the Dutch and the Irish, occasionally annoying: "If I travel by ship again, I will go first class. There is nothing more disgusting than people who do not eat properly . . . I think the Germans are the most proper eaters, except for those Englishmen from the better classes, who would probably rather starve than eat fish with a knife."

Bosch the sociologist had an easier time with national eating and drinking habits than Bosch the rationalist did when it came to comprehending the behavior of a large group of young girls traveling to an American convent—their cheerfulness, their unquenchable desire to help one another bothered him. "Among ten people it cannot be that they are all suited to one another and like one another, despite the proverb 'children, love one another.' Are they broken beings who do what they are supposed to, but not out of feelings of duty? They do not look broken. Is it all hypocrisy? It would not be nice to assume such a thing. But why do so many women get along so well with one another? Among ten there must be at least one who does not harmonize with one of the others; if both do not play the hypocrite then there must be friction. I, too, love and respect my fellow human beings, but if one of them does not suit me he will certainly realize it right away, and if he is an honest chap then we will get along pretty well together, but not because we butter each other up, but because we steer clear of one another . . . Could it be that Jäger's thesis is applicable to nuns, namely that the way to a peaceful household is found by kissing as often as possible? But I must stop, or my thoughts will make me seasick!"

On another occasion he philosophizes that "women can do so many things at the same time. I know a good example of this. One of the sisters takes a walk, knits, prays her rosary, and perhaps thinks all the while, too. These are four things which a man would find very difficult to manage all at once. For example, if a man sits at an inn and drinks, smokes, talks, and thinks, that is also four things, but as a rule one of them isn't worth much. For example, if he drinks a lot, then it can be assumed that he is not saying much that is intelligent, and then drinking and smoking are pleasant activities, at any rate more pleasant than praying or knitting. I do not think I need to illustrate my point any further, for the facts and the curfew violations speak for my theory."

Naturally the homilies of this chatty journal can only be viewed in terms of their psychological implications; they give an early indication of one of Bosch's lasting characteristics: the logical play with paradox and the development of argument based on sense impressions.

His observations contained occasional looks into the time that lay ahead. Somewhat surprising was his realization shortly before his arrival (the pilot brought newspapers on board) "that it would be a bad turn of events for me if Germany were to go to war. Should I turn right around again? I think everyone who knows me well will know better than to accuse me of cowardice, but to return to Germany under such circumstances, perhaps to allow oneself to be shot and crippled and to have to say at the end that one cannot take responsibility for such patriotism in one's own mind, because one has destroyed one's own happiness and in the end helped the fatherland very little or not at all, now would that be rational? In this struggle between rationality and the heart, I think the latter won out in the end . . ."

He had embarked upon the trip with an air of confidence. He was "almost envious of the fish-blooded Dutchman and the certainty with which he believed in his coming good fortune. But where a Dutchman can hope, a Swabian can too!" The days just before the landing betray a suppressed uneasiness: "I am curious as to how far I will get with my recommendations, whether I may really have to start from the bottom after all. It could set me back years if I were to have to start work as a waiter or a baker's assistant. We've laughed about the prospect many times, but when one is faced with it, it is not quite so funny, and laughter won't get you very far. But I always believe that my luck will not desert me, and even if things do not go smoothly, I just keep at it, whatever happens. Perhaps it is better if I have to suffer a bit; that way I think one more quickly becomes what the Americans call 'smart.' " The next day there was a stolid pep talk: "I want to do whatever it takes to get ahead, and it would be extraordinary if I could not hack my way through in a land where so many have made something of themselves without ever once having good intentions, and I will certainly not be lacking in those."

On the first few pages of the little book, which discuss encounters with departing and returning ships, is a modest sentence imbued with a deeper meaning: "It is nice to outdistance others." The new arrival was not able to get much taste of this in the New World, and he never did become what the Americans call "smart." But things did not begin altogether badly. Before Bosch departed, Professor Dietrich had sent him to Munich, where an engineer by the name of Wilhelm Seubel, who was at the time outfitting the town theater with electrical lighting under contract with the Edison Corporation from America, was to advise him. He put a few letters of recommendation in Bosch's pocket, and one of them helped Bosch rapidly allay any fears of having to start out as a waiter. The Fates did not intend any such romantic flourish in Bosch's life. The letter was addressed to Sigmund Bergmann, who, after Wilhelm Fein and Sigmund Schuckert, was the third pioneer in the young field of electrical engineering that Bosch encountered. With a salary of eight dollars a week, he commenced work in America as an engineer.

Sigmund Bergmann, ten years older than his new employee, was already a success. A locksmith by trade, he had left his home in Thuringen in 1869 and had found work in Brooklyn as an engineer. The workshop manufactured ticker-tape machines, and it was there that he was discovered by Thomas Alva Edison, whose youthful inventive genius was just beginning to develop in a more systematic and industrial direction. Edison could use responsible and clever people, young people like himself for whom no task was too great if it meant tackling a new invention and successfully completing it. The Germans seemed especially well suited for this. Working for him in his factory in Newark he already had Krüsi, a Swiss German, and Schuckert, from Nuremberg. Bergmann was the third member of his staff of closest assistants.

They were all young people who experimented and puttered about in his factory in the early 1870s. Edison, their leader, born in 1847, was already going beyond his improvements in telegraphy, en route to new areas in electrical engineering. He had made preliminary studies for the phonograph and was already in the process of revolutionizing lighting with the incandescent filament bulb. Bergmann formed his own small-scale workshop in 1876 on friendly terms with Edison. In 1880, he expanded the business, with Edison supporting him as a silent partner. After the sensational success of the incandescent lightbulb introduced a new era of lighting technology, the business grew rapidly. Bergmann became the most important designer and producer of accessories, switches, fuses, shunts, and so forth. It is well known that Bergmann, perhaps influenced by Schuckert's example, began to sever his American connections in the early 1890s and founded a new business in Germany. It blossomed rapidly and quickly went beyond its first specialty, the insulating tube (already invented in America), to the building of engines. When Bosch arrived at Bergmann's in 1884, they made Hughes recorders and telephones, arc lamps and lighting fixtures, gramophones and telethermometers—in short, everything that was in demand.

In retrospect, Bosch did not have a very high opinion of his own work, and it seemed to him that he had missed the chance to acquaint himself with important things present in America, from grinding machines to cylindrical grinders; at the time, he had been oblivious to how important they would one day be to him: "I have to say that I didn't approach matters of business with the seriousness they deserved. At any rate, I learned very little that could help my career, outside of what I picked up by being an engineer. It wasn't pleasure in my work and career that made me work. Looking back, I get the feeling that as an engineer I was never much more than average."

This sort of matter-of-fact attitude and skeptical opinion of his work capacity in his younger years surfaces repeatedly. He qualifies it by saying that in the end he must not have been so very average, because ultimately he was well liked everywhere. This was not exactly the case with Bergmann's foreman. When there was a lull in the work, Bosch found himself among the first to be thrown out in the street. This had been preceded by a one-man campaign for higher pay. He recollected later, "In Germany, I would have walked away from the job before it would ever have occurred to me to help myself in such a way." It happened like this: When word got out that a large order of Hughes type-printing telegraphs had arrived, Bosch arranged for a friend from his apprentice days in Ulm to get a job with Bergmann, who paid his friend two dollars a day. Bosch himself was not getting more than eight dollars a week because the foreman wasn't allowing him to advance. So Bosch approached Bergmann on his own, and Bergmann agreed to a raise of one dollar. Bosch was to inform the bookkeeper, to whom he instead unabashedly related the news of a two-dollar raise. "The next day they came to my work station together. Bergmann looked at my work and in departing said, 'Well, give it to him.' I had already adjusted quite well."

The same coworker from Ulm had been a fellow apprentice and, as he was an orphan, had often spent time with the Bosch family. Now Bosch latched on to him. "Leonhard Köpf had always been a model engineer, in my eyes. I probably had a better overview of the whole. Köpf was an extraordinarily clever and order-loving man who was extremely hard-working and also became successful later on back home." But their temperaments were clearly very different. Köpf was not made of the same stern stuff, and was not much concerned with the general interests that began to fascinate Bosch more and more. Nonetheless, there was an element of home and youth in the human contact, which gave them both an anchor against the Americanism that surrounded them; their Swabian suspiciousness prevented them from being caught unawares by it.

While he was employed at Bergmann's, Bosch also encountered Edison on several occasions. He relates the following anecdote in his recollections from 1921: "One day a tall, thin man in a blue-and-white-striped smock rushed into the workshop. He rushed over to one of the motors and got oil all over his hands, just in time to greet a few gentlemen of whom it was said that they were to be worked on to purchase shares in the company. Otherwise Edison never dirtied his hands with oil at our workshop. His experimental workshops were not in New York, but in Menlo Park, New Jersey, where he later received the younger Rathenau and my brother-in-law Kayser, and tried to sell them on his magnetic ore separator patents. When I told Kayser about my earlier observations, he said that now several things had become clear to him." These few sentences, with their ironic twist, were not Bosch's last words about Edison. Ten years later, in 1931, he granted him an obituary that was a veritable homage full of a kind of emotion that was highly unusual in its writer: "You have to think back to the way people felt in those early days, sixty years ago, and imagine this country, with its unimaginable developmental potential, if you want to understand how a man like Edison could develop, and could create and produce with such Leonardic abundance. Edison's life was not only wonderful and worth living because he grew old enough to see the fruits of his life's work mature, but also because he had the good fortune to live in a time when science and technology created the tools with which he was able to accomplish something as great as only the greatest of men have managed to achieve." The paragraph gives an overview of Edison's work and experiments, the successful ones and the ingenious but problematic ones, and continues: "When I worked at the Edison firm in New York almost 47 years ago, my coworkers told me of Edison's incredible capacity for work. When he was absorbed with a problem he threw himself into its solution completely. He could stay in the workshop for days; his bed was a few wool blankets on the floor. Edison was the quintessential and best kind of American. Never was personal gain the motivation behind his indefatigable industry. It was the creative spirit of a titan!"

Bosch's stay in America brought him into his first close contact with the organized labor movement. Nothing has come down to us about it from the time he spent working in German workshops and growing factories—undoubtedly he viewed the various workplaces only as passing events, more or less, and did not seek out closer ties. One must also bear in mind, in looking at those times, that the Anti-Socialist Law went into effect in Germany at the end of 1878. It was directed against the political tendencies of the Social Democratic party and not actually against the workers' unions. But the police force did not make the distinction quite so precisely in the beginning, so that even the first modest attempts at trade unionization were either officially disbanded or fell apart on their own.

In the early years of American history, there was a colorful variety of social theories and social experiments in which quite a few Germans participated. The large, history-less country seemed better suited to be the training ground or laboratory for a wonderful future than did the Old World with its hardened social and political forms. The Christian Communist Georg Rapp from Swabia and the Welsh social reformer Robert Owen had both carried out their experiments with some success and some failure, and Magdeburg journeyman-tailor Wilhelm Weitling, who greatly influenced Bosch's philosophies, looked there for an answer to his call for justice. After 1878, radical German Socialists shifted their propaganda work to the burgeoning new area of industry. It could not be said that they were exactly warmly welcomed there. For quite some time an American workers' movement had been forming in its own right, and it did not want to have anything to do with Marxist ideology, although, at the same time, it was full of practical and tactical contradictions. Ultimately, a type of union styled mainly after the English model was established in America, and the specifically political development of groups of proletarians remained within modest limits.

In the early 1880s this was still an open question. It looked as though the Knights of Labor, founded in 1869 by Uriah Smith Stephens, a tailor in Philadelphia, might become something of a force, for the organization was growing rapidly. The Knights of Labor was created as a secret society, with Masonic rites and organization and strong bonds to secrecy. Feelings of insecurity toward employers and caution toward government officials seemed to justify this approach, just as the romanticism of its rituals may well have appeared useful as a kind of spiritual bond between the members who had been thrown together. In 1882, the group had finally gone public. Bosch contacted them. His memory of the circle, "which talked a lot about brotherhood," is colored throughout with the skepticism of an old man grown anti-Romantic. "One time," he writes, "we discussed at a meeting that there was no sense in the unemployed offering themselves for hire, only to allow employers to hire them at lower wages and fire the higher-paid workers. I made the suggestion that every employed worker should give up some portion of his earnings, so that the unemployed workers would not be reduced to such actions, but I received no support whatsoever." It is difficult to say whether the odd coloration of the circle had any other influence on him at the time. The Knights of Labor, after a rapid surge to a membership of over 700,000 in the mid-1880s, bringing the group to the top of all the workers' unions at the time, lost ground to the expanding trade unions, which had existed alongside and independent from them for a few years. What gave the Knights of Labor its very American flavor was its tendency toward temperance—brewers and similar tradesmen were excluded—its hesitancy to strike, its emphasis on arbitration, the organizational intermingling of the professions, and the radical fight against land speculation by the great railroad companies. We do not know whether the young Bosch was exposed to Henry George's 1879 book *Progress and Poverty,* which considered rent for the land to be the root and cause of all social ills. But he moved in a circle in which the effects of transportation policies on the price of land, and the creation of land monopolies, had become a foremost concern (one must bear this in mind three decades later with regard to Bosch's position on land reform within the context of building a regional transportation network).

The Knights of Labor can only be included in a limited sense under the heading of socialist movements. It is true that its program remained unclear, and its mistrust of revolutionary radicalism grew all the more vivid when in 1879 a group of exiled Germans tried to revive the movement among the American workforce. Bosch, admittedly, was not part of this group, but this was the time when he was making an effort to become clear about a better socioeconomic order. It is hard to say whether and to what extent this incipient interest was influenced by the political tradition of his family and the political atmosphere of his father's house. The theoretical head of the Swabian Democrats, Ludwig Pfau, had studied early French socialism in his years in exile and had translated the work of his countryman Pierre Proudhon. In the process, Pfau brought an unusual lack of preconceptions about issues of power and property into the generally bourgeois environment of the old Swabian democracy.

At the time, Robert Bosch was also concerned with these issues. His old apprenticeship friend, Köpf, who pursued his work diligently and found adequate security in the habits of town and church, summarily dismissed his fellow countryman as a Social Democrat. But this is exactly what Bosch was not. What was he, then? He voiced his beliefs in his letters to Anna Kayser. The correspondence, which went back and forth between New York and Obertürkheim, and which penetratingly discussed questions of religious belief and the status of women, has as much biographical and psychological weight as it has interest as a document of the period. The twenty-three-year-old's socialist credo can also be found there (April 18, 1885):

"Now I want to turn to more serious matters, and I will not stop until I have told you at least some of what you must know in order to understand me. You see, I am a Socialist. If at this time I am not able to practice all of the teachings that I adhere to, you must not take me to task, because in my present-day circumstances I would have to relinquish you and with that also the entirety of my love and happiness in life. And even if the best and most pure thing a person can do is set his own pursuits and interests aside in order to serve humanity, I am much too human and egotistical to do such a thing—so, you asked me about a way to do away with wealth and poverty. Think of it, everything, land and soil, fields and woods, money and goods, all belonging to the state, i.e., to us, the citizens, managed by elected officials, whom you must not think of as descendants of a family of bureaucrats and thus endowed with a suitable dose of clannishness, but rather as people who have just been producing shoes in some big workshop, or working as field hands. Right now it is harvest time and there is a surplus of fieldwork, certainly not to the point of threatening their health, and certainly not more than they can stand quite well, because we all have machines that lighten our work load, and the state will not ask whether their purchase is profitable from the point of view of the cost, but will ask only whether the machine saves work. And we have enough workers, because everyone must work if he wants to eat. For a certain amount of work you receive a certificate, which is valid in any state warehouse, for the equivalent of an hour's work. If, for example, I make a hat that requires six hours of work, I will receive a pair of trousers that were also worth six hours of work. Nevertheless, you must not take this literally, because working in a large hat factory I obviously do not make a hat from start to finish, but perform only one particular part of the process of making many hats. It is difficult to try to put oneself thoroughly in that frame of mind, because one applies the standards of the present. Also, no one can yet say how the details would be best worked out, one can only establish a general plan and let the rest develop later. For example, it has been statistically determined that two to three hours a day of work per person, i.e., men and women, would be sufficient, and with the further development of machines it would be even less. Money in its current form can no longer be allowed to exist, and with that also no accumulation of capital, and, as a result of that no bribery, no robbery, no theft, etc . . . No person will have reason to do a disservice to another person, for our current means of winning power is money, and without it no one can hire others to be productive, that is, to do their work for them. The most capable person will be put on top, and clearly only the most capable, because he alone offers people an advantage. (Here in America they also elect their president, however the best man does not usually win, but rather the person who pays the most.) If our official breaks the law, he will be removed immediately, but actually he will have no reason to break the law, because he cannot grow rich by it or save up money to live on afterward. If he were removed today, tomorrow he would have to work somewhere else again. But note that even the most powerful leader is also a worker.

"Everyone must work as long as he is capable of it. If he becomes ill, the state cares for him. Nutritional problems and hunger will plague no one, because so much is always grown that everyone has plenty, and since everything will be international, Europe will help America, and America, Asia, and so on. You must admit that it is no injustice for a worker to work toward the socialist state. If you consider that, though our fellow humans did not invent machines only for those people who can afford them, and that every day technology grows more advanced, still more and more people go hungry, it is impossible to fathom how someone can resist the idea there must be a fundamental change. Shall the person who has no money starve?"

And after a quote from Heine's verse to the effect that only those who have, have the right to live, Bosch's protestations turn back to the lesson at hand. "If I wrote above that everyone will have to work every day, it is not to be taken literally, because supposing I want to take a trip for my enjoyment, I will simply work longer beforehand, until I think I have the necessary number of hour-checks, and then cheerfully proceed on my journey with my money. I will never save, because if I become ill tomorrow, the state is there.

"Until now I have only spoken of material things. When we begin to talk about ideals, then we definitely have the advantage. Think of it, one person as good as the next, i.e., externally, because naturally internally there will always be some difference. No man will be able to distinguish himself unless he does it in a fashion that benefits his fellow man. Petty and mean passions will be sharply reduced. But that is enough for today, because you will not be able to understand everything so easily. It took a long time before it became clear to me. Only one more note—perhaps it will give you some predilection for socialism. If we had a socialist state, nothing could keep us apart, but now if I am unfortunate, well—but that cannot happen. Just think, though, that could happen to someone, and are not circumstances in which good people are unfortunate through no fault of their own to be remedied at all costs?"

The long letter then turns to religious and family matters, but it comes back to socialism again at the end, and Bosch asks his bride not to immediately assume that he is incorrect, for this is something that one cannot simply explain in a few pages: "Socialism is something great and noble. To explain and justify it thoroughly and exhaustively would require volumes, which do exist but are banned by our government and as a result are not easy to obtain. If you cannot warm to it right away, then reserve your judgment, and just think that I haven't taught you well. I will clarify it all for you orally. Don't say anything to anyone, except Eugen, of course, because you might easily run the risk of having to defend me against unjustified attacks, and if one does not know something well it is difficult to defend."

These explanations, with their peculiar mixture of sober instruction and cautious but serious and impassioned pleas comprise the earliest surviving document that attests to Bosch's internal debate on the problems of society. The debate will often repeat itself, and, with experience, maturity, and responsibility, will undergo some transformations. But two elements of tension can already be sensed in this conversation of a lifetime. The development of technology is intended to make people's lives more bearable, and for him this generally meant shortening the workday. His utopian comment that "it has been statistically determined" that a two- to three-hour workday would suffice would be reflected in an essay that Bosch would write when he was much older (in March 1932), in which he wanted to discover the cure for worldwide economic crisis. The other noticeable element is his realistic sense of fairness, which not only accepts but also recognizes a socialist struggle of workers that results from the conditions of their existence.

This socialist system, which allows cash to disappear, and, as the letter explains, substitutes certificates for a quantity of work, with which one can buy the equivalent in state warehouses, is the creation of Wilhelm Weitling. One cannot necessarily assume that his *Guarantee of Har-*

mony and Freedom, or *Poor Sinner's Gospel,* fell into Bosch's hands, because these works of the 1840s were, like their creator, either almost forgotten or in the process of being rediscovered as curiosities of literary and intellectual history. Yet one cannot overlook the fact that Weitling lived in New York from 1851 until his death in 1871. In the beginning, he was rather influential, since he published *The Worker's Republic,* which was not without its appeal. Later he became resigned to the failure of the Socialist movement and abandoned his political and social calling for the practice of astronomy. Yet Weitling evidently knew how to be effective, and how to transform the warring realities of today into the happy certainty of tomorrow in a wonderfully simplified way. He gathered a solid circle of believers around him, and when his legacy began to dry up, his followers kept it flowing in narrow streams. This is probably the way Bosch heard about it. It is rather touching that Weitling's view of the world, with its poetic jumble of romanticism and rationalism, which has been sneeringly and jokingly dubbed "errand-boy socialism," found this belated follower.

Young Anna Kayser in Obertürkheim read Bosch's explanations with the greatest of interest, albeit with a reasonable skepticism about whether one could apply such general rules to human nature. Nonetheless, on one occasion after she had heard a lecture on the social structure of the Aztec civilization, she reported on it—wasn't it something like a socialist order despite its system of sharp social divisions? The fact that their future son-in-law declared himself a socialist—something which spoke for him, in his eyes—caused some consternation in the Kayser household. Robert Bosch's brother Karl was given the task of allaying Anna's mother's fears. "He has a way with older women," Bosch wrote to his future bride, "and hopefully he will be successful." In a letter dated April 6, 1896, he wrote, "At the time in New York, I once considered that if you did not love me I might devote myself to the cause. Under the circumstances, if I had done so it would have been quite dangerous for me . . ." The cause remained a mere interlude, with all its insistent discussions and plans, but it does shed some light on the young man's spiritual state.

The democrat's son had come to North America with all sorts of illusions. It is not clear whether his trip was intended as an extended apprenticeship or as a longer venture. Bosch remained for a year. In retrospect, he does not make clear whether his return was precipitated more by his engagement to Anna Kayser, which had taken place by letter, or by the persistent business crisis as the country continued to feel the backlash of the long-lasting depression of the 1870s. "I have been unemployed since April 27 and I will probably not find any more work here . . . Of the nearly thirty engineers I know, some ten are out of work," he reported on May 5, 1885. On May 13, the Lloyd Steamer left Hoboken. It did not take him directly to Germany, however, but to London. His *Life Recollections* include the following summary statement about America: "But as a person of enthusiasm and ideals, I didn't like the country, which lacked the cornerstone of justice: equality before the law. I once wrote that to my brother Karl." Later, Bosch occasionally visited America and had very personal experiences with the law and jurisprudence of the country. He clung very tightly to the impressions of his youth and was forced to learn to find a new perspective for the country's later great accomplishments.

6

———

WAY STATIONS

Bosch's stay in England, which lasted from May to December 1885, and where, after some searching, he found a position manufacturing instruments with Siemens Brothers, merits only one sentence in his *Life Recollections:* "There I found a system of production that, in contrast to New York, was set up according to the German system, but that was very old-fashioned in every way."

His letters indicate that he soon felt at ease in the new environment. "I like London very much," he wrote. "It has very pretty parks with wonderful spring-green chestnut trees. The contrast between England and America is extraordinarily great in every respect, and even if I couldn't agree with the Englishman yesterday who maintained that England was the best country in the world, I do think I could really like it here." His English was praised; he related that he spoke "pretty fairly" and was "naturally quite proud" of it. He was in generally good spirits, and mentioned that he thought the English surpassed even the Germans in their drinking. Though there was no lack of Germans in the city, he cheerfully quoted the saying "There are still a damned lot of Englishmen in London!" His friend Eugen Kayser soon became one of the Germans living in London. But the old cheerful harmony from the time when they had been soldiers together had begun to show signs of strain. Bosch had the impression that his friend did not want to put his knowledge to work; in the letters that went back and forth to Obertürkheim, his friend and future brother-in-law appeared as a sort of problem child. Although Bosch had defended him against his family's grumbling, now that they were together he was disturbed by his friend's lack of determination in pursuing a career: "In 'student-ese' we would call it 'loafing' or 'foolishness.' At the same time he thinks he is a capital fellow . . ." (November 8, 1885). There were discussions about a plan to start a business together, an electrical factory in which Kayser would be the designer. But Kayser himself realized that such a venture would "carry the seeds of its own death within it, because we did not have the necessary capital or experience." It was precisely this, the fact that Kayser did not make the effort to try to gain experience, that Bosch criticized his friend for, commenting that "It would hardly occur to me to start something with him in which he has no experience." Bosch thought he himself knew enough about the manufacture of telegraphs, which was what Kayser had in mind. His own money would suffice, and it would be cheaper to hire a stranger than a friend to do the design work. Their discussions were very open and frank: "Yesterday we discussed all each other's faults, which is the privilege of friendship, and naturally he knew his own quite well." But during these conversations the plan they made in London, and which Anna Kayser would very much have liked to see become reality, fell apart. She herself sensed where the more disciplined goal-setting energy was coming from.

Bosch was satisfied with his work and wages at Siemens Brothers: "Right now I have to work 12 hours a day, since there is a rush, and 10½ hours on Saturdays. My salary for 54 hours is 36 shillings, but at the moment it is 45 shillings. I can get along quite well on that. I am living with a colleague, actually more in the country, which I like" (June 8, 1885). Because of the piecework, there were extra earnings; his weekly expenses were twenty-five to thirty marks. His original plan had been to stay for a year, but after Eugen Kayser concluded his fleeting, unproductive visit to England in December, Bosch suddenly felt lonely, even though "he had had him around long enough." He was expected in Obertürkheim, and so he quickly gave up his "asinine insistence" on his resolution to remain another three months and went home at Christmas.

From this point on, he was occupied with the question of his final choice of a career; he wanted to settle down and raise a family. Bosch had spent more than a year and a half abroad, and he had had his fill of it. "It is certain that I would only settle in America if I couldn't do it in Europe, or better, Germany," he had written in June, just after he had arrived in London. Now he had to learn the lay of the land. It was not like him to begin his search in Ulm, sitting around his mother's house. He found a position in Magdeburg. The people there asked for "recommendations from firms where I had mounted lighting fixtures on my own," which he could not provide, but he made it "as plausible as possible that they could find no one better suited for their purposes, a fact of which I am convinced myself, by the way" (March 4, 1886). The firm mainly produced gas motors, tachometers, and speedometers, which were quite popular, but it also accepted orders for electrical engineering, and Bosch's first position of responsibility would be to install, with an assistant, electrical lighting in the Gerlobogk sugar refinery in Anhalt, which he accomplished to everyone's satisfaction. At the time, it looked as though he would choose this as his specialty and become an inventor in his own right: he constructed two variations on an arc lamp regulator and submitted them for patent approval.

Eugen Kayser, who visited Bosch that summer, helped him finish the drawings (the documents describing this particular invention are no longer available). The central patent office requested more specific details, since the solution that Bosch suggested was very similar to the ideas of an American. Nothing came of the whole matter, or at least Bosch did not pursue it any further. His reports to Anna Kayser, which contain the information about it, indicate, without much ado, that he hoped this work would help him eventually get started in his own business.

Until that time, Bosch had never been in northern Germany. He did not lack the common prejudices of his Swabian countrymen, and for the most part, he found these prejudices to be confirmed at work. The impression he got of the relations among the boss, engineers, masters, and workers was so deeply engraved in his mind that he wrote a memorandum about it decades later. His individual experience was subsumed under a more general judgment ("a manner that is not infrequently found in the north, and elsewhere"). What happened was that a master requested him to supervise the behavior of one of the engineers and then report to him about it. Bosch turned down this "alliance," as he called it, only to find out later in an argument with his boss that the latter was not ill-disposed to such things, since in this way he learned everything. In this atmosphere of mutual spying and minimal openness, Bosch felt so uncomfortable that he gave notice in the early fall, although the company would have liked to keep him on as a member of their workforce.

But Bosch had set his sights on the future and on independence. As he said to his boss in parting, his future business should bring in at least 3,000 marks a year. "That will take you a long time," was his boss's response. There was still a bit of uncertainty in Bosch's plans for that summer. Should he attempt to make a go of it alone? He had given up the notion of working with Eugen Kayser, but one of the engineers in Magdeburg suggested that they become partners. He was a wool advocate, and his adherence to Gustav Jäger brought them closer together. Bosch's apprenticeship friend from Ulm, Leonhard Köpf, had returned from America and was trying to convince him to go with him to Furtwangen. The Black Forest watch industry would certainly provide plenty of work for electronic installations. The landscape was alluring, but wouldn't the loneliness be too much of a burden on his wife if he had to go off doing installations? His brothers stepped in with advice and encouragement. Albert, who at the time was working on the construction of the church in Öhring, had come to the conclusion that Heilbronn was just the place for a new business. Karl had discovered a position in Cologne which in his opinion was full of potential, although perhaps it should only be an intermediate step. In any case, he warned Robert to "think about it three times over, before you associate yourself with someone, no matter how favorable things may seem." He knew something about this, because his far-reaching activity did not find a sympathetic echo in his brother-in-law and partner. For a while, Robert Bosch was greatly tempted by Cologne, with his brother and two sisters living there; at the same time, he was slightly concerned about his ability to develop freely there, when he remembered, as he had once written, "what wonderful letters of comfort and encouragement my brother Karl bombarded me with. Brothers are great at patronizing, particularly once they have become success-ful . . ." His feelings toward his family were a mixture of defensiveness and gratitude.

On July 4, 1886, he wrote to his fiancée: "Recently I have been think-ing more often about the idea of establishing myself in Stuttgart, and I cannot actually see any reason why I should not do it. Stuttgart does not have as much industry as Cologne, but as a matter of fact that will prob-ably be irrelevant to me, because for the most part I will have to send most of my products out . . ." A few days later, he writes: "My business will probably one day be carried out by the firm 'R.B., Mechanical Work-shop, Specialty Electrical Items.' And if it should get big, it can be called a factory. I do not intend to have any stores. I am quite glad to be able to do without them, for then I will be less tied down."

7

———◆———

FIGURE OF A
YOUNG MAN

There is a portrait of young Robert Bosch that clearly illustrates the fundamental inclinations of his nature: candor and defiance. The brow is high and proud, the nose aquiline, the mouth and chin vigorous. The dark eyes have a steady gaze—they will later take on a sharply searching and slightly mistrustful expression, sparkling with anger or beaming mildly with relaxed amusement. But there is still a long time before age will mellow him. The young man in the picture is not naive. One can hardly tell that below the surface lie feelings of, or the longing for, happiness, mirth, or earthy humor. The mouth does not yet betray a trace of sarcasm. Bosch's dark hair is somewhat unruly, and one stubborn lock refuses to be ignored.

His proud head rests on a slim, athletic body, more delicate than robust. No sooner did he hear about it than the avid gymnast took up snowshoeing, and he could often be seen as one of the first to astonish bystanders in the Swabian highlands or the hills around Stuttgart—in his mid-eighties! But he was never a sportsman. In his younger years he did not have the time to devote himself to such activities, and although he was ambitious, he never coveted the honors that were bestowed or recognized by others. But in the years he spent among strangers in strange lands he had learned to set expectations for himself that went beyond childlike games. He was very much aware of the defects in his education and his theoretical preparation. It comes through in his letters from that time: "I would have liked to have studied and at the same time have had a practical career, but the two things cannot be combined . . . Whether I will be equally well off with my half year of studying remains to be seen" (December 9, 1885). He set his own standards for what he wanted to achieve, and he set them high. His ambition grew into a sense of pride in his accomplishments, a quality he possessed instinctively and that awakened in him as he began to develop and assume growing responsibility, forming a combination of rational and ethical purposefulness and fundamental perceptions, the unified basis of his self-confident, mature character.

In looking at the symmetry of Bosch's young face, one senses the tensions that would accompany, and occasionally oppress and threaten, the rhythm of the years that followed. He was very much aware of the fundamentally contradictory elements of his being—if he wanted to highlight them, he would occasionally indulge in self-mocking irony—but what is more essential and characteristic is the argumentative scrutiny, the logical method he employed even in his observations of himself. This habit of observation continued to be one of the rules of his self-discipline. Although he was a very active person, Bosch possessed a tendency, even a need, for reflection, the origins of which are unclear. The writings of his later years—a bit unsystematic, it is true, but always to the point—are filled with it: some explanation here, a little justification there, and occasionally an outpouring of accumulated emotion or directives born of a restrained maturity. His letters to Anna Kayser make a statement about how he saw himself and how he wanted to be seen by his future wife. He had gained her consent to marry by letter, but now he was concerned as to whether she had the right knowledge about him. At times these discussions seem like studies for a self-portrait, varying with the mood of the moment and sometimes cheerful, sometimes serious, here with a flair for coquetry, there with a pedagogical emphasis that tries cautiously to convince.

Here, above all, are the temperament, the brusqueness, the self-confidence: "It is true that I am not overly humble or respectful even toward quite elderly people. I have a rather fresh mouth, as all of us in the Bosch family do. The others only have more reason for it, perhaps, than I do as the youngest" (April 18, 1885). "You think that it is conceited of me to say that I am the most respected of all my siblings. Yes, dear, unfortunately I am conceited, and I know it quite well. I think, though, that I am better than I used to be, unless I am flattering myself again. In any case, what I mean to say is more that I am the one who is on the best terms with everyone, and there is really nothing about that that would be worth boasting about, at best I can be pleased about it. One of my worst faults is that I am hot-tempered, but I immediately regret it, and have at least gotten to the point where I ask forgiveness if I have done something wrong. I do not think that I am stubborn in the usual sense of the word. I give in readily if someone convinces me that he has a better answer. One thing that seems to be dwindling in me is my taste for making a ruckus and causing scandals, and I do not know whether that is good or bad. At times I can sit for hours without saying a word, and yet I enjoy singing if I am in the right company, but then I can act quite differently in other circumstances. It makes me feel rather old sometimes. Earlier I was always the big-mouth, but now I almost have to be persuaded to speak" (July 7, 1885). A year later, he provides a further variation on this theme after finding his own behavior decidedly rough: "On the one hand, my brusqueness—to my mind, criticizing where I have no right to is a form of brusqueness—comes from the thought or intention of saying what I think, or in other words, of fighting against conventional lying, and it is justified as long it does not become rude" (July 8, 1886). Anna would discover that "it is not at all difficult for me to ask for forgiveness when I have done something wrong."

When his bride tried to please him by writing to him about the impression he had made on one relative, that he looked like he was "clean-scrubbed, inside and out," she promptly received the request that she "never again tell me about a good opinion of me." She should, however, let him know about the bad ones. Until now he had had so much luck, and had received so much praise and flattery, that he had gotten into the habit of letting people he did not think well of feel it without a second thought, and being short with those he was indifferent to, so that it was "not good" for him to hear too many good things about himself. She was welcome to express criticism, just or unjust, so that he could act accordingly, "but if you hear something positive, it is all well and good, I do not need to know about it, since I do not need to change" (November 9, 1886). In these casual sentences there is a great deal of the older Bosch, who easily grew nervous and cross when he was praised, and, if he suspected any such thing, for the most part left the offending document unread.

He did not have any illusions about his temperament, and if he had been reminded of these youthful protestations when he was an old man, he would have noted that the improvement he saw then had been approximate at best. But how did he see the basic structure of his being? "I have often asked myself what I actually am, and I am not yet quite clear about the answer. Recently I actually wanted to study my characteristics through phrenology, in order to settle it, but nothing came of it. It is very difficult to get to know oneself, and yet it would be so good and advantageous if one could say why one acted or thought a certain way. I think very definitely about certain things, and very realistically about others, and I have no objections to plain talk with dinner. But in other respects I am the exact opposite . . . I am not clear, however, whether I have acted with self-confidence, in my realistic manner of thinking, or simply idealistically like a man in love . . . You will forgive me if I talk about myself so much, and not think it is conceitedness. I do not want to be conceited, because then all my self-confidence would be weakened by my conceit, and then I might be a conceited idealist and I do not want to be that. Even less good would come of that than if I were a materialist of the first water . . ." (December 9, 1885).

But his tone was not always so self-assured: "With all my self-confidence and with all the praise I have received, I am still always weighed down by one thought, and that is, what if I were not what I appear to be, if I were not capable of securing a position that would allow me to bind you to me, if misfortune were to befall me later on. Tears come to my eyes too easily, too, Anna, but in this case I will not be ashamed of them." Bosch once said of his father that he had had a rather soft character but had not wanted to admit it. Certainly his son was cut from stouter cloth, but he had inherited one thing, namely, the habit of hiding his weaker impulses. These impulses are only rarely voiced in his letters and then only when amid his own feelings of happiness he becomes aware of the helpless suffering of others. Then there is genuine and immediate emotional power. The idea of encouraging sentimentality was foreign to his nature. There is an amusing entry to that effect in his journal from his return trip from America: "Lovely on deck this evening. Wanted to feel sentimental. Sang: 'Down Below by the Millstone.' Did not work, led right into: 'In My Stein at the Green Wreath Inn.' Voice is all wrong for sentimental stuff."

In this vein of self-portraiture that runs throughout the letters of his youth, the greatest number of pages, after the professions of belief in socialism (and sometimes intermingled with them), is given over to religious themes. This was in part because of Anna's opposition, an opposition that she defended and that he both anticipated and respected. There are pages and pages of religious discussions between the two young people, who had experienced different family atmospheres and who maintained their own beliefs as they sought to define their positions, but at the same time to recognize, respect, and preserve the beliefs of the other. "It is a matter of great importance," he starts out right away in his first letter (March 21, 1885), because Anna has said that without complete mutual understanding she could not imagine a happy life together. His lapidary words follow, "The high point of my religion is summed up by the motto 'Be just.' My God is humanity, or rather the entire universe. If I insult one of my fellow men in any way, then I have sinned. I deny the criticism that I am robbing the poor of their God, or of the punishment of sins and the reward of the afterlife. The greatest injustice in the world is that there are rich and poor. Every person who is born is entitled to all the fruits of this earth by virtue of that fact alone, whether it be the child of a beggar or a millionaire. By claiming that I want to take away the poor man's only comfort, the ones who make the criticism prove that it is invalid, because they imply that the rich need no comfort to be happy in this world."

Anna Kayser's objections led Bosch to take up this theme again and again, and to present his arguments with new embellishments. "The Christian faith is just as much a religion of the wealthy as any pagan religion," he wrote. "If this falls away, the entire situation has to change. The religion of true, practical—not just sermonized—charity is socialism. Forgiveness of sins is nonsense, one must be responsible for what one does. The forgiveness of sins creates criminals, c.f. Italy with all its murderers and so forth. Besides, assuming we have a personal God, who is better—the person who begins to doubt the rightness of our social order out of a certain striving for justice, and who no longer believes in God, but is accountable only to his conscience, and takes his human frailties to heart and attempts to make up for them, or the person who in all his good faith allows himself to be forgiven for his errors, because he never has second thoughts about such things? Must not God more readily forgive the one who has doubts (the nonbeliever, only because he made the mistake of reflecting)? There is no system at all in the entire Christian faith, which says 'Belief alone makes blessed.' . . . A rich man, if he has no conscience and no charity, can believe whatever he wants and feel satisfied, but it is greatly to his advantage to allow the poor their faith in God; that is why the higher up on the ladder, the more you are tied to the Church, and once again: our religions benefit the privileged . . . admittedly it is also psychologically preferable to suffer injustice than to commit it. There is a third choice, however, more practical and noble than either of the other two, and that is: courageously and actively to prevent injustice from occurring. In our beloved country they have usually taken away the cross, only to replace it with the gallows. As bad as that is, it seems an improvement. The cross is to the gallows what a monk is to a soldier: the first are the instruments and the second the henchmen of the spiritual and secular despots" (July 10, 1885).

The vehemence of his vivid imagery, which forms the high point of the letter, sounds like an echo from contemporary pamphlets. Wilhelm Weitling had also carried on his discourse on the Church and Christianity at the level of antithetical ethics. But Bosch's basic position had not yet been influenced by outside forces. He seems scarcely to have been exposed to, or concerned with, the philosophical materialism of the popular school of natural science, for example. Nor is there any later indication of leanings in this direction. The crucial thing is his unusual striving for freedom from all obligations, for he felt that all religion is obligation and the consciousness of being obligated. He had an intrinsic drive for freedom, very much directed at the present, which saw things that were the result of historical conditions as no more than a part of past history. His was a wakeful mistrust; he was always prepared to attack or oppose the world of traditional forms and laws, easily regarded as mere convention and thus requiring a rational critique. The letters discuss the organization of the Christian doctrine with a lively interchange of logical objections. Why does the God of love permit his creations to misuse each other so? Why does he require "such complicated teachings, for his followers to be able to sustain their belief in him?" And Jesus? "Jesus Christ was a talented man, one of the noblest men who ever lived, but now he is six feet under. He died for his convictions, and whether these convictions were identical with the ones that are taught today, or different, is irrelevant" (April 18, 1885). In another observation he has Christ, if he returns, cast the money changers out of the temple once again, because they ("the priests, the usurers, and the rest of their sanctimonious lot") have created the Christian religion the way they wanted it to be. "To them I say: why should Christ necessarily have hit upon the right thing? And besides, what comes directly from him; do you really believe he was the son of God? And therefore he would have to know what is right and wrong? Then why did he only preach? And not write it all down right away? Why did he allow his apostles to elaborate on the whole doctrine at their own discretion?"

Anna Kayser maintained her opposition in the face of this torrent of questions and arguments; indeed, her initial wavering gradually changed to greater steadfastness. She herself, as she wrote, tended "toward rather liberal views," but thought that "it is not right of me," and found it terribly difficult "to return to my old way of thinking, which, if I look closely, I realize I have ultimately abandoned out of convenience. It is very difficult to live this way, but I can see that a woman with such modern ideas cannot survive in this world." Has our religion not stood the test for many years? But belief and reason do not coincide: "I am lacking in inner tranquillity; I am not at one with myself . . . And if I were to succeed in returning to our religion, I am tortured by the thought that we would no longer agree in our thinking. But is it not true, dearest, if we each try to do our duty we will be one in deed?" (March 25, 1883). To Bosch's questions about the idea of eternal life and belief in God she responds very movingly: "Do you think, then, that God takes pleasure in it [that human beings mistreat each other]? He could not create machines, because if it were taken for granted that people had to be good, then there would be no particular virtue in it. This way man has the freedom to choose between right and wrong. But mankind is not perfect, and unfortunately often chooses the wrong thing . . ." (April 6, 1885). Anna's concern that their different positions on religion might harm their relationship is refuted by Bosch: "I do not hold it against you that you cannot agree to my godless ideas; on the contrary, it would not seem at all right to me if you were to let me persuade you. That is precisely what I meant, you should have your own opinions . . ." (May 27, 1885). What mattered to him was to make everything clear from the beginning, but precisely in this area he wanted to respect boundaries. The following sentence sounds somewhat banal at first, but in the end it goes right to the heart of Bosch's independent consciousness: "I allow the Jews, the Turks and the Buddhists to remain faithful to their God or gods; as long as they are good people, I love them. For myself, I hope to go through life as peacefully as they, and perhaps to know more precisely what to do in specific situations, because I must come to terms only with my conscience" (April 18, 1885).

This ethical rigor forms the center and foundation of his religious life, if one may speak of it as such. Perhaps the word puritanism can be applied, without its religious connotations, to suggest the consequences that follow from this basic predisposition. His nature, which was focused more on his present occupation, on earthly fulfillment and satisfaction, could not have been conscious of the fact that he lacked the capacity for transcendence and a sense of the power of history. Later, he would listen closely and with slightly dubious surprise to the opinion that in his position, in his personal and public life, he had achieved a very personal form of secularized Christianity.

The portrayal of these youthful discussions of religion is necessary in order to show the passionate seriousness with which Bosch defended his position of separation from the Church and Christianity. Not until much later, in 1908, did Bosch follow through with the outward consequences of his position and sever his traditional ties by leaving the Church. However, he found no contradiction in supporting Christian and church organizations, to the extent that he liked their representatives personally or approved of the goals of their work.

The spiritual individualist, at his own risk, aware of his masterful internal strength and liberated from all dogmatic beliefs, also had a very dim opinion of creating new conventions and dogmas based on the opposite assumptions, much less joining them. A telling anecdote from his later years relates that when he, who was estranged from the Church, was asked to join and support the Atheist Association, he asked the question: "But are you really certain, then, that God does *not* exist?"

The bewildered canvassers responded with embarrassed silence. They were dismissed with, "Well then."

PART II

BEGINNINGS AND GOALS

8

—•—

THE ECONOMIC
DEVELOPMENT OF
SWABIA

By 1870, Stuttgart had joined the ranks of the German metropolises. The census of 1885 produced a figure of more than 125,000 inhabitants. Construction had begun to spread beyond the valley floor and bowl, climbing the slopes and seeking a path eastward into the Neckar Valley. Big business was not well developed within the city limits, due in part to the hilly landscape, but due more to the lack of an uninhibited entrepreneurial class. As a result of the energy of bold and inventive individuals, such growth had begun to make itself felt in other parts of the country, in some of the former free imperial cities, as well as in very isolated areas. Some businesses had been founded as far back as the beginning of the century. The 1850s and 1860s had witnessed a lively development, but this only extended in a very limited way to Stuttgart itself. The town had a strong middle class of tradesmen, but the city's image was essentially stamped by the presence of the court and the government, the central bureaucracies. The life of the tradespeople was somewhat affected by the literary brilliance that had emerged in Württemberg at the end of the eighteenth century, and that had survived in Stuttgart into the middle of the nineteenth century. In printing and related trades, the great publishers, such as Cotta, and daring newspaper founders such as Hackländer and Hallberger, had captured the top positions and accompanying status for the entire southern part of Germany. For a while, it might have seemed as if the pharmaceutical and dyestuff industries would win leading positions, but the departure or merger of the firms involved turned these economic hopes into mere interludes. The building of musical instruments, especially pianos, assumed particular importance, and the long-standing tradition of carpentry grew into a furniture industry that quickly gained a more than regional market for itself. The textile industry was represented by a number of firms with important specialties. As for machine construction and metalworking, larger firms in this industry were almost entirely lacking. A few young installation businesses and handicraft workshops were just in the process of being formed.

But this view of Stuttgart as a site of industrial production, based on the statistics from the professional census of 1882, does not reflect the actual significance of the city as the capital of a business activity that was just beginning to stretch its limbs. For several decades, Württemberg had been developing busily. It had found its way from times of severe need back to an optimistic and active sense of itself, and was struggling—evidently flying in the face of all calculations based on rational theories about industrial location—to make the connection with capitalist industrialism, which was then fatefully entering and beginning to dominate the world. This industrialism, in its early years, lived almost entirely on steam power and drew its nourishment from iron and coal. What could it possibly mean for a region that had no coal and only a little iron; that had only one large river cutting through its heartland, which was navigable for only a short distance thereafter; that consisted of a maze of mountains and valleys and could only be opened up to traffic at great expense? Ruin at the hands of more powerful competition would be the outcome. The competition was threatening and, above all, endangered the spinning and weaving of linen, which was carried out throughout the area, often as a cottage industry on the small peasant farms. From England and Belgium, but also from Saxony and the Rhineland, came cheap textiles produced by the new machines. Labor power was being set free, but there was no work available for it to do—cottage industry, which continued to limp along, had to be satisfied with sadly reduced proceeds.

What was left but emigration, which had already relieved the population pressure a few times previously during periods of poverty?

Here the government of Württemberg intervened, and the way in which it did so represents one of the most remarkable chapters in nineteenth-century German domestic economic policy. Mercantilist thinking and the willingness to take advantage of basic liberal economic theses came together in a most remarkable fashion. King Wilhelm I, an eminently practical man, had created state organs for the improvement of economic performance shortly after assuming the throne in 1816. When the various efforts of the voluntary associations to advance the trades stalled after achieving only limited success, the monarch created the Central Bureau of Trade and Industry in 1846. The mining specialist Ferdinand Steinbeis, who had already distinguished himself as the reorganizer of the mines of Fürstenberg and Stumm, was assigned to this governmental organ as its technical adviser. In 1855, he became president of the newly created bureau. Steinbeis has been called the actual creator of the industry of Württemberg. Such a remark must naturally not be interpreted too narrowly. Even before his entry onto the scene, there existed factories of some importance. There were the fine-metal works of Gmünd and Heilbronn; there were important paper mills. On the western side of the Swabian highlands, near Ebingen, the production of wagons and measuring instruments had been flourishing for half a century in the wake of Philipp Matthäus Hahn, the pastor and mechanical inventor. Voith had already built his workshop in Heidenheim into a larger enterprise, and the Machine Factory Esslingen was assuming its leading position under Emil Kessler. In Reutlingen and its environs, Gustav Werner had begun to realize the plan—conceivable only in Württemberg—of creating a Christian factory, which at first would provide jobs for part-time workers, and later would adopt the principles of technical and economic rationalization. All of these had been only isolated beginnings. Now a united will drew them together with other scattered efforts.

The complete reversal in Steinbeis's basic political-economic stand exemplifies the change that he initiated and for which he was essentially responsible. When he assumed office in 1848, he represented Württemberg at the congress on political economy in Frankfurt that was supposed to transmit its will, in general terms, to the National Congress. At that time and in that place, Steinbeis demanded protective tariffs. He knew that in taking this position he was following in the footsteps of his fellow countryman Friedrich List, who had demanded a unified protective tariff for Germany in opposition to the more developed industrial countries until such time as the German trades would have been educated to greater productivity. Thirty years later, in 1878, when Bismarck began his policy of protective tariffs, Steinbeis took a position as one of its most vehement opponents. On this occasion, the polemics of the man, for all his air of calm superiority, were not free of passion and bitterness. How did this come about? Without benefit of the tariff that he had once desired so ardently, he had found other methods of education and now feared that the result would be endangered by a protectionist policy among the German states. The fear of foreign wares in his own territory had been replaced by the worry that the products of Württemberg, which had succeeded in breaking into the world market, would be choked off by opposition from outside. This swing of the pendulum exemplifies the historical transformation of a generation.

Steinbeis's promotion of the trades was popular pedagogy of the most magnificent sort. It recalls Christian W. Beuth, whose activities a couple of decades earlier had had a similar significance for Prussia. Steinbeis, in his more limited area, appears as the more flexible of the two. It is wonderful how he intervenes everywhere, personally giving advice. At the same time, the whole fascinating image of his activity is built on simple and lasting tenets: the state will help you if you are willing to help yourself, but the state will only help you if you also allow others to share in the product. In the process, Steinbeis approached things in a way that was completely nondoctrinaire. If foreign countries enjoyed a competitive advantage, the thing to do was to look and see how they achieved it, how they maintained it—so he studied the Belgian situation thoroughly and with insight. Naturally that situation could not be transferred to Württemberg, but there were machines in Belgium that could also run in Württemberg. Where was it written that the Irish make better linen than the Germans? Steinbeis simply hired some Irishmen as employees of the state and sent them to give courses throughout the province. He bought newfangled machines and put them in the hands of trustworthy individuals. By making regular payments to the state they could become owners themselves, but on the condition that they must show the equipment to every interested person who might also dare to make the transition to a new method of work. His keen sense of discovery led him to the places where new technical inventions were being made; he collected different models and tested ways in which they could be used. The Central Bureau gave scholarships for trips abroad, especially to visit industry fairs, and encouraged people by awarding prizes. But above all, Steinbeis brought the industry of Swabia together in a single trade association, which maintained a permanent display of samples in Stuttgart, and he insisted that Württemberg always be represented as a single unit. Within two or three decades he succeeded, thanks to good selection and presentation, in impressing not only Germany but the whole world with this conviction: Here is a business territory of rare productivity that you simply have not heard about yet!

The fact that the result may, on occasion, have seemed hasty or improvised did no harm. What was essential was that a spirit of daring confidence had arrived in the province. Honors were brought home from London, Paris, and Vienna. People were proud of Steinbeis for turning down the Legion of Honor medal offered by Napoleon III because the emperor, in order to annoy the king of Württemberg, had cancelled several medals intended for Swabian products. In the space of a quarter of a century, Swabia had acquired a sense of cosmopolitanism. It was not the same thing as the old Swabian wanderlust, which naturally did not die out, and it was different from the daring or despairing attempt to escape from a bare and miserable existence. Instead, it was a proud and self-confident awareness of the region's advancing technical abilities.

As change progressed, however, many people, including Swabian natives, were faced with a puzzling situation. In the last several centuries, the particular mission of the province had been thought to rest with its poets, philosophers, and theologians, who seemed to have been born to increase the fame of their homeland and, thus, of all Germany. Now Swabian names were turning up in the strange newfangled area of modern technology. This process does not seem so strange when viewed from a long-term historical perspective, and the ventures of Steinbeis and his colleagues would have remained nothing more than an artificial or desperate attempt to satisfy an obvious socioeconomic need if they had not reawakened old powers that slumbered within the populace. Swabians had always been hard workers, particularly in agriculture. Moreover, the division of the arable land that had resulted from the liberalization of property transfer laws had forced the inhabitants to wring whatever they could from the little scraps of fields and vineyards. Now, with the collapse of the market for "home work"—that very guildlike activity of spinning and weaving—the village workforce was seeking new employment possibilities and was increasingly willing to reach out and strive for the top. In thousands and thousands of cases, Swabians demonstrated these qualities as colonists in foreign territories, making it easier for their children to escape from peasant homes or from those trades that had been doomed to decline over the years by industrial production. It also became clear that, in addition to the virtues of hard work and a modest and economical way of life, they possessed a clear-eyed eagerness to take up their new tasks with thoroughness.

One can observe how the first successful securing of a certain branch of industry led almost organically to its expansion. The newly founded textile industry—which at first had been dependent on imports—was soon followed by the production of looms and industrial machines. Food processing created a significant supporting industry; the various means of utilizing wood for furniture and tools awakened the need for specialized new machines, which could now be satisfied within the province itself. People were innovative and inventive; demand created new needs. These supporting trades, as well as their marketable end products, applied the highest standards of human excellence to overcome Swabia's lack of coal, iron, and transportation. The ascent could not be accomplished with cheap mass-produced goods or with semifinished products produced by the trades but only with finished production and specialized services of high value; hence the economy's sensitivity to questions of trade policy.

Another remarkable aspect of the early phase of this economic development—as distinguished, for example, from the rhythm of development on the Rhine—was the relatively minor role played by finance capital. Lending institutions were naturally not completely absent as investors in industry, but the countryside, and Stuttgart, too, entered this period relatively lacking in banks, and the period of rapid industrial development after the early 1870s saw only a few brief, painfully unsuccessful attempts.

It was not until the last two decades of the century that finance capital, in its search for interest or dividends, would penetrate firms that had until then owed their growth to personal success and protective family policy. Naturally, these ventures did not live entirely on savings; the state had lent them its financial support—which as we have seen was quite limited—at the beginning. But within this geographically rather circumscribed area, what counted was the supportive power of personal credit, whether in the form of bank credit or informal private loans among a circle of acquaintances. People knew each other, they were familiar with the borrower's diligence, his way of life. This was more important, at least at that time, than research on economic cycles, market diagnoses, knowledge of specialized branches of industry, or the state of the stock market.

The Swabian character draws its essence from a tension between speculative imagination and a slightly pedantic precision when it comes to calculation. In the particular circumstances under consideration, this was now transformed into productive power serving the new industrial activity. The skill and patience in making things, the stubbornness in trying them out, the thoughtful tendency to get to the bottom of things combined with the ambitions of a few individual men who were determined, without benefit of any significant capital backing, to advance their cause ("If it should get big, it can be called a factory"). In the 1860s, such factory owners were occasionally found in mid-sized and smaller cities, and sometimes even in the countryside. They came out of handicraft production and were somewhat uncertain, at first, where their business would lead them and where they would lead it. Their adaptability allowed them to try a number of things until a saleable and often market-dominating specialty emerged.

At first, these were individuals who were themselves skilled in their specialties. They were practical, full of inventiveness, and capable of lending a hand and teaching others. But the last task had to be fraught with difficulties as the demand for workers rapidly increased. What to do? It was one of Steinbeis's profound insights that, sensing the actively expanding movement all around him in the province, and concerned about the individual people, he also knew that the encouragement of the entrepreneurial spirit must be followed by the careful training and cultivation of the workforce. Thus, adapting Belgian experience to accord with the situation at home, he became the creator of the system of continuing industrial education. For the Sunday schools that had sprung up here and there, he substituted evening classes. When he began his first attempts in the 1850s, this type of school was a novelty for Germany. With some variations, it would become the model for the general development that followed. For half a century, it was based on voluntary participation. Steinbeis did not want any use of coercion; rather he placed his trust in the ambition of the best elements of the populace. With considerable sensitivity, he devoted himself to the schedule of classes and laid the groundwork for acquiring a suitably skilled body of teachers. He gave instructions for the publishing of special textbooks and the production of teaching materials, models, model drawings, and so on, always concerned that continuing education not become merely formalistic but remain fresh and in tune with the changing, growing needs of the trades. A few trade schools devoted to particular branches of industry round out the picture of a magnificent industrial educational system. Naturally, this new education encountered many forces of stasis and inertia, but it was the start of the astonishing, rapid transformation of the productive capacity of Württemberg's economy, and its emerging industrial workforce in particular.

When Bosch returned home in 1886, Steinbeis had already been retired from his beneficial official duties for six years. He died in 1893 at the age of eighty-six, but the tradition he founded lived on. It is worth noting that with his lively eye for individuals who have it "in them," as he put it, Steinbeis played a role in the fate of a man who created a whole new field of endeavor in Württemberg's industry with his astonishing achievements, and whose growing strength would later have some importance for Robert Bosch: Gottlieb Daimler. The ambition and skill of the eighteen-year-old journeyman gunsmith from Schorndorf had caught the attention of the technical instructor at the provincial trade school where he had gone for further training. Steinbeis gave Daimler a state scholarship to the Grafenstaden factory in Strassburg and offered him advice on how to acquire the scientific knowledge that would give his practical experience a firm foundation. The Central Bureau of Trade and Industry made it possible for Daimler to attend the Polytechnic School in Stuttgart at no cost. Seldom have insight and human trust borne such immediate, thousandfold fruit.

The transformation of the economic basis of the province of Württemberg, beginning in the second half of the nineteenth century, also produced some worried observers. Conventional thinking regarded agricultural production as the essential, hereditary source of the people's nourishment. There was concern that the small territory of the province, where the good and productive land was interspersed with many much poorer tracts, was incapable of resisting the constant population pressure. Emigration was accepted as sheer fate. But then came an obvious turning point. If one considers the growth of the population to be the most noteworthy and significant historical event of the nineteenth century, then Württemberg plays a rather unique role in this phenomenon. At first, it was still contributing to the growth statistics of other regions, including foreign countries and continents. But as it developed industrially, it began to keep its young people at home, while keeping at bay the potential excess pressure of overpopulation. In the decades during which the province was gaining in strength, it was still giving up some of its talented sons. How greatly American technology and the American economy benefited from the achievements of men like Othmar Mergenthaler, the inventor of the Linotype machine, or Hermann Frasch, the oil and sulfur expert! But the era of mass emigration was a thing of the past. The saying that products, not people, should be exported has nowhere demonstrated its pertinence and accuracy more forcefully than in the province of Württemberg.

The important thing was that this process, which led the province out of a recurrent social crisis linked to small-scale agricultural production, took place without creating the new crises that almost inevitably accompany rapid industrialization. At least this was true of the overall situation. Naturally, production sites that were dependent on the larger market felt the effects of the swings of the pendulum during industrial cycles; sometimes they felt them more strongly than the producers of raw materials. But even during periods of stagnation in trade, or of declining orders, Württemberg suffered none of the painful emergencies that were the fate of other highly developed industrial areas. This resulted, not least, from the decentralization of the firms and the frequently beneficial mixture of varied branches of industry: textiles alongside small iron mills; woodworking side by side with canning. This made it possible, depending on the situation, for resources to be reallocated when employment declined in one of the industrial branches. The dispersal of the industrial population in small towns and the semiagrarian environment allowed workers to maintain their links with the small plots of arable land from which, in their free hours, they could produce as much as they were able to for their families. Every peasant's son, grandson, or wife had acquired a piece of farming land, a meadow, or a garden through the process of unrestricted inheritance. Though rational experts in agrarian policy may furrow their brows at this leisure-time activity on tiny parcels of land, calculating the wasted trips and losses for the market, this phenomenon unique to Württemberg provided the people who had to work in factories with an atmosphere of psychological relaxation that was both positive and important.

The industrial working class in its early years only gradually revealed an identity distinct from that of the small peasants and petit bourgeois tradesmen from whose numbers it had sprung. The boundaries were unclear, often crisscrossing within a single family. The possibility of becoming independent, even if the result was modest, was seen as life's goal. In the new industrial sites—still half villages—it was not uncommon for the factory owner, who had spent his childhood there and attended public school along with his contemporaries, to have cousins and nephews among the foremen and workers he hired. The result was neither patriarchalism nor feelings of suppressed envy. Rather, the mutual relationship rested on a relaxed sobriety; occasionally a shared Christian outlook lent the relationships greater warmth.

Thus the province did not offer a favorable breeding ground for the idea of class struggle. Social Democracy was only gradually able to establish a foothold, and in the beginning even trade unions had a difficult time making progress, with the possible exception of book printers, with their specific traditions, and bookbinders. For the 1880s, naturally, the effects of the Anti-Socialist Law must be taken into account. It is true that the law was applied more gently in Württemberg than in other places. As one result, the Social Democratic Party moved its leading party press (Dietz) to Stuttgart, and the most radical representatives of orthodox Marxism, Karl Kautsky and Clara Zetkin, made their homes there too, in an environment that was unsuitable in many other respects. After 1890, the social and political views of the young Robert Bosch developed in debates with them in a spirit of friendly opposition. When trade unions began to be founded, after the defeat of the Anti-Socialist Law, the organizations that would be the most important—metalworkers and woodworkers—also moved their central offices to Stuttgart, regardless of how small the local base may have been. Württemberg's right to freedom of association, as it was applied, may have prompted this decision. It lent future developments a peculiar tension—problematic aspects which would later have an impact upon the fate of the Bosch firm as well.

9

————

THE WORKSHOP FOR PRECISION AND ELECTRICAL ENGINEERING

November 15, 1886, is considered to be the date on which the Robert Bosch firm was founded. It is the day on which the official permit arrived approving the opening of a Workshop for Precision and Electrical Engineering in the rear building on Rotebühlstrasse 75B. The modest rooms on the ground floor had been occupied and the machines installed on November 11. The furnishings, at first, were spare indeed; they were intended to adapt to the firm's needs. There is no surviving list of the original working inventory; its expansion can be traced through the entries in the firm's books. According to these records, purchases valued at around 1,100 marks were made in the first year; one of the most important was a lathe from Boley-Esslingen.

The firm's prospects were hard to predict. Well-meaning acquaintances found the decision to enter this line of business without significant capital backing, with the intention "namely to build electrical engineering equipment," remarkably bold. It was obvious that the large firms, new and old, with their specialized experience and unmistakable drive toward expansion, could make life very uncomfortable for the newcomer. But, as Robert Bosch told one skeptic, the large firms could not make everything, "and after all, there are still things in which personal trust plays a role."

Electrical engineering, at that moment, was going through a remarkable and promising transition. The development of the telegraph system had occurred almost a generation before; people were already accustomed to it. In the early 1880s, the telephone, as a result of Heinrich Stephan's energetic intervention, had been assigned to the government-run post office. Stuttgart native Fein had improved on Bell's construction, and for a time it seemed as if his venture, which had set itself such varied tasks, might specialize in low-voltage technology. In addition to the public facilities, the need for home telephones was growing. But even this invention was already a sensation of the past; electricity as a source of light was occupying people's imaginations and absorbing the technical interest of the specialists. The task itself was not entirely new. Experiments with metal lightbulbs and arc lighting went back several decades, and H. Goebel had already constructed an incandescent vacuum bulb. Except for its occasional use for theatrical effect, however, this whole sector had not entered ordinary daily life—the generation of power by means of "elements" was simply not technically or economically cost-effective. Werner von Siemens's discovery of the dynamoelectric principle changed all that with a single stroke. In 1876, Sigmund Schuckert made the first attempt to light up the Kaiserstrasse with arc lamps, and a year later their blinding light was illuminating factory halls. Achieving technical perfection for the new product would occupy mechanics for a long time to come; its significance was lessened by the further development of the incandescent bulb, which was developed to the point of marketability by several technicians simultaneously and which became a worldwide success in the version invented by Edison. The Paris Exhibition of 1882 took place under the sign of the lightbulb. Primarily, it was there for purposes of illumination, but any practically minded person had to realize instantly how much more important its mild light would be for average human needs than the cold light of the arc lamp. One of the first people to really grasp this was the electrical engineer Paul Rieser, from Stuttgart, who immediately purchased a complete set of equipment and the license to sell it in Württemberg at the Paris Exhibition. In the history of electrical engineering, he is remembered as the first man to equip a house, and then a whole block of houses, with incandescent lighting. The power had to be provided by a special steam engine installed in the cellar. The fact that this small, private power plant already had two motors mounted on a single block gave an indication, in model form, of the developmental possibilities that awaited it.

During the months Robert Bosch spent in Magdeburg, where he, too, had been given the task of inventing a lighting device, he had developed as a mechanic. He had tried to construct a patentable regulator for an arc lamp, and for a time he had believed that as a result he would soon be able to achieve the independence he sought. But then his initial development turned away completely from the question that was generating so much interest at the time. This is not surprising. For the installation of electric light was dependent on access to a power source. Experiments with power transmission were necessary before power generation itself could assume a significance of more than private dimensions. Essentially, this occurred in 1891. Toward the end of the century, Bosch entered the business of installing lighting systems and engines. His venture, although he may not have been fully aware of it, had already taken a turn toward specialization.

It was almost inevitable that Bosch's small craft workshop, which had opened in the fall of 1886 with one mechanic and an apprentice, would have something tentative about it. It had no specialty to offer and was prepared to accept any order it could get. There is an almost touching testimony to this fact in the advertisement that Robert Bosch inserted in the democratic *Observer*, his father's favorite paper, on February 2, 1887:

Telephones, in-house telegraph. Professional testing and installation of lightning rods. Installation and repair of electrical devices and all jobs requiring precision engineering.

The books reveal that sales of electrical equipment from the factory in Erlangen made up a considerable portion of the early business. Among 66 customers listed prior to the end of 1887 there are 21 doctors and medical institutes, including some with orders of between 400 and 900 marks—a significant factor when one considers that total gross sales were 5,000 marks. Naturally, Bosch was responsible not only for making the sales, but also for installing and then maintaining the devices and their batteries. To his dismay, the impressive numbers were not always accompanied by similarly impressive methods of payment.

When Bosch opened his workshop, he bought a ledger in which to enter income and expenses. He carefully removed the page that was traditionally inserted in the front of such books and that bore the words "With God!" This was a characteristic act; Bosch wanted to be responsible for success or failure himself; he did not want to appeal to a God in whom he did not quite believe. Naturally, it was clear to him that without careful notes he would soon lose his overview, and the undertaking would not prosper. But however varied the challenges might be, the opportunity to display his knowledge of bookkeeping was very modest, given the limited amount of business coming in. Entries were made but not totaled, and private and business accounts were mingled. He managed without a balance sheet that would have shown the value or depreciation of his assets or the balance between profit and loss. It was hardly worthwhile, and he did not take much pleasure in it; he felt that the time could be better used for other purposes. The method sufficed, ultimately, as a means of maintaining an overview of the current business. Until February 1891, Bosch served as his own bookkeeper; then another handwriting appears, which, however, soon vanishes, only to turn up again a couple of years later. We may surmise that the bookkeeping was not entrusted to a regular staff member with business responsibilities, but rather was assigned to someone who took care of it as a spare-time assignment. From time to time, the residents of the front building were asked for advice on how best to handle the entries or the bills of exchange. A tobacco merchant located there was particularly helpful.

From the ledger entries, shipping records, and accounts of products and wages, Otto Fischer was able, in 1942, to piece together the financial situation of these early years. Based on the bills and other documents, he succeeded in painting a picture of the flow and organization of the business despite the gaps that sometimes made it necessary for him to resort to estimates. Bosch, recalling this period, once commented that "for a long time it was terrible drudgery," a comment borne out by the books. In 1895 or thereabouts, there was freedom from the pressure when the installation business experienced its growth spurt due to the construction of the municipal electric plant in Stuttgart. Simultaneously, the workshop assumed the character of a small factory when it came to some of its specialties. The first workshop had soon grown too small; in the spring of 1890 it had moved to Gutenbergstrasse 9. In the fall of 1891, a still larger workshop at Rotebühlstrasse 108 was added. Before there was time to look for still larger quarters, however, Bosch faced a bitter setback.

The founding capital, representing Bosch's share of the paternal inheritance, had amounted to 10,000 marks. But this base was not broad enough for a business that could acquire regular customers only gradually. Nor could this sum support a man who, despite all his personal modesty, wanted to get ahead and was always ready to invest increasing amounts in machines in order to be in a position to meet all expectations. In 1889, a mechanical drill, bellows, and soldering device were purchased; in 1890 a gas engine, milling machine, revolver, and engine lathes; the total expenses for the year amounted to 7,000 marks. These expenses—in the form of bills for 1,900, 1,700, and 2,000 marks—could not be covered either by the original capital or by the profits. By 1888, the gross receipts had grown to more than 9,000 marks; by 1889, to 15,000 marks. Among the 119 customers recorded during this year, 20 percent still only brought in sums of less than 5 marks, but manufacturing, at 8,100 marks, had now surpassed installation, at 6,900 marks. There were also 19 customers from outside Stuttgart. Bosch's assessment of this situation was rather optimistic, hence the quick move to perfect his machine shop. It was risky, for in 1891 Bosch had basically reached the limit of his financial strength. His mother loaned him 3,000 marks, then 10,000 marks, and his brothers-in-law helped out, as well, once briefly with 1,000 marks, then with 2,500, and in 1893 with 5,600 marks. In addition, he had a line of credit secured by his relatives with the Stuttgarter Gewerbekasse; its upper limit was reached in 1893. The situation remained tense, even after a customer base of sorts had been established. In 1895 it again assumed crisis proportions, for it was not possible to count on regular orders. Bosch himself liked to tell a story about the time there was no money on Saturday for payday; in order not to have to be late with the workers' wages, he had to ask for help from a neighboring fruit seller. The latter realized that he would not lose any money on this particular borrower.

It is remarkable that in the business's third year the sales of the manufacturing department already surpassed installation. This would remain so, with the exception of the years 1895 and 1896, when the electrical power plant came on line, bringing a series of orders for the man whose punctual and careful work had already made him a name. Among these orders were telephone and bell systems in the Hotel Marquardt and the Conrad Merz department store. The more important question is what kinds of things were leaving Bosch's workshop?—one must be careful not to speak of a manufacturing program, or anything of the sort. The factory delivered whatever a customer desired and it believed it could produce, for example, an ignition device for a motor. Here was something connected with electricity, and since the young entrepreneur wanted to win his spurs in this new field, work of this kind was welcome. There was evidently no market for such a thing, or at least not yet. He was happy to have the opportunity to acquire some early experience, which might lead to improvements and cost reductions if the orders were repeated. In addition, there were jobs that were quite far removed from electrical engineering. Bosch recounted that many things were brought to him as an inventor, and how he experimented with them: a petroleum lamp with improved illumination strength; self-closing water faucets; the "Triumph point" for cigars, including "mechanical removal of the stump"; a typewriter for the blind and one that wrote musical notes, as well as ink wipers, fountain pens, games of patience, cigar lighters, and more. The items were faithfully produced on demand but remained trivial matters that made no lasting impact. Bosch went to great pains to construct a contraption for a photographer that would enable him to produce "full-size snapshots with flash lighting." Much time and a good deal of money were wasted on this attempt, for the photographer was unable to pay. More realistic, if prosaic, were orders like the construction of catheters or forms for noodle presses. Here Bosch appeared as a producer of specialized products for industrial firms.

The production and occasional installation of remote water-table measurements was something that took on greater significance toward the middle of the 1890s. A float was attached to a contact, and the water level was indicated by an electrical line. The device had been developed as a result of repeated experiments, according to Gottlob Honold, at the time serving his apprenticeship. Bosch took it to an exhibition in Karlsruhe, probably in 1894, for the first time. The Bureau of Metallurgy in Wasser-alfingen had already placed the first order. The purchase and installation of the apparatus cost 726 marks, and it appears that Bosch, who had begun to place occasional advertisements outside Stuttgart, also made this item more widely known after the trade show in Karlsruhe. Thus, in 1894, it was possible to send telemeasurement devices to Halberstadt and Fiume, Kassel and Rheine. The books bear witness to eighty-nine similar orders in the years before 1899, among them Skutari and Pavia, outside Germany. But the core of the orders consisted of the water system for the Swabian highlands, which was being greatly expanded at the time, and to which a similar system was later added in the Black Forest. Naturally, no real market could develop for these services, which were generally required by government agencies, but they played a significant role in sales. The orders from Bosch's home territory, in which he was given responsibility for the entire installation, were an important source of his reputation for good work. He had to have people on the outside whose performance he could rely on. Anecdotes about the period tell of him riding through the countryside on his bicycle, when the railroad failed him, in order to supervise the work being done at distant locations.

This legendary bicycle, which in those days could still be considered a semiluxury, turns up among the purchases of 1890. Bosch was a modern craftsman who bought himself a telephone as early as 1899, for an annual fee of 150 marks. He had brochures printed and had been a subscriber to the *Central Journal for Electrical Engineering* since 1888. This fact shows that he tried to keep up-to-date on all new developments; it was the time when many experiments were being carried out involving conductive materials, insulation, and techniques of measurement. One proposal followed another. Along with the difficulty of combining theoretically correct knowledge with economically defensible and technically solid practice arose the dilemma of finding a suitable workforce. Every new technology, when it appears, attracts people from the nearby professions who think they are capable of mastering it. Locksmiths, plumbers, and blacksmiths offered themselves for this kind of work, and Bosch was involved in many angry incidents when he was asked to help repair a job that had been bungled or he saw that competing small tradesmen, whose execution *had* to be of poor quality, were getting jobs at low prices. He himself certainly did not turn down any orders, but even a small one had to be well done, and then it had to be well paid. This principle applied even in the beginning years of the business.

The size of the workforce varied in the early years, as did its quality. The growth in the number of regular employees is reflected in the quick succession of new workshops. In 1897, the firm would move for the fourth time, and the enlarged machine shop would have to be reinstalled yet again. This time the move took them to the rear building of the house at Kanzleistrasse 22. It was still not a proper factory, and the years 1895 and 1896 would see yet another situation in which the space became too small, due to the increase in orders; it would not take much longer before Bosch would begin to look around for a place that would permit practical organization and perhaps even further expansion. There are no statistics concerning the number of employees in the early years. In 1891, the number was once given as ten: six journeymen, two apprentices, and two helpers. In the next year, the group grew temporarily to more than twenty, but the financial setback made it necessary to lay most of them off. Under these circumstances, it was hard to train a solid core group, so necessary if a proper manufacturing business was to develop. A note from the year 1896 mentions a staff of sixteen people all told.

More important than the numbers, however, was the fact that even during the firm's beginnings as a small craft business, several names turned up that would later go down in its history. In 1888, Arnold Zähringer arrived from the Black Forest, nineteen years old and descended from a family of carpenters and peasants in Furtwangen. He had completed an apprenticeship as a mechanic in the town—famous for its clocks—where Leonhard Köpf had once wanted to take his fellow apprentice in Ulm; but Zähringer had wanted to move to a new place. It proved to be not too distant; Bosch offered him a job. Zähringer stayed for a couple of years and then moved on, to Strasbourg, where he was employed at the town's new power plant. In 1890 he returned, and Bosch was glad to have this hard-working and skilled man who was both independent and full of ideas. The young proprietor of the business had to be on the road quite a lot, and so Zähringer stood in for him. Bosch had had a series of bad experiences with workshop managers; they failed to adapt to the tone of the company and were soon let go. So he decided to put the young journeyman in this position. It followed almost automatically that Zähringer became a kind of representative for jobs that involved manufacturing and became the de facto manager of the company to the extent that this term can be applied to such a small group of people. The two men, Bosch and his representative, were equals in the seriousness and detached strictness with which they took on the task of training.

In 1891, a fifteen-year-old boy had been sent to Bosch to serve as an apprentice. His name was Gottlob Honold, and he came from Langenau, from a family of teachers. Decades earlier, his father had been in friendly contact with Servatius Bosch, from the nearby village of Albeck, and he wanted to put his son, whose enthusiasm had been aroused by the marvelous reports of electrical power production, in the hands of someone he trusted. This was not possible right away; Bosch did not take more than two apprentices at a time, and so the Honolds, father and son, had to wait patiently for four months until a place became free. The wait was worth it; later, after the turn of the century, the one-time apprentice would become the chief technical manager of the firm. Inventing and experimenting were already part of his nature—Bosch once caught him trying to make a small electric engine during working hours. The apprentice was afraid that there would be a terrible storm, but there was none. After a reminder about doing his duty came the offer to use the workshop after-hours for his experiments; he could come and fetch the key at home anytime he pleased. The older man's sharp eye recognized and respected the underlying impulses of this shy adolescent. He also noticed the vivacious, clever, participatory cheerfulness of the young man who succeeded Honold as apprentice in 1894: Max Rall. Rall came from the flatland, where he had already tried his hand in another workshop without finding satisfaction. Now he became a kind of adjutant who helped his boss with the drawing of sketches and the calculation of orders. Bosch himself taught his apprentice to ride a bicycle and permitted him to accompany him—and soon even represent him—on his trips around the countryside. People's amazement at the fact that such a young fellow was sent to see them did not trouble the master. He knew he could rely on the ambitious young man's eagerness, practical flexibility, and undaunted good sense.

The responsibility of teaching was one that Bosch approached in an extraordinarily serious and conscientious manner. When Honold's father wrote to him, in 1893, to ask whether his son might have a small allowance, he received in return a detailed description of the whole situation, complete with expenses per staff member and a vivid picture of what Gottlob had just finished making—twelve door contacts which, as the work of an apprentice, cost one mark to produce, while they could be bought for eighty pfennigs. After this description, the letter continued with an important testimonial: "Now, however, you will say, either Gottlob isn't doing any work, or you aren't teaching him anything. But the reality is quite different. If I wanted to make G. work in a way that would make money for me, I would allow him, for example, to use molded parts, instead of making the contacts out of sheet metal, which is what I had him do. But so often nowadays I find that mechanics may be perfectly capable of making something, as long as you give them directions and a certain number of castings. But ask them to make something from raw materials, say from sheet metal or a brass rod, and not one of them knows what to do. I am trying to prevent this by making the work fit the apprentice. My apprentices are only allowed to do jobs like polishing screws, or turning screws on the lathe, or as long as it takes them to learn how. If I wanted to exploit them, I could fire two helpers, one of whom makes 10 marks and the other 12, and take on two apprentices instead, thus saving 22 marks a week. That is how it is often done." The teacher from Langenau must have been happy to receive this answer.

The memories of the Bosch years after 1890, as they were later written down by Honold and another worker, Richard Schyle, give a general impression of spirited activity. After a couple of missteps, the young entrepreneur became cautious. He hired people on probation, something not everyone was prepared to put up with, and a rough Swabian argument would sometimes ensue. But those who managed to stay on liked it there. Bosch attempted to keep the capable people, even when the orders were few and far between, and it was a difficult thing for him when he was forced to reduce the number of workers in the actual workshop from twenty-four to two. Fortunately, the sudden crisis did not last long, and Bosch paid well. Trained workers made a base salary of twenty-one marks, and as much as thirty-five marks with piecework; a particularly ambitious worker who didn't mind overtime might receive as much as forty-eight marks. In 1894–95, at the instigation of the workers, the working day had been reduced from ten hours to nine. According to Schyle, Bosch hinted that he might introduce the eight-hour day, if "the competition would reduce their work hours from ten to nine. He said he would like to take the lead and be a good example." Both writers also reported that there was much singing on the shop floor. "Sometimes there was disagreement over the texts of the songs, because two different political viewpoints were represented. But most of the time the more conservative Christian tendency had to give in." The songs were also a means of limiting Bosch's "often annoying supervision"; for the workers had discovered that as long as they sang he would not leave his office. Evidently he did not want to seem to be interrupting them. Schyle tells an anecdote about how Bosch—at a time when the workforce had been reduced to a quartet of four men—once asked whether they could sing pianissimo, rather than forte, so passersby on the street wouldn't think the place was a conservatory.

It all sounds a little like an old-fashioned German idyll, but it was not. Bosch insisted that all duties be strictly performed. He was the first one there to open the workshop in the morning and the last to lock up and leave. Work discipline and order were strongly enforced—woe betide the apprentices if the machine tools were not thoroughly cleaned by Saturday evening. At the same time, even in the craft workshop, consideration had been given to ways of making the manual work easier, and on oppressively hot days Bosch didn't mind sending his workers off into the greenery with full pay.

Personal documents for this period—letters, diary entries, and the like—are almost completely absent. The young craftsman was completely absorbed in his work. He did not play any perceptible role in public life, which was tense enough, with the struggle over the Septennat in 1887 and the new course in imperial policy in 1890. A note from a letter dated April 26, 1887, reports: "This afternoon I am thinking about closing up shop to go to the Uhland celebration"; Bosch's local pride in his homeland is perceptible when it comes to celebrating the one-hundredth birthday of his esteemed countryman.

His main concern was starting a household, and with all the worries about finding a place to live, he succeeded in August. "We can move in and set up the furniture any time. I wish we could do it today" (August 18, 1887). The first apartment was in the Schwabstrasse, close to the workshop. On October 10, 1887, he was able to bring Anna Kayser home from Obertürkheim. Two daughters, Margarete (1888) and Paula (1889), and a son, Robert (1891), were born. His socializing, to the extent that he needed and wanted it, was done with a few comrades from the student Hut Club, whose evenings he continued to attend for a couple of years, and in the circle of his wife's family, the Kaysers. Anna's mother in Obertürkheim formed the center of a closely knit clan with a warm emotional life, and the new family member, with his critical awareness, did not adjust to their emotional temperature right away. In the letters he wrote her during their engagement, Bosch may have expressed the thought that the young woman might prefer to remain close to her familiar circle, rather than starting her new life in Cologne or Furtwangen. In the process, he revealed his fear of convention and a characteristic kind of preventive pedagogy: "There, however, your contact with your girlfriends could no longer be intimate, at least not with the ones who move in bureaucratic circles, since we don't fit in there, as you know."

The breadth of his contacts during the early years in Stuttgart is demonstrated by his relationships with two such different types as Karl Kautsky, who was just about to become the official author of the program of the Social Democratic Party, and the young mining student Paul Reusch. The meeting with Kautsky was a chance occurrence, but it is not without charm. In 1891 Bosch, whose growing family needed more room, moved into the second floor of the house at Rotebühlstrasse 145. Kautsky, who had just returned from London, moved in on the third floor as the editor of the scholarly journal of the Social Democrats, the *New Age*, published by Dietz. In the rooms directly above the Bosch family, the Erfurt Program was being written. Bosch, who was acquainted with the journal before he got to know his new neighbor, was not immune to the latter's intellectual influence; the overly logical thought processes of his social criticism were related to certain aspects of Bosch's rationalism. But as often as they may have had discussions within the context of a neighborly friendship between their families, their natures were elementally and completely opposed—Bosch sensual, Kautsky abstract and blind to natural phenomena. The socialism of the young craftsman was emotional and ethical, while Marxism, in Kautsky's interpretation, reformulated these basic ethical forces in a dialectical interplay of economic interests and technological conditions.

Bosch acquired a good knowledge of Marxist ideology. The utopianism of his American years seemed to have fallen away completely, but familiarity with the subject also gave him the strength to draw a clear line of demarcation. From a fundamental rejection of the theory of surplus value followed, for him, a questioning and ultimately the rejection of the basic economic theory of Marxism. His political sympathies for an aggressively democratic policy were not, however, tarnished by this intellectual separation.

Kautsky, dogmatic and schooled in conventional forms, approached the evidently very independent-minded and searching craftsman with interested tolerance. He was seven years older than Bosch.

Paul Reusch was six years younger. They met in the circle of the Hut, which Bosch had joined in 1887–88. Bosch and Reusch had in common the enjoyment of hiking, a love of their homeland, and the habit of observing nature. A youthful comradeship was formed that would solidify into a lifelong friendship. The young Paul Reusch was not interested in hearing much about socialist ideologies; he was attracted to Bosch's human quality, his easygoing manner and independence from convention. Their paths would later lead them apart, then back together again. Reusch's career in mining, which took him first to the Tyrol and then to Moravia, eventually elevated him to a leading and influential position in the Ruhr region. Then the two men would stand in opposition to each other as captains of industry in the sectors of heavy industry and the manufacturing of finished products. Occasionally, they confronted each other with fundamental political beliefs that were quite antagonistic, exchanging views with clarity and directness, testing their temperaments but also subordinating questions of objective fact to a serious consideration of broader issues and responsibilities. In this way, the unsentimental but open and loyal youthful friendship would be a source of lasting gain for both.

The portrait of Bosch as a young craftsman has a touch of rebellion and romanticism about it. The slenderness of the young man's face has been replaced by a certain expressive strength, a result of a great, full beard. The elements of his nature have not quite come into balance. One is tempted to see a softness, perhaps an excess of imagination, but the solid shape of his head also betrays will and decisiveness. Its unusual aspect is underlined, for the modern observer, by the clothing—it is the cut that Gustav Jäger designed for maximal heat retention by the body, and that Bosch faithfully continued to wear for decades. A dark, broad-brimmed carpenter's hat covers his head. As he pedaled his bicycle through the city to check that his people had laid the wiring for the door-bell correctly, or done a good job of supervising the installation of some medical apparatus, people might more readily have taken him for a missionary or a preacher than for a pathfinder in the age of electricity. As for Bosch himself, he did not much care what people thought he was.

10

ENGINE AND
IGNITION

The development of electrical engineering was characterized by a peculiar
contest with illuminating gas, which sometimes served as a hindrance,
sometimes as a spur, to progress. The use of the gas, which could be produced cost-effectively, especially for lighting, had a fifty-year jump on
electricity. Considerable public and private resources had been invested
in gasworks, and many people saw their dividends threatened by the new
technology. The low-voltage systems, the telegraph and the telephone,
were not affected by this contest. But when the first arc lamps and, soon
afterward, incandescent bulbs began to illuminate streets and private
homes, a certain defensive insecurity arose, which was somewhat alleviated at first by the fact that throughout the 1860s gas was gaining in significance not only as a source of light, and increasingly of warmth and
heat, but also as a fuel for the generation of electrical power. The gas-
driven engine had been discovered and developed, and there was a brief
interlude—the all-encompassing and reliable transmission of electrical
power was still untested—when it seemed as if the gas-driven engine
would actually serve as a useful auxiliary source for the production of
electrical power.

There is a strange, comparable rhythm common to both gas and electricity in the way their significance moves from lighting, as their main use, to machinery. Something similar also applies to petroleum as a product for mass consumption. Because it has been around for such a long time, there is a tendency to think of petroleum as an old-fashioned resource superseded by modern technology, an assumption that is not correct. It was not until the end of the 1850s that the systematic exploitation of the great reserves of mineral oil began, with its refining and preparation for industrial use and its worldwide transportation into every village. In the recollections of his youth, Robert Bosch mentions the impression it made on him as a child when the candle was "shunted aside" by the "triumphal march" of petroleum. At first, it was welcomed and was used as a source of light, but it was not long before people also recognized its industrial value, and a new resource appeared in the form of gasoline. Its full significance could not yet be reckoned but would be proven in barely two decades.

In 1859, the first oil wells began producing in America; in 1860, the Frenchman J. J. Etienne Lenoir developed the first "gas-power machine"; in 1867, Werner von Siemens discovered the dynamoelectric principle. The dates lie close together. Lenoir's invention represents the first type of internal combustion engine; it brings a mixture of illuminating gas and atmospheric air to combustion, i.e., explosion. The expansion pushes the piston forward, the atmospheric pressure pushes it back again. With the regulated introduction of a combustible gas mixture, the requisite exhaust, and properly functioning ignition, a new possibility of producing power, and hence motion, had been created. The challenge would be to develop the dependability of the combustion process, and to secure the effectiveness of the connection between power generation and the transmission of the propulsive force, with a minimum of gas usage and a maximum useful effect. The extraordinary gain that this made possible is obvious at first glance: medium and small industry, for which the installation and repair of a steam engine would be too expensive, now had access to a source of power that was quite adequate for the average need and that did not require elaborate preparations. True, its installation was dependent on the existence of a nearby gasworks. But did illuminating gas have to be used for the explosive mixture? In Nicholas Otto's first unsuccessful application for a patent in Cologne in the year 1861, he spoke of using a combustible gas that was to consist not of illuminating gas and atmospheric air, but of the vapors of liquids containing hydrocarbons, especially spirits of alcohol and atmospheric air.

Otto, in other words, intended from the very beginning for his device to have a certain mobility and flexibility. Alcohol could be had everywhere in unlimited amounts. The towering achievement of this man, who was a technological outsider, a bookkeeper, was not that he loosed the combustion engine from its moorings, but that he, together with an openminded and inventive engineer from Cologne, Eugen Langen, constructed a gas-powered machine that lived up to its performance potential. Illuminating gas was the material at hand for their experiments, and he stuck with it for economic reasons. In this way they gained the first steady customers for their engines. These modest beginnings were followed—in part only after the death of their inventor—by enormous expansion. The most important machine Otto constructed, which, after many attempts, achieved patentability in 1876, was the so-called "four-stroke" engine. This, according to the patent application, was a means of "designing the working of a piston that was cranked in such a way that with two revolutions of the crankshaft the following things would happen on *one* side of the piston: a) the induction of gases into the cylinder; b) compression of the gases; c) combustion, and action of the piston; d) its exit from the cylinder."

When the new engine had been developed to the point of practical application by the Gasoline Engine Factory Deutz, which in 1872 had succeeded the firm of Otto & Langen, engineer Gottlieb Daimler was the technical leader in charge of the company, which was enjoying a brisk upswing. With him he had brought into the firm Wilhelm Maybach, a man whose technical powers of invention he had learned to appreciate during their previous collaboration. Four talented men, each critical and ambitious, were in charge of the new machine; Eugen Langen also took an active part in improving Otto's original invention. The work they shared could have gone well, but it did not. Decades after their separation in 1882, when all the participants had long since died, scholars and historians were still struggling over the parts the various men had played in the work, and over the name Otto engine or Daimler engine. This much is clear: Otto had begun work on the basic (if imperfect) idea of his solution decades earlier, but it was Daimler's developmental work, above all, that prepared the way for the decisive result—the introduction of a whole new phase of transportation, along with the faster engine, even if this did not mean that it was *his* internal combustion engine that had been created.

One of the points of contention between Otto and Daimler was the question of ignition. This was, after all, not an unimportant issue. In his memoirs, Carl Benz called it the "problem of problems." The challenge was to ignite the mixture of gas and air at the moment when the piston compressed it and the cylinder approached the maximum compression point. Electrical ignition had already been utilized for other purposes. Werner von Siemens reports in his *Memories of My Life* that in 1848, as an artillery officer, he had improvised a barrier against the Danish army by laying ocean mines in the harbor of Kiel. The explosive charges were attached to an electrical line, which was admittedly not designed to function automatically. In 1866, Siemens tried "to perfect the functioning of electrical ignition with the help of a cylinder inductor." These efforts preceded Siemens's discovery of the dynamoelectric principle. At that time, he developed a device with magneto ignition. Another method was to make a platinum wire glow through the use of galvanic elements.

Otto had also worked with an electrical ignition device in his first attempts in the early 1860s; it is not known what type it was. The "atmospheric machine" of 1866, when it reached the stage at which it was ready for introduction to the market, used an open gas flame, which, applied to the cylinder, brought the compressed gas mixture to explosion through a small opening. Naturally, this was only a temporary solution, because the opening, no matter how artfully the lid was designed, still permitted part of the propulsive force that had just been developed to escape, and the flame itself always remained subject to too much pressure. By regulating the combustion created inside the lid, it was possible to achieve a rate of 140 to 180 revolutions per minute, depending on how powerful the engine was, and this limited the work it could do. After the design of the four-stroke engine had been worked out (its first version was still designed for combustible gas), Langen turned to Siemens because of the latter's magneto inductor with the double-T armature. Otto encouraged the test, for electrical technology had progressed a great deal since his earlier attempts. But it seems that the result did not live up to their expectations, at least not immediately; Daimler, at any rate, remained dismissive and skeptical on this point, as little satisfied as he was with the type of ignition that had existed until then. He himself would find a solution that would make the ignition process independent of valves and control systems, while at the same time making use of the basic material of the operation, whatever kind and proportions of gas that might involve.

Naturally, this technical issue was not the decisive factor in the sharpening conflict at the Gasoline Engine Factory Deutz, or the uncomfortable personal relationship between Otto and Daimler, which could no longer be held in check by Eugen Langen. In the summer of 1882, Daimler turned down an offer of compromise from the firm, which terminated his employment, and he left. Now the engineers at Deutz turned once more to the ideas of 1877, with the aim of advancing the technical and formal development of the process Siemens had proposed. Since 1884, the gas engine factory had been producing a magnetic ignition device; the previous "pneumatic" ignition was not entirely abandoned, but the new principle had been recognized. This ignition device became an independently manufactured product, although a secondary one, in the context of the overall production of the factory.

Robert Bosch met Daimler shortly after the precision engineering workshop was founded in Stuttgart. One may say that it was a fateful encounter. His memories, in their sober way, give an impressive report of the event: "In the summer of the same year (1887), a small machine-builder had approached me and asked me whether I could make him a device like the one the Gasoline Engine Factory Deutz was using in their gasoline engines. I drove over, and there I found the low-voltage magneto device with firing points. I asked Deutz, just to be sure, whether anything about the device had been patented. To this question I got no answer. I found no other signs that the device was patented, and so I built one, which I demonstrated to Gottlieb Daimler, who happened to be in Canstatt in the process of designing his internal-combustion engine for stationary machines, which was considered to have high rpms, at about 600. After I delivered the one device, I immediately made three more, which were picked up, for the purpose of testing, by the existing factories of gas motors that were thinking about building gasoline engines. Through ads, I discovered that the well-known firm of F. Martini & Co. in Frauenfeld was also looking for magneto devices. I delivered one, which, following the Deutz model, was equipped with twelve magnets bent over the milled edge. I went to Frauenfeld myself, where I quickly became convinced that no technically effective machine could be built with the twelve fragile magnets. I remembered the harvester from Schäffer in Göppingen, and there I bought magnets with a diameter of 40/20 millimeters, equipped them with pole shoes and a base plate, to hold the thing down, and suitable side plates. With this, the ignition device for stationary machines was created; though at first it sold very modestly."

The firm's books from the early period reveal that the small machine-builder was the firm of Schmehl & Hespelt, from the town of Möckmühl in Württemberg. It also purchased the second ignition inductor. It was charged 216.5 marks for the first one and 181.3 marks for the second. The delivery was made in 1888, in which a total of nine ignition devices were sold. The connection with Martini-Frauenfeld made itself felt; of the annual sales, which exceeded 9,000 marks, more than a sixth (1,546.5 marks) were tied to this product for which an average of 180 marks was being charged. The next year saw the number of sales climb to 24 devices for 6 customers; with 3,500 marks they now accounted for more than a fifth of the total sales of 15,000 marks. The year 1890 saw the percentage rise further: of 19,000 marks in sales, 8,000 marks were attributable to the ignition devices. This was the point at which Robert Bosch was expanding his machine shop with a fine optimism and was putting a gas engine in his own workshop. As early as the 1880s, the construction of gas engines, and soon gasoline engines, had attracted more and more entrepreneurs. There were long court battles directed against purported imitators, leading to the discovery that a watchmaker in Munich had built a comparable machine completely independently, before Otto, without ever thinking about its legal protection or industrial use; thus Otto & Langen had lost their claims to a patent. Alongside the Deutz firm, which was the market leader, other factories were springing up, and an expanding and apparently dependable market was beginning to develop. With sales of 14,800 marks out of an annual total of 25,500, the ignition device had come to outweigh everything else in the business by 1891. Of the 130 units produced, 72 went to Hille;

the price, listed at 135 marks in 1890, sank to about 100 marks for bulk orders. It may have been during this period that Bosch told the tobacconist who served as his adviser, "I should have only weeks like this!" He had been able to ship five ignition devices.

The tendency to specialization became marked, but it was not pursued further. In the very period in which the ignition device was on the way to becoming the dominant article in manufacturing, the demanding experiments with the long-distance water level gauge began. The fact that of the 151 customers listed for 1891, 11 bought ignition devices—accounting for 58 percent of sales—undoubtedly brought much-needed relief to Bosch. There were plenty of small things to manufacture, as well, and this always made it necessary to remain conscientious.

It is understandable that Robert Bosch, for all his daring, did not rush into specialization. For the leap that the ignition devices had made between 1890 and 1891, from 55 to 130 units, did not continue at that pace. A certain stagnation set in. In the following years, the number would hover between 136 and 157 units; in 1896, it climbed to 263. This was the year that also saw the powerful, if temporary, jump in the installation business. Bosch was freed from material cares. During his early years, Bosch had done his banking with the Gewerbekasse. Now this connection was severed and he transferred his business to the Vereinsbank, which played a leading role in the industrialization of Württemberg. The new customer did not come as a prospective creditor; he was the possessor of a large bank account that soon grew larger.

Among the purchasers of ignition devices, the shipping ledger of August 1893 lists Carl Benz in Mannheim. He had been struggling with the ignition question for a decade, but his first experiments with the product from the workshop in Stuttgart led nowhere. Almost a year later, Bosch made a special trip to Augsburg to help inventor Rudolf Diesel install the ignition device. But its usefulness for this purpose, at the time, was an illusion.

11

—

THE MOTOR
VEHICLE

It is unlikely that Gottlieb Daimler in Cannstatt was particularly interested in the device Robert Bosch had demonstrated for him in 1887 which was modeled after the sample from Deutz. Daimler had already seen something similar in Cologne and had decided that the solution was not effective when it came to the question that had occupied him so intensely for many years. In 1882, after his separation from Otto & Langen, Daimler had returned home, where he succeeded in interesting Wilhelm Maybach in continuing their collaboration. In Stuttgart, he hoped to have an easier time finding the skilled workers he needed; in 1872, after all, he had imported a whole colony of Swabian masters and journeymen because he was dissatisfied with the level of performance he was getting in Cologne. At that time, his inventive imagination was completely focused on producing a high-speed engine. For only after the revolutions per minute were increased would it be possible to think sensibly about making the increased rotations serve the means of transportation.

The task itself was not a new one. Automotive history is replete with predecessors—a gallery full of clever, awkward, or bizarre examples. To begin with, there was the series of English attempts: during the first half of the nineteenth century, the nation that invented the steam engine had produced all kinds of rail-less variations. These had already achieved a degree of practical importance, only to be throttled in parliament under pressure from the railroad companies. When England capitulated, the challenge was taken up by France, where the first experiments were also based on steam power. The internal combustion engine was also beginning to play a role. Lenoir, who had constructed the engine that ran on illuminating gas, began by equipping his own factory with one. These various attempts were certainly not useless; they helped the participants to gain experience with timing, gears, and brakes. Still, they remained more or less curiosities. Much depends on whether the automotive history one consults was written in England, France, or Germany—the emphasis varies considerably, as do the roles assigned to individual nations and the credit received for the revolution in industry and civilization that followed in the wake of the new technological invention.

The decisive contribution was made by two Germans: Gottlieb Daimler and Carl Benz. History tells us that well before them, in 1875, Siegfried Markus of Mecklenburg had made a vehicle run in Vienna with a gasoline engine that even had electrical magneto ignition. But this experiment remained only a footnote, a quasi-successful experiment that would have no further consequences. Certainly, the first inventions of Daimler and Benz soon began to look like museum pieces themselves, and to us today they may appear either naive or outlandish. The key thing is that continuous development was now possible. At a decisive moment, Robert Bosch was to play a role in it. The early history of the automobile and, after it, of air travel, can be reduced to a few men from the southwest German countryside.

The peculiar duality repeated itself. Just as Otto, working in Cologne, and Reithmann, in Munich, did not know anything about each other when they were developing the four-stroke engine in the 1870s, so Benz and Daimler experimented independently of each other, although they were virtually neighbors. The two men whose names history has linked together never saw each other and evidently did not feel the need to meet. There was no lack of posthumous argument about which of them deserved the actual, larger credit for the creation of the automobile. When Benz, in a circular, was identified as the inventor of the automobile, Robert Bosch confirmed in a letter to Paul Daimler dated January 4, 1933, that "it was the high-speed engine that made further development of the automobile possible . . . It is more or less an argument over semantics, whether Gottlieb Daimler or Carl Benz is the inventor of the automobile. That the work of your father and Wilhelm Maybach paved the way for the automobile in its present-day form is beyond any doubt whatsoever, and no one can question it."

Benz's work placed greater emphasis on overall planning, on the questions of cooling, weight, transmission, and steering. In this he was close to Maybach, whose ability to conceive the task they confronted as a structural unity surpassed even that of his master, with whom he enjoyed a close and devoted working relationship. Daimler's contribution was to find a way to increase the piston engine's revolutions per minute; for it was only with this advance that the notion of the individual motorist took on real, practical significance. It is characteristic that Daimler's first car was a horse-drawn carriage with its shafts removed and an engine mounted on it, and that his first commercial successes came not from the new vehicle he had designed for the roads but from motorboats. This fact expresses both the limits and the universality of his contribution. At the experimental workshops in Mannheim and Cannstatt, the fuel, in both cases, was gasoline. In Cannstatt, the process that regulated the vaporization of the gasoline and its mixture with the air was perfected in 1893.

The Daimler engine's decisive innovation was as simple as it was clever—the invention of a new method of ignition, the glow tube. In the Otto motors, an ignition flame was steered into the combustion chamber by a sliding device. Daimler replaced this clumsy mechanical apparatus, which also limited the revolutions per minute, by introducing a little tube made of porcelain (later platinum), sealed at the back, into the cylinder wall near the dead center of the piston barrel. When the tube was heated by a flame from outside, it took in the gas mixture and made it explode. Daimler's theoretical calculation was that the degree of heat created by the explosions would maintain a sufficiently high and steady temperature in the tube. Even though this expectation did not hold true under all weather conditions, and practice later revealed many incompatibilities, as well as the sensitivity of the ignition point, nevertheless the invention represented an extraordinary leap forward in the very area that was most important to Daimler: increasing engine speed. With this, regardless of the immediate practical consequences, a new technical beginning had been created for further development.

Carl Benz had stuck with the same type of battery ignition Lenoir had already used in his test drives with a gas-driven automobile in 1864. Since 1878, Benz had been trying "all possible experiments," as he wrote, "sometimes with small dynamos and battery ignition, sometimes with hydrogen phosphide and catalysis." Naturally, the arrangement of the elements caused some difficulties; still greater difficulties were caused by the fact that batteries were still in their infancy. Regardless of its other problems, the disadvantage of this system was the fact that it imposed a time limit on the engine—the battery had to be charged frequently. But at least, thanks to the number of revolutions that were now possible, it could produce the necessary sparks in the cylinder by means of a circuit breaker. Battery-driven ignition stood alongside the glow tube as an independent form of development. Then magneto ignition made both of them obsolete, until battery ignition made a comeback under new conditions, including the introduction of electric headlights and the invention of the starter motor, and was perfected to such a degree that the risks and weaknesses of the early period faded from memory.

It is rather well known that at first Daimler's and Benz's work met with little interest in Germany—there was some local amazement, but also mistrust and rejection. Actually, only the use of the motorboat found quick acceptance. The early connection with France proved fateful for both men. The licenses they gave, and the motor vehicles they were able to sell there, laid the foundation for their fame. In France in the late 1880s and early 1890s, there was real public enthusiasm for the motor vehicle. The choice between the improved steam engine and the internal combustion engine would still have to be fought out; it was decided at the first great road race of 1894 by a Daimler engine.

It is consistent with this picture that, in Robert Bosch's case, the interest expressed by foreign countries—or at least by a foreigner—turned out to be a decisive factor in his turn to the motor vehicle engine. The Englishman Frederic R. Simms came to Bosch in 1893 seeking a connection. Even before that there had been some contact between Bosch's magneto ignition, which was actually meant for stationary engines, and the new motor vehicles; Benz had ordered a device for himself in 1893. In 1894, several ignition devices had been installed in the motor vehicles of the newly founded Thuringen Motor Vehicle Factory in Neustadt on the Orla. This attempt, which was led by the engineer F. P. Teichmann, could have made history. But the new venture ran into financial difficulties in 1895. In the same year, attempts were made to mount an ignition device— it bore the number 718—in a Benz car, and it worked, since this was an engine with low revolutions per minute. In 1896, Bosch tried to construct an ignition apparatus for a motorcycle made by the firm of Rüb & Wegelin, in Augsburg, but the result was unsatisfactory due in part to the way the model was constructed. Earlier efforts to arrive at a solution by means of a high-voltage inductor, for the firm of Hildebrandt & Wolfmüller—then one of the leading firms in the young motorcycle industry—were abandoned. "What worked in a room was a long way from being good enough for the highway," is one of Bosch's later recollections of this period. Experiences like this were an often disappointing refrain for the engineers competing in the new field.

Frederic R. Simms was quite an important figure. He was in contact with Gottlieb Daimler as early as 1888, and had been his representative in England since 1893. There he was a leading contender in the struggle to bring down the outmoded parliamentary laws that held back the development of the automobile. Together with another English finance group, he was responsible for exploiting Daimler's patents on British soil, and in the process he had gained decisive influence over the personal relationships, then at a low point, in Cannstatt. Daimler had had a fight with the financial members of his company, which had been formed in 1890, and had reverted for several years to his earlier activity as an inventor and builder with no industrial ties. The Englishman's character was not entirely transparent. He was an engineer of some technical acumen, but was lacking in any solid educational background. He was prey to enthusiasms, but first and foremost he was a capitalist businessman, and one who was not too particular in his advertising methods. The English syndicate with which he was connected was interested in virtually *all* innovations that had to do with engine technology, either in order to utilize the patents themselves or to sell licenses based on these patents. The ignition device Bosch was offering for stationary engines may have seemed to Simms to be appropriate for this purpose. His ultimate goal was more far-reaching: if electrical ignition proved to be suitable for motor vehicle engines, too, then he would reap an even greater benefit; if the sales of Daimler engines in Britain were to increase, he would make an additional profit from the sale of the Bosch devices. To test out this theory, Simms took a detour, posing a challenge to the workshop in Stuttgart that would ultimately be of decisive significance. It would also bring Bosch into contact with a product made by the most interesting French builder of motor vehicles, Count de Dion.

Although he had no technical background, de Dion had at first become involved with steam-driven cars simply out of a sporting interest in showing their ultimate absurdity in comparison with the internal combustion engine. Thanks to his restless activity and inventive mind, he made sure that the new product gained acceptance among the aristocracy, as well as popularity among the masses. He was the power behind the enormously important French road races of the 1890s, and was responsible for the founding of the French automobile club. In the process, he became something of a technical expert and had independently begun to develop an internal combustion engine while the leading French firms of the time were pinning their hopes of success on licenses from Daimler. De Dion created a small, high-performance engine that he mounted on a tricycle. The ignition was provided by a dry cell battery.

Simms now sent such a de Dion tricycle to Bosch with the request to fit it out with a magneto ignition device. The engine, according to the information that accompanied it, had a speed of approximately 600 revolutions per minute. But when the Bosch engineers started up the motor in Stuttgart, they noticed that this did not seem to be accurate. How could they find out the correct number of revolutions per minute? The solution was straightforward: on the road to Wengen a section was measured out; the time it took to drive along it would be timed with a stopwatch, and from this it would be possible to calculate the engine's revolutions per minute. There is a famous anecdote about how the young Max Rall volunteered to carry out the experiment and drove the test run without waiting to receive any instructions. It went well, but confirmed the suspicion that Simms's numbers were incorrect: the estimate was 1,800 revolutions per minute. To provide the number of ignition sparks

.it required was something the magneto inductor was unable to do even in its developed form.

In its existing form, the double-T armature swung between two permanent magnets. A swinging motion caused by a bell crank on the steering shaft of the engine generated adequate electrical current with sufficient voltage. In the compression chamber of the gas mixture, a center electrode (spark plug) had been attached, together with an ignition lever and flange. At the moment when the electrical current was strongest, the connection linking the electrode and the lever was suddenly separated, breaking the contact, and an ignition spark was created. But this method had only been tested on stationary engines, and an engine speed of 250 revolutions per minute was sufficient for the industrial uses they served.

Should they give up in the face of this new challenge? As they tested and considered various possibilities, Arnold Zähringer came up with the crucial idea: Instead of the heavy coiled armature, a sleeve would swing back and forth between it and the pole shoes and would be used to attract the lines of force. This sleeve was driven by a bevel gear transmission, which also served to set the correct ignition timing. The principle of the breakaway gap between the electrode and the lever naturally remained—the whole system was based on this concept—but now, by taking advantage of the invention's increased power-generating ability, it was possible to achieve a much faster sequence of sparks, and therefore of explosions of the gas mixture in the combustion chamber. Bosch's colleagues installed the new ignition device on the de Dion tricycle. Success had been achieved.

There is no doubt that Bosch and his colleagues must have sensed the significance of these moments. They had made the connection with the motor vehicle industry. This was not something they had pursued passionately, but they had nevertheless paid attention to it throughout the various experiments they had carried out for firms in Neustadt, Munich, and Augsburg. The new discovery was patented, and Zähringer received a share in the patent. Young Rall had also made his first invention during the preparatory work, when he suggested a fireproof, weatherproof enamel, in place of asbestos, for the insulation of the electrode; he was given a bonus of twenty pfennigs for his efforts. In the beginning of January 1898, Simms's tricycle was delivered; by the end of February, Daimler was knocking on the door with his first order. Simms had evidently carried out his plan to interest the Cannstatt factory. He did not approach the inventor, whose return to the factory he had supported so actively, but apparently chose to approach the company via a member of the board of directors of the Daimler motor vehicle company, Duttenhofer. Gottlieb Daimler had the Bosch ignition installed in a car and took a test drive to the Tyrol. Although it was satisfactory, the technical experiment did not initially have any further impact. Simms made sure that the board of directors, of which he was a member, decided to enter into negotiations with Bosch. It is not entirely clear what degree of seriousness these negotiations possessed. They were handled by the technical and sales directors, Wilhelm Maybach and Alfred Vischer. Could Bosch be bought out? That was a question of price. But Bosch did not want to give up the independence he had just achieved; if the cooperation did not work out, he wanted to be able to say good-bye without regrets.

Fundamentally, Bosch's inner sense seems to have been a negative one. He seemed to feel that the other parties to the negotiation would be pleased if he came in with rather high demands—in this case, the failure of the negotiations would be Bosch's fault! Would Bosch be prepared to give the Daimler Motor Company the exclusive sales rights for the device? Bosch countered with the question: What security would they have that in the future only the Bosch ignition would be used? Maybach had to consult with Daimler, and Bosch, in the next room, heard his words: "The person who would tie his fate to an invention like this in the space of a day would have to be a lousy inventor or engineer." The direct link was dropped. But what were the approximate limits of Daimler's willingness to buy? Maybach thought not many, perhaps 100 units, with approximately 150 the following year. But the previous year, answered Bosch, he had sold 1,200—that had to demonstrate to the gentleman that a restrictive contract with the Daimler Company was not something he could consider. With this, the negotiations over whether Bosch would become a subsidiary of Daimler had to be broken off.

However, an unexpected order for the Cannstatt factory would bring the neighbors together after all. The occasion on which this occurred is one that has symbolic importance. After many theoretical experiments,

Count Ferdinand von Zeppelin was just starting, at the beginning of the century, to build his first airship; the new internal combustion engine made it possible to give this bold venture a chance for practical realization. Daimler had been convinced of this development ever since he had built his engine; he had made proposals—unsuccessfully—to the Prussian War Ministry and had built engines for the balloon experiments of Wulfert and Schwarz. It was practically self-evident that Zeppelin, whose manufacturing operation was then located in Stuttgart, would call on Daimler for this task. Before they were installed in Mainzell, the engines were still being equipped with the glow tube ignition, although the count, for obvious reasons, was interested in keeping the risk of fire to a minimum. Thus it finally came about that when the first Daimler engines were installed in the first Zeppelin dirigible in 1900, they were newly equipped with the Bosch low-voltage magneto ignition.

The relationship between Daimler and Bosch, with all its personal character, had its problematic aspects. In a memorandum that Bosch wrote only a few days before his death, and in which he made additions here and there to the earlier *Life Recollections,* stands the sentence: "Daimler hated me and caused me all the difficulties he could." When he had invented the glow tube long before, he had not wanted to admit that magneto ignition could be of any benefit to his engine. Naturally, Bosch recognized Daimler's splendid accomplishments, as he confessed in his letter to the inventor's son Paul, but in human terms he could not but feel a strong sense of alienation from the man, who was almost thirty years his senior. The judgments he made when he spoke about Daimler usually had an undertone of rejection. Later he would find that Maybach's share in the creation of the automobile was greater than historical legend suggested. Like Bosch, Daimler had a thick skull and a stubborn will. He had a sense of what he had accomplished and did not ever get a chance to enjoy it in a relaxed way. The experiences he had had when he separated from the Deutz factory, and the friction with the financial people who founded his company in 1890, had made him sensitive, even mistrustful. The affection and emotion of which he was capable had been sealed off. In his somewhat coarse and very clever face are carved the furrows of work; it is the face of a man possessed by his factory. What did he care about this young man whose stuff his board of directors was trying to talk him into buying? He had dealt with these ignition schemes two decades before. Bosch's demanding self-awareness, teamed with his technological superiority, could cause him to be rather undiplomatic. Yes, he wanted to do business, and the link to Daimler had to be important to him, but it could wait.

He did not need to wait long before the Daimler Motor Company, not Gottlieb Daimler, found its way to him. This did not represent a technical capitulation but was the result of a commercial consideration. The connection between Daimler and Bosch, which Simms had failed to achieve, was made by another outsider. The General Consul for Austria-Hungary, Emil Jellinek, who lived in Nice, had participated in the general enthusiasm for the automobile that overcame wealthy Frenchmen who did not have a great deal to do to occupy their time. As an interested amateur, he had gotten to know various makes of engines. He had found that the Daimler engines were the most reliable, but that the construction of the auto body and the safety and attractiveness of the design left a lot to be desired. He came with a proposal: if his demands could be fulfilled, he would like to take on the sales of Daimler automobiles on a grand scale. His suggestions were reasonable, for they responded to drivers' needs. There were difficulties, but Maybach and the young Gottlieb Daimler were able to find solutions. The car, which was named Mercedes after the young daughter of the Austrian, would catapult Daimler to the top not only of engine performance, but of the automobile business as a whole, within a decade.

Jellinek unintentionally became something of a fateful figure for Bosch's manufacturing business. For his notion of sales was based less on the trained professional driver—the profession was still very new and its quality uncertain—than on the private amateur motorist, and he wanted to offer him the greatest possible safety. Thus he laid down a condition: the car could not have a glow tube. And he backed up this demand with a public journalistic attack on the serious danger of this technology: "The glow tube will make every car burn at least once. I do not mean to say that as a result every car has to burn up. It is not necessary for a car to turn over for the gasoline to catch fire; a powerful shock that damages the connecting tube to the combustion chamber is enough to cause a fire. In my own long experience, my cars have caught fire innumerable times . . . Hopefully greater insight among manufacturers, or, if it cannot be achieved in any other way, a law will do away with the use of glow tubes for automobiles, since with the spread of the new means of transportation the consequences of this dangerous ignition device are impossible to predict."

The worried appeal to the lawgiver had to be the strongest argument. Naturally, there was the option of battery ignition, which, after all, had improved in the previous two decades, but if the goal of the new automobile was to be greatest possible lightness of weight, safety on long journeys, and reliability, then the decision for magneto ignition was to be recommended. Arnold Zähringer was brought in on the discussions. "Gnashing his teeth," he reported, Gottlieb Daimler had told Jellinek that he would give up the glow tube.

But by then Daimler was already a sick man. He died on March 6, 1900. A few weeks later, on April 2, the negotiations with Jellinek were brought to their final conclusion. On March 2, Robert Bosch had bought the property at Militärstrasse 2 in Stuttgart, with a garden that was bordered by the Hoppenlaustrasse, with the idea of building a factory. Like many encounters between strong personalities, the relationship between Daimler and Bosch is interesting. Daimler, after his initial hesitation, would become quite important for the excellent start that Bosch's products received. For the triumphal successes of the Mercedes brought the fame of Bosch's work with it. In the workshop in Stuttgart, they could tell themselves that reliable ignition was a precondition of the racing victories that gradually began to awaken the interest, and finally the enthusiasm, of the Germans, too. In the first years of the improved low-voltage magneto ignition, foreign countries led the way in sales—a consequence of the agreement with Simms. Among German firms, Theodor Bergmann's factory in Gaggenau and the Benz factory took their place alongside Daimler for a time. Carl Benz had personally inspected the new invention in Stuttgart, but initially there had been no sharp rise in orders. The number of ignition devices produced for motor vehicles in the years 1898–1900 was 132, 406, and 1,015, respectively. Among the ignition devices produced, the larger share still belonged to stationary engines. Naturally, production of the one-thousandth ignition device in 1896 had been an important event. This was celebrated by a company picnic in Geradstetten, a fact indicating Bosch's awareness that the rhythm of his growing success—

which was quite clearly evident at this point—would be determined by this product. But the numbers also show how limited the overall demand still was. They hesitated to speak of a market that would justify volume production for stationary engines, although there were naturally some regular orders. It was even more difficult to predict the future of automobile ignition.

The fact that automobiles and motorcycles would have revolutionary significance was something that anyone, finally, could see. Whether one thought the great races, organized by the French with a great deal of press fanfare, were worthwhile, superfluous, or even questionable, almost every one had brought a technological surprise. Anyone with any imagination at all could see how things might continue. After all the experiments, certain aspects of the various constructions had begun to be accepted as a unified type: the location of the motor at the front end of the frame; the low construction, which broke with memories of the horse-drawn carriage; the decision not to use belts for the transmission of locomotion. For the steering and the gear box as well, comparable basic forms were being developed. After 1890, pneumatic tires, which the British doctor John Boyd Dunlop had developed to the point where they could be industrially produced, gained general acceptance, at least for lighter vehicles. The convenience of quick changes using spare tires, or rather spare wheels, was not offered until 1907 and 1920, respectively. Concerns about lubrication and cooling were still unresolved; the issue of lights was still very troubling, and all kinds of intermediate solutions to this evident embarrassment were found—from stearin candles behind glass chimneys to petroleum lamps to lamps that used the newfangled acetylene gas. Every day, one could expect to discover something new— or be subjected to it! This was what occupied Bosch's mind: wasn't it dangerous to make the turn toward specialization? Was he already thinking that this type of ignition might be as ephemeral as a mayfly?

At any rate, there it was, and they had to let it fly. Bosch decided to show it at the Berlin Exhibition of 1890, and he spent several days at his booth explaining the complicated device. That he had no great success with it may have been his own fault, for he was certainly not a good salesman, and was probably only successful when he could argue in front of a knowledgeable person. There was also no opportunity to demonstrate his invention in operation. Hence the bronze medal was a consolation prize of encouragement, and Bosch, whose nature needed no consoling—he was quite conscious of the product and its merits—was more annoyed than pleased by the award. The exhibitions of the following year, in Nuremberg and Vienna, brought him the gold medal.

Magneto ignition had begun to win acceptance within the still-limited circle of automobile enthusiasts. People in the field followed the innovations with the type of passion characteristic for sports, and passed on word about them to each other. Here, among all the many uncertainties and disagreements that surrounded the drivers on every hand, was an element of dependability. Bosch ignition was something drivers desired even before the automobile manufacturers were ready to offer it. Thus, in practice, its introduction often followed the pattern of being installed in existing or used cars. This was not an easy matter, but it was instructive. Bosch was now providing the ignition, but the linkage had to be constructed by some other person, and there was no more a unified plan for performing this operation than there were fine mechanics capable of doing it. The different kinds of engines, their placement in the automobile, and the equipment of the driver's seat were quite varied, and as yet there was no thought of a norm. Thus the good results also brought problems. Bosch himself had to make people available to settle things here and there; people had to learn that it was not *his* products that were responsible for the disappointments, but rather the way in which they were installed. In the course of all this, Bosch gained experience and realized that the task would not really be solved until he and his colleagues succeeded in creating an ignition device that was independent of the changes in engines and engine mountings, and of the variety of linkages. But even now it had to be an advantage if the design of the engine and low-voltage magneto ignition were coordinated with each other.

Systematic exploitation of the new product for manufacturing was precisely what Frederic R. Simms had in mind when he suggested to Bosch that he take on the task of representing magneto ignition in England, and that he form a company for that express purpose. The decision was a doubly weighty one for Bosch. If he were to find a secure customer for a whole country, or perhaps for several countries, then he himself, as far as his production was concerned, would soon have to go into mass production. Until that point they had produced some semifinished devices for the warehouse that were destined for stationary engines, for here it was possible to reckon reliably with a growing market and the danger of having to sit on their product had receded. In addition, the connection with Simms was the first big step into the field of capitalist business with an international division of labor. It had to be good for Bosch's self-esteem to be approached by an Englishman who trusted that he could do business abroad with products of the still-modest Stuttgart factory. That might impress Daimler, or even Carl Benz, both of whom were finding it difficult, if not impossible (in 1898), to divorce themselves from the form of ignition they had been using up until then. In 1899, Simms became Bosch's largest customer, even if the figures for the first three years—87, 318, and 230, respectively—were not exactly overwhelming.

Bosch called his English representative of the time a "complicated character." In their preliminary negotiations he had not quite succeeded in finding out what actually made the man tick. "The Englishman is pleased when the person he would like to use for his own purposes is doing, let us say, rather well." The sentence was meant to express a general maxim; it is found among Bosch's remarks about Simms. But it also meant that they could be satisfied with the prices and with the sales. Still, there was never-ending friction, for Simms wanted to retain control of the business; for him Bosch was only *one* of the automobile deals in which he was engaged. This divergence of interest made the work for and with him occasionally tricky. "Again and again," Bosch wrote in his *Life Recollections*, "he tried to block my way with patents," and then there was mutual indignation, which was volubly expressed.

Simms did not merely open up the English market to Bosch (where the ignition device, according to contract, was presented under the name Simms-Bosch); what is more interesting, and more important, is that he also brought the product its independent recognition in France. In 1899, he convinced Bosch to join him in founding an English company for the French market—the Automatic Magneto Electric Ignition Company, Ltd. Simms invested 1,000 pounds, and Bosch contributed his patents, basically the patent for the Zähringer sleeve device. The business contract specified Simm's share as 50 percent; he was also in charge of the business management. In the beginning, their plan was to have the work done at a French firm, but the first tests aroused apprehensions, and Bosch was concerned that the final product might not bring honor to his name. The conclusion of the German-French patent union made it possible to import the devices. But Simms was not making such good progress. The English engineers whom he had entrusted with carrying out the project failed, and he could thank his lucky stars that Max Rall, who had long since completed his apprenticeship with Bosch and was eager to go abroad, was willing in 1900 to drop his other plans and go to Paris. The development of the Paris firm would be his real accomplishment; he was already established in a significant position when Bosch decided, a few years later, to dissolve the connection with Simms.

PART III

THE EVOLUTION OF A MAJOR FIRM

12

INDUSTRIAL
BEGINNINGS
AT HOME

On April 12, 1900, Robert Bosch wrote to his old school friend Burck-hardt: "I am a property owner; and I am happy, though not particularly because of the property, even though I don't think I have made a bad deal by buying Militärstrasse 2B." The workshop in the Kanzleistrasse had been too small for some time, so that Bosch had had to rent additional rooms in the rear building of Kasernenstrasse 61 as a temporary solution.

The contract was signed on March 2, 1900. The property was a solidly constructed apartment house with a garden that extended as far as the Hoppenlaustrasse. The purchase price was 140,000 marks, of which 40,000 were paid within two months, with the balance remaining as a mortgage. For the purchaser, the most important part of the new property was naturally the garden, as the construction site for the factory. The choice of location shows clearly enough that what was planned can hardly have been a major firm; on the contrary, it is more likely that the installation business, which in 1900 was responsible for 63,700 marks, or 21 percent of overall sales, influenced the choice of an easily accessible location in the city. The area, which was located at the outer edge of the old city, had been developed a couple of decades earlier. With a *Liederhalle* designed by Leins, a garrison church, a trade hall, and a *Gymnasium*, it even showed signs of becoming a showplace in the new Stuttgart. A more confused and awkward use of the available space can hardly be imagined. In the midst of the formless riot of house façades and apartment buildings one stumbles upon the idyllic splendor of the Hoppenlau cemetery, the last resting place of Swabian poets and artists. The expansion of the city had divided the district into neat rectangles as far as the point where the hills began to rise from the landscape, but the cemetery had resisted. The Hoppenlaustrasse forms an acute angle to the Militärstrasse, which had once provided something like a bypass that followed the city wall. Vintners had moved in, with their modest homes; the corner building still housed an old wine cellar.

It is amid this odd mixture of self-consciously historicizing north German architecture, neat tall apartment houses, fanciful tree-shaded Romanticism, and old, half-countrified houses that Robert Bosch settled, and in looking at this first factory building one is impressed with his unembarrassed willingness to project his own individuality on to this mass of contradictions. One would not want to argue that the building's form was especially successful, and there is something touching in the way it introduces itself in letters that run vertically up the length of a tower wall as an "Electr. Engineering Factory." But the building is extraordinarily important, not only because it would become the site of significant decisions and developments, but because Robert Bosch learned from it. It would be completely wrong, in his case, to speak of a passion for building. He built only what was necessary, although once the decision had been made he did it with verve and a complete lack of embarrassment. When it became impossible to overlook the limitations of the building that had been completed in 1900, there were many complicated questions to be solved. His mistrust of architects, whom he liked to accuse of emphasizing the façade to the detriment of practical questions of floor plan organization or considerations of hygiene, led to his involvement in the technical details. His ambition became the creation of excellence. He not only learned to read construction drawings with a critical eye, but he also watched over the construction with tireless energy and understanding. How many construction managers had to suffer through his instruction in the field of their expertise! As he sought in 1900 to move out of the rather stately, two-story rented rooms in the rear building, with their electric lighting, his main concern was to create bright, well-ventilated spaces. Hardly a decade and a half had passed since the new process of combining iron and cement invented by the Frenchman Monier had been introduced into Germany (at a time when it was already not so new in France), and the architects were somewhat hesitant about using the new technology. Whether Bosch was aware of G. A. Wayss's Monier leaflet, in which the technical and economic advantages of the method were described, is unclear. But he later felt a certain pride and gratification that this building, with its external façade of stone and brick, was "the first in Württemberg or at least in Stuttgart to be built with reinforced concrete . . . For this reason it was also regularly inspected or at least visited by the building inspectors during the first years of its existence."

The move took place on April 1, 1901. The great gain was the ability to separate office rooms and workshop space. Previously, the separation had been somewhat makeshift and until the Kanzleistrasse had never been satisfactory. Up until 1900, Bosch had still been technician, correspondent, salesman, all rolled into one. He needed to be relieved, and the business required a division of labor. This division began at a point where the problems were the most urgent: with a consistent, no longer episodic management. Embezzlement by a company accountant had already sounded a warning note.

In October 1900, Hugo Borst arrived from Esslingen. He was nineteen years old; his mother was a sister of Anna Bosch's, so a certain family trust smoothed the way for the collaboration. Six months later Ernst Ulmer was brought from Ludwigsburg; he took over the accounting department in 1901, and his calm, reliable manner placed it on a firm basis. While Borst was fulfilling his military service (1901–02) and a stay in America (1904–06), Ulmer headed up the business end of the business alone. Bosch quickly realized his value, and in 1902 granted him limited power of attorney. Both men were deeply involved in the development of the factory. After his return from America, Borst introduced a systematic organization of both the business and the manufacturing activities, characterized by a clear, strong style. His other principal accomplishment was to build up the German and foreign sales organization under constantly changing conditions.

There were also the beginnings of a sales staff, but Bosch may have been wondering whether the business with the factory wasn't too risky. As a secure and wealthy man, he was now beyond having to worry about money. To construct the factory he had been approved for a loan of 40,000 marks, and later 60,000, without any difficulty. But wasn't it possible that the building was too large? At the time of the move into the new building, the entire staff numbered forty-five. It is good to make a mental note of this number, as it gives a measure not only of the history of the factory, but also of the state of the auto industry at the dawn of the new century. Despite the intense public interest in the popular races, the breakthrough of its revolutionary consequences was still some time off. Forty-five men, and the building in the Hoppenlaustrasse was designed for two hundred! Although the increased demand for the sparking devices seemed assured, no one could guarantee that it would be satisfied by Bosch alone. No one was forbidden to try his hand at making the new product; perhaps one of the existing large electrotechnical firms would hit upon the idea of assigning it to their factory and laboratory workers—a move that would not be particularly desirable. Bosch was in favor of free competition, but he did not feel that he was particularly well-equipped for price competition in a market still in the process of formation. In fact, a competitor did arrive: the engineer Ernst Eisemann had already founded a workshop in 1884 and had attempted for several years, with some success, to develop low-voltage ignition.

At the time, Bosch thought briefly about renting out two floors of his newly constructed factory building so as to make full use of it. It was possible to avoid this decision, which would have been a difficult one for him, as the history of the firm took a surprising, if characteristic, detour when Robert Bosch began to construct machine tools and also considered building up a widespread installation business outside Stuttgart. After the turn of the century, electricity had begun its conquest of the countryside. Sources of water power were being harnessed, although the examples were still few and far between. It was a task that required skillful negotiation and adaptability, but, with the delivery and installation of engines over a wide geographic area, it promised to provide a dependable source of income that was not sensitive to business cycles.

The production of machine tools had begun almost by accident. A master named Schärer, a Swiss who had worked first in ignition manufacture, owned the patent for a rear lathe for milling machines. Bosch agreed to his proposal to apply it commercially in the factory. His *Life Recollections,* which are sparing in words of praise, call the man "extraordinarily able," and indeed it looked as if something important would come of the matter, the more so since Schärer also developed a grinding machine. The task itself appealed to Bosch; he later commented that only a relatively small number of German machine manufacturers of the era really accomplished good and useful results, and if the production of this kind of machine was not really the kind of thing his background had prepared him for, still, the wealth of possibilities that lay in store here appealed strongly to his technical sense. But Schärer, as he devoted himself with skill and circumspection to the development of this department, after a few years inevitably came into conflict with the overall rhythm of the firm's production program. He felt that this business could not be carried on as a sideline. Bosch was confronted with the question of whether he should expand the newly established program into an independent department. One can sense from his description that he hesitated in his decision; it took place during the period when the arguments with the Englishman Simms were tormenting him. Perhaps it would be possible here, after separating from the existing factory—this was hotly debated, back and forth—to open up a new field for his endeavors. Finally, in 1906, the solution was found, as Bosch passed the ownership of the entire machine tool department to Schärer, who now founded an independent factory in Karlsruhe. It soon acquired an outstanding reputation and remained a preferred supplier for Robert Bosch's growing and changing needs.

A new man was needed for electrical engineering. The day-to-day management of the firm, particularly for ignition, was in the best hands with Arnold Zähringer. But if the installation division was to be expanded, someone had to be there who could represent Bosch. It was fortunate that at this time Gottlob Honold completed his studies at the Technical University in Stuttgart. After his apprenticeship, Honold had worked for a year for a specialized factory in Frankfurt that produced electrical measuring instruments and had then gone to the university as a special student in mechanical and electrical engineering. His studies were interrupted a couple of times—by practical work in the electrical engineering department that the Machine Factory Esslingen opened in Cannstatt, and by a year of military service, which Honold, like Bosch, spent with the engineers in Ulm. His enthusiasm and hard-working independence made an impression on his fellow students, who benefited from his desire to be pedagogically helpful, a trait he had inherited from a long line of teachers. In the spring of 1901, Professor Dietrich invited him to become his colleague as an assistant at the Institute of Electrical Engineering. That was a great honor, but Honold declined. For one thing, he had not completed his *Abitur*, but only had a middle school certificate, and this would be a hindrance to a scholarly career. It was at this moment that the former apprentice and master encountered each other again. Bosch, on whom Dietrich's opinion could not fail to make an impression, asked Honold if he would like to work with him again. Honold's affirmative answer was fated to have a big influence on the firm, both directly through his own contribution, and indirectly through his ability to attract future colleagues.

Admittedly, what Bosch had in mind in his search for a new coworker was not Honold's strong suit; the tasks connected with installation held little charm for Honold, and an additional staff person soon had to be hired for this purpose. The position was filled by Heinrich Kempter. Honold continued to work with ignition, and it was his influence in shaping, or rather reshaping it, that would give its still unclear development a decisive direction: specialization. The very specialization Bosch had wanted to avoid would now be forced upon him by the needs of the market, at least as an important transitional phase in the firm's overall development.

During the months when Honold was laying the groundwork for a new solution, Bosch found himself confronted with a business consideration that—even if it did not have any concrete consequences—is characteristic of the reputation that his business enjoyed even then, and also of his own view of it. The Berlin firm of Mix & Genest made him an offer to enter into a closer business relationship and asked to see the records of the firm's sales, fund balances, and profits. In the context of the expanding electrical engineering industry, they were evidently interested in gaining a firm foothold in southern Germany. In his answer,

Bosch declined to give detailed information. His profit was relatively high; he did not have to worry about large machines, and the installation business, which he was expanding by taking over Bergmann's sales business, was especially lucrative, "since I have only good customers." Two days later, on September 12, 1901, he followed these modest remarks with a more thorough presentation of his position: "I have become convinced that the joining of our interests, or their going hand in hand, could only be brought about through a very loose or a very intimate connection. One possibility would be for me to remain entirely my own boss; I could not subject myself to the supervision of an employee of your firm, which you have characterized as essential. It would be nothing short of miraculous if the gentleman in question and I were to get along well, something that would happen only under the rarest of circumstances. I am not suspicious by nature. But I would not like to guarantee that I would always approve the reports your man would make to the firm, and the result would be a disagreement. . . . But the relationship that would be created by such a contract seems to me, after further consideration, to be untenable. So it could only be a matter either of my retaining complete freedom of action and responsibility, or of your company taking over my business. Apart from the fact that I do not assume it desires to do so, I myself would only give away my company if I were placed in such a position that I could leave you, in case it became necessary, without regrets. That means, in other words, that I would have to be paid a price that you, or the stock company, either could not or would not pay. Even when business is bad, I have a good living from it, because I do a lot of work for good private customers. . . . The price that I would be forced to ask for my business is one that I would not demand of anyone, and for the management of a southern German subsidiary you can find less expensive people." The anecdotal charm of this letter lies in the fact that the suspicion he has about his own nature—based on sound knowledge of his own temperament—hides behind the assurance that he is not at all suspicious, and behind the factually and historically accurate fact that even at this point in time Bosch regarded the "good private customers," in other words the installation business, as his security against the vagaries of economic cycles.

While the boss, in his office, was taking stock of the state of his firm with these words, his young technician sat in a room that had been furnished as a test laboratory. He filed, fiddled, wound wires, tested materials, experimented with electrical current and static electricity, mulled over insulation materials, and based on previous experiments with low-voltage magneto ignition, tested out the possibility of creating a high-voltage magneto ignition system, which would be free of the problems associated with linkage. For despite the fact that machinists were becoming more and more skilled, the problems could only increase, since the engine industry was rapidly making the transition to multicylinder engines. After all, every cylinder needed its own ignition apparatus, and they had to be synchronized to keep up with the increasingly rapid sequence of explosions and piston movements.

When Honold, instead of taking care of the installation orders, devoted himself completely to this task, Bosch did not object. A year before there had already been sporadic efforts to come to terms with this problem without success. Now an attempt was under way to develop Arnold Zähringer's solution by changing it from a sleeve that oscillated around a fixed armature to a rotating sleeve. Honold explained the technical state of affairs in an essay in the *Automobile Newspaper,* albeit with a certain skepticism about whether the change being worked on would hold up in practice. It was necessary to seek out and find a new way. Who knew what clever minds might already be busy working on this problem somewhere else? The program was formulated collaboratively by the two men working together; then Honold withdrew into his lab, occasionally bringing in a skilled worker or getting practical and critical advice from Zähringer. It was a very systematic process that was able to identify failures and could occasionally produce surprising results. By December 1901, Honold had progressed so far that a test model was ready for demonstration.

At the time, Bosch happened to be visiting the Paris Automobile Exhibition with Albert Hirth, who had gone off on his own a few years before, and whose skill as an inventor made him a most instructive and stimulating travel companion. Max Rall, who had remained in Paris on behalf of Simms-Bosch since the fall of 1900, was able to lead him to the stand where a French firm was demonstrating a high-voltage ignition apparatus they had dignified with the fine-sounding name *la Comète*. Bosch remarked that "This will certainly be a surprise for Honold." The discovery was not particularly worrisome for Bosch, for various tests of a version of his own ignition apparatus that had been undertaken by the French had not left him with a particularly high opinion of their competitiveness. After Bosch's return, when Honold was able to show him the results of his labors, it was his turn to be astonished: "You have hit the mark." Few words were wasted in their conversation with each other, but coming from Bosch's mouth the comment was significant. He recognized what had been accomplished. There was no need to say anything more about the Frenchman, who had chosen a more symbolic name for his product than he realized—it appeared and disappeared again after blazing briefly across the sky.

Gottlob Honold gave a report in the factory paper *The Bosch Spark Plug* on February 28, 1921: "How was the Bosch arc ignition created?" His description can serve as a model for specialists, thanks to the vivid and forceful style in which he describes the various steps and their expected and unexpected results. Beyond its technical research aspect, it also goes some way toward revealing a brand of humanity that, where success is concerned, maintains a straightforward objectivity along with a sense of gratification. The essence of previous ignition methods is described in simple words. In the case of low-voltage magneto ignition, the spark is created at low voltage (50–100 volts) by the mechanical separation of the moving contacts; here a spark appears of relatively great size and duration. With high voltage of the sort used for batteries of several thousand volts, it jumps between spatially separate but motionless electrodes and is thin and short.

The task was to find an apparatus "that would produce a *hot* spark of relatively *long* duration (arc) with nonmoving electrodes." The paths and detours that led to the goal do not need to be recounted here. The decisive question, after various preliminary attempts using different sources of electricity for the high and low voltages, was to create a common power source. This was accomplished by a division within the armature coil itself: a short part for the induction coil, the entire coil for the arc. And here the result was "that in the winding of the magnetic apparatus high and low voltage were generated simultaneously." To follow this insight through to its practically useful conclusion required the most careful labor. By no means the least important thing was to find a suitable isolation material: lacquered Chinese silk. Honold himself wound the first test armature. The basic solution, to create the spark between the non-moving electrodes of the ignition device magnetically and not by means of the transformation of chemical into mechanical energy (as in the case of batteries), was followed by the painstaking construction of the parts necessary for the installation of the mechanical devices that would connect it to the motor and the ignition. The task at hand was to create an apparatus that could be made available to machinists as a single unit.

The immediate fate of Honold's invention was strange enough in several respects. The people who specialized in engines hesitated to touch it. But the preliminary work had been well and thoroughly done. By the end of August 1902, Honold was able to report to Robert Bosch that a trial visit to Leonberg had gone off quite satisfactorily; a couple of weeks later Daimler, too, ordered its first ignition device in order to find out what it was all about. But overall, the reserve was striking, and was not immediately overcome even by the demonstration at the Paris Exhibition that autumn. As strange as it may seem, the reason was appearance. People did not believe in the igniting power of the short, thin spark compared to the "fat" one generated by touch-spark ignition. All kinds of tricks were invented for the doubters—burning silk paper, melting copper wire. Frenchman Louis Renault's decision to use the new ignition apparatus in the Grand Prix race—which he won—was the signal for a complete reversal of public opinion.

In the meantime, Honold had a rather difficult struggle to go through with regard to the legal recognition of the patent on his invention. The application of January 4, 1902, was formulated in this way: "magnetic electrical ignition apparatus for internal combustion motors, characterized by the fact that by means of a break in the coil the voltage that is induced reaches a level that is sufficiently high that by interrupting the shorted armature coil of a part of said anchor coil the voltage induced in the coil rises so high that between two end points for current that have been introduced into the inside of the cylinder in the familiar manner, isolated from each other, and attached to the ends of the armature, a small arc is created." The patent office refused to recognize the practical usefulness of the procedure. Honold's arguments with the appeals department led him to delve even more deeply into the process and its problems. Years before Bosch had taken him on as his apprentice, Honold had volunteered in the studio of a local photographer. He had continued to practice the art as a hobby; now this hobby proved to be very useful. He constructed a clever apparatus by means of which the creation of the spark could be photographed. This, along with numerous demonstrations in the testing division of the patent office, helped to convince the critical bureaucrats. Two and a half years later, in June 1904, the patent was approved.

Now, however, it would be shown that the reservations of the National Bureau of Patents—for reasons that were not clear to the responsible official himself—were not without some objective justification. The dispute went on for such a long time because the usefulness of the new construction was at issue. That the production of high-voltage ignition by means of magnetic induction represented an idea that was new in principle had been taken for granted. But this was not accurate. A competitor was able to discover something that had remained as unknown to Honold as it was to the specialists from the patent office—that in the year 1887 an engineer in the Deutz Gas Engine Factory, Paul Winand, had been granted a patent formulated along related lines. One is reminded of the fate of the Otto four-stroke engine, although there the circumstances were admittedly somewhat different: Winand's construction obviously remained on paper and never got to the stage of realization. Robert Bosch, with his deeply rooted misgivings about all formal legal processes, which to his temperament were nothing less than torture, did not go the way of Otto & Langen. He simply let the patent expire, failing to pay the fees. The entire matter was handled discreetly, and it was left to competitors to continue their imitations; Bosch was not interested in pressing the matter. Others could try as they might to equal him. In making this decision, Bosch sensed that the *essential* things could not be taken over so easily. By this time, a whole crew of people had been trained for this very subtle and intricate work, and their skill and reliability represented an asset of his firm that could not be duplicated easily. The words "Bosch product" had begun to be recognized all over the world.

13

———◆———

THE MARKET
EXPANDS

On the client list of the firm of Bosch, the names Fiat, Austro-Daimler, Skoda, Pöge, Presto, and Protos appear for the first time in 1900. The automobile is now becoming a factor that causes new industries to be founded or product lines to be expanded. Two types of automobile entrepreneurs are characteristic of Germany. One group comes from the engine manufacturing sector, which in the past had built gas- or gasoline-driven engines that were mounted in place. The other group had previously manufactured bicycles or sewing machines; their machine tools and workforces could easily be adapted for certain facets of the new task. The motorcycle sometimes served as an intermediate link in the process; the bicycle factory Rüb (later Heinle) & Wegelin had been one of Bosch's most important customers between 1898 and 1900.

Soon Opel in Rüsselsheim and Kleyer in Frankfurt would appear on the market with their inventions. For an undertaking like Bosch's, these young firms had the advantage of not being linked to a tradition of early inventiveness on the part of their founders, as they had become active at a later stage of development. Since their particular contribution was to make technical and economic adaptations to the process, they could become involved in new projects whenever it seemed advantageous and in keeping with the dictates of rationality. A certain basic division of labor became evident and, with some exceptions, would continue in the future. Along with the key firms, which supplied engines, chassis, gearshifts, steering mechanisms, and so on, came the manufacturers of auto parts. This division of labor was not entirely clear when it came to the body of the vehicle, the shaping and equipping of its outer shell and seats. But here, too, independent firms were emerging that exerted a significant influence on the development of the designs, especially of passenger cars. The tire industry clearly occupied a special position, and ball-bearing production—not limited to the automobile—created its own industrial niche, while the various kinds of equipment developed for oiling engines and gears were located somewhere in-between. The fact that the ignition industry crystallized as an independent business sector was Bosch's first achievement. Through his initiative, the new industry developed independently from the automobile but received a powerful stimulus from its growth.

In the powerful expansion of the ignition industry after the turn of the century, and the fantastic proportions it assumed after 1906, one can also see the reflection of a more general boom. The automobile lost the character of a luxurious plaything and was transformed into a tool that revolutionized transportation. A new industry was created. Robert Bosch surely owed much to the automobile's importance, which the industry's pioneers had foreseen and which aroused fear and envy in petty bourgeois Babbits even as it was overlooked by many government offices. An impartial assessment of the overall situation also shows that in the long run Bosch had more to give, and gave more, than he received. The ignition device meant more than simply perfecting a technical means of increasing the revolutions per minute of an engine or linking its multiple cylinders. Over the next decades, almost the entire production program of the firm would be determined by the motor vehicle, as Honold and his co-workers focused on the remaining auto parts. The creative contributions of the workshop in Stuttgart not only increased the automobile's technical effectiveness, but also gave drivers the security and ease that were required if the motor vehicle was to win mass acceptance and true popularity.

The increased speeds desired of motor vehicles were dependent upon the smooth functioning of the ignition inside the engine's combustion chamber. These early rates seem, in retrospect, quite low. The Daimler engine that took part in the great road race from Paris to Bordeaux back in 1895 was the easy winner with an average speed of 24.5 kilometers per hour; a Mercedes created a sensation in 1901 with 75 kilometers per hour. But only three years later, the world record already stood at 156 kilometers per hour. It was the era of the great auto races. The restrictions on weight and cylinder capacity continually challenged the engine builders, and the profile of the tires was consistently studied and improved. The importance of regular and reliable ignition was also confirmed. In 1903, a Belgian, Camille Jenatzky, had won the Gordon Bennett Race with a Mercedes touring car that was not even new—the new models had been destroyed in a factory fire. The race car still had the old Bosch low-voltage ignition. This victory was so important that a stylized picture of the head of its breakneck driver was chosen by an advertising firm as the subject of Bosch's first poster, the Red Devil.

The increasing commercial exploitation of the automobile, which had been developing in Germany, began at Daimler-Benz with the signing of licensing contracts and the setting up of dealerships in foreign countries, crucial for this early period. Demand was stronger abroad, despite the fact that industrial diversification had begun there earlier. At any rate, in 1902 the German National Bureau of Statistics recognized the production of motor vehicles as an independent branch of industry, and a new listing, the automobile, turned up in the statistics on foreign trade. It had previously been included under machines. For the next twelve years automobile exports would continue to be several times greater than imports.

For Robert Bosch, too, the first large-scale commercial link had been with foreign countries in the form of the Simms contracts. As early as October 1898, the engineer Eduard Denes, in Budapest, was given the job of representing the firm in Austria-Hungary. Later, he opened the firm of Denes and Friedmann in Vienna, which was given responsibility for all of Italy as its sales territory. A sales outlet and repair shop in Milan were among the first outside offices to be set up, at first under different names. No thought had yet been given to Germany itself. The few buyers at the other firms knew what was going on, but the situation might change as competitors came into the market. It was not Bosch's style to issue loud propaganda, and even the residents of Stuttgart did not have a very clear picture of what he produced—the city's chronicles mention him for the first time in 1913. Bosch was worried about the danger that could result when better-capitalized firms became aware of an article whose developmental possibilities and requirements he himself had not fully explored. When Honold's arc ignition was introduced, there was a brief moment when it seemed that the Daimler firm, which had immediately ordered a sample, might be seeking a closer relationship. They had made a car available to test it, and when they saw that the new ignition mechanism did a better job of responding to the increased revolutions of their engines, they proposed to Bosch that they be given a monopoly on its distribution for a certain period of time. Bosch declined the offer but was prepared to deliver the first 500 pieces to Daimler with the condition that the new ignition be put through the toughest tests on several vehicles over a six-week period, because its real practical utilization over extended periods of time was not yet a reality. They got no farther than an agreement in principle, and Bosch remained unfettered in his decision-making ability.

In this situation, Bosch was not displeased when August Euler sought him out in the spring of 1903 and presented his plan to open a sales operation for the automobile business. Until now, Bosch had taken care of sales himself. Here was a good opportunity for some relief, and he agreed. Euler, too, was happy to make a deal, for even if the commission of 2 percent could only be regarded as modest, Bosch would guarantee him 20,000 marks a year in commissions. This was enough for a start. He himself once commented on how much the "business card" was worth to him. His background was the bicycle—he had become a famous bicycle racer, and represented the firm of Reichstein, from Brennabor in Brandenburg, as a traveling salesman. Then he turned his enthusiasm and nose for business to the newly popular automobile. He worked for Bosch (although not exclusively) for five years. Bosch was satisfied with his profits in purely commercial terms, although there were differences of opinion, for Euler was self-confident, stubborn, and touchy. Euler would drive through the countryside in his car and had friends from his sport-

ing past everywhere—he was knight and traveling salesman all rolled
into one. Their separation came in 1908, and took the form, at first, of a
complete break. They were simply no longer compatible. (Later, however,
they would reconcile their differences.) In that same year, Euler had
taken to the air. Although he himself was not mechanically adept, he possessed a strong mechanical instinct. Since German airplane construction, in spite of Otto Lilienthal's pioneering achievement, had remained
backward, he purchased a Voisin double-decker, learned to fly, and
founded the first school for pilots in Germany (with the exception of the
independent experiments of Hans Grade). In this way he entered the
early history of flying in Germany in a very honorable way, as a teacher
and propagandist. From 1919 to 1921, he occupied the post of under-
secretary of state in the National Office of Air Travel.

When Bosch separated from Euler in 1908, the structure of the
Stuttgart firm had already undergone some fundamental changes. The
conscious differentiation of its various goals had been strengthened. Both
personal and professional motivations had played a role in this development. North America began to build automobiles shortly before the turn
of the century—somewhat later than Europe but on a more massive
scale. In 1899, Henry Ford, after long and careful preparations, sent his
first car to the market, a car that was not designed for the snob, the sporting gentleman, or the rich man—they could continue to order luxury
models from Paris or heavy, solid speedsters from Germany—but for the
middle-class citizens of that vast country, businessmen and farmers
alike. It was a good, strong piece of equipment, and was meant to be
affordable and even inexpensive. Ford could succeed in this endeavor
because from the very first design of the production process, his automobile was always intended for the masses. Production and sales rose
immediately into the tens of thousands. With the country's great oil
reserves, the natural conditions for inexpensive operation were at hand.
Hugo Borst had been in America since 1904, perfecting his sales and
language abilities. He had crossed the Atlantic after Frederic R. Simms
had broken his promise to take him on as a member of the staff of his
London office. Although it is true that Borst had nothing to do with the
auto industry while he was in America, he did keep his eyes open and
cleverly collected the addresses of all the American manufacturers, deal-

ers, and builders of combustion engines. He brought this packet of information back to Stuttgart with him in 1906, along with his now cooling anger at Simms.

In Stuttgart, however, he ran into a situation in which the Englishman once again figured prominently. Simms had made quite a place for himself in the automotive and motor vehicle business. At the firm of Robert Bosch, his technical ability was not held in terribly high esteem, but it was obvious that he knew how to make an impression and stimulate interest. He had turned to manufacturing and had brought out a six-cylinder Simms engine. In 1901, one could find pictured in German magazines the "Simms war car"—a vehicle on the order of a gunnery tower, armored and equipped with light arms, which was meant to run on railroad tracks and be used for security and the defense of railroad property. This was a remarkable idea by any standard, especially at a time when few military leaders were thinking about motorization. The fact that Simms was making a name for himself, and that he prided himself in being the real manager of their joint ventures in England and France, was something that weighed on Bosch's mind. The decisive contribution had been made by people from *his* operation, and, besides, it was annoying that while in other places people were already beginning to talk about Bosch ignition as a well-known brand name, their products appeared in France and England under the double name Simms-Bosch, as had been specified in the contracts.

And what contracts! It was one thing for Simms to have taken over the sales in his country in 1898, but he had also been formally given the option of purchasing the patents for 50,000 marks. He could then begin to manufacture ignition devices himself, in and for England, as a licensee. In the company they had cofounded in 1899 for the French and Belgian market, Simms's stake of 1,000 pounds had represented 50 percent of the capital, but this fifty-fifty arrangement had been cleverly altered by Simms. In a word, he had tricked Bosch by giving the English managers in Paris, with Bosch's assent, 1 percent of the firm as a bonus for good performance. At the next suitable moment, he challenged Bosch to do the same. Bosch did not want to be any less generous and followed Simms's lead, without immediately seeing that this voluntary renunciation had played into Simms's hands. But if Simms, who exercised control over his English employees and thus represented the majority, were to buy the patents and thus become their owner, he could also force the company to begin manufacturing in France. This, in turn, would bring a concrete advantage—the possibility of access to government and military orders that were closed to imported goods. The danger that he sensed in this process tortured Bosch. He later expressed the opinion that his fear had been essentially unfounded; Simms's cleverness was probably a sign that "he wouldn't want to separate from me as long as he had a good profit and as long as his vanity did not suffer." At the time, he saw the relationship as much more worrisome, and he did not like the business style of the man who wanted to force people to buy from him in order to "rob them." These methods seemed to Bosch to be an obstacle to building up a business on a grand scale, particularly in England. But because of the restraints imposed by the contracts, his influence was limited. Thus he sought through a codicil to gain some assurance that delivery from Germany would be guaranteed, at least for a period of time. That would have meant that Simms would have been held back from starting his own production, if only for a limited time initially. But Simms declined. "We pulled each other this way and that for a few years," says Bosch in his memoirs. The joy of working together had been thoroughly dissipated, and one thing, at least, seemed certain: Simms would fail when it came to the prospects offered by the young American market. He had not so much as touched on the possibilities he had of exploiting it, although America was also included in the contract.

In 1905 things took a surprising turn. Simms proposed buying the entire company from Bosch, offering him 5 million marks in cash. With this, Bosch would have been free to start something else. But despite the fact that after almost twenty years of intense work he must have been tempted to devote some time to his hobbies, he was not well suited to retirement. He was not looking to engage in competition, but perhaps he could envision running the machine-tool department that had been built up by Schärer. In the last few years, when they had had to purchase various machines of this kind, it had become abundantly clear to him that in comparison to America, Germany was lagging. The plan to found a joint venture with his stepbrother Eugen Kayser, who had been busy gathering industrial experience in Berlin, surfaced again. In other words, he felt a fundamental readiness to separate himself from the firm if it meant becoming free of the irksome tie with Simms. For him to act as a manager under Simms was already beyond the realm of psychological possibility. Honold and Zähringer, who each received a payment from the firm for every ignition device of their design that was sold—one mark for each device—and thus had a strong interest in the continuing positive evolution of the firm, wanted to continue in their positions even if the firm should change hands. Although they had no desire to fight things out with Simms themselves, Honold knew an excellent person for that job, a comrade from his student days, Gustav Klein. If he could be brought into the firm's management, the deal was possible. Klein was interested, and the meeting between Klein and Simms, in December 1905, was satisfactory. The planned separation could go forward. But now Simms no longer would or could pay Bosch the 5 million marks in cash—Bosch was supposed to remain in the circle as a stockholder. Everything remained up in the air.

This whole episode, however, had an important impact on the company. Bosch invited Gustav Klein, who had come to his attention as a prospective manager of the Simms venture, to join his own firm. At the same time, Hugo Borst had returned from America to take up his old position with Bosch.

14

———

PROBLEMS OF WORK AND
THE WORKERS:
THE EIGHT-HOUR DAY

Based on various surviving records, it can be established that when the Bosch firm moved into its new building in 1901, there were 45 workers. For 1904, an average of 261 is mentioned, and by 1906 there were 560 staff members. These numbers reflect the speed of the industry's growth. As a quick preview of things to come, the number of employees in 1912 totaled 4,500.

Behind these rough statistics, however, lay serious concerns about human needs, technical realities, and even aspects of personal life. The early employees had been hired by Bosch himself, on probation at first, which was not to everyone's liking. He observed them, and if someone was hard-working and able Bosch gave him a chance. Anyone who proved himself was allowed quite a lot of freedom in his manner of work. Cleanliness and careful handling and organization of all required materials and tools were carefully scrutinized. The catchword "rationalization" was not yet in vogue. Just as Bosch, in constructing his first building, seriously considered the importance of hygiene for the protection of the workers' health and productive energies—reflected in his concern for light and ventilation—so now he proceeded with care when it came to organizing the installation of machines and the location of work stations. There was, as yet, no such thing as timekeeping, but there should be no wasting of time, either. Sloppiness and nonrational methods were frowned upon. As Ernst Durst, who would later become a technical manager in the factory, said, "At Bosch, they don't pay you for picking things up." The management style at the new establishment was consistent and frugal. It was not Bosch's manner to push people to the limit. Bosch was happy when there was a cheerful atmosphere in the building, when there was singing and whistling. That he was fully capable of interrupting it in a sudden storm of anger was something everyone knew. In addition to reliable work, it was expected that people would get along with each other. In later years, when Bosch had long since given up handling personnel matters himself, and conflicts in the company were brought to him—a complaint here, an objection there—he paid the most attention to the human relationships involved and would often suggest a change of work station or a different composition of the working group. He had no hesitation about letting workers go who could not get along with others, no matter how good their technical abilities.

The enduring significance of this transitional period between craft workshop and large industrial firm may be that the demanding, closely observant, decisive man—always present, always eager, alert, tense, and objective—exerted an unusual educational influence through his attitude as well as his actions. It is not as if his influence shaped a certain type of personality. Among the men who were gradually maturing toward their independent responsibilities in the business office, or as engineers and masters on the factory floor, there were very definite and diverse personalities, and powerful and self-confident workers particularly attracted Bosch's interest. A certain kind of awareness was being developed, at first quite unsystematically, toward the work and the workers, which was shared by the leading technicians and factory foremen and which permeated the different levels of responsibility for the company's operations. In these years when Bosch himself acted as a teacher meting out praise or criticism, he created an intellectual and emotional tradition that would continue to live in many individuals and be handed down over the years, even after the firm's growth to gargantuan proportions removed him from daily contact with the workers and made him almost a legend. Later, this force would be called the "Bosch spirit."

The question of workers arose soon enough. Where could he find the trained people? Stuttgart was not an inconsiderable reservoir, but it lacked specialists in fine mechanics, who had to be brought in from outside. When the space became too small and new workshops had to be built, Bosch himself noted that one of the reasons he remained in Stuttgart despite the high price of real estate was that it was easier to attract people from outside to come to the big city than to a suburb or small town in the vicinity. Commuter travel was, as yet, poorly developed. Additions to the workforce continued to come from the surrounding area of Württemberg. With few exceptions, these workers were essentially farmers.

Gradually, however, the work itself inevitably underwent a transformation. The rapidly growing demand forced a change in the form of production. The statistics on the production of ignition devices give an idea of the order of magnitude: in 1896 the number reached 1,000; in 1901, 10,000; in 1906, 100,000. The growth of the workforce corresponded to the increased utilization of machines. The time when things were produced on order was past; it was now possible, without too much worry, to work in volume and stockpile the products despite the seasonal variations that affected industrial customers. But this procedure, too, almost immediately became outdated; the products were being snatched from their hands. In 1905 it was necessary to adopt the expedient of double shifts in order to make full use of the machines, an experiment that would have far-reaching consequences.

This period was not without a certain embarrassing quality of apprenticeship, not only for Bosch but for all of German industry. Its practitioners became aware that America, which until recently had lived on the import of ideas and organizational structures from Europe, was on the brink of gaining the advantage along a broad front. At issue was not the accomplishment of individual geniuses like Edison, but a new industrial principle. The introduction of machine tools, including high-speed steel, turret lathes, grinding machines, high-speed drills, and even robots, meant that the care required to do the work assumed a different character from traditional craftsmanship. Not all the older trained people responded eagerly to the innovations in which mechanical precision competed with their sensitive craftsmen's skills. Implementing the transition was not a simple matter.

At Bosch, they had worked according to the piecework method from the very beginning. Based on experience, temporal norms for familiar work processes were established; when new processes were introduced, the master had to help out, at first, by making estimates. The time study, the scientific method of determining piecework norms, had not yet been invented. But it was known that even the most capable and eager worker, following the best piecework scheme, would not thrive if his tools were outmoded or were not properly cared for. The struggle to obtain the best tools, and the unrelenting effort to educate workers about the care of these tools, was not only a matter of economics but also represented a core element in the social policy of the Bosch firm: people were expected to do good work, but the factory was also expected to provide them with what they needed to succeed and thus enable them to make a good living.

In the tool shop with its constantly changing tasks, the work was at first permitted to remain free of piecework. Wages were high and varied according to the degree of responsibility assumed by the worker. In the production shop, there was group piecework at first. Columns of workers were formed for particular tasks, and the percentage share of the total wage allocated was calculated on the basis of the importance of the individual task. As a transitional practice, this was a very educational means of discovering and developing individual abilities. Unfortunately, this method had the disadvantage of placing an additional burden on the masters and chaining talented individuals and their unusual productive abilities to the average. From the year 1908—the business had already grown substantially—norms were established by a special piecework office. It became evident that straight piecework, which freed the individual from the limitations of the group, led to an increase in productivity.

By the time this phenomenon was noticed, an important decision had already been made: the refinement of the piecework system and its results were linked to the reduction of the workday. In 1894, Bosch had already introduced the nine-hour day and had given an indication that the eight-hour day was not far off, as soon as the competition would cut its hours to nine, something that had not occurred. The question remained as vivid in the minds of the older workers as it did for Bosch. One must recall that at the end of the last century the length of the workday stood at the center of public sociopolitical concern. The Paris Congress of the Socialist International in 1889 had proclaimed a work stoppage on May 1 as a demonstration in favor of the eight-hour day. With this, the demand took on an overtly political character. The German protective legislation of 1890 had legislated maximum workdays for women and children. Since that time, parliamentary discussions about the permissibility or desirability of legislative intervention in this aspect of German employee relations had continued without interruption. This issue also occupied the British House of Commons. Legislators hesitate, they are grateful to be relieved of responsibility by a decision that is freely arrived at by the people who are directly involved. But in this case the workers themselves were in a state of complete confusion regarding their opinions. When Heinrich Freese, a manufacturer of Venetian blinds from Berlin, originally offered his workers the eight-hour day in 1889, his proposal was met with rejection. He introduced it in 1892 as the first large manufacturer in Germany to do so. In Britain the eight-hour day had been decreed in 1891 for the army staff and the admiralty. Although these bureaucracies lay outside the purview of capitalist competition, still, the decision could not help but have a broader influence.

The research that Lujo Brentano published in 1893 on the relationship between the workday, wages, and worker productivity provided the impulse for Ernst Abbe, the founder of the Carl Zeiss Works in Jena, to turn his attention and later his decision-making to this complex of questions. His intervention had resulted in a reduction of the workday from eleven and a half to nine hours; then, in 1900, he reduced it still further, to eight hours. The workforce had grown to more than 1,000. In a factory that enjoyed world renown thanks to the scientific preeminence of the man and the generous legal structure of the firm itself, this was a highly impressive occurrence.

To what extent Robert Bosch was already taking an interest in the specific cases that reflected this general development cannot be established with any certainty. Later, from a human perspective, Ernst Abbe would have a strong influence on him. Bosch may have felt his temperament to be akin to Abbe's in his brusque sense of freedom, sensitivity in questions of justice, and unease when confronted with questions of state power politics. Despite the differences in their ways of life—Abbe undermined his own health relentlessly—the two men shared many similarities. Their point of departure was not identical. Abbe the scientist was more deeply influenced by socioeconomic factors and was simultaneously more doctrinaire than Bosch, the developing entrepreneur whose passionate youthful dreams had been tempered by the sober business of mastering the concrete tasks at hand. But the deepest impulse behind their sociopolitical behavior was the same. Both also remained free of Christian religious coloration or nationalistic sentiment. The ethical and humanitarian element that both of them inherited was mingled with a biological approach to the human capacity for work. Ernst Abbe, after careful studies, had argued that such a position could be justified from a socioeconomic or business point of view. Robert Bosch saw this confirmed by simple experience.

The biological point of view had already appealed to Bosch as a follower of Gustav Jäger, who had not only studied clothing and the body's caloric systems but had turned his early investigations to the topics of human work capacity and the forms of fatigue, exhaustion, and recuperation. Jäger's views were certainly not unimportant to Bosch, but they were not what led him to the decision to shorten the workday. In Bosch's environment, many decisions that history would later color with the pathos of conviction were simply the result of a realistic insight into the situation at hand. In the year 1905, orders were coming in with such rapidity that even overtime would not have been able to help. The new buildings had not yet been erected, and the number of machine tools would have to remain limited. Hence there was no other expedient, if they were to come anywhere near meeting the delivery deadlines, but to introduce a double shift—after all, the machines were willing and able. Thus they introduced shifts of eight hours each on a temporary basis. The result was instructive. On the whole, production remained the same, and the piecework rates earned in the shortened work period remained at comparable levels. At the very least, they recognized that with the help of an easily introduced organizational or technical adjustment or two, the degree of work intensity could be secured for the firm, with a savings in electricity and a gain in free time for the workers. Work regulations were posted to the effect that beginning on August 1, 1906, the eight-hour day would be adopted. Along with Freese and Abbe, the firm of Robert Bosch was the third fledgling large industrial firm that voluntarily came to the decision considered by entrepreneurs of the time as a revolutionary point of view.

Among the days on which work would come to a halt, the list, between Easter Monday and Ascension Day, included May 1. This was the origin of the phrase "Bosch the Red."

15

INTO THE
WIDE WORLD

On March 1, 1906, Gustav Klein and Hugo Borst, who had rejoined the firm, were sitting and talking. How could they realize Bosch's desire to separate from Simms? It was not easy to come to any agreement with the man. Bosch himself was tired of all the letters, which in peaceful periods began with "Dear Bob" and assumed a confidential tone, but in times of crisis addressed Bosch as "Dear Sir." Borst had been treated hesitantly by Simms in London; later the Englishman wanted to win him over again, in combination with Honold. But the letter had failed to reach its addressee, who was in America at the time. Of the three, Klein was the least inhibited by the situation, but the picture it presented to his interventionist temperament was clear enough. The problems that so distressed Bosch—overly high prices and unfair stipulations—bordered on fraud, and according to all the experts, they also hindered the development of the French and English sides of the business. They simply had to be corrected. The danger remained that Simms would start his own production in France. Bosch himself had the feeling that his partner was taking a hostile attitude toward the construction required in Stuttgart, and was hoping that these heavy investments might lead to financial difficulties.

So the contract and the correspondence were studied in detail by Klein and Borst, but they found nothing that would enable them to get a better understanding of things. They then turned the whole matter over to a man who had had nothing to do with it until then—a hiking companion of Robert Bosch's named August Jung, who had recently started work in the bookkeeping department. It was possible that his unprejudiced eye might be useful. In fact, he discovered that in all the complicated contracts (in 1900 they had been renewed for a period of fourteen years) concerning the sale of the products, the option to purchase the patents, and the calculation of the profits, there was not a single line about a requirement to make deliveries. Simms had relied on the fact that the Stuttgart firm, which at the time was still poorly developed, would be happy to deliver its products. This now served as their point of departure, and when Rall, in consultation with those in Stuttgart, resigned from the Simms firm, it could only mean that the Bosch firm was ready to force the issue. Simms had just received some large orders from Renault, and he was now left sitting on them. Under this kind of pressure even he became tractable and he was willing to give up his ownership of the French company. The deal he made in the process was not at all unfavorable. Seven years before, he had invested 1,000 pounds; now he was bought out to the tune of 600,000 marks. Bosch was freed from the worry that production might begin in France without him. By June 1906, he was the sole owner of the Paris company; Rall stayed on as the technical manager, and thanks to his superior technical experience and skill in human relations, combined with the firm's new freedom from constraints, the firm entered a period of ascendancy under his leadership. In October 1906, Rall was joined by Hermann Fellmeth from Mettingen, near Esslingen, who became sales manager.

Perhaps Robert Bosch, in spite of the annoyances of the past years, would have hesitated to force the break with Simms; after all, the latter enjoyed some status in England, where his general position in the automobile business gave the impression of a certain grandeur. But it was discovered that in the course of the Paris deal Simms had made an error of 100,000 francs in his own favor, and this heightened the tensions. In his contract for Britain, Simms had no production rights; on several occasions he had already been caught manufacturing ignition devices and trying to avoid paying the fee to Bosch. The matter had been smoothed over with excuses and payments, but now, in the summer of 1906, Bosch went on the offensive. The French company, now independent and set up according to British law, appeared in the British market as a seller and was greeted quite cordially by firms that had had enough of Simms's pricing policies. At the same time, the gap that existed in that part of the contracts where the delivery requirement might have been stipulated was brought to bear on the situation. Bosch himself led the final negotiations in London with the "absolute scoundrel, who is finally afraid that I will saddle him with a lawsuit" (from a letter of July 27, 1906, to his wife). The material was potentially damaging to Simms's social position—"he has become a fraud." The Englishman caved in and ceded the right to be the sole representative. He received a free license to all the existing patents, but he had to give up the name Bosch. At their separation, Bosch had to pay a compensation fee of 17,000 pounds. Simms's attempt to make the transition to the independent fabrication of magneto ignition devices in Bloomfield, Illinois, ended a few years later in bankruptcy.

Now Bosch appeared on his own. At first, the French firm took the lead; then followed the founding of Bosch Magneto Company Ltd. in 1907. The English automobile industry, which was just entering a period of rapid growth, was happy to have access to quality German products. The prophecies of Bosch's serious British friends were fulfilled. The experience was also instructive in a larger sense. In his correspondence of the previous few years, Bosch had urged his English partner not to dissipate his planning energy, not to go too far in his experiments in producing engines. But this had been to no avail. Simms's restless activities as the founder of the new business made him unpopular with customers with whom he was, at the same time, eager to compete. By 1907, when he closed down the engine and car manufacturing business, he had recognized the fact that perhaps the base was too small after all, but the insight came too late. If necessary, Bosch only had to think of Simms in order to be reminded of how *not* to expand. To the many frequent suggestions that he should also start building engines, he always responded that he could not allow himself to think of competing directly with his clients. The breakthrough to contractual freedom in the French, Belgian, and Anglo-

Saxon markets, and the extraordinary phase of development that followed, was initially intimately tied to the name and achievements of Gustav Klein. In a memorandum in the spring of 1921, when discussing the
events of 1906, Robert Bosch remarked, "After that I took Klein into my
own employ, and here I had the man I needed. He had every imaginable
skill and was as mobile as it is possible to be. He was constantly active
everywhere, in the best sense." Bosch's relationship with the man he
"needed" is not fully reflected in these words of sober acknowledgment.
Their colleagues found Klein to be the only one of their group whom
Bosch really loved—quite apart from the value he attached to their
achievements, which in Honold's case, for example, were never questioned. Decades later, whenever he spoke of the colleague who died so
young, whether he was talking about his humanity or his business acumen, his voice and eyes would betray his emotion.

Gustav Klein was a conqueror by nature, a catcher of men, one of
those cosmopolitan and ambitious Swabians who are able to feel their
way into a situation with sensitivity and adaptability and without losing
themselves in the process. Armed with a solid and positive sense of himself, he immediately felt at home everywhere. He charmed his friends
with his free spirit, sociability, and wealth of entertaining stories. Yet he
was not merely the cheerful, respectable man about whom anecdotes
would be told for years to come, but also an extraordinarily hard worker
and sharp-eyed practitioner in technical matters who gave encouragement and knew how to define what needed to be done. Honold would see
to it that it was somehow carried out—that was his job. Klein was not
much interested in political matters or weltanschauung, and for him the
social problems of the workers' world were finally reducible to a strong
and even rough camaraderie in which he participated as often as it
seemed necessary. In setting goals at work, he proposed the highest possible requirements, which people followed because he was the one making the demands. His own enthusiasm and pride in the work carried them
along; they knew there would be no lack of thanks and celebration afterward. At the firm he was Klein, whereas his colleagues addressed the
somewhat shy and self-absorbed other manager as Herr Honold.

When Klein arrived at Bosch he had already had a taste of the wide
world. The son of a strict stationmaster with Pietist leanings and small

means, he had earned his middle school certificate in Stuttgart and had then been sent as an apprentice to the Machine Factory Esslingen. After a few years there he made his fortune in a peculiar and characteristic fashion. A machine that had been delivered for a molding mill had been breaking down repeatedly. By chance, Klein was assigned to its repair. The clever and self-confident way in which he discovered and fixed the problem so impressed the owner that he voluntarily offered his apprentice money if he wanted to continue his studies. Klein accepted. From 1896 to 1898, he attended the school for the building trades and simultaneously became a special student at the Technical University, where he met Honold at the Saxonia fraternity. After his compulsory year as a soldier—where he served well, albeit without any genuine sense for the military—he returned to the electromechanical department of the machine shop in Esslingen. In 1900 he set off for South America, where there was an opening for an engineer to build and supervise a power plant. Klein stayed in Argentina for three years. From the management of the electrical power plant he transferred to a similar position at a large silo complex. He was in the process of becoming a sought-after engineer, one who was also adept at building construction. At home, they thought he would stay "over there" and make his career. But one day in the fall of 1903 he returned, and in an extraordinary way. He drove in through the factory gate in a horse-drawn carriage. He had driven the horses from Genoa, across the Alps and through the hill country. This is the famous, often retold story of Gustav Klein's return from the outside world. Perhaps he had read from the book of life of one Friedrich Wilhelm Hackländer, who had returned to Stuttgart in the same way to find his fortune. Klein's friends understood him very well—he still had the youthful arrogance to make a bet that he could drive his horses across the ocean. Of the five steeds he had brought onto the freighter with him in America, three had been sold to pay for his passage and for the wagon he bought after he arrived in Italy. Nor had he lacked pleasant company on the journey—at least until he arrived at the borders of his home territory.

The factory in Esslingen was glad to have him back. But in 1904, when the position of manager of the electrical department became available and he was passed over, he resigned and joined the firm of Lahmayer, in Frankfurt, as a field representative. This was at a time when the construction of electrical power stations offered a tempting opportunity for men who were skilled at negotiation and had a knack for giving practical advice. Klein's 1906 decision to accept Bosch's offer may have been partly affected, among other things, by his strong attachment to the place of his birth. At the same time, as a member of the group that had conducted the Paris negotiations of 1905, he had also had a chance to see the scope the firm had assumed during his absence. Just as Bosch was impressed by Klein's ability to quickly assess a complicated situation, so was Klein impressed by the depth of Bosch's trust as well as the broad latitude he was willing to grant for independent activity. Klein became the head of the sales department, thus relieving Bosch of a very important burden. Until now, the care and cultivation of customers had rested largely on Bosch's own shoulders; he had considered it sufficiently important, even though he would not have said that it appealed to his inner motivation or nature. He was more concerned, at the time, with the problems of building new factories.

Klein's first independent task of significance was to explore the North American market. Robert Bosch had watched its development with a certain ambivalence. He had been annoyed that Simms had talked about developing it but then, despite his urgings, had not done much of anything about it. When the Simms crisis came to a head, Bosch and his colleagues actually felt rather glad that Simms hadn't appeared "over there," perhaps ruining their chances with his pricing policies. Now, admittedly, there was no time to lose, for Simms, who had been closed out of the French market and was coming under pressure in England, and who was well capitalized as a result of the buyout, might decide to rush into the territory he had previously neglected. In the summer of 1906, Klein traveled to America, accompanied by a mechanic. On the other side of the ocean he was met by a German-speaking salesman whom Borst had gotten to know during his stay in America.

The name Bosch was not completely unknown in America. At that time, wealthy Americans, attracted by the highly visible auto races organized by U.S. publisher Gordon Bennett, still preferred high-status automobiles of the type built by European firms. Those with the best reputation were outfitted with Bosch ignition systems. But beyond that, the automobile had become a means of mass transportation with a suddenness that was overwhelming. In that huge country with its great territory, the automobile's appeal as a sporting activity, along with its snob appeal, soon fell away; here, from the very beginning, the automobile was an implement of middle-class and business life. It is well known that the toughness in design and the socioeconomic vision of Henry Ford had created a new situation with regard to technical processes and pricing policies, and that Ford was forcing his competitors to follow suit; differentiation did not set in until later. In any case, the mass demand was already there. "Fortunately," Bosch writes in his memorandum about Simms, Simms "had not done anything prior to the time when I was able to arrive in the United States, and I can say that our appearance there took on aspects of a triumphal march . . . There were times when people would take an old car and build a Bosch ignition system into it that was worth almost as much as the car itself."

The point of departure was the list of approximately 100 addresses of specialized businesses that Hugo Borst had compiled in America; the businesses were sent well-designed English-language brochures in the mail, and one-fifth responded immediately. After a few weeks of traveling, Gustav Klein had collected orders worth $1 million, and by the time he left for home, a sales office had been rented on Sixth Avenue near Broadway, and the Bosch Magneto Company had been formed with starting capital of $25,000. It is interesting to note that Klein cleared up a very troublesome matter of tariffs on his very first visit. At the customs bureau in New York, a certain Harvey T. Andrews held the position of general appraiser—a man who would become very important to the firm of Bosch in a different context several decades later. But first the firm got to know him from his unpleasant fiscal side. The ignition apparatus was subject to the ad valorem duty system, and this meant duties of up to 45 percent of its book value! Klein, who had brought along a quantity of goods of different kinds, lodged an appeal. A court case ensued in which the son of Carl Schurz appeared as the Bosch firm's attorney. The trial was decided in their favor after the accounting documents were hastily assembled in Stuttgart and rushed to America. The way was now clear. Klein had asked a colleague from Lahmayer, Otto Heins, to move to the Bosch firm with him. He had been keeping his eye on him as the future head of the company's Brussels office, which, following the separation from Simms, was also in the process of becoming independent. Klein noticed Heins's practical manner and his skill with languages and had him transferred to America. There he was joined by sales director Günther Jahn, who was recommended to Klein by Borst and who would later be the main pillar of the American venture in times of crisis.

But for the moment no one had thoughts of anything ever approaching a crisis. The American business grew by orders of magnitude that were simply uncanny. Only a few years later it was decided that it should have its own manufacturing plant. But even before that, the Bosch performance and name had become known to Americans. Bosch himself told a story, which he had heard from Klein, about a music hall in Arizona. A musical clown appeared and could not say enough about the wonders of his instrument. As his last trump card, he threw in: "And it even has Bosch ignition." This kind of comical advertising was not at all the type of thing the firm was accustomed to, but it suited the new environment and could only be welcome. It made the name Bosch into a concept, a standard of value per se. This would later lead to highly unexpected, if not actually paradoxical, results.

The year 1906 marked a serious turning point. Only a few weeks before his death, Bosch remarked in a letter to Eugen Diesel, "In the year 1905 I was still going through a lot. From 1906 on, things went more easily. I gradually found people who supported me. But that is almost saying too little; they were and became more and more capable colleagues. Until that point, machine tools had eaten up all the money; I still had to save" (January 2, 1942).

The development during the coming years was marked by the same grandiose rhythm that had come to be typical of Bosch's creation. His liberation from Simms, followed in 1908 by the separation from August Euler, the sales representative for Germany, marked the beginning of the building of the business organization, which took two different forms: Existing businesses were given a franchise to represent the products from Stuttgart in a country or a group of countries; or Bosch decided to build his own sales outlets, subsidiaries, and repair workshops abroad. The Austro-Hungarian and Italian outlets had already been joined in 1903 by one in Holland—Willem van Rijn, of Amsterdam—and in 1904 by one for all of Scandinavia—Fritz Egnell, in Stockholm. In 1906, South Africa, which had been part of Simms's area, became independent. In

1907, a subsidiary reporting directly to the parent company was opened in Brussels, which until then had been served by the French firm. In the following year, the sales outlet in Milan was taken over, but retained full internal autonomy. Things continued in this vein. In 1908 came Spain and the leading countries of South America. In 1909, an independent office was set up, at least provisionally, in Berlin. In 1910, a Bosch sales office opened its doors in Geneva. Russia, Turkey, and, after 1911, even Japan had joined the great network through firms that represented Bosch. The network itself became more tightly woven with each passing year. Even the smaller countries joined in. The French subsidiary expanded within its own country, opening an office in Lyon, and the American subsidiary put down roots in Detroit and, as early as 1910, crossed the border into Canada. In the brief eight years of expansion before the Great War, the globe was almost completely encircled with outposts of the Stuttgart firm.

At the time, the technical administration of this task was essentially in the hands of Hugo Borst. He approached the organizational structure with a preference for theoretical clarity. Klein's spirited suggestions, which arose from his close contact with the changing practical requirements, not only affected the production program but also had implications for the general policy of the firm. Through Borst's thoughtful consideration, they acquired a rational basis and a certain stability and orderliness. For Borst, who was still a young man, it was a splendid thing to think in terms large enough for the gradual expansion to grow into them, and to set up a clearly delineated sales structure. He was also responsible for the first conscious forays into the area of advertising. Robert Bosch had been very restrained in this area—his pride and his ambition made him feel that the quality of the product would be its own best advertisement. But now competitors had joined the fray. It was a matter of necessity that something more had to be done. The advertising of the year 1906—for example, a touching letterhead with statistics of races that had been won with the help of Bosch ignition—had had a rather accidental quality until this point. Now, thanks to Hugo Borst, it became more significant and ambitious.

The thrust of this development was determined by the powerful will of Robert Bosch, who established its direction. He knew by now that magneto ignition had become his fate, and as the growing number of machine shops were fitted with the best machine tools, his determination to fight for the leading position was apparent. The ignition apparatus was being refined and simplified by Honold's ingenious and never-satisfied nature; during these years he came up with a new spark plug, which, if it had been invented a few years earlier, would have saved many a detour. Bosch's satisfaction with his overall success was mixed with a thoughtful concern: Would the solution of the ignition process, as he had developed it and brought it to the highest degree of perfection, hold firm? Would not technology one day find an entirely new solution that would devalue their apparatus and experiences? The factory's statistics record the symbolic dates and figures: 1901 saw the ten-thousandth magneto ignition; in 1905, there were 50,000; in 1906, 100,000; in 1908, 250,000 on the market. When they succeeded in reaching the 500,000 mark, the occasion was celebrated in a very characteristic manner among the workers, whose number had already passed the 1,000 mark some time earlier: work-free Saturday afternoons were introduced. The first million mark was reached in 1912, the second at the beginning of 1915 when the war had already broken out. The comparison of the numbers and time periods gives a vivid picture of the tempo and rhythm of growth.

The motor vehicle was now in the period of its most powerful development. The notion that it was a rich man's plaything, or essentially an excuse for sporting events with all the social activities accompanying them, was on the wane. On the streets, the first trucks appeared. Noisy, puffing, and awkward, with wide axles, they were quite annoying to automobile drivers at first, but with their advent even the slowest observer could see the revolution in transportation. And this first decade of the new century brought something else, as well—the motor-driven airplane. People may not have imagined, at first, what joy and terror these clumsy boxes—moving through the air only for their amusement—would one day hold for them. Technical and economic considerations led to the setting of new goals and tasks. While the ignition device remained the centerpiece of the high-speed internal combustion engine, at the same time many specific questions having to do with reliability, safety, and convenience arose out of the practical needs of automobile traffic. These included, for example, tires, suspension, the construction of the chassis, and the structure of the axles. A specialized industry was the result. But some areas were still not at all or were insufficiently advanced, such as the whole system of traffic signals or the methods used for early evening and nighttime lighting. The increase in the number of cars on the roads and the increase in the average speed clearly led to problems in these areas, which were now of utmost concern. What tasks awaited Honold's eagerness to apply his precise scientific knowledge to the secrets of optics and acoustics! In the next decade and a half he would celebrate new triumphs.

A chronicle of this era must not overlook a sideline of Bosch's which, although it did not become a very important concern and was either closed down or in some cases sold off after a few years, testifies to his two-pronged approach in which entrepreneurial thrust was combined with caution and diversification of risk. In 1911 Robert Bosch purchased the waterworks in Munderkingen, on the Danube, developed the electric power station, and began to build power lines, install transformers, and fill the sheds of the peasant villages of Upper Swabia with engines. The figures may once again provide an instructive indication of the contrast: In 1910, the first U.S. factory had been built, with the goal of technically and economically securing the production of magneto ignition in the New World; 1911 was the beginning of the invasion of the Upper Swabian idyll. This was not an area in which Bosch invented anything original. The construction of electrical plants associated with water-power stations and the provision of electricity, in the form of light and power, to the countryside had been taken in hand since the beginning of the century, after municipal initiative had been awakened by the great experiment in power transmission in Lauffen-Frankfurt. The old firms from Berlin, Frankfurt, and Nuremberg were the most important in this development, but the entrepreneurial spirit of millers, whose mills were located next to waterfalls, also played a role. When it came to the exploitation of natural resources, the local municipalities and administrative districts staked their claims early on, and societies that combined public and private interests came into being. For Bosch, the issue was to give his installation department, which had been separate from factory production since 1904 and led a somewhat shadowy existence, a new and objectively important job to do. The purchase of the Ulm installation firm of Köpf & Bantleon, which had been led with great industry and technical reliability by Leonhard Köpf, created a geographically convenient outpost for the venture. Undoubtedly, this step also reflected the need to become associated, in both a learning and a helping capacity, with the process that would lead to the technical and rational transformation of the agrarian areas, but compared to the orders of magnitude that characterized the main business, this excursion into Upper Swabia played a secondary role. Nevertheless, Bosch the world wanderer undertook this little stroll through his familiar neighborhood with the liveliest of interest, particularly since he came up against forces that opposed the power of the semipublic corporation to that of his private industrial will. The friction was an incitement to struggle.

When, in 1905, Bosch—tired of the fights with Simms—was firmly determined to give the Englishman his factory, a purchase price of 5 million marks had eventually been negotiated. Simms had not been willing or able to pay the cash price they had settled on. The success of the firm of Robert Bosch was achieved without outside money, except for the investments Simms had made in the joint venture they had founded in Paris. But occasional financial pressures still existed. Even as a young craftsman, Bosch's eagerness to succeed had led him to purchase one machine after another, actually outstripping his capacity to do so. But if earnings were good, so were the savings for new acquisition and construction. The people from Daimler had once made tentative inquiries as to whether the young venture might be for sale; it remained an inquiry. The Berlin firm of Mix & Genest was thinking about how to gain a southern German outpost, and Bosch sensed the threat to his independence. Still, he had once written in a letter to Simms, "I have, myself, been thinking about turning my business into a stock company, and if we do not come to an agreement about France, I shall take steps in this direction" (October 1, 1904). Was this just a tactical threat, or was he serious? As it became evident that the business was gaining momentum, capitalists from other branches of industry came to him with offers to invest in the firm, making mild threats that they would start competing. They had patents—wouldn't it be smarter to work together? Bosch turned them down.

The flood of orders that began after 1906, especially from England and America, brought the firm such liquidity that the great investments in factory construction and new machines, which occurred in the years 1909 to 1911, could be paid for from current income without any reliance on outside credit. In an era in which the formation of companies often followed the policies of banks—nearby Daimler had become the model for this—Bosch retained his independence. He wanted to be accountable to himself, not to anyone else.

16

FIRST
PHILANTHROPY

Bosch once told an acquaintance that it had been his dream to be far enough along by his middle forties to be able to free himself from business and devote himself entirely to his hobbies. Dreaming was not actually his forte, given the type of man he was, and if his words did not contain an element of irony, they may have been romantic self-deception to the extent that the word "romantic" is appropriate anywhere in his vicinity. In referring to his hobbies Bosch might have meant botany, zoology, or basic questions of biology, and it is hard to imagine him as a research scientist patiently striving for pure knowledge, trying to catch the fullness of life in the abstractions of scientific laws. His basic nature was much too pragmatic for that.

Bosch had a very realistic conception of man's responsibility as a citizen. He was uncomfortable when he heard someone use idealistic views to blur the hard realities of workaday existence. If the purpose of work is to secure life, then that life will be guided by the degree of security that is desired. There are no hard and fast formulas for this. Individual preference, family tradition, the habits of class, religious beliefs, and customs all work together. Robert Bosch came from a wealthy peasant-bourgeois family that had never known want. The family had worked their property actively and had maintained a sense of frugality. It was natural for them to include those who were less fortunate, and they did so with a matter-of-factness that came from an inborn goodness or good nature. A lifetime of work should be followed by relaxation, rest, and well-being. The son would later come to the conclusion that his father, Servatius, had done this a bit too early.

In the early period of the craft workshop, the Bosch family strove to sustain a secure and well-tended household in the bourgeois sense. Actually, they rather frequently found themselves in financial straits. Things were not always easy for the young wife, especially since her husband was very particular in his wishes. The word "savings" was emphasized from the beginning. The debts they owed his mother and his brothers-in-law were not particularly onerous, and he was confident that he would one day be able to take care of them. But it was a good feeling, after all, to be rid of his debts and in a position to help his circle of relatives. Rather than such luxuries as culinary delicacies, which did not fit with Bosch's principles of hygiene, he sought pleasure in hiking, traveling, and sight-seeing. "For the first six or eight years I didn't dare to be away from the shop for long periods," he wrote. "Every Sunday and holiday I used to take long walks. In the middle of the 1890s, I went to the Alps for the first time, and from then on I was crazy about hiking in the high mountains" (1921). As the children grew older, the family began to go to Upper Bavaria or Tyrol on their summer vacations.

The trips to the high mountains did not make Bosch into an alpinist in the technical sense of the word, but he was capable and sure as a climber. As he exercised in solitude, he refreshed himself and cast off the burdens and petty annoyances of the day's business. There in the mountains, Robert Bosch also became a hunter, although as the result of a business-related venture. The Englishman Simms owned a piece of land on which he hunted chamois, to which, beginning in 1900, Bosch was invited on several occasions. These seemed to Bosch like useful opportunities to get to know this important and enigmatic man, to observe him among the peasants in an atmosphere free of contracts and delivery problems. As psychological experiments, these visits revealed little of Simms's nature, but they did have an effect on Bosch, as he was now gripped by a passion for hunting. In 1904, he leased his first hunting preserve in Magstadt, near Stuttgart. "I often went there completely alone and when I could I would spend the night in the hunting lodge, for example, after I had been locking horns with Simms and was quite in need of relaxation." Simms had provided the recipe that Bosch used to recover his psychic strength. The fact that Bosch's love of hunting came about through his English partner and opponent is surely accidental. In later years it would play a large role in his reflections; he justified the expenditure of time, mental energy, worry, and sacrifice as follows: "Today, in my 60th year, I am indebted to hunting for a certain physical and I might also say mental agility and decisiveness" (1921). Or another time: "The advantage of hunting for the person who is in need of relaxation is that it prevents the hunter from giving free reign to his thoughts. It distracts him."

The fact that he had begun to hunt gave a certain direction to his social life. Several of the members of the firm began to imitate him. First came Gottlob Honold, then Ernst Ulmer. Gustav Klein, who feared other colleagues would follow suit, resisted: "To go after a leopard, well, that might be appealing, but to sit there waiting for some poor little deer to come along . . ." Ultimately, Klein had to accept his colleagues' interest in hunting, although he may have grumbled when the schedule of business trips and conferences was adjusted according to the hunting seasons.

In the years during which the business was gaining strength, Bosch remained aloof from public life. There are no documents from that period that indicate his feelings about the questions that confronted his country, but it is not difficult to imagine them. It is quite certain that even then a continuous inner debate was taking place over questions of current tariff policy, the expansion of the army and navy, and the arguments over constitutional issues. He was not a member of any party, and it would not have suited his style to have to assume leadership on tactical questions. He was antigovernment and oppositional to the core, tendencies that were revived as soon as he cast a glance northward, past the boundaries of Württemberg. His critique of the social order no longer had the clarity that it had had in his letters from America twenty-five years earlier, but he was still displeased by the social atmosphere—the casual acceptance of obvious injustice, the hardening of social prejudice, the conceit of the educated, and the evident class hatred. He did not conceal his sympathy for those groups who struggled to expand their living space, even if the theories they used to justify their claims might be false.

These were subjects he had once discussed with his neighbor, Karl Kautsky. The two men kept within their respective boundaries when having such discussions, for although Bosch enjoyed masculine conversation and logical argument, he was too down-to-earth to be tempted by abstract economics. His thinking was not influenced by theoretical Marxism, and he had long since formulated his arguments disproving the theory of surplus value. It had been a few years since he and Kautsky had lived in the same apartment building. Although Bosch had built a home of his own in the Hölderlinstrasse, and Kautsky had moved to Berlin, their family contacts did not cease altogether. Through sheer coincidence, Bosch's household continued to be linked with the circle of individuals who were the theoretical leaders of Marxism. Frau Anna Bosch wanted to have her adolescent daughter's portrait painted by an artist whose strong, colorful work had impressed her at an exhibition. The painter was Friedrich Zundel, one of the leading organizers of the Stuttgart Artists' League. Along with the portraits, in which dark coloration alternated with transparent brilliance, Zundel also created paintings that presented a version of the modern worker. A measure of proselytizing spirit was mixed in with the realism of the painting. The painter was a socialist and the husband of Clara Zetkin, who was living in Stuttgart at the time and was the editor of the women's newspaper *Equality*. The initial encounter between Anna Bosch and the Zundels grew into a friendship. Clara Zetkin was a speaker of explosive temperament who possessed not only the vehemence of the hatred that in those days seemed to be directed primarily against the "revisionist" Social Democrats—the leaders of the faction within the Württemberg *Landtag*—but she also had a thorough historical training and a sensitivity to form that, if not native and original, was at least intellectually schooled. She became an influential factor in the Boschs' circle. This encounter with a personality so active in the political party apparatus would later have an important objective impact on Bosch.

The immediate effect, admittedly, was of quite a different sort. Friedrich Zundel's interest in helping his artist colleagues in Stuttgart succeeded in awakening in Bosch a friendly and supportive involvement with their work. Bosch's relation to workers in the visual arts was not a natural one. He liked some things and not others; he was mistrustful of estheticizing value judgments, no matter how eloquent. But he appreciated skilled craftsmanship and straightforward thinking, and he was ready to offer his help where he thought it was deserved. Collecting, whether from a desire for possessions or more from a feeling of historical connectedness, was completely foreign to him in every area. He did keep his hunting trophies, at least the most important pieces, but when someone proposed that since he had become such a connoisseur of rifles and shotguns he should put together a collection that would demonstrate the development of their various designs and forms he refused. Now, however, Zundel's encouragement led him to acquire artistic works of the leading Stuttgart masters of the time: Pleuer, Reiniger, and later, Landenberger and Goll. For the most part, the paintings that found their way into his collection were landscapes, although he was particularly fond of artwork that evoked an element of personal experience. Among the older masters, for instance, he owned works by the animal painters Braith and Mali, and one senses his interest in the subject matter. In later years he once wrote a few characteristic sentences to Eduard Gebhardt, the friend of his youth from Ulm, about his purchase of art. "For some time I had been buying pictures from living artists," he wrote, "and primarily, as much as possible, from Swabians. I bought only a very few older pictures, and then only for particular reasons. I do not buy any expensive old pictures, but tell myself that instead of giving a dealer 10,000 marks for an old picture, I would rather give 10,000 or 15,000 marks to a living artist and make his life easier and more possible" (1937). In this way, a rather impressive series of works was assembled; Bosch's personal inclinations toward art took on firmer contours and limits within the context that this collection provided.

In 1911 the appropriate framework for the collection was established when Bosch bid farewell to the streets of the town and had a large residence built on the ridge of mountains that marked the southern boundary of the city, at the spot where the ridge turns eastward toward the Neckar Valley. It was not so much the location that attracted him—he later remarked that the sunny slopes on the opposite side of the bowl would have been more appealing—but up there in the Heidehof he had found the most splendid woods. His pride and joy was to show his guests the luxuriant growth of the most beautiful, and in some cases rare, species of trees. It was touching to see how he would consult the botanists, in long detailed letters, about a diseased tree. Here, almost entirely surrounded by the city, he lived inside a protected nature preserve that had its own bit of history. The creator and first owner of the park had been the writer Friedrich Wilhelm Hackländer, whose fate in the early 1840s had driven him from the Lower Rhine to Swabia into the service of the court. He possessed a cosmopolitan talent of comprehensive scope, and not only wrote novels, travel books, and plays with ease, but also advised the crown prince of Württemberg on a thousand matters. Hackländer also built for the crown prince the park that surrounds the villa, which was designed by Christian von Leins. The elderly King Wilhelm had made the dilettante Hackländer, with his fund of useful information, the director of the palace garden. Thus he had left his mark on the city landscape of Stuttgart. Up above in the Heidehof, where the vintners of Gaisburg had their vineyards, Hackländer had first begun to experiment with his hobby, as recounted in his *Novel of My Life,* which also tells of the loud and lusty gatherings that occasionally annoyed the local residents. Such anecdotes had almost vanished from memory, as the property had changed hands a couple of times and was not often used. Now, as the Bosch residence, it became the site of a princely residence with outlines borrowed from the early Renaissance. The owner, as passionately as he concerned himself with the details of all his factory buildings and workshops, restrained himself from involvement in its design. One is tempted to think that once he had made the decision he let the matter take its own course, for in the period during which the building was being completed he made a trip to America. The trees, in all their splendor, would be waiting for him when he returned.

Part of the park, where the old avenue had been, had previously been open to the public. The fact that a high wall now transformed the entire property into an island of seclusion did not please everyone. The man of whom people saw so little was soon the subject of much talk—talk that ranged from envy and admiration to fairy-tale fantasy. What could he expect from all of this talk? Two sentences in a letter of April 1912 read: "Really, nothing at all surprises me any more, and thus I am not surprised that it is said that I wanted to build a school for my administrators here in the city. Naturally this contains no truth whatsoever."

The first large contribution with which Robert Bosch had introduced himself to the public in 1910 was the occasion for a colorful run of rumors. It was the beginning of his virtually incomparable philanthropy, and it was directed at the technical sciences. Earlier, there had been smaller, although not insignificant, sums. In 1902, he had made a gift on the anniversary of the Engineering Association of Württemberg; he expressed a loyalty to the Hut through considerable contributions for the construction of a clubhouse. Now, as the first decade of the new century came to a close, he was occupied with the notion of funding an experimental school of air travel and technology in Friedrichshafen. But, as the government of Württemberg did not believe that it could assume the long-term obligations the project would entail, his readiness to be involved had to find another outlet.

Carl Bach, a professor of machine building at the Technical University, was also an international authority as a researcher and writer on the subject of all elements of machines. He came from modest circumstances and represented a rare combination of scientific rigor and practical, pedagogical energy. In him Robert Bosch had found an individual whose advice he willingly followed. It was not only that the life story of this scholar could not fail to impress him—as a locksmith's apprentice with no family background he had made his own way to the top—but Bosch also knew that it was Bach who had made practical craft training a requirement for admission to the Technical University, creating a model that would soon be adopted by the other provinces. This was in accord with Bosch's fundamental instincts. In addition, Bach, who fought tirelessly for the status of the engineer in public life and government, was also concerned about the relationship between factory engineers and wage workers. He was worried about the dangers of a fundamental division between designers, for example, and those who worked with their hands.

Bach came to Bosch with his concerns, and the businesslike exchange of letters between the two men continued in a lively fashion for decades. It would not be possible to speak of intimacy, but each man knew what he had in the other. Bach's memoirs mention it, but Bosch, among whose gifts flattery surely occupied one of the least prominent positions, wrote to the scholar on the occasion of his retirement from his professorship in 1922: "What you have accomplished in your profession goes well beyond general praise. It belongs to the history of technology." Bosch was generally sparing in such praise in individual exchanges. Now, in the summer of 1910, Bach was describing his troubles—how inadequate the financial provisions for the annual support of a number of institutes were when it came to enabling them to conduct actual research. The sums varied between 5 and 8,000 marks. At the Institute for Material Testing, one of Bosch's favorites, the budget was only 1,800 marks. Wilhelm Dietrich, Bosch's former teacher, got wind of these conversations and hastened to ensure that electrical engineering would not get short shrift. He was reassured by the fact that on November 20, 1910, Bosch wrote a letter to the rector that contained the motives for his decision to fund the school and a detailed listing of the various budgets. "These sums, so far as I am informed, have scarcely sufficed for the satisfaction of the immediate needs; it is as good as impossible to conduct scientific research with them. As a result, the fertile influence such work can have on teaching has become practically negligible. I consider this state of affairs to be inappropriate to the tasks and goals of a technical university, and have therefore decided to contribute to the Technical University of Stuttgart the sum of one million marks for a Robert Bosch Foundation." The foundation would support and cultivate the physical foundations of applied technology, particularly machine engineering, through research and teaching, and would include both electrical engineering and construction. In both lectures and practical courses, the foundation would work to secure the physical foundations, as defined above, in theory and practice. A charter, which defined the share of the capital that was to be used for the various purposes, also described Bosch's conditions. Among the formal rules it was stated that government contributions were not to be reduced as a result of the gift. Whatever increases would have been required at some point, without the existence of the foundation, had to be continued. The foundation board consisted of the rector, the heads of the institutes, and Bosch, who might be succeeded after his death by his son, assuming that he had passed his twenty-fourth birthday and was willing. The heads of the institutes were free to use their portion of the income as they saw fit, but to draw on the principal of the endowment required the agreement of the founder.

These conditions were devised with the help of the responsible professors, with the clear aim of reducing bureaucracy to a minimum. In the first years the income was used primarily to increase and refine the stock of instruments; later, systematic research projects were added. The prelude and postlude to the document have biographical significance. Bosch had asked that the matter be handled in a way that would be as painless as possible for him, that there would be no academic honors, torchlight parades, or honorary doctorates, for it would only demean the title to link it to a financial transaction. The rector took due note of this, but when the foundation charter had been filed and the formal act was completed, the university senate passed a unanimous resolution to give Bosch an honorary doctorate. He was in an awkward position. Taking back the foundation was not a possibility. Should he offend the academic body with whom he had just established this relationship by turning down the title? Not wanting to offend, he submitted to the honor. He often regretted it, for as he feared and as may have been the intention of the professors, other financial supporters of scientific institutions seemed to come to expect academic recognition. Bosch, who found this quite undignified, occasionally found himself in the vicinity of people with whom he was not comfortable. Personally, he made the most limited possible use of the new honor. In the firm's internal operations, he disdained the title of doctor, which is much more broadly used in Germany than in the United States. He remained simply Herr Bosch.

He was more successful, both then and later, in fending off the government, which had to approve the foundation. The fact that any medals or titles it might give would arouse little joy in the recipient had been communicated, at any rate, by the rector, and the minister of culture, Fleischhauer, therefore expressed his regret that Bosch's "rare modesty" prevented the king from giving any particular expression to his grateful recognition, which he would so gladly have done. Bosch must have grinned when he realized that the danger of being councillor of commerce and the menace of the Friedrich Medal had passed him by. The minister was not quite accurate when he wrote "modesty," where in fact pride and a contemptuous disdain for all external state honors were at work. Bosch might find them acceptable for others, with a slightly scornful indulgence, but never for himself.

The one-million-mark contribution of 1910 had made Bosch's name known even in circles that were far removed from the technical sciences or the automobile business. In Germany, private support in areas traditionally funded by the state was not as common as in the Anglo-Saxon world. The only truly impressive event along these lines had been Werner von Siemens's creation of the National Institute of Technical and Physical Sciences. The founding of the Kaiser Wilhelm Society for the Sciences and its prudent management by theologian Adolf von Harnack, and Oskar von Miller's diligent collecting activity for his Deutsches Museum in Munich, were the first acts that effectively tempted people to act according to a sense of noblesse oblige. Bosch's own decision was completely independent of this rather professional and soon somewhat officious trend. Perhaps, as a hopeful comment by the ministry in Württemberg said in December 1910, it would "break the spell against doing something of the kind in heavy industry." For Bosch, what mattered was having the desire and the ability to give concrete assistance. He desired neither honor nor honors, neither power nor influence, and he was not motivated by a sentimental desire to do good deeds. The splendid freedom with which Bosch, over the course of the coming decades, would make available both small and very large sums for purposes of the common good sprang from his sovereign attitude toward money and from the sense of his duty as a citizen to make his growing wealth fruitful for the welfare of the people, in the broadest sense. Bosch's contributions were unsystematic at first; later, they came to reflect a certain type of giving. Considering that his funding was kept within certain psychological bounds, the breadth and variety of what Bosch accomplished is astonishing.

Naturally, the goal here cannot be to catalogue the various generous gifts Bosch gave to individuals or organizations, as the list would necessarily be incomplete and rather dull, and it would be difficult to gain a clear overview. It is appropriate, however, to recognize those contributions which allow particular insight into Bosch's judgment. Bosch could not have realized the commotion that would be caused in the German press following the announcement of the foundation's creation. He would have been horrified at the prospect of a virtually endless procession of supplicants. The Leitz binders of the period are a burial ground of fates—begging letters alongside attempts to explain special interests. Modesty and boldness are all jumbled together. All of Germany, from the Memel to Lörrach, sent its greetings. Individuals in need presented themselves along with needy institutes and inventors looking for a chance to patent their discoveries. Bosch could have set up a special office just to deal with the vast number of requests from people involved with the development of the airplane.

In order to organize the flood of requests, Bosch began a search for a capable assistant. It was quite clear that among the unimportant things that overflowed from his desk after every mail delivery there were genuinely valuable and sensible suggestions. There were emergencies that could be alleviated by a gift, a piece of advice, or a show of interest. Bosch needed to save time for himself and his coworkers, who were pressed into service to help with the replies. He wanted to find another hand—someone who would bring an independent imagination and sensitivity to the task—to help sort out the requests, weigh the merits, and advise him on this sphere of his activity, which was emerging alongside his more narrowly business-related or technical work. In 1911 he found Hans Walz, a twenty-eight-year-old salesman at the time, the son of a teacher from Stuttgart. It was one of the most important personnel decisions Bosch ever made.

One of the amusing events from the first years of Bosch's philanthropy was his relationship to his hometown of Albeck, which was planning the construction of a new schoolhouse. It occurred to the mayor that they could approach the village's most prominent son about the costs, and the idea was not without merit. Bosch was receptive, on condition that nothing should appear about it in the newspapers. Could the municipal council and the head of the school guarantee this? They said so in a solemn written declaration that was signed by all of the town councillors. But Bosch did not quite trust the situation—wouldn't one of them start boasting over in Göttingen, or in Langenau, about how easy it is to get a schoolhouse in Albeck? The contribution of 10,000 marks had a condition attached to it: if anything appeared about it in the newspapers, each member of the city council and local school board would have to pay a fine of 500 marks! As Bosch well knew, this was a threat that would make Swabian peasants hold their tongues.

The first large philanthropic gift, soon legendary, had a somewhat bizarre side effect, as it was used against him by his business competition. In April 1911, Bosch wrote to a friend that in Italy it was held that "a person who made charitable gifts and paid taxes naturally had to demand high prices for his products. This made it very difficult for my representative to conclude any business deals there." As far as the difficulty of concluding deals in general was concerned, it was probably not so tragic; but Bosch himself reacted very sensitively to questionable acts on the part of his competitors. He was glad to accept the accusation of high prices from those who wanted to attack him by underbidding. He was aware that he had the best product, and if someone wanted to have it he had to pay for it; if that person was satisfied with less, he could gladly go to the competition. But Bosch defended himself, as he demonstrated frequently and in a variety of circumstances, whenever other motives were brought into these discussions.

17

———

THE NEW PROGRAM OF WORK: SEMIFINISHED GOODS AND PARTS

In January 1908, Eugen Kayser wrote to his brother-in-law from Berlin. "To judge by your widely diversified program," he wrote, "there is a large-scale industrialist in you. There is something uplifting about this thought of creating industrial values, and as a true son of Swabia I must add: especially in one's home territory." Should he follow this call? He had the impression that Honold, Klein, and Zähringer would not be pleased if he did. The letter continued, "It seems that, as far as the question of my representing you is concerned, you are thinking more of someone to assist you with new ventures."

In the 1880s, Bosch had often considered the possibility that he would later join forces in business with the close comrade from his soldier days in Ulm, the man who later became his brother-in-law. Sometimes this seemed almost inevitable, but there were some rather negative factors to consider. Kayser seemed to Bosch to take too long when it came to making real decisions, not exactly dawdling but a bit spoiled and overly demanding in his expectations. Eugen Kayser, for his part, had taken his time; he did not want to be corrected and ordered about by his critical friend. He had made his own way through Berlin's big industries.

For some years he had been a close associate of Emil Rathenau at the
AEG, he had had leading positions with Löwe and Daimler Marienfelde,
and he knew his way around German and international big business. But
Bosch knew that Kayser's desire for independence was still alive.

As early as 1905, when he was almost at the point of selling his ignition factory to Simms, he had thought about starting something new with
Kayser. Now, the possibility arose once again. Had Bosch planned to hire
Kayser as his actual representative? Probably not, and Kayser's thinking,
to the effect that some of the leading men in the firm would not necessarily welcome the addition of a new, older leading employee with background and expectations, could not be dismissed. Bosch had thought of
this himself, and before he developed his plans he had worked out his
ideas with Klein, whose agreement was important to him. He described
Kayser, whose only failing was the fact that he was his brother-in-law,
and Klein wanted to have a look at him. This investigation took the form
of an all-night drinking session involving Klein and Kayser, who showed
up in the office at eight o'clock the next morning, where Klein observed
that it was possible to work out their agreement quite objectively and
without any difficulties. Bosch liked to quote Klein's laconic summary
after he returned home: "We can use Kayser. I have tried him out."

The task that awaited the new man may have been Robert Bosch's
most far-reaching decision, and the one that had the most significant
consequences. He wanted to make himself independent, for economic
and technical reasons, from the suppliers of magnets. For this reason a
new factory was founded to serve the ever-changing needs of the core factory (stimulated by the continual evolution of ignition devices) and to
develop its own marketing policy. This prospect could tempt Kayser. He
had achieved a certain amount of wealth himself, and would have liked
to have a financial stake in the business, but he understood that given the
size of the financial requirement, Bosch's participation would always
have to be very large. Thus a financial partnership might easily be a
source of irritation. More important to him was the fact that the structure
offered him a degree of objective independence—something that Bosch,
with his liberal insight, offered every employee he trusted. In this way
Eugen Kayser, following Bosch's basic plan, became the real creator of
the new factory, which was first called the Press Works, and which later,

with the expansion of tasks and technical procedures, became known as the Metal Works.

But before things reached this point, Robert Bosch himself had his hands full, as it was necessary to begin building on a large scale. Although building was something he had always taken personal charge of, it would be wrong to say that he had a passion for building. In the early years of the firm's development, he was quite hesitant to construct new buildings, and more than once the tempo of demand took him by surprise and forced him to make compromises. Even today, the core of the building complex in Stuttgart shows signs of interrupted development. It had been a residential area with gardens and courtyards; the properties did not come up for sale all at once, and the new buildings had to accommodate the old property boundaries. The price of land was naturally very high, which made it necessary to take advantage of the space by building vertically. This situation would have made it difficult, under any circumstances, to achieve a unified, objectively clear organization that would also be pleasing to the eye. In order to understand Bosch, it is necessary to understand the intensity with which he occupied himself with each of these construction projects from the very first, influencing them, learning from them, and finally becoming something like a teacher. Bosch once noted with grim pride that some experts had admitted actually having first learned how to build from him.

Bosch had a poor opinion of architects and construction specialists in general—a judgment that he occasionally expressed in drastic terms. He blamed esthetic formalism, which he felt was encouraged and promoted by the way in which the universities were run. There was almost nowhere, to his way of thinking, where the craft tradition had been so thoroughly dismantled. What good was it to create more or less successful façades— this seemed to him to be the particular ambition of academic architects— if one had not taken the trouble to objectively study the conditions under which the residents lived and worked! Compared with these stylish experiments, he found the sureness of the old untrained masters, with their sense of proportion and reliable work, to be far superior. Bosch often complained about this, and he was quick to recognize the weaknesses of the merely artistic. His opinions sometimes seemed unfair. He often ignored the ongoing conflict between tradition and the search for an adequate expression, and he had little time for the questions about materials and techniques that confronted the construction business, for which tradition provided no clear answers. When a new addition was being constructed, Bosch was a constant presence at the site, not to speed up the tempo of the work but to reassure himself about the quality of the material and the solidity of the construction. If he found sloppy work, there was trouble. If a site manager talked to him in a superior tone about statics, the manager was sure to be thrown by a few pointed questions and observations. Although it was not easy to build for Bosch, it was ultimately profitable for those who approached it intelligently.

From the beginning, the things that were of particular concern to Bosch, along with good lighting for the workplaces, were the temperature and ventilation of the rooms. Lighting posed some nearly insoluble problems among the crush of the narrow, tall buildings, but questions of heating and ventilation were approached and carried out with all possible thoroughness. The Schreiter method of supplying fresh air from the ceiling and removing stale air from the floor was new at that time, and Bosch became a propagandist for the method, regretting that most factory managers paid so little attention to this question. He knew what the proper answer meant in terms of his employees' health and capacity for work. The additional costs, which were not inconsiderable, had to be both socially welcome and economically justified. It is no wonder that Bosch pursued the development of the idea of regulated climate control with intense interest. Gustav Klein's brother, Dr. Albert Klein, would later become one of the pioneers of this new technical solution based on his experiences in America. The fact that Bosch always pursued the latest goals of hygienic and ergonometric perfection so enthusiastically caused the Academy for the Building Trades to invite him, the precision engineer, to become an honorary member of their society. One may assume that among all the various forms of recognition that managed to reach the recalcitrant honoree, this was the one that really gave him pleasure. He believed that the construction business needed a reformer, and although it was not his goal to be that person, exactly, he did want to play an initiating and quasi-pedagogical role.

The year 1908, with its new plans, forced Bosch to make the important decision to look for a new building site. The Stuttgart property would do for the precision engineering work, which did not make any noise and which was profitable enough to justify the high real estate costs. It was also possible to perform such work on several floors. The production of semifinished goods, however, would give the manufacturing process a different rhythm. Not wanting to be caught unprepared, Bosch began to look for locations large enough for future development. The town of Feuerbach, a northern suburb of Stuttgart, offered such locations. There it would also be possible to bring in a rail spur, something they had felt they lacked in Stuttgart from time to time. A large piece of property was purchased in 1908; here it would no longer be necessary to build upward. Sheds and factory halls were now possible.

Bosch by no means thought it necessary for everything that was needed in the manufacturing process to be produced in-house; he did not tend to think in terms of vertical integration. He himself, if one may express it this way, was satisfied for years to manufacture parts of the whole. It was not until very late that finished products for the consumer market became part of the production program, and these came from a branch of industry other than engines (radios, refrigerators, and so on). As long as the market satisfied his needs for magnets, in terms of quantity and type, he was happy to purchase them; it could be useful, from a price standpoint, to take advantage of the competing offers. But from time to time there were instances when the free market failed, either because insufficient numbers were available for delivery or because the producers could not or would not supply the particular types required by the refinement of ignition techniques. The producers hesitated to make special investments for orders whose total extent they could not foresee. This led to the consideration that it would be good to be independent of them. It could also be advantageous from the standpoint of price; the firm's own needs were sufficiently large to make a large-scale investment in mass production cost-effective. At the same time—and this was not inessential—the new factory in Feuerbach was not to function exclusively as a supplier for Stuttgart, but would seek to bring its products to market. It was this independence in matters of business policy that attracted Eugen Kayser: it was not merely a matter of serving Stuttgart; he was supposed to seek out other buyers and create products that could earn a place for themselves on their own merits. This would influence the share that the products to be delivered to Stuttgart would have in the fixed costs; it would ease the calculation that was necessary in order to meet the underpricing of the competition without somehow lowering the standards of quality and work performance.

The basic task of the Metal Works was to provide interchangeable magnets whose material and precise shape would be of reliable, unvarying quality. This soon led to the mass production of the other parts required for ignition systems by the die process, a form of manufacturing that was in its infancy and that was extensively developed by Bosch, using metal, aluminum, and zinc alloys. The complicated business of pouring, which requires either a large number of molds or a great deal of patience when there is a rush order, was replaced by dies. The steel forms of the molds and dies might be expensive, but *one* set sufficed to produce quickly by machine what was needed. Although the basic idea arose out of an immediate practical need, once the factory for semifinished products and individual parts had been created, it evolved according to its own magnificent logic. Over the years, it grew into an important institute for scientific and technical research and development, taking its cues from the increasingly complex requirements posed by the work of the factory. Above all, it was insulation materials, so crucial for the spark plug, that were conceived, tested, and newly created here. A ceramics factory joined the Metal Works. Its goal had to be to make the durability and reliability of the spark plug adequate to meet the demands posed by increasing engine speeds. The design bureau in Stuttgart and the materials office (if one may term it such) in Feuerbach spurred each other on in a process of questions and answers.

The Metal Works occupied a peculiar, marginal location among Bosch's creations. It grew out of the technical and economic needs associated with the production of ignition devices, and it gradually assumed an independent life that was only indirectly connected with the concept of parts. The lubricator, the first new technical problem Bosch addressed from a manufacturing standpoint, after ignition, went through a similar development. The engineer Eugen Wörner, in Cannstatt, came to Bosch in 1909 with a central lubrication system he had developed. Its purpose was to take care of the lubrication needs of those parts of the automobile that needed it by means of a carefully thought-out and constructed system of individual pumps that would be simple to understand and regulate. The fact that Bosch responded to this idea is of fundamental importance. For now he was tying himself to the automobile on his own initiative; the development of ignition devices had basically come about as a result of suggestions made by others. Admittedly, the new step seemed to be destined to failure, as fruitful as Wörner's basic invention may have seemed from a technical standpoint. Only a few automobile factories, including the Horch and Tatra factories, adopted the new system. The goal—to provide a new and lasting impulse for car manufacturing in this important and sensitive area—was not achieved. The cheaper system of circulation lubrication developed elsewhere was accepted so quickly that further efforts on behalf of a lubrication system based on individual doses were pointless.

But there were not only automobiles. Everything that involved cylinders and pistons, wheels, ball bearings and supports, gaskets, levers, and valves required regular maintenance with lubricating oil. Reliable maintenance is essential for the function and life of an engine. It was an appealing challenge—to save human labor and to steer clear of its inadequacies, such as forgetfulness and fatigue. In fact, Wörner's central lubrication system proved to be effective, in principle, for both steam and internal combustion engines, so Bosch decided to continue experimenting. The factory history of 1936 describes these experiments, as they searched for a practical form for the lubricator, a way to control its functions and make it adaptable for the most varied types of machines. For a long time, the whole matter remained problematic, and some people felt that it was a kind of foreign body in the midst of the manufacturing program since it led away from electrical engineering, the center of the firm's achievements. The project consumed substantial investments; in the beginning, the foundry that had been added in Feuerbach was almost entirely devoted to this department. It was not possible to even think about volume or mass production, because the needs of the various types of machines were too diverse and the advantages of a central lubrication system only gradually became apparent to customers. After the war, the scarcity of lubricating oil had the effect of encouraging people to save it, and the replacement of old, worn-out machines gradually made people more willing to fit them out with this part.

The lubrication department, despite successful solutions in individual instances, had developed only with difficulty, and for a long time it did not bring in much profit compared to the cost of the experiments. In 1920 Karl Wild suggested getting rid of the whole thing. Bosch disagreed. To do so would have been to admit that after almost a decade and a half they had not achieved their aim, that there might be reason to doubt their own accomplishments. From a technical standpoint this was not true at all. Profit and income were not as important to Bosch as undiminished prestige and the certainty that patience and repeated attempts would pay off. His tenacity proved to be justified. Whereas in the first twelve years a total of 50,000 lubricators had been sold, now, in 1912, the annual production stood at almost 20,000. Although it continued to be subject to the vagaries of the business cycle, the lubrication system as such was accepted. It had already taken over locomotives and was now being used in the engine rooms of large oceangoing vessels. It became specialized for machine tools, and gave birth, in a manner of speaking, to a grease pump for machines that were located out-of-doors or in dusty rooms. The name Bosch had taken hold in new areas—in rolling mills, brown coal mines, and halls filled with looms. It had earned the right to be at home in all these places.

It had been a long journey measured against the tempo with which the ignition devices had achieved international recognition. The lubricator had at first reached a primarily German group of customers, although the factory history records the fact that in some years sales to foreign countries were as much as 40 percent of the total. But the name Bosch became more closely linked with *the* new product being developed in those years, the product that attained the highest degree of popularity: lights. Here was something you could *see*. Ignition and lubrication were hidden somewhere in the interior of the automobile, protected, familiar to the specialist but a bit unknown to the lay person. But when lighting systems and headlights began to be mounted on automobiles, encased in well-thought-out, tightly designed forms, the notion was confirmed everywhere: So this is what Bosch makes! Later, the other parts were added—horns, turn signals, windshield wipers—which also immediately awakened associations with Bosch.

In the automobile's early days, lighting was no problem—one simply drove during the day. And if one had to drive after dark, there were candle lanterns styled after the horse-drawn carriages. That was sufficient, as long as there were only a few motor vehicles on the roads and the speeds were still modest. But this primitive circumstance could not last for long. Soon permanent kerosene lamps were installed. Then a seemingly excellent solution was presented in the form of the invention of acetylene gas. One could either mount a water vessel with a calcium carbide container—a miniature gas plant—on the automobile, or one could carry bottled gas. Acetylene gave off a bright, sharp light. But it created many problems for its owners, not only when it was blown out in the wind, but also because the headlights rapidly became dirty and there was an element of danger in their use.

As the number of automobiles grew, their average speed increased and their use became part of normal life and human interaction that could not be restricted by the angle of the sun; lawmakers began to take an interest in the matter. It is characteristic that this first occurred in Württemberg, the birthplace of the automobile. An ordinance from the year 1902 had required that "brightly burning lanterns of white glass" be mounted on both sides; in 1906, it was further required that these lanterns "cast their light on the roadway in such a way so that the driver can see it for a distance of at least 20 meters." An early insight into an emerging concern that would become very important later on is shown by the prohibition of "excessively powerful floodlights." The Württemberg ordinance was made nationally binding in 1909 by a regulation passed by the Bundesrat and applied to the entire area of the Reich. This minimum standard, however, would soon become irrelevant.

Naturally, the question of electric lighting had arisen quite early. It had been used sporadically since 1905. The difficulties had to do with the production of the electricity. The battery had certainly been further developed since the time of its creation for battery ignition, but there was still the necessity of charging it. The lightbulb with a carbon filament had its problems as well: it did not last long on bad or bumpy roads, and the projection of light was imprecise; on the roadway the image of the carbon threads jumped in the light. There were two tasks to be solved: to design inexpensive, small headlights with a strong forward projection and adequate lateral dispersion, and to provide a steady regulation for the electrical current. Connecting them to the motor as a source of power was obvious enough but did not solve the problem because the light was needed at precisely those times when the engine was idle, when the vehicle was standing still, and second because the number of revolutions and the strength of the current produced by the dynamo varied, while the lights required a steady voltage. At Bosch Gustav Klein was pressing to find solutions. He himself would not be the one to point the way, but he wanted to see something created that was not dependent on the battery, an instrument he both hated and distrusted. But how to do without it? The searching and testing consumed a good deal of time.

Gottlob Honold, the amateur photographer, was looking into optics, studying the laws governing light, refraction, and reflection, and he was accompanying his study with practical experiments directed at discovering a suitable, stable reflector that could serve as the socket for the headlight. His goal was not to gain scientific knowledge or to discover an apparatus that would be suitable for specialists, but rather, he was looking for something weatherproof, sturdy, and more or less dirt-resistant. Naturally, Honold's experiments suffered from the fact that the available lightbulbs had been conceived as more or less stationary. The transition to metal filaments did away with the problems of short-livedness. The really splendid aspect of Honold's accomplishment was the creation of parabolic metal mirrors, the identification of the proper place to mount the bulb, and such apparently quite simple but convincing ideas as the installation of the headlights from the back, without opening the glass, a solution that removed the most frequent cause of problems. The development of the parabolic silver-coated and polished mirror, and the discovery of the proper placement for the bulb, were decisive accomplishments. A normal twenty-five-candlepower bulb that was available on the market could now accomplish at least as much as the stronger floodlights that had been built before; it was also much cheaper. Now, in innumerable experiments, Honold turned his attention to the treatment of the slightly curved glass, trying to find a way to press grooves into the glass to help regulate lateral diffusion. One consideration led to another, such as special provisions for fog or the creation of movable searchlights. The greatest challenge was the prevention of the dangerous blinding that could occur when two autos met. Various solutions were tried. Attempts were made by using two lights of differing strength, or by installing a movable cover. Finally, although Honold himself would not live to experience it, the experiments went in a direction he had suggested. Osram developed the Bilux-bulb, combining two different intensities of light in a single bulb.

Bosch's entry into this new, previously uncharted territory had to be seen as particularly daring because Germany already possessed a highly developed optical industry that had naturally been interested in headlights for some time. In the memorandum he wrote during the last days of his life, Bosch recounted how the leading personalities in Jena and Berlin first made fun of the matter. When Honold had discussed it with Paul Görz, the founder of the firm that later became Zeiss had literally laughed at him and his metal headlights. This is not so surprising, for to these optical firms, most of whose work served military purposes, a floodlight was an instrument that threw blinding light many kilometers into the darkness—a task diametrically opposed to the one Bosch and his people had set themselves. They wanted to light up the nearby space, a distance of no more than 300 to 400 meters. The distance to be illuminated was fundamentally related to the braking distance in an emergency, and depended on the speed at which the vehicle happened to be traveling. Carl Zeiss, who had become interested in automobile lighting, made a proposition: Forget about headlights; we will provide them, and you will give us your electrical systems. Bosch refused. It was clear that if he had decided not to continue with this venture, other firms would have appeared with cheaper metal headlights to compete with Zeiss. Besides, the products were ready to be marketed, and there was the competition in America to consider, where electric lighting was already quite developed. There was no need for this comparison to make him anxious, but it was instructive. In an essay from the year 1927, Bosch wrote a few characteristic and revealing sentences: "In order to establish a documented basis for our deliberations in the firm, we once mounted an American headlight and one that we ourselves had produced on a special shaking machine of the type we used to test our products. The result: after 10 hours the American light was in pieces; the German one was still in good shape after 200 hours. Debate and decision: it is not necessary for our products to last longer than an automobile, but their effectiveness must not be reduced. So we cut back and cut back. Only the wages had to remain such that the worker still earned the same amount . . ."

Honold's most successful exploratory mission into the realm of optics, if one may use this term for his long and difficult series of experiments, would have been incomplete, however, if he had not simultaneously addressed the question of generating the light itself. The apparatus they developed should be able to be offered as a single unit, if possible. That way there would be no arguments over responsibility in the case of failure. The new task led back to the core areas of electrical and precision engineering. The goal was to create a light-producing machine that would be driven by the motor while the automobile was in motion, and would simultaneously charge the battery, which would have to provide electricity for the light source whenever the vehicle was either moving slowly or was standing. The essential thing was to find an independent regulator that would provide a stable and unvarying current under varying conditions and with differing levels of electrical voltage. Many a theoretically conceived plan foundered on the shoals of practice before the goal was attained. Actually, it was never attained, for practice itself continued to present new and different requirements, for instance, for large trucks or for light or heavy motorcycles. Sizes varied, as did the combinations of different systems. A journal entry that noted the situation in 1936, a quarter of a century after they had begun work on this problem, may give some idea of the differences. The smallest light generator, with a diameter of 76.2 millimeters, weighed 2.47 kilograms; the largest, with a diameter of 203.2 millimeters, weighed 61 kilograms.

At that time, in 1910, Bosch and his colleagues were keeping a very sharp eye on America. The market there was growing so rapidly that a separate manufacturing operation was started. Once "automobile madness"—as Bosch once called the utterly incomprehensible boom—had broken out in America, the "self-driver" had become the rule, while in Europe the professional driver was still the rule, often a trained locksmith or mechanic who had adopted the new profession of chauffeur. America demanded equipment that did not break down and that was designed to be convenient and comfortable to use. People in the United States were making more energetic attempts to resolve the issue of electric lights for motor vehicles, and they had also reverted to the battery, rather than magneto ignition, because it was cheaper, especially for automobiles. In addition, there were hundreds of experiments aimed at technically simpler ways to get the motor running.

In the early days of the automobile, this had seemed like a secondary concern. The driver placed himself in front of the vehicle with a hand crank and started it with an energetic winding motion. This was necessary because the internal combustion engine requires an external source of power in order to begin operating. It required a certain amount of practice, along with physical exertion. Older people can still call up an image of times when the effort was in vain, for one reason or another, and remember the bystanders' malicious satisfaction as they enjoyed the victim's annoyance. The task was to make the starting of the motor independent of human effort and to create an apparatus that would enable the driver to set the vehicle in motion from his seat. A competition organized by the Automobile Club of France in 1905 encouraged technicians and inventors to create a usable starter, but nothing of value resulted. As obvious as the idea may have seemed of installing a separate source of electrical power, the costs seemed too high for a device that would only be used for a moment.

The Bosch firm had begun to explore the creation of such a device independently in 1912, with discussions and experiments focusing on an inertia starter. It did not immediately reach the stage of marketability, but was picked up again decades later when it was utilized for diesel engines. At any rate, they had made a start. The improvement of the batteries, and the creation of the overrunning clutch by Fichtel and Sachs in Schweinfurt, made it possible to invent the foot step switch. Once again, as had happened so often in the past, there were concerns that the cost of the parts, as a result of expensive special fabrication requirements or unusual installation costs, should not work against the tendency of automobile prices to fall. In America, where the most diverse methods had been tried, Bosch's subsidiary could serve as a good observation post.

When a new electric starter came out in 1913, Bosch's firm got in touch with the inventor. Bosch's *Life Recollections* had this to say about it: "In Europe, people did not want to take up this matter [the starter] for a long time. The road toward making this kind of starter had been heavily blocked by Americans and their patents. But we finally found a workable way that was quite good. An American, Rushmore, had a patent that seemed better, and we bought it, along with his firm, after only a few days of negotiations." With this, Bosch had secured an immediate head start as far as the German market was concerned. The international use of the invention, as a result of the World War, would soon come to a halt. At any rate, the apparatus that the Europeans "did not want to take up for a long time" was soon viewed as unquestionably essential. It, too, went through various alterations, refinements, and decreases in price. Bosch had taken the leading role in order to remain the leader.

The factory, which had made decisive beginnings in the years between 1907 and 1914 on products as diverse as semifinished goods and insulation materials, lubricators and starter motors, headlights and light generators continued to experience changes in the area of ignition, particularly in relation to the spark plug. But this time there were mature competitors like Ernst Eisemann, who demonstrated considerable originality in technical matters as well as careful implementation. Eisemann had an inventive mind, and the drive to expand awakened in his colleagues as well. Eisemann began to open sales offices, respectable in scale though not in Bosch's style, and they also went overseas. An ambitious American firm had guaranteed that it would carry everything Eisemann produced, and an American company was founded. In France, Panhard and Levasseur had become regular customers, so that sales increased and Eisemann attracted the interest of finance capital as well. He came out with a high-voltage device. In principle, Bosch welcomed competition. He mentioned it often, and if customers were dissatisfied with his conditions for delivery, he simply told them: Fill your needs somewhere else. Bosch's basic position on economics was liberal; every capable and ambitious person should be given the chance to move up in the world. The fact that in Stuttgart itself, a design office and workshops were working away to find better answers to the same questions would help to assure that Bosch's employees in the Militärstrasse and the Hoppenlaustrasse remained technically alert and constantly tested the manufacturing process. With Eisemann Bosch succeeded in reaching an early agreement about sales requirements, mutual protection of customers, and so on. The relationship could not remain completely free of friction, but conditions were created early on that would later make it possible for them to merge completely.

But there were other competitors who caused Bosch's tolerant curiosity to vanish instantly. The thought, for example, that certain firms had been created so that he, Bosch, would buy them "to keep the market clear" was not at all to his liking. Just what he needed—to have somebody enter the ignition field with the notion (or the intention) of making a nuisance of himself and then being taken over by Bosch! Thus it was with a certain anger that he followed the development in Feuerbach of the "Mea" firm, a factory for magneto electrical devices founded in 1908. The ignition device they were producing had been offered to Bosch shortly before for only 5,000 marks. Honold found the device, which involved a bell magnet and could therefore achieve a greater range of variation in the setting of the ignition timing, to be interesting. The decision was reached, however, that the production of the bell magnets would result in higher prices; the device also seemed overly sensitive. The history of the Mea became a strange zigzag of optimistic expectations and financial difficulties; it had to be refinanced more than once. The figures of the capitalists who filled the leading posts came and went. Again and again, they came to Bosch with merger offers. Among them was the well-known German-American beer brewer Adolphus Busch, who turned up around 1910. In 1897, he had purchased Rudolf Diesel's patents for the United States, and he wanted to become active, with his powerful capital resources, in the engine business. Bosch got along quite well with this unusual man; their correspondence is characterized by a certain cordiality. But they remained separate. An anecdote has come down to us to the effect that Busch, in a play on the similar sound of the two names, said that one-syllable names were the privilege and sign of important men. Bosch made the witty rejoinder, "Hence the name Öchelhäuser!" referring to the head of Dessau Gas, a man who was an important personality in Germany's industrial development at the time. After the war, the Mea became part of the AEG in Berlin, which was then seeking to establish a base in southern Germany, making it once again a matter of concern for Bosch's marketing policy.

Thus it was not only technical issues that kept Bosch's specialists on the move, but considerations of business competition as well. At the same time, there was pressure, if not from technical necessity then from force of habit, to make certain adjustments in the core business. Bosch had become great through magneto ignition. With the light generator, which also required a battery, the question of battery ignition had once again become acute. It was cheaper and it was in demand, especially in America. In addition, battery technology had developed considerably over the course of twenty years. Hence the problem of this combination was taken up once again at Bosch. Several years before, using mass production techniques, they had begun producing in-house the actual spark plug, which they had first purchased from others. The combination of battery and magneto ignition, to which they now turned, left the original Bosch ignition with the market for heavy trucks. Another would soon be added—the airplane.

In 1912, Bosch traveled to North America in the company of his wife and twenty-year-old son. This time he did not keep a journal like the one twenty-eight years before, in which ironic comments about himself, wise observations about the world around him, homesickness, curiosity about life, and self-confidence were combined in a way that was naive and rather charming. He was in his fiftieth year. As a young man, he had been only moderately impressed by America. The state of the workers' movement, to which he had then felt he belonged, had disappointed him. The lack of a craft tradition, the rapid growth of its population with its diverse origins, and its large territory had moved manufacturing toward work-saving machines and mass production. This had also begun to have an effect on Europe; Bosch was one of the individuals who, in his farsighted and daring way, had always brought the newest American machine tools into his factory. There had been things to be learned, and he had learned them. But he did not feel like a student, for it is not the machine alone that is decisive, but man and the leadership of men. If Bosch had not been thinking about his technicians and workers for the last quarter of a century—perfecting, designing and rejecting, challenging and testing them—he would not have been arriving in this country as an economic conqueror. Americans did not love him, but they needed him.

Two years before, Bosch had decided to start production "over there," in order to save transportation costs and customs duties. In the search for a suitable location, he had settled on Springfield, Massachusetts, because a large engine factory was located there, and it therefore seemed likely that it would be relatively easy to find suitable metal workers. The property, which was located on a flood plain, was not the best choice; it would later suffer considerably because of its location. But that did not concern Bosch as he traveled to the United States to visit the concern that bore his name. Although the Bosch Magneto Company was now making the transition to manufacturing, the president continued to be Otto Heins, whom Gustav Klein had recommended for the leadership of the sales operation some years previously. The manufacturing division was headed by Karl Martell Wild. He, like sales manager Hugo Borst, came from Esslingen, and was the son of a teacher. After completing his study of electrical engineering at the university in Stuttgart, he had gone to Siemens & Halske, but hadn't felt particularly at home there. His connection with his fellow countryman Hugo Borst brought him to Bosch. In January 1909, he began working for Gottlob Honold, who introduced him to work in the laboratory and to the current design tasks. Tradition has it that a friendly argument broke out between Klein and Honold. Honold wanted to keep Wild; he saw him as his possible successor. But it seemed too soon to Klein to be concerned with this question. Klein needed a man with technical imagination, open eyes, and a tenacious will, so Wild went to America, too. The factory there was designed and built in the years 1909–1910 by Albert Klein, who had specialized in industrial reinforced concrete. They were able to build this large facility with current funds, and when Bosch arrived, he felt confident that his American subsidiary would prosper.

18

———•———

THE LABOR MOVEMENT
AND THE
WORKERS' STRUGGLE

In the spring of 1913, Bosch experienced a partial strike in a crucial department, to which the management, after an unsuccessful mediation attempt, saw itself forced to respond by closing the entire factory. The first decade of the new century had been filled with political and social tensions. It had begun with the violent struggle over the increase in the grain tariff, which had given the Social Democratic Party a great boost in the Reichstag elections of 1903. True, in 1907, when the elections turned on the issue of colonial credits, there had been a serious reversal, but it was corrected in the elections of 1912, which advanced the Socialist faction to leadership in the Reichstag.

These external developments of the Social Democratic Party were accompanied by powerful internal struggles. The party factions in the provincial parliaments of southern Germany, which had achieved a certain amount of power after the democratic constitutional reforms, resisted the tactical guidance of the party leadership in northern Germany. The hopeless opposition to which the Socialist movement was condemned by the electoral laws of Prussia and Saxony had radicalized the Socialists. Even more profound was the division that had begun to appear between the political and the trade union tendencies. Slogans like "Party and Trade Unions United!" tried to smooth it over, but with very limited success. The Social Democratic Free Trade Unions, although superior in numbers, saw themselves confronted with emerging craft unions of other political persuasions, unions that charged dues and became negotiating partners. Their leaders also sensed that the tough fights over specific issues such as the legal position of workers in the factory, wages, and the workday were difficult to reconcile with some global claims of Marxism, such as the theory of pauperization or the sharpening of class struggle. In practice, they were engaged in continuous truces and pledges of peace, hence the efforts of the trade unions to distinguish themselves from the specific needs of party politics in the struggle. In the 1890s and the early years of the twentieth century, there had been powerful offensives aimed, in many cases, at awakening the sense of solidarity in struggle; now the union leaders were on a more cautious path. There were treasuries to be administered and money to be lost, and in specific industries collective bargaining agreements had been reached that had to be protected, as contrasted to those industries—for example, parts of heavy industry— where the *individual* labor contract was regarded as the basic legal form, even where the masses of the wage earners were concerned. The union statutes had developed as a kind of field regulations for the organization of the social struggle, characterized by pedantic, quasi-military order and mistrust of all irregular forces. This mistrust was concerned, above all, with the party's political claim to power. It was especially strong in Württemberg, where the relative calm of the political situation had recently been interrupted by extreme radicalization. At the time Karl Radek, the Polish-Russian Socialist who a few years later would become one of the most influential promoters of Bolshevism on the world stage, was performing his editorial experiments on the Swabian workers of Göppingen. He met with little success of any significance, but the rapidly growing workforce at Bosch might provide suitable raw material for his experiment. A not untalented, but unscrupulous, agitator named F. R. Westmeyer took a particular interest in the Bosch workers, whom he isolated in factory groups.

There was an additional factor: the development of machine technology and its effect on the wage system. Among early Socialist theorists,

Karl Marx had been an exception in that he had come out in favor of technological advancement and the progress of the machine. After all, machine power, the early concentration of production it created, and the liberation of workers who could join the "industrial reserve army" were among the central tenets of his theory. This was not insignificant. In contrast to the craft-oriented radicalism of the "machine stormers" and utopian social reformers, Marx accepted technological rationalization as a part of his theoretical construct. But the discussion was not free of contradictions. Theory recognized the increasing productivity of the machine; practice had to deal with its effect on wages, as well as on the health of the workers. Depending on the type of activity, the product, and the production process, regular wages and piecework wages diverged to a greater or lesser extent. From the beginning, the organized workers' movement fought for an hourly wage that was adjusted according to age, and condemned piecework, which grew out of payment based on the individual product. Despite its objections in principle, in practice the movement learned to live with piecework. This was no simple matter. For the piecework rate was not a stable value; it was subject to the influence of technological changes. New machine tools, for example, challenged the assumptions that had been applied on the basis of previous experiences. The period around 1900 was beginning to take up this whole complex of questions once again and to refine the answers based on practice. From America, the principles of "scientific management" had been introduced as a kind of new gospel, and the name of F. W. Taylor had become a buzzword that stood for business ambition; he was also a figure who inspired fear. Workers and employers alike were forced to alter their thinking, and managers were also becoming accustomed to operating with new concepts. The idea itself looked newer than it really was. Things that had been taken for granted had been elevated to a conscious and systematic level, and this, along with its word magic, gave the theory its power as a lure and as a threat.

Individually and in combination, these various factors had an effect on the origins and course of the workers' struggle at Bosch. This test of strength reflected not only Bosch's individual personality and tactical decisions but also the tenor of the times, and it possessed elements that can only be understood as part of an evaluation of more general problems. The period saw plenty of labor struggles that went beyond individual companies and involved an entire branch of an industry in a particular region. On October 9, 1910, for example, Bosch wrote to his wife concerning a related industry: "The automobile factories may be angry with me for not taking part in the lockout, but I can't be concerned about that." The power struggle at Bosch, which lasted throughout June and July of 1913, had a deeper impact on all of Germany than almost any other battle over wages and the length of the workday. The public followed its various phases with a kind of passion; rumors and tall tales spread. For Bosch, the struggle, in human terms, was a psychological shock and burden.

With the growth of the company, the structure of the workforce had naturally gone through various phases. The core of older employees was expanded to include the necessary reinforcements. They were not uniform. The reputation for good pay and for offering particularly good opportunities to anyone who was an able worker attracted capable individuals from throughout the region. No advertising was necessary. The other factory owners could complain all they wanted when they lost trained men to Bosch, but it was by an irresistible process of attraction. The reservoir of Stuttgart itself did not suffice; the whole surrounding territory sent people to Bosch, and similarly to Daimler. A half-peasant element, including workers whose training was widely disparate, came with them. These individuals had to be trained. The new stratum, with its fluctuation, its commuting between home and workplace, represented a sociologically uncertain factor, in the beginning, and provided unformed raw material for trade union and political propaganda. The division of labor began to give women, who up until then had worked primarily in the textile industry, a place in the metal industry as well.

Bosch knew the people who had grown up with the company, and he knew what he could expect from them. Even in his later years, when he returned to the factory, his excellent memory allowed him to recognize individuals, and as he greeted them old memories would come back to him. Zähringer, who was responsible for the division of labor within the company, also had strong personal connections with the basic core of the workforce. But now the workers had to be divided into departments and hierarchically organized groups. The masters came from the old core or were selected from among those new younger people who were eager for opportunity. This was no different at Bosch than in other similar businesses. The masters, who were in charge of the quality of the output, its tempo, the assignment of the piecework, and the calculation of the piecework rates, bore a growing share of responsibility for the internal rhythm of the business. The exceptional position of the masters would play a large role in the struggles that followed. In selecting his masters, it was claimed, Bosch had given preference to men who could be considered the unions' best shop stewards, thus robbing the workers of their best immediate representation and even creating contradictions within the company. This objection did not worry him particularly. If the capable individuals had been active in the trade union movement, their professional advancement would not require that they divorce themselves from their previous convictions and insights. When there were complaints, Bosch would have the case brought before him, but he was not squeamish if the grievance happened to be about the brusque tone of one of his masters. "However, I must permit myself one more question," he wrote in November 1912, to the German Metal Workers' Union, "whether the offended parties do not occasionally use worse expressions. So far as I am acquainted with the tone of conversation here, this is the case." The local leadership never responded to this letter.

Ultimately, the union leaders had small reason for conflict with him. For over the years a work-based cooperation had gradually been worked out between the company and the union, with which both parties could be, and were, in fact, satisfied. Bosch did not ask whether or in which trade union his workers were organized. He had once organized a workers' committee himself, to settle internal issues, but he had been disappointed by the group's vacillating position when he asked for moral support in the struggle against the damage being done to tools, damage that was having an economically deleterious effect. The committee had avoided coming to a conclusion about this actually rather innocuous issue. There was not much to be done with such a position; Bosch had at the very least expected some advice. So the committee was abandoned, and questions such as these were taken up with the leaders of the German Metal Workers' Union. About 95 percent of the workers, according to a note of Bosch's, were organized in this union. In other words, the opinion of the partisan representatives would probably be authoritative. Things went quite well, and Bosch recounted: "Most of these people were endowed with a sharp intelligence. For several years I negotiated everything with the union that needed to be negotiated." But there was a sense that this procedure was gradually taking on a new tone. The union representatives themselves were followed and watched by stewards from the shop floor—they were beginning to be mistrusted. Political radicalism was trying to establish a foothold from which it might be possible to mount a test of strength.

The point of departure was not easy to find. One could not resort to slogans from the usual labor battles, about wages or time off, to attack a factory owner who had introduced the eight-hour day, closed the factory on Saturday afternoons, and paid for the overtime required in boom times with significant wage supplements and extra vacations. Perhaps some evils had developed in his social programs that were just waiting for criticism to be brought to light? Whoever went looking for such things looked in vain. For the very institutions that were generally equated with social services in large businesses—housing, insurance programs, convalescent homes, and so forth—were completely lacking at that time. A characteristic anecdote is that in 1913, on the occasion of the twenty-fifth anniversary of Kaiser Wilhelm II's reign, a book was being prepared for publication in which the noteworthy social activities of German industrialists were to be presented. The authors turned to Bosch with the request that he send information and photographs; his colleagues might not be pleased, but in a work of such representative character it would be quite wrong to omit this "socially minded" employer entirely. Bosch answered that there was nothing to photograph at his company; he did not engage in any "charity" toward his workers. But what was not accessible to photographic representation and what the authors of the planned publication might not have wanted to repeat was something that lay outside the framework of the question: the company paid the premiums of the individual workers' health and disability insurance. This was almost in the nature of an incidental benefit, which the workforce had already come to expect as if it were automatic. In 1912, the not inconsiderable sum of 300,000 marks was expended for this purpose, including some 20,000 marks of special payments for the vacation fund.

In those years, Bosch felt much more strongly rejected and attacked by other employers than by his workers. In his *Life Recollections,* long after the period had ended, his thoughts were sometimes suffused with bitterness, as if at the time he had suffered from a certain isolation. As far as his inner feelings were concerned, things were probably not so bad. Part of the problem was his lack of social ease, which led him to shy away from, rather than seek contact with, the circle of industrial leaders. "I was not connected by personal relations with any of the leaders of any of the large electrical firms. I was always in a somewhat isolated position," he wrote in July 1913. At the AEG, with which he carried on a lively exchange of letters, he was "personally completely unknown, i.e., I do not know any of the leading gentlemen from the AEG by sight." This was the period during which Bosch could already be regarded as a worldwide business, and this fact is astonishing, but also revealing in terms of the image being formed of the man from Stuttgart who had become a great industrial power within the course of only a decade.

For a while, Bosch may have been unconcerned with what people were saying about him, namely, that he was a "radical Socialist." Let them be annoyed that he had been first with the eight-hour day, and had not fared so badly with it. He did not deny that he "sympathized" with the Social Democratic party. This expression is taken from his own *Life Recollections.* When he read in a newspaper that "important figures like Clara Zetkin were frequent visitors" in his home, he may have found it exaggerated, but not sufficiently to cause him to set the record straight. It may also not have been unknown that, through the intervention of Clara Zetkin, whose husband had been a Russian Socialist, he had taken political refugees into his factory and had given them work and bread after the Russian Revolution of 1905. His bitterest enemies, in the midst of the most difficult battles, expressed their admiration for this, although admittedly not out of any love for him. But he gradually became uncomfortable about all the rumors and written remarks. He had discovered that they were encouraged by the competition and that in the long run it would be detrimental to the business. In 1911, he had already made a statement in the committee of the Union of Automobile Industrialists to the effect that he had never made a contribution to a Social Democratic electoral fund. The following year, an angry Reichstag candidate from

Stuttgart, a member of the National Liberal Party, declared that a certain individual had caused his defeat by giving 100,000 marks to his Socialist opponent. Everyone knew he meant Bosch. Following Bosch's energetic letter of protest, the person who started the rumor had no alternative but to retract his statement. And in January 1913, after the first difficulties had occurred in the factory, the Frankfurt *Central Gazette of the Motor Vehicle and Bicycle Industry*—not exactly an insignificant organ— contended that the strike (it was not a strike) had "been settled in the meanwhile because Herr Bosch has become even more Social Democratic and has agreed to the majority of the demands." So that was the way the wind was blowing! When the conflict broke out, the right wing press experienced something like pangs of joy. The Social Democrats themselves had to learn to apply their vocabulary to Bosch as well. This was not immediately successful. They railed against the behavior of the masters, they supposed that Bosch himself might not be accurately informed, they tried to uncover the guilty parties by making puns based on the names Klein, "little," and Borst, "brush." Finally, however, they concluded that the "former master locksmith," the rich man of today, had cast off his "social camouflage" and was even worse than some nameless "agitator"—"the most hard-boiled, crafty employer, for all his socially minded claptrap." The sarcastic tone hurt Bosch more deeply than one might think. He refused to have any personal contact with the representative of the German Metal Workers' Union who had previously served as his principal negotiating partner and who had now suddenly, bowing to deeper political currents, become abusive, as if the habits of many years had been nothing.

Near the end of 1912, a demand had been raised for a 10 percent increase in the hourly wage. That was more of a feeler, to which the union felt pushed from the political side. Stuttgart had just been through the excitement of a direct popular mayoral election. Social Democracy's hopes had been disappointed; its internal contradictions were becoming more acute, and the radical wing, under the leadership of F. R. Westmeyer and Clara Zetkin, was increasing its agitation; discussion of the "guilt" for their defeat needed to be drowned out. At this point, the union, which was primarily concerned with reaching new members who were streaming in from other areas, did not take the matter very seriously. The company's reminder that its wage level was exceptional among all the companies in the industry rapidly defused the demand. Indeed, a few weeks later, on December 12, 1912, broad general agreements were reached about wage levels and the management of piecework rates; in the case of the possible failure of internal factory commissions, the participation of the German Metal Workers' Union was foreseen as a last resort. Regulations were drafted concerning grievance rights and layoffs. The company should not be unduly constrained, but the rights and interests of the workers should be regulated in a pragmatic way. It looked like a peace agreement in the making. There was no reason to think that the union was preparing for a battle. It had to know that at that time the company was not in a period of seasonal demand, hence pressure would have no effect. It was more likely that there would be layoffs.

That, indeed, is what did happen. On January 17, 1913, eight men were laid off at the Feuerbach factory, among them a shop steward. The members of the department laid down their tools, and about 40 percent of the workers—the decision went back and forth—left the plant before closing time. Bosch announced that anyone who did not return to work, or who in the future left his work without the permission of the factory management, could regard himself as laid off. The union was uncertain as to how it should respond; it successfully opposed the call for a strike but saved face by permitting a blockade of the Feuerbach factory— everyone was to be kept out. Bosch answered this fighting gesture by calling off all agreements. If he had come to a contractual agreement with the union, then it should not be able to be broken at the first opportunity without the union calling its people to order. But the union no longer quite dared to do that. In their meetings, the union officials had already felt themselves to be on the defensive. The issue was resolved two weeks later. Both sides accepted the arbitration judge's offer to mediate. Bosch participated unwillingly. He was irritated, and one of his letters to the arbitration judge contains the remark: "Better a happy war than a rotten peace!" He had no interest in this war. The discussions that had begun with the fight over a master irritated him. That mistakes were made in his firm was self-evident; then the union had come, and the two sides had talked things over. But the firm had stayed within the terms of the contract. Now, he thought, the union wanted to strong-arm him. Bosch decided to replace the agreements with his own order, which departed from the agreements in only one specific: the establishment of the piece-work rates was relegated to the calculation bureau. The union did not object. The two sides assured each other by mutual agreement that in the future they would try to settle their differences through negotiations. The cause of the struggle, the layoffs of the eight men, no longer played any role in the resolution; they were accepted. Evidently Bosch believed that peace would now reign. To distract himself with new impressions, he took a trip to Algeria that lasted several weeks.

The skirmish provided the excuse to put together some comparative statistics, which were presented by the Professional Association of Precision Engineers, Section IX. Their results may have been astonishing even for the Bosch people; in any case they certainly provided a satisfying affirmation. The figures for the year that had just ended, 1911, showed that in the entire sector, 23,384 workers were employed; of these, 3,423, or 14.65 percent, worked at Bosch. Of the total wages, which amounted to 31,360,500 marks, 6,850,950, or 21.85 percent, were paid by Bosch. And the average wage looked like this: 1,341 marks in the sector; 2,011.44 at Bosch. The difference of 660.44 marks in the Bosch workers' favor amounted to 49.25 percent. For the year 1912, a few months later, while the struggle was still going on, an even better wage ratio could be observed. The average wage of the precision engineering sector was 1,259.07 marks, while at Bosch it was 2,044.41—a difference of 62.37 percent. Even more remarkable were the official figures on accidents, for they offered an unspoken argument against the thesis that the work tempo at Bosch was particularly dangerous for the workforce. The number of reimbursable accidents in the sector was 112, while at Bosch it was 8, or 7.14 percent of the total accidents; the insurance payments in total amounted to 155,991.64 marks, while at Bosch they were 3,055.85 marks, or 1.96 percent. In the area of medical insurance, for every hundred insured employees Bosch had 37.7 cases of illness that resulted in lost work time; the other companies in the sector had 58.8 cases. These sober official statistics actually should have served as a very eloquent defense, but they did not succeed.

The unrest in the Metal Works did not cease completely, even after the blockade was lifted. April brought a few new layoffs; the fact that a

Social Democratic committee member was among them was considered a hostile act. There was nothing to be said against the rationale for this action, given the situation in the relevant department, the more so since the man in question had only recently been hired. Technical changes had led to reductions in the piecework rates for several work processes. Business was rather slow overall, and the company therefore had to look more closely at the rates at which the competition was offering its products. By now, the tensions in the factory had begun to affect Bosch's family as well. There were passionate discussions between the daughters and their father. The father had to convince them that he was in the right, and he was happy when he succeeded. "At least now I do not have to find that I am attacked at home, as well," he wrote in a letter to his wife on May 19, 1913.

Actual conflict broke out again on the morning of May 30. It was quite dramatic. Two people were to be laid off in the tool-manufacturing department. The steward in the department demanded that the pink slips be taken back within a quarter of an hour. The manager said no, and fired the steward as well because of his behavior. The latter then gave the department the command "Down tools." They obeyed, and the factory stood still. In the specialized vocabulary of the social sciences this was a so-called wildcat strike. It broke out in a location that was less important for current business than for overall production. Since the supply of parts in the warehouse was not inconsiderable, management thought they could manage for a while by having the grinders who finished the products take over the work of the toolmakers for a few weeks; they would then decide what to do next. But the grinders refused to do the work of the toolmakers. It was impossible to continue work. The factory had to be closed. Bosch resisted calling the decision a lockout; instead he spoke of the pressure that was forcing him to shut down. From the union's point of view, the more or less technical cause of the struggle was also in contradiction with the rules. A typical orderly work stoppage would have required negotiations and a prior vote. The fact that there was none relieved the central leadership of the German Metal Workers' Union of the duty and the right to become involved in the matter. They were quite evidently happy about this. They saw a political advantage in the affair and would not have been displeased to see it fail. Leaders like Alexander

Schlicke and Scherm were tired of the constant agitators, but were themselves too much administrators and formalistic tacticians to have risked an offensive against the incursion of party politics.

The leadership of the struggle lay in the hands of the unfortunate local union leaders, who only four months earlier had described and averted a strike as a financial catastrophe. Now they saw the full burden falling on the local treasury, and they were soon made to feel how fragile their authority was. They implored the young people to go elsewhere, but they did not want to go, as they feared losing their jobs at Bosch altogether. What had they paid their dues for? The strike fund had to appeal to the solidarity of the other metalworkers. But there they were to discover that the desire to help the Bosch workers through the medium of the local union treasury was not very great—they had earned so much that surely they could hold out for a while! The workers, who had found themselves in a very bitter, unexpected, and for the most part unwanted struggle overnight, found that they lacked the moral backing of the members of their own class. The Social Democratic newspaper had to try to make the conflict with Bosch seem more acute, and to compare the "former" Bosch with the current one. The *Metal Workers' News* was more cautious and printed sociological essays in place of alarms; its final comment almost detachedly called the struggle a "strange conflict."

Indeed, it was that. The union and the public were confronted with a strategy that was very unusual for such struggles, and that was led by Bosch himself. The first thing he did was to announce that he would pay all those workers who were affected by the forced shutdown, and who were not members of a union, the same amount of support the union members were receiving. That might have sounded unwise, for it almost appeared to be a special contribution to an auxiliary strike fund. But the decision weakened the moral position of the union, for it was a gesture of willingness to help. The records of the battle give instructive insight into the labor practices prevalent during the period. Offers from everywhere poured in to help Bosch procure workers ("First-class bureau for strike matters," etc.)—all the agencies in this strange line of business contacted him. He did not respond. The German Metal Workers' Union tried to make contact and received no answer. Through the Social Democratic faction in City Hall, they attempted to involve the newly elected chief mayor as an intermediary; Bosch thanked him for his willingness to be involved but declined to take advantage of it. The rather odd situation gave birth to all kinds of rumors. The company denied that it was engaged in sales negotiations aimed at handing the entire factory over to an American consortium.

The members of Bosch's staff were somewhat informed about how things stood on the opposing side, what sums had to be withdrawn from the bank accounts, what bad feeling was caused by the local surcharges. They also knew that the head of the union, Alexander Schlicke, had declared in the beginning of July that the whole thing was "completely hopeless and a great embarrassment for the union and the workers." If Bosch reopened, they must "unconditionally return to work." Even more drastic opinions could be heard from Schlicke's close colleagues. But the opposition had their information, too. The open labor struggle created a deep conflict within the Bosch family; no longer were they merely having theoretical discussions about what was "the right thing." The daughters rebelled against their father's decision, pressured him with their wishes, and let no one in earshot doubt that they, with all the passion of their young hearts, stood on the opposing side. Although that caused Bosch grief, it was clear to him that the struggle had to proceed according to its own laws.

But Bosch would be the one to decide what these laws would be. On July 12, after the factory had been lying idle for six weeks, the time seemed right to him to end his reticence. He announced through advertisements that he would soon be opening the factory again, and he requested written applications. "The wages that have been paid until now for workers in my plant will not be reduced." True, in the future health and disability insurance would have to be paid by the workers themselves. However, the company would not keep the amount it had previously paid for this purpose, but would set it aside for the workers' benefit. The factory opened its doors on July 16; the day brought a public declaration by Bosch that he did not care whether or where the individual workers were organized. They could do as they pleased. With that, the shutdown or lockout was at an end. In social science terminology, the strike now began. For the union warned its workers not to respond to his offer, and sent pickets even to the railway station. Nevertheless, three days later, on July 19, Bosch was able to announce that 1,120 people had come to work, not counting masters, apprentices, and other staff. This continued for days; the people of Stuttgart found it quite American that they could read announcements on the kiosks and in the newspapers about the growing number of people working at Bosch: 1,296, 1,436, 1,607. This method of proceeding, intended to lure workers back, amazed people. When the *Swabian Daily Watch*, the Social Democratic newspaper, doubted the accuracy of the figures, they were invited to check them at the factory. The paper sent an editor; Bosch brought in a notary public for the occasion. The study naturally proved him right. The German Metal Workers' Union was as furious as it was helpless at this turn of events; it was forced to recognize that old union comrades preferred going back to their machines to constantly attending meetings, and since a not inconsiderable portion of the polemics now had to be directed against these traitors, there was not much animosity left for Bosch and the company. The struggle had been lost. Even the radicals, however exercised they might get in their speeches, could make no mistake about that.

Bosch himself naturally saw that ads with suggestive numbers, as useful as they might be, were not the soul of wisdom. Should he attempt to found a "factory association" that would remain independent of the larger trade unions? Numerous suggestions about how to do so came fluttering onto his desk. Yes, if something like this were to occur spontaneously, then one might consider it. He declined to exercise any influence in this direction, either personally or through his staff, and denied the rumors that the founding of a "yellow" association was planned. Yet on July 23 he made the demand that the workers elect a factory committee in which nonunion workers would also be represented. He suggested proportional voting. The committee was to be independent in its representation of the workers' interests, but was also to know how to prevent arbitrary acts like the shutdown of individual departments.

When this was announced, the most important decision had already been made: Bosch had become a member of the Union of Württemberg Metal Industrialists. This decision gave a completely new tactical dimension to the struggle. It helped both parties to find their way out of a confusing situation and seal the formal conclusion of a struggle whose end was close enough to touch. The German Metal Workers' Union acted as if this solution was quite welcome. For the moment this was certainly accurate. A neutral and somewhat familiar space had been offered that the representatives of the association could now enter. The office of the Metal Industrialists took the formal steps to open negotiations on July 25, which occurred without incident. Bosch confirmed what he had already stated publicly, that the workday and wages would remain the same as they had been, and that he regarded the issue of vacations within the context of the willingness, in principle, to work overtime. He would naturally not make this dependent on the behavior of individual workers, as had been claimed by agitators during the struggle. When it came to rehiring, the striking workers would be considered first, in accordance with their suitability. "Other measures will not be taken by either side, the blockade is lifted by mutual agreement." The end of the strike was voted by a meeting of the workers with only two opposing votes.

The defeat of the German Metal Workers' Union was complete, even if the concluding memorandum gave it the possibility of saving face. The struggle had cost the local leadership hundreds of thousands of marks—the estimates vary from 500,000 to 700,000 marks. It had to expel the strikebreakers—a printed list contains almost a thousand names, and this action created bitterness. The overall loss of members was even greater. The number sank from 15,000 to 9,000; in other words, the flight went beyond the immediate participants. It was not until years later, in a world that was very different, that the union was able to recover from this conflict. The radical wing of the Social Democratic Party, which had played the role of agitator, was humbled, and this gave the more thoughtful forces, who were more restrained in their agitation, new self-confidence.

Robert Bosch himself took little pleasure in his victory. "What I suffered at that time, particularly toward the end and in the first weeks after the opening of the factory, I do not want to describe." His *Life Recollections* also criticize the tactic, so effective at first, of returning to work with a partial workforce. For this had been the "only lesson" that the struggle had held for him: that after a strike one should not reopen the factory until a meeting of the entire workforce had voted to go back to work. For in the eyes of the others, those people who had accepted the public invitation to return to work remained "strikebreakers—God only knows for how long." This, however, created a psychological division among the workers. It might have suited Bosch, had he looked at the situation from the standpoint of power politics. But that was not his style. He also knew that the union leaders had not wanted the strike, something they later told him. But as a result of this experience, he remained skeptical about the freedom of movement of the workers' leaders in economic questions: Did they follow their insights and really lead, committing themselves personally? Or were they measuring their advice and decisions against the vacillations and uncertainties of the formless mass?

The thing that caused Bosch the most suffering was the fact that the strike had become "a great triumph" for those employers who had attacked him for his position on labor issues. The "social enthusiast" and "card-carrying Comrade" could read reports laced with scorn, irony, pity, and smug satisfaction every day in the *Post* and in large sections of the right-wing press. He had beaten the workers, but he experienced this victory, which could have been predicted with certainty at the beginning of the struggle, as a defeat when it came to his relations with the employers. It was the radical Socialists who had brought about this situation. As Bosch noted in his *Life Recollections* of 1921, "The employer who had social sympathies was nothing but a nuisance. It had been written that the philanthropists held the movement back. They had to be opposed more strongly than the agitators, for *they* at least helped increase the tempo of the class struggle. They helped reach the final goal. Yes, the left agitated against the right, and the right agitated against the left, but both of them agitated against the middle, and that was me."

When Bosch became a member of the Union of Metal Industrialists of Württemberg, it was the outgrowth of a certain resignation. He had convinced himself that it was not possible for an individual company "to hold out against the union's lust for power." In any case, and this much was clear, he would not allow himself to be pressed into any molds. "Membership in this association," he stated in the public announcement of July 19, 1913, "in no way prevents me from remaining true to my past behavior toward my workforce. Hence, I shall remain faithful to my point of view, now as before, and am concerned to place myself on as good a footing as possible with my workforce." The workers were assured of the same wage possibilities and the same workday, their grievances would be treated "as before, in a just and sympathetic manner." But he also expressed his willingness to protect those members of the workforce who had now left the union. Up until this time, the union had been permitted to collect dues, distribute information, and carry out other organizational chores in the factory itself, although not during working hours. This kind of convenience now came to an end. The relationship had entered a new, more sober phase.

The situation had no further consequences. Those who expected Bosch's conversion were disappointed. The National Association Against Social Democracy, which was suddenly enjoying a certain popularity, was politely informed that he did not intend to join (June 24, 1913). He did not want to allow the foolishness of the Stuttgart radicals, as profoundly as he might have been hurt by their tone, to force him into a position that was not compatible with his true nature.

Otherwise, his membership in the organization of the metal industrialists, which he had decided upon out of a certain tactical necessity, was not at all burdensome. The leadership, particularly after it was assumed by Albrecht Fisher, who had been a factory inspector, was not at all intent on struggle or tests of power, but focused on the attempt to arrive at a feasible compromise. Large-scale wage struggles could generally be avoided, and the social atmosphere remained free of serious storms. Bosch himself had taken a very prominent role in the summer of 1913, and the struggle upset him deeply. Now, after the whole situation had been transformed into a union contract and its technicalities, he withdrew from the day-to-day leadership of this complex of questions. He handed it over to Ernst Ulmer, who had had no part, as yet, in the disagreements and conflicts, and was actually quite far removed from these matters of social engineering. But Ulmer's human qualities, the goodwill that his personality radiated, his obliging manner, his humor and straight-talking reliability of character—these were the best preconditions for overcoming the legacy of the struggle. For a decade he would be Bosch's representative to both the employers' association and the union; he would preserve an internal tradition among changes that transformed the external situation.

19

———

EDUCATION
ON THE JOB

The year 1913 was a time of profound tensions for the Bosch company, but it was also a year that saw the implementation of an idea that had been under consideration for some time and that would always enjoy Robert Bosch's special concern and affection: the Teaching Workshop. The bitter power struggle had reached its last phase when on July 15, 1913, August Utzinger, who had just arrived from Berlin, stood in a room that had been cleared out inside the factory and began considering the best way to apportion the space for the installation of lathes, grinding machines, and the like, at which some thirty apprentices would now be working.

The problem of finding new employees had suddenly caught up with the world's large and growing industrial businesses, insofar as their production depended on well-trained skilled workers. The latter were simply too few and far between. At one time they had been trained by the crafts. But would the crafts be able to survive, and was it their job, ultimately, to train young men so that they could later help to destroy the small businesses whose decline and fall the authorities were predicting? In the meantime, the situation was such that wherever a good mix of crafts continued to exist, there were always new reserves available from which to draw skilled workers, foremen, and masters. Where the crafts were lacking, the general development required new forms, and forcibly created them. The mechanization of the production process, the thoroughgoing specialization of machine tools, the division of labor, and automation all grew out of the polarity between the growing demand for products and the decreasing numbers of skilled workers. This would shape the fate of North America, which had been able for so long to fall back on the journeymen who had been schooled in European workshops. European industrialization put a stop to this type of emigration. But the colonies had no broadly developed and mature craft tradition of their own. Naturally, the lack was noticed. The trained workers who had been selected according to F. W. Taylor's methods and had been schooled to carry out specific tasks did not replace the old skilled workers with their—at least in theory—universal education and experience within their particular branch of industry. Consequently, given the unevenness of public education, the large enterprises began to help themselves by expanding their programs to include apprentices.

In Germany, under different conditions, similar conclusions were being drawn. The problem at first might not have appeared to be so pressing. There, they had a proper system of technical schools, as well as the general vocational schools for continuing industrial education, the very type of school, based on Belgian models, that Ferdinand Steinbeis had developed and strengthened in Württemberg. Steinbeis had remained committed to voluntary participation, but in 1895 a special law had been enacted that required middle school dropouts to attend. The central task remained to create as close a link as possible between the practical apprenticeship in the factory and the teaching in the classroom. The great difficulty in getting started, especially when it came to new techniques that were on the verge of rapid and startling development, was finding suitable teachers. It is therefore no accident that the first training workshops with some degree of systematization were created in the young electrical engineering industry—in 1890 at Sigmund Schuckert's firm in Nuremberg.

As the head of the Precision Engineering Workshop, Robert Bosch, in his early years, had personally taken charge of the education of his apprentices. He continued to harbor grim thoughts about his own bad apprenticeship in Ulm, where he had been sent to a master who was busy taking things easy. In his workshop, the young people should learn something. They were severely tested, but their labor power was not permitted to be misused. And when Bosch came across a young man who was clever, eager, open-minded, and happy to lend a hand, Bosch quickly gave him a chance to prove himself. The role that the young Max Rall played in independently representing the young company, installing, demonstrating, even negotiating and practically taking part in the calculations of profit and loss, went beyond the norm of what was usual for apprentices. That was the early period. As the business grew, the situation changed. Now Bosch himself was no longer able to take charge of the individual apprentices. This task was assigned to the masters, whose qualifications were a matter of general knowledge. Many of them had themselves gone through the school of the workshop, and had kept up its traditions after it had become a factory. Bosch's extraordinary memory for people continued to be a personal and influential factor; he would intervene critically or express his appreciation in a few words, even after the company numbered in the thousands. The young faces that turned their somewhat shy and uncertain gazes in his direction as he walked through the spacious halls were not familiar to him, but it was precisely *their* future careers that occupied his thoughts. Were they learning the whole range of electrical engineering skills and techniques? Did they know something about the natural physical processes that were to be technically manipulated by the work? This had become virtually impossible since the factory had been divided into a series of departments, and even the masters, following the rhythm of an uneven, but on the whole quite tempestuous production program, had become highly specialized—this one in ignition, that one in light generators, and so on. It was simply not possible to send all the apprentices to the most comprehensive area, which was installation. True, they could learn very well there, if they intended to open their own shop one day, but how many of them might be thinking of that? And the issue of training qualified, skilled workers who would be imbued with insight and an overview would not be solved that way. Bosch discussed the matter with Honold, who responded with a profound sympathy for its importance and for the sentiments that motivated his concerned colleague. Thus it was decided to open a workshop for apprentices. The goal would necessarily be the closest possible link between practical work and theoretical schooling, along the lines of the program Professor Carl Bach had insisted upon for the education of engineers. In 1908, the Association of German Engineers had founded the German Committee for Technical Schooling. This was the beginning of the effort, which would later be so productive, to bring encouragement, support, and a systematic spirit to this whole field. The leaders at Bosch respected Bach's experiments, but it was not Bosch's nature to approach the new task with a clearly defined pedagogical-technical program; he was aware, on the contrary, that its spirit and shape would depend on the individual who took charge of it. This individual was the person he sought. Bosch would not find him in the factory itself; it would have to be someone whose career would be made in *this* particular area. In January 1913, Bosch ran an advertisement in the *Electrical Engineering Gazetteer.*

As he leafed through the application letters, Bosch came across a familiar handwriting: his coworker from the year in Nuremberg at Schuckert was writing to let him know that the challenge appealed to him. For Bosch, from this cautious query to the solution was no distance at all—what good luck if they should succeed in recruiting August Utzinger for this responsibility! Bosch's colleagues had to be convinced that he was the right man. As it had been Klein's job in the case of Eugen Kayser to "try him out," now it was Gottlob Honold who had to play a role in the testing. It went very well; the two men had various shared scientific interests and a comparable skill in coming up with technical solutions.

August Utzinger was a Swiss who came from the canton of Zurich and was six months younger than Bosch. They continued to address each other with the informal *Du* of their early relationship. After an apprenticeship in precision engineering in Zurich, Utzinger had attended the *Technikum* in Winterthur. In the factory in Nuremberg, he stood out by virtue of his theoretical knowledge, which he was willing to share with anyone who desired to learn. In their correspondence in 1913, Bosch reminded his former colleague of the lectures he had given for his colleagues at the age of twenty-eight, and suggested that in addition to the training program for apprentices he should also think about continuing education courses for adult workers. In his previous activities, Utzinger had not been employed in the plant. He had been involved with the question of apprentices in a marginal way, for the management of the Nuremberg factory had chosen him as a member of their school committee and had entrusted him with reporting on its activities in the workshop. He had spent most of his working years in the laboratory, primarily working on the development of light measurement techniques. In 1904, after Schuckert and Siemens merged, he went to Charlottenburg, Berlin, to become the head of the department conducting scientific and technical studies of lighting; here he gained a leading position as an innovative designer. But life in the hectic climate of Berlin did not appeal to this rather thoughtful man; his more reticent character made it difficult for him to gain broader recognition. He took refuge, to a certain extent, in his hobbies, for example, astronomy. For all his commitment to engineering questions involving light, he remained true to his origins in electrical engineering by building and designing clocks with much patience and skill.

Bosch always regarded the hiring of this friend of his youth as one of his most important and best decisions. For as critical, occasionally mistrustful, and sensitive as Utzinger could on occasion be, he exuded objective certainty and an eager love of the task he had undertaken. "The person who did not take pleasure in technical and mechanical things under August Utzinger had best stay away from the technological professions," Bosch wrote in Utzinger's obituary in the fall of 1921. "He was at the same time a capable precision engineer, a thorough scholar, and an unsurpassed teacher." Their friendship must have blossomed again when it came time to plan and implement their project in the summer of 1913. It would be correct to say that there was no department to which Bosch, right up to his last years, so constantly devoted his personal attention and concern as the Teaching Workshop. In creating it, he was clearly aware that an example needed to be set in this area. And for Utzinger it was a wonderful and fulfilling challenge to be able to spend large sums on the creation of a small center with its own life, a center that was not a mere appendage of the practical work of the factory but was accorded its own dignity from the beginning.

Bosch's workshop for apprentices soon came to enjoy a strong reputation and a special status, and was not without influence on the numerous

similar workshops created during and after the war of 1914–18. The
technological transformation of victory on the battlefield had suddenly
demonstrated the extraordinary military importance of skilled metalworkers. Bosch's new creation possessed a number of special features
that distinguished it. The apprentices were not required to go on to work
in the Bosch factories after the conclusion of their apprenticeships,
which generally lasted three and a half years. It was only recommended
that they do so as a means of acquainting themselves with the rhythm and
idiosyncrasies of industrial mass production. In the Teaching Workshop,
none of the Bosch products sold on the market were produced or were
made the object of special study. The workshop remained committed to
the individualized work typical of handicraft production. The examinations were given at the Chamber of Handicrafts, and part of the general
education and theoretical teaching took place within the framework of
the city's continuing education program. Practical considerations led to
the organization of virtual "Bosch classes" there. This is not the place to
describe the curriculum, with its progression from simple manual tasks
to more complex assignments, its mixing of older and younger apprentices for larger projects. The essential thing at Bosch was that the
apprentices were not lent out to the factory from time to time to participate in production, as was customary, but worked only in the Teaching
Workshop. This procedure also found its critics, who considered this an
exaggerated and overly long isolation from the actual industrial milieu, a
kind of spoiling of the apprentices. This opinion was held by people who
had themselves once experienced what it was like to be an apprentice in
the negative sense, and had later come to regard the unfortunate experiences of their youth as beneficial. But it was not as if the apprentices
were simply producing some useless stuff just to learn manual skills, or
to make a show of it later. The apprentices did not work in the factory but
worked *for* the factory. The workshop was first and foremost a tool shop
that made everything from the simplest to the most complicated items; it
then produced the instruments for the departments engaged in scientific
experimentation; last but not least, it also made everything that Utzinger
needed in the way of models and demonstration apparatus for the workshop's own theoretical classes. Psychologically, everything was geared to
the eagerness and pride of the young men, the fact that they themselves

had to calculate, refine, and install the models with which they or the students who followed them would learn the physical sciences. Utzinger's wide-ranging scientific and technological interests, and the new suggestions and needs that continuously came from Honold's department, assured that the tasks would never become routine. The students did not limit themselves to individual parts, but shifted from electricity to optics, from mechanics to the study of chemical substances. Occasionally the result was work that led rather far afield, at least from the standpoint of Bosch's own manufacturing. When a wall clock was needed for the reception room of the new administration building, Utzinger was proud to construct it and polish its every part in the teaching workshop. This sort of thing made Robert Bosch happy. Naturally he knew about the inevitability of specialization and the dictates of mass production, but he never overlooked the human *and* objective gain that resulted when an all-around education free of immediate calculation of profit and loss taught the mental agility that would later enable the journeyman—or master to be—to approach new tasks not with anxiety but with daring insight.

The questions of industrial pedagogy, which Bosch had addressed on a large scale with the founding of the Teaching Workshop in 1913, would occupy him continuously from now on. What was required for the training of an elite? Maintaining quality would seem to depend on whether the students possessed certain attitudes and were able to communicate them to others: accuracy and the proper care of tools and materials. But these alone would not make the difference. Among the notes that Bosch occasionally made in his last years, there is one concerning the fact that for the manufacture of "unspecified quantities of interchangeable products" the invention of the grinding machine and the development of finer and finer measuring instruments had been a fateful agent of change. For now it was possible, indeed necessary, to fabricate things using so-called "trained" workers. Their numbers were growing, and as a result, the task of industrial education had changed. It had left the realm of all-around pedagogy behind and, except for transmitting certain manual skills or making the workers familiar with specialized machines, it had become a matter of psychological leadership, of the atmosphere of the factory. Pedagogy, wage policy, and the workers' welfare and security became intertwined.

Bosch later continued to turn his lively and supportive attention to questions of general public education; his interest was directed less at specialized professional questions than at issues of humanity and citizenship, as he understood them. Occasionally he would take a public position. The confidence underlying this was the experience he had gained in the factory. A few basic ideas can be discerned: work and life experience are better teachers than school and theory. Despite an occasionally surprising credulousness regarding the powers of pedagogical influence, he remained skeptical about ordinary schooling, and particularly about any privileges that might result from it. Academics, just because they had completed university schooling, did not impress him one bit; one can sense a certain irritability in his rejection of claims based on theoretical knowledge or the passing of examinations. The schooling that occurred in the workshop was more important to him, specifically when it came about through work that was intended to be serious. Volunteers who only wanted to look around and do a bit of learning here and there were never taken in at Bosch. And even students performing their practicum, who were required to prove that they had done a year of work in a workshop prior to their examination, were only accepted very late in the program, and then only if they agreed to work an entire year at a time and not gradually collect the required twelve months during unconnected stints broken up by vacation periods. This may appear to be a matter of secondary importance, but it is characteristic. Praxis should not be play, but should be a period of seriously demanding objective work. There is also one apparently unimportant matter on which Bosch repeatedly turned to the public in essays, even entering into a polemical exchange with the government of Württemberg: not only professors and certified engineers should be permitted to attend the courses for future teachers of industrial subjects, but also craft masters. If the latter proved themselves as teachers, they should also earn the rank of regular professors and be remunerated according to the administrative pay scale; they should not merely be visiting faculty teaching specialized classes. The castelike objections of the trained pedagogues or the concerns about administrative law were ridiculous in Bosch's eyes. Methodology and the necessary minimum of theory (which was all that mattered) could be learned in courses. A man who learned in this way would make fewer embarrassing mistakes in front of the apprentices than a professor of industry lacking a skilled background in a craft. As Bosch wrote in 1926, "there is no need to worry about a capable craftsman *of charac-ter*—and every teacher must have that!—having an unfavorable effect on his students in terms of building their character. Morals and ethics are not *taught* most effectively to young people of the age of the industrial students; they must be demonstrated by *living* them in front of the students; in other words, a person will have a greater effect through his entire manner, his example; less through words" (1926).

The mistrust of theory, or at least discomfort with it—the words he used were sometimes quite crass—marked the limits of Bosch's own nature. Naturally, he understood and supported the necessity of abstract, basic research not tied to specific purposes, but he maintained a certain shy distance from the mental processes involved. More than was necessary, he smelled the danger of "over-education," which would make a young person either useless in life or insufferable as a result of intellectual arrogance. When an essay was published in 1929 in the Socialist *Swabian Daily Watch* on the topic "Higher Education Does Not Guarantee Success in Industry and Crafts," he found it "so worthwhile and so accurate" that he felt "compelled" to write a letter to the editors expressing his "cordial thanks" for the fact that the author had addressed this question is such an excellent way. He felt confirmed in his own experience, where capable masters with elementary school educations were helping to drive the work forward. Utzinger, too, had repeatedly expressed similar observations, even stating in a 1919 essay that "the better student [he meant the young person who was a product of a 'so-called better school'] is usually petulant and condescending, while the public school student is moving up into the trade, and is fresh and cheerful."

Bosch was not concerned, in general, with the question of the extent to which the public schools should be transformed into professional schools. When Gottlob Honold, who had made some money, made contributions to outfit the middle schools of the province with more and better apparatus for the study of the natural sciences, Bosch heartily supported his actions, if only for the example and the precedents Honold might set. In a memo late in his life, he instructed his estate administrators to continue Honold's initiatives if it should be necessary. If circumstances warranted, the firm should take an interest in the Technical University and the Machine Building Institute of Esslingen. Given Bosch's basic position, it is not surprising that he approached the humanistic education of the *Gymnasium,* which in Württemberg could look back on a broad, unbroken tradition, with reservations if not with outright rejection. Bosch never took a public position on the matter; he would probably have felt that this would exceed his abilities. But with his unphilosophical tendencies, he had a keen nose for things that were abstract and speculative, and he feared the arrogance of the educated even more. Classical antiquity had had no role in the formation of his life and character. Even later on, he remained unmoved by its relics, with the possible exception of an interest in building construction on his trips to Italy. He did not want to hear anything about the special educational value of the *Gymnasium.* When Paul Schmitthenner, the architect from Stuttgart, once stated in a lecture that well-prepared university students only came from the *Gymnasium,* or possibly its modern version that stressed foreign languages, his listener (although he was grateful for the high value the professor ascribed to the crafts in general) contradicted him. If Schmitthenner were correct in his judgment, this might be due to the fact that in the *Gymnasium* the students *and* the teachers were better, as he, Bosch, had been assured. But it was not acceptable to presume that a more realistically oriented education must be geared toward materialistic thinking. Bosch then made the comment, as lapidary as it is personal, "My opinion is that the teaching material that is used in the instruction of Greek and Latin makes the students into cynics and egoists, and that Julius Caesar, for example, was by no means a great patriot. But on the other hand, I am convinced that our German classic writers, above all Schiller, are well-suited to educating human beings of character and love of the fatherland. And our great scientists! Were they materialists? Does one not become more and more modest, the more knowledge one acquires about the material forces of nature? I can only remind you of the 'Ignoramus Ignorabimus!' (My Latin, as a non-Latinist, may be faulty.) It is the motto of a person who knows his limitations, and is conscious of the inadequacies of human beings."

This quote, from January 1934, was a statement from Bosch's late years. But it was in keeping with his consistent view that the natural sciences, with their logic and their compulsion for exactitude, possessed educational advantages that were no less than those recognized in ancient languages and cultures. But the study of nature and technology should be kept separate in the minds of young people. "By the way," he wrote in a letter from January 1930, "I find it extraordinarily regrettable that the young people are only concerned with these technical things and do not take any interest in the nature that is all around them. But one does not have to look far to find the reason for this; the parents themselves, for the most part, are completely alienated from nature, and now the little ones are surrounded by so much technology, to which they are attracted from their childhood, that they can scarcely get interested in anything else." He speaks of a twelve-year-old boy who tells him "that he is busy with the design of an airplane"; he finds this a trendy, disagreeable story. "At some point, young people should take an interest in our animal and plant life . . ." (They did not exactly need to go to Lapland to do this, however, for which someone had just asked him to give money!)

Robert Bosch would probably not have objected if someone had wanted to talk about the impact his education had had on his character. But if his conversation partner had tried to reflect on the essence of this education, it is by no means certain that the two would have reached agreement. For his insights and the convictions he held more or less as articles of faith were sometimes contradicted by his character and his spontaneous reactions. What Bosch brought with him in the way of unquestionable long-term educational commitment was a generally positive notion of the educability of man. It is even possible to speak of a measure of abstract love of mankind, which did not quite seem to fit with his sensual, concrete nature, and which he himself, if he had thought about it, would have seen as an inheritance from his parents—an element of traditional responsibility. Rousseau's "Man is good" would have sounded convincing and familiar in his ears, at first, and he would have nodded. But after some thoughtful reflection he would have added sarcastically: yes, but with the exception of this person and that person and that person . . . The optimism with which he approached people had suffered quite a few disappointments.

In his late writings, Bosch made something of an attempt to bring some method to his practice of handling people at the factory, if not as a

commitment to pedagogical principle, exactly, then as an emphatic recommendation to his successors on the managerial side to act in approximately the same way. These notes contain important biographical and
psychological information, as well as historical data on the history of the
firm, but they are not pedagogical principles that can be separated from
his person. He detested conferences and meetings that only involved
people who had nothing to do with the subject being discussed, and
which were therefore just a waste of time. And if by chance notes were
taken for the files, to which people could refer later if they wished, then
the door to bureaucracy had been flung open. Bosch had the habit of
dropping in on his colleagues in their offices, unexpected and unan-
nounced, to discuss current concerns and take care of them on the spot.
"I got to know my people better than if they visited me at an appointed
time." Psychologically, this is undoubtedly correct; whether it was
always fortunate from a technical point of view in terms of the best use of
work time may be open to question. He did not consider that his arrival
might be awkward or intrusive for some piece of work just being completed. In this way, from impressions and inquiries, sometimes followed
by directives and decisions, he gathered an overview, in his wonderful
memory, of the technical and business problems. As far as what his colleagues might think of the overall situation, or what picture they might
form for themselves of the course of events in related departments (something that was often necessary), that was their problem. They should
inform each other and reach a mutual understanding. This naturally also
took time and led to memorandums, which led to written agreements. But
if this meant that something resembling red tape arose after all, out of
sheer necessity, it occurred anonymously, so to speak. Bosch himself did
not have to bother with it. Since, because of the nature of his character he
was not one to hesitate once something was under way, he kept the pace
of business dealings fresh and lively. That was a gain, and may have been
the goal; but the psychological cause was Bosch's hesitation to chair
meetings, even in a small group. He, who was always driven by his own
particular tempo, was a miserable moderator—impatient, nervous whenever a speaker made detours that might in themselves have been quite
sensible but seemed superfluous to him at that particular moment—and
he was conscious of his weaknesses. Therefore, out of his hesitation to

take part in meetings, when his leadership was needed and all he had to offer was displeasure and unease, he constructed a pedagogical virtue: individual encounters.

Here is where his power to mold individuals came into play. His employees were not children, but were rather fully developed individuals. He communicated to them the enormous objective seriousness with which he treated even matters that appeared secondary while not neglecting the central issues. He was able to portray the things he was familiar with, such as questions of plant biology or hunting, to a lay person if he sensed that that person had a serious thirst for knowledge. But his actual dealings with people involved questioning. The *way* he posed the questions, his intensity, was—if one can see in this a rational consideration and not simply an instinctive behavior—the most impressive pedagogy. It was not always comfortable for his conversation partner, especially for the person who might be intimidated by the unexpected. A younger acquaintance who had known Bosch quite well both personally and professionally once commented that after every conversation with him he had the feeling that he had been taking an examination. The exam went like this: If someone told Bosch, "I don't know that," he was satisfied (unless it was a piece of factual information about work that the individual had to know). Bosch himself knew a great deal, although he was no polymath and was conscious of his limitations. But woe betide the person who might have said quite harmlessly: "I believe that this is the way it is." Then he would receive the emphatic reply: "I don't want to hear what you *believe*, but what you *know*." Perhaps he was thinking back to a saying of his mother's: "You shouldn't have opinions, believe, or think! Smart people know for sure."

To some degree, this process of inquiry and detailed questioning was a kind of pedagogical technique. Bosch did not only want to find out *what* people actually knew—naturally it was often enough just a question of filling in the gaps in his own knowledge with the help of someone who he thought might be particularly clever—but he also wanted to get a sense of *how* that person would respond to and perform in a jousting match of this kind. If it went well, Bosch would be satisfied; he loved not only the objectivity but also the jousting match quality, if his opponent knew how to parry and thrust, of the conversations. But if the human circumstances were not favorable to clarity and precision, if the conversation took a turn toward murky claims or, even worse, emotional assurances—his unsentimental love of factuality was particularly sensitive when emotion entered into the conversation—then things could get ugly or end quite embarrassingly. This happened in a number of historic conversations.

In general, Bosch considered himself to be a good judge of people. In fact, when it came to recruiting his closest associates, he not only had the famous lucky touch, but arrived at his decisions after very detailed and conscientious testing. With a good eye for what was essential, he put the available people in the right places. Then he left them the freedom to develop. His bossiness was consciously kept under control whenever there was someone with a will like his own who was developing under and then beside him, and he allowed every kind of individuality—even if it contradicted his own nature—its opportunity and freedom. They were to seek and hire their own colleagues, and they should also participate generously in the growth of the firm when it came to their own incomes. One requirement, if their job was done during regular hours, was punctuality in coming to work, so as to curtail loafing or prevent criticism on the part of the workers. The leaders of the departments had to be models for their workers, both in human terms and in matters of work discipline. Bosch expressed respect for accomplishment, essentially through the trust that he gave; he was sparing with direct praise. This was something that sometimes brought disappointment. When he visited the new sales building in Frankfurt am Main, its director expected a word of recognition about the way it had been set up, but all he was told was that a water faucet in the washroom had been installed incorrectly. Bosch's critical eye had noticed it at once. Indeed, he saw everything, even a lightbulb that was not turned off in a hallway. Such a discovery could lead to a sudden argument. Only one who misunderstood Bosch's character would call it petty. This was not merely a calculation aimed at saving money, rather it was the will to make sure that attention was paid to unimportant things, too, so that similar care would be taken for granted in important ones.

Naturally, as he wanted to let others grow, but had at the same time an intense drive to exercise power, there were tensions and even sharp conflicts. This was inevitable. Bosch tortured himself with doubts about whether he had been wrong in his judgment of a person, or whether he had been deceived, and sometimes the strain caused him to reach the breaking point. The fine judgment of men that Bosch, with his critical eye, was certain he possessed may appear less obvious to the impartial observer who reviews not only the beginning, but also the end, of a relationship. One would not exactly want to emphasize the number of people Bosch was taken in by, although often enough his closest colleagues and advisers, in addition to the objective influence they exercised, had understood how to hold him back or distract his attention. But when one looks at this political connection, or that support of an economic initiative, or at some of the far-reaching medical research one encounters very astonishing human connections. In Bosch one finds an almost intimate, active willingness to help individuals who are instinctually quite far removed—even alien—to him. Here his agreement with an objective goal, for example, the political movement to create a unified "Pan Europe," or his sudden enthusiasm for some perhaps arcane medical idea, led not only to a financial but also to a mental concern of such intensity that the person examining his correspondence or the nature of his partners asks himself in astonishment: Could this really have gone on for so long? Bosch must have had some sense of whom he was dealing with! Here his own obsession with the subject matter overcame the skepticism of the mistrustful observer, which was not at all foreign to him, or drowned out the warning voice. The files from this segment of his life are full of dramatic and audible final curtains, doors being slammed shut to correct errors of psychological judgment and to create a temporary emotional balance.

Among the numerous gifts with which Bosch was endowed by nature, one was completely lacking: the gift of deception. This is not meant as a moral judgment. Even if he had wanted to dissemble, he would not have been able to; the mental and physical response would have failed him. This lack, if one may call it that, did not cause any disadvantages in business, but could bring about occasional difficulties when it came to certain technical matters. At the beginning of his rise to prominence, Bosch had before him a model of the art of dissimulation in Frederic R. Simms. Naturally, he learned from him, painfully, that in negotiating one must wait and sometimes remain silent, that for a man of his character the very difficult art of patience almost required a kind of training. Here hunting, and the contact with nature in general, was a wonderful school of character. Must one be conventionally polite? Yes, one must, but it is impossible to do so if it is only done because of convention and goes against the grain psychologically. This must be distinguished from unforced cordiality among friends, where there is no need for caution and where the need for a large space in which one can breathe freely—in both a physical and a mental sense—is not suppressed.

The fact that Bosch was unable to dissemble, that the honesty was not merely a moral category but a basic fact in his emotional makeup—this was the decisive element in his pedagogy. Similarly, those characteristics that were so important in his professional life, his unfailing appreciation for good work—for the best work—and for essential materials and appropriate forms, were nothing but reflections of this *one* fundamental force. In encountering it, the people who met him were educated, consciously or unconsciously, and felt gratitude, shyness, or denial. Some were broken by it, for it was not a school of sensitivity. But in the process, a type of personality was formed that became the source of an influential tradition.

PART IV

POLITICAL
PRESSURE

20

———◆———

BEFORE THE
STORM

During his rise, Robert Bosch's financing strategies had been about as unproblematic as one can imagine. In the early years there had been frequent cash shortages; relatives had helped out with loans and security guarantees, a typical example of the personal credit that played such an important role in the development of midsized industry in Württemburg. Neither the offers made to invest in his developing factory nor his own thoughts about the possibility of forming a joint stock company came to fruition. Besides, it seemed almost impossible to express the worth of the company in numbers in a period of such rapid growth. He no longer needed the money of the strangers who approached him, and a certain autocratic instinct made him hesitate to depersonalize the business. The huge investments in buildings and machines, which had continued without interruption after 1906, could be financed from current income. He also refrained from making any of the industrial investments about which he was approached. "I cannot decide to spend 25,000 marks to buy into things all over the place. I could die one day, and I cannot bear the thought of leaving my surviving relatives with a hodgepodge of small debt claims" (July 20, 1912). His words are formulated somewhat sentimentally, but he was not very interested in investments as such unless they involved companies that also interested him technically and economically, like the question of peat utilization that he took up in 1913. In such situations, he did not believe in doing things halfway.

One thing, however, that was and remained a half-hearted attempt was Bosch's venture into electrical power production and transmission. It occurred as a result of his above-mentioned endeavor to give new impetus to and to set new goals for the installation division, which had been organized as a separate accounting unit in 1910 and 1911. The experiment with water power in Munderkingen had some business potential, although it did not have the broader possibilities that had already become apparent in the electrical industry. Bosch's share of the upper Swabian business was somewhat more than half a million marks. The technical manager of the department, Ludwig Kilp, who had come to Bosch from Kellner, hoped that by combining with a factory in Geislingen they could play a central role in development of the Swabian highlands, which was then on the horizon. Both Bosch and Gustav Klein were prepared to go along with this. It would require patience; they would first have to educate and win over the peasants, and those who, being "progressive," had already purchased gasoline or oil engines would have to be convinced to sell them back. As early as 1912 there is evidence of Bosch's impatience and questions about whether he should divest himself of the whole installation division. The volume of customer sales for the year 1912–13 was approximately 973,000 marks. Added to that were installation contracts for his own company that were valued at 259,000 marks. In itself, this did not look bad, and it is important to note that Bosch did not give the department any monopoly on contracts within the factory, but opened them up to free competition. His purpose was both economic and pedagogical: the Bosch firm should and would not profit from itself; the rules of the free market should apply there, too. But when it came to actual transmission of power, things were not quite so simple. For just before Bosch, as the successor to the firm in Ulm, had begun a modest conquest of some new business, starting from the Munderkingen factory, which had been expanded through the purchase of several new sources of water power, government officials in Upper Swabia created a special association for the purpose of electrification: the Regional Union of Upper Swabian Electric Companies. It grew quickly under energetic and intelligent leadership, and enjoyed the support of the provincial government. The area that Bosch had secured through his contracts was now surrounded, in the most literal sense of the word. Although it seemed large enough to sustain a modest undertaking, a glance at the map revealed that it would always remain scattered, with endless squabbling over the borders, and with the threat of fights over rates. His opponents held the stronger cards in their hands, not only because of the geographical superiority they possessed, but also because of the remaining reserves of water power that waited to be developed on the Iller, access to which was barred for Bosch. It was soon clear to Bosch that he must find a good way out of this situation. His legal adviser undertook to mediate, which was difficult enough because Bosch's present willingness in contrast to his earlier obstinate stance was interpreted by the other side as weakness. He complained angrily about the leaders of the Regional Union, with whom one could not reach a settlement the way one could with "businessmen in a more strict sense." "I have already racked my brains," Bosch wrote to the arbitrator, "about where this comes from, and I think it stems from the fact that public officials think they are diplomats, while members of the nobility rank doing business alongside horse trading. Naturally, neither is the correct attitude for conducting business today . . ." This angry letter, dated January 8, 1914, attempted to explain the restraint that he had decided to exercise. A few months later, on May 4, 1914, the parties arrived at a contractual agreement after all, through which Bosch's ownership interests were handed over to the Regional Union. The installation division's monopoly of manufacture and delivery in the area was safeguarded during a transition period. Financially, the affair was not unprofitable for Bosch, who had not been forced to give up his holdings. But his accommodating schedule of payment resulted in a significant portion being devalued by inflation, with the usual bitter arguments over the recalculation of their value. In this matter, however, his interpretation of the law prevailed.

The events of Munderkingen were of minor significance, but they were not without fundamental implications. Bosch, well aware of the challenges and duties that are likely to inspire private pioneering efforts, intervened in a number of areas that represented essential aspects of

public administration, for example, transportation policies and the cultivation of moorlands. He retreated from the electrical industry with clear
decisiveness. This was true not only in the case of Upper Swabia; he also
dissolved other ties in which he had a supporting role, and declined to
pursue new suggestions. He had had enough "unpleasant experiences"
with this "fairly dangerous matter" (March 1914). He had beaten a
retreat in 1914 following his insight that the unification "of electrical
transmission for the whole region was beneficial, and even necessary," as
he formulated it in a legal writ. With this, he recognized the objective
superiority and justification of public corporations. There was no more
special role for private initiative. The installation division continued, but
Bosch viewed it with increasing cheerlessness. When the financial structure of the entire business was reorganized in 1917, the division was separated from the company complex and was made into a fully independent
business.

Such a reorganization had been the subject of consideration and suggestions for several years. Gustav Klein, quite aware of what he meant to
the firm, had been longing since 1911 for a way out of his position as an
employee. He wanted an open general partnership in which the most
important colleagues, Honold, Borst, Kayser, and himself, would participate without regard for Bosch's capital superiority. A few draft contracts
were requested from leading commercial lawyers. The idea did not make
any real progress, however, and Klein decided in December 1912 "to ter-
minate the currently existing contract." He could count on the fact that
Bosch would not give him up. The negotiations began to move more
quickly—they would be interrupted, for a time, by the labor struggle of
1913, but would also take on a new psychological meaning as a result of
this struggle. The questions of business organization and financial policies touched on the tragic human circumstance that had shadowed, even
darkened, Robert Bosch's life for several years. His only son, Robert,
born to him as his youngest child in 1891, suffered from an illness that
all the powers of medicine could not cure: torturous episodes of paralysis
that could be relieved to some extent with varying treatments at medici-
nal baths but always reappeared, worse than before, and cruelly dashed
any hopes for recovery.

Bosch could recognize the legacy of his own nature in his children—
the sense of independence, rebelliousness, and practical idealism. He

saw the things that moved him being taken up again and developed by the younger generation as part of their desire for self-sufficiency. His oldest daughter, Margarete, studied the social sciences, and in his second daughter his interest in construction seemed to resurface. His son mirrored his own youthful passion, his intense and lively interest in the phenomena of the plant and animal world and mineralogy and geology. Thanks to his more favorable circumstances, the young man's somewhat dilettantish endeavors had been able to develop a systematic bent; his father supported this inclination with joy and pride. In his old age, he nostalgically recalled the independent conclusions the boy had drawn with his observant sense of nature. It was taken for granted on both sides that the son would follow in his father's footsteps. There was no need or desire to rush things. After his *Abitur,* Bosch's son entered the workshop as an apprentice, and his father was not displeased to learn that young Robert felt at home there. But due to his illness his training had to be interrupted several times. Nevertheless, it was decided that Bosch should bring his son along on his trip to America in 1911; the new experiences might help raise the frail young man's spirits. It was a daring venture and one that worried his mother. In the coming decade, it was she who would bear the burden of her son's care, which utterly consumed her physical and emotional strength. Anna Bosch grasped at every ray of hope, but her husband saw things more clearly. The letters that were sent to the spas and convalescent homes are full of encouragement, and there is something touching about them, especially when Bosch wrote about his bird-watching journeys or plant classification, or once when he wrote to the sick boy for pages on end about a great ichthyosaur whose excavation and preservation he had made possible. His nurturing responsiveness to the active interests of his son, who continued his scientific education from his sickbed, does not conceal the painful realization that there was no likelihood of recovery. His son had a hopeless case of multiple sclerosis. The factory that Bosch had created appeared to have been denied a male heir of his own flesh and blood.

The strike of 1913 tore open the whole painful problem of the future of the business from yet another angle. Gustav Klein and Gottlob Honold grew alarmed because of the positions taken by Bosch's two daughters. The two men—one with a stormy and outgoing personality, the other more thoughtful and inclined to cheerful tranquillity—were not very interested in politics; they followed their own mature instincts and found "live and let live" to be adequate as their slogan. Bosch's social and wage policies, which did not affect them personally, were perfectly all right by them. They saw that these policies had never restricted the flow of business, but rather had helped to increase it. Klein was popular with the workers, although he could be relentless when it came to job performance, and Honold was respected. Neither of them concerned himself with the opinions of the political parties. Now their life's work was suddenly thrust into the midst of an ideological fight between political parties. This did not suit them at all, and they wanted absolutely no part of it in the future. But what would happen if Bosch were to die? They knew quite well that, when he gazed at his sick son, the unpleasant prospect had also occurred to him, only to be pushed aside. Bosch's daughters' opinions made them worry that political influences outside the business might gain influence in Bosch's absence. The leading men did not want to take that chance. They disclosed to Bosch that they would only remain in the company's employ if there was an organizational provision to prevent the possible danger of such a development. This was not meant as an ultimatum, exactly, but it was not far from one. And Bosch did not hesitate for a moment to recognize their desires and demands, as difficult as the decision was that they were asking of him. Above all else, the thought of separating himself from the men he trusted was unendurable: "I would rather sell my whole shop to a Jew than work with new people!" The security they demanded, however, meant the reorganization of ownership they had been talking about for two years.

Gustav Klein kept pushing for an open partnership with unlimited joint liability for the partners; however, the lawyers counseled against it because of the possible legal consequences if one partner were to leave the firm prematurely. The real difficulties were obvious. Even if the coworkers in question had already become quite wealthy, the sum of all their possible holdings would not add up to the superior capital position Bosch occupied. Similar considerations might apply in the case of a partnership with limited liability. Bosch's legal counsel, Dr. Paul Scheuing, suggested the form of a joint stock corporation. With a joint stock corporation, provisions could be established for the new partners to grow into their stock holdings. Naturally there were misgivings about this type of corporation: through testamentary succession, shares in the business could become alienated, so to speak, or could even end up on the capital markets. This possibility disturbed Bosch the most. Some provisions were made to guard against this: registered stocks, which could not be sold freely, but for which a right of first refusal was established for the founding stockholders. But in what proportion? The initial idea had been to exclude the possibility of a majority vote by Bosch's heirs in the event of his death. The question remained undecided, particularly since Klein, primarily for tax reasons, resisted the joint stock corporation. The outbreak of war in 1914 caused it to be dropped entirely. When it was brought up again later, the angry mistrust, which had been temporary, had dissipated.

The year 1913, which saw an important addition to Robert Bosch's staff in the person of August Utzinger, also brought the resignation of his earliest coworker. As stated in a letter of February 27, 1913, "Zähringer will have to take a six-month leave. He has already had to do so once before. He is simply worn out, and one can no longer count on him in a serious way." The six months was extended, and Bosch and his colleagues finally had to get used to the idea that Zähringer would give up his position entirely. His formal departure was announced for the end of 1914. The business manager had aged prematurely, and his heart could no longer maintain the pace that had been required in manufacturing for the past few years. The former master's technical inspiration had helped put low-voltage ignition to practical use in nonstationary engines. That had been important enough. Although the man was not a design engineer in the true sense of the word, he had considerable technical instinct and skill. Even Honold would call him over to look at his inventions when he wanted the sensible advice of an expert craftsman. When the Hoppenlaustrasse factory was opened, Zähringer, who had already lived next to the "windery" (where the coils were wound) when the factory was located in the Kanzeleistrasse, moved into the new complex. He kept watch over the factory "like a garden spider" from his apartment. He got on well with Klein. His relationship with Honold, whose special demands were increasingly frequent, remained more distant. The quasi-student tradition that Klein, Honold, and Kempter kept up, in a friendly fashion, was quite alien to this frugal and rather difficult man.

In the meantime, Guido Guttmann had become one of the leading fig-

ures in the business. Gustav Klein had made his acquaintance while working for Lahmayer in Frankfurt am Main, where Guttmann had headed the
materials purchasing department. Typically, he wanted to bring Guttmann
to Stuttgart with him immediately, in 1906. By 1907, he had talked
Guttmann into it. This turned out to be an important decision, which also
relieved Hugo Borst organizationally. To meet the enormous demands
posed by the surge of business in the next few years they had now created
a single source of market information about raw materials and semifinished
products. With the help of their new, scrupulously cautious colleague they
garnered a wealth of knowledge and experience that would prove to be
invaluable when the war-related shortages of materials occurred.

But who among this circle was thinking, in 1913, about the threat of
war? True, the world had grown increasingly troubled since Italy's grab
for Tripoli had unleashed the Balkan campaigns against Turkey and then
Bulgaria. The engineers were able to observe that intensive use was
made of motorized vehicles. This fact was also duly noted at Bosch, but
the numbers were still modest and seemed insignificant in terms of sales
volume. It would not have been wise to use the words "business boom"
when having a discussion with Bosch about war; injured indignation,
even contempt, would have been showered on the speaker. This would be
followed by the rhetorical question: What could the potential military
demand possibly mean, measured against the markets that had
conquered the world over in the last eight years! As recently as the spring
of 1913, Bosch had called together all the leaders of his sales outlets,
as well as independent representatives from all over the world, for the
first time, in Stuttgart. It was the first "Bosch parliament," full of enthusiasm and optimism. The men were shown the new kinds of generators
and starter motors that were now ready for fabrication and would
soon be made available to them from the expanding factory halls in
Feuerbach.

Here was no room for dark forebodings or prognoses. A festively optimistic atmosphere embraced the foreigners, and everyone did his part to
make sure they felt at home in their Swabian surroundings. If there were
hunters among them, Bosch might issue a personal invitation; Gustav
Klein might take them along to the charming and delightfully comfortable
country house he had built for himself in a secluded valley of the Black
Forest near Teinach, or he might bring the group to Lake Constance.

There, in Reichenau, Honold owned a summer residence, and Klein had settled in Allensbach; they both found relaxation in motorboating.

Lake Constance not only offered a magnificent landscape to introduce the foreigners to Germany's beautiful side, it was also the setting for quiet bays where one could take refuge from the daily grind. And it was a workshop for things to be—Count Zeppelin was building his airships there. At this point it was no longer a question of a stubborn eccentric's forceful, self-sacrificing efforts, beset by misfortune and disappointment, which one might greet with respect, irony, or sympathy. It was a broadly conceived big business bursting with daring plans through which the winds of the wide world were blowing. Naturally this could also be sensed on the lower lake. The visitors to the country house in Allensbach followed what had been conceived and executed on the upper part of the lake with a lively interest, but they also viewed it with a watchful technical skepticism. Since the Westphalian industrialist Alfred Colsman had made common cause with Count Zeppelin in 1908, bringing his unsullied enthusiasm, organizational ability, and propagandistic verve to the business, the firm had had big plans. Klein and Colsman, with their similar qualities, particularly the quick imaginations and their boldness, had quite a bit in common.

There can be little doubt today that in the popular imagination the moral and political figure Count Zeppelin cut on the national stage exercised a very one-sided influence on the German debate over the conquest of the air. Otto and Gustav Lilienthal's airplane experiments did not receive the public acclaim or support that they deserved. In the fight over lighter than air versus heavier than air, the second, more promising slogan emigrated from Germany to achieve its first sensational accomplishments in America, France, and England. These achievements were soon adopted and significantly developed in Germany, but the memory of the early German ventures into air travel was not revived until much later.

Without any effort on his part, Robert Bosch had come into contact with airship travel earlier. It had happened very simply: When a Daimler engine was installed in the Zeppelin airship in 1900, it had been discovered that Daimler's glow tube ignition was something of a fire hazard. The result was one of Bosch's early triumphs, and one that he fully enjoyed. From then on it had been taken for granted that the motors would be outfitted with Bosch ignition, but it was always only a matter of a few pieces.

After the Wright brothers' flights and Louis Bleriot and Hubert Latham's successes, there could no longer be any doubt that air travel would have a future. In 1910, before Bosch made his donation of millions to the Technical University, he had considered the idea of using the money to found an experimental institute for aeronautics, to be located in Friedrichshafen. Nothing had come of it at the time. Should he seek closer ties to Zeppelin? The count's tenacity had impressed him, and yet Bosch held back. In his *Life Recollections,* Bosch writes that in 1910 he had declined to make a contribution to a Swabian flight for which he was approached (a matter of 30,000 marks), because he "didn't care for" that sort of endeavor. He thought this might have created bad feelings in Friedrichshafen. In the summer of 1912, Alfred Colsman tried once more to awaken his interest. He invited him to accept a position on the supervisory board of the German Air Ship Society. Although Bosch was in the habit of promptly declining all such requests to join supervisory boards, in this instance he seems to have wavered. He then said no after all. "This decision has not been easy for me," he answered Colsman on June 4, 1912, "but when one of my directors took me aside and posed the question of whether perhaps I already had enough responsibilities, it became clear to me what I had to do." One seems to hear the voice of Gustav Klein, whose thinking was already moving in a different direction.

In May 1914, Zeppelin and Bosch did finally establish a personal connection and a business understanding. Zeppelin came to see Bosch with a plan for a great airship made of steel, which would have a capacity of 80,000 cubic meters and would be ready to fly to America in two years. He thought he had the right engineer for the job in Claudius Dornier, who had worked in statics in the experimental division at Friedrichshafen since 1910. Zeppelin wanted to direct the matter personally, and not through the Zeppelin Air Ship Construction company, where there were already too many people who wanted to have a say, and where problems might arise. But he had had little success until then in raising the money for the project, the cost of which he estimated at one million marks. So he found his way to Bosch, who was intrigued with the technical problem, and so infected with his visitor's faith that he pledged half the estimated amount. But—and this was his sensible condition— the people from Zeppelin Air Ship Construction should not be excluded.

Zeppelin would have to settle for that. When Gustav Klein heard about Bosch's obliging generosity he made it clear that he was less than pleased about it. The airship seemed outdated to him; he had become an advocate of the airplane. The automobile, bound to the earth and faced with end-less obstacles, seemed to him—although he was a very fast driver—to be too slow. If he was in the mood, he could produce pictures of a future when people would fly from the roofs of their houses to the seashore for an evening's enjoyment. There they would have their airplane hangars and their own airplanes.

The first technical and business contact between the Bosch firm and the new sport which, like the automobile a quarter of a century earlier, was on the verge of becoming a powerful industry, occurred on foreign soil, in France. This is not so remarkable, considering the situation at the time. However, things did not go quite the way Bosch had hoped. Louis Bleriot had ordered a magneto ignition device for himself, and as a con-dition of acceptance had demanded problem-free continuous operation for a period of thirty minutes. In the twenty-ninth minute the overtaxed contact breaker spring broke! This was bad luck, but the misfortune could not hold up the course of development. In the same year, 1907, the engineer Hans Grade, who had already made a name for himself in the manufacture of motorcycles and as a racing driver, successfully made the first German flight in his triple-decker plane. The year 1909 brought him victory in his monoplane in the Lanz Prize for the Air. Grade had used magneto ignition from Bosch.

This was particularly important because Grade decided to establish a flight school near Bork in der Mark. For the first generation of flyers who went through his school, especially the north Germans, the Bosch device had unquestionably become one of the crucial parts of an airplane engine. In those years, Grade helped make flying popular by means of demonstration flights in the big cities of Germany. When he visited Stuttgart, Bosch was on hand to watch one of those flights, and there is a priceless photograph of him as he placed himself, accommodating the wishes of the photographer, with very unusual friendly ease beside the young pilot. What Grade meant for the north at that time, August Euler meant for the south. From 1903 to 1908, it will be remembered, Euler had been Bosch's sales representative for Germany. The separation, instigated by an angry Klein, had been carried out in dramatic style, accompanied by a small lawsuit. Later on all the parties were reconciled, and were able to agree. There is a nice story about how Euler once introduced Klein by saying: "*He* threw *me* out at Bosch." In retrospect, Euler probably did not see his forced separation from Bosch as a bad thing, for his next task gave him a much more distinct historical profile. With a Voisin airplane, for which he acquired a license, he opened a flying school near Darmstadt.

The group in Stuttgart also acquired some local sporting connections. In 1911, twenty-five-year-old Hellmuth Hirth, from Heilbronn, began his flights, which were triumphal for their times. In 1908, he had assisted August Euler with his experiments, and he had continued to pursue the things he had learned with daring and a rare gift for technology. Bosch had already been associated with his father for years. Albert Hirth was one of the most important and stimulating figures in the industrial life of Württemberg. He was extremely imaginative, a near-genius as an inventor, and was able to turn his hand to many tasks, constantly initiating new projects. He may have lacked the professional steadiness to be a real businessman, but he founded industries and, as the owner of more than 100 patents, had developed excellent instruments. According to a late comment by Bosch, the development of precision work using skilled workers would have been unthinkable without Hirth's instrument to measure "minimeters."

Although an intimate relationship never developed between these two fundamentally different natures, they each thought highly of the other's accomplishments. They went to industrial exhibitions together, and during peak business periods, when he ran out of space, Bosch was able to use the ball-bearing factory that Hirth had built as a temporary workplace. On his part, Hirth had been able to convince Bosch to become a member of the Union of Metal Industrialists of Württemberg, which was created in 1907. Hirth, with an alert, somewhat fitful sense of public relations, had been the driving force behind the founding of the group and had then become its first chairman. All at once, his son had now made flying truly popular in his homeland of Württemberg, and in one year, 1911, he held the speed, altitude, and flight-time records for all of Germany with his Rumpler-Taube. His successes gave a signal, the more so since the younger Hans Vollmöller also quickly rose to the top ranks of German pilots. Young Swabian engineers were captivated by their breathtaking example: Ernst Heinkel and Hans Klemm—their names are recorded in the history of aeronautics.

Hellmuth Hirth, who was not only a daredevil sportsman but also an imaginative designer (and who later proved to be a brilliant engine builder), had introduced Gustav Klein to flying. Together they had dreamed up plans for the future and had sent the new form of transportation all over the world. Why shouldn't it be possible for a plane, built to the right specifications and outfitted with capable motors, to cross the ocean and drop in on the Americans? Willhelm Maybach, too, thought it would be possible. When they were in Monaco together at an athletic meet, in May 1914, they pledged to work together for this purpose. Small wonder, then, that Klein was not very enthusiastic about Bosch's pledge to support Count Zeppelin on something he felt was as outmoded as the airship.

The energy Klein devoted to this problem helped the Bosch firm to solve the technical questions. An engine is an engine and needs ignition, but an airplane is no automobile. At the same time that people were changing over to battery ignition, in combination with a generator and a starter motor for their automobiles, the old magneto ignition was proving to be particularly well suited for the airplane. Here there was no need for a starting motor that could be operated easily in all the difficulties of congested city traffic. An apparatus was required that was as problem-free as possible, that was reliable and relatively lightweight. Battery ignition was therefore excluded; in fact, the former low-voltage magneto ignition came back into special favor. The program was clear, but with the development of specialized airplane engines and their varying cylinder counts there were more and more new challenges confronting Bosch and his designers. These increased following the national Campaign for Flight of 1912, which collected millions from the entire nation to make it easier for motor industrialists and daring inventors to catch up with what they had missed out on in Germany until then. It was unmistakable that the sporting and sensational aspects that had been a part of all flying in past years were quietly fading, to be replaced by military considerations.

21

THE FIRST
WORLD WAR

In the political view of the world that had been instilled in Bosch at home, and to which he had added his own personal touches, there was no appropriate place for war nor for the idea that it was necessary or even possible. The task of politics had to be to make war avoidable, and hadn't a peaceful settlement been achieved for more than four decades, through all the crises, at least among the great powers of Europe? Those four decades had transformed the face of the world's peoples, perhaps altering their fundamental makeup as well. If they were not happier, they were at least richer. Their military capability might be greater, but the interests at stake were incomparably larger than before; they were also less clear, as a result of economic interdependence, and more sensitive to violent disruption. The campaign in Tripoli and the Balkan wars could be seen as symptoms of an unstable world situation, but could not be taken as indicative of the kind of war that could be created by the collision of powerful capitalist industrial nations.

It was not Bosch's style to become overly concerned about the prospect of war. His involvement with public affairs was directed at domestic policy and social questions. That same year, in 1914, he had become close to Friedrich Naumann and decided to give vigorous support, not to his party's aspirations, but to his plans for political pedagogy, which extended beyond the party framework to encompass literature, training courses, and schools. If there were ever to be a German left that was both objective in its work and politically reliable at the national level, then all kinds of other concerns might be alleviated—for example, the problem of the Kaiser. Bosch never could stand him, and it was only quite late that he learned to judge him with a certain degree of tolerance. Like others of his generation, he had not formed a view on foreign policy, but the war would bring about the most drastic change in his interest. Diplomacy was quite foreign to him; he did not know any diplomats. He also lacked any relationship with the officers' corps. He had never sought such ties, and at the time it would have been ill-advised for officers to have dealings with "red Bosch." Had he had such a connection, he might have learned more of the military forces and preconditions that could decide the outcome of a war. He might have been told that Chief of the General Staff Count Alfred von Schlieffen had declared that a long period of war with a strategy of attrition would be impossible, if the upkeep of millions required the expenditure of billions, and he would not have been unhappy to hear it. Old Field Marshall Helmuth Moltke, it is true, had feared war for quite some time. His successors, specialists in campaigns and battles, had not given sufficient weight to the profound influence of social and economic factors.

Who did? Actually no one in the world. The next generation, which learned such an emphatic and painful lesson, has forgotten this fact when it talks about inadequate preparedness. Had a business that was already as significant as the factories in Stuttgart and Feuerbach prepared for war? Bosch would have contradicted with astonishment the claim that his was a national armaments plant, although Krupp and Mauser were, as well as Suhler and a few others. Bosch's was a technological specialty business that served the whole world. The interrelatedness of economic policies and the military situation had certainly been discussed during the fight over grain tariffs. The advocates of such tariffs saw them as security that in the event of war the country would be independent in the production of food; their detractors feared the exodus of workers and industries that would result from a period of industrial stagnation. Lujo

Brentano and Karl Oldenburg's arguments about the numbers of able-bodied men in the countryside and in the cities were concerned with the relationship between military power and economic structure, but their discussions remained marginal. It seemed utterly impossible to form an idea of how a war would affect the commercial life of the nation. When the radical Social Democrats defended the plan to respond to war by calling for a general strike and thus making war impossible, old August Bebel, who had indeed done some thinking about military policies, responded that it made little sense to try to force anything by means of a strike, since the factories themselves would be forced to close their doors for lack of markets and raw materials.

The secretary of the interior at that time, Clemens Delbrück, is to be credited with having tackled the problem of the mobilization of the economy in the spring of 1914, in order to arrive at an overview of supplies and requirements from a *single* office. The questions of nourishment, distribution of raw materials, and administration of manpower were to be investigated and answered administratively in terms of gross requirements. This undertaking, before it was able to produce the desired clarifications, was overtaken by the fact of the war, and the war itself then became the lawmaker for a thousand new tasks that were sometimes elastic, at other times inflexible. Robert Bosch was called up by Delbrück to serve on the industrial advisory board.

On July 31, 1914, Bosch wrote to his wife: "In principle, I have not yet given up my hope that it will not come to war." Admittedly, he found it worrisome that it was not possible to ascertain whether Austria would relinquish its territorial claims against Serbia and whether Russia would then refrain from invading. The mobilization of the latter would force Germany to take the position "either you stop or we will begin. France will be scratching itself behind the ears and saying: We sought protection from Russia, and now we have to enter into war because of a pan-Slavic affair, at a time that doesn't suit us at all, and all because of a matter that suits us even less . . . More than anything, I am counting on the fact that in case of war we will not have the enemy in our country. We should be able to hold back France and Russia. It is another question, if England were to get involved, whether we wouldn't suffer from hunger. Naturally it will take some time . . . If one knew for certain that a war was coming in the foreseeable future, it would perhaps be better to make a pre-emptive strike. Since one does not know, however, whether war may yet be avoided, because it is conceivable that Germany and France and England could come together one day to fight the Slavs, in my opinion a delay is preferable." In the midst of turbulent times, this is an almost tranquil calculation; its immediate purpose was also to have a calming influence on Anna.

The war came after all. "It was fortunate for me," he noted in 1921, "that I was and am convinced that we were attacked." The question of responsibility for the endless human suffering that overwhelmed the nations would later worry and upset him; he sensed the political weight of the right answer and wanted to come to terms with it. At the time, in the summer of 1914, such thoughts were still far from his mind. Since politics without a definite ethical foundation was unthinkable to him, he felt he could safely assume one existed, if not in the Kaiser's nature, then at least in that of Chancellor Bethmann Hollweg.

Bosch's first reaction to the fact that they were now at war was very immediate and simple: There will be need, and one must help. Thus he invited Stuttgart's Mayor Lautenschlager to visit him on August 4, and pressed 100,000 marks into his hand, to use at his discretion. There would be plenty of opportunity to alleviate suffering. The city leader was happy about this initiative. Collections and public appeals would not become common until later, and as soon as he was back at the town hall he wrote Bosch a well-formulated thank-you letter. It was not well received, however. The addressee answered: "I have just received your letter of yesterday and cannot help saying that it is very inappropriate for you to be wasting your working hours writing thank-you letters, which are out of place and which you could reserve for more opportune times. I do what I consider to be my duty, and it is most displeasing to me that you should waste your labor on such trifles. I do not misunderstand your good intentions, and I hope you will not take offense at what I have just said. I only want to say that in these times you have more important things to do than write thank-yous. I say this in regard to future situations, as it would serve no purpose otherwise!" Lautenschlager, who did not yet know with whom he was dealing quite as well as he would later, was slightly amazed at the gruff lecture to which he was subjected. But it was something he could put up with. He also did not miss the "in regard to future situations." When they occurred, he was in for some astonishing experiences!

This spontaneous act in the early days of August was the precursor to very widespread relief activity instigated by Bosch and largely made possible by his means. Its significance could not be overlooked. For Bosch, it was not only a matter of the noblesse oblige of a man of means that led him to assume a share of the general responsibility, it was also a matter of the heart. As brusque as he might seem and as unsentimental as his true nature was, he also possessed a virtually limitless capacity for sympathy in the face of innocent suffering. The theme of not wanting to make money from the war, which was causing humanity to suffer, would come later; at first he may have felt worried about the business side of things rather than being particularly optimistic. At the same time, he very consciously went his own way. He saw how the activity of the public service organizations also generated a carnival of vanity, and he feared that with the many untrained volunteer workers who had entered the lists, things would be done in the next-best fashion, without factual or administrative knowledge. He denied his help to the Red Cross with pedagogical obstinacy because he had encountered more good intentions there than clear organization and calculations; they should not get the impression that people could simply come to Bosch whenever they needed something. In general, his contributions should not be discussed; he did not think so highly of his good example, but rather feared that his contributions would give others the excuse that their own generosity was now no longer necessary. He declined on principle any requests from organizations or individuals outside Württemberg; he wanted to be able to keep an eye on things and make sure the funds were being used wisely. The only exception was his participation in the campaign to aid East Prussia.

The important result of his initiative, to which he made a start-up contribution of 300,000 marks, was the War Assistance of Trade and Industry; additional contributions followed. Bosch personally assumed the chairmanship and influenced the basic decisions, out of concern that the operation should remain flexible and not get bogged down in bureaucracy. Implementation was primarily the responsibility of Hans Walz.

The responsibilities that the war brought with it quickly elevated his private office to the level of a cabinet, with a versatile staff of advisers and assistants who were not only capable of turning Bosch's suggestions and directives into reality, but also, as Bosch himself wished, became a source of independent planning rooted in the firm soil of personal and professional trust.

Bosch's second charitable deed at the beginning of the war was to offer and equip his newly completed factory halls in Feuerbach as a field hospital, and he made sure that the right people were hired to manage the kitchens and laundry. Years later he still remembered with pleasure this undertaking, in praise of which the doctors and the wounded were united. For the careful consideration of lighting and ventilation that had been designed to make the industrial work process easier proved their usefulness here as well. Bosch's pride was combined with the satisfaction of being able to ease the fate of those who were suffering. Reinhold Nägele, the Swabian master, captured the bright inner space of the great factory hall in an amusingly inviting photograph. True, the whole episode lasted only a few months, until the moment came when the beds were forced out by machine tools. The boom had begun.

It had never been predicted. In response to a friend, Bosch had written in December 1912—when the Balkan crisis was threatening all of Europe—"I prefer to pay ten million marks, if by doing so I can prevent a war." It was not, or not merely, an emphatic outburst of feeling but a calculated judgment. What awaited him in the way of worldwide sales and development—especially with the important innovations, generators and starter motors, that were on the way—approached or may indeed have surpassed this order of magnitude. Eighty-eight percent of the goods produced in Stuttgart were sent across the German borders! Now most of those borders would probably be closed—certainly those of the hostile nations.

Slightly over half the workforce of the factories had to serve in the military, among them the leading administrators Gottlob Honold and Hugo Borst. To his annoyance, Gustav Klein found no employment with the military, not even as a truck driver. The administration of the factory did receive some reinforcement, however, as Max Rall and Hermann Fellmeth returned from Paris. Thanks to the training they had received abroad, they would grow into roles in the central leadership. At first, they simply went on working with reduced resources. Many young people were hired at the request of those employees who were leaving, and who wanted to see their sons trained at Bosch. "Many, many more people were hired, throughout, than should have been," Bosch wrote in a May 1915 letter in which he declined a request for an apprenticeship. The problem of workers was not pressing at this point. In the first few months, certain aspects of how the factory would be utilized were not entirely clear. A storm of indignation was aroused when Bosch, after the available raw materials had been used up, had imposed a 10 percent price increase on spark plugs, in keeping with the higher production costs, "so that people would only resort to using Bosch spark plugs for airplane motors and in other particularly important cases. While I was consistently implementing the prices that had been set, my competitors were underbidding each other" (to Director Berge of the Daimler Engine Company, June 1915). Bosch attempted to continue doing business according to the principles that had proved themselves in the past, from a cost-benefit point of view, as well; the firm stood by the eight-hour day, which had produced achievements of the highest quality despite many speculations to the contrary.

The greatest problem of the new business policies was export. Of the 88 percent of their products that crossed the borders, 82 percent had been absorbed by countries that were now hostile. England alone had purchased 200,000 ignition systems in the previous year. It was clear that these countries must now be in a predicament, particularly with regard to their air forces. It was with some satisfaction that the Bosch firm heard about the opinion of the French pilot Roland Garros, the first man to cross the Mediterranean in 1913: "If the Bosch magneto did not exist, it is certain that aviation would be several years behind." But could this achievement be easily replicated? No wonder foreign countries continued to want Bosch products. "We are of the opinion," Bosch wrote on October 6, 1914, to the Swedish representative Fritz Egnell, with whom he was on friendly terms, "that we would prefer to lose a rather large portion of our business in the future than to support the nations that are at war with us by delivering devices that they could use for airplanes and the like." At Bosch, they happily made note of anecdotes, such as the one from France about the automobile owner whose Bosch ignition had been requisitioned for army purposes, and who, dissatisfied with the substitute, demanded additional compensation because the Bosch piece had been so much better, whereupon the judge awarded it to him. Or the half-joking contest between the German and English pilots in Flanders. The Germans had thrown down leaflets saying, "Give us your flares!" And the Englishmen had answered by the same method, "No problem, if you give us your Bosch magnetos!" The interruption of direct delivery was unavoidable; it was followed by the ban on exports to neutral countries after it was observed that goods delivered to Italy, then still neutral, were being resold to France. Only at a later date was a controlled and limited export of spark plugs once again permitted; they served as a means of exchange against the demand for nickel in Germany.

Bosch accepted the French and English attempts to discredit Germany's industrial achievements with characteristic equanimity. He did not think much of getting involved in noisy polemics in front of the whole world. "It is better, on the contrary, to say as little as possible about it. One can accomplish much more against such attacks with good products and correspondingly good prices." In the same letter, dated October 3, 1914, and addressed to a leading man at the Continental Company in Hanover, he wrote: "I do not think it very appropriate, as a businessman, to goad the national passions." It did not seem sensible to him to "make a public display of patriotism"—the gentleman and Gustav Klein had been feuding on the subject.

Such considerations from the early months gradually faded, as the war, contrary to the original expectations and hopes, turned out to be a historical venture of long duration and began to unfold its own inherent laws, which imposed their rhythm on the Bosch factories as well. The war of technology and materials along stationary fronts displaced mobile field maneuvers, and with it came a need for munitions that far surpassed those already in existence, along with an absolutely enormous attrition of war materials. The factories were converted into arms workshops; the state was the principal customer, with a thousand demands that required adjustment and changeover. Bosch's leading men, Honold and Borst, took their uniforms off again in order to take up roles as designers, supervisors of the finishing process, negotiators, and organizers. Once more, skilled workers began to fill the halls of the factory; new ones, trained and untrained, joined them. The items that had initially made the factory famous naturally remained prominent in their manufacturing—automobiles and airplanes were now among the most important, indeed indispensable, tools of the military. But how many other things were added, and how many new demands were imposed on these very crucial items in Bosch's production to meet the new demands during those years of development. In this period, Honold, according to Bosch's later assessment, "accomplished the greatest achievement of his life," to the extent that he—the contemplative, scientific inventor—also found within himself the energy and the organizational flexibility that it took to be a leader of men.

The fact that they were at war may have taken its toll on Robert Bosch's soul, but he had an easy conscience, as a German, about its origin and significance, and he allowed his confidence in a not too distant and positive conclusion to be bolstered by popular opinion. There are a few telling examples of this in his letters, which are rather touching in the light of historical experience. It should be mentioned that the letters were going to foreign countries and thus indirectly may have served the purpose of providing support to readers who were sympathetic to Germany. "If I now express to you my conviction that we will force the majority of our enemies into retreat, I am only expressing the general conviction," he wrote on September 28, 1914, in a letter to Fritz Egnell in Stockholm. "We will attack England and the English on their own territory. This latter point, by the way, is not everyone's conviction, because there are people who cannot comprehend such a thing and consider such an event to be impossible. I am, however, as I said, convinced that we will do so and that we are capable of it. But once we set foot on English soil, I believe peace will not be far behind, for once the English have been made to realize that they are not inviolate simply because they were born in England, then they—who have never found it necessary to defend themselves with weapons in hand—will soon lose their courage, I am convinced. That it will cost us great sacrifices, particularly of human life, is beyond doubt. Perhaps you have read that the German chancellor has declared that under present conditions Germany will only agree to a peaceful settlement if things have reached the point where it can create conditions that will make Germany invulnerable in the future. In so doing, he has voiced what the vast majority of the German people think. The conclusion of peace will be a very difficult matter. It will require great decisiveness combined with great restraint, if lasting good relationships are to be created. I should like to say that I am glad I do not have to set the terms of the peace." The letter was written at a time when the serious strategic setback on the Marne, in September 1914, was still being concealed from the German people. The military fate of the channel coast was still undecided. In January 1915, Bosch wrote in a letter to Otto Heins, the director of the American factory: "We all are counting on and are firmly convinced of the fact that we will achieve a favorable peace. Let us hope that this will soon be the case." How often he ended his letters and conversations with this expectation! The skepticism that at times surfaced within him was always suppressed. Bosch was aware of the responsibility that necessarily adhered to his opinion, his statements. The pent-up tension made him very ill—he suffered a serious dilation of the heart that put him out of commission for months; he would continue to suffer the consequences for years afterward.

In the meantime, Gustav Klein had begun the task that had jolted him out of the ill-humor he had felt during the first few months of the war— "The things that have to be done in design and production only Honold can accomplish." For Klein, a man of such country-hopping mobility, there seemed to be no other meaningful way to satisfy his will to work. The military had passed him over.

Alfred Colsman relates in his memoirs, *Airship to the Fore!*, how a few days before the outbreak of war Zeppelin approached him with the suggestion that the Friedrichshafen shipyard should now build a great airplane, which could drop destructive bombs in enemy harbors. The leader of the shipyard could only turn him down; the pressing contracts they had already received would require all their space and manpower. Colsman was also mistrustful of the prediction about the explosive effect, and, in addition, who had enough experience to take responsibility for such a job? But the old count did not let go. It almost seemed as though the airship, which had hitherto been the main purpose of his life, had suddenly become unimportant. He wanted to give the world, or at least his warring fatherland, the large load-bearing airplane. Had a sudden doubt arisen in him, now that the use of his airships in the war was impending? Would they be too easily damaged?

Colsman knew about the plans that Hellmuth Hirth, Gustav Klein, and young Wilhelm Maybach had discussed in Monaco a few months before. Their purpose was not destruction; their giant airplane was to fly to the 1915 World's Fair in San Francisco and be a sensation. Maybach had undertaken the task of building the engines that were required. Would it not be possible to combine the two projects? Colsman knew that if there was a person who could be considered for the job of improvising something, grabbing hold of people, and galvanizing them into action, someone who could bring together imagination and technical reliability and not slack off when it came to overcoming obstacles, it had to be someone like Gustav Klein. Colsman advised Zeppelin to seek out Bosch and ask him to release Klein from his service. As Bosch knew of Klein's plans, he knew he would not be able to hold him if an opportunity of this kind arose, and he released him. Zeppelin and Klein quickly came to an agreement. Klein took over the overall leadership of the new venture, and Zeppelin used his influence to get the workforce released from the military.

And so they began, with enthusiasm. The army administration, initially astonished that a weapon of war was to be produced as a result of a private initiative, nonetheless gave Zeppelin and Klein a chance to come up with the necessary workers from the airship works and the Bosch factories. When things did not go according to the time periods they had in mind, they grew impatient, but that summer when the first test flights were successful they took an active interest in the new creation, perhaps even more than the original organizers and engineers would have wished. For since the War Ministry had traditionally feared the accusation that they promoted the creation of monopolies, licenses for the construction of the giant airplane would have to be given out to other large firms as well. The first phase of the work was completed in a rented hall in the Gotha Railway Car Factory, where the false designation of the first R-Airplane as a Gotha originated. Later the operation was transferred to the well-suited Staaken airship hangar in Berlin. It took all of Klein's persuasive powers to mold a kind of unity out of the various individuals who had been brought together. The main design work was handled by a serious scientist, Professor A. Baumann from the Technical University of Stuttgart, assisted by flight experts such as Hirth and Vollmüller, and for a time, Ernst Heinkel—it was a regular Swabian colony. Klein, Erich Hoch, and Anton Diemer all came from the Bosch home office. Later, Gottlob Honold's younger brother Fritz, who had previously worked at Körting in Hanover, was brought in from the field to become Klein's right-hand man for statics. It was not so simple to come to objective agreement with the pilots—"exceptional people," in Klein's opinion—or with the young officers sent to him. The individual sporting self-confidence that was part of those early days of aeronautics often had to be broken and forced into the dispassionate discipline of work. This was no easy matter. Klein himself had to curb the élan he had brought with him; with all his high-spirited insistence, his nature was too responsible to approve things that had been rushed or were half-finished. That summer, when Hirth and Klein brought the airplane to Friedrichshafen, proof of the capability of the new creation seemed to have been given. Even the difficult and highly instructive emergency landing they were forced to make on the return flight could not disturb their well-deserved confidence, as much as it may have been contrary to their plan.

That first test airplane of early summer 1915 left all previous standards for international flight far behind. Outfitted with three 240-horsepower Maybach engines, it had a wingspan of 43 meters and could carry a payload of 3,000 kilograms. Certainly it must seem utterly ancient today (it is pictured in E. Offermann's detailed technical monograph, *Giant Airplanes*). During the war its capacity was further increased, and the number of motors rose to four and then five, the horsepower to an average of 1,250. The altitudes increased, and the climbing time decreased. The demands from the front lines, first in the east, then later against English harbor installations, influenced the types that were developed. Naturally, their useful effect in the war remained limited, because the air force consisted of only a few dozen of these giant planes. Nonetheless, the history of aeronautics views them as the predecessors to the great commercial airplanes, as they would later be developed by Hugo Junkers and Claudius Dornier from different technological perspectives. The foreign experts showed their respect for these German pioneering experiments after 1918 by forcing them to close down.

All the time he was pressing ahead with the construction of war machines, Gustav Klein had never forgotten the transoceanic flight that had been planned in the spring of 1914. Now there was certainly no World's Fair to visit because German-American relations had suffered one crisis after another in connection with submarine warfare, and in the early months of 1917 the situation had reached a level of acute tension. The two countries were still at peace, however, and Klein did not quite want to believe that war was imminent. Now, as he discussed with Robert Bosch at a meeting in Berlin on the evening of March 9, he was planning a 2,000-horsepower airplane to fly to America. Unfortunately, Zeppelin would no longer be able to experience it; he had passed away one day earlier while undergoing surgery. At the funeral service in Stuttgart, they would both say farewell to the old man who, despite all their differences and all his eccentricities, had won their affection with his extraordinary energy and personal integrity.

On the following day, March 10, Gustav Klein was dead. In the fall of 1914, Bosch had made it a condition for Zeppelin and Colsman to make sure that Klein himself did not fly. The imposition was undoubtedly intended to protect him, but it was no more than wishful thinking and not at all compatible with Klein's nature. He took orders from no one! It was completely evident to him that he would be the one to test the viability of a thing for which he bore the responsibility. Hence he had taken part in some flights, and on March 10 he climbed into the airplane once more. It was a nasty, cold, windy day, and instead of ten o'clock it was two o'clock before he was finally able to take off; the gates of the hangar were stiff with cold. But Klein and the others did not want to put off the attempt.

The attempt failed. The airplane, returning from its turn around the field, collided with a corner gate of the hangar and broke apart on impact. The pilot, young Vollmöller, was killed instantly. Klein, mortally wounded, died after several difficult hours. Three accompanying mechanics also died in the tragedy. The issue of blame, as is so often the case, was never answered satisfactorily. Had a control mechanism failed? Was the course too tightly figured, did they underestimate the wind, to which they were suddenly exposed as they glided in for a landing and emerged from the lee of the hangar? As he lay dying, Klein kept repeating the warning cry, "Vollmöller, left!"

Colsman was forced to relate the bad news to Robert Bosch, for whom this death was a terrible blow. He knew that Klein would be irreplaceable, in a certain sense, when there were peacetime problems to be solved. Klein's expansive thirst for action and entrepreneurial sense were the strengths that had helped pave the way into the world for the precision work and ethos of accomplishment that Bosch brought to his factory. At the moment, however, this was not the most important thing. Bosch wrote to his nephew, the chemist Carl Bosch, on March 24: "The loss is even greater for our fatherland than it is for my company." But the death of this colleague also made him poorer both personally and within the business. Where Honold's more sensitive, reserved nature had a tendency to back away and withdraw from Bosch's occasional brusqueness (as Bosch himself sensed), Klein had approached him with uninhibited self-assurance. And that was something Bosch valued, even if Klein could be frank and rough at times. Each of them knew and respected the other's living space; neither of them was a Philistine. In the company history, Gustav Klein's name was not linked with particular manufacturing innovations, as Zähringer's and Honold's were, but it had a kind of special aura that remained alive; Klein was already a figure of half-legendary status in the eyes of those among whom he had worked. Bosch, too, was fond of referring to the deceased: Klein would have understood me right away; Klein would have done it that way, or certainly differently than what you are suggesting! Or the reverse: If Klein had been here to discuss things, this decision about production, that conclusion about personnel, would not have been made; the dead man came to represent an imaginary standard.

Everyone had loved him, and the sorrow ran deep.

When the city council of Feuerbach informed Bosch in June of 1917 that a street had been named after him, he wrote back to them with the suggestion that the other street bordering the factory should bear the name of Gustav Klein. They followed his suggestion. Only later did the echo that Klein's death had had among his friends abroad become known. There were many of them, particularly in England, where he had been invited to join the Royal Automobile Club many years before. Amid the terrible atmosphere of the war, which made human and professional recognition of the opposing side a rare exception, it was a remarkable event that a club obituary memorialized a friend, with honor and melancholy, who must now be counted among the enemy.

Following the devastating accident, Bosch forbade his leading officers to take part in any flight. It stands to reason that this prohibition gradually slipped from memory after air travel had grown so rapidly that it became an everyday event. But Bosch himself never set foot in an airplane! That is how intensely and lastingly the shock of the unhappy events in Staaken affected him.

"When the war came, and with it the military orders, on which people made money even when they had no idea how to manufacture products, I felt oppressed by the profit I was making while other people were losing their lives. I decided at the end of 1916 to use the profits I made from the war to set up a fund for the construction of the Neckar Canal." With these sentences from his *Life Recollections,* Bosch notes the action that left the strongest impression on his contemporaries, and that, at least in Germany, has yet to be equalled. Bosch's contribution to this project represented a sum of 13 million marks, followed by more than 7 million marks for other purposes.

This contribution, in which Paul Scheuing, Bosch's trusted legal adviser, was intimately involved, was not only unusual in its size and purpose but was also quite characteristic in terms of the conditions under which the state of Württemberg was allowed to make use of the funds. The question of building a canal for the Neckar, which runs through Württemberg, and making it passable for large ships so that it could be connected to the inland navigation system of the Rhine, had been at the center of public debate in the province for several years. Although agricultural circles were reserved, and partially opposed it, the trades declared that the cost reduction in freight for such essential raw materials as coal would be a decisive benefit in the attempt to establish and progressively expand their competitive position—despite their unfavorable geographic location—on both the German and the world markets. Visionary foresight saw the river canal as the centerpiece of a daring crossing of the Swabian highlands, where it would connect with the Danube.

Naturally, there were many technical and financial difficulties. The most urgent was political. At the time, transportation policies were the responsibility of the individual provinces of the federal state. The lower course of the Neckar belonged to Baden. This stretch, marked by the beauty of its landscape, had very little industry above Heidelberg; industry had not really begun to build until the valley widened out, near Heilbronn. In Baden, the city of Mannheim had a great interest in the expected rise in harbor trade, but the remainder of the province had scarcely any. The traditionally cool relationship between the provincial governments of Stuttgart and Karlsruhe helped to assure that negotiations didn't get beyond a noncommittal distance. In Württemberg, meanwhile, they were hard at work producing drafts, expert opinions, and cost benefit estimates through an independent committee that finally led to the establishment of a company. After Heilbronn manufacturer Peter Bruckmann began to take an active interest in the question, it really began to pick up speed.

Bosch took a serious interest in the planning from the very beginning. From a business standpoint, he was only marginally interested in it; the freight issue for raw materials played a negligible role in his sector of production. But he enjoyed the powerful business impulse that he felt around him, and he was annoyed by the fiscal hesitation and petty political war between the two provinces. At the very least he wanted to get rid of this pretext. It sounds rather fantastic, but at one time he considered the thought of "turning the Neckar into a canal by myself; but I turned away from the idea, because I could see that it would cause great difficulty for a private citizen to do it." The total cost of the building of the Mannheim-Esslingen canal was estimated at 53 million marks. The fact that a quarter of this sum would no longer need to be taken from the public treasury was meant to provide the stimulus needed to get past the preliminaries. The savings in the cost of construction could later be passed on through freight charges.

But the province was not to receive the money until the completion of the Mannheim-Esslingen stretch was established by law and construction had already begun on the various sections in such a fashion that the proper continuation of the work could be considered guaranteed. Bosch also made it a condition that the right to expropriate land along the canal be established. If the conditions—the beginning of construction and the law—were not met by December 31, 1926 (or if the state of Württemberg declined to accept the contribution), the contributed capital, but not the interest, would revert in its entirety to the German Reich for research in fighting devastating epidemics.

The capital without the interest! In this way the government would not be tempted to pursue the clever notion that it could drag out the settlement until the established deadline, so that in the meantime the sum would have increased by a few million due to the accumulation of interest, a return of 5 percent from a government bond. The beneficiary of the interest that would accrue until the capital was transferred to the province would be the city of Stuttgart. It amounted to 650,000 marks per year, which was to be administered as the Robert Bosch War Fund by a special board. War emergencies and needs that were not adequately met either by the city budget or by private donors were to be considered first. The mission was interpreted broadly, however: not only various kinds of social assistance, but education and training, housing and transportation, health care, and the beautification of the city were to be taken into consideration. To guard against the hoarding of interest, there was a provision that the city must have spent the contribution in its entirety by the end of 1940.

The foundation charter is dated December 25, 1916. On January 14, 1917, the district councils of the state capital decided unanimously, in a closed meeting, to bestow honorary citizenship on Robert Bosch. The mayor then visited the Militärstrasse to personally convey the news of this act and to inform Bosch about the impending creation of a specially designed certificate of honorary citizenship. Bosch listened to Mayor Lautenschlager calmly, but insisted on forgoing any document, no matter how well intentioned or decorated; the matter was over and done with, and he would have nothing to do with such stuff. His emphatic reprimand was unambiguous, and the mayor had already had some experience with this man. No document, either plain or decorated, was drawn up in what is possibly the only instance when such a ceremony was carried out with enforced informality.

This is not the place to write the history of the Neckar Canal. Bosch, who had once been pleased to discover the story of the Fossa Carolina ("over 1,100 years ago, Charlemagne already pursued the idea which is now gradually being realized through our efforts on behalf of the Rhine-Neckar-Danube Canal," January 14, 1916), was deeply involved in the technical issues of hull sizes and sluice and hoisting works. A long-drawn-out correspondence with Paul Reusch attempted to draw on the experiences of the Good Hope Mine in South Africa. The political and financial conditions from which the canal contribution resulted had changed radically within a few years: the Weimar Constitution removed waterway policies from the jurisdiction of the member states and transferred their development and administration to the Reich. With this, the conflict between Baden and Württemberg lost its significance. The contribution itself, which had begun with such promise of local assistance, became immaterial, for inflation ate it away almost entirely.

Naturally, its historical and moral meaning was, and is, not affected by this fact. Bosch could say that his decision of December 1916 had had a profound effect on the public consciousness, which remained palpable in spite of the changes in the legal and financial situation. As the representative of the Friends of the Canal, he also held himself responsible for the progress of the work. His angry journalistic polemics against the Heidelberg professors Carl Neumann and Richard Thoma all during the 1920s were striking. Some ill-considered remarks about the motives of certain Württemberg industrialists and their methods had so infuriated him that, although the remarks were not addressed to him, he felt slighted and equated his reputation with the cause he served and the position of his colleagues.

In the summer of 1917, when it seemed to Bosch that the canal business would probably be taken care of by the state, i.e., the Reich, without ever taking advantage of his willingness to help, he wrote to Paul Scheuing that perhaps they ought to look around for another cause, "because it goes without saying that I cannot permit it to be said about me that I backed away from my commitment to use my war profits for the common good" (June 7, 1917).

His supposition was incorrect. But the war continued after the end of 1916, and there were plenty of causes to be supported, particularly in the area of health care. The beginnings that had already been made before the war were confirmed for Bosch, but were not brought to a conclusion; they would find their magnificent culmination almost a decade later.

Other activities took place during the war. In the deed of gift for the canal, the provision about the right to expropriate land was a direct result of Bosch's wishes. The state, the communities, or public service organizations were to be given the right to expropriate land up to one kilometer on either side of the canal. The purpose of the demand is clear: The canal would inevitably lead to an increase in the price of the land that bordered it; this was not supposed to be simply funneled into the pockets of the people who happened to own the property. Particularly not if, for example, the new businesses founded there were to be accompanied by apartment houses, and the higher price of land was to be translated into higher rents. This is a manifest expression of Bosch's adherence to the principles of land reform. If the state wanted to take his contribution, it would have to support those principles, even if only within a limited geographical area. At the very least, private speculation should become a very risky undertaking.

Bosch was a land reformer sensible enough to see that it was not a social panacea, but well-intentioned enough to support Adolf Damaschke's incessant campaigns even though he was occasionally annoyed by the latter's imprecise way with detailed information. The housing question seemed to him to be an aspect of public hygiene. But he himself very consciously declined to build housing for his workers or staff members, because, as he once explained, it was repugnant to him "that the workers should be limited by such good deeds in the freedom of their employment."

His position on the *general* encouragement of housing construction was different. The impending urgency of such construction could already be felt in the second year of the war, when things had begun to slow down; the slogan "Homes for Soldiers" was used to promote construction. Bosch did not care for this limitation; he wanted to see his participation as being of use "for the less well-off classes in general," as he explained to the minister of the interior in January 1918. The way to do this was through the construction of public housing, while simultaneously promoting an interest in individual home construction and preservation. In order to move things beyond the stage of eternal debate, he made possible the foundation of the Swabian Housing Association, which was formed in December 1915. He supplied it with one million marks in seed money on the condition that "people on the outside do not find out about it . . . above all so that others will not think that there is nothing left to do." The Swabian Housing Association achieved many good things by bringing about the creation of public-interest housing associations throughout the country, helping to procure money and advising about plans. Bosch's wartime initiative was not the only reason the half-urban, half-rural housing development was more strongly emphasized in Württemberg than elsewhere, giving the province its particular reputation for stability in a crisis. Yet it is hard to conceive of the development without Bosch's efforts. In Bosch's mind, the government's participation was to be less financial than administrative and organizational. There should be no centralization and no complicated official channels between the various offices—if the state wanted to help, it could provide a supply of cheap building materials (with wood from state forests), and in this way recognize its financial obligation. At a later stage, in 1930, the Robert Bosch company did in fact give building loans to a limited circle of employees who wanted to build, and who thus became part of the general phenomenon of public housing construction.

Along with his interest in housing policy and his concern for the public health system, Bosch played a partly supportive, partly leading role in setting the goals of cultural policies (in the broad sense of the word) during those years. Bosch's work in these areas rested on his connection with two men who were quite close to him at the time: Ernst Jäckh and Theodor Bäuerle. Jäckh, a cousin and brother-in-law of Hugo Borst, had left his job as a journalist in his hometown in Württemberg for the directorship of the Alliance of German Craftsmen in Berlin, and at the same time had stepped up his political attempts to strengthen German-Turkish ties. With his rational and persuasive way of putting things, he was able to win Bosch over to both of these areas, which might otherwise not have been of immediate interest to him. The far-reaching projects that the Alliance of German Craftsmen was now able to carry out were largely dependent on Bosch's financial assistance. More important to Bosch personally was the area in which Bäuerle would contribute both content and richness over the next two decades. As a seminar leader, Bäuerle had already been concerned with continuing education. Philipp Stein of the Frankfurt Institute for the Common Good, whose fundamental position and activities so fully reflected Bosch's own goals, helped point him toward this developing local talent, and Bäuerle became Bosch's most trusted aide for a multifaceted and fruitful involvement in popular pedagogy. The workplace education that Bosch himself practiced grew to include the areas of adult education and promotion of the gifted and talented, which had suddenly been recognized during the war as an important issue of national policy. Under Bäuerle's circumspect and flexible leadership, a complex system of broad and independent education and training programs was created for Württemberg. It was Hans Walz's job to keep this entire philanthropic, future-oriented activity, with its projects to encourage and initiate, consistent as it grew up alongside Bosch's business responsibilities. Walz gradually assumed the role of chief of staff for these campaigns aimed at numerous areas of community life, just as he had formerly administered Bosch's concern for and assistance to individuals.

The year 1917 brought a very significant change in the ownership of the Bosch firm. The change had been initiated in 1913 but had not yet been completed because those involved could not agree on the form it should take. The illness of Bosch's son, followed by Klein's death, could not fail to have an influence on the form that would be selected, assuming that they wished to continue pursuing the idea of incorporation.

On Scheuing's advice, the form of a joint stock corporation was chosen. The existing firm was divided in such a way that the parent firm, including the foreign branches and the factory that had been built in Feuerbach for generators and spark plugs, would go by the name of Robert Bosch AG. The Metal Works in Feuerbach became independent as the Bosch Metalworks AG, Feuerbach. From the very beginning, it had occupied a unique position as a supplier of semifinished goods for outside companies. Eugen Kayser had been a particularly strong proponent of this separation; he personally had a vested interest in the Feuerbach company's growth, and by giving him 49 percent of the shares the possibility was created, in the event he should outlive Bosch, that he could acquire enough additional shares to secure the majority for himself. The installation division was broken up entirely in the reorganization, and was transferred to the newly founded Electra G.m.b.H. Bosch remained a partner in this business, along with the technological and business directors.

Bosch's recollections of the founding of the corporation differ in their emotional temperature. In 1921, he explained with a certain equanimity: "After Klein died, we resumed thinking about the subject . . ." It remained to be seen whether the incorporation was the right thing to do. It had accomplished its goals, but probably not for long, because "it is impossible, in itself, to do things of this nature in a way that is correct for all time, so to speak. Circumstances change too much for that." As a result of such changed circumstances, Bosch's judgment in 1930 sounds almost bitter, as if the incorporation had occurred against his will. As a result of the dilation of his heart in 1916, he wrote, he had been "apathetic" and "incapable of doing anything." "I am only aware of one fact: the hour in which the incorporation occurred was one of the most difficult in my life."

This judgment was undoubtedly colored by the friction that had been inevitable, given the organization and the specific nature of the personalities involved; however, it did not reflect the actual atmosphere of the founding period. At the time, under the strain of illness and states of intense agitation followed by exhaustion and fatigue, relief from Bosch's immediate responsibilities had not been unwelcome. He had even thought fleetingly of pulling out of the business altogether. Perhaps the poor condition of his heart was a sign that this was the right time to carry out the plan to "secure the firm after my death against inappropriate objections or intervention by my heirs" (1930). The factory had grown to a size where it had its own momentum. If he did not want to separate himself from it, or it from him, then the appropriate solution had to be to give it a relatively objective status through the participation of leading individuals; this would also guarantee that his creation would not simply be subsumed under the rules of the industrial-capitalist world. The idea of a complete separation from the business was not foreign to him in 1917, as it had been at the time of the conflict with Siemens in 1906. Perhaps the AEG would be interested in the company.

The change in ownership occurred in such a way that Robert Bosch assumed control of 51 percent of the original capital, estimated at 12 million marks, 2 percent of which were transferred to Paul Scheuing in trust; this 2 percent was to be available for purchase by the members of the board of directors (Honold, Borst, Kempter, Kayser, Ulmer, and Rall) after Bosch's death. In fact, this solution was extraordinarily accommodating for Bosch's colleagues. He had set them up with large salaries and a share in the returns; they would earn a great deal. When Gottlob Honold once offered to give back the special premium of one mark with which he was credited for every high-voltage ignition device that was sold, Bosch refused; he valued the accomplishments of his colleagues. Although their participation in the ownership of the stock was graduated—Honold, with 25 percent, owned the most—they were not necessarily in a position to take over the shares allotted to them. Bosch made this possible by granting certain loans.

Bosch himself took over the chairmanship of the supervisory board, on which his brother-in-law Eugen Kayser and Paul Scheuing also sat. The formal relinquishment of power over the day-to-day businesses, which Bosch had permitted to take place in the reorganization, did not immediately change the existing situation very much, if at all. Even before then, Bosch had not interfered in individual questions of departmental responsibility, where he knew that men with talent and zeal were at work. With his excellent memory and critical intellect, he never lost his overview of the business, and with his dominant will he would also remain the leading force in the future. The extent of his involvement would be up to him. Besides, the incorporation papers specified a large number of areas in which the participation of the supervisory board was required (buildings and real estate holdings of significant size, changes in the manufacturing program, important hiring contracts, and the like). Bosch could now more easily avoid the numerous personnel issues that had sought him out in the past. The mention in his correspondence that he was "no longer responsible for that" sounds more like relief than regret, and yet he never completely escaped his worries or interests. If those in the plant were not exactly pressing, he created plenty of others on his own.

The agreement optimistically assumed that the primary stockholders would get along and would continue the business policies according to Bosch's principles even after his death. This was something that might hold true. After all, with the exception of Kayser, the stockholders were all young people, with an average age of forty. They were not free to sell their shares; potential buyers would have to be approved by a general meeting of the stockholders. The fact that the inheritance laws were not mentioned, however, presented a certain risk. The heirs of the directors, whom Bosch did not know, would occupy a much stronger position than his own heirs. Who could say anything about their suitability for running the business appropriately? This consideration had to become more prominent in Bosch's consciousness as the psychological and political motive for the reorganization faded farther into the past. This would not be without its consequences.

Indirectly, the war had changed Bosch's position vis-à-vis the general public, for the public had gotten used to being concerned about his affairs. He liked his position in the public eye very little, and still held firmly to the fictitious idea that he was a private citizen. With a mixture of shyness and pride, he declined to show his face in the marketplace. The newspapers that wanted to print his picture received the polite request that they refrain from doing so, even if, to the despair of the editors of one illustrated magazine, he was the only one missing from the complete board of directors of the Motor Vehicle Association. With implacable persistence, he refused to sign petitions or declarations when they became all the rage in Germany. Even during the National Campaign for Flight, in 1912, he refused to lend his name to it. The committee must have been quite astounded, but it still had to take into account the fact that he had already donated many thousands of marks for experiments and competitions. Bosch feared that he might turn up among commercial bigwigs and be linked with things whose outcome or implementation he could neither pursue nor influence.

This position, which is officially considered admirable modesty and privately called annoying obstinacy, was a headache for the authorities, too. They were of the opinion that something had to happen—some sort of acknowledgement of his business accomplishments and charitable deeds. The feelers they put out about titles or honors were always answered with a more or less brusque no. When they sent Bosch the Iron

Cross on a White Band in the spring of 1918, they did not inquire ahead of time; they knew he could not give this distinction back during wartime. However, he was not exactly pleased to see the war decoration given to a civilian, either. There is a telling anecdote, going back to the period before the war, when Bosch was to be honored by a visit from the king of Württemberg. Wilhelm II, himself no great friend of the formalities to which his position obliged him, was ready, willing, and perhaps even curious to make the acquaintance of his remarkable subject and visit him in his factory. Bosch was ready and willing to receive the head of state and show him around, but curious he was not. Various middlemen came to feel things out; they were told that the king was welcome to come. But, Bosch informed them, he would not put on a dinner jacket! The dinner jacket became the subject of three different negotiating sessions. Bosch, who was getting quite annoyed, told Mosthaf, the president of the Central Office, that the whole thing was becoming too ridiculous for him; what did they take him for, with all this diplomacy? A compromise was proposed, and Bosch agreed to wear a black suit jacket. The visit never took place, however, because Bosch fell ill. Later, when the new head of the cabinet, Neurath, wanted to revive the matter (he did not even request the black suit jacket), the king's visit was dropped. One could not be completely certain about the mood among the wartime workforce. This story is not a page from the slim German volume *Proud Men Before the Throne*—Bosch simply had a better feeling for style and tact than the ministerial and court bureaucracy, and he did not want to tour the plant with the king in front of his workers in a kind of masquerade.

The road to public life, while it did not lead through the public forum, did, in a certain sense, make a detour through Berlin. During the war and as a result of it, the capital of the Reich became the decision-making center, even for questions of second- or third-rate importance, irrespective of the federal constitution and to an extent that was not anticipated or appreciated by most Germans. The manufacturers were constantly on the road, attending meetings called by war offices or advisory task forces. Bosch was not tempted to take part; he preferred to leave such duties to Honold or Borst or some other appropriate representative of the firm. But he by no means shirked his obligation to visit the more important offices on behalf of his factory, and he sensed that his word carried some weight.

People there treated him more openly and dispassionately than his compatriots in Swabia, where his rise in the world had been surrounded by a
legend not entirely free of jealous gossip, until finally, during the war,
this gossip, too, began to abate. To the people of Berlin, he was the leader
of a business with great potential and absolutely reliable performance.
This reception also made Bosch more uninhibited and self-assured. In
Berlin, he found a circle he enjoyed frequenting. Moreover, if he had formerly been emphatic about limiting his financial support exclusively to
ventures in his home region, he now expanded his horizons to include
German matters in general.

The gift he presented to the political and intellectual circles of Berlin
was a former private palace in the Wilhelmstrasse, with beautiful rooms,
which he purchased and made available rent-free to the German Society
of 1914. This represented Bosch's well-intentioned and initially effective
attempt to give the consciousness of the nation, which had overcome the
traditional contradictions between parties and classes at the beginning of
the war, a place where it could come together in human terms. Secretary
of State Dr. Solf became the director of the organization. Germany did not
have the political clubs of the Anglo-Saxon world; they were now to be
imitated here, but in an inclusive rather than an exclusive sense. Conservatives and Social Democrats, industrialists and scholars, artists and
officials, landowners and trade union leaders could meet here, freely and
uninhibitedly, so long as they strove to transcend the narrowness of their
professional interests and exhibited a certain measure of distinction in
their personalities. It was assumed that the members would have a fundamentally nationalistic attitude, which they could grant even to those
who were pursuing different goals. The organization meant more to Bosch
than social opportunities with a greater or lesser snob appeal; these did
not interest him in the slightest. But he took the organization very seriously as an opportunity to tear down the half-rotten barriers between
groups active in political and intellectual affairs and to give political
opponents a chance for fair, human interaction in Germany. Later, he
looked on disapprovingly as the organization lost its deeper purpose and
began to degenerate from its German starting point into a rather incidental Berlin affair. Then he gradually retreated, not without making a number of additional sacrifices. But the beginning of the venture must be

understood as having been very important to him. The fact that he kept a small apartment in the house alleviated the discomfort of his frequent travels. He did not feel like the lord of the manor, but he was treated like one. He got to know people, to view German history in its transformation, to see how people behaved outside their offices and professions, to see their susceptibility or capacity for resistance to rumor and affectation. It was an observation post whose yield of insight and judgment, for a man with such a sharp eye, could not have been insignificant.

And yet, in Berlin Bosch remained a private citizen without a position. The fact that in 1916 he gave up this role, which he had maintained so carefully, and accepted an office in his Swabian hometown, shows how greatly his sense of public duty had been heightened by the war. Bosch agreed to take over the chairmanship of the Union of Württemberg Metal Industrialists, as Albert Hirth's successor, in April 1916. He had already been its formal representative for quite some time. One may judge the importance of the position he held in different ways; the fact that Bosch ventured out of the circle of purely self-interested politics, as exemplified by his work with the National Union of the German Automobile Industry, and assumed new responsibilities of a more general industrial and geographical scope was simply a result of his sense of duty. "I have always been conscious of the fact," he wrote to the manufacturer Ernst Lilienfein after holding the position for a few years, on February 6, 1919, "that I am not cut out to be a chairman, quite apart from my nervousness, and I have expressed this at every opportunity, and have asked that another chairman be chosen. I do not possess a shred of personal ambition, so it seems easy for me, indeed it would be with a sigh of relief, that I would give up my post. Unfortunately the answer I get is always that there is no suitable replacement." So that "sigh of relief" was some time in coming. Twelve long years passed before he was relieved of this burden in 1928. The very capable and knowledgeable managers, whom he personally trusted, made it relatively easy to bear. But it was not his nature to view his position as purely decorative. Even if he did not need to concern himself with the day-to-day affairs of the organization, he insisted on conscientious reports and above all else on a tight budget— it was other people's money that was being managed. There were hardly any economic or political conflicts to settle within the organization. The

general nature of Württemberg's industry, with its concentration on processing, was relatively unified in its direction. But the fact that a man
like Bosch was at the head of the organization would be important during
the years of turbulent social problems. His unselfconsciously powerful
yet objective and moderate manner would come to have a very positive
significance for the general situation in Württemberg.

The course of business in the Stuttgart and Feuerbach factories was
determined entirely by the needs of the war; the superficial observer
would not have found anything amiss. The factories were operating at
maximum capacity. Compared to August 1, 1914, the workforce for the
fiscal year 1916–17 had doubled in Stuttgart and had even tripled in
Feuerbach. New buildings were being erected at the Metal Works. A
hydraulic rod press had been installed alongside the various kinds of
machines necessary to manufacture their present products, and a new
foundry was erected—enough effort and responsibility for the cautious
men directing the business. Total sales in Stuttgart reached "the very
extraordinary level of 69 million marks," and in Feuerbach "about 20
million marks." These numbers were cited in order to give a sense of the
overall volume, and were not connected to any particular feeling of satisfaction. It was "overwhelmingly" a matter of goods which had come into
production and manufacture only after the war had begun. "These products," stated the report of the board, "vary greatly among themselves, and
are also, for the most part, of a very different nature than the usual Bosch
products . . . Our situation forbids us to say more on the subject. But one
can already say with certitude that after the end of the war we will have
to reorganize completely the greater part of our manufacturing equipment, which is now concerned with that portion of the business." But
then how would things stand with exports? "We have been made aware
that with the long duration of the war the manufacture of our peacetime
products, in part through the use of our own expropriated patents, has
assumed considerable proportions in both the hostile and the neutral
countries, so that we will be faced with tremendous challenges and
expense if we want to engage in competition on the world market again
after the war." This insight helped lead to a very well-considered policy

of financial reserves. It was also clear that many of the raw materials and unfinished goods that they needed to buy at painfully high prices for the specific munitions production in Feuerbach would be next to useless for the plant after the war, not to mention the fact that the machines would be worthless as well. The development in the coming business year, although it was still a war year, highlighted these concerns, which were evidenced by a slight decline in the net profit along with an increase in the workforce. The figure for output had increased; that for cash reserves had shrunk. In 1916–17, they had been able to assign an annual dividend of 10 percent; by the last year of the war, they were not able to pay any dividend.

Because the future of exports would be full of unknowns regardless of the outcome of the war, the Bosch firm did not want to pass up any opportunity to expand its position in central Europe. Vienna and Budapest were given their own sales branches with repair and installation workshops, in keeping with the wishes of the Austro-Hungarian authorities, primarily in order to assure smooth handling of army supplies. One of the most successful ventures was the creation of a showy business office in Berlin, in the middle of the war, on the Bismarckstrasse in Charlottenburg. Until then the Bosch firm had gotten by with makeshift space. Max Dehn, a school friend of Karl Martell Wild's, was appointed head of the Berlin branch; like Wild and Borst, he came from Esslingen. Dehn brought with him a specialized knowledge of the trade, having begun his career with the Mea. He would conduct the business of his forward post with tact and circumspection throughout the difficult decades to come.

The cautious way in which business policy was conducted during this period, while Robert Bosch was donating millions upon millions of marks from his private means to charitable causes, was colored by the insight that in order to survive the firm must prepare for the future. It is difficult to say when, in Bosch's worried reflections, he began to seriously consider the possibility that military victory might elude Germany. The magnificent accomplishments of the armies at war, and the fierce, still unbroken energy of the war organization must have had a tremendous influence on this man who experienced the suffering of the war so vividly.

At first, his imagination caused him to nurse the most audacious expectations; hadn't he believed in a successful plan to land in England in the fall of 1914? The respect for the expertise of the military leadership that the Germans possess to an almost excessive degree, was not unfamiliar to him; his skepticism was aroused when he recognized what he saw as an undesirable confusion of military with political goals. This first became evident in the latter phases of the great struggle. He was only too happy to be infected by optimistic statements. So, for example, he wrote to his wife in August 1916: "One hears from the front as well as for example the Foreign Office in Berlin that the war will not last much longer. The English have seen that they cannot break through, and the French don't have the men for it, either. I hope that may prove correct." And in April 1917, also in a letter to his wife from Berlin: "Hindenburg is supposedly of the opinion that they will start peace talks in July. It is strange that here people's mood is so terrible. At the front, by all accounts, the mood is excellent." The information about Hindenburg came from "the highest possible source," as well as the information that "the only shooting on the Russian front is where the English or the Japanese are giving the orders." Myths like these were widely disseminated. "If the English haven't had enough one day soon, then I really do not know what they want. Although the business with the submarines must continue." This was at a time when submarine warfare was threatening enemy shipping routes with very high sinkage rates and seemed to be able to protect against America's active engagement on the European mainland. In late 1917, in a letter dated November 17 that he sent to his friend Egnell in Stockholm, Bosch was counting on this weapon: "We cannot foresee what the revolution in Russia will bring for us. That the war will not be prolonged as a result seems certain, but it still depends on what England and America will do. I think that the effects of submarine warfare on England will be of more decisive importance, after all, than our actions in Italy or the revolution in Russia."

Such opinions were typical of the time more than they were a reflection of his individual opinions. Bosch knew the Anglo-Saxons, through both good and bad experiences in his business dealings. Like almost all German commercial leaders and industrialists, he tended to think of them as businessmen who generally thought logically and with whom one could talk reasonably when the occasion presented itself. The native instincts to exercise far-reaching governmental rule were completely foreign to his own nature, and so he never had a sense of their peculiar demonic power. He looked upon the ideological arguments as a propagandistic accompaniment and misjudged their effectiveness. During the war he saw for the first time their dangerous effects and recognized the need to take emphatic countermeasures. He therefore attempted to create an instrument to represent Germany's interests, and their justification, through Switzerland in the form of the Rhine Publishing House. At the time, Friedrich Naumann had written a great memorandum entitled "Freedom in Germany," in which, as Bosch wrote to him in a letter dated September 25, 1917, he had "clearly and convincingly" painted a picture, in the face of hostile propaganda, of Germany's special intellectual and social values and particular accomplishments. It was to be included in the new publishing program. But the attempt faltered because of the organizational inadequacy of René Schickele, who had been recommended to Bosch. Even before that, in conjunction with Gustav Klein, Bosch had made possible the expansion of the magazine *German Politics*, which had been founded during the war by Paul Rohrbach, Ernst Jäckh, and Philipp Stein.

It would be impossible to outline anything resembling a well-defined foreign policy for the war years, at least not in the sense in which Bosch later conceived and publicly expressed such a policy. His friendly respect for Naumann brought him close to the concept of *Mitteleuropa* and he subsequently helped Jäckh with his policies toward the Orient. The sums he made available for the education of young Turks were considerable. With one large contribution, he made possible the plan to create a Friendship House in Istanbul, which led immediately to the construction of a great building. This provided the occasion for Bosch, whose health had been more or less restored, to undertake a long journey with Jäckh to Istanbul in the spring of 1917. After this journey with its wealth of new impressions, a sojourn of several weeks on the Princes Islands in the Sea of Marmara finally brought Bosch the relaxation he needed. As a preventive measure, it was announced before the journey that Bosch would decline to receive a Turkish decoration, which certainly must have been an unusual pronouncement for the government on the Golden Horn. There were many celebrations and receptions. The goodwill of the young Turks from the ruling class was acknowledged in Bosch's letters home. The letters contained little in the way of political reflection; ethnological, botanical, and zoological observations predominated. They were his greeting to his sick son.

Bosch's position on the question of the developments within Germany itself was very different. The political truce between the parties did not seem to him to be only a tactical expedient; it was a matter of conviction. Bosch was of the opinion that the spiritual balance of the nation could be maintained only if people were willing to focus on its common elements. This explains his sharp reaction to the intrigues against Bethmann Hollweg's chancellorship on the part of both the left-wing Social Democrats and the right-wing opposition. Here Bosch abandoned the reserve he had generally maintained in matters of day-to-day politics and made himself available to Count Botho von Wedel's National Committee, which attempted to lend moral support to the government's policies. "The National Committee," he wrote to his wife on August 10, 1916, "wants to support the Chancellor of the Reich against the people who want to attack him on the issue of voting reform and bring about his fall from power. They reproach him for weakness, which they say puts everything at risk. In reality, it cannot be a matter of us conquering more than we already have. The fact is that England has our colonies, and in order to regain them we would also have to give back Belgium, even if one were to set specific conditions and try and avoid incidents like the most recent ones." Bosch stuck to this general line. When Hans Delbrück undertook his publicity campaign against Pan-German demands, he found in Bosch a vigorous supporter.

More psychologically interesting is another event that occurred during the same period of time. Until then, Bosch had always voted for the Social Democratic ticket, but would never join any political party. Once, during the war, when he was asked about his political affiliation in a survey, he wrote that he was "Naumannish." This was an expression of fundamental sympathy rather than of party membership, however. Bosch would later express this sympathy on a magnificent scale by securing the possibility of a political university, the political and pedagogical venture that Naumann had been preparing since 1916 as his main objective for the postwar period. In 1917, Bosch purchased a building suitable for this purpose on the Kronprinzen Canal in Berlin. As different as Bosch and Naumann may have been in temperament and religious background, the two men were united in their belief in the capacity to educate mankind for good. One of the assumptions on which all these considerations were based was the notion that the fundamentally positive national convictions of Social Democracy would and must remain a historic force in the postwar period, as they had proved to be during the early phases of the war. Bosch and Naumann were therefore concerned lest the leading circles among the Social Democrats be threatened by a radicalization of the base. The unexpectedly long duration of the war and the worsening supply situation only exacerbated such fears. When Bosch heard about the financial difficulties that afflicted Stuttgart's Social Democratic newspaper, the *Swabian Daily Watch,* he decided to offer them a loan, which was accepted and recorded as a mortgage in the amount of 60,000 marks. Barely three years had elapsed since the great strike, when Bosch had read angry words about himself in the paper. That did not matter to him. For objective political reasons, it seemed to him a good idea to alleviate the newspaper's critical situation. It goes without saying that at that time the event was of a confidential nature. But in terms of the man's exceptionally unbiased stance, there are few things that are so telling. The agreement was made without any strings attached.

The illusion of a political truce faded during the course of 1916. What followed was an era filled with confidential memorandums about war objectives, about the future of Belgium and the ore deposits in French Lorraine, about the later political organization of the Russian border areas and their relationship to Germany. The Russian Revolution in early 1917, while its significance was difficult to gauge, had a great impact. The chancellor thought he would be able to prevent an undesirable influence on the spirit of the masses by immediately tackling the new course that had been announced at the beginning of the war, rather than putting it off until an uncertain peacetime. The central element of this plan was the elimination of the Prussian three-class voting system. At Easter time, in 1917, Bethmann Hollweg was able to win Wilhelm II over to the idea

of announcing the voting reform as the program of the Prussian government. This ushered in the dawn of a period of open political hostilities
within Prussia, since the opposition of the Prussian Conservatives was
clear and unshakable. The situation was further confused by tensions
that arose over military policy and included the political assessment of
unlimited submarine warfare and the military assessment of North America's entry into the war. The differences between the military and political leaders were revealed quite openly in public. Bethmann Hollweg
became their victim. Bosch regretted the chancellor's fall from power, but
he suffered under the establishment of the feuding fronts. The grudge he
held against Tirpitz, which he occasionally expressed in very strong language, arose from the fact that the latter had put himself at the head of
the Fatherland Party. Now Bosch, too, began to declare himself more
definitively. He wanted to avoid the heightening of tensions that was
threatening. The Representative Professor von Schultze-Gävernitz discovered as much when Bosch rudely rebuffed him, on March 26, 1918,
for his statements that the biggest war profiteers on the right were financing newspaper propaganda for the war: "This type of struggle goes
beyond what I consider acceptable. With all my profound distaste for the
exaggerations of the Pan-Germans, I still think it is very risky to make
this kind of public assertion that some Pan-German has an interest in the
continuation of the war and is whipping up the passion for war in the
newspapers, to prolong the war with the goal of increasing his profits." As
far removed as Bosch felt, particularly at this time, from the tendencies
of west German industry, whose overarching press policy could be traced
back to Alfred Hugenberg, his sense of justice prevented him from
impugning unfair motives to an opposing view simply because he disagreed with it. Just a short while before, in the fall of 1917, he himself
had been briefly involved, admittedly on the opposite side, in a matter
having to do with the press. At issue was the attempt to purchase the *Vos-
sische Newspaper* in order to free it from the unreliable editorial policies
of its leader, Georg Bernhard, where the war was concerned. The plan
was carried out by a political group in Berlin, and Bosch was prepared to
lend them sustained support. Admittedly, he did demand that the question of staffing be cleared up first; Friedrich Naumann was to take over
the management of the newspaper, which was very influential among the

educated classes. Naumann declined. His health had already suffered so terribly under the privations of war that he could not with good conscience agree to another time-consuming responsibility; in addition, he was already overburdened with the campaign for *Mitteleuropa* and the preparations for the political university in Berlin. An indiscretion then brought the entire plan to an end.

The winter of 1917–18 only appeared to have resolved the inner crisis that had been made public with Bethmann Hollweg's fall, followed by the clumsy interlude of Michaelis's chancellorship. The government of Count Georg Hertling, Friedrich von Payer, and Friedberg, which had been created after negotiations between the crown and the political parties that autumn, enjoyed some degree of support in the Reichstag. It was not, however, able to gain any independent authority in its dealings with the army High Command, which, without having any formal responsibility, effectively exercised political leadership. The army High Command had attracted the stronger-willed personalities; its history of world-historical achievements had made it virtually undismissable. The Kaiser sensed this, and Secretary of Foreign Affairs Richard von Kühlmann experienced its power in tactical run-ins with the army. Nothing, perhaps, is so indicative of the fluctuating condition of actual power in Germany as the strange attempt, in the spring of 1918, to gain direct influence on the quartermaster general's military decisions. Professor Alfred Weber, who was employed at the Reich's treasury, sent a memorandum to Erich Ludendorff on February 12, 1918, which was signed first by Bosch, then by Weber, Naumann, and Jäckh, and then by the leaders of the three trade union associations, Legien, Stegerwald, and Erkelenz. By that time the German armies had marched westward. Ludendorff believed he would be able, by dint of great exertion, to jolt the front lines out of their stationary positions and then, once he had succeeded in reestablishing it, defeat the enemy in mobile warfare. At this point, the suggestion was made that he should give up the military offensive and should instead initiate a political offensive with his defense at full strength, or allow the political leadership to conduct one. The contents of their plan were to be the following: renunciation of any claim to Belgium, and recognition of the Reich's rights to Alsace-Lorraine. The goal of the action would be to bolster internal unity by emphasizing its defensive character, and, at the same time, to give the tendencies that supported peace a chance in England, where the question of Belgium was seen as central. In January, Bosch had already attempted to influence his Swabian countryman, Vice Chancellor Payer, to "say a public word" about Belgium. Payer "admitted," according to a letter from Bosch to a childhood friend, "that my opinion was valid, but naturally as a statesman he had to take various things into consideration." These "things" were the opinions of the military, hence his absolutely paradoxical decision—although one that acknowledged the seriousness of the situation—to make Ludendorff, and not Count Hertling, the addressee of this petition. The fact that Bosch was the only industrialist who stood on the side of the labor leaders corresponds to the special position he occupied among the leaders of industry on policy questions regarding the war aims. The letter, as one might suspect, had no effect. Ludendorff's answer was a soldier's, pure and simple: "Only action produces success. Attack has always been the German mode of fighting." The army was looking forward to getting out of trench warfare. At the time, the general did not address the political considerations (to which he would turn in a few months) at all. Bosch was severely disappointed by the rebuff. His later judgment of Ludendorff was full of bitterness and rancor.

22

———•———

THE CONCLUSION
OF THE WAR

In October 1917, Bosch wrote to Paul Reusch: "We are all very preoccupied with the war, at least those of us who really take it to heart and cannot just be glad to be making a profit from it." In the months that followed, his worries and agitation would increase. It was fortunate that a long stay at a health resort in Wiesbaden had alleviated some of his heart problems. In those days Bosch often visited Austria and was struck by the low standards of nutrition that prevailed in the countryside and the smaller cities. He found a certain ambivalence about the war, and his remarks were full of bitter mistrust of Kaiser Karl, although not of him alone. Count Ottokar Czernin's resignation from the foreign office of the Austro-Hungarian Empire deeply disturbed him.

He was more emotionally and directly moved by events in Germany and the terrible struggle on the western front. Ludendorff's powerful offensive, which was meant to bring the war to a victorious conclusion, had come to a standstill after strong but limited initial successes. The expected result remained elusive, and repeated attempts to achieve it during the early summer, at differing locations, were not successful. At the same time, in Berlin, a political struggle was raging, complete with all the fine points of parliamentary procedure, over the reorganization of the upper house in Prussia and the electoral law, which was to be brought into line with the rest of the Reich, particularly the southern states of the federation. This aroused all of the hostile instincts Bosch had inherited from his father. Of course, Bosch was never what one would term a particularist, but he was quite convinced of the unusually fine qualities of Swabia, in the manner of, say, the aesthetic philosopher Friedrich Theodor Vischer, and he was quite proud of his home province. The Prussian claims to superiority had no effect on him! But now he had become sensitive. When an Organization of Loyalists to the Kaiser was organized, his initial sentiment was that the Kaiser should quickly put an end to it. "If the Kaiser sits back and looks on while people who claim to be specially loyal to him start sowing justified doubts about his word, then the most terrible fruit will grow from this seed," he wrote to Berlin. And: "It would be quite fitting to speak out from time to time on the subject of how irritating it is for us southern Germans when people promote a specifically Prusso-German credo." A few months later, he declined the paradoxical proposal that he take part in a large wine shipment for the soldiers; technically it was hardly possible at that point, and furthermore he did not believe that an initiative from Württemberg "would find many imitators in Prussia . . . And why, at this time, should we incite the Swabians, who are accused of being strikebreakers, to shed their blood alone, perhaps in vain? . . . If the spirit which lives in us Swabians were also alive in Prussia, the war would not have occurred in the first place!" (October 24, 1918).

When this bitter sentence was written, the fate of Germany had already been sealed when the army High Command forced the leadership of the Reich to declare a cease-fire. In the same letter, Bosch assessed the situation as follows: "It seems that the front line could be convinced to hold out for a few more weeks, and might be able to hold the line at the Meuse, in order to provide somewhat more favorable conditions for the peace negotiations. More than this I do not think possible." That the war could no longer be won militarily was something about which Bosch had not had any illusions for months. By now, especially since Ludendorff's push for an immediate cease-fire had been followed by the entente's breakthrough in the Balkans, and Austria-Hungary's peace offer had

made it necessary to open up a new southern front, it had to be clear to
any clear-thinking observer that the war on the battlefield had been lost.
The official spokesmen for the general staff had hidden the deadly seriousness of the situation from the public for too long, and the reaction to
the news was that much worse when it did come.

Bosch experienced the crisis and all its troubles with a sort of inner
emancipation. "It is very peculiar," he wrote on October 24, 1918, to the
newly appointed Secretary of State Conrad Haussmann, the leader of the
Württemberg Democrats, "but the awareness that we had an iridescent
soap bubble that was about to burst, and that the overwhelming majority
of the people saw our situation as good and hopeful worried me so much
this summer that at times I did not know what to do with myself. But now
that the soap bubble has burst, I have grown relatively calm." Once outside the world of uncertainties, half-veiled truths, false assumptions,
opinions, and rumors he felt he could breathe more freely. His clear
recognition of the situation, which he wanted to see openly expressed,
seemed to him to demand quick and ruthless action. Perhaps *political*
decisions could prove helpful to the overall situation in Germany, before
a military catastrophe occurred that would affect an entire people.

Conrad Haussmann had asked his fellow Swabian for his support and
advice. Bosch responded to the call. In three detailed letters, written during the second half of October 1918, he laid out his conclusions, his
anger at the "underhandedness of the former Foreign Office," as demonstrated by the conflict with President Woodrow Wilson over submarine
warfare. "In the business world, and particularly in the world of big business, dishonesty and unreliability are two of the worst things a businessman can be accused of. The small shopkeeper lies, the businessman is
frank and honest." This was also true of politics; he thought he could cite
Bismarck as proof of this: "History is certainly not my strong point. Nevertheless, I can remember that in his memoirs Bismarck speaks about the
fact that the Czar's trust helped him a great deal. But I say to myself, if he
had the trust of the Czar, then he must have earned it, and only a man
who is open is capable of earning trust, and therefore I cannot believe
that Bismarck thought his strength lay in a diplomacy of cunning." Bosch
had the impression that the new government had not grasped this yet,
since Secretary of State Matthias Erzberger had just pronounced that the

offer of peace was by no means an indication of Germany's weakness: "Once a person has tried to mislead others, they will always assume that he is only trying to mislead them, and even the most full-throated declarations of conviction won't do him a bit of good." There was no sense in trying to conceal the state of affairs from the other side. "They see it for themselves on the battlefield, and they hear what our prisoners have to say." One should tell the enemy that they should beware of "driving us to extremes . . . only a little less than a hundred years ago the world could see what a people driven to despair is able to accomplish when it is fighting for its freedom" (October 15, 1918).

But this motif, of counting on a popular uprising, dissipated after a few days. Walter Rathenau had mentioned it publicly in an article; Bosch's correspondence with a friend in Berlin speaks of an attempt to play the "German Gambetta." "I do not think it will be possible for us," Bosch wrote to Conrad Haussmann on October 24, "to carry out a national defense on a large scale, in part because what we would be able to offer would not be attractive enough. There is no grand idea behind it." On the other hand, the national concept was not secure enough: "Broad segments of the people are lacking in national consciousness and material appreciation of the state . . . Unless one could bring larger considerations to bear, considerations of such revolutionary magnitude that an extreme left government might be able to accomplish something. Our current and—please excuse the expression—much too tame government will hardly be in a position to carry out such a popular uprising." The same theme appeared on the following day in a new variation: "A popular uprising like that of '14 [sic] is unthinkable, because technology plays far too great a role nowadays, and manly courage, even if it is the courage of despair, cannot perform heroic deeds the way it could a hundred years ago. Machine guns are too powerful. Our concern must therefore be to make the army, as it stands in the field today, capable of resistance in the event that the conditions imposed upon us for a cease-fire are aimed solely at rendering us harmless so that we can subsequently be raped."

His question and his advice were: "Why don't the people whom our soldiers trust—trade unionists and the like—go to the front, without delay, and explain to them there what the issues are that confront us?" (October 24, 1918). And on the next day: "But one would have to send out people who are very far left. Still, perhaps it is possible, after all, to present the defense of the 'fatherland' as a goal that people can respond to . . ."

It was a question of gaining time. Because "if we are humiliated, we will undoubtedly experience a social revolution like the Bolshevik one in Russia . . . even the people who occupy the leading positions among our enemies, at least those in France and England, must be afraid of this . . . I will not conceal the fact," he confesses, "that I am very far left and that I would not consider a more extreme revolution than the one we are experiencing now to be undesirable. But I cannot imagine that such a more extreme revolution could succeed without overshooting the mark, if the people take it into their own hands the way they did in the Russian Revolution. Only by opening far greater safety valves can we escape a catastrophe that will bring more misery than good along with it . . . the further left we go, the sooner we will be able to make an impression and avoid a catastrophe."

This theory was predicated on a change in the traditional position of the officers' corps. Bosch was impressed, based on stories he had heard from soldiers and particularly sailors, by the gulf that had opened up between officers and their troops, particularly in the way they lived. He reported on this to Haussmann: "It means a complete turnabout in the way soldiers think, if nowadays giving orders is no longer synonymous with leadership."

Naturally he was also observing the enemy camp: "Today we have no choice but to hope that Wilson will really prove to be the honest man who will bring us the League of Nations, and who, if he succeeds, will become the greatest man in history. In his day, Napoleon I, if he had not had the ambition to rule the entire civilized world of his time, could have played a role similar to the one Wilson is about to play, if he is the man we hope we are able to recognize in him" (October 15). This would be repeated later: "It is possible that Wilson wants to be an honorable man. It is possible that he will be able to assure we are treated relatively well, namely if our side understands how to present the danger of Bolshevism in the correct light." The uncertain role that the American president would play in the preliminary conference of the Allies in Paris a few months later would stamp his "It is possible" as a dubious proposition. But at the time, to an observer who was keeping an eye out for the best prospect, this could still be an open question.

The problem of the Kaiser concerned him only vaguely in those weeks, as was the case for many Germans. It surfaced in a general but vividly telling comment in which he revealed how totally alien and removed he was from the fundamental ethos of the monarchy: "What we were lacking was a good housekeeper, someone who would walk around the house and peer and sniff into every corner, to make sure it didn't stink. The appropriate person, by his calling, would have been the Kaiser. After him, people thought Hindenburg was this kind of good housekeeper. It was said that he had gotten a lot of things organized in the field. But in the long run he does not seem to have been up to the job, either" (October 25). Should the Kaiser remain? "Does someone think he will have an impact on the working classes? The bourgeoisie seems to have extraordinarily little fondness for him . . . Prussians, it is true, are very special creatures." Bosch admits that he does not know "what we would put in place of the Kaiser, so perhaps it may be best that he stays where he is." But the proposal to "install the grandson, too, with Prince Max of Baden as the regent, seems like a good suggestion. . . . It leaves the Prussians their Kaiser and does not force us into a republic. The upheaval is less and can be accomplished more easily."

A few days later, the problem appeared more urgent to Bosch. The Austro-Hungarian offer of peace made him look with anxiety toward the southeast, where there would soon be Italians on the Bavarian border. On October 29, he wrote to Friedrich Naumann that "it would probably be appropriate if in one way or another it were possible to get the biggest obstacle to peace, the Kaiser, to leave." His grandson could be his successor: "It would be much better if this were to be taken care of by the Reichstag now, rather than waiting until in Bavaria, in all possibility, the desire for separation makes itself heard." When Bosch made this comment about his neighboring province, he could not have known that just a few days before, on October 25, the Munich government had already presented the Prussian ambassador with its wish for Kaiser Wilhelm II's resignation. Naumann, who was himself expressing the notion that the Kaiser should personally resign in order to save the obviously endangered monarchy, had to explain the legal, political, and personal difficulties to his impatient friend.

Bosch received a confusing firsthand impression of those difficulties when he traveled to Berlin in the early days of November, as is reflected in a letter to his wife dated November 5. Arguments are quoted pro and con, worries about a delivery strike in the countryside, uncertainty about the position of the army in the event of an uprising. "Does the abdication, which four weeks ago might have made sense, serve any purpose now, its opponents ask? Now it is being forced upon us by our enemies, and only encourages them to make further demands." There were rumors that the terms of the cease-fire had already been handed over but were still being kept secret, which Bosch thought was senseless if it were true. "That we cannot keep fighting is clear to everyone; I have not heard a single dissenting opinion on this point." His stay in the place where these decisions were being made was intended to give him greater certainty than could be gleaned from letters and personal accounts; instead it gave him "a sense of his own powerlessness." Bosch announced that he would return home the next day: "One really cannot accomplish anything, and, in the end, there are others who are as smart as I am."

The events of November 9 essentially held no surprises for him. Only a short while before he had hoped that it would be possible "to hold the front, somewhere around the Meuse, until winter creates difficulties for the large-scale operations of our enemies. If we could manage that, at least we might still hope for a reasonably fair peace." The ill-fated way in which the request for a cease-fire was made, the boost it gave to the enemy's military leaders, and the spiritual confusion that threatened the German people, who were not at all psychologically prepared for the impending situation, endangered the foundations on which these expectations had been built. The military events on the Macedonian and Italian fronts, and the repercussions they had on the political structure of Austria-Hungary, destroyed these foundations. All considerations about how a political and psychological reorganization could relieve the tense war situation appeared to be nothing but speculations reflecting the observer's own worried state, and were soon overtaken by the force of events. Not for a moment did Bosch nurse any illusions about the real socioeconomic consequences of the lost war. Politically, in the long run, the profound changes in Germany's affairs did not seem to him to be entirely devoid of hope if the German people could survive the lesson they were being forced to learn.

A few years later, in 1921, when Bosch began to set down the notes for his *Life Recollections,* he wrote: "I would prefer to write nothing at all about the war," and concluded about Wilhelm II: "The Kaiser did not want war, but he did not understand how to avoid it. On the contrary, his personal behavior contributed a great deal to provoking the war and making possible Germany's encirclement. Wilhelm the Second was no proper leader for a world-class company! That sounds insolent, but is not meant that way. The person who occupies such a high post cannot be vain, nor can he be spiteful; he must be a serious man, always aware, in every situation, that not only he, but in certain circumstances an entire nation will be held accountable for his actions . . . Under a serious person, for example Wilhelm I, we never would have experienced such terrible things." Bosch's critique of the political and military system had "unfortunately turned out to be true."

Elsewhere, he complained about how many people, particularly among the highest ranks, had lacked the consciousness "that what was important, above all, was to win the war." He noted that there were also those who "saw the war as lost from the very beginning. I cannot agree with that." At the time he wrote this sentence, the opinion had already been circulating that the war could have been won if the homeland had not failed. "The German people," Bosch wrote, "fought for four long years in a manner and with a devotion that simply borders on the inexplicable. This is all the more true when one remembers that the leaders always put themselves before the cause, so to speak. Hence the misdeeds of the Ludendorffs and Tirpitzs are all the more vile, and it is unbelievably impertinent for anyone to talk about having been stabbed in the back at the front."

23

—◆—

REVOLUTION

The war had been lost, and defeat had taken the utterly defenseless old government and the bearers of its authority down with it. It was in poor taste to disguise this event as a victory of the people, for revolutionary will was only to be found in a tiny minority, who lacked a compelling leader and whose political and socioeconomic view of the world was decked out in borrowed terminology. The masses were both spiritually and physically exhausted. The upper class, which only a few months earlier had been deceiving itself about the tragic tensions of the war situation, with the help of illusions provided by the general headquarters, was stunned. Although the apparatus of the nation's administration may have continued to operate in the usual manner, what had become doubtful was the rationale for giving the government ultimate power. Only years later would it be possible to create the myth that decisive intervention by those German military leaders with actual and juridical powers of command on the home front could have imposed a different rhythm on the course of history. The fact that such decisiveness was lacking everywhere had a more profound cause; the men sensed that they could not, at this point, whip up the garrison soldiers' battle weariness for tests of domestic political strength.

This was true in Stuttgart as well. For Bosch, who on November 6, 1918, had returned home from Berlin and the depressing uncertainty of the decision-making (or non-decision-making) process with great misgivings, the local development in the coming weeks became the center of his emotional involvement. Berlin was now far away. One could clearly see that a struggle over the form of Germany's future, which was difficult for outsiders to unravel, was being carried on there among Socialist groups. One could hear many new names of people about whom one knew nothing. One could sense how this big city, in a state of prolonged agitation, sought to influence the improvised government of the Reich, as if the local ambitions of the city of Berlin were the vehicle for the fate of the entire nation. The task that Stuttgart faced was interpreted as follows: to protect the province against the confusion that was threatening from Berlin, and at the same time to shield it from the tragic burlesque that had been started by the radical Socialist Kurt Eisner in the neighboring state of Bavaria. Similar things were occurring elsewhere. With the continent shattered by this world catastrophe, people sought to find spiritual security on a smaller, more comprehensible scale where they might preserve or create real order.

Bosch had not previously concerned himself with the details of Württemberg politics, but during the war he had become a public figure as a result of his contributions to the province and his chairmanship of the Union of German Industrialists. It was no longer possible for him to be so reserved when men in leadership positions sought him out. He had begun a kind of respectful and confidential relationship with the newly appointed minister of the interior, von Köhler, a man whose experience extended beyond the borders of the province. In Stuttgart they had attempted to form a government in which experienced party leaders would work alongside some of the official ministers; tradition was not to be destroyed, but instead was to be made flexible enough to deal with whatever the future might bring. It was the sort of solution Bosch seemed to have desired, yet it remained a mere interlude. The events of November 9 extinguished it. King Wilhelm II himself cleared the path by offering to abdicate, with the clear insight that after the events in Berlin and Munich the monarchy would not be able to maintain itself on an isolated basis in Württemberg.

For a man of Bosch's strictly rational way of thinking, the demise of the monarchy did not mean any personal or emotional loss. He had never denied the last king of Württemberg his respect as a person, but now there were urgent matters to take care of, and there was no time for sentimentality. There were negotiations among cabinet ministers, the military, the mayor, and the party leaders, accompanied, at a tolerable level, by loud and restless masses in the streets. These negotiations, at which the participants decided the course of a revolution that was essentially nonexistent at that point, had no direct effect on the public consciousness. The Stuttgart mayor, Carl Lautenschlager, was conscious of the discrepancy and understood the danger of false rumors. He decided to invite a loosely organized group of men from various professions and social classes to visit him on November 12 and to report to them about the proceedings in which he had played a considerable role because of his position; at the time the police force was still under municipal control. Here Robert Bosch stood up to talk. It was probably the first time he had ever spoken in public, and it resulted in coverage by the press. The text of his speech, which the mayor found echoed popular sentiment in its temperate solidity, has come down to us. Bosch asked a few detailed questions concerning raw materials for the war, tabled for discussion at a separate meeting, but the most important thing was probably Bosch's statement that the returning soldiers would be reinstated at their workplaces, a statement that must have had a calming influence. The mayor's request "to place themselves willingly and with all their strength behind the new form of government would be followed without reservation by industrial circles."

It was not Bosch the private business proprietor who was speaking here, but rather the chairman of the Union of Industrialists. His statement was a liberal interpretation of his leadership role. The immediate effect was apparently quite powerful, but its dependability was subject to question. For in a meeting that took place on November 13 at the Ministry of Labor, the fearful voices of the opposition were also raised. Bosch rejected them, saying that more was at stake now than petty business concerns. There was a revealing exchange of letters on the subject. A young industrialist who had just returned from the field implored him to get even more involved in the leadership of business, particularly the

metal industries, in order to "bring in a breath of fresh air." Bosch was
pleased about the expression of encouragement ("unfortunately it has
been the only one so far"), but he could not become more involved; his
health prevented it: "For example, a short speech in the town hall, which
admittedly moved me very deeply, brought on another small dilation of
my heart." The leitmotif of the coming times was touched on in the young
industrialist's long letter dated November 14, 1918. The trade unions
would have to be honorable in their methods, and above all else must
avoid withholding labor's productivity under questionable slogans. The
employers, who "have used the same kind of dishonest means," would
have to cease such behavior: "I am of the opinion that an employer's first
duty is to be decent." The letter made Bosch "most extraordinarily"
happy. If he felt rather isolated in his position, even in his more immediate home territory, and if, on occasion, he liked to exaggerate his unique
position with a certain bitterness, here he thought he heard a voice of
comradeship based on a shared mentality. In the months and years that
followed, he listened closely to the younger breed of industrialists, and a
few years later was quite satisfied to say that among them he had often
found more open-mindedness about labor questions than the older trade
unionists demonstrated in their attitudes about political-economic and
even social needs.

The political fronts in Württemberg had hardened quite rapidly toward the end of 1918, and would admittedly be put to a very difficult test
in 1919. At the head of a coalition government of Social Democrats,
Democrats, and the Center was the former Socialist parliamentarian Wilhelm Blos, who, as a knowledgeable historian of earlier revolutions, had
very skeptical notions about revolution, even the one that had elevated
him to a territorially limited but still significant position of statesman-
ship. He was going on seventy at the time, and had put ambition behind
him. He was a man with a clear, open character who combined a certain
old-Germanic dignity with a tendency toward joviality. He did not hesitate to assume, out of a sense of duty, the office that he had not sought,
and he fulfilled his duties with composure. Bosch never became close to
him personally; when after Blos's death he provided the lead contribution
for a tombstone to be erected for the deceased, he wrote to Blos's widow
that he felt "dejected" about him (and Friedrich Ebert, the "deputy of the

people"), "because I did not express my gratitude or recognition of both men often enough." Bosch's health, shyness in groups, and the pressure of work had made his human contact in the postwar years very limited. "The fact that both of these men, above all, have earned a memorial, is something I have often said and will continue to say in the future."

Friedrich Ebert, who in those difficult months had begun to assert himself amid the chaos of opinions and political leanings in Berlin, could not have been a clearly comprehensible phenomenon in Bosch's eyes. The events in the capital of the Reich would first need to be clarified; Bosch was not immediately concerned about them. Walter Rathenau, the industrialist and politician, made the attempt to bring a Democratic Popular Union to life in Berlin, and he was counting on Bosch's cooperation in doing this. On November 20, 1918, Bosch had given his hearty assent to the plan, but wished to see the program expanded in the section defining "the socialization of society as its goal." He only wanted clarification about how the tempo of development differed from that of the Social Democrats. An agreement about the speed of development would be possible as soon as the Socialists felt "the honest will to act" on the part of the bourgeoisie. It was up to the bourgeoisie to "intellectually broaden and deepen the materialistically restricted demands of the Socialists," to justify socialism ethically and "transform it intellectually into social idealism." The bourgeoisie itself would be spiritually renewed by such a task. It all sounds both very definite and at the same time somewhat abstract. A second letter from Bosch, dated December 12, 1918 (Rathenau had meanwhile limited his political plans to an Organization of Like-Minded Individuals), encouraged Rathenau "to offer stimulus and backing to the forces of leadership that are pressing forward, and to unite the youth struggling to achieve a social standpoint." The most important thing seemed to him to make possible a "lively person-to-person exchange," first in a small circle where the decisive questions would be clarified "in serious and penetrating intellectual work." Next they should "work particularly among youth and women." Rathenau's plans were soon forgotten. Bosch would later make attempts to construct such a circle with Professor Philipp Stein and August Müller. His goodwill was unfailing wherever he saw the potential for taking a stand, transcending party stereotypes, and coming up with objective and decisive formulations. One fruit of those efforts was the founding of the Württemberg Society, which he engineered. What the establishment of the German Society of 1914 had meant within the context of the rise of a sense of national unity the Württemberg Society now meant to do for Bosch's home province. The new organization, in which he initially played a significant role, was very dear to his heart, and it seemed to help create an equalizing atmosphere. Unfortunately, the crack in the soul of the nation, an unavoidable result of the war, was already visible to the perceptive observer. This new organizational initiative would never assume a really comprehensive character.

Did Bosch, with all his passionate involvement in the events of his times, actually want to enter politics? By no means. He had repeatedly talked about how ill-suited he was for public appearances, which were precisely the kind of thing associated with the new style of political leadership. Bosch had little interest in the questions of constitutional law now coming to the fore, and he had no great understanding of the dynamics of governmental legal systems. Instinct and knowledge told him that all economic thinking and planning in the foreseeable future would be linked to the simple facts of foreign and domestic politics. Who could draw a picture of peace, starting from the state of military impotence that reigned during the winter of 1918–19? "President Wilson's offer of mediation," Bosch wrote on December 13, 1918, in response to an American newspaper agency, "raises such demands that it makes one ask whether it is even possible for someone who is so close to the events, and for whom the impression of these experiences is so fresh in his mind, to carry out his mediation in an unprejudiced and impartial way." He then assured the American rather suggestively: "The German people, who are order- and freedom-loving, will quickly overcome the internal crisis, if they are given an opportunity to rebuild their economy, and will be among the most responsible and valuable supporters of the League of Nations."

When Bosch wrote these words to his American interlocutor, he was naturally quite clear about the fact that the foundations of his economic optimism were anything but secure. The same optimism applied to his own ventures. The armament contracts ceased; the raw materials, semi-finished goods, and machines that only yesterday had been vitally important for running the business were now nothing but a burden, a useless waste of space that only required cleaning. They had been preparing for this moment in their thinking and in their fiscal policies, although it is true that they had expected it to be accompanied by more favorable circumstances. A long-term view might conclude that the war, as such, could not retard the age of motorization, but on the contrary, could only accelerate it. The war had proved, particularly in Germany, to be a kind of teacher. The lack of uniformity of German manufacturing had had a very deleterious effect on repairs and on the replacement of parts. Attempts to achieve standardization, although halting at first, had begun with the experience of the war. Bosch's products had proved themselves to the highest degree. But now what? The biggest source of contracts, the war, had vanished. When, and to what degree, would the private customers be able to assume their previous role? It was possible to detect quite early that, as German industry reorganized for a peacetime market, some factories that had primarily been producing weapons of war would move into the sphere of transportation. Weren't people already saying that Krupp would build heavy-duty trucks in place of mortars and howitzers? Bosch might welcome new customers, but there was soon other news, as well. The AEG in Berlin, it was said, was going to expand its manufacturing program to include ignition devices. That meant getting ready for some serious competition. Bosch was not fearful, however; a few decades of experience were worth more than millions in capital.

The question of foreign countries was more worrisome. For after all they had been *the* market, particularly for ignition devices. The anecdotes about the French driver who had successfully argued in court for higher compensation for his requisitioned Bosch products, or the English pilots who asked their German comrades for Bosch ignition, had been very colorful. But the seriousness of the situation was of a deeper hue. During the war, the Bosch firm had kept an eye on the efforts foreign countries were making to create their own manufacturing establishments or to expand existing ones. The Bosch patents had been annulled in England, and the large Vickers factory had begun manufacturing ignitions. In America the Bosch Magneto Company was sequestered; the foreign property administrators sold the entire complex to an American company, which gave the firm the name American Bosch Magneto Corporation and in a bombastic proclamation declared: "Only the ownership has changed . . . I am an American!" It was to be expected that the United States would protect the invested capital by imposing import prohibitions or prohibitive tariffs. But apart from that, if the practice of free trade were to continue as it did in Belgium, wouldn't the public boycott German goods out of hard feelings created by the war? Similar noises had been coming from Brussels, where Bosch had occupied a preeminent position since erecting the firm's building there. And, as if that were not enough, the neutral countries, ill-served all these years by the warring countries, had become richer and more ambitious since the boom and were attempting to found their own specialized industries. This was true of both Switzerland and Sweden, and the reports Bosch received from these places were discouraging at first, although the situation would undoubtedly clear itself up in time, and then they would see. The Bosch firm looked difficulties straight in the eye. First of all, the patents and logos that had been linked in part to the name Bosch had lost their value. The multifaceted Gottlob Honold became a graphic designer and created the new company logo. During the war the firm had been content with simply impressing or engraving their products with the letters *RB*. Honold suggested they end that practice. The previous logos, a flaming magnet and an igniting armature, were designed entirely around ignition, which had now been joined by a number of other items. Honold broke with tradition and designed the magneto-armature in a circle; it had the same amazing sureness of proportion and form that gave all his designs their intuitive as well as logical quality. His sketch, which was made at the end of November 1918, was an apparently unimportant event, but it proved to be a smart and significant move. Even during those terrible weeks of confusion, it was absolutely clear to Bosch and his workers that they wanted to get ahead in the world once again, and the clear new emblem would greatly benefit their campaign.

Next they busied themselves with clearing the domestic market. Bosch had retained his usual rates of profit and loss and his tried and tested price policies. Although this created considerable difficulty in the beginning, people ultimately realized that they could not do without him.

His competitors, who could not match the quality of his goods, sought to stay in business by underbidding him. Ultimately there was a general perception that his prices were excessively high, and so the company made the decision to institute a price reduction of 20 percent on January 1, 1919, a decision they themselves regarded as a risky venture ("very unbusinesslike—based on emotion"). It was meant to set an example and indicate an encouraging concession to both the general buying public and the business customers. What seems remarkable about this price policy wager, in retrospect, is how much the company underestimated the revolutionary influence that the lost war and the uncertainty of the peace would have on prices, even if they did see that "without question we lose money on every contract we sign under these circumstances." It only took a few months before the increase in living expenses forced them to take back their well-intentioned decision. They began to learn the word "inflation," and became aware that the decline in the value of the currency, which was slowly setting in, was destroying or at least endangering the very substance of the domestic markets. This phenomenon also led to an unmistakable decline in products intended for export.

Another difficulty became apparent in the abrupt decay of the entire culture of buying and selling. This did not only affect Bosch, of course, but he was particularly sensitive to it due to the system of representatives he had built up so carefully over the years. The entire automobile branch was derailed. In attempting to judge the terrible setback to which the German motor vehicle industry was subjected after the war, and from which it did not rouse itself without a series of crises, the disorganization of the market, caused by the unregulated dumping of automobiles and motorcycles from the army stores, played an important role. Naturally there were also other elements involved—changes in income strata, questionable or misleading technical initiatives, and uncertain or crude tax policies—the ramifications of which would not make themselves felt until later. At present there was much aggravation and displeasure about profiteers selling products acquired from the military or through middlemen, who, as they introduced their own pricing and sales policies, ruined the business for salespeople in the neutral foreign countries. Bosch was irate with the military administration, which seemed to have come apart at the seams. It would be more than a year before things were once again under somewhat reliable control.

The manufacturing situation turned out to be somewhat better than the Bosch firm had first feared. The total workforce, which had numbered 4,210 on August 1, 1914, had reached 6,420 by March 1, 1919. In addition, more than 400 employees of the plant were expected back from the service or from prison and internment camps. Their positions were held for them. There was no lack of orders; the desire for goods had made itself felt among the civilian population. "The situation here is relatively good," Bosch reported to Reusch on February 1. "Thanks to the fact that this winter has not been exactly dry, we can work longer, despite the lack of coal." There was much complaining and struggle over the issue of coal. For a time, Bosch felt quite self-sufficient—to keep the plant going, he had peat brought to Feuerbach from his Upper Swabian factory in Ostrauch. But throughout all of 1919, Bosch workers were frequently forced to take off one or two days a week because there was simply not enough coal. These events, or, more significantly, the various walkouts— in which the situation was no longer relatively peaceful—did not have an immediate effect on profits, but did threaten Bosch's reputation for good work and especially for timely delivery. The labor struggles had a particularly negative impact when they were depicted by hostile commentators.

During this period, with its unstable currency and accumulated demand for products, a very powerful trend emerged to undertake expansionist business policies. Having material assets of various kinds at one's disposal could seem like security, like a way to bolster a position of power. Even Bosch allowed himself to be convinced that there was a real task and opportunity for him here; the private founding of the Hiranie company provided the framework. However, this became a cheerless matter for Bosch, from which he reaped more annoyance and losses than satisfaction or profit. He did not experiment at all with the business policies of the factory.

When Conrad Haussman, in September 1918, implored Bosch to write down some of his experiences in business for the manuscript collection of the Prussian State Library, he wrote, along with other observations: "To negotiate a contract without ulterior motives, and to fulfill it absolutely punctually, is an act of the greatest intelligence in business. I have always acted according to the fundamental principle 'It is better to lose money than trust.' The inviolability of my promises, and the belief in the value of my products and in my word, are far more important to me than any momentary gain." If Bosch stood firmly by this basic principle, then what he had to achieve, above all else, was to guarantee the precision of the work to the ultimate degree, and to make sure that no product was sent to market that did not stand up to the closest scrutiny. That meant a difficult and uncompromising struggle to keep up morale in both sales and production, not always an easy matter in those months when political discussions and credulously hopeful and artificially or honestly disappointed voices echoed through the halls of the factory. In those months, it was also necessary to keep a strict and merciless watch over production while the workers argued themselves blue in the face over the nature of the socialism that was to come. Any slackness or carelessness in the use of raw materials that was overlooked might mean an immediate profit, but could become a danger at the next moment. If there were to be something like a Socialist government, then the Bosch emblem should not be responsible for even the slightest diminishment of value. The fact that Bosch stood firm on this issue, amid all the sacrifices that the end of the war brought with it, and in all the crises that necessarily flowed from Germany's domestic and international situation, not only saved his enterprise but also created a firm foundation for a new, much more difficult conquest of the world.

It was obvious from the beginning that one legacy of the war psychosis would be that the national policies of the former enemy nations would do their utmost to keep German products far from their markets or would erect almost impenetrable barriers in the form of high tariffs. To plunge ahead would only create psychological disadvantages. But the issue took a surprising turn. Bosch did not need to send any scouts to foreign countries because they sent their interested parties to him; these representatives could not exactly be called traitors! As early as February 1, 1919, Bosch was able to report to his friend Paul Reusch that "I received a letter in which a Frenchman is applying to represent me. As an automobile driver for the army, he became convinced that none of the substitute products could hold a candle to my ignitions." One of the old Bosch employees, who had returned home from internment in England, brought with him the opinion that Vickers & Company, which had purchased the individual Bosch patents from the British government, would also be applying for recognition as a representative, since they "couldn't make it on their own." This put them in a more hopeful mood than before, even if soon afterward, in April, the Board of Trade extended the ban on imports. Patience was essential—at least there still remained some neutral ground. At the first motorcycle race after the war, in western Switzerland, 90 percent of the participants used Bosch ignitions, including all of the winners. When Holland put on an air travel exhibition in August, Germany was not invited because of pressure from the entente powers, but the Bosch representative, a Dutchman, exhibited under his company name and achieved unqualified success. On this basis old ties were renewed. A few months later, on October 7, 1919, Hugo Borst could write to Bosch in Stockholm that a German-American had come to him with the request that he should return to the United States. The products distributed by American Bosch Magneto were poor, and their business methods no better. "The most important news, however, is that two people from Peugeot have been sent by their management to reestablish contact." In Italy, the old firm name had been back in use since October 1, 1919. Thus, the foreign relationships seemed to be returning to normalcy remarkably quickly, but it only appeared that way, for given the uncertain currency situation, one could not really speak of order. "Business here in the firm is moving along excellently," Bosch wrote to Fritz Egnell at the close of 1921, "but naturally one cannot be exactly happy about it, knowing on what the strength of the business is based. At any rate, the prospects are better now than they were three years ago, and perhaps some day we will have order on our planet." The great and difficult struggles on the world market would not be necessary until after the mark was stabilized. By then, the ring of attempted defamation surrounding Germany's products would also have been broken.

What the world desired, above all else, was the ignition devices and spark plugs that had made Bosch famous. Shortly before the war, the starter and lighting system had been added to the list; really big sales of these items were only just beginning. The years ahead would show that Bosch was becoming the trend-setting business, in a more comprehensive sense, for motor vehicle accessories. In certain ways, the war orders had alienated the firm from its industrial focus. Now, after the war, since the overall situation was still somewhat uncertain, they were looking for all kinds of products that might find a market and support the core of the skilled workforce. They built typewriters, fountain pens, wrenches, and the like just to be able to have work in an emergency. But it remained a temporary expedient. The Optical Factories of Stuttgart-Feuerbach, which were founded in August 1919 with a starting capital of 300,000 marks, offered more substantial prospects. Bosch had stumbled into this in an odd way. One of the factory buildings that had been purchased during the war was not stable enough on the upper floors to support heavy machinery. The firm was considering mass production of eyeglass lenses. Honold wanted to take charge of the matter personally, since his own work on headlights had brought him into such close contact with optics, and things did not go badly at first. In 1920, they purchased the existing firm of Julius Faber, including the name, which was already well established. But interest in the new product did not last; by 1922 they were content to retain only 49 percent of the ownership, which they sold back to the Faber family in 1926. They would not reach out securely to take on new manufacturing tasks with all the difficult technical and organizational issues they entailed until later, after a new generation of coworkers had come to the fore.

Gustav Klein was not the only victim the war years had claimed among the leaders of the factory. Heinrich Kempter, who had been a close friend of Klein's before his fatal accident, suffered a physical breakdown from which he never recovered his earlier strength. He was only forty-eight years old when he died in the fall of 1919. Among the strong temperaments of the firm's leaders, he was the one who stood for objective mediation. He took things seriously, and he had a tendency toward pedantic orderliness that was the perfect complement to Klein; he was also a tireless worker. Earlier, the death of Eugen Kayser had had an even greater impact. Kayser, bowed by family suffering, appeared to be completely shaken by the outcome of the war, which seemed to have destroyed his life's work. He took his own life in December 1918. Fate had dealt him terrible blows: the war had robbed him of his two eldest sons; his wife and his mother had died. His cheerful soul sank beneath the weight of these burdens. Gloomier and more indirect than his younger colleagues, his rather gentle nature realized that there was no way out of the situation. He no longer trusted his ability to give the Metal Works, which he had established and led with flexible, experienced intelligence, strong leadership in the times of crisis that lay ahead. Honold had to step in for him. But Honold's leadership role was intended only to be temporary. The man who could relieve him from the additional burden was perhaps already on his way home: Karl Martell Wild. Wild had been the technical director of the factory in Springfield, and like the other leading members of the American venture he had been discharged following America's entry into the war; his return was now anxiously awaited. The date of his expected arrival was delayed through the end of 1919. In the spring of 1920 he assumed his new responsibility. Hermann Bosch, a son of Robert Bosch's oldest brother, came to work with him on the business side. Since 1901, Hermann had been in Japan working for the Hamburg export firm of Illies & Company, the leader in German-Japanese business. He had had the good fortune during the war to be able to get to the United States, and from there to Germany. It was not entirely easy for him to adjust to the customs of his homeland once again after such a long absence in foreign lands, and his relationship with Robert Bosch was not a warm and human one, but his world-traveled versatility was a stimulating factor.

Ernst Ulmer, who had borne the main responsibility for personnel policies since the great workers' struggle of 1913, brought in Hermann Borst to work with him. Borst built up and systematized the professional staff organization, and understood how to make it develop freely in a lively sociopolitical way. He was a man who combined a strong capacity for sympathy with strictness and objectivity. His relationship with the workforce, as could already be sensed, would be put to many a difficult test in the excitement of those times. What the circumstances required was the kind of strength that inspired trust but also remained firm in the face of unpleasant responsibilities. The factory newspaper, *The Bosch Spark Plug*, whose first issue appeared on March 15, 1919, was founded essentially to secure this relationship of trust, although not only for that reason. The idea of creating a newsletter, or something similar, had already been tossed around in the years before the war and had basically been approved. The rapid increase in the size of the workforce made it difficult to maintain a secure sense of tradition. But Bosch declined to implement the plan as long as the right person was not available. He sensed how dependent something like this would be on the person who ran it, if it were not to be done according to some boring scheme. Hugo Borst believed he had discovered just the man in the months he had spent in Ulm as a soldier, at the beginning of the war, and he made sure of his availability after the end of the war. Otto Debatin, from Baden, was thirty-seven years old at the time. After an education in the natural sciences, he had entered the publishing house and editorial offices of the popular sculpture magazine *Cosmos*. He found the prospect of this new publication enticing. The suggestions he submitted to Bosch, after he was wounded and returned home from the war in 1916, combined with his uninhibited self-confidence, immediately won Robert Bosch's approval. His written comment was: "If we ever wanted to put out a factory newspaper, he would be the right man to do it." To get the hang of things before the plan became reality, Debatin started his new job in September 1918.

The Bosch Spark Plug was not some accidental appendage to the big firm, nor was it mere decoration. The history of the Bosch factories can simply not be imagined without it. The old issues have long since earned the honorable title of "chronicles"; they are useful as a source of information, but one must read them with contemporary eyes. When one does this, one very quickly becomes aware of how much the newspaper and its editor helped form what would later, with a depth of emotion intended to express high expectations, be termed "the Bosch spirit." More was at work here than editorial cleverness. Not that the latter was lacking in the mixture of useful and entertaining material, the educational descriptions of the development and purpose of the firm's individual products, the reports on the general business environment, or the outlook for economic legislation and the like. An essential element was the willingness with which the newspaper opened its columns to the expression of concerns inside the plant, in controversies that sometimes took on a bitter tone. The newspaper staff was determined not to be prudish, and to permit harsh words here and there, but they also knew when to use harsh words in reply. The leading men in the company were asked to participate, along with workers who needed to express themselves, and even Bosch occasionally took up his pen. On appropriate occasions, the newspaper staff liked to commemorate the special individuality and accomplishments of remarkable men, in a felicitous combination of familiarity and respect. In this way everyone felt included. And if they had had enough of the solemn tone, there was room left for friendly satire and irony. All in all, the paper was a masterful feat of public relations, with a willfully individual tone amid all the workplace newspapers that had appeared or were beginning to appear. Bosch took great joy in the creation of the newspaper, because the combination of familiar Swabian elements with the rhythms of the wide world, the coexistence of explanatory scientific and technical reporting with ethical and pedagogical comment, corresponded to his own nature.

24

THE ORGANIZATION
OF INDUSTRY:
SOCIALIZATION

In early December 1918, the Württemberg Ministry of Labor, which at the time was led by Hugo Lindemann, asked Bosch to take part in the Commission on the Preparation for the Socialization of Industry. Bosch felt that although his capacity to work had been "greatly diminished . . . he should not shrink from the task," even though his doctor might soon forbid him to continue. Not much came of his work with the commission, because the entire committee never got beyond well-intentioned clarifications, assessments, and appraisals.

The Württemberg socialization commission was not the only one of its kind; similar groups were being formed everywhere. They are a part of the picture of the times, and even then they must have seemed, to the careful observer, like the result of an objectively awkward situation. The goal of socialization was the overthrow of the current political powers. Men who were Socialists, or who at least called themselves by that name, occupied visible positions in government at the national and provincial levels. But suddenly, it seemed, they no longer knew what socialism really was, or they had had the insight that the utterly uncertain status of the German economy, which could be detrimental to Germany's recovery and probably even dangerous to the reputation of the vaguely conceived socialism, was ill-suited for experiments. "Socialism is only possible when the smokestacks are smoking." Hesitation and caution became the watchwords. Those who were more impatient could only respond: If socialism is the superior economic form, then it will assure that the smokestacks start smoking again! The fundamental question argued and fought over in the committees, to the extent that they took their assignment seriously, was this: Which way offered a guarantee of higher productivity? And there was another, more obvious question: Which sectors of industrial production distinguished themselves by their basically monopolistic character or their method of production, so that it would actually be possible and even desirable to treat them as special cases at the level of national policy? In other words, the committees were seeking to determine which businesses were ripe for socialization, whereas the concept of socialism remained vague and undefined. The practical results of these efforts were few, and their theoretical gains soon faded. It was politically interesting, however, that the representatives of the Social Democratic party were more than once divided in their opinions. This indecisiveness when it came to the central programmatic question crippled their will. For an impartial observer, the psychological background of the situation could not remain hidden for long. It was not at all the forces of socialism that had propelled the country toward revolution. In the military and political collapse, an individualism had been unleashed that pushed against constraints, regulations, and authority and did not allow itself to be reined in by old formulas couched in abstract Marxism. Hence this period became a whirlwind of misunderstandings, in which people fell prey to unsatisfying slogans.

Bosch was fundamentally too serious to look at the entire complex of questions from a merely tactical point of view, as many people were then doing. Something would have to happen, some concessions would ultimately have to be made to the desires of the workers, preferably of a temporary nature, until the excitement died down again. Bosch took seriously the debate about what could properly be called socialism. He did not view the demands being put forward with the eyes of a concerned business proprietor, nor was he infected by the agitation, which, notwithstanding his emotional sympathy for the disappointed masses, he regarded with a very critical eye. Rather, he saw it from the standpoint of the entire people, of Germany's capacity to survive within the framework of the international economic order. The idea of socialism as a matter of national policy was difficult for him to conceive of if it meant that the country would distinguish itself from the rest of the world as a separate type of economic system. Bosch considered the Russian experiment, which at the time was completely unclear and weighed down with political slogans, to be at best negative evidence. It was lacking in all conclusive force, at least for Germany. For Bosch the term "socialism," to which he had turned in the utopian conviction of his youth during his years in America, had nothing frightening about it, even now when it was suddenly being spoken of as a present-day possibility. "I guess I can regard myself as a Socialist," he wrote on March 27, 1919, to Eggert, a leader in the metal workers' union to whom he wanted to express his support for the moderate statements of the socialization commission. "Even if I do not admit to being a Social Democrat (just as one can be a Christian without going to church), but, precisely as a Socialist and out of that socialism, I find the rage for socialization, which despite the deterrent of the frightful Russian example has seized the radical circles in our nation like a fever, quite disastrous." When Bosch declared his adherence to socialism in this remarkable letter to a man whom he had recognized among his opponents during a strike six years earlier—quite unwillingly, since Bosch liked him personally—it indicates that his thoughts were turning to the "general welfare." This is a vague phrase, and one will certainly not find any more specific or dogmatic answers among his various notes from that period.

The basis of Bosch's thinking continued to be a realistic feeling of responsibility. The material and political emergencies of his homeland had to be accepted as fact, like the permanently capitalistic structural foundation of the nations with which Germany had to compete economically. Any unwise socialization in Germany would "cause the greatest damage to the idea of socialism," and it would also cause Germany "to lose a significant portion of its capital and economic intelligentsia to foreign countries." Socialization could not mean that "for those in leadership positions, who drive our actual progress, all internal and external incentives would cease." "The capacity to earn" and "room for the development of personal initiative" must remain. National financial policy

Robert Bosch in 1931.

Robert Bosch, the twenty-five-year-old
founder of the firm, in 1886.

(ABOVE) The first workshop, Rotebühlstrasse 75B, Stuttgart.
(BELOW) The first advertisement published by the firm in the
Stuttgart daily newspaper *The Observer*, 1887.

Robert Bosch visits his customers on a bicycle, 1890.

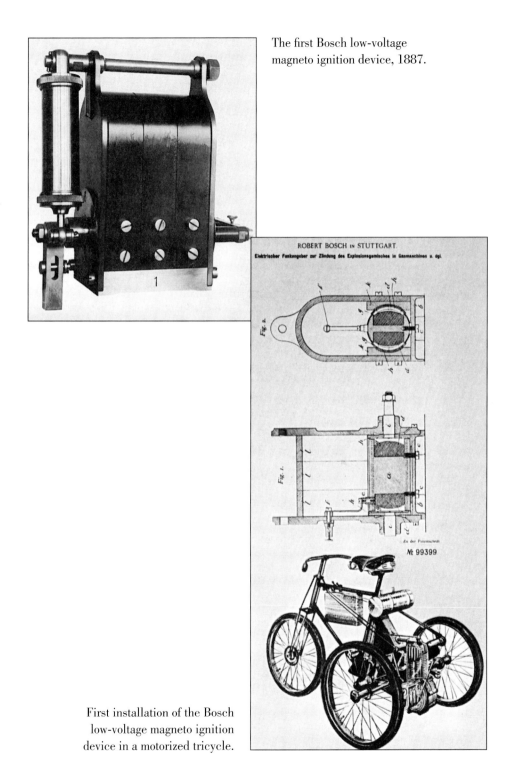

The first Bosch low-voltage
magneto ignition device, 1887.

ROBERT BOSCH in STUTTGART.

Elektrischer Funkengeber zur Zündung des Explosionsgemisches in Gasmaschinen u. dgl.

№ 99399

First installation of the Bosch
low-voltage magneto ignition
device in a motorized tricycle.

KAISERLICHES PATENTAMT.

PATENTSCHRIFT

№ 99399

ROBERT BOSCH in STUTTGART.

Patent from the year 1897.

Bosch writes in a letter
about his purchase of
the property in Stuttgart
on which he will construct
his first factory building.

In 1901 Bosch moved into the factory building in
the Hoppenlaustrasse, Stuttgart.

(ABOVE) Drilling pole shoes in one of the Bosch workshops for magneto ignition devices, 1906.
(BELOW) The administration building of the Bosch sales operation in Auteuil, Paris.

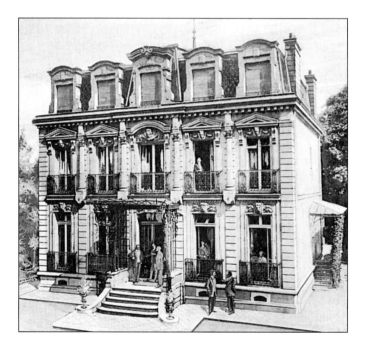

Arbeits-Ordnung

der Firma

Robert Bosch, Stuttgart.

Die nachstehende, auf Grund des § 134a der Gewerbe-Ordnung erlassene Arbeits-Ordnung ist rechtsverbindlich für Arbeitgeber und Arbeitnehmer.

§ 1.

Die tägliche Arbeitszeit währt 8 Stunden und beginnt

im Sommer (1. April bis 30. September)

Morgens 7¹/₂ Uhr und endet Abends 5¹/₂ Uhr,

im Winter (1. Oktober bis 31. März)

Morgens 8 Uhr und endet Abends 6 Uhr; Mittagspause von 12 bis 2 Uhr.

Bezüglich der Arbeitszeit für jugendliche Arbeiter wird mit Genehmigung der Kgl. Kreisregierung vom 9. Juli 1906, Verfügung Nr. 7449, weiter bestimmt:

1. Die durch § 136 Abs. 1 der Gewerbe-Ordnung vorgeschriebene ¹/₂stündige Vormittagspause kommt in Wegfall, dagegen ist den jugendlichen Arbeitern gestattet, Vormittags während der Arbeitszeit ein Vesperbrot zu sich zu nehmen.
2. Auf körperlich schwächliche, d. h. nicht gut entwickelte junge Leute, oder auf kränkliche jugendliche Arbeiter findet diese Bestimmung keine Anwendung.

§ 2.

An den Tagen vor Ostern, Pfingsten und Weihnachten tritt der Schluß der Arbeitszeit Mittags 12 Uhr ein. Am Neujahrsfest, Erscheinungsfest, Karfreitag, Ostermontag, 1. Mai, Himmelfahrtstag, Pfingstmontag, Volksfesthaupttag, sowie am ersten und zweiten Weihnachtsfeiertag ruht die Arbeit vollständig.

Die Arbeitnehmer haben weder für diese Tage, noch für die vor Ostern, Pfingsten und Weihnachten ausfallenden halben Tage Anspruch auf Bezahlung, wie überhaupt nur die Zeit, in der tatsächlich gearbeitet wurde, bezahlt wird.

§ 3.

Wird infolge von Betriebsstörungen, Inventur oder aus sonstigen Anlässen, welche den Arbeitnehmern tags zuvor mitgeteilt wurden, nicht gearbeitet, oder ruht die Arbeit auf Verlangen eines Teiles (mindestens drei Viertel) der Arbeitnehmer, mit Einwilligung der Fabrikleitung, so kann kein Arbeitnehmer Bezahlung verlangen.

§ 4.

Die Abrechnung des Lohnes erfolgt wöchentlich für den Zeitraum von Mittwoch Früh bis Dienstag Abend der folgenden Woche. Die Lohn-Auszahlung findet am darauffolgenden Freitag Abend in bar in Reichswährung vor Geschäftsschluß im Geschäftslokal statt.

§ 5.

Bei Versäumnissen steht dem Arbeitnehmer ein Anspruch auf Lohn auch dann nicht zu, wenn er durch einen in seiner Person liegenden Grund ohne sein Verschulden für verhältnismäßig nicht erhebliche Zeit an der Arbeit verhindert wird.

§ 6.

Jeder Arbeitnehmer, der im Geschäft Aufnahme findet, hat die Quittungs-Karte über die zur Invaliden-Versicherung gezahlten Beiträge, sowie sein Arbeitsbuch, soweit er zur Führung eines solchen noch verpflichtet ist, vorzuzeigen.

§ 7.

Beim Eintritt in das Dienstverhältnis erhält jeder Arbeitnehmer einen Schein, den er dem Meister, welchem er zugewiesen wird, zu übergeben hat. Beim Austritt erhält der Arbeitnehmer nach ordnungsmäßiger Fertigstellung seiner Arbeit und Übergabe seines Werkzeuges an den Meister von diesem den Schein wieder zurück, worauf ihm gegen Aushändigung desselben sein Lohn ausbezahlt wird.

§ 8.

Eine Kündigungsfrist besteht gegenseitig nicht: die Arbeitnehmer haben jedoch das Recht und die Pflicht, angefangene Akkord-Arbeiten fertigzustellen.

§ 9.

Vorstehende Arbeits-Ordnung wurde im Einverständnis mit dem gesamten Personal aufgestellt, und tritt mit dem 1. August 1906 in Kraft. Sie ist von jedem Arbeitnehmer durch Unterschrift anzuerkennen.

Stuttgart, den 16. Juli 1906.

Robert Bosch.

Work rule notice from 1906: Robert Bosch
introduces the eight-hour workday.

(ABOVE) The Bosch subsidiary in New York, 1910.
(BELOW) Front view of Robert Bosch's residence in Stuttgart, in a sketch from 1909.

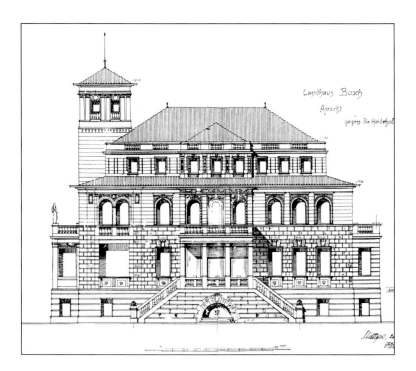

(ABOVE)Bosch representatives on a trip through the Black Forest
in the summer of 1913; Robert Bosch is behind the wheel.
(BELOW): Bosch talking with aviation pioneer Hans Grade, 1910.

(ABOVE) A forest of transmission belts in a Bosch workshop, 1920.

(LEFT) Bosch horn and Bosch headlights, 1921.

One of the first Bosch injection pumps installed in a passenger car with a diesel motor, 1927.

The Boschhof, south of Munich.

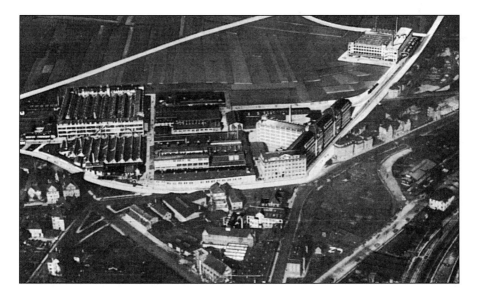

The Bosch facilities at Feuerbach, Stuttgart, 1929.

Bosch at the Berlin automobile exhibition in 1931.

(ABOVE) Bosch on a hunt in 1931.
(RIGHT) The first Bosch refrigerator
at the Leipzig Fair, 1933.

Bosch inspects the work of an apprentice at the sales
office in Frankfurt, 1936.

Bosch converses with Chief
Mayor Strolin during an
inspection of the Robert
Bosch Hospital by the
Stuttgart City Council.

(ABOVE) Bosch at the Ignition Works, 1941.
(RIGHT) Letter from Bosch to Theodor Heuss, dated March 4, 1942, thanking Heuss for sending his biography of Justus Liebig and asking whether he would be inclined to write his biography.

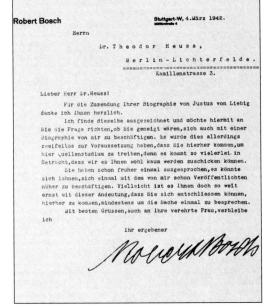

must not lose sight of this either. Among the observations made in Bosch's letter to Eggert were some fundamental formulations. The prologue reveals an unusual depth of emotion. "The deepest yearning of a freely associated human community must be to bring all of the good, valuable forces of the individual to development and effective use, and to bring all these forces to the highest possible level of attainment in every area of life. This includes the economic system. This uppermost and leading principle of the highest possible productivity must be ranked above all other thoughts and desires in the building of any economic plan or structure. The highest possible yield is the basic demand for an economic order that is understood to be both reasonable and free. It is not only important that goods are produced in the greatest possible measure, but also that they are produced as well and as cheaply as possible."

Inasmuch as the "capacity for work" appeared as the "greatest economic asset of the German nation," he seriously described the importance of its care and development. Only the highest level of performance, as some people nowadays had forgotten, would enable them to surmount the difficult times ahead. But good work capacity also demanded "resources at its disposal that are as ideal and plentiful as possible," the best work methods, and the most expedient organization. In that respect, Bosch felt that Germany was in control of its decisions, although not of all raw materials, auxiliary materials, or machines. For those, foreign countries were needed, but they would only provide them in exchange for financial consideration. The fateful question for the future was whether it would be possible to remain competitive in quality and price. To satisfy the needs of the populace with what was produced inside Germany was not difficult, but a surplus was needed to purchase raw materials and foodstuffs. Bosch's essay closed with the observation that all socialization plans must be weighed against a single question. "In which businesses, always with the end goal being the highest possible yield and quality, combined with the lowest price, is the *collectivist* form of economy more expedient and necessary, and in which businesses should the *capitalist* form of economy best be continued, irrespective of later developments that may lead in a different direction?"

His antithetical statement contains a number of ideas quite characteristic of the period, which tended to equate socialist thought with collectivism. Later, this link became weaker for Bosch, and his rejection of the bureaucratic and controlled economy lent a greater emphasis to free capitalist responsibility to oneself. His socialistic side found fulfillment in his involvement with the structure and ethos of work.

Because of the sufferings caused by the war, Bosch, in a departure from his earlier principles, began to develop an active welfare policy for the employees of the plant and their dependents. He was particularly concerned about the fate of those who returned home disabled or unfit for work. In the years to come, the care of the needy grew into a new task. Previously, because of the high wages he paid, he had consciously distanced himself from anything that smacked of welfare or might create feelings of dependency. He would continue to avoid such programs in the future, but the consequences of the war had left behind situations of individual need, and he personally assumed the duty of assuaging them.

The question at the forefront of the struggle and debate over social policy at the time was something that did not need to affect him at all. The law that had been enacted to officially declare the eight-hour workday, as of November 23, 1918, did not exact any changes from Bosch, who had implemented this practice years earlier and had held fast to it despite difficulties. If the eight-hour workday was a central tenet of socialism, then he could indeed regard himself as a socialist. The decree may have initially given him a real sense of satisfaction, but he felt no gratification in the fact that his competition was now forced into the same position. For he had fared so well with the shorter workday that he had been in first place all along. True, he was not entirely lacking in criticism of the law, which could be interpreted too formalistically. The man or woman who was harnessed to the continuous production process should not be equated with those who were only on call, without steady physical and mental labor. Later, Bosch would express his opinion on this subject at some length.

In those months, when threats of leveling the highly articulated wage system were being made, at least in theory, it was absolutely crucial that piecework and the piece-rate system of wages be saved. In 1919 and 1920, Bosch would experience the revolutionary agitation that caught up with him, so to speak, and sent shock waves of unrest through his own plant. But by then these matters were no longer subject to debate. Their significance and justification had been firmly recognized among the

employees. Bosch expressed his critical opposition to plans that sought
to overcome the social crises by means of industrial conscription or profit
sharing. There might be something to say for agricultural conscription,
and it could also be implemented legally, he wrote on February 22, 1919,
but it seemed doubtful to him that its usefulness would justify the effort.
Most young people would not make it past the early training stages. But
more important, experience had shown that forced labor with negligible
pay would result in "very insignificant" productivity. His counsel against
profit sharing was more emphatic. There existed no "direct, somehow
calculable" relationship between the performance of the average worker
or staff member and the profit of the company. It was the indirect relationship, expressed in "skill, hard work, and accuracy," that "should find
expression in the graduated nature of fair wages." Should a good worker
who was employed in a business that happened to be doing badly be
socially disadvantaged as a result? Was it sensible for the wage earner to
be focused on an uncertain, fluctuating surplus of income, for whose rise
or fall the management was responsible, rather than the general situation
of the times? And wasn't there a danger that any surplus not paid to the
workers would be viewed with mistrust, and that this would pose a danger to the accumulation of reserve capital, depreciation, and even investments? Any distinction between responsible leadership and the desire to
have a voice in specific business decisions would be lost. The "raising of
the absolute level of wages and the refinement of the methods of wage
payment" seemed to him to be more profitable for the workers, as well,
than "shifts that could be economically detrimental both to individuals
and to the nation."

When Bosch, in a long commentary to an Augsburg industrialist
dated April 15, 1919, counseled against an attempt at profit sharing, the
question of what influence employees or their representatives should
have on the firm's business policies had already been widely debated in
Germany. It occurred under the slogan of the so-called "factory councils." The struggle over the councils reflected the ideological, tactical,
and very practical power struggles through which Germany gradually
managed to recover from its revolutionary situation. The system of councils seemed quite useful as an improvisation for the creation of revolutionary groups. Russia had produced the model and the term "Workers'

and Soldiers' Council," to which were soon added farmers' councils, a council for intellectual workers, etc. Those people in Germany who wanted to adopt new forms during the military and political collapse had no ideas of their own. The paradox was obvious. The councils, which pretended to be the power holders even if they did not actually feel that way, were locked in a struggle for power with coalition governments based on the old parties—parties that were themselves undergoing a process of transformation. The strongest of the proletarian parties, the Majority Social Democrats, was uncomfortable with the new formula. It threatened the party's traditional vision of democratic leadership in government and administration, to the extent that this was at all secure. The workers' councils wanted to create a more flexible type of democracy under continuous collective control by providing that their elected representatives could be recalled or be given binding instructions at any time. It was not hard to see that this had to lead to leadership by the determined, active minority. The debate between Mikhail Bakunin and Karl Marx, and the experiment of the French commune, were to be continued on a different plane. Anyone who wanted to advance the revolution had to seize upon the notion of the councils. But the idea of the councils suffered a peculiar and confusing fate, as conservative intellectuals also seized upon it, and, sensing its explosive antidemocratic force, attempted to imbue it with the old corporate ideals of German Romanticism. The decision rested with whatever elements of real power remained or were regrouping; it was the army and the police, and their point of view, that carried the day. This occurred in various guises, amid crises, in forms that varied from one region to the next. In Württemberg, the beginnings of a new governmental authority seemed to have been created through the decisive and courageous will of Reserve Lieutenant Paul Hahn, a graphic designer who established a security force made up of reliable army units.

Bosch had followed the political phenomenon of the councils with discomfited interest. They attempted to lay claim to him in a brazen interpretation of his radicalism. One day he read that he was a member of the central committee of the Council of Intellectual Workers of Germany. Such mistakes were not unusual at the time, and Bosch himself may have given encouragement to the false notion that he had been co-opted by the group when he participated, in contrast to his usual reserve, in a public protest over the assassination of the left-wing Socialist Karl Liebknecht in Berlin in 1919. This participation was certainly not motivated by sympathy for the fanatical Liebknecht but rather by anger over the breach of the legal process. Now he vehemently refused to be used as an advertisement without his consent. He sensed the danger of becoming associated with the radical literati, to whom he was not the least bit suited. The task he had defined for himself consisted of exerting an educational influence outside the firm; at the time, this meant in the social sphere.

He was able to take on this educational task after the ideal of the workers' councils had been robbed of its politically revolutionary significance and ambition by the provisional national constitution, and had been transformed into a problem of industrial structure. This occurred in a very peculiar fashion, as the politicians of the left began to wax enthusiastic about the socioeconomic significance of the councils, while the trade unions, which had been more unsettled than overjoyed by a rapid influx of new members, would have little to do with them. The political view won out. It was prepared to cooperate and anchor the notion of the councils in the constitution; what the result of this decision might be in terms of the power structure within the Reich meant little more than a vague promise for the future. For the present, the demand for the councils was diverted to the industrial plants where it became an element of social policy. Basically, it was a question of obligatory blue- and white-collar workers' committees whose structure, rights, and obligations were to be defined. The constitutionally organized factory, the model for which had been produced and tested in Berlin years earlier by Heinrich Freese, was to be legally mandated throughout Germany. In the process, admittedly, it would have to shed its individual flavor and become something with more of a schematic nature.

At the Bosch firm, they had been determined from the very beginning to tackle the question of the factory councils positively, however discouraging the memory of their own earlier workers' committee might have been. Their experience at that time had revealed a failure to follow insights with the courage to assume independent responsibility. The shop stewards had not really become sources of authority within the plant. People could get more done with the help of the trade union officials. The bitter conflict of 1913 had disturbed the traditional relationship, but a balance had been restored during the war years. Now a new body, closer to the workers in the plant, was to be created; certainly its power would depend not only on the paragraphs about voting and jurisdiction but also on the men who, in the process, stepped forward. There had been problems earlier with their quality, and there was no certainty now as to whether the right people would be in charge. In these confusing and noisy times, it was not the honest people who pushed their way to the fore, but the loud and active ones. In the Stuttgart region, the unrest was centered among the Daimler workers, whose numbers had swelled tremendously during the war. Now they experienced a feeling of uncertainty. As early as January 1919, there had been unrest in Stuttgart, with street demonstrations that attempted to foment a belated revolution. The situation worsened in March. Even at Bosch there were wildcat strikes against a background of expectations linked to the magic word "council." Both supporting and dissenting voices found a vivid outlet in *The Bosch Spark Plug.*

In those days, Stuttgart was experiencing its own special brand of social reformer. Rudolf Steiner, who had been called in by several industrialists who were members of his Anthroposophic Society, happened to be in Württemberg, where he was speaking at gatherings throughout the province. With his ideology of the "tripartite organization of the social organism," which did not acknowledge the essential role of power residing in the state, he was looking for a testing ground for his theories. The flair for the speculative that was native to the Swabian population, seemed, for a moment, to suggest prospects for a broader impact. An interesting anecdote from the period recounts how Bosch, under pressure from some zealous followers of the anthroposophists, invited Steiner to lecture Bosch workers on the solution to society's problems. Steiner's personal attempt to win Bosch over could only be termed a complete failure. Bosch felt embarrassed at the way his visitor was speaking to him about the rights of the employer, and interrupted him gruffly: He "did not speculate on this subject." As Bosch wrote in a December 31, 1919, letter, "Steiner himself told me in a conversation: 'people criticize me because the workers pick the raisins out of my cake; why don't you do the same thing?' I do not have time for such thinking." Given the nature of the two men, the relationship Steiner desired was a human impossibility.

The Bosch circle drew back from Steiner. His activities in Württemberg, which never developed to the point where they had any effect on matters of state, ended soon afterward, leaving behind nothing more than a bit of spiritual bewilderment.

The day-to-day political, ideological, and finally parliamentary fight over the factory councils dragged on until February 4, 1920, when a law was passed in the Reichstag to the accompaniment of frenzied street demonstrations. Bosch had already sent a letter to the leadership of the National Union of German Industry in which he defended the specific suggestions of the Württemberg Socialization Commission. He expanded upon the commission's suggestions with his personal comments "on cooperation between employers and employees": "The fundamental attitude of struggle between these two groups must be abolished. In order to achieve this, it is necessary that trust be as widespread as possible on both sides. But such mutual trust will only be possible if each side gets to know the other better. The factory councils that are provided by the law can be useful for this purpose. In such factory councils, white- and blue-collar workers will have to be granted the right of codetermination in internal business matters, as well as in the hiring and firing of workers and lower-level professional staff." Bosch felt that cases involving higher-level staff might warrant an arbitration committee. There must be no specifically determined right to codetermination by the workers "in any purely business or technical questions, insofar as they are concerned with the construction, price, or type of goods being manufactured, etc." In such cases, it would not be possible to spell out precisely the employer's duty to provide information; that would have to be a matter of trust on both sides. "Hence it will depend on the degree of the employer's skill and tact, as well as that of the factory council, how far they will be able to go in this direction with information. The criterion for the skill and tact of the employer would be the extent to which information is provided. The more extensive the information that can be given out, the more productive their cooperation will be and the more the factory will flourish." Here, too, in doubtful cases an arbitration committee could be given authority to decide grievances on both sides. "The introduction of factory councils, in itself, is something I deem necessary." Parts of this statement were printed in *The Bosch Spark Plug* of July 5, 1919 (no. 5).

Bosch's expert opinion on factory councils was directed at the National Union of German Industry, on whose board he served. It required a bit of getting used to before he felt relatively at ease in his new surroundings and with his new position.

The groundwork for a comprehensive organization of German industrialists had been laid during the war in the War Committee on Industry. The earlier contradictions between the Central Union and the League of Industrialists, between the producers of raw materials and semifinished goods and the manufacturers of finished products, which had been focused especially but not exclusively on the area of trade agreements and policy, had lost their meaning within the context of the war. Trade policy in the traditional sense no longer existed, but it would return one day, and then what would be the emphasis? Bosch had always been an opponent of the political alliance between heavy industry and large-scale agriculture; thus he counseled against maintaining the war alliance or solidifying it by means of an organizational merger. Such a merger had been provisionally introduced in December 1918 and was being heavily promoted by the men from the Central Union. "Is this," Bosch wrote on February 1, 1919, "because the Central Union, after its recent experiences, feels that it no longer has any solid ground under its feet?" He did not consider the joint federation to be "appropriate," and exchanged thoughts on the matter with the leader of the Carl-Zeiss factories in Jena, Dr. Max Fischer, to whom, since he was unable to participate personally, he had entrusted the task of carrying on the negotiations in his name. In the end, the new entity was created after all, but it was not a simple fusion. The powerful formations of the chemical and electrical engineering industries were added, as well; until then the business leaders in these sectors had been satisfied with more narrowly defined industrial associations. Bosch also reconciled himself to the merger, although he found it wrong that "people make it necessary to take such hasty actions."

In fact, things developed rather better than Bosch feared at the time. On the territory into which he now ventured there gradually grew personal relationships that later became important to him, for example, that with Dr. Hermann Bücher, who had originally been a botanist in the colonial service, and had left the foreign office to take over the directorship of the National Union of German Industry. A shared love of hunting helped pave the way for a trusting, although occasionally combative, friendship. But in the first few years, more than anything else Bosch sensed the political conflict with the men from the Ruhr Valley in matters of both domestic and international policy. Where personal trust existed, he overlooked it. Years before, when he and Reusch, who had directed the Good Hope Mine, had a difference of opinion, Bosch had reassured him: "I am in a position to respect the political convictions of a third party." Bosch had given his friend "the promise that our personal relationship will not be affected by it." But a man like Hugo Stinnes, although he may have interested Bosch, was not his type. As long as the tone of the discussions was determined by the traditions of heavy industry, he found them "unpleasant." He reproached the iron-producing industry for being too indulgent with that great iron consumer, agriculture, for selfish reasons. "At times I feel quite alone," he wrote to Ulm industrialist Philipp Wieland on June 15, 1922. "I do what I can in order to preserve our position. Unfortunately, I am not very skillful, and, perhaps more importantly, I am not in Berlin often enough. And then, it is no small task to stand by one's guns around people like Hugenberg, etc." Later he softened his judgment somewhat. "With time, even in heavy industry the more thoughtful people also came to see that one cannot accomplish anything by force when one has no force left. This is just as true of relations with labor as it is in politics," he wrote retrospectively in 1931. And: "By the time matters had gotten to that point," he wrote, "I was far less isolated, with my point of view, on the board of the National Union. I should say that the right had moved quite a bit closer to the left wing, which I had earlier represented essentially by myself." But the feeling of strangeness and the awareness of a contradiction did not leave him in his later years, even if he no longer said, as he had in 1920, that he was "the most hated man" in industry circles. In 1938, when a Berlin magazine published pictures of leading figures taken in their youth and old age, he remarked in a letter: "It seems odd to me that I am shown with Kirndorf, of all people, who in terms of social issues was always my opposite number, as it were." Bosch's personal involvement in the deliberations of the National Union's leadership was negligible. "I held myself back enormously," he wrote. "I got immoderately worked up when I did speak once . . ." But his indirect influence had increased over the years; industry had learned to count on his tough, strict argumentation, free of inhibitions. Through the years, in this context too, he was a stronger force than he himself knew.

25

———•———

MAKING PEACE
AT HOME
AND ABROAD

In a memorandum from the year 1931, in which Bosch described his differences with the "leaders of heavy industry," he stated: "I always maintained that we were powerless, and that we should shrewdly use our weaknesses as strengths. This was not the attitude of the north, however. There they were convinced that defiance, even the defiance of the powerless, would get them somewhere." Behind these sentences is the sober insight, born of many hopes and disappointments, that making peace on the continent and achieving the inner calm they longed for would not be possible with a politics of pure prestige that refused to recognize the fact of their political and military impotence.

Shouldn't it be possible to smooth the way for the return of a simple moral attitude of decency and goodwill between peoples, which had been destroyed by chauvinistic passions and defamatory hate propaganda on all sides? If this were not feasible, at least it would be important to attempt to uphold the standards of a policy of unsentimental honesty, both domestically and abroad, in these confusing times. One should not harbor any illusions. The conditions of the cease-fire demonstrated quite clearly the harshness of will that was bound up with the entente's late victory in the war. The uncertain domestic situation in Germany—with the Spartacist agitation and the growing particularist sentiment—inhibited any feeling of confidence that the Reich and the nation would be able to remain internally united politically, in spite of their external impotence. As unclear as the developments on the opposing side might be, it was clear that difficulties, discrepancies, and conflicting goals and interests necessarily had to arise there too, given the great number of tasks that had to be addressed. For the moment, it could only be a matter of developing Germany's stand on the issues, if possible, before it took on the characteristics of a response to opposing views. This was the goal of the Heidelberg Union for a Politics of Law, founded by Chancellor Prince Max of Baden. Professors Max and Alfred Weber and Richard Thoma in Heidelberg, and Lujo Brentano in Munich, were the moral and intellectual backbone of this attempt. Robert Bosch took part in the founding discussion in early February; it was so important to him that he stayed away from the discussion on the future of the industrial associations, which was held at the same time, in order to participate. From this encounter he gained a number of connections that would later prove fruitful. Some of the men who belonged to or sympathized with this circle—Hans Delbrück, Max Monteglas, and Paul Rohrbach—immediately addressed an issue that would assume great significance in the political debates to come: the clarification of the "war guilt." Bosch himself naturally did not take part in the debate, but he followed it closely, supported its intensification, and agreed with its results in the hope that some good might come of it. Neither he nor any of the other participants could have known that the struggle over war guilt (and the outcome of the war) would be completely ineffective in foreign policy, and would later become a thoroughly irritating weapon in the hands of the feuding political parties.

Soon enough, Bosch got a very vivid and rather embarrassing sense of the difficulties involved in finding a relatively compelling formulation for the German position. The Heidelberg circle was not "pacifist" by nature—Hans Delbrück and Max Weber understood the influence that power had on the lives of the people. As passionate and suffering patriots, they also understood the destructive danger of nationalistic hubris. To a certain extent, they were militarists. Bosch was not. His humanitarian rationalism clearly tended toward pacifist ideology. And because he felt that the time had now come to speak his piece without any reservation, it was not difficult to convince him to participate in a conference that had been called by the peace organizations in Bern in March 1919. The appearance of one of Germany's most important industrialists—a man of worldwide renown—could not fail to have a special impact in the international arena. The whole affair was a terrible disappointment for Bosch, who felt as though he were being "led around by the nose" by the people who had requested his presence. Among those in attendance, there was not a single Frenchman, only one American, whom Bosch judged to be of Galician origin, and two Englishwomen. The rest of the group was almost exclusively German, mostly young intellectual-style Jews who fought among themselves or "put forward pure ideals." "When it came to the question of disarmament," Bosch wrote in an ironic and aggravated letter from Bern on March 12, 1919, "I am surprised the proposal was not made that no more iron should be allowed to be mined, because weapons could be made out of it. As you can see, I am already quite taken with the idea . . ." But his humor was bitter. He saw the emphatic mistrust, occasionally justified, with which those who were already pacifists greeted people who were just beginning to take a stand; he sensed their jealousy and concern about being pushed aside. He met people who were quite evidently making pacifism into a business, and he was ashamed of the Germans who made professions of self-accusation and maintained that "everything in Germany is just the same as it was before."

The only thing Bosch gained from the Bern congress was his contact with Lujo Brentano. Brentano, too, had been brought to this conference by his unrelenting desire to have an impact, in order to speak about the circumstances affecting the postwar international economy. His goal was to create the conditions for founding a free trade movement; he believed that this would not only smooth out the economic confusion, but would also relieve political tensions. The two men, very different in their flexibility and mental makeup, got along famously. Bosch fit the ideal type of employer Brentano had imagined in his early studies on the workday and worker productivity and in his writings on unions and wage contracts, and Brentano attracted Bosch's attention through his practical political will. They were very much in agreement about goals, and in the coming period Bosch often referred to Brentano, particularly when he was exam-

ining the way the causes of the war were treated in the press. He was prepared to adopt Brentano's thesis on free trade, which would overcome the
boycott of German goods imposed in Paris in 1916. A few months later,
the Treaty of Versailles transformed his naive plans into utopian castles
in the air.

When the terms of the Treaty of Versailles were made public, Bosch
spoke openly in favor of its rejection. It filled him with satisfaction that a
few of the leading pacifists, like Ludwig Quidde and Walter Schücking,
who knew how much the Treaty of Versailles contradicted the idea of
peace itself, took the same position. Opinion in Württemberg at the time
was deeply divided, and the division went right through the parties,
which was hardly surprising. For a question of such world-historical
dimensions could not be answered by a party line but only by an individual historical instinct. The concern spread throughout the country
that a "no" vote would be followed by the violent secession of southern
Germany from the Reich, a move that would find disturbingly ready support in both regions. This objection did not particularly impress Bosch,
for despite his discomfort with and disapproval of the previous imperial
style of government, it was quite clear to him that the historical development toward national unity was irreversible. His calculation was based
on the idea that rejection was the weapon with which to activate the powers of reason in the enemy camp, which had been suppressed by the
delayed military victory and the popular desire for revenge.

The decision went the other way. For a man like Bosch, with his realistic view of the world economy, there was no mistaking the fact that the
reparations policy, with its still undefined sums, would disrupt trade and
credit relations in general. It would be difficult for the firm to survive, in
terms of the calculation of profit and loss and production technology,
until such time as the whole procedure would have revealed its absurdity,
with wounds and suffering. Until then, should they accept the condition
as given? He thought not. They would have to seek a way to change the
character of the terms of Versailles from the inside out. There was a limited basis for doing this; even the thought seemed utterly hopeless. But it
was pointless, once the facts of the case had been established, to perse-
vere in mere defiance or protest. These considerations led Bosch to participate actively in the efforts to begin to reform international relations,

beginning with the League of Nations—a better organized League of Nations than the one that had been created in Geneva. When the German League for the League of Nations was formed, Bosch supported it with an initial contribution of 300,000 marks. Without underestimating the psychological difficulties, he wanted to promote the insight, at least in Germany, that there might be another method of politics, after all, than resolution by brute force with weapons. His father's idealistic legacy came alive in him.

His support of this group, which wanted to participate in the anticipated international debate with its own studies and proposals concerning the rights of nations, also amounted to a rebuff, in practice, of the professional pacifists. The Bern Conference had left a bad taste in Bosch's mouth; he would grow angry if anyone praised Professor Nicolai, for example, and openly displayed his extreme distrust of Friedrich Wilhelm Foerster. But he tried with almost surprising and tenacious devotion to find his way among the different tendencies, and remained much sought after both as a personality and as a potential supporter. In the end, he withdrew.

There is a remarkable correspondence that continued from the end of 1919 through 1920 between Bosch and the Württemberg pacifist journalist Fritz Röttcher. Although there would later be a very abrupt break between the two, Bosch expressed himself with astonishing intimacy to this man whose lack of merit bothered him greatly some years later. Röttcher's penetrating and rather clever style of argumentation knew how to appeal to Bosch's elementary sense of justice; he sought to gain Bosch's support for individuals who had been misunderstood historically or were currently being ostracized. The result was the strange suggestion, which Bosch did not decline, that he should familiarize himself in those confusing months with the political ideas of the half-forgotten Swabian philosopher Carl Christian Planck concerning the organization of the state along vocational lines or with the "federative" theories of Bismarck opponent Konstantin Franz and the ideologies of Friedrich Wilhelm Foerster. Not much of real value could come of this correspondence. Bosch was not able to follow the abstract terminology of the intellectual schemes; he saw the concrete individuals before him, and the odd legal existence with which they imbued their vocational groupings appeared to him as a legitimization of simple economic interests that endangered state and national unity in fundamental ways. The political parties, which were not yet worn down by their failure in the face of excessively difficult tasks (one of the consequences of the postwar policy of Paris), and externally not yet so divided as they would be a few years later (a result of the system of proportional representation), seemed to him to be the better, necessary way to form a sense of nationhood from below and national leadership from above. But aside from that, although Planck's idea of basing the nation on the closed trades may have been more or less appropriate in his time, "the world economy today has outgrown that." The world economy, however, was an economic war—pacifist protests against a war of weapons would not help much on this front, only free trade could do that. Throughout these debates ran a thread from the simple formula of the British Bright-Cobden slogan: "Free trade and peace." Brentano, who loved and occasionally believed in this, may have discussed it with Bosch.

Röttcher, with his pushiness and lack of inhibition, once tried to win Bosch's support for Foerster's candidacy for the presidency of the Reich, before Friedrich Ebert's provisional appointment to that office was extended to five years by the National Assembly. Although the episode is certainly only a detail, it is a good piece of historical reminiscence, for Bosch named names (April 10 and 29, 1919), and his list has a charm that is more than anecdotal. He did not want to comment on Foerster. Wasn't he a renegade who had therefore lost his credibility in matters of faith? Was it even possible to think about a professor in this position? "It is one thing to think up systems, another to seek out people to implement them. Professors can control ideas and perhaps things, as well. But the control, i.e., leadership, of people toward a *single* purpose and a *single* end is not a part of their experience, at any rate, and whether Foerster has the natural aptitude for it is questionable." Foerster's one-sided stance opposing German militarism (as if there had been no militarism in France) did not commend itself to Bosch either. "An Englishman considers such a man to be a fool or a toady, whose toadying is meant to lighten his lot under false pretenses." In a later letter, Bosch dropped the objection against Foerster's one-sided self-incrimination, "but would Foerster be more than a man of the study?" Who else could be considered? At the time, Adolf Damaschke was pushing his candidacy, but Bosch feared that he was "incapable of seeing anything except land reform" and "did not have a powerful enough personality . . . Hindenburg certainly is a personality, but he is old; he is a soldier and will die as one. I would say he is not for the republic, either, and I think he would regard himself as the administrator of the throne for his imperial master. At his age one no longer learns new tricks, if one has character; it is no longer worthwhile. Hindenburg is also no politician . . . Of the soldiers I could only possibly consider Gröner . . . I have a certain weakness for people with a sense of humor, and Ebert has one. He has also accomplished a great deal. I still cannot give up on Ebert in favor of Foerster. Above all else, they would have to come up with someone who I am certain knows people and understands how to manage them."

His words appear, in retrospect, like the variations on the theme of a prelude in the performance of which Bosch would later produce powerful chords. At the time, the debate was nothing more than an addendum to the discussion over whether pacifism could or should be accorded a role in the leadership of Germany. Röttcher complained about how much pacifism had to suffer as a result of preconceptions in Germany, but he failed to notice (or remained silent about) the fact that it was precisely the German pacifists who were endangering the efforts of honest friends of peace in the Anglo-Saxon world. "Pacifism is good," Bosch wrote on February 24, 1920, "but it is only a part, not the whole. It is a result, not a cause . . . Pacifism is quite a good thing, like any religion, one might say, only her priests are often bungling, incapable, and also careerists. Naturally, among its priests there are also some very honorable, competent people who accomplish much good. I find, however, that many pacifists are neurasthenic, hysterical, feminine, cannot exercise self-restraint, and sometimes do not foresee the results of their actions and speeches . . . Do you think that any decent Frenchman would demand the explanations that the people of this type have produced? Brentano, Monteglas—these are men, in contrast to so many others. So all due respect to pacifism, but it is something to be encouraged through education and training of the people. To support it as such would mean having to defend oneself constantly against the reproaches that would then be made against the mistakes of those who have no goal or dignity." Bosch did not want to allow himself to be coerced into that role, to be made responsible for phrases or foolishness or noncommittal enthusiasm. In a letter dated December 31, 1919, he wrote, "Earlier on I was an enthusiast myself, but today I think about how I can help."

Bosch never got beyond a certain contradictoriness, as he held back the support that was requested of him despite zealous campaigning for his participation. He wanted to serve the cause, but the individuals who sought to act as the tools of (or benefit from) the cause were not to his liking. Later he used his strength where he believed he could tackle concrete, well-defined tasks for the policies of peace, although once again he was not always fortunate in his choice of the groups to which he lent his name and his support. His connection with the pacifists who had had such a lively exchange with him in 1919 and 1920 ended in a radical break. Röttcher, who had moved the offices of his magazine *Mankind* to Wiesbaden, received one more letter from Bosch at the end of 1926, in which Bosch declared he was "pacifistically inclined out of the most profound conviction," but "the self-incriminatory style that issues forth from some of the pacifist circles is not only repulsive to me personally; I also hold it to be objectively wrong." Röttcher was bold enough to respond that it was due to the "influence of their milieu," but by then Bosch had already given up on him. When he was asked, in early January 1928, to sign a statement supporting Röttcher after he had become involved in a trial for treason, he declined. He felt that one could no longer speak of pure motives stemming from Röttcher's weltanschauung; this was a man who "for years served only his fanaticism and his blind dogmatism . . . just as Foerster did." The political climate had changed completely.

Any attempts to prepare responsible opinions and practicable legal forms for the shared life of the nations were pointless so long as the German people were still threatened by the danger of civil war. For civil strife would only exacerbate Germany's external weakness and undermine the beginning effort to win back the foundation of the nation's existence through hard work. Bosch saw the two polar extremes of the difficulties: the agitated radicalism of proletarian groups, and the uncomprehending resentment of bourgeois circles. He personally experienced the test of strength in his own business in the spring of 1919—a sudden strike lasting several days, which threatened the management and paralyzed the unions. At the time, Bosch was in Bern, and it was suggested that he prolong his stay. The government was initially unsure, as the unrest spread, whether it had sufficient force at its disposal, but it was able to restore order. In industry circles there was a growing mood in favor of taking drastic measures. Bosch counseled against them. "The reticence of the Union of Industrialists of Württemberg, I am not ashamed to say, has been caused by me," he wrote in a letter to a manufacturer pushing for stronger action. "Each one of us should work within our own circles, and each one of us should honestly attempt to bring about an honest, open agreement." There was nothing to be accomplished by meeting at that moment. "Who wants to subject himself to the aspersions that the incomprehension of the masses of industrialists would certainly launch against this speaker? The masses do not want to hear the truth . . ." In another letter to the same man he wrote: "As for myself, I emphatically deny that it would be correct for one of the employers' organizations to play a different, harsher tune. Even the government can only proceed with caution, if it does not want the entire china shop to be smashed. Usually I am a man who prefers the end, with all its terror, to terror without end. But in this case I am of the opinion that decisive action will surely bring about chaos, i.e., Bolshevism, whereas this way it is possible that the intoxication will be followed by a hangover before everything is destroyed . . . I remain convinced that it has been good to wait until some resistance to Bolshevism can be felt among the peaceful contingent of the workforce." In another section of this correspondence with Ernst Lillienfein of the Fortuna AG, he writes: "I am, for example, not convinced that a republic is the best thing for us, but I take it to be a great mistake that remarks are being made against the republic by the bourgeois party in the National Assembly. To go against the republic now means creating strife, and I think that more than anything else we must come to an agreement *right away*. To want to work up enthusiasm for the monarchy now is to create chaos just as much as what the Spartacists are doing. Once the house is on fire you extinguish it with swill, if you have no water. This is only meant figuratively. I personally am of the opinion that we should stick with the republic now that we have one."

He maintained this position on the basic form of the government, knowing full well, as he wrote to a more right-wing friend in early January 1923, "that even the republic is not the decisive thing, in and of itself." As emotionally far-removed as he may have been from the monarchical, much less the dynastic traditions, he also placed little value on the republican form of government as such. But now suddenly the republic had become the shelter of German history. "We Germans must show that we are capable of leading a good republic, despite the depravity in which we find ourselves. In the end we must clean up shop. Unfortunately, our citizenry does not want to hear much about it. Which does not, however, speak for the monarchy as such, but solely for the lazy thinking and indolence of our citizenry."

His critical tone stayed with him and occasionally intensified when he thought he sensed wariness or a narrowness born of class prejudice in the face of necessary social reform. Later, a portion of his criticism would be redirected at the schematization of this very same governmental social reform. Now the workers' leaders felt the sting of his reprimands, as did the administrators of the health insurance and the communal agencies, which it seemed had lost all sense of thrift. Some of the budding dreams of his youth—that one could and should no longer talk about class struggle, that the national idea was all embracing and above special interests, that there would be a lessening of bureaucracy and control in the life of the community, that groups would relate to each other through free and frank contractual agreements—such hopes and wishful thinking had to fade.

All the worries that Bosch had expressed in 1919 about the undesirable consequences of a sharp reaction on the right seemed to him to have been justified by the events of 1920. After the rioting of March 1919 had been quelled, Württemberg experienced a certain period of peace. The province was not seized by the excitement that ensued with the senseless right-wing Kapp Putsch in Berlin in March 1920. But the long-range effect of the disturbance made itself felt later in the summer as the opportunists of revolt once again found an audience among workers, particularly since the Metal Workers' Union had gradually come to occupy the favored position in the power struggle among Majority Social Democrats, independents, and Communists. In midsummer of 1920 this led to a very risky maneuver on the part of the workers' movement, for which the Bosch and Daimler firms were to provide the testing ground. In the course of the national financial reform, the new law provided that a tax should be imposed on income. The first time this tax became due, the workforces of Bosch and Daimler demanded that the business management ignore the measure. A completely nonsensical attempt, a last rebellion by radicals who wanted to regain the leadership that had slipped away from them—the assiduous advice of the business management was spoken into the wind. The result was a work stoppage. The government took charge of the struggle in a simple and effective way: it closed both plants and to prevent acts of sabotage occupied them with police. This lasted from August 26 until September 5. Then the uproar was over—a bitter pill for those who believed that the young democracy had already implanted any awareness of mutual responsibility for the government into the German consciousness.

Bosch did not get involved in the active life of the political parties. With the sudden death of Friedrich Naumann in August 1919, he lost the man whose opinion had provided the orientation for many of his own decisions in recent years. Bosch had expected Naumann to provide the vision and participate actively in creating a national life that would link personal freedom with the self-evident authority of a governmental order, not an order that was imprisoned in legal paragraphs but a living social order in the minds and souls of the populace. The temptation to play a part in political activities, if such a thing could have been possible, came in October 1919 when Conrad Haussmann was sent by the German Democratic faction to propose that Bosch join the cabinet as minister of reconstruction. At the time, this ministry was intended to have the task of organizing the reconstruction in the areas in Belgium and northern France that had been laid waste by the war; other tasks would later be included, as well. The idea was to fill this highly visible position with a man of international rank, whose history in business spoke for his seriousness of will, energy, and organizational ability. Haussmann added, touching a sensitive spot in Bosch, how happy he would be to see a southern German in this particular position. Bosch did not hesitate for a moment to decline, but not out of inappropriate modesty: "In order to show you that I know what would make me appropriate, on account of my name there would certainly be something to be said for me" (October 15, 1919). He explained that he was not at all in a position "to be able to conduct tense negotiations for even two days in a row, particularly such important ones as those in question." For that he lacked the necessary skill and confidence in the foreign language. Finally, he thought that a man with a knowledge of structural engineering would be better suited, someone who could also put together a staff based on his own experience. He suggested one of the leading men from the large construction firm of P. Holtzmann. Bosch felt Walter Rathenau to be the right man for the negotiations, although he knew that a suggestion to this effect "had failed because of the government's unwillingness . . . I do not want to experience the kind of failure I would create if I were to take the matter on" was his final conclusion. Bosch possessed too clear a sense of the limitations of his aptitude to continue to play a role in pursuing this plan. The practical realism of his judgment and his hands-on will would have been an asset to such a task. But his nervous inability to deal with the unavoidable business of meetings, combined with his temperamental outbursts, which he himself mistrusted but to which people in the circles around him had by now grown accustomed, would only have made him unhappy and would have served the purpose poorly. He could not picture himself in cabinet meetings or in front of parliament.

Nonetheless, the year 1920 brought him a public, semipolitical position that he did not decline; on the proposal of the government of Württemberg, Bosch was named a member of the transitional National Economic Advisory Board. The group had the right to review and propose economic and social laws as provided for in the Weimar Constitution. The composition of its organizational structure was left for a later legal process to decide, but this never took place. There was a desire to somehow accommodate the ideology of the councils that had been pushed out of the political arena, and to comply with the sudden fierceness of demands for representation by profession. The decision was a tactical one that was made in the hope that this attempt, once it had become reality, would be able to justify and maintain itself due to the substance of its accomplishments. The actual influence of the National Economic Advisory Board remained negligible compared with the dynamic of the political parties, which, though themselves hampered in their intended task, gave little chance to their competitor. Bosch answered the call, especially since he was not classified among the industry representatives, but rather as one of a group of expert consultants. That was as he wished; it offered him the opportunity to use his influence freely. For the most part, however, this influence retained its personal character; Bosch never appeared as a speaker in the plenary sessions, although he took part in the work of the social policy committee to which he had been assigned. His significant contribution was the 1922 expert opinion on the legal regulation of the eight-hour workday. Bosch felt quite at ease in his group, which, as he said, should serve to "tip the balance of the scales" among the representatives of the various interest groups: "I can say that among these men I really got to know some fair thinkers." Coincidence would have it that his seat was next to that of Karl Kautsky, his neighbor of three decades earlier. In addition to political discussions, Bosch reminisced with Kautsky about old family stories, which he could then take home with him. Their political discussions were no longer the well-intentioned lectures that Kautsky had given to the young, open-minded tradesman in the Schwabenstrasse in Stuttgart around 1890, but friendly tests of strength between the man of ideas, who offered an endless series of calculations and expectations, and the man who had gathered much worldly and personal experience. Kautsky had to admit that German Social Democracy lacked men with the necessary knowledge of government and economics. Austria, he thought, was another matter. If it were, countered Bosch, what good did that do us?

The work methods proved to be "too clumsy and expensive," and Bosch was quite happy "when there were enough applicants for free train tickets" so that he was able to resign his position gracefully a few years later. After 1921, he was seized by a certain restlessness, which did not make his constant travel from Stuttgart exactly a burden—the excuse of needing or wanting to go to Berlin for meetings was not always unwelcome—but it became repugnant to him to participate seriously in the meetings themselves. Still, his memory of the time of his participation was generally more pleasant than that of his chairmanship of the National Union of German Industry, for example. One could both learn and teach through the exchange of opinions. His final conclusion (in a memorandum from 1931) was that the National Economic Advisory

Board had proven itself to be "very serviceable," because it was in a good position, much more so than the Reichstag, to initiate studies on economic matters of all kinds. At the beginning of its existence, when the issue was dealing with socialization in its most far-reaching form, the National Economic Advisory Board was very effective. It forced employers and employees to sit at *one* table and was probably the first time that serious consideration was given to the question of what socialization meant. The results are well-known. "The mountain labored and brought forth a mouse."

PART V

REBUILDING

26

THE MANUFACTURING PROGRAM
AND BUSINESS ORGANIZATION
OF THE POSTWAR YEARS

Working for war needs had turned large segments of the Bosch workshops away from their original tasks. The factory management and workers remained uncertain, in the transition period, about whether the earlier state of affairs would return. The question was raised repeatedly in workers' council meetings as to what the workers would be given to do. *The Bosch Spark Plug* had reported that foreign countries were trying to block the import of Bosch products by implementing tariffs or even outright bans. In Germany itself many firms were beginning to produce articles similar to Bosch's. All this was incentive for serious thought about what direction the factory should take. One new area that had developed was the production of artificial limbs for wounded war veterans. Although this production was not part of the main thrust of the company, it is worth noting. Robert Bosch took a special interest in this question, and he watched with satisfaction as a cleverly adjustable arm was developed; it was one more way in which his workshop could alleviate the individual suffering caused by the war. The experiments, which wore on for a long time, ultimately never got beyond the model stage (partly due to the stubbornness of the inventor), and the project remained a curiosity. The arm had become too heavy and too expensive. Bosch himself had invested tens of thousands of marks in its development.

They had adopted a certain theoretical guideline "for the adoption of new products." They would make nothing that was already being produced in Germany "in adequate quantity and quality." Thus they passed up the typewriter, in order not to compete with customers like Adler and Wanderer. "Our attention," the 1921 business report stated, "is therefore directed to undertaking the production of such items as have, until now, chiefly been imported to Germany from abroad; with this, it is true, we are limited to a smaller selection." That sounded quite convincing. Bosch and his colleagues could only surmise that the worsening of the currency would restrict the import of high-priced finished products from abroad, and would thus create an unsatisfied demand, but reality took a completely different turn. Bosch was compelled, in the short term, to return entirely to his previous specialty—delivering accessories for the motor vehicle industry, soon to be followed by items for the airplane industry. The concept itself was expanded in one extremely important way. Of all the experiments with products that lay outside their industrial niche, only one was developed to the point of marketability. It was an adjustable screwdriver, a well thought out, practical tool in a handy form. It had nothing whatsoever to do with electricity, and the manufacturers of machine tools were more than a little astonished when the name Bosch turned up on their territory, claiming recognition. There was probably no one in the entire Bosch firm who had an inkling that this ordinary, sturdy item would, after thorough technical development, be the unsuspecting predecessor of a group of new products.

The situation was simple: Foreign markets were asking for Bosch ignition; private customers, in particular, wanted their reliable products back. They might have read in the newspapers that it was patriotic to buy only French and English devices, which were at least as good as the ones from Stuttgart. But when one found oneself sitting in a car by the side of the road, stymied by a ruined or dirty spark plug, one remembered the way things used to be. The openness with which such matters were discussed in letters to the editor, for example in England, was the most effective form of advertising. Official government efforts in these countries to secure the start-up costs for the young industry—in Britain they amounted to 33 percent, in France to 45 percent of the value—were to no avail. As inflation increased in Germany, France went as high as a value tariff of 180 percent! This, too, was a form of acknowledgment of their success, albeit an undesirable one. At Bosch, they had the sense that their name commanded respect even during the embarrassing inspection visit by the Allied Military Commission. ("They treated us quite considerately," Bosch reported in March 1920 to Fritz Egnell in Stockholm.) The most important thing may well have been the revival of international racing, which started up uncertainly after the war, and which was especially popular in Italy. There is no question about the significance of these races for the early days of the motor vehicle. They made the automobile popular over all objections of Philistinism or snobbery. The winners' names became celebrated; designers at the individual firms were faced with the never-ending task of surpassing their latest accomplishment. By now the use of motor vehicles in war had come to be taken for granted, and trucks were a banal reality; the automobile had long since lost its aura of sensationalism. From a strictly objective point of view, the return to the testing of speed and reliability, of the skill of individual drivers, may appear to have been superfluous. There were many critics over the next few years who thought automotive development had taken a wrong turn, or at least an avoidable detour, by devoting countless hours responding to the special needs and wishes of automobile racing. This was especially true in Germany. Henry Ford's magnificent accomplishment—partly appealing, partly depressing—which had suddenly become widely known, had been achieved entirely *without* this kind of record-seeking. Be that as it may, in Europe they were having automobile races once again, and at Bosch they had every reason to be pleased about it. It became clear that even when the postwar mood prevented German drivers from competing, the vast majority of racing drivers demanded Bosch ignition for their non-German cars and won by using it. In 1921, at the Targa Florio race in Sicily, the spell was broken. Once again, German drivers appeared at the starting line. For Bosch the day was a triumph. Thirty-one of thirty-seven cars used his equipment, among them the five winning cars—four Italians and a German. This was the beginning of an unbroken string of victories. The international racing press, albeit unwillingly at times, could not disregard this fact, and the foreign representatives who had begun to reestablish themselves had a very useful argument at their disposal.

The Bosch firm had already decided to pass up any opportunities to acquire new territory, at least for the time being. The future of the economy was completely uncertain. The victorious Allies were experiencing their first crises and labor problems; in the neutral countries, which could be considered war profiteers, demand appeared stronger. Spain in particular was a country to pay attention to. The situation in Germany was still in flux and subject to political events. Attempts to stabilize the market were sometimes apparently successful, then sometimes utterly hopeless. The economic history of these years, with its abrupt alternation between apparent boom and sudden stoppage, reduced hours, layoffs, raw material shortages, and constant price revolutions, brought almost daily confusion for anyone involved in it. In retrospect, although it must have been a ghastly time, there was one thing that everyone soon sensed: the era of the automobile had dawned, and the era of the airplane was not far off. Tax and tariff policy might have some influence on their development, holding it back in one place, helping it along in another. It was possible to look at the automobile with joy or mistrust, or—as occurred in all countries, both understandably and foolishly—to see the whole matter as an essentially fiscal question that revolved around new taxpayers. The automobile helped determine the rhythm of the times. In North America, within the space of a quarter of a century it had become *the* most comprehensive industry and the most important in terms of jobs. The international statistics looked discouraging for the Germans: the homeland of Daimler and Benz lagged far behind when it came to the statistics for motor vehicles per inhabitant. In 1921, the number of privately registered cars reached the level it had been in 1914, so powerful had been the impact of the war. (Trucks, it is true, had tripled.) There were reasons for the slower development in Germany: the extensive railroad network and a frequently unfortunate attitude on the part of various government offices. It was quite uncertain whether and at what pace the country, cast down by the war, would catch up with the more fortunate countries. These considerations had to be of great concern to Bosch and his people, if they were not to be misled by the "false boom" of those years (words that turn up often in Bosch's *Life Recollections*).

Now, in 1923, foreign countries were once again absorbing 65 percent of the firm's production. Would this continue if it became possible to reduce the discrepancy in the rates of exchange that had resulted from the decline of the mark? In that case, the state of the domestic market would assume greater importance. But here they had to reckon with increased competition from other German factories. In any case, they tied their fate even more closely to the motor vehicle industry, in the belief that the force of events would overcome the hundreds of difficulties. When it did, they wanted not only to be there, but to help decisively.

In the fall of 1921, after a hiatus of ten years, another German Automobile Exhibition was held. The experts could observe many improvements or refinements that had been made to traditional Bosch products. The ignition device, whose basic elements were already in place, had spawned more and more new types. The increase in the speed of the engines demanded constant adaptations, including changes in the insulation material that was exposed to heat. Along with the passenger car, the motorbike had become popular; its ignition and lights required their own special design—small but sturdy miniature ignition devices and spark plugs. A number of changes had been made in headlights. The lowering of the bright far beams, which created such difficulties in urban traffic, had been technically simplified. Now there was also a "little brother" (if the term is permitted)—the searchlight. It was affixed to a handy lever with swivel joints so the driver could use it whenever the lateral dispersion of the front headlights was not sufficient for him to find his way in curves, crossroads, or other difficult places. The great innovation that could be seen and, above all, heard in 1921 was the signaling instrument that earned Bosch even greater mass popularity than the earlier products of his factories: the Bosch horn. The name, with its echo of the post horn, may have had something to do with it.

Gottlob Honold was the creator of this instrument, too. After his all-important creation, the high-voltage ignition device, and his successful experiments with practical optics, he had turned to acoustical questions. In 1919, he took up the obvious task at hand. With the increase in traffic on the roads, and the ever-increasing speed, drivers and pedestrians faced growing dangers unless the approach of a car or motorcycle was made known early enough. The historic bicycle bell did not suffice.

There was a whole string of signaling instruments: horns with rubber bulbs, which were sounded by hand; sirens; shrill whistles; bells. The resulting cacophony of street noises was amusing but was more confusing than helpful. And some of the instruments were awkward or difficult to use. The principle that Honold applied was not in itself new. The electric bell was based on the same idea: instead of a clapper, a membrane (made of steel) was set in motion, with its own specific vibration, and the sound was amplified by a specially designed megaphone or horn. In their experiments, they had come up with a strong, deep sound but had discovered that people had a hard time knowing where it came from and how far away it was. The problem was solved (after they consulted an ear doctor) by introducing a second membrane that was not attached to the anchor and produced more rapid vibrations, thus adding a higher note.

With this, a signal had been found with a sound that carried well and was also musical. It also lacked all of the shock effect produced by other horns. The Bosch horn was given a harmonious form. Later, when the trumpet was moved under the hood and the horn shape, in some cases, had been replaced by something resembling a box, it kept the name horn. There were also some other improvements. For inner-city traffic, for example, a mechanism was provided that lowered the noise level. A button attached to the steering wheel made it comfortable to use with a minimal expenditure of effort. At Bosch, they were very satisfied with the impression the new horn made in traffic. "It stood out again and again," said Debatin's introductory essay in *The Bosch Spark Plug* (1921, no. 241). "Let us hope that the opposite will soon be true: that the Bosch horn will be the rule and others will stand out."

This, in general, is what happened. From its inception, the design, development, and manufacture of the horn were aimed at mass production, a complicated matter since the horn was composed of 130 parts that required 1,300 different work processes. In Germany in particular, where the authorities took pleasure in passing irritating and rather fruitless regulations, the new item soon became popular. The police also welcomed it. Official studies and even court opinions brought recommendations that were not sought after but were not unwelcome either. There is a curious and amusing story about the head of the Frankfurt City Council using a Bosch horn in turbulent meetings. When a motion to do away with the noise-quelling device was defeated, this unanticipated use was legitimized, so to speak. After two years, they had already produced the hundred thousandth piece; in order to get a sense of the order of magnitude involved, one must recall that in 1921 in Germany there were only about 60,000 automobiles and 30,000 trucks on the roads (and they had naturally been fitted out with some kind of signaling device before this). Foreign countries soon grew fond of the Bosch horn, as did the competition, which came out with all kinds of imitations. In 1929, the statistics on the manufacture of Bosch horns showed that the first million had been produced.

A similar anniversary was celebrated in the same year by a newer product from the workshop: the electric bicycle light, which had been introduced to the market in 1923. This could be regarded as something of a digression for Bosch, for along with the motorbike, the Bosch firm was now also concerning itself with the engineless bicycle. The insights they had gained in perfecting light generators had lured them in this direction, one that other firms had already explored. The principle was simple enough: the cyclist himself, through his pedaling motion, activated the light generator, and the power of the light depended on the speed with which he was traveling and the number of revolutions per minute. The Bosch design, which contained nothing new, was characterized by lower weight, smaller size, practicality of use, and low price. It was conceived as a mass-market product and cost only eighteen marks.

In the following years they devoted their imagination, drawing on past experience, to ways of increasing driving safety and comfort. The experts had learned to expect new refinements from the Stuttgart workshop, and they were not disappointed. Among the new ideas were some that were very cleverly thought out but never had a significant practical impact. For example, there was the Bosch bell (1923), not an electrical but a purely mechanical instrument that was mounted on the rim of the wheel and touched the tire with a sensor. If air began to escape from the tire, the tire became deformed under the weight of the vehicle and the lever would set off a switch that rang the bell. Tire damage could be prevented in good time and an accident avoided. The simple device was rather clever, but it never became popular. Years later, they developed a mechanism in which Bosch was involved not as the inventor but as the manufacturer, and which was not named for Bosch, but rather for the firm of Eisemann,

with which they had developed a close relationship. This was the Eisemann Tire Tester (1927). It was a handy spring pressure device that when
pressed against a tire recorded its atmospheric air pressure on a scale.
This was a convenient way for the driver to monitor his air pressure.
Bosch had purchased the license from the French firm Repusseau, thus
acquiring the right to produce and distribute it in Germany and several
other countries. Shortly before that, Bosch had purchased a shock
absorber from the same firm. It was connected to the vehicle's springs
and was aimed at absorbing and reducing the shocks that caused serious
difficulties for both cars and drivers, especially on bad roads. Neither of
these items was the type of laboratory work done at Bosch. But it is characteristic that as soon as Bosch and his colleagues became convinced of
their serviceability, they accepted them into the manufacturing program.
Even more important was the purchase of the manufacturing rights to the
so-called "servo" or power brake that had been developed by the Belgian
engineer A. Dewandre. It came onto the market in 1927 after an
extended period of technical development. With the growing use of automobiles, their increasing speed, and the traffic they caused, the rear-
wheel brakes that had previously been the rule had been replaced by
front-wheel brakes, which made it possible to absorb the mass and speed
of the vehicle more rapidly, but also required considerably more physical
effort and could be tiring on winding roads or in the sudden traffic congestion of a big city. Dewandre's design took the vacuum of the engine as
its source of power. When the driver put his foot on the brake pedal and
sensed the degree of braking, he could press softly or firmly without
additional effort. This mechanism was the starting point for much more
elaborate designs of brakes for trucks.

The new products that appeared in 1926, windshield wipers, and
1928, blinkers, led back to Bosch's "own" area of electrical accessories.
Both of these items, like the Bosch horn, were successes and rapidly
assumed the status of things that were taken for granted. The battle
against raindrops and snowflakes had been joined early, after automobile
travel had begun to be something that people did in bad weather; closed
cabins were now popular. Wiping the precipitation away by hand was as
awkward as it was dangerous and exposed the interior of the vehicle to
the weather when the windshield was being snapped up. Mechanical

windshield wipers powered by the vacuum of the carburetor were unreliable and ran slowly when the car slowed down. Bosch created windshield wipers with a little electrical motor that set the wipers in motion with a worm gear transmission and was not dependent on the running of the car's engine, since it was fed by the battery—a radical change. The blinker, which was supposed to indicate a change in direction by the driver, had already been thought of as a possibility in the regulations on motor vehicle traffic, which referred to a "mechanical device" that could be used, although it was assumed that the normal thing to do would be to stick out one's arm. Naturally this was a temporary situation. Precisely when changing direction, it is useful to have both hands on the steering wheel! For this reason, directional signals had already been invented, for example, a round disk that protruded from the car with a red arrow that pointed left or right and flashed against a dark background. The solution chosen at Bosch was more primitive but more effective. When needed, an arrow snapped out on the desired side so that it was unmistakably visible as part of the profile of the car. In the darkness it appeared as a glowing red strip of light. A handy lever was attached in front of the driver's seat, and a way was found to make the blinker snap back automatically into its protective housing after eight seconds, without any additional hand movement. Another new design aimed at increasing safety was the brake light. Installed on the rear of the vehicle, it was supposed to indicate to those who followed that they should now slow down or stop. Signaling by means of a raised arm was of course completely outdated. There were already a multitude of mechanical signals with optical effects. What was so pleasant about the design that Bosch introduced to the market in 1928 was the combination of the brake light with the brake pedal by means of a switch; the signal, a red glowing triangle on a round disk, was given automatically.

This period, in which a wealth of new accessories was being developed in quick succession, also brought a significant advance in an area where serious obstacles had existed: the lubricator. The Bosch lubricator had quickly achieved acceptance for stationary machines. An important milestone was the willingness of the government-owned railroads in Württemberg to participate in experiments with the lubricator in which its design simultaneously provided both the pistons and axles of the locomotive with the lubrication they needed. For the personnel, this meant an enormous reduction in the workload, which still required, for example, that the axles be lubricated with an oil can. It made the prevention of premature wear and tear of the metal virtually automatic. Württemberg's railroads changed over to the Bosch lubricator. The most important state, Prussia, remained closed to Bosch; the government had adopted another system. But the unification of the German rail system through the creation of the German *Reichsbahn* in 1919 created a new situation. For very understandable reasons, there was interest in getting away from the different types of lubrication and attempting to establish a national norm, if only to simplify repair and the installation of replacement parts. In the course of these efforts, the lubrication question came up once more. The experiences and wishes of the *Reichsbahn* administration and the design ideas of the technical experts would have to be brought into line with each other. Among the many efforts to find the best and most reliable solution—a process in which the lubricator factory in Stuttgart was naturally not the only applicant—the proposal that had been developed by Bosch was found in the end to be the most practical. The perseverance Robert Bosch had displayed in this sometimes unpleasant matter and his faith in the design technicians were rewarded. For now the Bosch lubricator, which had changed quite significantly since the earliest plans, had become a factor in an altogether different sphere of the transportation industry. Because of the nature of their use, the products of the lubricator factory never became popular. Most people would never know that Bosch products are hidden inside countless locomotives, but the work that had been done and the experiences that had been gained would prove to be profitable in a later expansion of the firm's manufacturing tasks.

It is one thing to invent and design something, quite a different thing to manufacture it, and yet another to sell it. The ingenious mind sitting in front of a problem—measuring, calculating, testing, comparing, rejecting, seeking one new solution after another until the right one is stumbled upon—may be so fixed on the goal that all considerations of cost, price, currency fluctuations, and marketability are ignored. What matters to the inventor and designer, if he is a good technician, is to use the forces and materials that nature offers him, in raw or semifinished form, to achieve performance that can be utilized, in the most perfect possible form, for human ends. What happens during the process of realization no longer concerns him directly. Fundamentally, it had become Gottlob Honold's dream to free himself from organizational pressures. He had been able to build a staff of younger scientists and a few excellent artisans from the workshop, who gave the experimental laboratory an independent life of its own. The manifold improvements and changes they made to old items, the various new things they produced, did not bear the names of their inventors and were, to some degree, the work of the collective. Robert Bosch understood the potential benefits of daring invention, and the workshop was always provided with a generous budget and honored with patience as the firm waited for something to ripen.

Making sure that inventions found their way into manufacturing, and that manufacturing became profitable through sales, depended in the first postwar years on an infinite number of fairly unpredictable factors in the international power struggle. Not only did tariff and trade policies play a role, but there was the virtually hopeless struggle for a viable currency, especially following France's occupation of the Ruhr in 1923, which had removed some of Germany's most important areas from its fiscal control. The early, optimistic attempt that Bosch had made in 1919 to set an example of restoring sound prices had been nothing but a brief interlude. It could not be otherwise, as nominal price increases for raw materials combined with wage increases to undo all decisions. There was no point in trying to determine the source of the problem—prices or wages—in individual cases. Cause and effect were inextricably confounded. Calculating sales figures for the internal market became an illusion. Things were somewhat different in the case of foreign sales, at least where it was possible to count on halfway stable exchange rates. For the most part, the history of the Bosch firm does not occupy a unique position in this regard. At Bosch, they were also compelled to make repeated additions to their capital base and were forced to present marketing statements the fictitious character of which was fully clear to the participants themselves.

The capitalization of Robert Bosch AG had been estimated at 12 million marks in 1917. In March 1917 the first increase occurred, to 20 million. At first they hesitated to continue along this path, hoping that the various stabilization attempts would ultimately succeed. The bond issue of the year 1921 was intended to help tide them over the cash shortage. They thought, finally, that they could get by with a sum of 20 million. Staff members and workers were given the opportunity to buy a portion of the certificates at the rate of 4.5 percent under preferential terms. In May 1922, they were forced to vote on a stock issue of 50 million marks; the dividend of 25 percent that had been announced for the previous year was not paid out but was treated as the down payment on the new stocks. The firm wanted to decrease its capital as little as possible. This was followed by a new bond issue, 30 million marks at 5 percent. Naturally nothing helped. In December 1924 the stock capital was increased four-fold. That was enough for the moment, for it seemed pointless to chase after the mark. At Bosch they were naturally forced to suffer all the unfortunate consequences of the fact that inside Germany the period of time between order, fulfillment, and payment had destroyed all sense of appropriate reimbursement. But the firm was in better shape than countless others because it had made a decisive reentry into the business abroad and was receiving foreign currency for its exports. In September 1924, the firm calculated the balance of its assets in paper marks, as required by law after the conclusion of the seventh year of business (which had been extended beyond September to December 31 to coincide with the end of the calendar year), and arrived at the tragically curious sum of 18,990,415,323,717,414,132.77 marks. Even at that time, when people were used to meaningless numbers, it is likely that hardly anyone would have been able to pronounce the amount without careful practice. The opening balance on January 1, 1924, reckoned in gold marks, restored some meaning and solidity to the calculation at 30 million gold marks. But it is clear that the disastrous times left many a difficult legacy when it came to resolving internal differences, for example in calculating German and foreign participation, or in deciding what standards of comparison for the long-term valuation of capital assets, goodwill, and so on should be taken as the basis for reconciling private and company interests.

An organizational measure that had been in the making for quite some time, objectively and in terms of personnel, occurred during this period of inflation: the Bosch Metal Works AG in Feuerbach lost its status as an independent business. The separate founding of the Metal Works in 1917 had occurred essentially in order to accommodate a personal leadership role for Eugen Kayser; it had also had the effect of publicizing the fact that the stamping and metal works was not merely an auxiliary operation for Stuttgart but a free agent with the ability to attract its own customers. Naturally this would remain so. But the Metal Works had become more and more essential for the special needs of the parent company in Stuttgart due to the growing need for standardized products from the casting and die works. The interlocking character of the two corporations had been expressed in their personnel policies through the exchange of board members. On October 30, 1923, Robert Bosch AG took a leasehold on Bosch Metal Works AG, thus simplifying the organizational structure. The Metal Works AG continued to exist as a corporate entity for some time, primarily in order to administer the real estate. Five years later, on August 5, 1928, the final merger was completed. The independent company vanished; from now on it would be the metal works department. With the merger, the sales tax also disappeared since there was no longer a sale involved; this had an important impact on pricing, for the stabilization of the currency and a shortage of cash forced the firm to calculate its profit margins very closely.

After 1923 the property in Feuerbach, where the headlight factory had been built, became the site of an impressive new facility. As early as 1914 Eugen Kayser, with the encouragement of Gustav Klein, had added a ceramics department as part of the stamping works. Robert Bosch's notion of being independent from the producers of magnets and semifinished products was felt once again, and they began to fire their own insulation materials for the spark plugs. In 1917 the Metal Works gave control of this subsidiary over to the Light Works, where it became an operating division, but the space there had been cramped for some time. In the spring of 1922 they decided to build a new facility for the Insulation Works. If its principal task until now had been to fire the insulation mass needed for spark plugs, and to form the insulation elements for generators, battery connections, and so on, now a new goal was formulated that had implications for the entire future scientific and technological development of factory materials—Bakelite! Here was an important new territory to explore. The continuing development of electrical engineering, with the enormous temperature demands it faced, led to additional intensive research on the subject of material resistance.

Basically Bosch had to deal with only one competitor in Germany, Ernst Eisemann. He was a creative mechanic who had been independent since 1884 and wanted to make inroads in manufacturing with all kinds of designs—he had been involved in a lawsuit with Edison over the phonograph—and he had begun to get involved with manufacturing spark plugs in 1899. In the design he was using, the magneto device generated a low-voltage primary current, which was transformed into high-voltage current through an external transformer. Although the form invented by Honold was more compact, this did not prevent Eisemann, too, from having his admirers. He had achieved a solid position in Frankfurt and the United States, and now he was beginning to hire representatives in Germany. But he was working with other people's money.

His financial backers were undoubtedly capable business advisers, but the fact that he was subject to the influence of the banks, which were gradually becoming noticeably restrictive, made it seem reasonable to approach Bosch, which one of the partners did. Bosch, with ten times the level of sales, was by far the stronger of the two, but he did not dismiss the suggestion of a merger. They had already had an agreement, in 1912, in the form of a mutual customer protection pact; it had led to Bosch's confidential participation in the business when Eisemann & Company was refinanced in 1916 as a joint stock company, Eisemann AG. The situation that followed the stabilization of the mark made it advisable to take the next step, an arrangement resembling the recent leasehold agreement with the Metal Works, the ultimate goal being a merger. The public announcement was muted for tactical business reasons. It stated that "the question of an agreement within certain limits" had been discussed, and had demonstrated "a coincidence of views." "In the short term," they were considering an agreement on types and forms of products, joint purchase of raw materials, and an increased use of semifinished products from the Metal Works and the Insulation Works. In practical terms, in the course of development the leadership of the manufacturing business soon came to be concentrated at Bosch, with Ernst Eisemann assuming the role of technical adviser. The Eisemann company, with its experienced sales apparatus, remained as distributor. It, too, had its own markets and customers, and the predecessor company was still engaged in lawsuits involving damages in the United States!

This agreement with Eisemann had gone fairly smoothly, in contrast to the long-term competition with the Mea factory in Feuerbach, the other Württemberg factory that had grown up in Bosch's shadow and was engaged in the manufacture of ignition devices. Founded in 1909 by a financier from a completely different branch of industry (who had also been interested in financing Bosch), the Mea firm led a rather turbulent financial life. A merger with Bosch was proposed more than once. He had come to the conclusion that the company had been formed and pumped up with capital for the sole purpose of being offered to him for purchase. He remained cool, but gradually Mea began to make its presence felt; Eisemann had also run up against it and had even become embroiled in a patent lawsuit with it. Mea launched a public relations offensive against Bosch in connection with battery ignition, which was making a comeback in America, and the game began—something that was rather unusual in the history of the firm—as the Bosch board issued polemical declarations against the neighbor who had settled in Feuerbach and had lured away workers. But all that was only tactical skirmishing. More interesting, from the standpoint of industry politics, was the fact that following numerous financial participants of varying capacity—the Rosenfeld, Scharrer, and Gontard groups and Max Wild—the AEG eventually emerged as the owner of the factory. The large Berlin firm wanted to gain a solid manufacturing foothold in southern Germany, as Siemens had done through its merger with Schuckert Nuremberg. Did they think they might win Bosch over to a closer cooperation, as Mix & Genest had planned two decades earlier? The AEG had recovered from the setbacks of its first twenty years, while Bosch had been more severely affected by the crisis in the German automobile market. The AEG believed they could discern a weakening of his position from the business reports, and it looked for a time as if a power struggle might break out, a struggle that could be avoided. Dr. Hermann Bücher had been brought into the leadership of the AEG in 1925. After the years of tension and friction between the two firms, his personal friendship with Bosch had a broadly beneficial effect. The AEG, following a proposal from Bücher that Bosch accepted "with goodwill," removed itself from the realm of the ignition and parts industries entirely. Bosch took over the real estate, machines, and facilities of Mea, but not its financial assets and obligations. He also paid a form of indemnification. The AEG renounced its rights to appear as a competitor for fifteen years.

Before things reached this point and a certain degree of clarity was achieved on the German ignition market, the Bosch firm had been forced to struggle hard to regain its world position, a struggle that for all its negative aspects was waged with a certain optimistic vigor. The period of time during which the design department was bringing forth new products necessitated the restructuring of the sales operation as well as the profound transformation of the manufacturing process itself.

In the prewar years, a particular achievement of Gustav Klein and Hugo Borst had been to develop a network of foreign representatives and showrooms, which were just beginning to be opened in Germany. The most important of these were located in formerly hostile territory and had been lost due to the war. The confiscation of the salesrooms and furnishings represented millions of marks in losses compared to which the obligatory compensation by the German Reich was small comfort indeed. Fortunately, the neutral countries provided a kind of springboard for regaining an international presence. Holland was particularly important—and also paved the way for a solution in Belgium. In Switzerland, Geneva was developed, but patience would be needed before business picked up there. In Italy, a leading member of the earlier sales staff was involved in the reopening, which was an advantage. Things were more difficult in France. Max Rall and Hermann Fellmeth were now in the headquarters in Stuttgart, and their experience abroad seemed important enough. Rall, for example, traveled to Prague to investigate the new territory there. But it must have been unthinkable, in the first years after the war, that a German might once again head up a Paris subsidiary. They had to settle for authorizing a Frenchman, Fernand Péan, to sell their products on the French market, supported by credits from Stuttgart. Until this was worked out, there was a struggle with the speculator who had bought Bosch's property, which had been sequestered at auction, and who wanted to extort half a million francs from Bosch before he would give back the name! Fellmeth skillfully succeeded in getting this overly ambitious gentleman to settle for a tenth of his claim. In England, matters went more smoothly. There was no struggle over the name, for the well-respected firm of Vickers & Company had bought the Bosch rights at auction there, and their own name seemed good enough. But what Vickers produced fell short of the expectations of his fellow countrymen. When better products gradually began to be manufactured in England by others, "American Bosch" tried to penetrate the market, securing a trademark for its name from an English court, and two former employees of the Bosch subsidiary in England announced their willingness to attempt a new start. The former technical director, Emil Schwer, had returned from internment and had begun to rebuild the most important sales office in Germany after Berlin—Frankfurt am Main. In London, the newly reestablished firm of J. A. Stevens Ltd. bravely and eagerly took over the Bosch business. A Bosch Magneto Company for Scotland was founded in Glasgow in 1924. The name was back on the market, but access to its products was more limited than it had been because Britain had introduced a protective tariff. Would it not be better to start their own production? Attempts to arrive at an understanding with Vickers in 1925 went awry. When they were finally able to move ahead with this decision, their most powerful competitor, Joseph Lucas, proposed that they avoid market competition. Not until 1931 was a decision reached in this matter, and by then a change had also occurred in Paris.

The reorganization of the foreign dealerships with all this entailed in the way of difficult contracts, building construction, and personnel decisions, as well as the full development of the German sales offices, rested, in those postwar years, on the shoulders of Hugo Borst. It was also his job to create an intelligible and unified system of accounting, billing, and advertising that would be elastic enough to adapt to changing circumstances. Only a few years later, a well-developed system was put in place in Europe, and in 1921 they once again risked taking an independent role abroad—their second invasion of the United States. In the same year, Robert Bosch decided to take a major business trip abroad himself. He was hungry for new impressions and wanted to be alone to breathe the air of the wide world. He was hesitant, wondering "whether I can be absent here, for example if the French were to make an incursion, is something I am not quite sure about" (February 8, 1921). But the head office was encouraging. In the spring of 1921 he traveled to South America on a Dutch ship. Naturally, the firm had long since had its established representatives there, but because of the long distance the personal connection with them was very weak. They were absent from the annual business or technical meetings, the Bosch "parliaments" at which slogans were announced and experiences discussed. Hence Bosch's visit also had a certain symbolic value. For the head of the firm, now in his sixtieth year, to subject himself to the rigors of the trip was an honor and an acknowledgment. He was thus properly welcomed and celebrated, but this was not what he had in mind. He wanted to see for himself with his own sharp eyes what kind of developmental potential existed in the countries in which the wartime business, despite certain obstacles, had paved the way for increased independence from Europe. He visited Rio, Buenos Aires, and Santiago. The business situation he encountered was not exactly encouraging, for the crises in European politics had reverberations here, too. But ultimately the counsel of his advisers contained a good measure of faith, and Bosch himself, who in his letters home to the family noted zoological and botanical observations, was impressed by the wide open spaces of these countries and the energy with which they were approaching the economic tasks. The fruit of the trip, from a business standpoint, was Bosch's decision to create a salesroom in Buenos Aires, which opened for business in the spring of 1924. The annual report for the year could state that "there are now 21 such salesrooms (11 of them in their own buildings), compared with 13 in 1914." The same report could list "new sales representatives hired in the year under review in Ecuador, Honduras, Jamaica, Persia, Santo Domingo, Trinidad, and several territories of East Africa." It sounds like a final harvest, and it was, for only five years after the end of the war the world was once again open for Bosch. Australia, which had long resisted the import of Bosch products out of political chauvinism, opened up in the summer of 1923 after a change of the country's leadership.

The business reports of those years could boast of new buildings constructed in Milan, Vienna, Prague, Budapest, and Stockholm, and branches in Rome, Turin, Glasgow, Chicago, and other cities. In Germany after 1925, the number had to be increased to include Eisemann's former offices. By the early 1920s the salesrooms were surrounded by a large number of smaller repair workshops, testing stations, spare parts warehouses, and so on. It was free competition American-style, whose slogan was "customer service," and it had given new and effective forms to the time-tested thrust of all sales—getting products to people who needed them. The new methods could not be adopted in Germany until the motor vehicle business revived and sales companies, acting as buyers for spare parts and accessories, began appearing alongside the small number of factories. Here they assumed a very large significance. Bosch, like Opel, had gotten involved on a large scale. The "Bosch service," which opened in large and then also in small cities, was well received, and only a few years later it was taken for granted; people missed it in the places where it did not exist. Setting it up was no small matter, however, especially when it came to finding suitable people. When he was unable to find people who had been trained in his own firm to act as his representatives, Bosch had to entrust his name to strangers. In most cases it was a matter of involving local experts, making them sufficiently familiar with Bosch's standards and getting them to understand how much depended on their technical conscientiousness and skill. It must not be merely business, but an honor as well to be able to put up the sign "Bosch service."

Although the Bosch service had not been created as an element of advertising, once it was there it became one of the company's most important tools. In the years of rapid development, there had been no advertising department, as Robert Bosch had then thought advertising to be a waste of money; the orders came pouring in on their own, and after the high-voltage ignition device was introduced it was almost impossible to fill them all. There was also a tactical business consideration. If they talked a lot about their specialties, they would only arouse the interest of the big capitalists in the field of electrical engineering. Bosch wanted to grow, but quietly so to speak, and by convincing people rather than talking them into something. But the Bosch representatives abroad may have expressed the need for advertising material more keenly than those in Germany itself. In the year 1908, after August Euler had given the sales rights for Germany back to the firm, they had begun to engage in direct customer advertising for the first time; they had a poster and an advertisement with a picture. Then, in connection with the full development of

the sales operation, Hugo Borst systematized it. He hired Lucian Bernhard, a graphic artist from Stuttgart, and with his own artistic sensibility
helped to develop a unified style that was on a very respectable level and
included posters (with and without pictures), type design, exhibition
booths, stationery, and the like. Bernhard used good spatial effects and
rather muted but clean colors to simplify the basic structure of the technical devices and produce an enlightening characterization of the individual processes. The art was never loud or garish. Their trademark, the
armature in a circle, had been drawn by Gottlob Honold in late 1918 in
a moment of inspiration and now took its place on all products from the
workshop, along with the Bosch name. Magneto ignition required the
least advertising. It was more important for the later products such as
light generators, headlights, the Bosch horn, and power brakes, so they
began to look around for a comprehensive advertising slogan. One American slogan was fresh enough: "Good, Better, Bosch!" It was soon
dropped. The staff was asked to contribute suggestions as part of a competition, and many strange phrases were concocted. The slogan that was
chosen was "Get ready with Bosch, and the trip will go well." The phrase
had a lilt that stuck in one's mind.

Bosch himself did not participate much in the initiation of the advertising, but he followed it with critical interest. No unnecessary decoration; clear, legible writing; text as simple as possible. In a letter to the
Frankfurt Newspaper of June 27, 1932, he made a few basic comments:
"That advertising is necessary cannot be disputed. One can have the
most diverse opinions about the amount of advertising that is needed. I
am aware, for my part, that my success is due more to the quality of my
products than to advertising. Others will have to take the opposite position and they will sell their products more dearly, the more they advertise." He completely rejected all requests and propaganda about buying
German products. It contradicted his belief in free trade, and he
brusquely rejected the "manipulation of public opinion" (July 11, 1922)
by means of a "united German trademark," in which a black, red, and
white flag was supposed to be used on sales to foreign countries. This
suggestion was "completely mistaken, not to say crazy. I am proud to be a
German and I claim to produce exemplary products, but I cannot make
up my mind to deck them out with the black, white, and red flag. First, for

political reasons: the German flag is black, red, and gold. Second, because I will and must sell my products, and sell them, among others, to people who prefer not to buy German products if they can get a non-German product of the same quality. And third, because there are also poor-quality German products, which I do not want to excuse by association with my good ones."

The description of the manufacturing accomplishments and organizational expansion of the 1920s almost looks like the reflection of an even development, a repetition with a perhaps somewhat flatter curve, of the firm's tempestuous rise between 1908 and 1914. Within this context, the increases in business capital and the issuing of bonds might appear as unclear reflections of the decline in the currency and nothing more. The reality was not at all like this. Robert Bosch embarked on the new voyage well equipped, it is true, better than many others even though he had given away his war profits in charitable gifts that ran into the millions. The substance could be found in the undiminished quality of his work, which was ultimately able to survive political bans, defensive tariffs, and imitations, but this survival had its very difficult days and aspects. The market situation, given the unstable character of the exchange rates and the differing rhythms with which economic uncertainty visited the various countries—the victors as well as the vanquished and the neutral countries—was subject to endless fluctuations. The period of inflation, to the extent that one was not concerned about the trick of balancing the books, or the losses that the poor record of payments necessarily imposed on the domestic German market, might seem halfway tolerable as a way of getting back into the business outside Germany. Bosch wrote to Wilhelm von Opel in February 1921, "Our export now makes up 15 percent" (as opposed to 90 percent before the war). This was an indication that German automobile manufacturers were misleading themselves about the level their exports had achieved. The latter, it is true, would grow very rapidly in the following year.

Bosch had to put up with accusations at that time that the increases he made to the base price levels that had been established after the war were too large. He rejected the claim: the 1,500 or 1,200 percent increases for light generators and spark plugs were significantly less than the 2,500 percent being charged elsewhere in the electrical industry. But there were repeated and rather testy exchanges with several firms that claimed Bosch was too expensive and that the share of the accessories in the overall cost of the automobiles was too large. These voices could not be ignored, for the efforts of the German automotive industry to make a new start were naturally of the greatest importance for Bosch too. But relations continued to be accompanied by friction for some time—for example, when the producers of motor vehicles, after the stabilization, began to call for tariff protection. This was understandable. On the one hand, it is true, the eagerness to found and build up new businesses had led to many mistakes. Here a reversal, although painful, would be healthy. Many merely speculative ventures vanished as quickly as they had appeared. As these things were being cleared up, the financial and organizational superiority of foreign competitors who had developed the small car was oppressive; many people feared it would be deadly. For Bosch the situation was not clear-cut. He had an interest in the revival and increasing strength of German automobile production, but he also feared that an exclusionary policy would call forth countermeasures from abroad, which would undoubtedly have less effect on the automobile manufacturers than on him and on related industries.

Bosch had always demanded good prices for his products, and when people complained he had answered that they were perfectly free to go elsewhere. His monopoly had not come about as a result of capitalist control of the market, or protection through patents, but quite simply through the quality of the work he did. And he could say to himself: Isn't the most expensive product you can buy, in this case, precisely the cheapest when it comes to using it? Reliable, durable, easy to repair; just because the cars themselves were getting worse or at least were not designed to have such a long life, did that mean he should lower the quality and prices of his products as well? He had no inclination to follow this kind of logic. The fact that Bosch was already thinking about later price policies during the inflationary time when business was picking up is nicely shown by Honold's words during a meeting of the managing directors on March 22, 1922: "We want to deliver the best, but it does not necessarily mean it has to be the most expensive!" The struggle over price had to be waged during the following years. It was carried out not so much on the market, via delivery contracts, as in the struggle over internal production costs and the changeover of the manufacturing process itself.

The continuing uncertainties naturally had an effect on the continuity of the workforce. If orders were not coming in, the work went into the warehouses. This seemed quite appropriate; at least the firm was creating definite value. It was a way to survive. But with the currency stabilization the problem changed in more than one respect. Suddenly there was a lack of business capital—it was tied up in the warehouses—and sales were slow. Germany's unsurprising lack of capital—disguised by a cloud of meaningless numbers—was revealed. Interest rates climbed, and it became necessary to calculate as closely as possible. Now the inventories were no longer a source of pleasure. The firm could not go on increasing them, lulled by easy optimism. The large new facilities (the Insulation Works) had been finished before the capital shortage. After the prices for raw materials had stabilized, problems arose in the wage account. It became necessary to reduce the number of workers; the statistics for these years show a constant up and down. Naturally the firm attempted to keep trained workers on. Reductions in hours, not necessarily in the whole factory but in particular departments, were necessary as a means of getting through the difficulties, but the firm did not reduce the general overhead. The full warehouses, which had previously been looked at with a certain satisfaction, were now the subject of suspicious criticism. At Bosch, because of the durability of their products, they were compelled to continue producing spare parts for models they already considered outdated; the customer who wanted them should not be disappointed. But at this very moment, under the mounting pressure of events, the changeover of the manufacturing process began, leading to new norms that reduced the number of work processes. Technical refinements led to more complex solutions, and the firm was forced by external pressures to adopt changes even in their core area, ignition. Working in the old style, for inventory, was now out of the question. If they did not want to stand still—something they could not do—then every further advance might lead to a devaluation of the inventory they had just produced. Thus the internal organization of the plant remained extremely tense for years at a time. This tension was reflected in the dividend policy as well. During the period of inflation they had held back the dividends on several occasions as a necessary means of increasing the firm's capital; now, quite apart from the year 1926, which showed a loss, dividends were discontinued for years at a time, and the profits were used to increase the undisclosed reserves. They were needed for the changeover, but they were not sufficient.

The leadership of the firm experienced repeated changes and additions during the early 1920s. Zähringer's departure in 1914 and the deaths of Klein, Kayser, and Kempter had created noticeable gaps. In replacing these men, the firm was able to rely on men who had been displaced from positions abroad where they had proved themselves. Thus Max Rall, from the Paris office, had already been named a deputy member of the board of managers when the stock company was formed in 1917, and then became a full member of the board in 1920, replacing Kempter. The "Americans" returned at the end of 1919 and the beginning of 1920: Karl Martell Wild took over the leadership of the Metal Works, succeeding Kayser. Otto Heins became a full member of the board in 1920. His area of responsibility was not specified; he had the opportunity to define it himself. Would he be able to fill the gap that had been left by Gustav Klein? The board of managers also welcomed salesmen Guido Gutmann and Hermann Fellmeth, who became deputy members. Fellmeth, who was charged above all with winning back the foreign markets, was adept at numbers and was a tough, realistic negotiator who concealed his scientific interests and artistic hobbies. In addition, there was Richard Hochstetter, who had spent many years in positions at Brown-Boveri, Lahmayer, and the AEG before returning to his Swabian homeland in 1914 to take over the management of the new generator factory just being completed.

Honold remained the unquestioned authority in the development of all technical experiments, although he felt that he was not altogether suited for this role. His personal ambition was to loosen his tie to the current business and to become a kind of consultant in his own laboratory. In this way his inclination toward scientific research and inventive experimentation might be able to develop in a way that would be more personally satisfying while remaining no less productive for the factory. This arrangement was never fully realized, as Gottlob Honold died on March 17, 1923, not yet forty-seven years old, after a brief illness. Objectively, it was the bitterest loss Bosch and his business had suffered since the death of Gustav Klein. And two years later there was another painful loss: Ernst Ulmer died of a heart attack on November 23, 1925. For almost a quarter of a century, he had devoted his tireless energy to the firm; he had been the first salesman other than Bosch when the firm was still small. After the strike of 1913, Bosch had entrusted him with all of the external relations with the Employer's Association and the unions, and he had always considered this to be one of his most fortunate decisions. Ulmer approached this task, especially tricky during the confusion that followed the war, not with the diplomat's tricks or the tactician's interest in advantages and small victories but with a warmhearted honesty. He viewed and approached his negotiating partners from the point of view of common interests. His weapons were argument and common sense, and he would somehow try to find a workable, just compromise among the contradictions. This occurred in a completely unsentimental fashion, for he was not lacking in roughness and, where necessary, severity. But he had succeeded in accumulating such a store of human affection that this alone became a source of strength from which could be built a tradition that went well beyond his person. Robert Bosch said at his coffin: "I trusted in Ernst Ulmer as he trusted in me."

Finding a successor for Honold was less difficult than might have been expected given the man's eminent importance during the previous two decades. He himself had "discovered" Karl Martell Wild in friendly competition with Gustav Klein, and regarded him as the person who should one day replace him. Since 1920 Wild had carried on Kayser's legacy in the Metal Works in Feuerbach. Now, in the personnel reshuffling of April 14, 1923, he was named a regular member of the board of managers. He was responsible for the overall technical leadership of the firm, to which, when it came to large tasks, he would soon enough add his personal note. If Honold had taught the engineers how to design, Wild taught them how to calculate. The needs of fabrication were brought into even closer harmony with plans and designs. At the same time, Fellmeth assumed his role as a full member of the board of managers. The attorney Emil Kirchdörfer, who had been brought in by Ulmer in 1910 as the head of bookkeeping, and whose flexible and energetic style and sense of clarity had helped that department adapt to the growth of the firm, became a deputy member along with Dr. Erich Rassbach. With this, a new man, one who had not been a part of the factory's development, entered the leading group. He was a German-American who had been educated in Germany and America, had earned his spurs at Siemens-Schuckert in the railroad division, and had been involved, above all, in their foreign business. In 1922, after several other jobs, Rassbach had come to Bosch. His task was the technical handling of the non-German foreign business; in a certain sense it was he who became the actual successor to Klein, whose familiarity with the world he shared. And for the work that awaited him it was a not insignificant convenience that he possessed a neutral passport. As a technician he had also studied the theoretical problems connected with economic matters and had concluded his studies with a Ph.D. in government.

No less than eight leading staff members, on both the business and the technical side, were given general power of attorney on this occasion. Among them was Ernst Durst. Trained as a mechanic, he had come to work for Bosch in 1904 at the age of twenty-seven after having had a look at various companies in Germany and abroad. At Bosch, as he himself tells it, he encountered piecework for the first time. His particular achievement in the business was to work through the labor processes in a manner that could be termed experimental. After he became a master in 1908, he replaced the work in columns, in his department, by completely breaking down the work process, with the effect that production showed an immediate and substantial increase. This achievement earned him his personal reputation. There were other masters whose names had already been written into the history of the factory. Adolf Krauss, whose skill and original inventiveness had earned him a place at Honold's side, was, after 1898, the most reliable practical participant in the many experiments carried out in preparation for actual manufacture. There was also Otto Grimmeisen, whose mental agility and numerous new ideas, in combination with his Swabian thoroughness, had supported Max Rall in Paris until Gustav Klein made him his closest associate. Ernst Durst, who had been a senior master since 1910, developed his particular expertise in organization—the acquisition and management of tools. The war made him the head of the training workshop. This task played a significant role in deepening his insight into the changing work methods of the manufacturing process. It in no way diminished, in his eyes, the importance that the craft element played in a comprehensive basic education for any of the skilled jobs; he later wrote a short textbook for precision engineers, in which, along with its skill at educating, one can get a sense of Durst's abilities. The challenge pointed him toward the mass production of parts. When a central manufacturing bureau was instituted in the year 1918, in order to prepare for the production of newly approved designs and to do some new testing of traditional ways of doing things, it was Durst who was entrusted with its management. From this vantage point he stayed in touch with the needs and concrete conditions in the individual departments. Robert Bosch watched and encouraged Durst's rise with deep satisfaction. What he accomplished was daily proof of the exaggerated claims of academia. Durst grew into the tradition of Arnold Zähringer within the context of the larger dimensions the firm had now assumed. He was keenly self-disciplined, and he imposed this discipline on his unsophisticated and trusting temperament.

With the creation of the two stock companies in 1917, Robert Bosch had made his most important colleagues into co-owners. All of them, with the exception of Eugen Kayser, were significantly younger than he was. In the background was the psychological situation that had led Gustav Klein in particular to come out in favor of this step before the war. The family tensions that surfaced during the great labor struggle of 1913 had long since become history, not completely forgotten, but faded, and the objective situation had been accepted. But the death of men who had been leaders in the creation of the factory, and later co-owners, reopened this whole complex of questions. There were heirs. Should and could they be granted a right to participate in business decisions? Was any claim to future participation in the leadership of the firm implicit in their limited participation? Bosch, with a certain mistrustfulness of the danger of nepotism, resisted the thought that the sons of his directors, merely because they were sons, wanted to and should be permitted to grow into the company whether or not they were really suited for it. Hadn't the solution of 1917, which had taken 2 percent of his 51 percent share and put it in trust for a later sale to shareholders, been a clear passing over of his own children in favor of untested, unknown heirs if one looked beyond the present generation to the next one? This was what Bosch felt, and it tortured him. The relations of ownership had become more complex in several ways, for there were shares that had been created *before* 1917 and others in which the firm and the private individual Bosch appeared as separate entities. That he would serve as a source of credit for the firm had already been foreseen in the founding charter and continued to be the practice, in varying degrees, depending on the situation. Finding a balance between the capital needs of the firm and the status of his personal ownership, particularly during the period of inflation when all valuations rapidly became illusory, and the period of time that elapsed before payment robbed transactions of any lasting substance, required skill and firm goodwill if appropriate solutions were to be found.

It was the concern about the settling of these matters, as much as anything else, that led Robert Bosch to appoint the director of his personal office as a full member of the board of managers in 1924. Hans Walz had been a member of the supervisory board since 1919 and was familiar with the problems of their objective situation as well as with the personal relationships. He had earned Bosch's fullest trust in the care of Bosch's nonbusiness affairs, and yet he had simultaneously maintained his independent position. His business responsibilities would be decided in practice, in relationship to Borst and Fellmeth. At first it was a matter of carrying out a certain reversal in the relations of ownership; the clause concerning the 2 percent was soon overturned. But the actual definition of his job occurred in a way that was quite unwanted. After Ulmer's sudden death, Walz assumed the ultimate responsibility for company-wide personnel management. On April 1, 1926, he was joined by Otto Debatin. The department of workers' affairs was combined with the economic office and became the economic secretariat, which now reported to him. For the moment, editorial control of *The Bosch Spark Plug* remained in his hands. The technical control of the private office was transferred to Willy Schlosstein, who had been a notary and would later become Walz's closest colleague. The responsibilities of Bosch's private office included public and philanthropic activities, as well as efforts in the fields of health policy and agriculture, which had assumed considerable importance of their own.

Professor Richard Stribeck took Walz's place on the board of managers in 1924. Bosch had called on his old student friend, after Stribeck had retired from Krupp's board of managers and returned home to Swabia, for advice on several matters close to his heart—the top-ranking expert in the field of ball bearings had become a silo builder! One needed, it seemed, only to give Stribeck a task and he would find the solution. Thus the company was glad to make use of him for special assignments. The metallurgist became an expert in ceramics; later on, when a solution needed to be found for diesel engine ignition, he was able to help the designers make the decisive breakthrough by drawing on his insight into physical questions. In inviting the friend of his youth, whose professional authority he was glad to accept, and whose outspoken, casual sarcasm he very much enjoyed, to join the board of managers of the factory, Bosch wanted to clearly express their renewed connection.

27

———•———

DEALINGS WITH
AMERICA

During the prewar years the American side of the business had been the most powerful force behind the rapid development of the company in Stuttgart. It was in large part thanks to the number of dollars coming from America that the Bosch firm was able to build the large factories in Feuerbach without outside capital. How lucrative would this market be in the future?

Bosch and his colleagues had been worrying about this question since 1917, when the United States had entered the war. Since then, a development had appeared there that would have a fateful effect on the industry of postwar Europe, particularly Germany, and specifically on Robert Bosch's factory: the debtor nation was being transformed into a creditor nation. At the same time, the war production, with its unvarying types of goods, gave a powerful impulse to the existing tendency in America's manufacturing facilities to replace human work by mechanical means. The face of industrial work seemed to be completely transformed. America was rediscovered in the first years after the war by professors of economics, technicians, and journalists. No one missed a chance to write about and expound on the words "assembly line," with either enthusiasm or a certain amount of apprehension. There was no immediate unanimity among those who tried to comprehend its possible social and psychological requirements and consequences, including its long-range economic impact on such things as international markets. Was this the specialty of a geographically large country lacking in skilled workers derived from the crafts, which was erasing, or at least evening out, all differences in a process of mass transformation that was therefore unthinkable for Europe, with its many cultural and national differences thrown together in a small area? Or, if one wanted to survive, did one have to recognize it as the model of a future that was inescapable and that must therefore be carefully studied?

The question did not catch Robert Bosch and his colleagues unawares. Bosch had always paid attention to the constant review of the best in manufacturing. Hugo Borst had studied F. W. Taylor and had explained his thinking in lectures, and although the firm had rejected the accusation, when it was expressed during the strike in 1913 that at Bosch, Taylor was in charge, the company did follow similar practices in the selection of people for specific tasks. It is not unimportant that at Bosch, for example, they attached great value to handwriting analyses of the mental qualities and especially the character traits of applicants. The refinement of piecework wages, which had been assigned to a special department, was in accordance with a basic direction that they were now forced to discover not for the first time. This whole complex of questions became urgent once inflation had been overcome and the insoluble problems connected with reparations and a repressed economy had worked themselves out. It became linked to the tensions in Germany's internal politics around 1930; hadn't the tendency to look to America been a deception, the American model a false one, the optimistic talk of the technocrats nothing but an unconscious mockery of human reason—rationalization as the road to growing human misery?

At Bosch they approached this question both practically and theoretically. Robert Bosch, Karl Martell Wild, Otto Fischer, and Otto Debatin participated through *The Bosch Spark Plug*. In the process, they clarified the lines of demarcation that separated them from the American model. They had drawn their conclusions from the American experience boldly and decisively, but the outcome had not been immediately comprehensible to everyone. Technical progress during a period of dangerous economic and social disorder had to be defended against its own supporters.

The discussion at Bosch in this area was only part of a debate that was being carried out on an international, even intercontinental, scale. Its economic and intellectual importance could have been historic had it not been confused by the undertone of the international political exchange, which alternated between fear and boastfulness, insight and nonsense.

At first there were narrower concerns that were linked to the course of North American politics. These concerns took abrupt, sometimes embarrassing, and occasionally bizarre turns, and went on for a decade. But at the end, after a number of formal defeats, they ended with a kind of victory that took the form of a peaceful agreement. This was the struggle over compensation for the Bosch Magneto Company, which had been founded by Otto Heins and Gustav Klein, as well as Bosch's struggle in the American courts to retain his name.

The sequestering and liquidation of German property in the territories ruled by the former Allied powers took different forms, although their overall tendency was the same. Sequestration always came right away; the pace of the liquidation, or sale, differed. The American law of October 1917 wanted to allow sales of German property only under certain circumstances; the later famous Alien Property Custodian, A. J. M. Palmer, had interpreted Congress's law of 1917 as intended to protect foreign property, and had characterized himself as a trustee: "There is absolutely no intent to sell or damage this property." This fine opinion did not stand up for long. It may be that the reports Palmer received from his European colleagues affected his thinking; more likely, his own desire for power had grown. He now pursued the expansion of his authority, with the effect that in March 1918 he was given the option of selling the sequestered properties. Only Americans were to benefit, however. On December 7, 1918, Palmer sold the Bosch Magneto Company at auction for the sum of $4,150,000. A certain Martin E. Kern was the buyer. The sale price may have amounted to somewhat less than half the actual value of the company.

The Treaty of Versailles had confirmed this wartime practice and had come up with the formula according to which the profit from German private property that had been sequestered, after the satisfaction of private claims against Germany, was deposited in a reparations account. The government of the Reich was given the responsibility of compensating its citizens; this empty phrase was meant to overcome the objection that taking away private property was in contradiction to international legal practice. This regulation created a wretched difficulty and poisoned the country's internal politics as well as the international discussion over the actual contribution, desire to contribute, and capacity for contributions by the defeated German Reich. The fact that the American Congress did not follow President Wilson but refused to ratify the treaty created a rather peculiar legal situation as far as the further treatment of German property in the United States was concerned. It had still not been clarified in the Berlin Treaty of August 25, 1921. But in the years that followed, in the course of the discussions back and forth about American claims (the costs of occupation and so on), the fate of German property developed into a domestic political scandal of great magnitude. True, it was never associated with a particular political party, but it came to serve as a kind of escape valve for much of the disappointment created as a result of Wilson's policies. This led to tough exchanges in public debates and to fights in both houses of Congress. Certain idealistic tendencies struggled to the fore, to the effect that Palmer had completely destroyed the meaning of sequestration and had begun a series of corrupt actions. Highly realistic interests also came into play, since large legal firms, which also understood how to lobby politically, were representing the injured parties. When the German parties offered to make a deal, the political situation was relieved through the use of semiofficial agreements, and after much uncertainty things reached the point by 1928 where a "bill of release" could be made out to the original owner at up to 80 percent of the sale price. The fact-finding process had to be carried out in long and difficult proceedings. On the whole, one can say that the fundamental state of American politics was affected by the new situation in which the country, as a developing creditor nation, found itself. In the future, the citizens of the United States would be creditors; their money would be invested in facilities all over the world, and these facilities might one day be in need of protection. In that case, their own practice in America should not be able to be cited as a model for the sale or dispersal of private property.

Bosch had made friends he had left behind in America, but the American Bosch Magneto Corporation (ABMC), as the company now called itself, had not understood how to maintain relationships or make new ones. It sounded quite optimistic when Bosch wrote to Fritz Egnell, in Stockholm, as early as February 21: "The news from America sounds quite positive. There can be no doubt that we will get our property back over there." This was quite premature, and they would still have to go through some rather unpleasant experiences with the ABMC—and not only in America, for its subsidiaries turned up in Copenhagen, Barcelona, Milan, and other cities in Europe, and even tried to penetrate the English market. It did not help that old customers complained about the quality of the products or the lack of cooperation on the part of the new firm. The ABMC was there, and it was a source of difficulty and misunderstanding.

After peace had been established between Germany and the United States, in the summer of 1921 Borst and Heins made a trip to New York. They simply started over. In September 1921, Otto Heins founded the Robert Bosch Magneto Company together with the German-American Günther Jahn, who had been the treasurer of the old company, and the lawyer Harvey T. Andrews. They received the sole manufacturing and sales rights for Bosch products. The economy was in a slack period at the time, and in Springfield, where 2,000 people had once worked, only 200 remained—and they were taking several days a week off! But when one looked at the number of automobiles crowding the streets it was obvious that one day there would again be a market for Bosch products.

This much was clear: the situation continued to portend struggle. In the question of the actionable character of the auction that had taken place in December 1918, Bosch and his advisers did not believe they had a basis for suing. It was a pleasure for the lawyers to discover that the purchaser from Alsace, Martin E. Kern, had an assortment of criminal activities in his past, and that he had been German at the time of purchase, but was now a French citizen. These revelations, which were given to the press, made quite an impression all by themselves. But he had only been a straw man; now there were solid American capitalists in the management, and they were not so easily upset by the revelations. For them, Kern was merely part of the stage set. But the fact that now, after he had already spent two years attacking their right to use the Bosch firm's name, this Robert Bosch was sitting in New York and was about to get in their way not only with his products but with his trademark and name as well—this was something the new owners would not stand for.

Harvey T. Andrews was not a stranger to Bosch. Gustav Klein had had dealings with him when he had arrived in America in 1906 with a suitcase full of ignition devices. At that time Andrews had held the position of general appraiser, the senior appraiser for factory tariffs in the New York Customs Office. Klein had had to engage in a legal fight with Andrews then, and he had succeeded. Andrews was already familiar, from a different angle, with the substance of ignition devices. Now, as the lawyer for the Bosch interests and as a cofounder of the new subsidiary, he really went to work. He mobilized public opinion to the point at which a government lawsuit was finally initiated against Palmer on the basis of his sales practices; then Andrews won over to his side the attorney who had been entrusted with the matter. The fight for Bosch's proprietary rights in the United States was carried on with considerable verve. In the beginning, flush with confidence, Andrews had financed it himself and he continued to do so unabashedly. Along with his business sense and an idealistic interpretation of the law, there was a measure of sporting ambition in the agility and flexibility with which he approached the changing circumstances of the battle. His manner and his influence had an impact on the fate of the laws concerning release of sequestered property in general.

On one legal question close to Bosch's heart, not only from a business but also from a personal point of view, the Bosch firm experienced a defeat before the Supreme Court of the State of New York. Bosch was to be deprived of his name not only for products that had been made in America, but also for those from Stuttgart! He could have had a good laugh and ultimately even taken pride in the fact that his name had taken on such objective significance in America that, independent of his person, it had become the symbol for a certain group of products of the highest quality. But he did not see it in an ironic or romantic light, and the capable attorney to whom he had entrusted the case didn't see it that way either. He was girding himself for a campaign that would take the firm to the highest authority. The decision had provided a starting point which, if skillfully exploited, could not help but make an impression on public opinion and on people's sense of justice, for the judge had scarcely been able to conceal his own inner uncertainty and had characterized the decision as "drastic and ruthlessly arbitrary, which could only be justified by the war, but from a national standpoint the war had in fact justified it." The directors of the American Bosch Magneto Corporation themselves had a sense of the uncertainty that characterized such a resolution, the more so since the press and Congress continued to be displeased over the cases of corruption surrounding Palmer, and there was the unpleasant prospect of a lawsuit against him. Thus, surprisingly enough, a proposal for an out-of-court settlement came from the party who had formally been declared the winner. Robert Bosch accepted. He detested court battles even in his own country, and the requirements posed by the unfamiliar legal process, with its hearings, depositions, and protocols, irritated him; he had been forced to suffer through it a couple of times before. Thus he may have welcomed the opportunity to free himself of these matters, which had been dragging on for almost ten years, as long as the offer was honestly meant and might lead to a reasonable result.

On October 26, 1929, the "peace treaty" between the man from Stuttgart and the partner in Springfield—which is how *The Bosch Spark Plug* referred to the deal—was signed in Paris. It comprised a number of parts. The ABMC withdrew its claims to the proceeds of the sale and agreed to work to speed up the release of the funds. The court cases were quashed. The core of the agreement was the decision on the question of the name: from then on the Stuttgart firm and its representatives were to have the uncontested right to appear in the United States under the full name "Robert Bosch." In the rest of the world the short form "Bosch" also belonged to it exclusively. The ABMC was permitted to sell its products in North America only under the name "Bosch"; if it crossed the border, it had to use the name "American Bosch." Robert Bosch AG also gave up the right to use the advertising figure of the red devil; this was not too difficult, since at the main office they had long since abandoned this early graphic attempt, although a few foreign offices might still be using it. But that was of no consequence. The parties to the agreement assured each other in a general clause that they would practice fair competition and would provide mutual support in respect to third parties.

It was a solution, but only a temporary one. The business report of Robert Bosch AG of June 6, 1930, already mentioned the possibility of new "more detailed agreements." These had meanwhile been prepared, and in a most realistic fashion. As stock prices were low during the period of the world economic crisis, which was now also weighing heavily on the United States, Bosch had begun to buy up stock in the ABMC. The result was a shift, and ultimately a change, in the majority ownership of the American company. In October 1930, things had matured to the point where a new contract was concluded, bringing about the merger of the American Bosch Magneto Corporation in Springfield and the Robert Bosch Magneto Company, Inc., in New York into the United American Bosch Corporation in Springfield. They omitted the "Magneto" because the factory in Springfield had already modified its program some time before, and had begun, among other things, to make radios. The "United" was meant to express the end of the fraternal struggle and the equal rights of the two merging Bosch firms. Robert Bosch AG transferred its representation rights in the United States and Canada wholly to the new firm and received the right to carry the American products in its non-American sales organizations. With this, Robert Bosch AG regained the freedom to use the unadorned name Bosch in the *entire* world, including North America, whereas the American firm was limited, in all of its products, to the brand name "American Bosch." Bosch could be satisfied with this result. Its success, admittedly, was a gamble on the future, for first they had to carry the losses that corresponded to the decline of the American economy.

In barely two decades, automobile manufacturing had become one of the key industries of the United States and had transformed the reputation of that great territory, as well as the rhythm of its life and the habits of its population. Those hardy adventurers of the postwar period who told tales of the assembly line naturally talked a lot about this invention. They did not miss an opportunity to repeat the rows of statistics about how many cars left, or could leave, every day for the market from Henry Ford's workshops in Detroit. Then there was the traffic congestion in New York to be described; with astonishment, they saw towers with traffic lights rising, colored light signals guiding drivers and pedestrians. On leaving the city they could turn into broad, asphalt roads, arterial highways that at night were bathed in the mild light of streetlights and covered great distances. Soon they came across gas stations at which they could get oil, fuel, and water, and where they could charge or change their batteries; they also found skilled hands that made quick work of any minor repairs their vehicles might require. These gas stations awakened the particular interest of visitors. Whether they were primitive or fully developed, they appeared, in their organizational form, to be one of the most astonishing peculiarities among the many novelties America offered. All the things that would later become banalities in Germany, too, were described and received, at the time, like fairy tales. Without a doubt, in the United States the motor vehicle had become a social force; people were making it serve their interests by serving it. And Bosch could say that he had a most active part in it, both in giving and in taking. But after the first turbulent upswing, the Bosch firm was forced to recognize that most of the new cars were not using the magneto ignition that they had so ardently desired only a short while earlier. They had switched to battery ignition, in which the Bosch spark plug might still play a role. Otto Heins had noticed this movement in the sales curve in a report as early as 1912. After the war, battery ignition had simply taken over as far as private automobiles were concerned. The same general conditions that had quickly covered the country with a network of emergency and supply depots had paved the way for this development. Ultimately, the decisive issue was price. Battery ignition was cheaper, and the overall development in America was aimed not so much at the greatest imaginable technical perfection as at the creation of a respectable average that would be affordable and easily serviceable for an ever-growing number of users. From the first moment that American automobiles began to penetrate the European market, they influenced the form of ignition, first in France, and later, after the stabilization of the currency, in Germany as well. Bosch was forced to consider how he would respond. Personally, it was not easy for him to let go, in a certain sense, of the magneto ignition that had replaced Daimler's ignition tube and had finally even won out over

Benz. But in the final analysis, it was not a question of being right in some ideal technical sense but a matter of maintaining the leading position in the motor vehicle industry. In the middle of the 1920s, Bosch began to develop battery ignition and simultaneously to improve upon it in connection with the light generator and voltage or current regulators; Bosch and his colleagues were not sure whether the new development would hold, or whether, as the business report for 1926 noted, magneto ignition might make a comeback as it was doing in England. A comment made in 1929 (*The Bosch Spark Plug*, no. 10) observed with a certain satisfaction that Bosch battery ignition "has not only rapidly gained acceptance in Germany; it is already used quite often now in American automobiles, as well." The final consequence of this technical and economic development was that Bosch, who had been obtaining the batteries from specialized factories, became involved in manufacturing in this area too.

The fate of various ignition devices is only a marginal phenomenon in the great story of the struggle with America, which continued for many years. The struggle can be summed up—and not only at Bosch—under the catchwords *standardization* and *rationalization.* Each of these concepts was surrounded by a peculiar atmosphere; they were used as objective statements of fact, as well as emotionally urgent demands, but they also had an undertone of cultural distrust and complaint based on social considerations. Didn't these words mean the beginning of the death of creative individualism? Wasn't the standardization of the world of products merely a prelude to the standardization of human beings? Didn't the recognition of the sameness of the masses threaten precisely those things that had been the source of the attraction and power of Germany's young industry—the skillfulness of its individuals and the thoroughgoing artistry that derived from its craft origins? And wouldn't this path, if it finally led to "automation," rob "human" work of its soul to the extent that this work was even necessary anymore; wouldn't it lead, furthermore, to the redundancy of skilled and decently paid work? These issues would be the subject of eagerly pursued and often tortuous conversation in the years to come.

During the war, the large number of models and norms that existed in the German motor vehicle industry had been considered a great hindrance from a military point of view. The consequences of this situation were drawn only inadequately and hesitantly. A national council on manufacturing was formed, but not much came of it except some studies and memos. More successful were the proposals of the norms committee of the Association of German Engineers, but since the association lacked binding authority, its effectiveness was limited. In the years after the war, particularly in the automobile industry, the numerous new businesses that were founded and independent experiments that were made created more confusion than simplification. The resulting accomplishments may have been interesting and technologically and economically significant, but they were too narrowly market-oriented to encourage the development of a unified manufacturing program. Bosch suffered from this state of affairs. The needs of his customers forced him to deliver customized solutions, to whatever extent he reasonably could. At the same time, it was clear that this situation basically represented a waste of labor and raw materials. To the extent that it was possible, Bosch began to develop norms for spare parts within his own operation, and in 1923, the Bosch firm informed the great conference of technical representatives of the far-reaching limitation of models that had been agreed upon. If the customers wanted to be able to pay a more moderate price, they would have to be taught to understand.

In America, things were simpler, at least to the extent that the number of firms was small compared to the level of production, and almost all of the manufacturers—led by Henry Ford—were aiming not at an ever-changing variety of compelling innovations but at a stable average quality. American industrial capitalism presented an utterly conservative face. It didn't run after the latest thing but held fast to tried and tested types in order to distribute them widely by means of an attractive price policy. In his memoirs Robert Bosch commented about this development: "America devotes itself to the production of mass goods with a—I would like to say—passion, such that only very extraordinary efforts will be able to make inroads against it" (*The Bosch Spark Plug* 1926, no. 10). What Bosch called "passion," in a tone that was halfway between irony and admiration, was not only the rational business policy of private industry but was also a function of insistent governmental will. Since most people in Germany did not want to give up the notion of the United

States as a territory ruled by wild, unfettered individual capitalism without any governmental intervention, it was some time before they noticed that the U.S. Department of Commerce was playing a role in clearing the market of dispensable product types in thousands of articles of daily use. This was accomplished—with success—by means of education and propaganda, but was also helped by weaker or stronger pressure in the form of government procurements at an annual cost that ran into the millions. In Germany, as they read the reports about the waste of half-used products and conjured up unhappy images of decaying automobile cemeteries, the idea of a kind of pointless waste became lodged in their minds. They failed to recognize the psychological guidance that was being given by the government and was leading to the most rational use of labor power and valuable machines in accordance with the law of the conservation of economic and physical energy. Over the years this German error in judgment gradually took on a tragic aspect.

At Bosch they saw the situation quite clearly from the very beginning. If they wanted to regain their former position in the world market, or lay claim to that status, they could not avoid taking the American competition as seriously as possible. In quality, their products surpassed those that were appearing on the market in America. Bosch once noted, not without satisfaction, that in the prewar period, when Ford was producing 250,000 cars a year, he subsequently installed 30,000 Bosch ignitions as replacements for the ignitions from Detroit. Bosch had the greatest respect for Ford's *organizational* achievement, for the totality of his production program, which included raw material and semifinished goods, metal ores, wood, and glass, as well as the finicky accessories; this was only possible once and "only in such a big, rich, young country . . . There is no contradicting the fact that Ford has done humanity a great service. He made the automobile available in large quantities. The only thing one can accuse him of is that in the last two decades he has not contributed to the technical improvement of the automobile" (*The Bosch Spark Plug* 1927, no. 1). What were the terms of the comparison? "Ford can build one and a half million ignition systems a year, Chrysler needs at least 200,000; all of Germany needs about 60,000 a year. In France and England I pay 45 percent and 33⅓ percent entry tariff, in Italy 30 percent, in the United States I have to pay 30 percent. All the European firms together produce about 450,000 cars a year. There are about 50 factories in Germany; one can add those of the other European countries. Most of these firms want special orders for their production lines. And now the German manufacturer comes to me and says I should deliver the products as cheaply as an American."

When these sentences were being written, Bosch was already in the process of fighting the Americans with their own weapons, in order if not to defeat them, at least to prevent them from gaining the industrial ascendancy that many people in the United States already believed they had won. He also confronted them with American money. For the first time in the history of the factory, except for the insignificant (measured in gold) bonds of the inflation period, Bosch took advantage of the credit market; in 1926 he took out an American bond in the amount of $3 million, at 6 percent interest, secured in a mortgage and repayable in twenty annual installments beginning in 1930. The purpose of this sum was to prepare for a new manufacturing project that the Bosch firm wanted to undertake for the diesel engine, and to help continue increasing efficiency with the extensive new machine tool purchases it required.

This had been under way for years, with the reduction of the norms for types and individual processes coming first. It had not implied any change in the work process itself but had brought a decrease in cost thanks to the more frequent repetition of the same technological processes and, indirectly, to a very noticeable simplification of warehouse management. This had some effect on overall costs, but what had a major impact in this area was the decision to reduce the costs incurred in producing every single item, by means of the greatest possible division of labor and the removal of all uneconomical time loss. For this, new factory facilities, new machines, a new division of labor, and new materials were often needed, along with—last but not least—a new way of thinking. Implementation was largely the responsibility of Karl Martell Wild, who had personally observed the beginning of scientific production in America when it was completely new, and who had a good feel for the limits of what was possible in the way of simplification without sacrificing quality. Along with the further division of labor, the Bosch firm also increased the construction of conveyor belts and the installation of tracks for hauling materials, as well as the number of testing stations. The more they relied on trained in place of skilled workers, the more refined were the testing methods developed for semifinished goods and finished products. Visitors to the factory were always commenting on how sensibly and carefully the products were tested before they were allowed to be sent to the delivery warehouse. Precisely in those cases where not only labor-saving machines but also new raw materials were used—for example tin plate, which they would have disdained as beneath their dignity a few years earlier—the customer had to be assured that the decrease in price, which did not displease him, was not achieved through a loss of quality. In this task, which took years, Wild was supported by Ernst Durst, who had thoroughly immersed himself in the task of "getting rid of dead time." In a lecture he gave to the Working Group of German Plant Engineers, Durst presented the transition to assembly-line production clearly and soberly. He was the practical expert who achieved savings of time *and* space from the proper arrangement of machines, the accurate supply of parts, and so on. The entire development, beginning with the earlier stage of individual piecework, was still in his blood; he was conscious of how profound the transformation was, but he did not view it pessimistically. He calculated the savings of space at 70 percent and the reduction of the time it took to manufacture something at 50 percent. Durst's optimistic conclusion about rationalization was drawn in 1926, when the use of it was still new at Bosch. Robert Bosch himself, it must be said, although in basic agreement with the new arrangements, was not at first fond of many aspects of the technical innovations; his basic instincts were those of an artisan. This pressing and stamping of tin was certainly no longer precision engineering! In a speech at an anniversary celebration, he once remarked that they had made his factory into a "tin hut," a better-quality "tin factory." He sounded a bit upset, and this was also upsetting to hear. Bosch had to be told that this did not exactly increase the employees' pride in their work. He did not refer to it again, for he could not and did not deny that the new products did their job as well as the old ones had.

The rationalization that was so actively promoted and discussed in the mid-1920s was nothing fundamentally new. Whether one views it as an increase in the effectiveness of human labor itself, or of the mechanical activity derived from it, the entire history of technology is a process of increasing efficiency, during which only the tempo actually changes;

inertia is replaced by rapid change until another position of rest is reached. The introduction of the steam engine, of electrical power generation and transmission, were revolutionary processes of rationalization. People had other names for it; they talked about the progress of technology and believed in its blessings, but always to the accompaniment of opposition by those people who suffered devastating injuries as a result of this progress, or who believed they were endangered by it. The larger scale of the intercontinental comparisons raised these processes to a higher level of consciousness. The mechanical loom had once been the target of curses; even locomotives had had their opponents. The first effect of such innovations was always to throw some people out of work; later the innovations proved to be powerful creators of new opportunities for work. However, it was not the people immediately affected by the changes who realized this fact; economic historians with their statistics pointed it out. The question became urgent once more, but this time in a world of organized labor, which was especially susceptible to being swayed politically as a result of the war and its consequences. It was a typical symptom of the times when the entire workers' council of Robert Bosch AG turned against "this system" (of rationalization) in the spring of 1926. They feared it would lead to unemployment, "which will have a catastrophic effect on the working class . . . The entire workers council therefore requests categorically that the German trade unions use their influence to see that this disastrous system be opposed with all available means."

The addressees, the leadership of the German trade unions, found themselves in an extremely awkward situation with regard to the growing struggle over this issue. After the stabilization of the currency, when there were difficulties in selling their products, which resulted in unemployment, they had hurled accusations against the employers whose majority, in recent years, "had severely neglected the technical improvement of their factories . . . As a result, the problem of the rationalization of work, on which the successes of the other countries, particularly America, are based, has remained unsolved." Hence the General Association of German Trade Unions demanded, in addition to democratization, "technical and organizational measures in the plants," and "a comprehensive rationalization of work." That was in 1925. But a few years later voices were raised that were scornful of the "fixed gaze at

America" and observed that "this whole magnificent arrangement is not possible given the German method of production and the small German market in a divided Europe."

Thus the struggle with America was carried over into the social sphere as well. It is not as if only the plant engineers were fascinated with the assembly line; the workers' leaders also studied the conditions of life and the wages in America and discovered the considerably higher real income—quite apart from the earnings of the skilled workers—and came back with the answer to the riddle: The higher wages had created a mass expansion of the market for consumer goods; this was the engine driving the economic boom. The purchasing power theory was born. It would create some problems in the future for Bosch, too, although he tended to concede that it had a certain justification, and practically speaking he had adhered to it in his traditional wage policies.

When he made a statement about this complex of questions toward the end of 1925 in the *German General Newspaper*, he emphasized, speaking to employers, the right of the workers to strive for higher wages. But he did not emphasize the effect this had on the economy in general; he was more interested in the personal satisfaction of the individual. He was interested in the question of how it was that in America rationalization had not run into any obstacles on the part of the individual workers, "that it does not occur to them to be opposed to increases in their effectiveness." On the contrary: The individual American was proud of working in a factory in which productivity was as high as possible. He was proud of the fact that he himself was able to be highly productive! How did it happen that the psychological situation in Germany appeared to be different? "It is not the individual worker who spontaneously holds back with his productivity. On the contrary: the individual worker is diligent, and he also loves to have a good income." But the worker was worried that his piece rate would fall if his wages increased; in most cases the employers held fast to the notion that "the worker should not earn more than a certain amount." This, then, had a depressing effect on the worker's will to work and on his sense of being an equal participant in the plant. "And I would particularly like to emphasize this point—that in the United States, factories are dominated by a spirit of equality and comradeship that one can scarcely imagine in Germany, and a very large part of the productivity of American industry is based on this spirit."

These sentences were not the result of some study in political economy but were addressed to employers and trade unions and were meant in a pedagogical sense; it was not until later that Bosch attempted to make a comprehensive evaluation of this complex of questions. His comments were characteristic of the situation at the time; they attempted to maintain a flexible viewpoint vis-à-vis the hardening of debate through the slogans being advanced. It was Debatin, in *The Bosch Spark Plug*, who provided the running commentary on the reorganization, its ideological defense against romantic objections about the soullessness of the work or the decrease in the work ethic. In the same publication, Otto Fischer, who had at one time administered the workers' council and who had been in Detroit for a number of years, gave vivid descriptions of the American reality, its enthusiasm and boldness as well as its very pedantic but highly effective methods of "scientific" market analysis and marketing. His sober observation distinguished things that had a lasting value from those that were speculatively dangerous—"consumption financing" was all the rage, in order to prolong the boom! He also examined the fate of those people who were discharged from their workplace and lacked any resources in the form of officially required security or insurance.

The debate about rationalization, for and against, was encouraged in *The Bosch Spark Plug* for many years. The firm not only justified it with arguments based on political economy, but it also encouraged the technical participation of the workforce. In itself, that was nothing new. The Bosch firm had always valued and appreciated the practical inventive skill of individuals—Honold frequently and willingly praised the many suggestions and ideas that came from masters and mechanics, for example, Adolf Krauss, and the debt he owed them when it came to the working out of his plans. Now the firm systematized the suggestions and emphasized the importance attached to making changes and improvements in the work process itself, the machines, the assignment of various parts, the construction of safety devices, and so on. The monetary prize was less important than the recognition: usable suggestions and their purpose were communicated in *The Bosch Spark Plug*. In this way the coworker relationship was made into something quite conscious.

The skilled worker remained central, although admittedly, with rationalization the number of trained workers, which had increased during the war years, grew in numerical significance. The Bosch firm had experience with training, but now it became important to have the proper hierarchy within the workforce, to educate a middle management that was not only exemplary and reliable in its own work but also familiar with the specific needs of the new work processes. The decision that was made in 1924 to send apprentices into the actual plant for an entire year may be seen within the context of these considerations as a means of making the apprentices more familiar with the nature of the unification of work processes, and at the same time with concerns about the timely completion of each element. The freedom of their later decisions about where they would work remained unaffected by this stronger direct link to the plant. August Utzinger's successor, Adolf Ottmann, was responsible for the management of the Factory Technical School created in 1924. He described its task as follows: "sticking as closely as possible to practical needs," "training qualified skilled workers, technicians, masters, calculators, and work analysts to be particularly well prepared, as employees of the plant, for the special needs of our precision and electrical engineering mass production." Three courses were created requiring a total of 270 class hours; they were limited to twenty-five participants each. There were a few scientific lectures but most of the courses of instruction were restricted exclusively to the concerns of the plant. Leading Bosch engineers were the teachers. The training period lasted one and a half years, and there were strict requirements for admission and graduation. It was a farsighted and fruitful decision to put education at the very beginning of the technical transformation, for it meant that when the new methods began on a massive scale there were trained "setup" and "adjustment" people available. The measure also achieved a secondary social effect. The successful graduates of the course became members of the professional staff, a process that was not without importance for the structure of the workforce. Thus the Bosch plant, in the course of its transformation, entered the field of international competition well equipped in terms of both facilities and personnel. But a tenacious will and a tireless process of adaptation would be necessary if it was to harvest the expected fruits of these labors. The senselessness of the reparations policy, which demanded money from Germany but blocked German products, and the collapse of the artificially inflated boom in the United States, saddled the world with a severe crisis that afflicted all countries and peoples by the end of the decade.

28

———◆———

BOSCH AND THE
DIESEL ENGINE

Bosch's relationship to the diesel engine, which would have such significant consequences, took shape in the 1920s. There was a prelude that
remained in Bosch's memory as an amusing anecdote. It had taken place
three decades before, and Rudolf Diesel himself had played a role in it.

At the time, Diesel was working on his great task, the creation of a
new combustion engine; he was engaged in a long series of experiments
at the Machine Factory Augsburg. Oil injected in the form of tiny parti-
cles into the air of the working cylinder, which had been heated by strong
pressure, was to be made to serve as the source of work and motion. It
was cheaper than gasoline, and its performance was better. It was also
less dangerous than the substances that had been developed for the
existing internal combustion engines. The principle by which the oil
spray would be ignited in the combustion chamber had been determined
a long time before, but there would be many failed attempts before the
theoretical knowledge about heat could be duplicated in practice, before
the fuel was ignited and the engine actually ran!

The moment arrived when Rudolf Diesel began to look around for
another method. In a certain sense it was a detour, a groping for a usable

form of exterior ignition. The fame of the workshop in Stuttgart was already so well established by 1894—a remarkably early date—that Diesel went to Stuttgart to have a look at the magneto ignition device Bosch had produced, which was at the time being produced for stationary Otto gas engines. After this Bosch repeatedly spent time in Augsburg. On one occasion Diesel's invitation caught up with Bosch as he was visiting his mother in Ulm. From there it was just a hop, skip, and a jump to Augsburg, and Bosch left at once. Once there he found that he had not brought sufficient travel money. Bosch liked to tell the story of how he was asked to join Diesel for lunch after the experiments, and how he accompanied him, secretly worrying that they would go to Augsburg's old hotel, the Three Moors. Diesel seemed like a fine gentleman to him, but his own purse contained only three marks, and he could hardly ask Diesel for a loan. Bosch was relieved when instead they went to a simple inn. The fact that this little story remained so unforgettable for him—it was his Diesel anecdote—is revealing.

Diesel's tenaciousness finally overcame all disappointments, false starts, and detours. The self-ignition of the fuel in the compressed air was achieved, the engine ran, and a new epoch in power generation was initiated. Its development lay outside Bosch's realm; the diesel engine quite evidently did not require the electrical ignition devices that the Stuttgart firm was providing for internal combustion motors of the most varied types. And the most clearly identifiable areas in which the diesel engine could be used—shipbuilding and power-generating machines in general—hardly coincided with the focus of Bosch's work.

Quite soon, however, the Bosch firm began to see things in a different light. What if the new combustion engine were developed in a way that would significantly restrict or even displace the existing internal combustion engine? A little imagination with which to paint a picture of the future, and the world of engines could appear in a thoroughly transformed light. There *had* to be attempts to use diesel oil for motor vehicles, perhaps for the airplane. It might be recommended because of its greater economy, for example, for trucks engaged in cross-country transport, or for airplanes because of its reduced flammability. Naturally, Robert Bosch and his colleagues followed the diesel engine, as they had the Otto engine, with the greatest of interest. In case electrical ignition should ever become unnecessary, even if only in some parts of the market, the Bosch firm wanted to be ready with parts that would be just as indispensable for engine builders as the things with which they were currently supplying them.

The diesel engine did require such an accessory—an apparatus, that is, that had to be designed and produced independently of the construction of the engine itself. The first builders of diesel engines had produced the *entire* product in their own workshops. Now, as production expanded to include all kinds of design variations, including attempts to create both larger and smaller engine types, it turned out that there was hardly any room for customized manufacturing, especially for items where the precision engineering aspect played a decisive role. This was particularly true of the mechanical devices such as valves and pumps that sprayed the fuel into the chamber containing the strongly compressed air.

The factory history written in 1936 includes a detailed description of the path that was taken beginning in 1922, and it is not sparing in self-criticism. By assuming the evolution of an engine that had not yet been developed, they were making demands on their own performance that were greater than those imposed by the state of engine technology itself. In retrospect, they were critical of the fact that the design engineers focused too narrowly on the multicylinder automobile engine with its higher revolutions per minute, for which it would need a unified system of several pumps; this already implied a certain kind of production program. At the same time, with the motor vehicle body in mind they had selected the smallest possible dimensions. But they had not examined the small, stationary diesel engines with *one* cylinder and moderate revolutions per minute that were in use at the time. If they had done this, they could have gained some practical experience. When they began to do tests, always thinking of the motor vehicle, they were unable to get their hands on a motor vehicle diesel engine; they struggled with reconstructed carburetor engines, were not satisfied, and planned to construct their own diesel engine for test purposes. Finally, in the fall of 1924 one of the diesel-driven trucks that Diesel had brought onto the market was available for purchase. By replacing its engine with one of their own, which they had single-mindedly continued to refine, they were able to see which aspects of their work appeared to be justified and where the sources of error lay.

Next, developments at Bosch took a different direction, a detour that may or may not have been necessary. Other people were working on the same problem; the Munich engineer Franz Lang had found a solution that included both an engine with an air container and the injection pump. The South German Engine Company was thinking about producing it and approached Bosch with the suggestion that he take on the production of Franz Lang's injection pump; they themselves wanted to maintain control over the production of the engine or its licensing to other factories. This was the ACRO (American Crude Oil Corporation) engine. The principal owner of the rights was the German-American Albert Wielich, whose two brothers held positions of some influence in the South German Engine Company: one was an engineer, the other the firm's legal counsel.

In November 1923, a preliminary meeting had been arranged in Stuttgart. Albert Wielich himself was present, and before long Bosch and his colleagues could sense that he would be the most important individual in the undertaking. Bosch took him, as he had taken Frederic Simms a couple of decades earlier, on a chamois hunt. Wielich repaid the favor by inviting Bosch to visit him the following year during the month of August, and to go with him to Canada to hunt mountain sheep and bear. This was a clever move, for Wielich had good reason to believe that during their several weeks together an atmosphere would be created that would be quite good for business, too. Bosch, for his part, did not see things very differently; his passion for hunting must have been awakened by the prospect of new and unusual quarry, and they would be able to talk about other matters during the evenings they would spend in the isolated tent.

Admittedly, the prospect of producing someone else's model for another engine factory, without being in touch with the actual consumers, was not much to Bosch's taste. That he, in a matter that might possibly assume major significance, should act as the provider of parts designed by someone else was not actually in keeping with the stature of his factory; if he were to get involved, he and his colleagues would have to find a way to direct and determine the work to the greatest degree possible. But it was difficult to gain a sufficiently clear picture of the qualities of the engine. The correspondence is full of impatience—they would like to have a chance to see the engine and pump in operation, to test it themselves. They were not thinking so much of the "earning potential *per se*" (from a letter in December 1923) "by which I naturally do not mean to say that the earnings are unimportant to us; but along with the businessmen a firm like mine also includes engineers, and by no means least of all." And from a letter written on January 24, 1924, "The contract can be settled when it is possible to gain a proper idea of the value of the invention, whether it is patented or not. One condition is that good and skilled work must be required for its functioning." Or the following: "It pains us that we do not know what we are dealing with . . . our customers are demanding information about the pumps. We ourselves are naturally convinced of the importance of this matter" (March 18, 1924). "As far as our participation in the ACRO, you are aware that we are willing and more than willing to participate in the matter. For this reason, your letter has put my mind at rest and I thank you for it very cordially" (April 11, 1924).

The tone of these remarks was rather unusual for Bosch; one may wonder whether from a business standpoint their intensity was smart. Wielich had to be saying to himself: This man wants to get his hands on the ACRO engine, and he will have thought about the interrelationship of supply and demand and already begun to calculate its impact on price. Wielich had no way of knowing that the board of directors at Bosch was not, or was only very hesitantly, inclined to go along with this step. Wielich's secrecy did not suit the technicians, who wanted to play it safe—and for good reason; the separation from the customers would not fit in with the scheme of things in their organization. A 49 percent participation in the South German Motor Company had been proposed during the negotiations, but that was a half measure. Bosch came back from the hunting expedition to Canada bearing Wielich's willingness to sell the majority of ACRO. This created a new situation: Bosch would be the owner of a new engine design but without wanting to build engines. . . .

One troublesome aspect of the matter was that the final decisions would have to be made in America, for only there would it be possible to test a functioning ACRO engine that had been developed more fully than the models they had visited in Munich. Bosch therefore made another trip in December 1924. Otto Heins was already there; Bosch and Wild followed. The engine they saw in Buffalo made a convincing impression, although the technicians did not achieve perfect clarity about the physical processes involved. They dropped their objections after Franz Lang, in a gentlemen's agreement, put the crucial design drawing on the table. Bosch himself had begun to waver in his confidence; during the psychological massage to which Wielich had subjected him early in their negotiations there had been all kinds of magic, including predictions of the future and horoscopes. These did not really fit his own style, but he had tolerated them for a while out of curiosity and goodwill. Now doubts suddenly arose as to whether they should agree to get involved in the matter, the more so since the business negotiations, which Bosch himself was leading, were going very slowly for the most part, with much finessing on both sides. Finally, they got to the point of draft contracts, which were drawn up a few months later in Stuttgart. Robert Bosch AG purchased the American ACRO company and the South German Engine Company. The rights to ACRO were formally transferred to a newly created ACRO Company in Küssnacht, which was to function as the overall licenser to Bosch. From a manufacturing standpoint, Bosch was only interested, it will be remembered, in the precision engineering work on the engine. He wanted to sell the production rights to the engine itself to third parties. If the engine worked, this would necessarily greatly encourage the use of diesel-driven vehicles, which would be both directly and indirectly profitable and would have economic and social benefits as well.

The ACRO engine was not, at first, able to meet expectations. The fact that its functioning during ignition depended on a certain minimum temperature reduced its utility for motor vehicles. As a result, there was disappointment and difficulty. Bosch concluded in his notes that "One should never send a committee; it is better to give the responsibility to a single individual." But now a committee, with him as its head, had made the decision, which in turn had been supported and affirmed by the technical management. There was a certain compulsion to find a satisfactory way out of these difficulties, the core of which they had not immediately identified. The purchase of the ACRO rights had not only required considerable funds but had also meant that the experts knew Bosch was developing a diesel engine. As it would not be to Bosch's advantage for anything less than perfect to appear on the market, they wanted to go ahead instead with work on the production of the ACRO pump. Its designer, Franz Lang, had been working at Bosch since the spring of 1925 but left again at the end of 1926. Forced to get to the bottom of the

engine itself, Richard Stribeck now took over Lang's role. He was no
engine builder; from the point of view of the industry as a whole, he
was the man responsible for ball bearings; for the Bosch factories he was
the man responsible for insulation materials. But his objective open-
mindedness, logical acuity, and the scientific thoroughness of his
experiments helped him to get things moving again. The technical consequences of what he learned made it possible to remove the engine from
the testing site, where it had attracted the gaze of so many unhappy engineers, and install it in an automobile. By June 1926, they were ready to
present the ACRO engine to the public in *The Bosch Spark Plug* as a new
product, along with its accessories the injection pump and the nozzle. In
addition to the automobile, they had begun to outfit a two-and-a-half-ton
truck with the ACRO engine for experimental purposes only. It ran to
Vienna and Berlin, Paris and Prague, on behalf of the factory. Beyond the
fact that it proved to be technically successful, those involved with it
made the impressive and highly effective observation that the savings, in
comparison with the gasoline carburetor engine, were about seventy
pfennigs on the mark (70 percent).

The advantage of the ACRO engine, compared with other versions of
the diesel engine, was the fact that from the beginning it had been
designed to achieve a relatively high level of revolutions per minute.
That recommended it for trucks, and this was the source of Bosch's interest. For the higher the rpm, the greater the requirement for fine work-
manship in the accessories, and *this* was where Bosch and his colleagues
saw the opportunity for the future. Once they had found the right principle, they could feel quite competent to equal, if not surpass, the work of
the engine builders who were creating the rest of the apparatus, as well
as any specialized competitors who might surface. It is therefore not surprising that they began to lose interest in the ACRO engine, because they
realized that their concentration on its needs resulted in a certain restriction of other types of engines that emerged. The business of licensing the
engine had gotten off to a good start; over the years, several dozen
licenses had been given out. But as early as 1928 the ACRO engine had
ceased to dominate experimental work in the field, and after 1931 Bosch
and his colleagues stopped paying particular attention to it. Other types
of combustion motors appeared, and it was like the early period of mag-

neto ignition when a variety of engine types each required special attention. They had learned from this process and were able to avoid looking at any one solution as final. But there was one difference compared to the earlier time: their own designs were made, from their inception, to be suited to the demands of mass production. If only things developed to that point . . .

A notice in *The Bosch Spark Plug* (October 1928) stated that on September 25 of that year the thousandth injection pump had been produced. The first test pump had appeared in 1925; March 1927 was cited as the date of the hundredth. Compared to the numbers of other items, this was a very modest event. But the demand was growing, so that the Bosch firm could now begin producing in volume. Indeed, it would soon outgrow modesty; May 1930 saw the ten thousandth and March 1934 the hundred thousandth injection pump leave the factory. They had not lagged behind the tempo, nor the worldwide effect, of the victory march that had characterized magneto ignition a quarter of a century earlier.

In a note from November 1930, Robert Bosch remarked rather drily, "The way things look today, it has been proven right, i.e., it was the right thing, that the ACRO business was taken over. It was expensive, but today Robert Bosch AG, with its pumps and nozzles, holds first place, according to the opinion of the leading gentlemen in the firm, and it is already doing nicely with sales of nozzles. Perhaps Herr Wild's statement will yet come true and Robert Bosch AG can have its old position back again in the diesel-engine business."

This is actually what occurred, and in Bosch's *Life Recollections* the result blotted out the feelings of disaster that had haunted him at various points along its crooked road to development. Bosch may have been periodically troubled by the feeling that he had been too trusting in a matter in which he himself could not form an assessment of the physical realities. On the other hand, he was satisfied with the tenacity he had shown in pursuing it despite many obstacles, plagued only by uncertainty as to whether magneto ignition might one day be technologically superseded. The comment about the mayfly that he had liked to repeat in the early days, with a certain mistrust of specialization and a great deal of respect for inventive genius, was repeated. True, this creature was alive, and it had been reproducing itself quite successfully for decades. But if Bosch magnetos and spark plugs were to find their way into the museum of technical history, at least the injection pump and nozzle would testify to the performance he had trained his colleagues to achieve. Then he tended to view their determined and ultimately successful engagement with the diesel engine as a second reconstitution of his firm.

There were soon some experiences not unlike the ones three decades earlier. Gottlieb Daimler had not been very pleased when the magneto ignition device had replaced his ignition tube, which at one time had been a clever solution. Now Bosch was greeted with skepticism by the diesel experts, for whom the Bosch firm, with its proven quality in electrical ignition, seemed an outsider in their field. Bosch came up with new ideas for the form of the injection pump, which had been developed using ideas from the first experiments, combined with suggestions that had been borrowed from Franz Lang's solution and then further transformed during the ACRO experiments. The type of injection nozzle and its connection with the combustion chamber differed from the norm. Would the whole thing hold up in practice? At Bosch they were quite confident, thanks to the broad and demanding tests they had performed on the most diverse types of engines. They could also count on the fact that they were now not a relatively unknown craft workshop entering the arena, but an international firm with a name people respected. There may have been some initial mistrust to overcome, but then it was the engine builders' turn, and they were happy, for the most part, that they could obtain a complete apparatus to transport the diesel oil from the tank to the combustion chamber. For the injection devices were joined by a diesel pump, which Bosch also produced, and finally by the Bosch filter. Since the nozzles, particularly in small motors with high revolutions per minute, had tiny bore holes calculated in fractions of millimeters, and therefore dirt presented a danger that could have all kinds of undesirable consequences, Bosch created a fuel filter. It was conceived of as a useful accessory for the diesel driver, but its appropriateness for general use was so evident that it became an independent item that was expanded beyond the specific pumps and nozzles the Bosch firm delivered.

The Bosch Spark Plug described the development of all these devices and parts, as they were created, in expert articles. The commemorative history of 1936 provided a summary. In those years the imagination expressed in the design process never flagged. For now it was the diesel engine's turn to conquer the world, in manifold new forms, from the smallest versions to the gigantic dimensions of stationary power generators and huge oceangoing vessels. The tractor became a requirement for the masses of people engaged in agriculture. In 1929, Junkers made his airplane fly with a diesel engine; the Italians followed suit, and next, in grand style, came the Americans. Despite obstacles that might have had a delaying effect in those years of threatening and then actual economic crisis, in the world of engine construction a mood of certainty reigned about the future. It was shared by the people at Bosch. As constricting as the worries might have felt at times, the people at Bosch believed in the capacity of technically perfect things to help; this capacity should be available once the world freed itself from its political sufferings and misunderstandings.

29

———•———

SOCIAL POLICY AND
SOCIAL WELFARE
IN THE PLANT

Bosch's social policies during the years of his rise can be summarized in a
few words: high wages and the eight-hour day (1906); to these were added
Saturday afternoons off and graduated vacation time (1910). Until 1913,
the firm also paid the workers' contribution to Social Security. Bosch had
a very simple remark with which to respond to foolish talk about his workers' earnings: "I don't pay good wages because I am rich; I am rich
because I pay good wages." That the shortening of the workday not only
had proved itself but was also profitable had been confirmed in practice;
Bosch insisted on maintaining it even during the war years. The care with
which he planned the lighting and air circulation in the new factory buildings, without sparing additional costs, corresponded to his original attraction to anything that promoted health as well as technological efficiency.
If he had been asked about it, he would have recommended that others
imitate it, but he would not have seen its implementation as essentially a
matter of social policy. For it seemed quite self-evident to him that one
should make working conditions as favorable as possible; it was a simple
human duty, and besides, it was economically profitable because sick or
easily fatigued workers are less productive.

Young Bosch, particularly during his year as a journeyman in America, had been strongly influenced by socialist thinking. Its utopian aspects had lost their appeal among the difficulties and struggles of his own craft beginnings. But what remained was his openness to the political and economic aspects of the workers' movement; it essentially outlasted even the difficult test of the strike in 1913. The right of workers to an increase in their standard of living and an expansion of their living space was something he had always regarded as necessary. It all depended on how it was done. Was it not possible for the employer to be a pioneer in this area? He would become one if he could provide the best and most durable working conditions. In that case, good business policy might be the best social policy; leadership was a part of it. Workers should be more than wage earners; they should feel recognized and appreciated as coworkers. The strict discipline in the workshop should be as natural to workers, within this context, as the secure sense of independence they felt in their civil existence.

Although Bosch had already given away millions for the general good, including many projects that by their nature involved social welfare, his own factory and its environs had remained unaffected. A kind of "plant patriotism"—the phrase had been used by Friedrich Naumann—might arise, but it should not be especially promoted. At Bosch, there was actually a hesitancy about welfare programs like those that gave several large German industrial firms a controversial fame. Welfare was anathema. Above all, there should be no sense of dependence! This did not exclude a willingness to help out in individual cases, and in such matters, the private office, where unsentimental goodwill and factual knowledge came together, might help by raising funds and giving support. The plant itself remained unaffected; there was no sign of anything that might have been considered patriarchalism in the more systematic sense.

The direct and indirect consequences of the war brought about a transformation, which, without any intent to abandon the original position, created an entirely different picture overall. The fact that during the inflationary years notices appeared on the blackboard about the sale of shoes or textiles to members of the workforce was merely a typical and irrelevant phenomenon of the time. The company, at a time when everyone was constantly on the lookout for scarce goods and prices were soaring above the purchasers' means, sought to make things easier for its people by buying things in bulk. That Bosch went so far as to add a retail outlet for clothing was a curiosity that was not entirely insignificant insofar as it reveals how in those days family concerns reached into the firm and found their way to Ernst Ulmer's kind heart. This, however, remained an isolated episode.

More important was the attention that was devoted to wounded war veterans and the widows and orphans of former Bosch employees. Special concern for the blind and disabled was taken for granted. The first statistical record of the postwar workforce, dated March 1, 1919, shows that the Bosch firm had employed twice as many seriously disabled workers as the law required. The main concern was with those who had been blinded in the war; there were six of them initially. Special devices were created for them in the testing departments in order to make use of their more finely developed senses of touch and hearing. With the help of these devices, blind workers were able to accomplish astonishing things; in an essay in the year 1920 the firm reported that the earnings of the blind workers were only 5 to 10 percent less than those of sighted unskilled laborers. A report from the year 1930 stated that a total of 222 jobs were occupied by the seriously disabled; the special devices to assist and protect them had been developed to the point where both amputees and blind workers were able to work at machine tools with excellent results.

Even though the firm was so large, these measures retained their individualized nature, since their goal was to protect the people for whom they were created from any sense that they were receiving charity.

The first social welfare program, developed in the year 1921, was completely different in nature. Robert Bosch was turning seventy; what should or could his colleagues give him as a present? The year had robbed him of his invalid son, but his memory—this was the suggestion of the factory leadership for the birthday—should be kept alive through a Robert Aid Foundation, which would provide educational assistance, on behalf of the factory community, to the children of war victims. In May 1922, the Robert Aid Foundation began its work. It was not set up as a foundation with a specific sum to use; the unstable value of money and the temporally limited purpose of the program recommended against this method of proceeding. There were 302 orphans (the number of employees who had fallen in the war or died as a result of their war injuries was 166). Their care was entrusted to honorary godparents from the factory, of whom more than 200 volunteered to report on the children's well-being, needs, and development. In this way a certain bond of friendship remained, though the assistance ceased when the child turned eighteen. As the group of young people became smaller, the foundation would achieve a certain savings, as it were. By 1932 it was also supporting the gifted children of other economically disadvantaged employees; the business report for 1934 cites the figure that had been set aside for this purpose as 12,300 marks. The Robert Aid Foundation's program remained at this level, and no restrictions were imposed on the professional goals of the young recipients.

Along with this early program, and complementing it in a certain sense, was the Bosch Youth Aid Foundation, which was created in 1938 with capital of 300,000 marks. It was aimed primarily at needy apprentices and young workers whose talents and demeanor qualified them to receive special support, for example, by enabling them to attend an advanced technical or business school. Support was also available for other family members of needy members of the workforce. Those who received this kind of attention were not required to work for Bosch later on, but it was expected that they would first offer their services to the firm. Not only the interest was to be expended for this purpose, but the entire amount was allowed to be spent within ten to fifteen years. The leadership of the foundation was placed in the experienced hands of Theodor Bäuerle.

The business report for 1923 is the first to mention the purchase and construction of apartment houses for employees of the factory. Until this point, Robert Bosch never appeared as an apartment builder. To link employer-employee relations with a landlord-tenant relationship contradicted his ideas about the two parties' mutual freedom to make decisions. Had he changed his mind about this question? Not at all. These first apartment houses simply *had* to be built, because the expansion of the factory required the removal of existing living space; a replacement had to be provided. This housing policy remained very modest in scope; it was connected to the purchase of real estate in Stuttgart and Feuerbach, for which the Bosch Housing Company, Inc., was formed in 1923. The accent was clearly on business; the element of social policy, for the person who might be looking for it, was only a weak echo.

The tone had changed rather radically a few years later. Beginning in about 1926, Bosch decided to assist those members of the workforce who wanted to build a home by offering construction mortgages. These funds were given as a final contribution when the applicant had solidified his plans with the help of his own means or through secured loans. The normal mortgage loan was a year's salary, at 1.5 to 3 percent interest. The low interest rate was the main attraction. The house builder was free in his choice of location; *The Bosch Spark Plug* offered good advice, including suggestions about furnishings. The order of magnitude of this program can be gleaned from the report of its activities for 1941: up to that date, approximately 600 construction mortgages with a value of 1.9 million marks had been given out. In later years, circumstances forced Bosch to construct homes himself. When Bosch and his colleagues began the decentralization of the plant that was required by the defense and economic policies of the 1930s, the sites of the new factories were in neighborhoods lacking any appropriate housing. The need to provide proper living accommodations for the employees, on an emergency basis, led to the decision to create the Robert Bosch Housing Complex, Inc. The investment capital did not come directly from the factory but from the Bosch Aid Foundation.

The planning of the Bosch Aid Foundation occurred during the period when the firm was beginning to make construction mortgages, that is, around 1926. The year had shown a deficit, and it was difficult to form a picture of the economic situation in general and the German motor vehicle industry in particular. But at Bosch they were pressing ahead with tenacious optimism to perfect their technology and were beginning to work on the new items connected with the diesel engine. There had never been such a thing as stagnation. But this period, in which Hans Walz also played a leading role, was characterized by a new activism in which Robert Bosch himself was personally involved. At issue was the creation of old age and dependents' pensions.

This had been preceded, for a smaller group, by the life insurance policies that the firm had set up on October 1, 1921, for longtime employees. When these took effect, the number of individuals covered was 222, the total value of the insurance 4.5 million marks; inflation was in its early stages, and inflation had also been the reason for this measure. At Bosch, people had earned well and had been able to save something. But now all their savings had melted away. Anxieties and cares surfaced; in lively exchanges in *The Bosch Spark Plug* the question was discussed whether and how they might create new means of security. Life insurance seemed to be the most decent form; it also did not require its own administration. The right to benefits began after ten years of service. (In cases where the insurance company declined coverage because of age or infirmity, the firm created a comparable savings account.) For the basic staff that formed the backbone of the work in the office and the workshop, this meant that the most urgent need had been met, at least as far as Bosch's intentions were concerned. Naturally, inflation invaded this space, as well; its effect on the oldest coworkers would be especially devastating. In 1925, therefore, Bosch assumed the costs of securing the full value of the policies in gold marks.

The business report for 1926 informed its readers—at the time there were 426 individuals with a right to employee support—that the firm was engaged in "subjecting the currently existing welfare programs to a thorough review." Robert Bosch had given the order himself. At Christmas 1927, Otto Debatin was able to make the happy announcement that there would shortly be an old age pension program that would extend beyond the professional staff. It would not be a pension fund with required contributions from the employer; there were already enough demands being made on him by taxes and government social security. For the year just past and for the coming year they had set aside a million marks for each. The Bosch Aid Foundation's plan took effect on July 3, 1929; the deadline for claims was made retroactive to January 1, 1927. The business report for 1928 explained the foundation in this way: "We see the creation of this support for older workers and surviving dependents not as an act of charity, but as an economic measure that is also in the interest of the firm and seeks to maintain and increase the goodwill of our workforce. At the same time it seeks to give expression to the mutual interdependence of all those individuals who are active with the House of Bosch."

Eligibility began with the fortieth year of an employee's life, after he had been with the company for an uninterrupted period of ten years (for the severely disabled this requirement was reduced to five years in 1935). The pension was calculated according to years of service, beginning with 20 percent of the normal income and increasing to 45 percent after thirty-five years of service (or in the employee's sixty-fifth year), counting from the date when the eligibility period began. There was no legal claim to it, since no employee contributions were involved. Detailed regulations were written concerning widows' pensions and educational assistance. The capital of the Bosch Aid Foundation was separated from that of the firm; in the case of the liquidation of the company, the capital was to go to the city of Stuttgart for a purpose corresponding to the foundation's mission. Those individuals covered by the earlier professional insurance were given the choice of retaining it or of joining the new program.

Detailed statistical research concerning the number and category of potential applicants, the rate of job change, and so on preceded the creation of the foundation. The workforce had reached the size of more than 10,000; if the foundation were to be continued over a lengthy period of time, it would require additional means. The most marvelous aspect of the Bosch Aid Foundation may be the way in which its financing was continued undisturbed throughout the crisis years that followed its creation. The goal was to reach a level of funding that would be as significant as possible as quickly as possible. This occurred in two ways: For a number of years, the firm assumed the cost of the pensions directly, from its current income, in cases where justified claims already existed. Year after year, even when the firm had not paid a dividend, an additional million was paid into the Bosch Aid Foundation; it would later be two million. The Bosch Aid Foundation was to be administered in a financially conservative way. It was foreseen that it might function as a creditor for Bosch AG; in this case the loans were to earn interest at the rate of no less than 6 percent. In case a dividend were to be paid that represented a higher interest rate, this rate was also to apply to the rates of interest on the loans. In fact, the Bosch Aid Foundation actually became quite significant as a kind of savings bank, providing working capital for the factory; this arrangement served the interests of both parties.

The order of magnitude created from Bosch's direct payments, plus the interest earned, was impressive. The "program report" of 1940 cited a figure of around 34 million marks. At the time, 533 individuals were receiving pensions; there were also nearly 10,000 who had already qualified to claim assistance. In the year 1939, the Bosch Aid Foundation was transformed, for tax reasons, into a registered association; its mission and the means of fulfilling it remained unaffected by the change.

Individual assistance and education for young people, and old-age security for all, were the two cornerstones of Bosch's efforts in the area of social welfare. This reflected his personal concerns. The man or woman who was earning well did not require any special attention. The task of leadership, economically and technologically, was to pay attention to these good earnings. Bosch's wage policy, which became more and more refined, retained its unique status through all the crises, collective bargaining agreements, and regulations. The nature of the work demanded extraordinary attentiveness most of the time, and there were times when the sudden influx of orders made it necessary to work overtime, a practice that was required. Here, the work discipline had to be strict, even harsh, for a large part of the firm's reputation hinged on the timeliness of its deliveries, especially on the international market where it had to measure itself against a competition with sometimes artificially inflated claims. Did Bosch demand more in the way of work than other comparable plants? The extreme productivity during the times of large numbers of orders might seem to support this opinion. It explains the half-admiring, half-impolite phrase about "Bosch tempo." Characteristically, the issue was discussed in the factory newspaper, including the period in the mid-1920s when Bosch and his colleagues were preparing to introduce the extensive retooling required for mass production, with its tests of machine tool suitability, mechanized transport of individual parts within the factory, refinement of wage procedures, and struggle against "dead costs." The term "Bosch tempo" was rejected; what they were doing was nothing but a "carefully prepared and thought-out, but quite normal division of labor . . ." The results of the statistics on hospitalization and injuries were unambiguous; the struggle to avoid accidents by means of education, warnings, and above all protective devices that were continually checked for effectiveness was one of the factory's early specialties and gained in significance with the increased use of trained and unskilled workers and the expansion of mechanization.

Naturally, it was necessary to review the whole complex of problems repeatedly, each time it arose during the review of piecework rates for new work processes, new machines or materials, changes in the parts that were bring used, and the like. A never-ending and precise process of testing was required before appropriate solutions were found that struck the right balance between the calculation of prices, in keeping with market requirements, the cost of materials, general considerations, and appropriate wage rates for the average good performance. In many respects this task was one of psychological education and trust.

The Bosch Spark Plug occasionally overflowed with frank and serious discussions. It encouraged people to speak out, so that unspoken complaints would not multiply, creating dissatisfaction. The paper talked about the responsibilities of middle management in the plant—the masters, calculators, and installers; the personnel department was always open to a review of individual grievances. But one thing that had been true before the war still applied: the wages of the "Boschlers" were well above the average in their branch of industry even if the standard was no longer set by the skilled craft worker.

A law had been passed introducing the eight-hour workday at other plants, as well. At Bosch, there were also free Saturday afternoons and paid vacations, guaranteed in the workers' contracts and graduated according to the number of years of service. One thing that was missing in the firm's benefits—intentionally so—was the Christmas bonus. At Bosch nothing was given away. The reward was already included in the good wages. The plant did not want to allow some half-sentimental claim to grow into something the workers felt to be their habitual right. Yet in the period of strong and steady employment the firm had been experiencing since 1934 the management decided, apart from the benefits for special purposes such as the Bosch Aid Foundation, to introduce general premiums for performance; it retained the right to set both the levels and the flexible measurements that defined them. This premium was not to be robbed of its voluntary character. The management was too acutely aware, after the lessons of the economic crisis, that large depreciation allowances and reserves were very essential elements of a *social* policy, the essence of which was the creation of jobs, i.e., work itself.

When the German Metal Workers Union did a study of the income of its members in 1927, the incomes of the workers in Stuttgart appeared right below those of the workers in Berlin, where life was so much more expensive, and Stuttgart incomes were ahead of those in Frankfurt, Nuremberg, and Hamburg. The study revealed that skilled Bosch workers earning hourly wages made 18 percent more, and those doing piecework, 13 percent more than the average for Stuttgart; trained workers in both categories earned 15 percent more than the average. Unskilled hourly workers earned 17 percent more; women earned as much as 23 and 17 percent more. This meant that Stuttgart workers made an average of between thirty-eight and twenty-two marks more per month. Comparisons between the average wages for all of Germany, as specified by contract, and the actual wages at Bosch, which were sometimes given for a period of several years, showed an even more significant divergence; however, these figures lack compelling force due to the absence of comparative data on the cost of living.

The relatively higher hourly wage of the Bosch workers was especially advantageous in light of the instability that affected the economy in general. More than once, in the decade and a half that made up the postwar era, the Bosch firm was forced to reduce the number of hours worked. The fact that the cause may have been a lack of electricity or fuel, for example in 1919, was soon forgotten. More troubling were the slowdowns in orders received that occurred as a result of the instability of the currency. Then, when stabilization of the currency took place, they had to be very flexible in the assignment of work. Spark plugs, for example, were always in demand internationally, while the generators required a certain time to gain acceptance. For certain jobs it was possible to reassign the workers, but this practice had its limits because of the number of workplaces and the specialization of the various work processes. The fact that as a result full employment existed alongside reduced hours, which were introduced out of cautiousness, required understanding on the part of the workforce. The situation never led to significant difficulties; the core staff of the factory was sufficiently educated to understand these necessities. It was an extraordinary accomplishment that, "admittedly not without widespread use of reduced hours," as the business report for 1931 stated, the workforce could be increased in this year of world economic crisis by 308 people to a total of 8,422. At a time when unemployment was depressing Germany's economic life and devastating the country politically, this fact reveals that the business policy of the Bosch firm was doing its part to demonstrate the much-discussed "depression-proof" stability of the Swabian region.

After the turn of the century, a successful association had been founded to promote group recreation homes for professional staff. Naturally the association came to Bosch, who had become known as a generous man, for a contribution. They received a rejection in March 1912. "It is my observation that the professional staff members in their vast majority do not prefer to visit recreation homes, since they have the understandable wish to meet people other than their colleagues when they are on vacation, and to see a different region than the one they see every day, or are otherwise familiar with." The exchange is unimportant, and whether Bosch's opinion was correct is irrelevant. His words reveal that Bosch, the exemplary individualist in his private life, could not quite imagine that human beings in their nonworking hours would want to seek connections with the familiar. As much as he may have wanted to assure that a certain comradely spirit reigned in his plant, the idea of worrying about what people did on their own time, or perhaps even influencing it, was foreign to him. Ultimately he would find that without any effort on his part something like an esprit de corps, which produced its own social groups, had emerged in the growing workforce. There were people who liked to sing and thought it would be nice if their comrades, and perhaps others, as well, knew that at Bosch they sang especially beautifully. Some had instruments whose sounds they liked to combine with others; surely, among the great number of employees, there would be comrades who were willing to learn the flute or the oboe or some other instrument—then they would have a regular orchestra. And couldn't one read in the newspapers that in Berlin or elsewhere soccer matches were being organized between plants—could Bosch be absent from these? As far as Bosch himself was concerned, he could perfectly well be absent, for the former gymnast used to point out to those people who thought he should give them an athletic field—this was now the modern thing and would make a good impression—that there were enough sport and gymnastics clubs in the city where they could amuse themselves. But one day the sports enthusiasts at the firm got together after all. They did not receive an athletic field as a donation, but instead the firm gave Stuttgart's largest soccer club a giant locker room, and in exchange the club let the Bosch employees use the facility on certain days. But the singers got their conductor, and naturally the orchestra musicians as well, along with their instruments. These things had developed out of the enthusiasm and goodwill of individual people. Once they had been created, they became a part of the collective life of the firm and were affirmed in a friendly way. The athletic enthusiasm took on a certain flair in the 1930s, chiefly as a result of the participation of several members of the board of directors. On the property in Feuerbach an athletic field and garden were created, and even in the big-city congestion of Stuttgart they carved out an opportunity for sport by using the old, little-used park around the Liederhalle. The new forms of concern for the community, which were an aspect of the ever-growing complexity of the mass of employees, which generated its own subcategories, earned the firm's support rather late, but it was all the more emphatic when it occurred.

Finally the firm decided to construct a convalescent home just for the factory. It had already been assisting tired and sick employees in choosing their vacation spots for some time. The firm had occasionally made long-term arrangements for members of the factory workforce; a special fund was also available. But in the 1930s, with the general increase in vacationing and its connection to winter sports, it became more difficult to find places to stay, and in 1940 the factory purchased a suitable piece of property in Riezlern, in the Walser Valley. It would hardly accommodate the growing masses of applicants, but it was evidence of the firm's goodwill. And in response to the difficulty young female employees and factory workers encountered when trying to find housing, a suitable apartment complex had already been purchased in Stuttgart and converted into a cheerful girls' dormitory for thirty residents. Social workers who visited the sick elsewhere had observed how dark and poor the places were in which the girls were often forced to live.

In introducing measures such as these, Bosch was not alone; others had gone before him. Factory lending libraries had been instituted by others, either before or simultaneously with Bosch. But the Bosch factory library—it was founded in 1919—deserves special attention because of the breadth of its subject matter and weltanschauung. It had a core of specialized literature, and the engineer or worker who wished to educate himself about his own or a related field would be able to find books here that were not generally available in other libraries. But the plan for this library was conceived, from the beginning, with a larger goal in mind: to satisfy intellectual needs and the desire for relaxation. (This goal also manifested in other respects. As early as 1919, the firm had organized good-quality orchestral concerts, even opera performances, for the work-force.) The unique tone of this factory lending library was a result of the complete lack of inhibition with which political literature was made available. If a person wanted, he could take out Bismarck, but Lenin was also available. A little note in *The Bosch Spark Plug* (May 1923) commented, it is true, that "strangely, there is no call at all for the writings of Lenin that are available." Library utilization was increasing rapidly, and a survey done of it notes that among the books that were "by far in the most demand," along with the stories of Ludwig Thoma, were such time-less works as Ludwig Raabe's *Hunger Pastor* and Knut Hamsun's *Victoria*! This would seem to reflect an astonishing level of quality. It did not last, however: a later statistical survey places the emphasis on the usual light fiction and popular literature of the day. Even so, the lending library was always furnished with a very large budget.

Cultural policy, of a fruitful kind with a generous admixture of Swabian local color, was also pursued by *The Bosch Spark Plug* in its literary compositions until 1937 when the regulations governing factory newspapers restricted them to directly plant-related events. Otto Debatin recruited the Swabian poets Hans Heinrich Ehrler and August Lämmle to work on it, and there was an excellent mixture of instruction and entertainment. In-house talents also contributed their witty lines, and the photography department was given a chance to show that it could take pictures of things that were not necessarily technical. The paper was always filled with upbeat and lively suggestions; with its rather personal approach it serves in retrospect as a reflection of the general intellectual movements of the times. Debatin had joined battle against the traditional business letter, with its stiff or affected style. This developed into a real campaign, a war that didn't want to end, and Bosch himself, who liked simple words, may have enjoyed it. The end result was disappointing. Debatin said in 1938 that "while the firm itself has actually made some progress in recent years . . . the style and writing of some people in the House of Bosch has for some time been getting not better, but worse." What was worse, all the sins that were enumerated were "homemade." Debatin's attempt to bring the firm's internal and external written communications up to the unquestioned standard of the factory's products was of secondary importance, but it is part of the portrait of a general pedagogical will.

The volumes of *The Bosch Spark Plug* are important today primarily as a chronicle of the technical development of the factory. The designers and department heads reported on new items, as well as changes and improvements to old ones. This was their most important task: to show the workforce, particularly those who worked on a part or parts of the finished products, what was being accomplished and how the final results worked. There were also reports on economic and social measures, the success of various Bosch products, racing victories, prizes, and the like—the Bosch worker should know how his performance measured up in the outside world. He should be proud of it and of the factory, but he should also feel that he shared in the responsibility for the factory's reputation. At this point, the Bosch name stood not only for good technology but also for good social organization. Its effectiveness, like that of all human endeavors, was constantly threatened by misunderstanding or ill will. If this accumulated, the atmosphere could be destroyed. Thus the factory newspaper reiterated its challenge to all and sundry to step forward with wishes, complaints, and suggestions for discussion. The opportunity was not taken all that often, but when it was, it was with a full and clear directness that was probably not to be found in any other factory organ. Issues were laid on the table, which did not necessarily solve things—the tensions inherent in the situation were numerous and were not to be underestimated. But after the critical events of the first postwar years had passed, things never again reached a point of fundamental difficulty. The inevitable individual complaints were smoothed out in fair and just adjudication. *The Bosch Spark Plug* was able to cite a very impressive statistic: Among the plants belonging to the Union of Metal Industrialists of Württemberg in 1930, a total of 258 cases were brought before the labor court. Of these, only two were from Bosch. In general this amounts to one court case for every 324 workers; at Bosch, there was only one in 4,823! And the two pending cases had been won by the firm. In 1929, the Communist paper *South German Workers' News* wrote angrily, if childishly, that the propaganda that the "yellow" *Bosch Spark Plug* published in support of the cooperation of capital and labor had done "immeasurable damage to the Bosch workforce." Such statements made people laugh. What had emerged is something they were beginning to call the "Bosch spirit."

It flourished among members of the old core group, who shared a tradition that went back, in some cases, to the modest workshop in the Kasernenstrasse. They were asked to tell their stories in *The Bosch Spark Plug*—what it had been like when Herr Bosch himself still took individual orders and worried about their fulfillment, or on sunny afternoons when he would simply close up shop and suggest that they continue work after it cooled off; those were idyllic times. Then there were the times when the entire plant went on a hike to the neighboring hills, with Herr Bosch leading the way; naturally he invited them for a picnic supper and a glass of wine all around; there was always some occasion to celebrate, some umpteenth magneto or the like. Now such events were no longer possible; a hike by the workforce would have blocked traffic. But the departments were encouraged not to let the old tradition die out, and it was finally expanded into a kind of community custom in which the firm handed out three or five marks to everyone who took part in the voluntary "Bosch Sunday." This could add up to a tidy sum.

Workers who had worked at Bosch without interruption for a quarter of a century could see their photo in *The Bosch Spark Plug*, whether they were members of the board of directors or were unskilled workers in the packing room. This honoring of anniversaries, which had started in a small setting as an occasional friendly gesture, grew into a massive job that required both tact and tactics. For in any given year, the factory had not a few, or a few dozen, but hundreds of employees with anniversaries to be celebrated. By now the photos were no longer possible, and neither were the little parties and receptions that would have taken the time of the members of the board of directors; events were organized monthly, then quarterly, then semi-annually, and finally annually with all the magic of a real celebration. Now the firm was glad to have so many singers and musicians, as well as in-house poets and artists. Robert Bosch was always on hand, and there were shared memories to be rekindled in conversations with the older folks.

The cost of these observances, which also included a monetary contribution from the factory, was borne entirely by the company. In 1938, an institution was created that was also supposed to express the internal cohesion of the staff members: a collective first aid fund in cases of death. The Bosch Aid Foundation, according to its charter, was limited to those who had already worked at the factory for ten years. Therefore, on January 1, 1938, the plant managers announced a regulation which stipulated that in any case of death five pfennigs would be contributed by each member of the workforce. At 20,000 employees, the number at that time, the result would be 1,000 marks, which would be advanced by the firm; this amount was only to be paid in the cases of those employees whose income was less than 500 marks a month. The firm calculated that each individual worker would be called upon to contribute a total of about two marks a year. A colleague of the deceased was selected to advise on the appropriate use of the fund.

In his later years, Robert Bosch no longer became personally involved with individual measures having to do with the plant's social policies and social welfare. A new vacation system was introduced, a full-time plant doctor was hired, the system of factory nurses was expanded, the firm signed a contract with day-care centers to help mothers who worked in the factory, and the connection with retired workers or their widows and children was deepened. But Bosch himself no longer became deeply involved in decisions of this nature. He stood behind them and approved of them, but they remained secondary. Along with his wish that the factory should always be top-notch in its manufacturing techniques, and hence in its scientific caliber—and not only in Germany—his most pressing personal concern was that the employer-employee relationship, the spirit that lived in the factory administration and workforce, should remain true to the ethos with which he attempted—successfully—to imbue it.

Bosch never developed a binding theory on the subject. His nature was more empirical than systematic; in other words, he knew that the sources of error in every system are rooted in human nature, and that one must make do with approximations. A phenomenon like Ernst Abbe compelled his respect, even his admiration. But Abbe's cleverly puritanical limitation of profit-seeking seemed to him to contradict a fundamental drive in human beings. He himself was glad to give his leading colleagues the chance to attain wealth; it would be up to them whether his example of standing *above* the money would one day bear fruit. He didn't care to lecture them about it. Theorizing (in a letter he once called it "waxing enthusiastic") was something he himself had once done as a young man. In 1932, after reading a book about Werner von Siemens as a social politician, he found "certain parallels" between Siemens's style and his own experiences. But one should not overstress the comparison, for Siemens's development had occurred in the time *before* protective legislation and the appearance of the organized workers' movement and its struggle for benefits.

Without wanting to create a compelling vision of the right social order, Bosch committed his opinions to paper quite frequently in letters, essays, and memoranda. Fundamentally, his concern was that the spirit of open comradeship should never be endangered or destroyed. That there had to be leadership in the plant was self-evident; without ever mentioning it explicitly, he was fully aware of his own leadership and the role of his will and decisiveness. But leadership had to be grounded in the acknowledgement of lesser contributions, particularly the ones that did not attract very much attention. Nothing was so irritating to Bosch as arrogance based not on immediate accomplishment but on titles, examinations, or family background. The use of titles in-house was frowned upon. In retrospect, it seemed that it had been a providential thing for the development of the factory that its first thoroughly educated scientist, Gottlob Honold, had himself been an apprentice there when a young man. Only a few years before, the men to whom he was now giving instructions had taught him his skills and ways of avoiding mistakes, and he had not forgotten this. Academics were required to prove themselves even more than others. As an example of this there was once the odd case of a nephew of Bosch's, an engineer, who refused to work under and follow the instructions of the head master, Ernst Durst. When the matter was brought before Bosch, he became angry: this was the last straw, that the interest of the factory should be made to suffer because of such nonsense! The man of the factory was closer to him than the scientist who carried out his experiments in the lab and quality control department, calculating, testing, and so on. Yes, he recognized the need for such work and he could be patient in waiting for results, something that was otherwise not exactly his most eminent virtue. The type of the pure scientist seemed more distant to him; it was lucky that he had, in his friend Richard Stribeck, an example of superior caliber to show him how knowledge is effectively transformed into reality.

He later liked to say occasionally that, until the workforce reached the size of 1,500 or so, he had known every single employee by name, style, and accomplishment. Bosch's extraordinary memory helped give a personal flavor to his relationships with masters and workers; even in the large plant this remained true of the older people. However, this trait should not be seen as a sentimental or emotional stereotype. Bosch's visits to the plant were more feared than looked forward to. If he came to Feuerbach, for example, word ran through the factory halls like tom-toms in the jungle—this in the words of someone who once experienced such a scene—and the workers at their machines took a firm hold on themselves. There was a certain tension. "Have you seen Herr Bosch yet?" "No, but I heard him." It might be a friendly greeting, a funny or caustic joke—for Bosch knew how to handle Swabian workers—occasionally, if it happened to be appropriate, a question about the family. This kind of thing might be interpreted as special recognition, even if it was not so intended. But the conversation could also turn into a professional inquisition about the work, either in the factory or in the design workshop, and this was less pleasant. For Bosch's incorruptible critical sense uncovered every oversight, every lapse of order, and demanded precise information from every worker about his or her methods of work and their technical significance.

At some point in the plant, "Herr Bosch" became "Father Bosch," pronounced in the soft accents of Swabia. The more correct form was reserved for formal occasions. It was a cordial and grateful acknowledgement from the heart, a consciousness of the man's consistent will to serve the welfare of the thousands whose fate was bound up with his life's work as challenge and responsibility. But it would be a mistake to see in the shy, affectionate name any unwanted familiarity beyond the respect and honor he was paid.

After the military collapse in 1918, when the representatives of the people had written the eight-hour day into law as an "achievement of the revolution," there was no excitement at the Bosch firm, no struggle about pro or con. They had already had it for twelve years. Nor did the subsequent law on work councils create any worries; except for a few innovations, it merely put into paragraph form things that in essence had long been customary at Bosch.

Matters were not very different after 1933, when new demands and realities were introduced in the areas of social pedagogy and social welfare. The formation of societies like the German Workers' Front, and movements like Strength Through Joy, Beauty of Work, and so on were for Bosch merely new names for old institutions and habits. And in January 1934 Otto Debatin wrote in *The Bosch Spark Plug* that "our Father Bosch already came into the world as St. Paul."

30

—◆—

SURVIVING THE
WORLDWIDE
ECONOMIC CRISIS

The susceptibility of the postwar decade to crises had many conflicting sources. It is probably correct that years of constant neglect of civilian needs produced an extraordinary hunger for products in virtually all countries. The demand was extremely large; the production sites might have sustained some wear and tear to their machines, but with the exception of a few devastated areas, they were still standing and were only waiting for raw materials. Then a recovery would begin.

This expectation, based on common sense and a few historical precedents, was not to be realized. It had been sustained by long-standing notions of an international market and an exchange economy with a free market in products and workers. This had never been fully realized, it is true, but through the English free trade movement it had achieved the status of a kind of ideal and had found broad acceptance in the form of "most favored nation status" in trade pacts since the 1860s. The protective tariff, however vehemently the arguments about it may have continued to rage inside France, Germany, or the United States, appeared over the long run to be more of a disturbance than a true obstacle to the overall rhythm of the world economy, which was gaining in strength. There were periodic ups and downs, recessions, reversals, crises; people played with the concepts of overproduction and underconsumption, looked at the effects of good and bad harvests on the most important crops, recognized the importance of opening up new territories that might serve as sources of raw materials or markets, fought over the meaning of the great increase in the exploitation of recently discovered deposits of precious metals, and calculated the influence that the amazing growth of traffic—huge and efficient shipping systems, endless railroad yards, and so forth—was having on the extent and value of trade. In general, this growth and development, whose beginning seemed to go back to the second third of the nineteenth century, was regarded with a certain credulous acceptance. The population was growing, but the English economist Thomas Robert Malthus's concern that it would grow in the direction of starvation was contradicted by all the facts. There were more living human beings, and they were living better, on average, than their ancestors had. That this "rise" did not occur absolutely smoothly, that the curve describing it was not without valleys, was part of the notion of a certain cyclical regularity with its ups and downs—the next up would always be a little higher given the presumed powers of the economy to heal itself. Its functioning could be influenced monetarily through the interest rate policy of the central banks; the supposedly automatic role of gold-based currency in the most important countries seemed to be an adequate tool for this.

This whole world of thought and deed had been broken apart in the war; the ensuing peace destroyed it entirely. To all appearances, it is true, the Versailles Treaty operated within the ideologies of the earlier period, and the innumerable conferences that followed it labored in the attempt to press the entire productive capacity that had disappeared from the international free market economy into the reparations demanded from Germany. Failure was inevitable, not only because of the order of magnitude conceived from the very beginning for Germany's burden, not only because of the years of continuing hesitation to assign this burden a final limit so that the debtor could ultimately rely on firm numbers, but also because of the purely power-political goals and methods that were superimposed on the economic and financial claims. The German currency, already highly susceptible as a result of the country's own war costs and credit financing, would be the first victim of this policy. All the attempts of the German government—some energetic, others hesitant— to bring order into public finance collapsed both psychologically and in actuality in the face of the political threats. These attempts had to reckon not only with the rigidity of French policy but also with the position of various interested debtors who owned tangible property. The extent to which inflation, by creating a currency gap that helped German products to appear once more on the world's markets, concealed the basic idea behind the Versailles Treaty was something its authors did not recognize until very late. The contradiction inherent in this situation collapsed in on itself with the invasion of the Ruhr, which led to the destruction of the German mark. This not only led to much emotional distress but was responsible for dislodging the German middle classes and creating the intellectual and social prerequisites for the profound domestic political turbulence from which, a decade later, the National Socialists would emerge to put their stamp on Germany's fate.

The intervention of the American financial world between 1923 and 1924, the attempts by means of expert opinions to clarify Germany's capacity to pay and to limit its payments could only provide inadequate relief. One could be of several minds about the numbers in the Dawes Plan or, later, the Young Plan, and could consider them halfway defensi- ble, largely exaggerated, or a cynical attempt to make Germany's depen- dence even more oppressive by "depoliticizing" it, but one could not deny a certain recovery and return of the entrepreneurial spirit. This soon became mired in failed ventures or disintegrated into a kind of megalomania. The period of inflation had ruined the public's sense for small amounts of money, and this also applied to some sectors of the gov- ernment administration. Germany's economy was beginning to run again, although it was not fully conscious of the impoverishment expressed in its high interest rates. It was inevitable that there would soon be a slow- down, however, for the other countries were not sufficiently willing to accept German products. The most profound contradiction in which the entire reparations system remained enmeshed consisted in the fact that the payments imposed on Germany could only be repaid if others would demonstrate their willingness to accept German products, and this will- ingness was lacking. During the war, countries that had been producers of agricultural raw materials had begun to build up their own industries, since manufactured goods were scarce. Now these industries were asking their governments for protection. And the new countries that had been formed from or had annexed large portions of the formerly unified tariff area of the Austro-Hungarian Empire continued to pursue the development of the industrial sites they had acquired out of a mixture of worry and ambition. In these cases, the notion of economic protection also took on aspects of military policy and military technology.

Germany's susceptibility to external and internal crises remained built into the country's foreign and domestic situation even after the Treaty of Locarno had begun to alter the terms of international commerce. Precisely those periods of relative calm, recovery, and growing strength that were needed in Germany if its former enemies were to receive their reparations payments also revived the fears of the other nations. These fears resulted from a guilty conscience or from lethargy. The effect was to encourage in these nations a rigid and small-minded policy of clinging to the letter of the Treaty of Versailles despite the fact that many observers had long since come to feel that it had become a liability. A cloud of political threats continued to hang over these short-sighted economic arrangements. The international conferences on disarmament were symbolic of the situation.

One must be conscious of all these factors in order to understand the background against which Germany's economy struggled to survive and renew itself. It suffered from constant, basically inevitable friction with a governmental authority that was forced on a daily basis to assert its authority in the face of external pressure and domestic recession and contention. Along with the loss of territory, the legacy of Versailles could be boiled down to damage claims by people who had suffered losses abroad, support for war victims, and poverty for everyone on a fixed income. In the meantime, the masses were struggling to secure their social welfare. Very robust interests were engaged in a mutual struggle; they were able to mount a joint attempt to oppose the state. Actually, quite a serviceable apparatus was created for the central government to regulate and integrate finance and public transportation. But the shortcomings of the Weimar Constitution and its misuse in forming a system of multiple contradictory and demanding provincial parliaments had a paralyzing effect when it came to creating a unified parliamentary will to lead.

In these difficult times, the decisions and measures taken at Bosch were affected not only by the worldwide political and economic movements but also by the specific crises that wracked the German motor vehicle industry. A whole extensive literature has been created about who was "guilty" for the fact that the German automobile industry was forced to suffer such harsh reversals, that it did not succeed in gaining the status it deserved to occupy in its country of origin. The most commonly heard reproach in this debate, which did not lack for polemics, was aimed at the United States, which had ostensibly imposed too large a tax burden on the German passenger car at the point of production and sales. This was ostensibly a result of social prejudice on the part of American proletarians and small farmers who influenced the legislators, or else of the desire by the United States to limit competition by automobiles with the highly developed *Reichsbahn,* which had been assigned a major portion of the reparations payments. This description of motives may seem exaggerated, but the existence of an added burden, in comparison with most other countries, was undeniable. The passenger car as an object of taxation is no more a German phenomenon than government sales of fuel; it was equally true of America, although on a totally different scale. In addition, the German government had for years also imposed a luxury tax on the heavier automobiles. The specialization of the production of parts, which meant that a number of different firms were often involved, increased the quasi-invisible but very real impact of the 2 percent sales tax on the final price (in contrast to Ford, for example). And the requirement that gasoline include a percentage of ethyl alcohol was intended as a gesture of support for potato farmers. Even before the industrial production of synthetic fuels had been introduced on any significant scale, first for reasons of foreign exchange and later for defense, the discussion about this unnecessary burden continued; it clearly had an influence on the designers.

At the same time, Germany's automobile designers were accused of an uneconomical passion for innovations and refinements that prevented the cost of motor vehicles from falling. Look how many fewer types of vehicles America managed to get by with, although it was so much big-ger and richer! Following the stabilization of the currency, and later during the period of deflation, Germany had to undergo a very painful adjustment. Numerous weapons companies, both large and small, had converted to the production of motor vehicles after 1919. They experimented with one specialty or another, as if it were a simple matter, and this may have been quite stimulating from a technical point of view. However, these new customers with their special requirements were not welcomed by the parts industry, for which the individualism of the old auto manufacturers had already been a burden. The new firms upset the process of standardization, which was also an attempt to lower prices. Robert Bosch's mood was clearly expressed in a letter to Wilhelm von Opel, who had sent Bosch his impressions from America. "The German automobile manufacturers have followed very different principles than the Americans," Bosch wrote on September 18, 1925. "For more than ten years, the German parts manufacturers, by whom I mean Tischbein, Sachs, and myself, have been telling our German colleagues on the board of directors of the National Automobile Industry Association at every possible moment what would happen. We were crying in the wilderness. The automobile manufacturers knew better. As long as they were making money, not one of them saw the future or looked beyond the border. They not only didn't look beyond the border; they didn't even see the parts factories in their own country . . . If you look you will see that in the German ignition industry people are working as hard and as efficiently as their American counterparts . . ."

The year 1924 and the period that followed saw the disappearance of dozens of new brands, but they had not yet hit bottom. Within the motor vehicle industry what was needed to jolt the economy out of its capital shortages and layoffs was either a large-scale merger of older plants or bold new plans that would lead to the sale of a practical and inexpensive passenger car. The relative weakness of the overall German position in the foreign trade negotiations created a situation where in Germany the protective tariffs for automobiles, compared with a number of other countries, were *less* than the differential in values that the German exporters had to overcome. As a result, foreign automobiles penetrated the German market. Sometimes they built their own plants on German soil; sometimes they invested their foreign capital in German factories. One odd result among the German manufacturers of finished products was that the automobile producers became supporters of protective tariffs.

The situation at Bosch was not simple. They could not simply go along with the complaints of the motor vehicle industrialists, whose weaknesses and ill-advised ventures they recognized. Bosch was irritated when he was criticized by people who said, in essence, "*We* would be doing better, if *you* were cheaper." The share of the parts in the final cost of the automobile had grown, along with their differentiation and expansion, to include brake lights, windshield wipers, blinkers, brakes, and so forth as a result of customer demand for these things, things that increased safety and comfort and had helped make the automobile popular. Bosch did not want to be perceived as the beneficiary of a motorization process that occurred all by itself, but rather saw himself as one of its crucial supporters. Price reductions? Yes, but not at the expense of quality. It was necessary to be patient and wait for rationalization to bear fruit. Bosch was not at all comfortable with the idea that propaganda for defensive tariffs might be the road to salvation. Although the welfare of the German worker was important, the world market was equally crucial to him from the point of view of political economy. One always had to fear that the call for industrial tariffs would be heard by interested parties abroad, and that they would take advantage of it to impose drastic measures aimed against German imports.

Although the continuing tariff threat to foreign trade was not directly responsible, it did play a role in Bosch's decision to add to the company's existing system of commercial representatives by building manufacturing plants in those countries to which they exported the most goods. This would not have been possible in the years immediately following the war, but by now the psychological obstacles had abated somewhat, even though they had not completely disappeared. The future would depend on how the manufacturing partners behaved. In 1928, the French designer and industrialist Count H. de Lavalette proposed a collaboration. In 1929, Bosch became a member of the Societé des Ateliers de Construction Lavalette, which immediately proceeded to open a large factory in St. Ouen, near Paris. The two men who had managed the prewar business in France, Max Rall and Hermann Fellmeth, joined the supervisory board of the new company. Experience showed, however, that even when their cooperation with their French partner went very smoothly, French officials were not able to free themselves from a narrow-minded mistrust. This was especially true of government contracts. This attitude had to be taken into account both in company policy and in the choice of company representatives.

At first, the development of cooperative ventures proved more difficult in England than in France. In true British fashion, opinions continued to appear in the specialized press that although they couldn't abide the Germans, the Bosch spark plugs were still the best, and so forth. The Bosch management in Stuttgart was glad to read comments of this kind; however, it would be years before they would gain acceptance. During the war, the English had been forced to begin their own manufacturing, and a firm had come out with a product that, as Bosch noted in 1940, "was not equal to mine in reliability, but at least it was usable." Since Britain had definitively turned its back on free trade, Bosch faced the question of whether he should start his own production there. His inquiries indicated that establishing the firm would probably be profitable, but it would be an uphill struggle. For this reason they were pleased to discover that their leading competitor, Joseph Lucas, who was an admirer of Bosch's work, was not terribly inclined to take part in an expensive struggle. "If the motorcycle manufacturers in Coventry knew how to behave," Lucas had once told the industrialists there, "they would long since have erected a monument to Bosch in Coventry." For Bosch's high-voltage magneto ignition had saved them from ruin. Bosch loved to refer to this anecdote, and in 1940 he summarized his view of the matter as follows: "Our friends were very generous businessmen and honored our contracts loyally to the full extent and in the full sense of the word." Bosch's connection with Lucas, which led to in-depth negotiations and the signing of contracts in July 1931, would prove to be extremely fruitful in the years that followed. The Birmingham firm of Joseph Lucas Limited had come to the parts industry through manufacturing headlights and bicycle lights. In 1914 it had merged with Thompson-Bennet Magnetos Limited, and after 1922 it became the leading firm in England. It became even more prominent after 1926 when it took over C. A. Vandervelt & Company Limited, in Acton, near London, a producer of electrical accessories designed primarily for heavy trucks. Bosch's negotiations with Lucas led to the formation of C.A.V.-Bosch Limited, of which Bosch owned 49 percent. The new joint undertaking was given the responsibility for electrical equipment in the area of commercial and diesel vehicles. In other areas, Lucas and Bosch concluded marketing agreements. Europe, for the most part, went to Bosch, the British Empire to Lucas; the rest of the world was free for friendly competition. At the same time, the two men agreed on an exchange of experiences, including the swap of engineers, masters, and workers over extended periods so that there were Englishmen working in Stuttgart, Germans in Acton. The agreements resulted in significant benefits for both partners. The workforce in Stuttgart apparently sometimes had difficulty in comprehending this—that English workers should be doing *their* work at a time when they were feeling the full impact of the world economic crisis; *The Bosch Spark Plug* undertook to describe the pressure exerted by tariff policy and to explain how important the overall strengthening of Bosch's position had to be for the workers at home. One may assume that this did not fail to have a certain influence.

The relations with Soviet Russia were naturally of a completely different sort from those with France and Britain. In the prewar period, direct sales to czarist Russia had been relatively insignificant. But the war had educated the Russians about motorization, too, and the planned economy of the Soviet system launched a powerful campaign to create state automobile and tractor factories, linking the country's national economic interests to the military-technical question of future tank manufacture. The Soviet Union soon became almost completely self-sufficient in the production of automobiles, although according to a report in *Pravda* in 1926 the wheel rims were imported from England and the magneto ignition from Bosch. The negotiations, as was customary, were conducted through the Russian trade office in Berlin; Bosch refused to send people to Moscow to build a manufacturing operation there. This particular customer may not have been easy to get along with, but Russia represented a significant sales volume, and the stability of its orders helped Bosch outlast the crisis, whose cycles were more pronounced in the free market economies.

The question of whether these fluctuations were avoidable or were inextricably bound up with the nature of capitalist production was one that

had been begging an answer for some time. The debate over "planned" or
"guided" economies, which in utopian visions had always come to a finely
regulated conclusion, had assumed a certain timeliness. It was not just
that literature on the subject began to proliferate; governments and parliaments found themselves confronted with tasks involving government intervention of a kind that they would have shied away from earlier. In
Germany, for example, laws were promulgated regulating coal and cab-
bage; other measures followed concerning cereal grains, flour mills, milk
production, and more. These laws were justified as being in the public
interest. On the one hand, they represented payments on account toward
an imprecise socialist ideology; on the other, they were drastic and prag-
matically improvised attempts to cushion the economy against the incipient crisis in agriculture. Along with state intervention, which reached its
high point in the support of banks and in campaigns to reduce farm indebtedness, the half-free, half-regulated market grew by means of cartels for
raw materials and semifinished products. The emergence of monopolies
and of monopoly pricing, which had been considered an extremely controversial and problematic issue at the turn of the century, now even extended
beyond national borders and was supported by international agreements
as a kind of sedative to calm the swings of the economic cycle.

The economic theorists were influenced by both the East and the
West. No doubt the extraordinary venture undertaken by the Soviet political leadership, the industrialization of the enormous Russian countryside through its Five-Year Plans, had begun to make a real impression.
This had long been considered impossible, the numbers pure fantasy.
But the Potemkin villages to which people referred gradually seemed to
be acquiring solid walls and foundations. The experiment, whether one
called it socialism or state capitalism, was on its way to becoming reality,
even if it was paid for with the sacrifices and low living standard of a generation. State planning in the Soviet Union provided orders and work—
couldn't this serve as an example for Germany? A glance westward
suggested a different answer: industry there was growing, or so it seemed,
not from the enforced impoverishment of life but from the freely expanding wealth of the masses. The motor of this powerfully developing commercial life was not mere satisfaction of existing needs, but the bold
awakening of new ones. A virtual science had developed through which

people in America were attempting to explore scarcely perceptible fluctuations in demand in order to adjust the supply accordingly. At the same
time, they were attempting to guide the desire to buy and were developing the psychological aspects of their sales techniques. America seemed
to have become exemplary not only in its systematization of norms and
types for the mass production of goods but also in the newly emerging
sales methods of commercial business. At Bosch they paid careful attention to this development; *The Bosch Spark Plug* carried detailed stories
about the special training of salesmen. In 1929, the firm concluded that
it needed to create a sales school. A department of market research was
added in 1930. These things were not overemphasized, but they did help
to provide quick information about emerging economic trends, particularly since the more intelligent people in Bosch offices all over the world
were asked to participate as observers and to write reports. Such ventures
were less significant when it came to the traditional products of the
Bosch factories, since they had plenty of experience with them and were
dealing essentially with a manageable group of purchasers—the various
types of motor vehicle and engine factories. But now they were crossing
the border into completely new territory, and here, the new methodology
proved to be very productive as a way of dealing with the economic crisis.

The "prosperity forever" that had been trumpeted in America went
astray in the late 1920s. The international financial agreements had only
temporarily averted the crisis that hung over Europe and Germany,
threatening to break out as long as political turbulence and the madness
of the reparations burden continued. The crisis was further exacerbated
when America's high defensive tariffs, theory of purchasing power, and
consumer loans finally began to affect the business cycle. The all-too-
easy equation that high wages equal stimulation of the consumer goods
sector had infected Germany, particularly influencing certain trade
union leaders. Robert Bosch had a natural tendency to see a kernel of
truth in this theory, which was reflected in his views and his actions, but
he warned about regarding it as the central means of fighting the crisis.
The example of Australia seemed compelling; despite high wages and
the government's highly developed social policies, it was staggering
under the weight of the world economic crisis just as much as other countries, whether industrial or agricultural. At Bosch, they were profoundly

skeptical about the approach that had become the main motor of the pro-longed economic boom and was now gaining adherents in Germany, as well—the seductive-sounding notion of "consumer financing," which had replaced the less impressive term "installment buying," basically meant the same thing. In the United States, the provision of credit for items of everyday need, charged against future income, had to be a tremendous stimulus to production, but the moment when the demand was satisfied finally arrived and the entire artificial mirage of the boom began to dissipate. Property was sold at bargain-basement prices, and unemployment, for which no official safety net existed, spread through-out the country, making it ripe for the experiments of the newly elected President Franklin D. Roosevelt. This had the effect of limiting the free market economy through central state interventionism in a manner quite foreign to the American tradition.

Bosch's course through the uncertain period of the years following stabi-lization can be charted, in rough terms, by the size of his workforce, which was detailed in the business reports at the end of every fiscal year. The comparability of these figures suffered from the fact that the firm was unable, despite numerous efforts and attempts to educate its customers, to change the seasonal character of its orders, which always caused the curve of the number of employees to rise between May and July. Overall, however, the numbers yield quite a bit of information. The firm closed the year 1923 with 10,546 workers and staff members, remained in the same general range in 1924, with 10,857, and then rose to 12,862. The year 1926—the first year to show a loss—brought a sudden drop to 7,031, but the low point did not last long, for now the Bosch firm began work on the diesel engine. As a result, the years 1927 and 1928 ended with an equally large workforce of just over 10,550. Then, in 1928, the German market first began to weaken, and 9,500 employees were listed. In 1930, 1931, and 1932, there were 8,114, 8,422, and 8,332; some of these work-ers were naturally working shorter hours.

    These apparently weak numbers are the most impressive testimony to the ability of the factory to withstand stress and stand as a silent witness to the business policy of those years. This policy was not content to hold on stubbornly to its position, but precisely during a period of general market weakness changed tack to take on new tasks with great flexibility. The statistics, it is true, do not quite speak for themselves. For example, the business report for 1930 stated, "In 1930, the average work week of our employees amounted to only 39.1 hours, and as a result we were able to employ 1,263 more workers than if they had worked 48 hours." For 1932, the average was 38 hours per week. In other words, the situation was not without sacrifices, but given the relatively high wages at Bosch, these sacrifices could be borne by the individual workers. In later years, buoyed by the momentum of a government-supported boom, Bosch sometimes reflected on these years as a period in which he felt particular pride and satisfaction.

Even during these harsh times, Bosch tended to avoid overly pessimistic judgments, particularly when people hastily concluded, as many did, that the rationalization of the industry had been responsible for mass unemployment. In a thoughtful lecture, "The Meaning of Technology," Karl Martell Wild explained the general situation as follows: "Germany was forced to maximize its efficiency very rapidly after the war and the end of the period of inflation if it was not to lose its export possibilities and, as a result, have to sacrifice jobs. We have between five and six million unemployed, who nowadays, in contrast to the past, are probably registered down to the last man. Still, compared to the prewar period— and this is almost always left out of any consideration—we also have the same number, that is five or six million, more employable workers. If we didn't have this increase in workers compared with the prewar period, then even in today's economic crisis and in spite of rationalization, we would not have any unemployed. Without rationalization there is no doubt that the number of unemployed would be higher than it is today, because then we would have lost our exports due to the high cost of production."

True, numerous firms had gone through rationalization with technically as well as economically positive results, only to suffer later, while Bosch did not. It may be that the most profound reason for the unbroken sense of security with which the Bosch factories came through this period lay in the firm's financial policy. Robert Bosch did not emerge as a war profiteer from the great boom that had begun for him—much against his wishes—in August 1914. In Stuttgart he had donated more than 20 million marks for the general welfare. Nor could he profit from inflation in any major way since he did not work with borrowed money, but for that very reason deflation did not hit him as hard as it did so many firms that had financed their expansion with borrowed funds. Except for the American loan of $3 million in 1926, there were no outside obligations whose interest payments could have caused difficulty due to the decline in income. After the years of inflation, when no dividend was paid, a dividend of 8 percent was announced for 1924 and 1925; however, payment of the 1925 dividend was delayed until 1929 and 1930 due to uncertainty about future developments. From 1926 through fiscal year 1932, no dividends at all were paid despite the fact that except for the years 1926 and 1931, in which the company posted a loss, there were some very substantial net profits. The Bosch Aid Foundation that had been formed in 1926 received regular payments from these surpluses, and a special reserve fund of 5 million marks was created in addition to the legally required reserve of 4 million marks. The main goal continued to be the renewal and expansion of the factory. To the extent possible, the plant, and especially the machine shop, was sharply depreciated; as a result, the firm was not burdened by old obligations when the time eventually came for technical changeovers.

Bosch was able to carry out this policy, which was solely directed at the welfare and liquidity of the company, because he had increased his ownership by buying back shares that had been given to the cofounders or their heirs. There were no bank representatives or opposition groups at his general meetings. The rules for joint stock corporations applied to him, too, but they were essentially denatured, for as interesting as the balances and business reports of such a large firm had to be for political economists, the factory occupied a strangely isolated position amid the turmoil that reigned in the worlds of banking and the stock market. It lived by its own brand of lawfulness, which was the character of its creator.

In the spring of 1932, Robert Bosch felt the need or the duty to take a personal position on the social and economic phenomena of the world economic crisis. This occurred in a paper he wrote, "The Prevention of Future

Crises in the World Economy." Previously, Bosch had written a rather lengthy essay for an anthology by Davis-Lüdecke bravely titled "The Solution to the Social Question." In his essay for the anthology, Bosch had stated his belief in the progressive achievements of a self-limiting capitalism, expressed his deeply felt anger at Oswald Spengler's pessimistic assessment of technology, and criticized as misguided the Lasallean "iron law of wages." But evidently this essay did not entirely satisfy him, for in the new work he revisited various motifs he had touched on in the previous essay and gave them a more systematic treatment within a larger context. The piece is prefaced by the following statement of goals: "It is intended to demonstrate that the progress of the development of technology, in the fullest sense of the word, plays the role of providing the greatest service to mankind, and that it is in a position to give mankind the greatest possible measure of the possibilities and happiness of life. It is intended to show that social struggle, or class struggle, is senseless, and that it only serves to hold down the standard of living. It is intended to point to the fact that free trade raises the standard of living of the earth's citizens, but that protective tariffs, on the contrary, rob every individual, even if he has barely been touched by civilization, of a part of his life's possibilities. Finally, last but not least, it will point to the fact that a change in the inner attitude of people toward other people and of the peoples in their mutual relationships is in itself capable of bringing about a fundamental change in the course of world events."

The goal was lofty enough in its definition, but Bosch the writer had less success with this than Bosch the industrialist. One may certainly make the case that this bothered him. Couldn't the *Frankfurt News* or the *German Economist* print the paper, as he would have liked—even if it had to be in installments—and then respond to his theories? The fact that journalists must respect certain rules of length, pacing, and organization when they serialize articles, and that they were in an awkward position when confronted with this—for their purposes—somewhat shapeless manuscript, was something he had a difficult time comprehending. He felt abandoned by people whose support or at least objective discussion he had counted on. Why didn't they want to listen to him? Did they think his openness on some points was out of tune with the times? The paper was privately published and distributed, and appeared in English and French translation as well. Bosch occasionally remarked on the fact that at least a few leading researchers like Carl Bosch and Köttgen had expressed their agreement, and he accepted the fact that, as he noted in June 1933, the paper "received no notice in the daily newspapers."

This odd essay is a peculiar mixture of personal confession and cool, sober argumentation. It begins with an apologia for technology and science, which had increased the average life span of human beings so significantly, and, with its means of transportation, would have driven famine out of the world if the "foolishness of mankind" had not prevented this possibility. This foolishness, one of the ancient scourges of mankind, was envy among individuals and among peoples. Envy led directly to protective tariffs, and "nationalism, which since the war has been growing like a weed, cries for autarky, i.e., wants to provide for itself." After rehearsing the theses of the argument for free trade, it continued: "The protective tariff, if one looks at it without preconceptions, is a hindrance for the world economy, which could not be worse . . . Autarky would strike Germany from the roster of progressive countries." It would be possible if Germany were divided up into small peasant holdings on which the populace would feed itself "as best it could, in an impoverished way." Germany's leading position in the world's economy—it had produced 50 percent of the Nobel Prize laureates—would be a thing of the past. The loss of freedom of movement for goods would be followed by the mutual exclusion of people at a time when the globe had become smaller as a result of technological progress. "We must commit ourselves to free trade," argued Bosch, even if "it may seem odd even to speak of it today," when the situation could not be farther from it. "But this state of affairs is precisely part of the reason for the worldwide crisis." Bosch believed that even in protectionist America he could hear voices that recognized this fact.

The war was not the sole cause of the acute crisis. The fact that wars leave behind a hunger for goods, which then creates an overheated boom and ends in a recession, appeared to be a typical historical phenomenon. During and after this war, however, the number and size of the production sites had not only been increased because of the conflict's dimensions, but the simultaneous "perfection of the means of product manufacture," whose advanced state had not yet been perceived by mankind, had fundamentally changed the situation. It was no longer possible to employ all the people capable of working for the number of hours that had customarily made up the working day. The point was to keep them all working, if possible, for "those who are unemployed must degenerate, physically and mentally." The radical cure was to reduce the workday from eight hours to six. In an earlier essay that preceded this paper, Bosch had suggested the possibility of a five-hour workday. Capitalism itself must take the lead in resolving this issue; it must adapt, for otherwise it would be justifiably accused of being responsible, and resistance would follow with the force of natural law. The opinion that the perfection of technology should be seen as the guilty party was not defensible; it was nonsense to pillory this blessing, which had freed mankind from so many burdens and labors, as if the opposite were true. All that was needed was to draw the pragmatic general conclusions from the facts that technology had produced.

These conclusions, as far as Bosch was concerned, included a break with economic nationalism, the limitation of struggle between peoples to decent competition, freedom of employment for workers, and recognition of individual achievement. Nor did the socialist state offer a means of preventing world crisis. Bosch expressed skepticism when it came to the suitability of human beings "to do their duty purely out of inner motivation, a sense of responsibility, or concern for the whole . . . Man only works under compulsion." However, he added, "it does not necessarily have to last many hours a day." When the Socialists spoke of world economic planning, he found the desire for such a plan to be quite understandable, but who should do the planning? "Governmental economic planning is already no good. In a state made up of bureaucrats, concrete personal responsibility is lacking, which is the only basis on which the highest achievement can be predicated."

Therefore the first proposed measure is the reduction of working hours from an average of 2,400 to 1,800 per year. This did not need to be followed blindly; it was only intended as a guideline. Plants that operated continuously could calculate suitable breaks between shifts. Ten years earlier he had been asked, as someone with particular experience in questions related to the workday, to write an expert opinion on the eight-hour day for the National Economic Council. At the time, the emphasis had been on a different question, namely the question of average work performance. His study had made a distinction between those individuals who were working intensively at a machine and those who were merely available for work, and had come out in favor of a certain elasticity within the plants and the various industries. Here he made a similar caveat to the effect that it was possible the six-hour day could only be introduced following a worldwide or perhaps European agreement; or perhaps it could be tried as an experiment in one nation or in certain sectors. In any case, it would be better than the present situation characterized by millions of unemployed throughout the industrialized world. Bosch abruptly dismissed one objection "made, in particular, by academics, that is people who are supposed to be at a higher level," namely, that the workers had no idea what to do with their free time. That was the same thing they had said before the introduction of the eight-hour day! The workers would learn how to use it in the same way in which they had said good-bye to the cheap alcohol that had accompanied the excessively long workday.

Shortening the workday, "along with its moral effect," aimed at employing everyone and thus creating more purchasing power. How high the wages were was not important per se. Full employment would immediately remove the deduction for unemployment insurance, and with good management much could also be saved in the area of health insurance. What was decisive was the reduction of the prices for products; "the relationship between wage rates and product prices is the determining factor." Since in many industries the wage level represented a large share of the production cost (in the coal mines, for example, it was 50 percent, and in industries producing finished products 25 percent), the creation of new purchasing power through wage increases was only possible in a very limited way, since the wage increases would be passed along in price. Fortunately, there were other possibilities available to achieve the necessary lowering of product prices, including "lowering the overhead connected with sales" and "better organization of production, through cartels."

Bosch thought that from an objective point of view the amount of advertising was nonsense. Measures that made shopping more convenient only made sense where they were economically justified; like so many other critics, Bosch was disturbed by the large number of cigar stores. The gap between wholesale and retail prices also seemed much too large. Bosch believed that a reform of the distribution system, including clearing out excess capacity, would result in lowering the prices of goods by 15 percent. Then one could create cartels in the various branches of industry in order not to set prices that would guarantee the continued existence of inferior producers and monopoly profits for good ones, but to stamp out those plants that had been left behind. Then the remaining good plants would be able to make full use of their capacity, i.e., deliver the goods most cheaply. There should be no "guild social- ism" with high workers' wages and high benefits to the owners, adhering to the slogan that "the consumer pays for everything." These cartels would have to plan and study the market, they would have to make sure their members were "top-notch when it came to manufacturing," and were fully utilized. Bosch assigned them the responsibility, in a notice- able departure from his earlier commitment to free trade, "to watch out that new plants are not constructed or old ones expanded unnecessarily." The cartel, if it is not to be derelict in its duty, must be supervised, but by whom? Perhaps by an organ created by its customers; certainly not by a group composed of equal numbers of workers and employers. Finally, the bureaucrat, whom Bosch had criticized as an economic planner or leader, turns up in Bosch's scheme after all, in his proper role as an inspector. "The only requirement is knowledge of the matter at hand . . . The bureaucrat must be independent." A superior authority may be intro- duced "if a cartel goes against the advice of the inspector."

There is also a more general consideration, namely, the eradication of the class struggle. With the further reduction of the workday, much of the bitterness that existed would evaporate. As productivity grew along with the improvement of mechanical processes, the moment would then arrive when the employer "must see that the worker, the producer, is also the consumer, and must take good care of him." The economic leader on whom responsibility for the progress of business, for the functioning of the world economy, rested would have no interest in keeping wages low. If this plan were not to seem utopian, it was admittedly necessary to restore trust and also to restore the health of the public treasury, as well as lowering the interest rates on foreign loans; otherwise the required means would not be available. The civilized world had "recognized that things cannot go on as they are. One may hope that even the politicians will go along at some point." What needed to be done, according to Bosch—this was in March 1932—was "through internal unity to earn the trust of the other nations . . . If our own political relationships are in order, then we will be able to say with complete justification that it is possible for all of mankind, at some point, to discover with satisfaction that the machine age has ultimately become a blessing for the human race."

In forming an opinion about this paper by Bosch, one cannot overlook the fact that its perspective was focused somewhat too exclusively on the sector of large-scale industrial mass production, ignoring the problem of agriculture, and that Bosch failed to recognize the potential of government regulation, which had already been discussed internationally for a number of years and was being practiced with growing success through government contracts, manipulation of foreign exchange, and interest rate policy as its chief implements. One could criticize the lack of attention to the complex of issues surrounding the development of new industrial materials and their relationship to foreign exchange policies, which had rendered some of the old formulations of the free trade argument invalid on technical grounds. The essence of the paper is to be found in the vehemence with which the shortening of the workday is conceived as the central task. It was seen not merely as a temporary measure with which Bosch himself had managed to survive the crisis in his own plant, but as a socially desirable and actually necessary long-term requirement, given the technological rationalization that had simplified the manufacture of products. Bosch's belief in the mission of technology to serve the happiness of mankind, and in the educational and motivating effects of free trade, considering the atmosphere that reigned a decade later, seem in retrospect like the swan song of an aging social liberalism, a song Bosch performed with conviction and coherence.

Bosch remained steadfast in his position. A business friend once posed the question to him, after circumstances had changed and the shortage of work had been replaced by a shortage of workers, whether he still believed in his earlier paper. Bosch reported this discussion to his friend Eugen Diesel on February 6, 1940, after the new war had already begun, with the words: "Naturally, I told him; now more than ever. But then I became interested in looking at my paper again, and now, having read it, I naturally say (as did Herr Walz, of whom I just spoke, by the way), now more than ever, and in a relatively short time perhaps even more so."

31

———◆———

ROBERT BOSCH, INC.

The business report for the year 1925, which was presented on August 13, 1926, was signed by eleven regular members of the board of management. A few months later, a memo was issued about changes in the company's leadership. In the future, it was to be composed of only three regular members (Fellmeth, Walz, and Wild) and three deputy members (Gutmann, Rall, and Rassbach). The number of attorneys was also reduced. This organizational measure was embedded in the general tendency toward rationalization, which was being aggressively pursued.

It was also something more than that, however, for some of the men who were now departing had been very closely associated with the history and rise of the factory. Otto Heins had held the first position in America; Hugo Borst, who was also Bosch's nephew, had been the leading force in articulating the company's internal sales organization and in building up its sales network both in Germany and throughout the world. Bosch's relationship with Borst had entered a period of difficulty, the ultimate cause of which is not revealed with compelling clarity in any sources. Did Bosch suspect that Borst's versatility, his significant and stimulating philanthropic interest in contemporary painting and sculpture, his cultured bibliophilism might alienate him from the firm at a time when it faced such fundamental challenges? The deaths of Gottlob Honold and Ernst Ulmer, who had also been present from the beginning, had somewhat reduced the old intimacy on the board of directors. There were a number of overlapping tensions, although for a time it seemed possible to transcend them, for example, by moving Borst to the supervisory board and giving him special responsibilities. Bosch, who was becoming increasingly obstinate and inaccessible, declined all attempts at mediation. He abruptly decided to separate himself from Hugo Borst, and also from his other nephew, Hermann Bosch.

The purchase of the ACRO engine and the development of pumps and valves for the diesel engine had been of fundamental importance for the firm. Bosch wanted and needed to remain in the vanguard of the production of ignition devices for motor vehicle engines; success would justify the costs and the effort, no matter how great they might be. When he began making injection pumps, Bosch had departed from the field of electrical equipment on which his reputation was based, as he had done once before with the lubricators, but he remained within the general framework of the overall program of providing accessories, in the broadest sense, for motor vehicles and airplanes. Continual variation had been the only constant. The transition to battery ignition, which was followed by the in-house manufacture of batteries, had presented new challenges. The growing average speed of automobile travel had led to the perfecting of brakes. The headlights, as they increased in strength, had been equipped with more refined low beams; special adaptations had been designed to assist the person behind the wheel when confronted with the dangers of fog. There was also a continuing concern with comfort; from a locked car, the Bosch internal-link searchlight could seek out highway signs and the like. A method was also developed to secure the vehicle against theft. And even the heating of the car had not been overlooked.

Then, gradually, appliances that had originated in an entirely different industrial world began to turn up in business reports and *The Bosch Spark Plug* articles. In 1928, mention was made of spinning pumps for the weaving of artificial silk. In 1932, the Bosch firm was able to report on a hammer and other tools; some people may have smiled at first when they saw that a machine for cutting hair was among these new products. A gas-driven switch was announced, and soon there was talk of radio parts and of a refrigerator, of products related to cinematic technology and experiments with television. The image of the overall enterprise underwent a profound change.

What was the cause of this expansion? In the factory history of 1936, there is a somewhat stereotypical phrase that often stands at the beginning of new sections: "In the search for new products . . ." In 1926, they had hit their stride with the changeover to mass production, but in the core area of their work they were confronted with a decline in business, so they looked for ways to utilize the increased capacity of the plant and to secure the positions of their employees. Some of the suggestions came from outside the firm. There was nothing more apparently obvious than that now more than ever inventors and designers should approach a firm like Bosch. This was the case with the spinning pump for artificial silk, or rayon. Basically, it was an engineering project that required a level of precision similar to that which Bosch had tested during the preparatory studies for the ACRO engine. The rayon industry was in a phase of powerful expansion; Bosch could count on good sales. But it remained only a brief episode, after all, and when demand receded as a result of the worldwide depression, the firm decided to drop this article; this was made easier by the fact that the lubricator factory, where the pumps were worked on, was fully occupied with the orders that were pouring in for diesel engines.

An extremely important decision was made in 1927, namely, to begin producing hand tools. It would be years before they would be introduced on the market, but once there they would achieve a leading position in a very short time. The objective was to introduce external power into movable hand tools and in this way to reduce or entirely do away with the exertion required of the person doing the work. The worker's efforts could then be limited to the appropriate and safety-conscious use of the appliance. The power was supplied by compressed air or electrical motors. In Stuttgart, the firm of C. and E. Fein, whose founder Wilhelm Emil Fein had stimulated so many varied experiments in the early days of electrical engineering, had become specialized in electrical tools, particularly those used for building construction and civil engineering. Bosch, too, was already using electrical tools for fabrication, which meant that the firm was in a position to gather experience about their use. Such power hand tools needed to be created both for circular movements (drilling, screwing, and sanding) and for linear ones (hammering, riveting, cutting, and so on). In many cases, there were already machines in use whereby the hand tool was often connected to the engine by means of a flexible shaft. At Bosch they felt from the very beginning that it was important to build the motor into the handle of the tool itself. This meant, because of the weight, that the work had to be minute in scale, particularly since it was necessary to devise a way to attach the apparatus to a power source that might have either a direct or an alternating current.

The modest hair-cutting machine, the Forfex, whose distribution had been passed on to the Eisemann subsidiary, seems, in view of the further history of this department, like a lighthearted prelude to a very weighty piece, which was given its solid and powerful rhythm in 1932 when Bosch purchased the sole production rights to an electric hammer with a swirl transmission from a Swedish firm. Bosch then reached an understanding with the firm of Ernst Heubach & Company, in Berlin, which handed over a number of patents for high-voltage electric tools. Heubach had accomplished some very important preparatory work in this field, but the growth of his sales was limited by the fact that his relatively young specialized company lacked a comprehensive sales organization.

Bosch appeared at the technical fair in Leipzig in the fall of 1931 with new items, and this was followed, as it had been after the automobile exhibition, by the expectation that in the future he would not disappoint people when it came to innovations and surprises. A student of Honold's named Steinhart, a man of great inventive flexibility, made sure that this notion was confirmed. Even if the company's offerings were nothing fundamentally new, they nevertheless immediately recommended themselves because of their ease of handling, high performance, and price. For even though the economic heavens were quite cloudy at that time, Bosch had immediately arranged to manufacture these products according to the principles of mass production; he optimistically calculated that these technical aids would be just the thing to increase and speed up workers' productivity and thus would reduce the factories' production costs per item. The potential number of customers was too large to estimate. In the big plants engaged in machine building, woodworking, or construction, on the docks and in the airplane factories, in fine metal and glass work (particularly engraving), people would be clamoring for just these sorts of work-saving precision tools. The small artisan, even if he had only a single electrical outlet—and by now almost everyone did—felt tempted to add to his supply of tools. If one viewed the electric tool as part of the great series that made up the general process of rationalization, it should and would be at home not only in the great factory halls and assembly lines, but in workshops with only a couple of journeymen as well.

Two types of tools were possible: those for direct current and single-phase alternating current, and those for three-phase current with higher voltage. Among the first group, the factory history of 1936 records the following: "hand motors, engravers, screwdrivers, sanding machines, polishers, metal shears, and hammers. As Forfex tools, we produce mainly haircutting machines and carpet and animal shears. The area of high-voltage tools essentially includes tools with a higher level of performance, such as drills, screwdrivers, threading tools, disk sanders, polishers, and metal shears in various sizes." Behind this list lay laborious efforts, for there were also disappointments, particularly with the hammer, which they had purchased from the A. B. Nordiska Armaturfabrikema. As cleverly as it had been designed, it had to be completely reworked when electricity was added. In the end, years later, they were very proud of this Bosch hammer whose force, depending on the material, could be adjusted marvelously. Conceived mainly as a percussion drill for stone and cement, but also useful for chiseling, stamping, the specialized riveting or chiseling of metals, and so on, it was a technical marvel that nevertheless had to be made simple and handy for the rough tasks it was designed to carry out. The Bosch firm began to export it relatively early, for the other industrialized countries, which at first had adopted rationalization only hesitantly, were now following the lead of America and Germany and were catching up with the introduction of work-saving techniques. A notice in *The Bosch Spark Plug* from 1938 was able to report: "In just a few years, our firm has grown to be the largest electrical tool factory on the continent . . ."

This branch of manufacturing was, and remained, a division of the main firm. The Bosch name became a prefix to the names of the most important tools. This was also the case for a new household appliance taken up as a challenge in 1929 and ready for market in time for the spring fair in Leipzig in 1933: the Bosch refrigerator. The consideration that led Bosch to undertake this new endeavor was rather simple, and once again America provided the model; the rest of the world followed. The use of electrical tools in the household, which the leading German firms had also begun to pursue, still had something of the character of a luxury, however. Vacuum cleaners, refrigerators, and the like were considered something for rich people with their many carpets and great stores of food! A glance at the prices of these sorts of items was sufficient to give an approximate idea of their sales limitations. Bosch's goal was to stretch these limits and thus create something like a refrigerator for the common citizen. The appliance should find a home in every small kitchen; it should be inexpensive yet have sufficient storage space. For the first type, the Bosch firm selected a drum form with a capacity of 60 liters, but after a few years, under the pressure of increasing demand, they began to produce two additional sizes that held 90 and 100 liters and by now had assumed the familiar rectangular shape. The fundamentals of the thermodynamic process were clear; the challenges lay in adapting the individual parts of the complicated cooling apparatus to mass production so that Bosch would be able to carry out the price policy the firm envisioned. The experts experimented for years on the body of the refrigerator and numerous times had to learn the hard way before they gained confidence in this area. Later, the cooling motor and the box in which it was housed were produced separately; cooling machines especially made to order gained considerable significance as export items.

A second excursion into the realm of housework would have greater consequences and be more interesting from the point of view of industrial policy—the gas switch. It led to gas-related products for industrial plants that used natural gas as a source of power and heat. In 1926, a designer had offered the firm a nonflammable gas valve. When the flame went out, the further escape of gas was supposed to be prevented automatically. At

Bosch they took a good look at the model but could not convince themselves of the practicality of the solution. The matter was set aside for a couple of years, but the temptation to find a better solution to a problem that had already attracted so many did not disappear completely, and in 1929 they went back to the original plan. Alfred Meyer, who had already worked on it in 1926, was the driving force. If something good were to come of it, they could count on a good level of sales. The competition between providers of gas and electrical power was in full swing despite the fact that both were being provided by public utilities, which made it easier for people to acquire their products. There was scarcely a new building in which the appropriate equipment was not built in. Piped-in gas was beginning to be supplied in midsized and smaller towns. Security against the loss of the unused gas, against the danger of explosions and accidents resulting from breathing the gas, could only be welcome. Not that such devices were lacking; this might be new territory for Bosch, but it had been thoroughly explored by others and was crisscrossed with patents. Nevertheless, Bosch succeeded in perfecting the gas valve. Now it was no longer necessary to wait minutes before the flame was lit or went out, as had been the case with the other devices; the process took only seconds. The principle of the gas burner was clever and simple, as described in the factory history of 1936. "It contains an expanding steel diaphragm with a small hole through which the gas flows to feed the flame. If the membrane is warmed with a match, it buckles out and thus opens a small valve, so that gas can now escape from the hole in the membrane. This gas provides the flame that warms the membrane and thus keeps the ignition valve open. Since the gas can now escape freely, the pressure is reduced in the pipe that feeds the burner and in one chamber of a casing that has been divided into two compartments by a leather membrane. The gas presses on only one side of the membrane, thus opening the main valve, which sits on the membrane, and this opens the way for the gas to reach the burner. When the ignition flame goes out, the steel membrane cools off, the ignition valve closes, and the pressure on both sides of the leather membrane is equalized, so that a spring can press the main valve closed and the flow of gas to the burner ceases."

How would the gas products industry react to Bosch's venture into this new territory? Its leading exponent was Professor Hugo Junkers in

Dessau. Junkers was a brilliant designer who some years before had turned his attention to the airplane, and had exerted a very strong influence on it as a result of his revolutionary boldness. But his early beginnings in industrial design had been in gas devices. The firm Junkers & Company ("Jco") had become a relatively well-established undertaking amid the rather inconstant evolution of his ventures in general. It had not achieved monopoly status, but in the case of the gas-heated bathtub, for example, its name had practically become synonymous with the product. In Dessau, where they were very proud of their own tradition, they were not very much inclined at first to pay attention to the Bosch device. They even raised objections about the patent. Bosch's offer to give them a license for the apparatus was rejected. The situation was becoming uncomfortable. At Bosch they hesitated to make an attempt to have the patent objection legally annulled but felt forced to do so in order to protect the work of the past few years. No trial was held, and in 1931 Junkers accepted the license.

For Junkers, who was mired in debt, the year would become a crisis year full of personal tragedy, as it was for so many hard-pressed German businesses. In order to become liquid, he was forced to divest and thus faced the decision of whether to separate himself from airplane manufacture or from the gas equipment business. He stuck with airplane manufacture, for this area had become more important to him and he believed he still had a contribution or two to make. At Bosch, when Meyer had begun work on the gas switch, they had been thinking about a more or less incidental expansion of their product line, but now a rather unexpected opportunity had arisen for a new and significant undertaking. An analysis of the technical state of the workshops in Dessau, which was prepared by Karl Martell Wild, proved on the whole to be satisfactory, and in the spring of 1932 the Bosch firm decided to buy out Junkers & Company completely. Bosch as an individual and the firm Robert Bosch AG were both involved in the purchase. They had made arrangements to produce the gas switches themselves in Stuttgart, as originally planned, but now they left the manufacturing at the subsidiary in Berlin. Its further development did not occur under the name Bosch but rather as the Junkers gas switch, which continued to be manufactured in Dessau and to be sold to independent producers of gas products.

Time-tested Bosch employees took over the management of the firm's business and technical departments. An experienced sales operation was in place, which extended to foreign countries, and Junkers already had a subsidiary in England. The main problem was that the capital base, at 3 million marks, seemed inadequate for larger tasks. When Bosch began negotiations with Junkers in 1931, the severe depression was affecting the entire economy; by the time the sale was consummated in November 1932, the Dessau factory had 725 employees compared with the earlier 1,100. For anyone who could hear beyond the political noise, the end of the terrible crisis was already perceptible, however, and this optimism was defended in the business report for 1933. They had "not been disappointed," but had decided to make the firm "active and resistant" by increasing its capital to 4.5 million marks in 1933; in 1934 it was increased to 5 million. Sales increased, although the movement of the curve was not regular. There were plateaus and valleys when the construction market declined in the second half of the 1930s or when the emphasis began to be on smaller houses that had no central gas supply. But Bosch was very satisfied that the efforts to expand the foreign market were bearing fruit. In 1937 it was reported that 44 percent of gross sales had been from exports. This favorable development was based on two preconditions in addition to the beginning of the world boom in general, and the German boom in particular. First, the intensive and thorough rationalization of the factory meant that Bosch's manufacturing experience was also transferred to this plant, with the dual result of simplification *and* falling prices for the products. Second, although the Junkers factory produced a surplus from the very beginning, Bosch went without a dividend for many years, returning the entire profit to the factory in order to strengthen it. In Stuttgart they did not judge Junkers according to the increase in the rate of return on capital but rather according to the requirements of the plant's own internal logic. Naturally, the purchase of the endangered factory was not a philanthropic gesture; it was an act that had been thoroughly considered from the standpoint of business policy. The factory's independence was maintained with the utmost conscientiousness; Bosch and his colleagues knew the name Junkers entailed both power and responsibility.

Thus the Junkers factory, which had come to Bosch's attention through a truly accidental event—the successful invention of a safety valve for gas switches—and which at first might have seemed to be a marginal venture, increasingly began to form a center of its own. To a much greater degree than when it had been run by its founder, it developed independent powers of attraction and expansion. This found its clearest expression in 1937 with the acquisition of the gas products department of the Askania factories in Dessau and Friedenau, Berlin, which was the second most significant firm after Junkers in this specialized area. In connection with this acquisition, Junkers's capital was increased in 1937 to 2 million, and in 1938 to 12 million marks. Its technical responsibilities were similarly expanded; along with hot-water heaters, bath-water heaters, and so on, they were now making gas ranges and other similar articles. The old well-known firm names remained. The individual purchaser was not aware that the Stuttgart firm, which was popularly associated with the motor vehicle, had now become the leader in gas-related products as well.

There is an anecdote from the early 1920s that begins with a birthday celebrated among friends on the Rotenberg near Stuttgart. The party guests were pleased to observe Robert Bosch coming down the path that led to his country home. They were sitting around a radio, to which a speaker had been hooked up; the guests who were enjoying the very newfangled present had probably read and heard much about this astonishing invention, and were now able to become personally acquainted with its wonders for the first time. A friend of the household, Eugen Kaiser, had ordered and assembled the apparatus himself. Decades earlier he had been Gustav Klein's master during the latter's period of voluntary apprenticeship, and he was on an intimate footing with the people from Bosch; now he was delighted to have the opportunity to introduce the invention to his great colleague. But things ended in terribly confounding disappointment. "So, you too have got one of those devilish boxes, so that it is impossible to have a sensible word with one another—in that case, I shall continue on my way!" Bosch did not even take off his hat; he simply kept walking in a state of irritation. Kaiser was despairing. "Herr Bosch, don't be that way . . . it will be a great thing, and it could be something for you." This on-the-spot advice, born of his embarrassment, became a prophecy.

When the first radio sets appeared, still marred by difficulties and imperfections, Bosch observed them neither as an engineer nor as a businessman. His first, very personal reaction was an uncomfortable rejection of the indiscreet instrument that would intrude into every home, where it would suppress intelligent, open sociability and threaten good, manly conversation. Bosch the supporter of technology and native outdoorsman was full of trepidation that a further area of human life, of space for man's soul, might become entrapped and dependent. If someone had told him about music, literature, or the like, his reaction might have been "Well, all right, but . . ."; the prediction of the power that this invention would place in the hands of private and public authorities would have made him truly mistrustful. On that late May afternoon, he simply wandered on alone through the vineyard with an irritated expression on his face.

At the firm they had quite a different opinion and in fact felt a responsibility to view it differently. They had had their eyes on this area since 1925. It was not easy to find their way, for the field was quite thickly staked out with patents, and the new item was in the throes of its general and technical development, with more and more new ideas coming forward from designers. For the moment, it could only be a question of staying informed about the whole question of the airwaves.

The first thing to do was to deal practically with a negative aspect of radio technology that came up in conjunction with aeronautics. Radio sets with receivers and transmitters were built into the new airplanes, but they did not hold up well alongside the electrical ignition devices and lights, and there were frequent problems until a protective mechanism was created at Bosch to shut out the interference. In the process Bosch's people were able to gain some insights, but they did not get much further than that until the final peace agreement with the American Bosch Magneto Corporation had been concluded. The central goal of this agreement lay in an entirely different direction; Bosch wanted and needed to come to terms with the annoying fight over the firm name. In the "peace treaty," they agreed to exchange manufacturing experience, and since the American Bosch Magneto Corporation had been engaged in the production of radios for many years, they were included. It was a secondary interest, but at least they had already gained a certain amount of hard-won experience. Bosch's managers in Stuttgart identified this as an area in which they could make a good start technically, and they tried to secure it as quickly as possible in order to avoid laying off workers—it was 1930! The immediate task was to find a link with one of the existing independent businesses, and Bosch found it in the Model Factories for the Wireless Telegraph, which had been founded in 1923 in Hohenschönhausen, Berlin. The Model Factories were not so much a comprehensive manufacturing business as an outfit that purchased the individual parts of the radio from subcontractors, assembled them expertly, and had made a good name for their Blaupunkt brand, with the help of a competent distribution department. With a capital of 1.5 million marks, they had made a profit of approximately 800,000 marks in 1929, with 64 percent of the deliveries going to foreign countries. In September 1930, a manufacturing contract was drawn up that made the Stuttgart firm the sole supplier of the radio parts. They had saved the jobs of a couple of hundred workers! As a result, the employees in the laboratories and experimental workshops grew happier about their new task. Naturally, Bosch did not decline to be a supplier of parts, but there was a tendency for the relationship to move in the direction of full, independent responsibility and control. The Berlin radio exposition of August 1932 had a Bosch booth for the first time, and thus announced to the world that this field, too, had now been tackled in Stuttgart.

By 1933 they were able to purchase the shares of the Model Factories. The management of the new subsidiary followed the same basic principles that had stood Junkers & Company in good stead: although the business was doing quite well, Bosch declined to siphon off the profits. Its capital was increased from 3 million marks in 1934 to 5 million in 1935, 6 million in 1936, 10 million in 1938, and 12 million in 1940. The increases had been necessary, above all, because in view of the heavy utilization of the space and machine capacities in Stuttgart, the firm had decided to transfer the entire operation to another location. The existing space in Hohenschönhausen did not meet the growing demand, and so a completely new, comprehensively planned factory was constructed in Wilmersdorf, Berlin, in the form of a shed. Bosch was gratified to see that the favorable business trend held even after a certain recessionary movement began to be observed in the German radio industry in 1937; the business report noted that in spite of this, exports had increased by almost 25 percent over the previous year. In 1938 Bosch was able to report an additional increase of 23 percent. The Blaupunkt brand had secured a definite position for itself, especially in South America. It existed in many languages, as Blue Point, Point Bleu, and so on, and this prompted the leadership to give up the rather bland name Model Factories. After 1938 the firm went by the name Blaupunkt G.m.b.H (its legal form was changed at the same time). The firm developed in an extremely promising way; along with large, very sensitive radios, it also developed models for use in both the automobile *and* the home—to be used, in other words, either with batteries or with an electrical outlet.

The radio exposition of 1932 had also exhibited an additional Bosch product that was related to the radio and was initiated as soon as the first steps had been taken in that direction: the Bosch record player. Within the overall production scheme at Bosch, this machine, with its handy and carefully thought-out design, remained a secondary affair, an offshoot of the general developmental work being done on the radio. Although it had gained a good place for itself among similar products, it was later abandoned.

The path to the gas switch and the radio had been determined largely by workplace policies that resulted from the crisis in the motor vehicle industry. This consideration played only a minor role when it came to the next decision to widen the firm's tasks by engaging in the production of film equipment, a plan that had already been conceived during the period of crisis. Ernst Eisemann, who always loved to tinker with the design of new product lines, had developed a machine to project double-eight film, and the firm was ready and willing to begin producing it—admittedly somewhat hesitantly because of their uncertainty about the market situation in this sector. A coincidental relationship gave the plan a new twist. Julius Faber, who was a member of supervisory board, was personally involved in an existing business in Untertürkheim, and as a result he had an opportunity to acquire the shares of Eugen Bauer G.m.b.H. in 1932, but the new ownership was not announced publicly until 1934.

Eugen Bauer, who had opened his own business as a precision engineer in Stuttgart in 1902, had also come across the question of film early on, albeit accidentally. In 1905 someone had brought him an early experimental camera by Pathé Brothers, and when he became familiar with the machine he began building on his own. The orders came in, his experience increased, and the workshop became a small specialized factory that found new, larger accommodations in Untertürkheim in 1928. Approximately 200 people were employed there. When his sound film camera came on the market in 1929, Bauer joined the ranks of the first companies in a rather wildly proliferating field; 75 to 80 percent of his production was exported to foreign countries.

There, too, in order to do justice to the plans for development it was necessary to increase the inadequate capital base of 13,000 marks to 2 million. At Bosch they greatly enjoyed the technical challenges, but their pleasure in the commercial customs that predominated in this field was considerably less, and there were many problems until the standards Bosch was accustomed to setting were established. The first few years resulted in losses, some of which were connected with the reorganization. Bauer had specialized in double-eight film projectors; now the production program became more all-encompassing and projectors designed for the normal motion picture theater appeared on the market. Great attention was also paid to projectors for instructional purposes, which were portable and were finished with a particularly reliable fire-proofing substance. The first year in which they operated without a loss was 1937. The report for 1938 notes that 50 percent of the normal sound film projectors were going to foreign countries. The fabrication process took place, in part, in the old Bosch workshops, but toward the end of the decade they were increasingly consolidated at the Untertürkheim plant.

The knowledge with which the engineers began to experiment came from the laboratories of the physicists; their skill paved the way for the move into more and more new industries. In this way, within only a few decades the moving, and then the talking, picture had emerged; after this voice transmission was liberated from the wire. Now not only sound but also images were being transmitted through the airwaves over long distances. It was a possibility whose theoretical range and realistic limits were still difficult to gauge, as was its ultimate significance, although it had to be very exciting to those who understood technology and were imaginative enough to recognize the potential of things still in their embryonic stages. In 1928 Karl Martell Wild and Erich Rassbach had been greatly impressed with the experiments conducted with television at Baird Television Limited. It was quite clear that they were dealing with something that could have a future. The two observers must have been excited about the possibility of channeling Bosch's powers into the developmental work that would be so essential, and they proposed to John Logie Baird that they collaborate. Baird was amenable to their plan, but he was no longer quite free, since there were existing agreements with Ludwig Löwe's radio company in Berlin. At the same time, he thought it would be objectively desirable, if they were undertaking a collective effort in the field, to attract an important optical factory that could provide helpful scientific knowledge. As a result, Television AG was founded in Berlin in 1929. The founding capital was set at a moderate level of 100,000 marks, with Baird, Löwe, Bosch, and the optical factories of Zeiss-Ikon in Dresden each owning one fourth. The modest sum indicates that they were not yet thinking in terms of producing anything themselves; the financing was for experimental projects. After a few years, it is true, these experiments required additional investments amounting to several times the original capital. At this point, the partners' shares shifted. Because the National Postal Service and the military, which naturally showed a lively interest in their results, desired that the capital foundation should be purely German, Baird left in 1935; his shares went to Bosch and Zeiss-Ikon. Löwe pulled out in 1938, and by 1938 Zeiss-Ikon had lost patience as well and had offered his shares to Bosch; Bosch now became the sole proprietor. The path that had been traveled in those ten years had required faith and a strong will, as well as a readiness to make sacrifices. "Profits are unthinkable for the foreseeable future," noted the business report for 1935; the sentence was written without any underlying tone of disappointment. The sparse notes discussed the planned continuation of the experimental work. After 1938 there were statements to the effect that the firm had been able to increase the production of usable products, and in 1939 the report grew more expansive, speaking of "rather large contracts" and "energetic" work on the development of a "standard television receiver." After ten years, the firm had outgrown the mainly scientific stages of early development, and for the first time the business was able to operate without subsidies. But millions had been sunk into this early development. And since they had approached the matter with daring and decisiveness, it had become an obligation toward science and their country not to drop it, for in the meantime it had become an object of worldwide efforts. The peaceful contest in which they had become engaged, with a healthy sense of the relative stature of their own hard-won skills, was interrupted by the new world war.

32

———◆———

PUBLIC LIFE AND
PRIVATE DESTINY

The conclusion of the First World War moved Robert Bosch to participate consciously in public affairs and to profess his opinions about political decisions, but it did not result in his becoming a politician. "Internally I am not robust enough to be politically active, and I have never been connected to any party. In my declining years I will not be able to make a change," he wrote in February 1932 to a member of the Prussian regional diet. He was aware of his limitations and ineptitude in public appearances, and his complete lack of ambition in this area was coupled with an uninhibited need for freedom; his eccentric tendencies kept him from confining himself within the tactical constraints a party would impose. And so he remained a loner, often sought out, occasionally feared for his biting criticism, and very reticent in matters of internal party affairs, particularly when he was called upon for financial assistance. After 1919 Bosch set quite a lot of money aside for political purposes but not for party organizations; he preferred to give to nonprofit associations whose goals or leaders he thought merited his support for some special and timely project. Nothing was more repugnant to Bosch than someone who thought he could count on his support, as so many people had accustomed themselves to doing!

In general it was openly known that Bosch, to use the traditional term, was a leftist. After the chaotic period around 1918, he had occasionally expressed the opinion that it would now be necessary to become conservative. But the term did not imply a party leaning, only an antirevolutionary desire for order that would help solidify the government that had been reestablished. In this sense, Bosch saw Wilhelm Blos in Württemberg and Friedrich Ebert at the national level as conservative personalities who now seemed rather meritorious. Bosch's escalating criticism of Social Democracy, which would grow noticeably milder in the early 1930s, was directed at a demagogic insecurity that sought to avoid the awkward burdens of assuming office, namely the need to make unpopular decisions. The notion of class struggle always seemed to Bosch to be incompatible with a sense of overall responsibility to the government and the nation.

Bosch did not view such limitations as being unique to the Marxist groups. The German Democratic Party learned that it could not count on Bosch's active sympathy if its policies did not enjoy the support of the workers. When the representatives of the German People's Party approached Bosch they were coldly rebuffed. The term "bourgeois politics," whether its use was intended defensively or offensively, was abhorrent to Bosch; people who used it were evidently not fully conscious of the degree to which they had been infected by traditional Socialist terminology. August Weber, a democratic member of parliament with whom Bosch got along quite well, succeeded in 1928 in winning him over to his "liberal unity," although Bosch declined to sign a proclamation with the argument that he did not want to be associated with people who, as he stated in a letter dated July 2, 1928, specifically naming German People's Party member Scholz, "play with fire when it comes to the monarchy . . . Our salvation," he continued, "lies in a social democracy that can also obtain the agreement and reinforcement of the working class, and our goal must be to at least reduce the social gap, if we are not in a position to be able to eliminate it altogether."

Throughout the years this remained Bosch's basic point of view, and he never tired of expounding it in tones that were by turns warning and pleading. His mistrust and avoidance of the bourgeois parties of the right, the German nationalists, was very clear, and was only multiplied by his personal distaste for Alfred Hugenberg and his henchman in Württemberg at that time, Wilhelm Bazille. When Bazille became the provincial president in 1924, Bosch made his participation in a celebration in Ulm contingent on the fact that he would not have to meet personally with this man, whose emotional tenor he found to be repugnant. He had a better opinion of Bazille's colleague, Minister of Finance Alfred Dehlinger, who was of the German national persuasion but was objective and levelheaded.

This is not to say that Bosch was fundamentally satisfied with the policies the leftist and centrist groups espoused. He complained that unions of every political persuasion pursued policies that were much too focused on the special interests of their membership; as a result, both the political leadership and the economic movement suffered. He completely saw through the interconnections between the competing groups. He also made plenty of remarks, particularly in the crisis years, to the effect that the Socialists in local government and the health insurance officials were too showy in their building projects. It aggravated him when the newspapers wrote about "exemplary" stadiums and the like, while business was struggling under the tax burden. Bosch did not consider such ventures to be particularly valuable as public works programs, and felt furthermore that they ruined the sense for responsible savings. The fight for votes among the parties seemed to him a necessary and tolerable evil, but he observed it joylessly and with growing anxiety. Bosch did not think deeply or in detail about the faulty design of the Weimar Constitution, which had halted the national historical avalanche in 1919 by dint of certain sacrifices and a certain amount of skill, but which was full of artificial provisions that hindered the development of simple rules by which to conduct the business of the state. He had not yet found the person he could trust. "I am of the opinion," he wrote to democratic leader A. Anton Erkelenz on July 28, 1930, "that Naumann, if he were still alive, would not be pleased with what our parliament and our unions . . . have produced and are still producing." Two years later, on September 19, 1932, he wrote to the same man with the harsh comments: "Who has brought us to where we are today with the Weimar Constitution? I say it is the dissolute lifestyle that the political parties have led in our parliament . . ." Elsewhere in this emotional correspondence, he wrote: "Only the fools, the Hugenbergs, seek to deprive the working class of influence on government and society . . . If things should reach that point, it would only be because Social Democracy has strung its bow so much tighter than it should that as the old adage goes action produces reaction . . ." And on August 29, 1930, "Social Democracy has no leaders who dare to put their finger on the festering wound." This would not be his last word, however. It is very characteristic that his criticism of the left was sharpest when he was speaking with one of its representatives, while he tended to judge it more mildly when an individual from the right castigated the same shortcomings. At the time, a Center for Bourgeois Policy had just opened under the influence of the German People's Party, which was campaigning heavily for Bosch's participation. He refused with the observation that "Herr Dingeldey is no crystallization point—jelly has never led to the formation of a crystal." This debate took place in the midst of the Brüning-Dietrich cabinet's laborious attempts to put the economy on a sound basis, attempts that were fluctuating between real success and psychological defeat. Bosch's response was to the point. "The Socialists," he intoned, "have grown to see that they have made great errors. For a long time now they have done everything they could to rectify their mistakes to the degree that this is possible, if only passively, by tolerating the emergency decrees. At any rate, they have done more to help the domestic situation than some hotspurs. In politics one can only try to achieve the possible, and what is possible is only a slow recovery."

Throughout these years Bosch followed the development of business and social policy with a lively skepticism. He was no advocate of the sort of government intervention embodied in ventures to assist the eastern provinces and reduce agrarian indebtedness, but he did not speak out publicly on these issues. His domestic political activity was limited to the support of a few groups that backed the republic and a few newspapers. He was deeply concerned that the Social Democrats should be able to continue publication of their independent reformist organ, the *Socialist Monthly*. He had met the most important individuals involved in this paper at a meeting of the national Economic Advisory Council, and he even sought support for the journal from among his own circle of friends. After Naumann's death he made it possible for a large number of copies of his journal *Help* to be distributed free of charge.

Bosch had come into much closer contact with the press in his home region after 1920 as a result of a decision that was by no means casual. Earlier attempts to make Bosch a force in newspaper publishing in Berlin had run aground; even to him this involvement had always seemed a bit foreign if not altogether odd. Now, after 1920, it seemed that Hugo Stinnes, at the peak of his political newspaper expansion, would make a breakthrough in Stuttgart as well. Bosch felt that this was something to be prevented. Through middlemen who were friends of his, and who kept their backer's identity a secret, Bosch acquired the majority ownership of the German Publishing Institute in Stuttgart. Since the institute was the principal owner of the firm that published Stuttgart's leading newspaper, the *New Daily News,* as well as the *Württemberg Newspaper,* both of these organs came under Bosch's control. Bosch's motive was precautionary. In general he was not terribly worried by the anxious talk of foreign infiltration. He found nothing horrifying in interlocking capital formations that transcended national boundaries; in fact, they might be helpful to the economic foundation of his peace policy. But there was one very telling exception to this point of view—public opinion in his home territory, narrowly defined, should not be allowed to become dependent on northern German influence! Thus, around 1920 Bosch became a force in Württemberg's publishing world. Still, he did not consider himself to be a press magnate, and he never issued directives. In general his opinion of newspapers was none too good, but he did have a healthy respect for individual responsibility. He did not want to see the reader's right to express aggravation diminished in any way, as it might have been had he not made himself personally responsible, however indirectly, for the statements of the press.

Was the entire decision, which on purely financial grounds Bosch would never regret, a result of his regional particularism? He was in the same situation as many Swabians in those years after 1918; intellectually they were in agreement with centralization, but emotionally they had reservations. In Bosch's notes there is no lack of outspoken expressions of annoyance with the northern Germans, Prussia, and Berlin, although one must not take these comments too seriously. If only the southern Germans had been more unified, they might have been able to offer more effective resistance! When Bosch thanked Oskar von Miller in Munich for coming out in favor of free access to electricity from the Bavarian Electrical Works he added, characteristically, "We Southerners should come together, in order better to express the individuality that is ours by rights. Until now, those of us in Württemberg have been both too small and too big for anyone to have felt the need to get together with us for this purpose. Too small, so Bavaria says we can't help them; too big, so Baden says, 'They only want to put our backs against the wall.' And yet we would be a greater force united than if we act alone." Bosch expressed his concern over this question many times, but he was aware of Karlsruhe's sensitivity on the subject of Stuttgart. When the *Cologne News* addressed the relationship between Württemberg and Baden in 1930, within the context of a discussion of national reform, Bosch found this "extraordinarily commendable," but at the same time expressed the opinion that "we (in Württemberg) will simply have to take a wait-and-see attitude, until the atmosphere in Baden has changed, partly from within, and partly due to a certain power of persuasion from outside." This view of the state of affairs resulted from Bosch's instinctive political sense. He did not involve himself further in issues of national political reform, and one should not attach too much importance to his support of the "Swabian Chapter," a well-intentioned attempt to lead the various Swabian elements within the southern German provinces to some sort of unity. This action may seem somewhat romantic, thus going against Bosch's basically rational nature, but it may have appealed to a part of his Swabian consciousness, which in certain circles had already become legendary. Once, in 1930, he actually had to deny the allegation that he only hired Swabians in his business!

Bosch was far removed from the parties' power struggle and shied away from taking a public position on domestic politics except for those questions that seemed important to him, and then only when he saw them as linked to foreign affairs. This was the case following the early death of Friedrich Ebert, the first president of the Reich, in 1925. Bosch had always had an understanding of Ebert's overall political position and appreciated his humanity, which had won Bosch's respect and sympathy in their occasional encounters; many years later he still spoke of him with warmth, bemoaning his demise as a loss for Germany. He honored the deceased at the time of the funeral with the decision to order a five-minute break in work in all of his businesses, less a political gesture than a human response.

Years earlier, in a personal letter dated 1920, he had once written about various individuals whom he did and did not want to see at the head of the Reich; at the time Ebert had seemed to him to be the proper man. The games the parties were playing with their candidates in 1925 revealed the absolute inability of the party factions to transcend their limitations. Ill will and anxiety destroyed the possibility of productive combinations. Thus the first ballot, with its multiplicity of party applicants, became a useless counting of votes, a sheer waste of energy. The nomination of General Field Marshal Paul von Hindenburg for the second ballot gave the process the political accent that the first contest had lacked. The willingness of the aged, apolitical military man to stand for election created some confusion and much disorientation among the opposing groups. In their confusion they agreed to recognize Wilhelm Marx, the representative of the Center Party, as their compromise candidate. It was not a happy solution, because Marx, although once in office experience might prove otherwise, had been rather outspoken on religious matters, in a way that made it difficult for some people to support his candidacy freely.

This was also true for Robert Bosch, although he did not hesitate to sign a proclamation for Marx. The myths surrounding Hindenburg could not move a character as sober as his; it actually tended to make him mistrustful. Bosch was concerned about Hindenburg's electors and feared the international repercussions of his election, which would have a negative influence on the international credit negotiations occurring at the time. "I still have hopes," he wrote in letter dated April 22, 1925, "that Hindenburg will not make it, and I am doing my part as best I can to see that this is the case."

Hindenburg was elected president of the Reich on April 26, 1925. The result of the nation's majority decision was not what most people had expected. As significant as the consequences of this event would be for Germany's history, neither the hopes nor the fears focused on his election were justified. The office of the head of state took on more representational splendor than Ebert could or would have wanted to give it, but the opportunities that the constitution offered to enhance its political power remained unrealized. Hindenburg had no desire to utilize them, for such a decision would have presupposed a goal in domestic and foreign policy for which he took personal responsibility, and he had no such goal. Although political decisions were sometimes made in response to his particular wishes—or in anticipation of his displeasure—the big questions were resolved by the same old forces in parliament. Germany's entrance into the League of Nations, the Luther-Stresemann policies associated with Locarno, and the transformation of reparations policy in the so-called Young Plan were stages in the difficult process of developing a foreign policy. Hindenburg backed them with the authority of his name. It seemed that some social and other tensions might be alleviated more or less automatically, for Hindenburg, as the former commander-in-chief of the Kaiser and as the representative of a royalist tradition rooted in both family and class background, was strictly committed to maintaining the dignity of his office under the constitution of the republic; in certain respects he even wanted to increase it. The relaxed and generally passive style of his old age made the parliamentary republic seem almost familiar, in a psychological sense, to many of its former opponents.

Bosch, who occasionally came into contact with Hindenburg at official functions but who never developed any personal relationship with him, was satisfied with this state of affairs. When Heinrich Brüning championed Hindenburg's renomination as chancellor in 1932, Bosch saw no reason not to support it just as vocally as he had *opposed* Hindenburg's candidacy seven years before. He responded to the derision and attacks that this occasioned with a very characteristic public statement in the Stuttgart newspapers entitled "Why Lacking in Character?" In 1925 he had been mistaken in his fear that Hindenburg would let his actions be determined by the goals of his backers. Hindenburg did not do what his backers wanted but instead saw the needs of the nation. "To admit to an error is not to lack character, but rather the opposite," wrote Bosch. "The fact that I can come out in favor of Hindenburg now surely gives me more satisfaction than those who previously supported him and are now fighting against him because he acts in accordance with his own view and conscience." Bosch went a step further and agreed to join the re-election committee formed by Carl Duisberg; this was intended as a public gesture that neither expected nor required Bosch's actual participation. He did attend a few meetings, and as his later writings make clear he got no pleasure from the proceedings. But Hindenburg's actual position *after* his re-election gave Bosch cause for concern. At the time, Bosch wrote to Georg Escherich, who had sat with him on the committee, with tight-lipped irony, "I do not have a very lucky hand with our friend Hindenburg . . ." The comment referred to the special action that had been ordered by President Hindenburg with regard to east German agriculture. Bosch's response was expressed even more clearly in a letter to Kurt Hahn dated September 20, 1932, in which he wrote, "Hindenburg's intervention on behalf of his class brothers in East Prussia has been a terrible disappointment to me. When all is said and done, it is not acceptable to want to help a small handful of people at the expense of the entire nation, particularly when this handful wishes to be helped in a way that is not compatible with the general well-being of the German people." In coming out in favor of Hindenburg he had naturally not foreseen the fatal developments that would begin with Heinrich Brüning's dismissal and the appointment of Franz von Papen. Bosch was uncertain: "One cannot see into the wings, does not know the leaders of the government, does not know what they are doing."

Bosch's chief concern in the postwar years had been—and would long remain—to reestablish German's position on a peaceful and secure footing by means of a foreign policy that was both objective and dignified. Among the leaders of the German foreign office, Bosch was most fond of Walter Simons, and in letters to Paul Reusch and others he spoke out in favor of letting him remain in office. The murder of Walther Rathenau, the Jewish industrialist and foreign minister, had greatly affected and upset Bosch, and it was a long time before he became accustomed to Gustav Stresemann, whose sentimental and theatrical brand of humanity was not to his liking. Earlier, in 1927, Bosch had written to an industry representative in Düsseldorf that he had been a follower of Hans Luther, but that the latter's "behavior in the question of the flag and other matters" had "cooled my feelings for him considerably." For that reason one had to be "very grateful" to Stresemann "for his leadership—extraordinarily grateful, in fact. Given his past history I was afraid he would not govern as well as he has." Bosch saw Stresemann as implementing what his former opponents had begun, an acknowledgement that was made without any warmth of feeling. In 1931 Bosch declined to help fund the cost of a monument for Stresemann on the grounds that this should be done by people who had been closer to him.

Bosch exercised his influence on the course of foreign relations in a rather roundabout fashion. He supported associations whose means of bettering international understanding were both effective and ineffective. He had broken with the career pacifists in the early 1920s, for he did not like the way they operated, their dogmatic polemics, or the nature of some of their more prominent representatives. They continued to woo him, and he continued to decline. As late as December 1930 he wrote to the German Peace Society to lecture them about their disingenuous methods of "fighting wordy battles with their opponents," and commented that "there is perhaps no idea better suited for a propaganda that seeks to win people over and convince them than the movement against war." In the same year he sent several thousand marks to a Commission Against Scientific Warfare.

More significant was his participation in several groups of likeminded individuals who sought either to nurture the exchange and understanding between peoples, in a process that was not necessarily linked to political ambitions, or to influence statesmen and members of parliament. The Carl Schurz Association, created in 1926 by the prodemocracy member of parliament, Anton Erkelenz, belonged to the first category; its founder even succeeded in convincing Bosch to be the chairman. This was a favor that Bosch continued for years, "for God's sake, as they say," while regularly reminding all concerned of how illsuited he was for the task. He was glad, however, to carry out the limited task of enlightening American students or other groups of travelers about German matters.

Bosch's solicitude was more lively in the case of two organizations that claimed more political clout but did not exactly coincide ideologically. The first was the New Commonwealth, founded by British coal magnate Lord Davies, who was a follower of Lloyd George. The second was Count

Richard von Coudenhove-Kalergi's Pan-European Union. Bosch must have realized that the efforts of the two groups not only did not coincide but to some degree actually contradicted one another. The British-led organization, which conceived of its rather utopian end goal as the creation of an international police force to bring peace to aggressive nations, was constructed on the assumption that Britain's navy and air force would be the primary driving force behind it. Coudenhove's conception, on the other hand, had a fundamentally anti-English bias, although this was disguised by geopolitics and various historical embellishments. His Pan-Europe was a leaguelike conception of a continent *without* Britain and *without* Russia. Both realms were viewed as alien to Europe, by nature and even more as a result of history. This conflict in the two organizations' basic premises did not bother Bosch. He focused on the goodwill that was necessary if the world were to be led out of the system created by the Treaty of Versailles. This was obviously not possible with the League of Nations alone, and the meetings and declarations of various pro–League of Nations organizations would not suffice. The New Commonwealth was concerned not so much with the legal interpretation of the Geneva statutes as with the notion of transcending Geneva and finding a new beginning. That seemed to make sense. Here, too, Ernst Jäckh was the go-between. Bosch's relationship to Lord Davies became more personal when he discovered that the Englishman also owned hunting preserves in the mountains. Bosch brought the lord to a chamois hunt in Allgäu, and this was followed by an invitation to Bosch to visit Scotland.

Even more intense and in some respects quite astonishing was Bosch's relationship with Count Coudenhove-Kalergi. The two men had markedly different characters. Coudenhove-Kalergi was essentially a member of the literati, a man of playful elegance with a talent for antithetical formulations. Eager for a public role and encouraged by his overly ambitious wife, he so overestimated himself that he was ultimately unable to make accurate judgments. He possessed the marvelous capacity, whenever difficulties arose based on concrete business interests or the more abysmal aspects of national historical consciousness, to let the magic of words work its spell, finding solutions for everything and enchanting or amazing even the most sober of realists. It would be too harsh to say that Bosch was duped by Count Coudenhove-Kalergi, for the latter's rationalist and optimistic belief in a European union was an element of Bosch's own inborn faith, although he had developed it quite differently. "More than thirty years ago," Bosch wrote on April 12, 1928, to one of the count's followers in Württemberg, "I occasionally expressed the notion that we Western Europeans have to join together in order to open up Russia and liberalize it." This outdated mission hardly corresponded to the goals of the present pan-European conception!

In any event, Bosch found Coudenhove-Kalergi's emphatic and moving apologia on behalf of technology to be quite compelling. He thought Coudenhove-Kalergi's writing on the subject "extraordinarily interesting and clever," and was delighted that two people with such different backgrounds "could be in such complete agreement as we two are," and that Coudenhove-Kalergi had come to conclusions "purely speculatively" that Bosch, as a practical businessman, had recognized or "experienced subconsciously, so to speak." "I am eager to learn what you understand by practical idealism," he wrote to Coudenhove-Kalergi on July 23, 1928. "You may remember my definition: The idealist is a materialist who is intelligent enough to see that he cannot prosper all by himself." One can see that Bosch kept up with the play of antitheses, although one might not want to weigh them too carefully. Without a doubt, at the beginning of their relationship Coudenhove-Kalergi had charmed him. In June 1929, Bosch even wrote to a number of acquaintances to publicize the count ("his books are really excellent . . . he excites even people who are none too easily excited") and to promote his organization ("I make no bones about saying that the money we make available to the count for his cause is money well-invested for us as Europeans").

Bosch remained willing to help sustain and expand Coudenhove-Kalergi's organization for quite some time. As a member of the association's circle of supporters, he also gave generously for specific projects, and in 1933 he decided join the group that was proposing Coudenhove-Kalergi to the Norwegian Committee for the Nobel Peace Prize. In a practical sense, what Bosch gained from his participation in this movement was his engagement on behalf of Franco-German understanding, which would remain the centerpiece of his thinking on foreign policy even after the end of his connection to Coudenhove-Kalergi. After Coudenhove-Kalergi came to feel, in 1932, that the important diplomats of the European nations did not attach as much importance to his activities with congresses and publicity as he thought he deserved, he conceived the completely illusory plan—lacking any knowledge of international political life at the popular level—of forming European parties in the individual countries. Perhaps through them he would be able to exert some pressure on the governments. Bosch counseled very emphatically against this, with the words, "It would be a great detour, if not a setback," and its success would be "extraordinarily questionable." In France and Germany, yes, one should "create a popular movement . . . If these two most powerful nations in Europe have come to an understanding and then declare, 'We are prepared to reach an agreement with all other European states,' and if they are wise enough to allow each of the other states the room it needs to live and maneuver, then the structure will quickly expand. I think Belgium and Switzerland and then probably Holland and Scandinavia would quickly join in, and the Poles and the Czechs will have no other option if France concludes the pact with us, not to mention Austria."

Bosch thus painted a direct and clear portrait of the possible results of a genuine agreement between Paris and Berlin. How would the English-speaking world react to this? Some of the acquaintances with whom he discussed it, believed, as did Ludwig Roselius, that the way forward could not bypass London. Paul Reusch warned Bosch in August 1932 against overestimating France's willingness, Coudenhove-Kalergi's stature in France, or his capacity for economic thought. Bosch, too, remarked in April 1928 that he thought it "tactically incorrect to exclude England from the outset." One would have to leave it entirely up to Britain to decide what position it wanted to take. "If one does not do that then there will be a far greater likelihood of an England that works *against* Pan-Europe than if some attention is paid to England from the outset." His objection was intelligent, but it had to be rather impotent, for Coudenhove-Kalergi's basic conception, whether one interpreted it narrowly or broadly, remained anti–Anglo-Saxon. It was in error that Bosch, in a discussion with Coudenhove-Kalergi in July 1931, assumed that there was no longer anyone in the Anglo-Saxon world who would "come out against the pan-European federation." He quite evidently did not understand the interplay of relationships and feelings that reigned in Europe.

All Bosch's efforts to give real encouragement to the easing of tensions between Germany and France, as initiated under the sign of Pan-Europe by the policies of Briand and Stresemann, were basically unsuccessful. They were threatened by the plan for an Austro-German tariff union. Bosch recognized the far-reaching psychological effect that this tariff union would have, but agreed with the government policy because at some point a beginning had to be made in trade policy. ("We have no time to lose," he wrote to Hermann Bücher on April 6, 1931.) In France his associates were not making much headway with the public mood. "Perhaps it was a mistake," Bosch noted in 1935, "that Coudenhove-Kalergi was primarily supported by Germany . . . Anything that is supported by Germany runs too great a risk of being seen as something that smacks of treason." Nonetheless, there was no lack of support. In December 1931 Bosch was able to thank the Parisian automobile industrialist Louis Renault for a letter expressing support for Franco-German cooperation. "Other industrialists were of the opinion," he wrote, "that this might be possible in 150 years."

It was natural that he should attach importance to the position of the capitalist upper class, for in the overall scheme of things it was international capitalist development that appeared to him as the greatest guarantor of peace. This notion was conceived along materialistic lines, although it contradicted the generally accepted Marxist thesis that expanding capitalism has an inborn tendency toward war. Once the continents were grouped together in great economic unions, with a world citizenry enjoying equal rights in every nation, "war will doubtless be unthinkable," Bosch had written to Coudenhove-Kalergi in 1928. Spinning out his utopian argument, he continued, "One of these days, when the people of Europe have reached the point where they are no longer stupefied by their dynasties, they will be even less inclined to start a war, because when it is a question of acquiring mineral wealth or forests, or whatever else they need, the capitalists will say 'war doesn't pay.' By then the capitalist interests will have become so interwoven all over the globe that war will be unthinkable for good capitalist reasons, and the dynasties will have been done away with long before then. In reality they have already been done away with, I would say." This, incidentally, was a theme he occasionally liked to expound upon. "The peoples are peace-loving; it is the rulers' ambition and desire for power that are the causes of war." It is unnecessary to point out that his interpretation was historically shortsighted and overlooked the fact that, even in the recent past, governments had been forced by "the people" to go to war against their better judgment, no matter what techniques of manipulation they used to gain influence over the masses.

In all these questions, Bosch kept his view focused mainly on France, despite his relationship with Lord Davies. He paid little attention to Italy's aspirations or the problems of Russia, and he encouraged any and all opportunities to increase the mutual understanding between the French and German nations. And so he happened upon Paul Distelbarth, the Württemberg businessman and farmer who became a sort of counterpart of Count Coudenhove-Kalergi's. Without an association, without grand phrases, without congresses or publicity, Distelbarth had begun to awaken an awareness of German concerns among the French, and of French concerns among the Germans. In the process, he had made contact with organized veterans' groups. His sole mandate was that given by his conscience as a German national, a humanitarian, and a Christian. Bosch, profoundly impressed by Distelbarth's intensity, afforded him the opportunity to keep this individual, almost private attempt free of everyday worries. In Distelbarth's case, one could not expect to influence any diplomats or any capitalists looking for investments. Distelbarth sought and found the bourgeois residents of the provincial towns—the workers, the farmers, the midlevel government officials. There was another way, from below, and it would not be ignored.

Bosch's life, outwardly happy despite all the troubles and worries of the postwar years—such as difficulties resulting from the early departure of important longtime colleagues—was plagued by a shadow of resignation tied to the private tragedy of his family. He and his wife had lived through the long illness of their only son in mutual fear. When they had finally learned the inevitable, the fact that there was no possibility of recovery, Bosch had girded himself in the harsh renunciation of his life's hope and filled his days, months, and years to the very brim with his duties toward the company and the community. Anna Bosch threw herself into the care of her son, which led her from doctor to doctor, from convalescent home to hospital, looking for any possibility of a cure.

Their son died at the age of thirty on April 6, 1921. At the time Bosch was on a trip through South America, where the news reached him in Buenos Aires. "As much as we had wished for a such a peaceful end to his existence, the fact that he is departed touched me to the core . . . He and we have been spared much. But the pain that this life that was once so full of hope is now gone is bitter, even though we have had years to get used to the idea and to prepare ourselves. How often I have asked myself why I continue to live and he, the younger, had to waste away? Life is hard, but one must live it. Must one? I think so." And the letter implores his wife to think of herself and her own preservation and recovery.

But still Bosch did not recognize how deeply Anna had been affected. Upon Bosch's return there were new tasks awaiting him. Above all, he had come away from South America with great agricultural ideas, which now solidified into broadly conceived plans. But with the death of their son, his wife seemed to have been robbed of her reason for living. Was the loss less difficult for him to bear? Surely not. But the attempt to come to terms with his fate was naturally different for the active man than for his wife, who was unable to stop grieving. She missed a responsive partner to share her experience. Bosch wrote to her about this in a few candid sentences at the end of July 1921. "Indeed I do not like to speak about Robert. I settle such matters best on my own. Naturally you had much more to do with him than I did, as the result of the situation. In the ten years his illness lasted I had time enough to accustom myself to the loss and to consider the consequences. For me Robert died gradually, and the end was the final conclusion that had to come. I am not able to wallow in the wounds and the pain. This is something I cannot change. I resign myself to the inevitable."

Anna Bosch could not resign herself. She had found her mission in the care of her beloved invalid and was almost completely drained by it. Now she herself, in delicate health and beset by spells of deep depression, required care, and began her tragic journey from convalescent home to sanitorium. Bosch accompanied her with solicitous instructions about how to come to terms with her illness, acquaint herself with the meaning of the doctors' orders, and follow them conscientiously and willingly. There is something moving about the almost pedantic instructions that filled his correspondence. His considerate yet sometimes firm arguments were intended to reawaken her will to get well. Was her illness an escape? The things she imagined in her anxiety attacks were so distressing that Bosch, who had usually filled his letters from the road with business concerns or plans, began to be quite sparing in his comments. In August 1924, when he went to America to resolve the ACRO matter, he wrote her about it only after arriving, so difficult did she find long journeys, even those of her daughters. Her pessimism may have abated, but her fear remained about returning to the duties of which she felt conscious but no longer capable, particularly since they had increased with the expansion of Bosch's position.

The stately house in the old Hackländer Park of the Heidehof became the setting for her personal isolation. Her relationship with her daughters, which had undergone such strains in 1913, had returned to normal, but the daughters had built their own lives, which were centered outside Stuttgart. Bosch suffered more under these circumstances than he would admit; he was plagued by an irritable unease, and he was often out and about, seeking diversion and a chance to express himself and listen to others. He had become quite lonely in the great rooms of their home, and it looked as though he would remain that way.

After a separation lasting several years, the couple came to the difficult decision to divorce in 1926. Robert Bosch entered into a second marriage with Margarete Wolz, the daughter of a family of Württemberg foresters. In her he found relief from the restlessness and concern he had expended on his invalid wife, as well as an intuitive and sympathetic conversation partner with whom he could intimately discuss the many worrisome problems and decisions he faced. In many ways he became more balanced and calm. He was able once more to invite friends to the house for the spontaneous and unconventional companionship that he so loved; on appropriate occasions, he was also a solid host. In many matters his wife became his colleague, relieving him of some things, advising for or against others, and serving as a go-between with the younger generation that was growing up in the firm and were getting ready to take on the challenges of leadership. Bosch's more relaxed state was also greatly appreciated by the leadership of the business.

But above all else, there were young voices echoing throughout the house, which for so long had seemed practically dead. Bosch had the joy of seeing two more children born to him, his son Robert in 1928 and his daughter Eva in 1931. The fact that fate, which had burdened him with so much sorrow and loss in the death of his first son, had granted him a male heir to bear his name and mission brought him joy in his old age. In the abilities, hobbies, and skills of the growing boy he was able to recognize traits from his own youth and elements of his own nature.

33

———•———

STUDY FOR
A PORTRAIT

In a conversation about Robert Bosch, one of his colleagues recalled the comment of a teacher whose job had taken him to the Swabian highlands and then back to the Neckar Valley. One of the experiences he recounted was the observation that the first words the children there learned to say were *noi, ette*—"no, not." The lighthearted reference was meant to indicate that Bosch had been and remained a proper son of the highlands. Naturally the story must be taken with a bit of the casual irony characteristic of dialect. The man of such extraordinary achievements was no negativist. Yet the anecdote reveals a quality of Bosch's, expressed in his very wakeful gaze, that many found intense and occasionally hurtful on their first encounter with him—his alert and occasionally abrupt readiness to contradict. Bosch was not a great believer in authority. As a young man he had commented on the fact that people sometimes accused him of harsh or brusque behavior. This would later abate after he had learned to respect certain limits when making judgments and decisions, but he always retained a readiness, if not an actual desire, for intellectual attack. Along with the pleasure Bosch took in sharp logical debate and quick repartee, he also had what might be described as a readiness to

453

defend himself. Once someone wanted to schedule his attendance at a reception where he would actually act as the host, something for which Bosch had absolutely no taste. The note he wrote in the margin of the office's response, dated October 1932, read, "Tell them I am pathologically opposed to such assaults on my personal freedom." It seems certain that the office must have found another way to express his refusal, however the sentence, with its tone somewhere between annoyance and self-reflective irony, sheds light on his fundamental nature.

He was made of the stuff of people who are better at giving orders than taking them, a characteristic he had inherited from his father. Servatius Bosch—farmer, beer brewer, and teamster in Albeck—had been recognized in his community as a gentleman and as a man who was independent, self-assured, and refractory despite his personal generosity. When Robert Bosch looked back at the rural background that was his heritage, he did not see idyllic village life or the miserable toil of small farmers; he set no store by the heightening of some romantic contrast between the formerly unknown, obscure family and the two men—himself and his nephew, the great chemist and organizer Carl Bosch—who emerged from it to link its name forever with Germany's industrial and social history. The family had its own proud tradition, which was neither assumed nor newly created. Nor did Bosch take a sentimental view of it. The members of his immediate family had followed their father on the road to urbanization; none of the later descendants remained on the farm. This migration to nearby towns was partly a phenomenon of the times. Bosch once discovered a fact that evidently interested him and was mentioned in one of his letters in 1931, namely, that in 1886 his name had appeared only four or five times in the Stuttgart address book, while now 105 Boschs were listed!

The masterful self-awareness of this son of a wealthy farmer, who as an apprentice and assistant sometimes rebelled against the demands imposed on him, had a peculiar other side: a shyness not merely in public, but whenever he was confronted with any kind of conventional behavior in dealings with people he did not know well. This shyness was an element of the great tension that characterized his nature. In conversation he commented, "You wrote once that essentially I am a shy person," and continued, after a thoughtful pause, "Actually you are quite correct." Bosch had seen much of the world, but he had never become worldly. He had come into contact with countless individuals from many classes and backgrounds, and yet he never lost a certain primness in his bearing and manner, an uncomfortable sense of restriction as soon as he found himself outside familiar territory where he could let himself go. This is a common Swabian characteristic; in Bosch's case it assumed its particular quality due to the sensitivity and actual physical repugnance with which he reacted to any kind of social pressure. "Letting himself go" was a relief and release; it was not exactly identical with the rather conscious lack of formality that is often encountered in Württemberg. Bosch needed people and liked to listen when someone had a good story to tell. He had a whole host of stories and anecdotes, some of them crude snippets of folk wisdom and folk humor, but he maintained a certain distance even in the sort of easygoing get-togethers he loved.

Bosch himself determined the measure of intimacy, never his conversation partner, unless it was an old friend. Paul Reusch tells how the two very temperamental men occasionally lost their tempers and shouted at one another. But they always got along again afterward because they had known, respected, and loved one another since childhood. Bosch did not have many friends; he was sparing with sentiment and once declared quite distinctly to an old schoolmate whom he did not particularly like that their youthful contact gave him no right to address him as a friend. But along with this rough streak he continued to feel an affectionate loyalty to the whole circle of his old school friends from Ulm, whose periodic get-togethers he never missed, even when he was expected at an executive meeting of the National Union of German Industry. He kept up an intimate correspondence with some of these former schoolmates, and he did not neglect to visit them on his trips to the city. But they had to be people of substance, and they should not be allowed to think that just because they had gone to school with him they had some special right to ask him for money. His comment on one such attempt, to a third party, was to ask how his friend could expect him "to pay for his wife's finery." He always demanded respect. Yet his desire for intimacy was frequently contradicted by his own abrupt manner, and he could be tough and bitter in his dislikes. In such cases his hardened feelings swept aside any arguments about fairness.

The extraordinary keenness of Bosch's critical acumen was directed at the material, the tangible, the visible. His powers of visual observation, which quickly seized upon impressions and retained them almost indelibly, were very unusual. This served him well in botanical identification. He could astound people when he traveled a certain route years later and was able to describe individual particularities of the landscape that they were about to encounter—its flora, geographic formations, and geological structure. These facts stuck in his memory like the precise markings on a film strip. Hermann Bücher tells the following story of a hunting trip they took together. "As we were climbing through the beech forest, I saw a snowdrop and called Bosch's attention to it: 'a Leucojum.' He immediately responded, 'Galanthus'; naturally it was a Galanthus and no Leucojum." Bosch had also read a great deal on the subject of natural science, although not systematically. What was most important to him was to see things, especially in the company of an expert on the subject whom he could profitably ask questions, so that any questions or uncertainties could be cleared up right away. He was thorough although not scholarly in any more ambitious sense. As soon as things approached the realm of mathematical formulas, and their visual vividness was replaced by language and thought of in terms of, say, the new theoretical physics, Bosch kept a respectful distance. Once, in 1941, when a young inventor praised his "biological vision" and sent him some publications of the Kaiser Wilhelm Society, he denied that he was qualified to pass judgment on them, "for actually I can only make 'educated guesses' about this kind of thing." When the translator of James C. Maxwell's groundbreaking studies on electricity and magnetism sent his manuscript to Bosch for his comments, Bosch responded candidly, "A fleeting glance at the book revealed at once that I would understand nothing except the Foreword . . ." In a letter to Eugen Diesel dated March 10, 1941, Bosch directed his affable irony at himself when describing an educational discussion with his fourteen-year-old son; the anecdote expresses not only aspects of his family life and biography but also the great changes that had transformed scientific inquiry and education since he had been an apprentice. Bosch had found a few magnets made of Alni steel in the boy's workshop, and had held a little lecture on how at Philips, in Eindhoven, they had come out with a new process by which magnets could be strengthened many times over by magnetizing them while they were red hot. "To which young Robert immediately replied, 'Is that perhaps connected to the fact that at absolute zero the molecules are completely still, so no electrons circle around the nuclei, in other words it would be easier to align the atoms in a heated condition than if they were cold?' When I told this . . . to my friend Stribeck, he shook his head and said, 'Whenever I hear something about electrons I run the other way,' to which I responded, 'You had better not imagine that I went into the matter any more deeply with Robert. I told myself that I could only embarrass myself.' "

Bosch spoke very objectively about how he had become involved in technology. His father had suggested it to him, and he had gone into it because he had not been particularly interested in continuing in school. His example, as he wrote in 1931 to a young man who had asked him for career advice, demonstrated that it was not necessarily so terrible "to go into a field without any great love for it . . . My profession never brought me any particular satisfaction, I always worked because it was simply required. My hobbies were always something separate." It had never been his ambition to invent anything, as he stated again and again when his name turned up among those of inventors—a frequent and well-meaning error. Such comments, however, should not mislead anyone into thinking Bosch had little profound engagement with technical issues. He approached individual questions practically and empirically, with a good eye for what was purposeful, economical, solid, and handy. When it came to civilization, he viewed the general phenomenon of technology optimistically. Problematizing the meaning of technology seemed to him more or less literary nonsense, an occupation for individuals who had never had anything to do with crafts and who took for granted all the results of mechanization while complaining about the corruption of mankind by machines; they talked about mankind's enslavement by technology without knowing or caring to know how difficult and poor life had been with sixteen to eighteen hours a day of work, work, work. In the final analysis, machines, if well used, meant freedom from need and toil.

The fact that Bosch's friend Paul Reusch was such a close friend of Oswald Spengler's and had such a high opinion of the man was something Bosch could never quite grasp. To him it was, as he wrote in 1941, an

"arrogance"—one Spengler "unfortunately" shared with his students—
when he permitted himself to make judgments on "things like technology, which is manual work and which he knows nothing about . . . To me
the question whether technology exists as a blessing or a curse seems
superfluous. If man has become a slave to the machine, it is *he* alone who
is at fault." In his treatise *Man and Technology,* written in 1930, Spengler
had given a pessimistic analysis of the current situation and predicted
the end of the idea of technology as such. Romantically and erroneously,
he thought he could sense the establishment of new values, or sought to
establish them himself.

Robert Bosch's concrete and experiential turn of mind could not have
been farther removed from the speculative or metaphysical interpretation
of social phenomena. He might perhaps view such thinking as a useless
mental game, but he became angry if it was linked to ethical value judgments in which technical progress was deemed a negative. This was the
reason he so often railed against Spengler's judgments. At the end of
1932, Bosch began a correspondence with Lili du Bois Raymond, the
biographer of the great Swabian engineer and organizer Max Eyth. Among
other things, she had written to him that despite all her respect for Eyth,
she did not share his enthusiastic opinion about the bounties of technology. Bosch went to great lengths in his sometimes moody letters to make
clear the extent to which she took for granted all the technology she was
so angry about, citing arguments describing the path from primitive tools
to X-ray machines and microscopes to a broadly based public health policy. At this point, in a letter dated October 25, 1932, he attacked Spengler.
"A certain Oswald Spengler, in a speech he gave at the Deutsches
Museum, uttered witticisms that are really the limit. One should not
believe that educated people can come to such one-sided conclusions
about matters that mankind has been working on for many thousands of
years, merely out of a certain short-sighted Romanticism, and because
they cannot see the means by which the long-awaited achievements of
technology can be made useful to all of mankind. There can be no doubt
that each period and cultural stage of humanity has had its appeal. But
what sense is there, ultimately, in complaining with such weltschmerz
about the fact that mankind has succeeded in producing food for itself in
quantities that were once unthinkable? How easy it is for technology to

prove that Malthus's fears were completely unfounded. I have never read a work of philosophy and I do not know what our philosophers have to say about the value of humanity, but I am of the opinion that human beings are here, that their task is to put the forces of nature to use, and that they have to civilize themselves and put themselves in the most rational position they can with regard to other living creatures, be they men or beasts. And if I take this point of view as my starting point, I must shrug my shoulders and ignore Herr Oswald Spengler's view that it would be better to aspire to the life of Achilles than to come to the cowardly conclusion that mankind is making cultural progress. By the way, I do not know what Spengler means by stating that it is better to live the life of a hero. I don't even know whether he sees Achilles as an ideal; it could be some other ancient Greek. Regrettably the modern heroes would look somewhat different in their armor, because nowadays they no longer could fight with a sword and spear. In my opinion, to survive nowadays when such powers exist demands more courage and greater endurance—if less muscle power!—whereby it would still have to be proven whether the muscle strength of today's population might not actually be greater than that of those heroes. Please be so friendly as to excuse me for philosophizing to you in a manner that is undoubtedly far from perfect in form."

Philosophizing was indeed not his forte, and when he wrote to an acquaintance in 1918 that he would get hold of Hans Vaihinger's *Philosophy of As If*, which the friend had strongly recommended, and that the book interested him "very intensely," one may have good cause to wonder whether Bosch's good intentions were ever acted upon. For as powerful as his purely logical ability was, his nature shrank from abstract concepts, and he lacked the gift of speculative imagination. Where natural phenomena were concerned, he relied on his sense of intuition, but was mistrustful of systematic natural philosophy, whether Romantic vitalism or mechanical materialism. He was hesitant when it came to any kind of dogmatism that claimed certainty or demanded belief. The closest he ever came to such thinking was probably as a follower of Gustav Jäger and Samuel Hahnemann, but he never permitted the space for his own search for knowledge to be hemmed in.

Bosch was similarly restrained when it came to religion. For his father, the meaning of religion may have consisted in its wealth of moral values and demands. The relationship of Bosch's childhood home to the Church was pale and conventional. His parents did not pay a lot of attention to it nor did they feel a need to come to terms with the issue of religion. As a young man, Robert Bosch was intensely involved in the questions of religion and the Church, although one would not want to say he was tortured by them, for metaphysical questions never penetrated the deepest levels of his consciousness. The positivism of his generation, with its rather optimistic answers, along with the urge to bring inner knowledge into conformity with external professions of faith, led him to leave the Church. It was the same process that influenced Ernst Abbe. Bosch did not want to appear to be something he was not, namely a church Christian—as much in his own eyes as in the eyes of others. But his religious instinct was not strong enough for him to struggle toward or clarify an independent position. He never expressed any rebelliousness against the Church. His youthful connection with the Church had not been powerful enough to lead to vehement contradictions; it was a simple separation. The urgency of dogmatic free thinking was as suspicious and alien to him as the question of confessional boundaries. In his philanthropic activities, he contributed both to purely secular and to religious ventures; his only requirement was that the project make good sense and be managed by reliable individuals. One day, not without a certain sense of astonishment, he observed that his closest circle of colleagues was made up of men whose fundamental sense of life was Christian, even Church oriented.

Bosch avoided conversations about religion that touched on questions of dogma and very rarely commented in writing about religious matters. There was no lack of people who felt that his work for the common good was essentially religious, and who tried to lead him back to the source of his actions by plying him with religious tracts. He declined such well-meaning attempts to lead him to religious instruction or edification in a friendly way, for example, in a comment in September 1931: "For me the concept of God is something so enormous that I don't believe there is a human being who can tell me what God is." The idea that he should read the Bible, which an old school friend who had been a free thinker had returned to, was surely "interesting," he wrote in December 1932, "but right now we have to read things that are important to know if we want to form an opinion of any kind about matters that are other than purely human." This was surely not written thoughtlessly. The Bible was a book of human knowledge and instruction, but Bosch was more interested in the secrets of nature, although he never sought or attempted to describe this with the magic of words.

In 1916 and 1917, when Bosch came to public attention with his great philanthropic contributions, a musician from Stuttgart had had the idea of expressing his respect by dedicating one of his compositions to Robert Bosch, a source of some embarrassment for Bosch. It was necessary to inform the composer that his intention was praiseworthy but that he was addressing it to the wrong person, for the object of his proposal was not at all interested in music. Bosch commented often that he was completely unmusical. In this way he was able to get rid of some petitioners, for he only wanted to help, as he noted in February 1936, "where there is a certain inner involvement in the matter." Nevertheless, when experts brought him young people who were deserving of support he made means available for their education, and asked to be kept informed about the results. When it came to music, he held back from expressing opinions in the definitive way that was his habit, for music was essentially alien to him even though as a young man he may have willingly sung along with his comrades, in or out of tune.

Things were different when it came to the visual arts, for Bosch was a visual person and was at the same time very much concerned with craft and technical issues in general. Eventually, he had to drop the hesitation to be photographed that often led him to turn down the press's requests for pictures after he was confronted with the desire to obtain portraits of him—paintings, etchings, sculpture—for one public purpose or another. He had his portrait painted a number of times, and several busts were made of him. He was not easy to satisfy, feeling that if he was to submit to the discomfort of sitting still the work should be carried out exactly! The subjective vision of the artist did not interest him very much. For example, when he was approached by a Swabian friend who was a patron of the arts and who insisted that Leo Samberger was the only ranking contemporary painter and must do a portrait of Bosch, the latter looked at a few paintings and very resolutely declined to be the object of such interpretation. A sculptor was once made aware of the fact, in January 1918, that "I have determined through taking measurements that the nose and ears on my bust are about one centimeter too long." Bosch's rather courteous and resigned comment that "I suppose there is nothing that can be done" was not always the rule. Along with grateful acknowledgment of achievement, for example, in the case of the Munich painter Carl Bauer, where one can also sense a shared human feeling, there were some rather rude criticisms. For artists, Bosch was no doubt a surpassingly interesting model, whose features betrayed a compelling and mobile tension, but he was not an easy one. His almost nonexistent talent for saying flattering things did not necessarily create an encouraging atmosphere.

Bosch never asked to be considered a connoisseur, however. If it is possible to speak of a particular love, one might find that Bosch preferred familiar landscapes, Swabian or Bavarian scenes, especially locations of which he was particularly fond. He was never interested in the historic aspect of artistic expression, nor in the ability of painting or sculpture to express ideas, much less allegories! All this was alien to him. In a letter dated February 21, 1918, he wrote a couple of sentences reflecting his very objective understanding. "B's sketch, in other words, would have to be accompanied at the same time by an explanation so that people do not puzzle themselves over it unnecessarily. But I do not think this is appropriate, for a picture should speak for itself and not require an explanation. This is my heretical opinion, but it is the one I recognize." In this sense, he was an unassuming friend of solid realism.

Especially in his later years, Bosch read a lot, but fiction and belles lettres played a rather small role. For him to have a particular relationship to lyric poetry is something no one who is familiar with his nature will be likely to expect. There is an amusing document in which he went to the trouble of correcting a long wartime poem by Caesar Flaischlen; he criticized both its language and its content with amusement and annoyance. Bosch seldom went to the theater; it is probable that his need for constant motion made it physically uncomfortable to sit for that long. He took a friendly interest in contemporary Swabian short story writers and supported them without making terribly precise distinctions as to quality. Here his approach was similar to that toward the painters of the Württemberg landscapes that appealed to him because of their theme. Anyone who knew how to make a poetic image of Swabian popular life, with its characters and customs, stories and traditional words of wisdom, could be sure of a friendly reception.

A great deal of Bosch's reading time, when he was not engrossed in natural history, was taken up by works on contemporary history—more biographies, memoirs, volumes of letters than critical surveys or monographs. He welcomed it when people made him aware of new publications in this area. He must have found a certain charm in getting to know the human side and motivation of people with whose activities he was familiar and who had occupied his imagination and his critical faculties. He was a particular connoisseur of illustrative anecdotes, in which a conversation, an encounter, or a pointed characterization might be more informative than a carefully conceived essay. Here Johannes Haller, the historian from Tübingen who had moved to Stuttgart, became a stimulating adviser during Bosch's later years. Between these two men with such divergent backgrounds and political stances there grew up a friendship of old age that was based on mutual respect, whereby no doubt each of them, with equal verve, threw in a dash of skeptical resignation when they looked at humanity's doings in the era of their maturity. In April 1939, after finishing Haller's book on Count Botho zu Eulenberg, Bosch wrote to Haller, who was one of the most vehement journalistic opponents of Bernard von Bülow's policy that he (Bosch) had "earlier already begun to vacillate somewhat in his judgment of Wilhelm II." Bosch's most lively exchange was with Eugen Diesel, whose literary production and interpretation of the tendencies of the times profoundly affected him. In Diesel's works Bosch found the sensibilities and ideas of his own subconscious brought to perfect expression. Is it possible that Diesel's attempt to convince Bosch of the writing abilities of Arthur Schopenhauer and his *Parerga and Paralipomena* might have succeeded?

Bosch concerned himself gladly and voluntarily with issues of language. For him, language was essentially a tool for precise and reliable comprehension in both oral and written exchange. Like a tool, language should always be kept in good condition and used with appropriate brevity. No one was safe from Bosch's unbidden critique if he made incorrect use of words such as "thereby" or "therefore"; lapses of this kind were considered impermissible sloppiness. His own speech was strongly colored by the Swabian dialect, whose expressions and traditional forms were for him a source of untainted speech. He had a vivid sense of the geographical coherence of traditional language; it bothered him, for example, if someone used north German slang in telling a Swabian story. The colorful expressions of Swabia seemed to him to be the true measure of good and correct German. There were times when he sent letters to the editors of newspapers that went so far as to remind them of their grammar on questions such as whether it was permissible to use the more northern German form "s" in giving the plural of proper names. "Why not use the regular plural form of names that are identical with well-known things?" he wrote in a letter dated March 11, 1918. "We southern Germans, unless we have become insecure in our feeling for language, due to the influence of the poor German of northern Germany, would no more say the words that way that we would say 'kids' for children; unfortunately it is not only uneducated people but southern Germans who can lay claim to some education who are saying such dreadful things and probably even considering it well-bred." He thought it would be worthwhile for the newspapers to give some ongoing consideration to these matters; *The Bosch Spark Plug* later did so with anger and wit and truly inexhaustible patience.

When Bosch himself picked up his pen, in the splendidly fluid, large handwriting he maintained even in his old age, he wrote confidently and vigorously, with a slight tendency to give in to sudden thoughts that might clarify what he meant to say. Naturally, he dictated a lot, especially letters. But then he was often dissatisfied with himself; once, in a letter he wrote to his nephew Carl in 1931, he commented that when he dictated "sometimes things turn out less well" than when he wrote them himself. In such cases there were postscripts or notes that explained, abridged, or weakened particular expressions so that the recipient didn't receive a distorted picture of what was actually meant. Bosch's correspondence is full of such attempts to lend an expression the precisely correct emphasis; generally they are weakened. A letter written in 1931 to the geologist Karl Hausmann, who had been a school friend of Bosch's before he moved to Berlin, may serve as an example: "As far as I am concerned, I have to be glad, because I must take the position, willy-nilly, that I have not yet carried out my mission. Do not stumble over the word mission; it is a task that has nothing to do with a higher calling." One can clearly sense how he comes to the word "mission" with full self-confidence but then is alarmed that it might appear to be false and presumptuous, reflecting his fear of emotion or sentimentality in private matters, a very Swabian peculiarity. Bosch is capable of being emotional or sentimental when confronted with general questions or human situations, in a few emotional or angry sentences, but this is rare. The strong feelings that often enough emerged abruptly in personal encounters were concealed in his writing.

Brief reflections, directives, or fragments of memoirs, written down in sudden decisiveness, took on the quality of dense objectivity; he liked to give his vocabulary some color by inserting folksy maxims or spicing up his explications with a dry sarcasm. "I am one of those businessmen for whom a good customer is more valuable than a bad supplier," he wrote in July 1912. Occasionally he found stronger and more vivid images. In a letter to his daughter Margarete dated August 1941, in which he developed his ideas about the war, the position of the United States toward Britain and the remaining Anglo-Saxon and Latin American world, he wrote: "The Americans are in the position of a young, very powerful people or perhaps we should say a young, powerful man, who shakes one's hand so hard you could scream and then wonders why you are not gladdened by this proof of his superior strength, out of unalloyed admiration for him as a hero." (This was written at a time when hostilities between Germany and the United States had not yet begun.)

In general, Bosch wrote the longer pieces with a certain ponderous fluidity and without a writer's concern for proportion. In 1930, when he again started working on the *Life Recollections* that he had begun during the ocean voyage to South America in 1921, he had a period to cover that was of great significance to both his business and his personal life, and that included his participation in the National Union of German Industry and the National Economic Council, the ACRO transaction, and various significant changes in the circle of his closest colleagues. But in the middle of all this, his memory went back to a hunting party in Canada, which he described in vivid colors and in which he detailed individual situations, to the point where this story took up almost one fourth of the entire manuscript; it is an odd and completely isolated element in the great survey of his life and work. The reader senses that the hunting trip was actually a rather secondary thing; Bosch went on plenty of other hunts without talking about them. But Bosch was not thinking of the reader; all at once these days of riding and hiking, the faraway mountains, the unfamiliar quarry, became so important to him again that he wrote it all down, objectively—no poet of the hunt or of nature making the attempt at imaginative enthusiasm or skillful description—and almost without humor except perhaps for witticisms that had to do with hunting. But the memory had him so completely in its grip that this experience seemed as deserving of detailed treatment as the entire ACRO transaction.

There is an anecdote about Bosch that must date from before 1913, for it is related in a letter written to Caesar Flaischlen in that year by the secretary of the weekly *The Selections* as a characterization of Bosch. In it, Bosch is on a summer trip and is asked to write his name in the visitors' log of the inn. The column with the heading "occupation" is full of honorifics like Commercial Counsellor, First Lieutenant, Consul, Judge of the Municipal Court, and the like. Bosch's entry reads "Human Being." Later he stopped doing this, out of a kind of truce that he made with this kind of custom and regulation. But the anecdote reveals a profound and original tension in his nature—that of his rebellion against convention. One might think it represented a kind of Rousseauian coquetry, but it did not; it was more a sudden annoyance that took an abrupt turn into humor, with the aim of giving later guests a drastic pedagogical demonstration that might cause them to reflect.

Bosch often reflected about himself, his natural abilities, his temperament, the reasons for his success. His self-confidence did not require confirmation by third parties. For a long time he found it thoroughly objectionable when the public took an interest in him; he refused to provide photographs, refused to become the object of autograph collectors. Some of his colleagues had the sense that he never even read the things that the newspapers and magazines wrote about him when there were anniversary celebrations; if he did, he was unmoved by praise and dealt tartly with errors of fact. When a writer approached him for documents for an essay on the "Locksmith from Albeck," he had already ruined his chances—Bosch was no locksmith, and said, "You seem to be more concerned about making a splash than about the truth." But Bosch was naturally pleased by recognition based on fact. For a long time he had expressed skepticism about the power of examples to inspire imitation, although he always felt that there had been "a certain improvement" in the attitude of employers after the First World War. "I was always a preacher in the wilderness," he wrote in July 2, 1930, to Gerhard von Schulze-Gäveritz, "by which I do not mean to say that I have done a lot of preaching. I have hesitated to make my opinion and point of view known and to state it openly; I have lived my convictions, so to speak, and yet I have the impression that I have gained followers." This feeling remained with him throughout the years of his old age.

On the margin of a request, he once wrote in 1937: "Turndown. I have no more urge to be active." This was not entirely true, for despite all kinds of difficulties and physical complaints the intensity of his temperament was utterly unbroken, and although it had been a long time since he had worried about the details of the business, his participation in public affairs and his concern about the plans that interested him were quite lively. Sometimes the mere fact that he was paying attention was sufficient to keep things moving forward. Years earlier, in 1919, he had written to his wife, "It is my habit to demand more than a little from myself and those around me. This is my peculiarity, which I cannot abandon without abandoning myself." This is how he remained; he did not abandon himself.

34

———•———

HUNTER AND
GAMEKEEPER

Within the context of Bosch's character and life, it is incorrect to say he was "also" a hunter. For this casual "also" is too weak a word to express the passion and sense of enjoyment with which he pursued hunting, or the careful planning and work that he devoted to it, particularly in his later years. If one were to measure the portion of his correspondence that is devoted to hunting preserves, personal anecdotes about hunters, arguments with communal authorities and other government bureaucrats, discussions about rifles and shotguns, hunting stories and trophies, one could say with only a certain amount of exaggeration that Bosch was a hunter who was "also" a factory owner. Bosch was forty years old when he first leased a hunting preserve; before that, in the most intense years of his working life, he did not have enough free time to hunt. Perhaps he also feared he might give the impression of inactive leisure time, either in his own eyes or in those of other people. But he soon discovered that hunting offered him just the source of energy he required in the critical years of his business. Ultimately, it would almost become an independent realm of his life, with claims and commandments that he did not merely impose upon himself out of a desire for recreation, but planned seriously and thoughtfully over the course of many years.

When Bosch was a boy, his father had allowed him to tag along on hunting trips, and when Servatius retired to the city of Ulm he did not give up his old hunting preserve. Young Robert managed to get his father to give him a Flobert rifle, which his father, in a moment of weakness, had promised to bring him from Stuttgart and then had intentionally forgotten. "Today," Bosch wrote in his *Life Recollections,* "I assume he did not want to encourage the passion for hunting in me." By dint of a perpetual bad mood, which his parents found quite difficult to bear, the boy managed to convince them to let him purchase a rifle with money he had saved from his allowance. Then he went after the sparrows in Ulm. His childhood games had always tended toward things that were related to shooting and required a sure eye and hand, for example, activities that used bows and arrows, slingshots, blowpipes with clay pellets, and spears, which he handled with a skill that became well known. Now that he had his own rifle, his shooting became systematic. "Perhaps my ability as a marksman results from this practice," he once remarked. "I began to hunt when I was about forty, and I was as good a shot with buckshot as with bullets, without having any idea that I was any better than anyone else. I was surprised when I won first prize in a target shooting contest; it was about thirty years ago, I think [this was probably written in 1936], during a summer vacation in Tyrol."

The recognition that "surprised" Bosch later became something he took for granted—he was a very good shot, if not the best. He was quite proud of it, and he was pleased that people in the areas where he had once hunted remembered his accurate shooting even years later. "In Berlin I heard someone say there had never been anyone in the Carpathian Mountains who was a better marksman than me." In the journal entries he occasionally devoted to hunting, he sometimes mentioned his bull's-eyes; the references have a tone of boastfulness that one seldom encounters elsewhere in Bosch's writings. "I never kept a record of my shooting. But years ago I remember series of 20 or more shots during which I had no misses at distances ranging up to 300 meters . . . Last year on a hunt I shot nine hares with nine shots, without a miss . . . Of five chamois bucks that I started shooting at a distance of about 200 meters, I shot three. The last one, i.e., the third, was at about 300 meters . . . In my life as a hunter I have surely not shot as much as two percent of my bullets into the trees . . . Even in pistol shooting, there was no one to compare with me.

Once I was at my friend Faber's hunting lodge when the caterpillar of a gold-tail moth let itself down from a tree on a gossamer thread. The moth was about 30 millimeters long and about 2.5 to 3 millimeters in diameter. I pointed to it and shot it from a distance of four or five meters."

His letters to his friends, which were written during relaxed, lonely evenings after a day spent at his "bloody craft" (as he once called it in a letter to Reusch), were filled with proud, happy remarks. "So far," he wrote to Dr. Eugen Bircher, his doctor in Zürich, "I have shot six deer at distances up to 300 meters with six bullets. Don't tell that to any hunters, though, especially if they are Swiss. No one will believe it who doesn't witness it. It cannot be done with the rifles one is required to use in Switzerland, and naturally not without a telescope, either; the latter is not forbidden in Switzerland, however." In Switzerland, rifles of relatively small caliber with high-speed ammunition, which were characterized by relatively high muzzle speeds, were not allowed to be used on the nobler quarry. Otto Mezger's study of hunters contains the following description of Bosch: "One of Robert Bosch's favorite hobbies is to drive up behind foxes in the winter in a sleigh and to kill them at 100–200 meters with a small-caliber bullet. In two days, in several hunting preserves in the Alps, he once shot 26 foxes with rifles in this way, an achievement that few hunters can rival; another year he shot six foxes in two days with a rifle, from a blind and stalking."

Practice and a sure hand do not suffice in themselves; success in hunting naturally also depends on the weapon. Bosch owned a whole arsenal of hunting rifles and knew that he was an expert in this subject, observing and testing innovations and improvements with critical passion; he was an outspoken critic of rifles and shotguns that seemed to him to be outmoded and inadequate.

However shooting, let alone shooting to kill, was by no means the main issue when he went hunting. The fact that he had such a good hand on the trigger, even when he was an old man, gave him a very pronounced feeling of superiority in matters of hunting. Skill was more important than statistics, and he was contemptuous of mere "shooters." When he first began to hunt during his vacations in the Alps, he was driven by the need for exercise, for outdoor activity and physical exertion to help drive out the residue of months spent in the city. In the process, his pleasure in observing the animal and plant worlds revived, and the intensity with which hunting involved all his senses provided welcome mental relief. Bosch ascribed the preservation of both his physical strength and his mental freshness to hunting.

In 1904 he had leased a hunting preserve, Magstadt, in the vicinity of Stuttgart, in whose modest hunting lodge he now regularly spent his Saturdays and Sundays, partly in order to relieve himself of the annoyance he felt over Frederic Simms. For a while he also owned hunting rights farther downstream on the Neckar, near Walheim. The genesis of his new passion had been in the high mountains, however, and that is where it stayed after 1906, when Bosch leased the hunting rights in the Hall Valley in Tyrol. In 1908 he bought a small piece of property that he called the "box," located in the Bavarian countryside in Scharnitz not far from the border. He succeeded in rounding out the preserve by leasing adjoining property. The fact that he had to deal with the bureaucrats in Tyrol and then in Bavaria was not always convenient, but he found ways to resolve things; the chamois growing up under his protection didn't care about the provincial borders either.

He later leased an extensive mountainous preserve in the Bavarian Allgäu, in the long Pfronten Valley with its forested slopes. This property, with its large number of valuable game animals, ultimately became his most cherished hunting preserve. He never failed to be there during the rutting season, to which he invited his closest hunting friends. For decades the preserve was managed by Franz Schöll, the chief hunter, whose thin figure with its long beard looked like the model for a popular novel about mountain folk. Schöll was an unforgettable figure for all friends of hunting—taciturn, sure of his knowledge, full of keen-eyed wisdom. Bosch was very attached to him; the two men had a mutual respect for each other's eccentricities. The Allgäu area had its own difficulties, for the peasants there are sly and not always easy to get along with. Schöll was there not only to care for the hunting quarry, or to act as a knowledgeable companion for the owner and his important guests; he was also a diplomat and the valiant manager of Bosch's right of exploitation. "He gets annoyed and worried with me," Bosch wrote on August 25, 1911. "If I didn't have him the whole thing would be ruined for me, too."

A visit to the Bavarian Alps was always an undertaking that required much preparation, even if the automobile did shorten the trip, so Bosch developed a smaller hunting preserve nearby, in the hills near Urach in the Wespen Valley. This area was mainly inhabited by deer and foxes. A very primitive hut, which was later replaced by a more livable hunting cottage, was the place to which Bosch withdrew when he wanted to put the city and his business behind him in a hurry.

Bosch felt responsible for these hunting preserves, with the purest of motives. He knew the areas intimately, not only geographically but psychologically, as it were; he knew the people who lived there, who was reliable, which neighbors and opponents were helpful and which were difficult. People who were acquainted with his hunting activities and were therefore able to form an opinion about it thought he was almost more engaged in protecting the property than in hunting on it. Whether a well-suited area was in poor condition or had even been devastated when he took it over was of little consequence to him; he would surely get it into top shape by protecting and taking care of it. He paid keen attention to making sure that there was enough feed and that it was set out in good time and in sufficient quantities. After hard winters, he reduced the number of kills that were allowed to himself and his guests. The preservation of a good population of wild animals to give pleasure not only to hunters but to hikers as well was as important or even more important to him than increasing his trophies.

Naturally, Bosch was tempted to get to know other hunting territories. But in this case they should be something unusual, with either quarry that was unknown to him or landscapes whose charms he had yet to explore. In 1913, in a letter to his nephew, he played with the idea of visiting the African interior and going hunting there; nothing ever came of this, however. The Swedish representative of the firm, Fritz Egnell, who was a close colleague of Bosch's, organized hunting trips during Bosch's trips to Sweden. Egnell knew that this created a good atmosphere for business negotiations. In September 1917, Bosch wrote to his son from Stockholm that he had been in the skerries hunting seals and would bring home a skull for him. The hunt that loomed largest in the memories of his old age was the one he undertook in Canada in 1924, at the age of sixty-three. He spent several weeks in the saddle, camping in tents. "I gradually accustomed myself to it and traveled about 300 kilometers in this fashion, sometimes without a path, but almost always on mountain tracks." They were hunting for mountain sheep, bears, and elk. Several professional hunters awaited the expedition at the place where the mountain sheep had been seen. "Then they gave me instructions—me who had already shot some 200 chamois, which amused me." Finally it was not the local residents, with their familiarity with the geography, but Bosch, the foreign guest, who sighted the herd and pointed it out to them with his good instinct; he was also the one who killed the ram with his first shot. His inner triumph at both occurrences was great. A second, even better ram, followed on the second day. He decided to forgo the mountain goats; he found their horns too insignificant. They then rode for another week to get to bear country. But all their searching was fruitless. Finally elk were sighted, and Bosch succeeded in killing a stag whose antlers had a span of 145 centimeters. From a purely sporting point of view the hunt had not quite lived up to Bosch's expectations, but he was satisfied because during the weeks of camping together in Indian tepees he had won his companion, Albert Wielich, over to his view of how the ACRO transaction should be handled although he would later have doubts about the wisdom of the decision.

Bosch often told the story of the hunt in Canada. His hunting exploits and some of his hunting preserves were also described by Otto Mezger, Hermann Bücher, and Georg Escherich. Bücher's tales took place in the mountains of Pfronten for the most part; he also gave a colorful description of an ibex hunt that occurred in 1930 in the Alps, at the Italian national park Val di Cogne. Escherich reported on the hunting preserve in Urach. In 1936, an invitation from Lord Davies took Bosch to the Scottish highlands.

The shared love of hunting formed the basis of strong human relationships, particularly with men who not only were fair hunters but also knew something about the world of flora and fauna, enjoyed a good conversation about these things, and could teach and learn. This was particularly true of Otto Mezger, who was in charge of food supplies in Stuttgart; it applied to Hermann Bücher and Georg Escherich as well. Bücher, who had worked as a botanist in East Africa before embarking on his political and later industrial career, introduced Bosch in October 1930 to the former African forester Escherich. The two men became fast friends in their old age. Bosch had probably listened with a respectful ear to stories of Escherich's activities in Africa, his service as a soldier in the First World

War, and his achievements as a forest manager in Byalistok, Poland. But Escherich the politician, the founder of the Bavarian Home Guards, the leader of the Orgesh, must have been quite foreign to Bosch, based on the legends that circulated widely in the years immediately after the war. Were they not indications of Bavarian particularism, hidden plots aimed at restoring the monarchy, military dilettantism—all things Bosch could scarcely abide? But the man he now met was cordial, bravely honest, and warm-hearted, with the capacity for enthusiasm. Bosch considered that Escherich had been fooling himself, no matter how pure his motives might have been, in thinking that there was a task waiting for him in politics. He saw Escherich as a friend and knowledgeable nature lover, and as a manager who had not been deformed by bureaucracy; he began to be very fond of him. They had addressed each other with the familiar *Du* since 1939, although Escherich was nine years younger than Bosch. His death in 1941 affected Bosch deeply. Escherich had been a regular guest on the hunts and had visited Stuttgart and the Bosch farm, while Bosch went to Isen every spring for the flight of the woodcocks. They had had a lively correspondence in which more general concerns were also expressed back and forth between Stuttgart and the forest house in Bavaria.

Among the staff of the company, Gottlob Honold and Ernst Ulmer had been gripped by Bosch's passion for hunting; Gustav Klein had sometimes complained ironically that decisions about business consultations were dependent on the hunting season. Honold's and Ulmer's legacy was later assumed by Alfred Knoerzer; Bosch was happy that the hunting tradition would not disappear from his circle of close colleagues, and he was glad to have a younger expert, a combination of adviser and student, at his side once again. Klein's worries had meanwhile become superfluous; he had accustomed himself to the habitual hunting dates. For Bosch himself, hunting remained a lovely, firm duty and occasionally a welcome escape. He was supposed to travel to Berlin for a meeting of the National Council on Industry, but he knew that in Pfronten Franz Schöll would be waiting for him! Actually, he had promised Coudenhove-Kalergi that he would take part in a Pan-Europe meeting—but why had they set the date so awkwardly, to coincide with the opening of the deer season?

Bosch was a generous hunting master, and his guests, particularly if he had invited them to the Alps to hunt, were given good quarry. But he was also demanding as a huntsman, and if he was not satisfied in this regard he could turn rough and rude. He made a clear distinction between hunters and shooters, and he was very selective in his choice of companions as soon as it extended beyond the narrow circle of his closest friends. There were no doubt numbers of individuals who waited in vain to be asked by him. But in such cases, even though hunting could be seen as a kind of social affair, he paid no attention to rank or position but only to a person's hunting reputation, and there were no doubt quite a few people who waited in vain to be asked back a second time! Bosch felt that on a hunt people really got to know each other—it was not without good reason that he began difficult business relationships during hunts, which offered such excellent opportunities to experience a person's professional and personal behavior. The others could also get to know him, in all his objective splendor and sudden abruptness. Hunting became the framework within which good friendships were formed; it was also, however, the occasion upon which old relationships occasionally fell apart in arguments.

35

AGRICULTURAL POLICY
AND PLANS

One can paint a sentimental, romantic picture: The factory owner, at the pinnacle of his industrial success, has fled the noise of the factory halls and returned to his nourishing mother earth. He wanders over the rolling countryside that is now his, thoughtful and at peace. He takes pleasure in the stand of rye, well grown and softly rippling, and directs his searching gaze to the signs of a storm brewing over the nearby mountains. Will they get the hay harvest, which is under way, safely into the barns? The evening walk homeward will bring him to the well-ventilated stalls, where he will cast an appreciative glance at the intensely powerful build of the breeding bull—it won a prize once, and a peasant takes pride in such things!—give a final parting word to the horses, who turn their heads in response as if they had been waiting for him. Does the scene awaken his childhood memories of the days when the teamsters unhitched their teams on the hill at Albeck and led their horses into the barn?

When Bosch in his *Life Recollections* arrived at the brief description of his interest in agriculture, he wrote that he "supported things for which my background must probably be held accountable," i.e., the blood of generations of peasant forebears. The dispassionate tone of this sentence should warn us not to view Bosch's interest in agricultural questions, or his own magnificently bold ventures into this field, with poetic lyricism. Here is no Rousseauian return to nature.

Bosch's interest was composed of several intertwined motives. First, perhaps, came his elemental attraction to the phenomena of the plant and animal worlds, which had remained a vivid memory from his childhood. His sharp eye observed, his sense of order compared, his love of knowledge sought to understand the connections. Otto Mezger tells how he was once looking through the books in Bosch's hunting lodge when he came across an old, shabby volume titled *A Guide to the Identification of Plants*. The title page bore the stamp "Robert Bosch, Mechanical Workshop, Stuttgart." Its owner had carried it with him years before on his Sunday walks; he always wanted to learn, not merely to enjoy. Later, he liked to quote the motto "Agriculture is applied science." In 1931, after he had already become deeply involved in his own farming ventures, he wrote, "Agriculture in itself is one of the most interesting branches of business there is. It is more varied than practically any other, for it overlaps with zoology, geology, chemistry, and meteorology in the most diverse ways." His innate sense of objective observation reverberates through sentences like these.

Soon after his youthful attraction to the field, Bosch became engaged in discussions about agrarian policy; with few exceptions these had a strong polemical edge. Bosch was a free trade advocate. It would be an oversimplification to assert that in this he was simply the speaker for an industrial special interest that feared the German policy of protective tariffs on agricultural goods might lead to repressive measures by foreign countries, and hence to a reduction of exports for Germany's own products. Naturally these feelings played a role, among others, as did Bosch's sense that the overall achievements of industry were not sufficiently appreciated by the government and the party groupings when it came job creation and tax revenues. That was not all, however. Bosch, as an opponent of all policies of government subsidy, refused to believe in the theory of the "needs of agriculture," which determined the rhythm of the tariff battles at the turn of the century and remained in force even *after* the trade talks of 1906 had increased grain duties. Certainly, this or that farmer might have a hard time if he had bought his property too dearly or his capital was insufficient to buy new equipment, or if he stuck to traditional ways without investigating the changing needs of the market and applying the dictates of science, but in general such a judgment did not apply. "I for my part am too closely related to agriculture," he wrote in February 1912 to an industrialist, "and so I know quite well that our agriculture is not in such bad shape as people claim. Thus I fail to understand why it should be necessary to pump our agriculture up artificially at our expense, as people are always nagging us to do . . . If it is a matter of spending millions on agriculture, perhaps more than all our farmers together pay in taxes, no one minds in the slightest, for agriculture must be protected."

Bosch was especially sensitive when it came to assumptions of this ilk. Later, one of his essays took the form of variations on the catastrophic slogan: "If the peasant has money, so does the whole world." In his letters and essays he was indefatigable in citing cases of peasants or owners of farm properties who got ahead in spite of the times and the public outcry about the suffering of the farmers, people who paid off their debts and increased their holdings simply because they understood something about what they were doing and made the effort. These farmers inspired the greatest respect in him; he only wished they would stop making the complaints that seemed almost to be expected of their class. When Bosch's friend Paul Reusch convened a committee of leaders of industry and agriculture, Bosch, who was already rather elderly, participated eagerly at first, feeling that intelligent discussion would be useful and necessary; later he became annoyed at hearing almost nothing but the same old stories and confined himself almost entirely to the role of listener. His anger spilled over into letters and memorandums, for example, in a comment he made in October 1930: "Whether I am just writing to rid myself of my misery or will actually make my experiences in agriculture public one day is something I do not know as yet, but I do know that the greatest enemies of farming are the farmers themselves."

It would not be realistic to expect from Bosch a systematic description of his views on agriculture. He never quite succeeded in writing enough to rid himself of his misery, for he lacked both the technical expertise and the patience to organize his varied thoughts and insights. In surveying his numerous comments on agriculture, which span several decades, one must be mindful of the fact that they stem from very different periods of time. Prices and pricing policies for various agricultural products were subject to considerable fluctuation in such politically unstable times. The basic tendency of Bosch's critique was to oppose the preferential government policies in support of grain production. He recognized that Germany led the world in productivity in this area, but he believed this had been achieved at the expense of increased diversification of the countryside. "It is odd," he wrote to Georg Escherich in March 1938, that it had been possible for such a long time "to convince our small farmers that they are in solidarity with the big grain farmers . . . Consider the fact that all the producers of milk and eggs, all the people who raise pigs and so forth have to suffer from the fact that we have grain tariffs." Then the letter launches with vehemence and vivid imagery into Bosch's favorite topic: What does the industrial boom mean for the development of the farm economy? "Here in Württemberg we have so many opportunities, for example when we are hunting, to observe that a region that has industry has lots of red tile roofs, and already had them before the war. Where there was no industry, there were no red tile roofs. I am thinking of Schiller's birthplace Marbach, for example. A sergeant once told me he had been stationed there on maneuvers, and he used the nice expression, 'The mice came running down the stage with tears in their eyes.' The towns that are located in the highlands 700 or 800 meters above sea level near the administrative center of Urbach have woodworking, bleaching, spinning, and weaving, and there the situation is completely different . . . Without industry we have a hard time, things are simply impossible. If we cannot export, they are also impossible. We must do away with the protective tariff and must do away with the barriers that stand in the way of complete freedom of movement for the individual." That this would only be possible within the context of international understanding was quite clear to him.

Bosch had familiarized himself with the thought processes of the leading agricultural economist Friedrich Aereboe. In 1928 he had read Aereboe's book *Agricultural Policy.* "It is very interesting, but not exactly easy reading and I have been occupied with it for some time now," he wrote on September 6, 1928. Bosch also consulted with Aereboe from time to time; he was impressed by his independent nature, which was unfettered

by ties to tradition, and by his organizational thoroughness, rich imagination, and capacity for unbounded enthusiasm. When Bosch's writings
and letters on the subject of agriculture dealt with the specialization of
agriculture along the lines of market requirements, or the rationalization
not only of agricultural production but of sales as well, these notions
reflected his encounter with Aereboe. What mattered most to him, however, was the unapologetic position that this scholar took when it came to
protective tariffs in agriculture. Bosch had called in Aereboe as early as
1924 to help him in the struggle against his "colleagues in industry," who
were "extraordinarily confused on this matter" and were only concerned
with "dead issues." Among the dead issues Bosch reckoned the argument about war, which supposedly could not be waged without a strong
agricultural base. Bosch would hear nothing of this objection. First, it
was one of the tasks of politics to prevent war, and second, a strong agricultural base did not consist of grain fields alone but included the production of meat, milk, and dairy products.

And the human beings who produced them! Bosch took a critical view
of farmers, and he responded with acknowledgment and gratitude whenever he met a peasant who was knowledgeable, active, thrifty, or daring
in an intelligent way; he was displeased when he encountered old ways of
doing things, laziness, or uneconomical theoretical organization that dis-
regarded real practical limits. This was an area, however, in which he,
too, had to gather his own experience. The personnel question seemed
more crucial in agriculture than anywhere else, for decisions constantly
had to be made with no one to supervise the actual organization of the
work—decisions about what crops to plant, about the harvest, about
sales—quite apart from the hundreds of details pertaining to fertilizer,
the care of equipment, and so on. What good was the best agricultural
land or the most favorable market location if the whole undertaking was
not carried out with insight, circumspection, character, and the willingness to lend a hand? The answer is obvious given Bosch's pedagogical
leanings and his faith in the influence of education: Build good schools
in the villages, found agricultural colleges, and make sure that the agricultural universities have a practical foundation and are useful for farming! In support of this conclusion Bosch pointed to both Denmark's
agricultural boom and the experience of Switzerland. The practical

impact of agricultural education was something that particularly con-cerned him. In all the crafts, as in business, the practical schooling of the young person came first and should always be seen within the context of immediate practical needs and responsibilities. For the farmer who might one day have large properties to manage, this link to practice was apparently not always considered a requirement. It is a subject on which Bosch often vented his anger and expended his proselytizing zeal—a commodity, to be sure, that he did not restrict to agriculture.

It was not until relatively late in his life that Robert Bosch, by an odd route, became a farmer. He had become a landowner before he had the intention of becoming a farmer. He had considered this once before, but had let the idea pass; this was in 1909, when he considered buying the domain of Klein-Hohenheim. "My wife's disdain for such things prevented me from carrying out this plan. I later regretted it." Anna Bosch may have been worried about the additional responsibilities and cares that might devolve on her during her husband's frequent travels if they were to move their residence there, as well; sometimes she may have found her hus-band's far-reaching ambitions oppressive and a bit frightening.

Bosch's agricultural interest had been awakened, however, and it could be transformed into something productive if the project were to extend beyond his private household. This explains why Bosch put sub-stantial funds at the disposal of an ambitious farmer from Lindenhof, near Eningen. His name was Otto Jäger, and Bosch had met him on a hunting trip; Bosch now enabled him to purchase the so-called "Eningen Pasture," a property consisting of approximately 400 hectares of pas-tureland at the foot of the Swabian highlands, and develop it through intensive cultivation. At the time, this event caused considerable con-sternation in Württemberg. Its economic feasibility was questioned, and since it soon became known that Bosch was the funder backing the bold experiment, he was inundated with reproaches that he was helping to destroy a natural treasure. A much-used hiking trail led past the pasture, with its heather, old groves of beech trees, and herds of grazing sheep, which lived as a friendly and idyllic memory in the minds of many visi-tors to the area. Bosch was more than a little annoyed that they were reproaching him, a well-informed friend of nature's beauties, in this way. "A field of waving grain and a blooming field of clover 20 hectares in size is as beautiful as a hillside of heather in flower," he wrote to his critics, and he did not let them destroy his pleasure in the economic success of the venture. Privately, though, he had a good deal less pleasure in the economic result of the experiment that he had undertaken with such generous means, for he became entangled in long and very unpleasant negotiations about its improvement. At their conclusion, in 1936, the province of Württemberg bought the entire area back from him at considerable expense. Decades earlier, before he had improved it, they had found it too insignificant to be of interest.

The path that eventually led Bosch into his own agricultural production was determined at first by quasi-industrial considerations. These were accompanied by a lively technical interest, and, as Bosch later remarked with the irony that is peculiar to dashed expectations, "the vile profit motive." At issue was the exploitation of peat bogs.

The industrial use of peat seemed to have entered a promising phase thanks to the development of a new technique. A Swede named Ekenberg had come up with it, and an English company began to test it and at the same time to advertise its licensing. It was a clever invention. An electrical countercurrent was to be used to remove the water from the moor, where it was stored in the form of hydrocellulose. When heated to a temperature of 300 degrees centigrade, this material exploded. The water was removed under pressure, in a filter, in the centrifuge; after that it was possible to make the flourlike residue into briquets. Theoretically, everything seemed to be in order. Bosch had managed to interest his nephew Carl, who at the time was in the midst of his work on ammonia and nitrogen production. Carl Bosch confirmed the favorable opinion that they had received from the description of the technical process. True, the commercial conditions imposed by the Englishmen, who demanded that in exchange for the licensing their partners found joint stock companies and give them 50 percent, did not exactly encourage Bosch to become involved with them. Better to keep an eye on the matter and see if it would prove itself—a test site had been established in Germany, as well. Bosch bought some stocks in the parent company, but no license. He was in no hurry. "At the time," he wrote in 1931, "I had a lot of income, and

I was intrigued by the transformation of swamps into productive land, particularly since it seemed to be possible to make great profits with the Ekenberg technique. The first thing I did was to buy up moors." In upper Swabia, in Ostrach, and in upper Bavaria, in Beuerberg, there was moorland for sale and he bought it.

Measured against its original intent, the purchase of this property was a complete failure. It engaged Bosch's attention for ten years, and even after that he continued to be interested in the various attempts to harvest peat more economically, and occasionally, in cases where a solution piqued his interest, he even lent his financial support. But his earlier experiences had taught him to be cautious. The Englishmen, using Ekenberg's patent, had built plants in Dumfries, Scotland, and had begun to operate them. But it never became possible to gain a clear picture of what they were doing and whether their technical success produced a corresponding yield. Some part of the apparatus was always breaking down, they were told; it seems that the plant only made a profit during the war, when the British government ordered and paid dearly for sulfur-free briquets to heat the trenches in Flanders. But Bosch had no interest in numbers linked to the war boom; the need for gasoline during the war had made even his own peat moor property profitable. The final conclusion, drawn from the expert opinion of a German engineer who had worked for the Englishmen before the war, was that the supply of fuel that could be gained from the Ekenberg technique, with all its problems and interruptions, was precisely adequate, on average, to produce the energy that had been required for its production! A little ammonia remained behind as the net gain. This was not worth the effort and expense; Bosch could be happy that he had not gotten more deeply involved in a matter that, while it may have been technically interesting, was ultimately not very successful.

As long as German coal production was insufficient to satisfy the need for fuel, during the war and the first postwar years, there was no problem with the exploitation of Bosch's moorland property. The use of the peat was prescribed by law, its purchase was guaranteed, and they didn't need to engage in any particular experiments or investments. "In the meanwhile, we are using the old technique, i.e., drying it in the sun and light, until we have something better. We are, however, going to great lengths to find something better," Bosch wrote in March 1920. Nothing better was found. When the day arrived that coal production and transportation were back to normal, the role of peat as a fuel once more became a purely local matter. The costs of transportation, measured against the peat's low heat production, were too high. The failure of the peat policy as an industrial concept was clear for all to see.

But had Bosch not been attracted by the notion of transforming swamps into productive land? He had written to Professor Carl Bach in March 1918 asking for information; would he please advise whether one of his students might be suitable for the peat moor business if Bosch were to take it up on a larger scale after the end of the war? The letter includes the statement: "The peat moor should be turned into meadows, which I can already see in my mind's eye complete with several thousand head of cattle. It is unlikely that I will live to see this dream realized in its entirety." Bosch would spend two decades on its realization, experiencing worry and elation, resignation and faith, defiance and pride. The dubious project of industrial peat production was transformed into a splendid, endlessly varied, boldly inventive and stimulating, even exciting, agricultural venture whose final results were imposing. There was in it an element of the Faustian drive to wring from nature its hidden or damaged fruitfulness, with the awareness that it would also be a battle *against* nature. Bosch gave this undertaking the name *Boschhof,* or simply, Bosch Farm.

The property lies about forty kilometers south of Munich, to which it is linked by the Isar rail line, which takes its time in doing its faithful duty. The rapid Loisach, a tributary of the Isar, arises in Lake Kochel and transports its rapid, dark waters through the region. The extensive moor area takes its name from the ancient community that lies on its northern edge—the Königsdorf Felt. Administratively, there is a slight inconvenience in that the area is bisected by the border between the counties of Wolfrathausen and Tölz. It is a landscape of pleasantly rolling hills; meadows give way to woods and the foothills of the Alps drop down to meet them. The picture is wonderfully framed by the mountains of the Benedictinerwand, the Karwendel, the Zugspitze. The whole area possesses a peaceful, quiet dignity; its amply framed simplicity contains an inexhaustible wealth of subtle tones.

The structure of the landscape is a product of the Ice Age; glacial moraines, rising above the moor, give it its character. They lie like islands in the plain; when a fog hangs over the dark, dank lowlands their tops emerge as if from a lake. These hilltops have been occupied by farmhouses for as long as anyone can remember; the mineral-rich earth on their slopes offered pasture and grain fields for one or more peasants; the larger hills could accommodate two or three. The earth is loamy and has baked-in stony pebbles from the moraine. Narrow, poorly banked roads connect these habitations to the external world.

Not much information is available on the history of the settlement. The entire property embraces seven farms: Fletzen, Nantesbuch, Karpfsee, Höfen, Mooseurach, Sterz, and Boschhof. The last-named settlement, after which the whole area in now named, was a more recent addition; it was developed from the factory building of the Beuerberg peat production company. Today it provides its administrative center and is the site of its great milking barn; it is situated favorably near the Isar Valley rail line, and has its own rail spur. Of greater historical interest are the old farms. The first four named above formed part of the old abbey of Benediktbeuren, which was founded in A.D. 740 and played such an important role in the early history of upper Bavaria. The abbey was responsible for the original settlement of the region. Old place names like Chunitzdorf, Wendenau, and others suggest that converted Slavs (prisoners of war?) may have been settled here, and later been absorbed by the Bavarian populace. In the chronicle of the monastery, set down by Meichelbeck, the farms are counted as having been among its original properties; they shared the fate of the monastery, which was devastated during the early Hungarian campaigns but then generously restored under Heinrich III. The tax rolls of the monastery, which go back to 1441, record the annual tithes of the various farms, how many bushels of rye, how many pounds of goose fat or butter, how many eggs, or how much honey had to be delivered at the end of every year. The farm products are translated into money amounts beginning at the end of the fifteenth century. A comparison with the assets of other monasteries indicates that the moor peasants were relatively productive.

There are few remains of buildings from the early centuries. In Nantesbuch there is a half-ruined early Gothic chapel, in Fletzen an old barn dating back to the sixteenth century. Impressive and beautiful avenues of oaks crown the hills, lining the important access roads; they may have been planted in the eighteenth century and bespeak a certain comfort and awareness of social status. In the nineteenth century, secularization apparently led to a situation characterized by occasional crises; the farms changed hands frequently. The purchasers included members of the lesser nobility, and an urban element appeared for the first time; for these purchasers agricultural production was no longer the main objective. Naturally, there had to be some attempts to make systematic use of the moor; the chronicle tells of a Swabian named Fischer who made his fortune in Australia and tried his luck in the 1860s, based in Mooseurach, but soon lost interest in the venture.

Bosch knew the area well from his trips to his first hunting preserve, the "box" near Scharnitz. Later on he would tell people that it was the colorful vegetation of the moor that first appealed to him, with heather growing in its non-arable places. Still, a lovely natural image that stands open to every hiker is not a reason to buy a piece of land. The stimulus to buy came, rather, from a complex of buildings that was less beautiful. Rather rough and clumsy looking, with a high chimney, it stood at the edge of the moor near the village and monastery of Beuerberg; it was the above-mentioned peat factory. Its founders had planned to produce ammonia by slow burning of the peat, which they wanted to harvest and dry; they had purchased enough moorland and built a big enough facility to accommodate a large business, but success was elusive. Perhaps they should have thought more carefully about the weather, for the area is truly blessed with rainfall, approximately 1,500 millimeters a year, so that drying peat in the air and sunlight is a matter of luck. There would always be enough fine days and weeks for local consumption, but for regular factory production, which has to reckon with quantities, fixed costs, and amortization, the venture was full of imponderables. In rainy years it was simply impossible to extract the necessary material for slow burning, and the business faltered. Bosch bought it in 1912. As soon as Ekenberg's method had been worked out in practice, he would no longer need to worry about the obviously unfavorable weather. The extraction of the water, which after all made up as much as 90 percent of the moorland peat, would be a consequence of the electrical heating process. Since the technique never really reached the point of mature development, Bosch—no longer as a peat producer but as a farmer—had to suffer through the difficulties of the peculiar weather zone for some time. Initially, his holdings had included both the peat company in Beuerberg, with its clumsy factory building, and its moorlands, which Bosch expanded. At the end of the war the property comprised about 1,200 hectares; over the course of the following years Bosch expanded it by purchasing various farms that became available until it covered a total area of more than 1,700 hectares.

The cultivation of moorland, including the production of peat, had been taken up during the war. Potatoes, rye, and oats were grown. One thing was clear: If they wanted their agricultural production to be oriented toward the market, the emphasis would have to be on animal husbandry and milk and butter production, perhaps with pig farming and eggs as well. The easy access to the large metropolitan area of Munich, the health resorts in the area, which included Tölz, Heilbronn, and so forth, would provide long-term marketing opportunities without the necessity of costly intermediaries. The geographical location of the property, in other words, proved to be economically favorable. One thing that needed immediate clarification was the reliability of the supply of feed. People had raised cattle on the hilly farms for as long as anyone could remember, but only on a limited scale. Given the heavy rainfall, a good hay harvest was more or less a matter of luck; there was not enough winter fodder for a large herd of cattle.

Bosch's trip to South America in the spring of 1921 had certainly not been conceived as an agricultural study tour. And although its business side had been rather symbolic, Bosch's personal motivation had been the wish to free himself from a number of psychological pressures by gaining new impressions. Nevertheless, it would become important for the new agrarian challenge with which Bosch saw himself confronted. In South America he encountered silos for corn; this meant the possibility of putting up and storing the feed grain without exposing it to decay. He quickly came to the conclusion that this was the means by which to secure his harvest of fodder in rainy years—by bringing the grass inside before it became woody and lost its nutrients. After his return, Bosch occupied himself with this question, which was still a relatively new one in Europe; as yet there were no large facilities. Shortly before, however, a method had been invented that involved using electricity for silo storage. Siemens & Halske had acquired it and had continued to develop it through a Dresden subsidiary, Elfu; it was Elfu that was selling the licenses.

This appealed to Bosch's technical imagination, and he was tempted by the opportunity for a pioneering achievement that might provide an example to agriculture. Ekenberg's system of heating the peat had not produced a satisfactory result; here was something that was simpler and easier to deal with. "The high cost cannot be the determining factor where I am concerned," he wrote on July 4, 1921, to his nephew Carl Bosch, who had provided him with some information about the new process. Since the land was so moist, he could not leave the harvest to dry naturally; without electricity it would not work. All that was needed was someone who would take the matter in hand and supervise it, and he found that person in Richard Stribeck, his old friend from their student days. Stribeck had returned home after his retirement but was soon persuaded to give up his retirement and take on this new challenge. Under his direction, they immediately began constructing the silos, each of which had a capacity of 120 cubic meters. Technically, the principle of using electricity seemed to hold true. When electricity is conducted through the densely compressed grasses it quickly raises their temperature to 40 degrees centigrade, at which point lactic acid bacteria begin to develop. These bacteria play the decisive role in the storage of the grass as fodder and also increase the nutrient value of the hay. The labor costs, or wages, are also lower if the grain is stored in silos than with traditional harvesting methods, in which human labor is repeatedly required. From the first spring cutting through the fall, one can harvest fodder for the winter and be independent of the vagaries of the weather or of labor.

True, one must first have the facilities! With admirable generosity, Bosch proceeded to build silos on all the farms of the property. They were linked together in rows, with airy roofs—characteristic architectonic forms that represented the core of the business, or its skeleton so to speak. With its fifty silos, the Boschhof is thought to have been the largest silo farm in Germany, or perhaps in all of Europe. In addition to its immediate significance for the fodder they needed for their own business, it became a very effective center of teaching and learning about this aspect of agricultural progress. Government agencies took a lively interest in Bosch's experiments and their results. It was necessary to gather experience with the silos, as well, and it led to a technical change that Bosch adopted only reluctantly. If the cost calculations were to work out, the electrical silos that Bosch had taken up with such programmatic determination would need to pay a lower price for electricity than was currently available. Nor was this the only consideration that led to a change in plan—science had established the fact that an optimal production of lactic acid is not only achieved at 40 degrees centigrade but occurs at 10 degrees centigrade when the so-called cold silo technique is used. Molasses, or a type of formic acid developed especially for this purpose, is mixed in with the grass as it is put into the silo. The work is done in cool weather and can even be done at night if pressed for time. It can be carried out quickly, reliably, and more cheaply than electrical silo storage; the enhanced quality of the fodder, which has a greater protein content than hay, is maintained.

The acres of green that had been wrested from the moorland were designed above all to produce winter feed for the silos, since the fields' soft earth and sensitive sod were not very well suited for grazing, and even then only during long dry periods. Traditionally, the slopes of the meadows and the mineral-rich earth of the farm hills had been considered grazing land. Later on, Bosch turned his attention to increasing the production of fodder from these areas, as well, by applying liquid fertilizer that he transported from a mixing trough by means of a system of pipes. The increase in the livestock herd, and especially Bosch's concern about maintaining its quality through breeding, led him, in the course of the reorganization of the farm, to lease a large property in 1931. The area was called Hohenburg; it was located in the Isar Valley and had a number of high meadows. The Boschhof already had some high meadows for summer pasturing, but they were too small, and the incorporation of the Alpine meadows with their exposure to sun, calcium-rich earth, and aromatic herbs proved extremely conducive to the health and breeding of the animals, as well as the quality of the milk they produced.

This lease of pastureland resulted from Bosch's more mature insight into the economics of the business. During the initial period, the central task had been the cultivation of the moor, and to this end the management adopted a plan to create 100 hectares of new cropland every year. This was a bold idea—too bold, for there was the danger that they would simply cultivate at any price in order to fulfill their plan and reach their statistical goal. It was not easy to accomplish this; the process is difficult and time-consuming and there are many unseen problems that can endanger success. The Königsdorf Felt is primarily high moor; in other words, the landscape has features that allow the water to flow off naturally into the Loisach, either through the natural slope of the land or through the streams that pass through it. No pumps are required. The first step is to free from dwarf pines, birches, and shrubs the land that has been set aside for cultivation. Then a deep trench or "outfall" is dug around it and narrow draining ditches are constructed leading into the area. This initiates the draining process. The outfalls and draining ditches are then made deeper, and pipes leading to the bottom of the trench are inserted at a depth of about one and a half meters. The water flows out slowly and continuously; the surface of the moor sinks one meter, then two meters; it is more or less safe to walk on now, and it is possible to use a plow attached to a tractor. Potatoes are planted as the first crop, followed by rye, oats, and hemp. The goal, after the earth has been treated by crop rotation, is to create a lasting plot of green that needs neither care nor cultivation.

The moorland's humus content, created by the decomposition of vegetable matter, is its greatest asset, but it is lacking in minerals. Carbon dioxide, phosphorus, and potash salts must be added. The question of more permanent fertilization containing calcium was something that occupied Bosch for a long time. Experience had shown that there was no reliable norm for cultivated moorland. Some fields suffered a relapse, if it could be called that, and in this case even the most strenuous efforts and the greatest expense were to no avail; the earth remained difficult to cultivate due to old roots, or became acidic again. The only option was to remove it from cultivation, plant it with alders, and use it as a spreading field. Bosch's aim had been to make the *entire* wasteland part of an extensive cultivation plan that would take many years to implement; within that goal, as a kind of voluntary conservation, some particularly typical sites were to be maintained in their original condition. The overall goal was not abandoned, but its pace slowed and the work was fitted in as a stopgap measure whenever they were not busy somewhere else. From an economic point of view, it had to be more advantageous to improve the cultivated fields located near the plant than to pursue the essentially statistical addition of newly cultivated hectares. An important goal had been to open up the extensive territory by providing roads to replace the barely visible tracks that disappeared into the moor. They made way for a system of roads that extended twenty-two kilometers and was secured with foundations; bridges required more complicated footings. A narrow-gauge railroad was built to reach the fields; it was also useful for hauling gravel, earth, or stone for the construction of roads. The railroad became indispensable for moving heavy loads as they improved the land. Originally they had the idea of transporting the milk to the central processing plant by rail, but this was clearly too much technical equipment, for after all, the business was not *that* large, and the terrain was difficult. Several "lines" are still served by a horse-drawn milk wagon; the others have become a weed-covered monument to overly ambitious planning.

The stalls were laid out with all of Bosch's customary attention to detail, and included all the means of waste disposal typical of a large animal husbandry plant. Here, as in his factory buildings, Bosch also considered the provision of fresh air to be one of the most important requirements. There were exhaust mechanisms that regularly expelled used air and delivered fresh air—the same things that had proved themselves when it came to the feelings of human beings would also be good for animals! The *Boschhof* acquired a charming reputation thanks to the birds that made their homes in its stalls, farm buildings, woods, and meadows, where they multiplied by the tens of thousands. This world of birds was hired on by Bosch, as it were, to police the insect population, which is overrepresented in moors. The ornithologist Staats V. Wacquant had been commissioned to introduce swallows and titmice; Wacquant, who was an expert on the needs and nesting habits of birds, succeeded to the fullest extent possible. The purpose was quite simple: to protect the animals from the previous torture of the flies, and to do something that would not only benefit the animals but would also be economically useful, since milk production increases when a cow is freed from the expenditure of energy needed to protect itself from this plague. Bats were introduced to work the night shift. For a friend of nature like Bosch, this avian protection was not merely useful; he was delighted that his property had become a landscape inhabited by birds. Not only the barnyards, but the roads and woods were thickly settled with nests and nesting opportunities (one hundred and seventeen species of birds have been identified here). Bosch also involved his neighbors in this cooperative venture. Specialists were hired for certain insect pests, for example, starlings for another dangerous moorland pest. There was something touching about Bosch's request to his boyhood friend Gebhard to send him a couple of jackdaws from the Munster cathedral for the old factory chimney before it was taken down during the war.

In 1930 a great milking plant was constructed in the central barn area; here they processed milk, primarily drinking milk for children and other high-quality milk for Munich, and churned butter. When the business was reorganized in 1931, special cheeses were developed that became familiar brands. The milking plant also processed milk from the surrounding farming communities; it was designed to handle 10,000 liters of drinking milk and 4,000 liters of milk for processing. The by-product of dairies, whey, is used to raise piglets. The raising of pigs and the mash used to feed them were only possible on a limited basis, since their feed has a different economic base. But the potato harvest, to the extent that it was not sent to market, could suffice for pigs. A butcher's shop was to process any meat products from animals not sold at market.

An unusual sight can be observed not far from the farm buildings. On the meadows and harvested fields are oddly constructed vehicles—chicken houses on wheels. Their location changes, and the poultry is allowed to go in and out and provide for itself at a kind of nearby automat that dispenses feed kernels. Naturally, great value was attached to the quality of the breeding. Breeding roosters became a market item, and several thousand hens (the number varied according to the time of year) were busy laying eggs. Bosch also arranged for an experiment to bring in varieties of fruit suited to the rough climate, but this could only be an afterthought within the overall plan; more important was the cultivation of fields of vegetables of various types. Also, in a business with such variety, a rather good-sized beekeeping operation could hardly be lacking! And when they had to excavate earth for road construction, might it not be possible to develop fishponds?

What about all these projects? In his writings Bosch had recommended that farmers become specialized. The breadth of the production program in his own ventures was not at all in keeping with this notion. Naturally it is evident that despite the overarching significance of grazing and animal husbandry, the huge property with its geological variety and changing surface characteristics was not really suited for a monoculture. But the diversification of risk, which Bosch later learned to appreciate as a counterweight to specialization in agriculture, was not the deciding factor. At the time Bosch felt driven to provide a highly visible example in food production and marketing policy. He had already integrated all the available technical and industrial means into his agricultural venture, in addition, it is true, to such "natural" ones as the raising of birds. Now he wanted to go a step farther in an organizational sense. The technique that had proved itself in his industrial works—the development of company-owned sales offices, the "Bosch service" in the most all-embracing sense of the word—was to be applied to his agricultural production as well. He took the brand name Bosch directly to the Munich victuals market; he even had surveys made of the costs of transport and traffic speeds in case he were to become involved in providing foodstuffs to northern Franconia and the industrial centers of Saxony. The customers knew that when they bought a product from Bosch, they were well served. It would start, shine, or beep at will; buyers were accustomed to knowing that the Bosch name was associated with the best; they paid for quality, reliability, and durability. These buyers should also know that they were receiving only the best milk, butter, cheese, eggs, vegetables, and sausage—or even the special bread baked with skim milk—and they should be confident that the produce was fresh and impeccable from the standpoint of good health. A sales center was built in Munich, with refrigeration facilities, and eight Boschhof stores were rented and outfitted. In addition, two milk bars were created. Boschhof had become a brand name emblazoned on large motor vehicles driving through the city.

The market quickly gained fame, and it lasted, but the plan to service the population of the big city directly, without middlemen, was abandoned. Naturally, the venture had produced some opposition. At that juncture, the politics of the middle class were easily swayed by sentiment or agitation—not that Bosch would ever have withdrawn in the face of such opposition, but the calculation was rather simple: the staff in Munich, the rent for the stores, the large number of employees lacking the self-interest of the small shopkeeper created more fixed costs than the sales volume could accommodate. High prices, which people might be willing to pay for an industrial product because the purchaser was also paying for durability, were not appropriate for foodstuffs unless they were luxury items. But this was precisely not Bosch's aim; he wanted his contribution to be of a more general nature, but the base was too narrow for a large-scale sales operation. The attempt to increase gross sales by marketing products from other sources had its limitations and was not in keeping with the basic plan. So from a purely commercial standpoint, Bosch had to give up his attempt to break into the market as an individual and instead was forced to link up with a large, well-known milk-processing cooperative, sharing its well-oiled sales machine while retaining his own brand name. The Boschhof shops remained a passing phenomenon; they had a positive influence on the hygienic habits of small grocery stores, which at first had felt threatened. This had not been Bosch's intention when he created the sales organization, but when he was told about the pedagogical side effect he had had, he was probably quite gratified to hear it.

In general, though, he cannot be said to have been very satisfied with the Boschhof. He had not initiated the venture as a hobby but with the serious goal of getting the maximum economic value from a rather unprofitable property. For this, he was aware that large-scale investments were needed, but the outcome put his patience to the test. Bosch was as far removed as one can imagine from the type of industrialist or successful banker who was eager, in the years after the war, to buy some kind of property in the country as an investment or for social reasons. In such a case Bosch could have sought out any number of more favorable opportunities. Nowhere in the entire organization of the barns, all designed for rationality with their structures and tools, was it possible to speak of luxury. The test of patience, however, took time, a lot of time, and the eagerness of the venture's technical directors (and of its owner!) cost money, a lot of money. Bosch didn't complain about it but took pleasure in the facilities and achievements; something had been accomplished after all. But he gradually sensed that with all the designing and experimenting what was at issue was less the productive capacity of the land than the financial capacity of its owner. This disturbed him, and it bothered him that the economic success of the venture, which had become evident despite several false starts, found no reflection at all in any personal profits. Where was the source of the problem? Being trusting and giving a free hand. Had he deceived himself so seriously about the quality of his people? Had he hired incompetents? He did not make things easier by seeking to blame others. He himself had approved everything; he had been inclined to be overly optimistic about the theoretical plans and had allowed himself to be carried away. There was no one to contradict him with courageous realism. As a result, Bosch's relationship with this creation that had been so dear to his heart had become particularly unfelicitous, and he felt that he himself was partly to blame. In 1931, he wrote that he would "discourage anyone from getting involved in agriculture who does not possess the necessary knowledge and have the time to become intimately involved with his business and to keep watch over his employees." Was this the end result? People came by to see the property, experts studied its facilities, the German Agriculture Society made an inspection visit in 1929, and people said nice things to Bosch about his great agricultural achievement. Ministers praised him and found it quite admirable that he had turned his social commitment to agricultural questions, as well, and was carrying out such instructive experiments. That was all very well and good, but not all the time. Occasionally Bosch thought he could hear the undertone: "Yes, *you* can allow yourself to do this. You don't live on agriculture. Your best cow stands in a stall in Stuttgart." This bothered him. Was the fact that he had gone over to the farmers actually something people held against him? Or, since the undertaking was subsidized, were his example and model finally misleading? The magnificent technical facilities did not only have admirers, they had their detractors, too, and along with admiring recognition of Bosch's willingness to make sacrifices and the stubbornness with which he held on to the business and continued to keep it going with new projects, a worrisome question occurred to him: Can an economic model be created in a situation where the business calculations are ultimately oriented to factors that are not agricultural in nature? For several years Bosch had quite clearly been aware of this situation. It had to be possible to bring his economic goals into line with the factors that influenced the business!

In the summer of 1931, Bosch entrusted the direction of the agricultural properties to a young farmer from Aereboe's school. Walter Mauk, thirty-two years of age, had had practical experience in Baden and Rhineland-Pfalz, Saxony, and Pomerania and had already managed large farms near Hanover and Mecklenburg. He was then managing a property in Brandenburg for the city of Berlin, and already had some experience with moor cultivation on the margins of his business, so to speak. The Boschhof, with its strange disproportion between freedom of investment and financial outcome, challenged him, as did the man who now stood before him and offered him his trust. Bosch was not the first individual from the world of major industry whom Mauk had encountered in his professional career; as a very young man he had been hired by Hugo Stinnes. The years of working for Stinnes had sharpened his sense of the differences between industrial and agricultural thinking and decision-making. On the whole, it had been quite a good psychological preparation, for things would not always be easy with Bosch, either. One could sense that despite his world-class accomplishments Bosch had come to feel uncertain about this piece of land that he had grown to love. Mauk accepted his offer. One of Bosch's notes from the first week of the new director's employment commented that he "appears to think like me when it comes to the education of the staff, and in economics, as well. Now I must put my trust in him and hope that he will manage the farm in such a way that it is worthwhile to continue the business. The beginning has satisfied me for now. But the difficulties that must be surmounted are great!"

These difficulties were naturally partially caused by the general economic crisis, which affected agriculture, too. The management of the Boschhof was spared the fate that was hanging over many landowners at that time—the struggle with creditors—but the collapse of produce prices ruined their prospects, too. The fact that it was possible, in the end, to create a balance sheet in which the return to profitability was expressed in hundreds of thousands was all the more astonishing and gratifying for Bosch. The most immediate concern was to reduce the expense budget in order to narrow the gap between expenditures and income. It was a difficult business. Which investments were uneconomical? The personnel budget, with a staff of managers and assistants for each individual farm, proved to be bloated. Did they really have to have their own veterinarian? Was it worth the trouble of negotiating special rates with the electrical companies and railroads? Who said they had to accept the agreements that had been made? It was not just a question of cutting back, however. The dairy, which until this time had focused almost entirely on the sale of fresh bottled milk, was transformed through the addition of a cheese-making operation. The Munich sales operation was put to the test; it was not yet declining, and indeed an increase in volume would bring it back to life for a time, but within a few years its limitations would become evident.

Bosch had to say good-bye to a number of his favorite notions. He did so almost with a sense of liberation, because now there was a will and a clear and unconstrained sense of responsibility for him to respond to. "The situation," he wrote in October 1934, "has changed as fundamentally as possible. Now it is a joy for me to visit the Boschhof, whereas before when I was there I constantly had to swallow my annoyance and other unpleasantness." Naturally, the transformation did not occur all at once; investments were required over periods of time, particularly when it came to developing suitable livestock. They began to renew their ties with the animal husbandry industry of Bavaria, which had been somewhat neglected during their experiments with black-spotted cattle from the East Prussian lowlands. The challenge of maintaining first-rate quality during the transition was met, and they had the satisfaction of seeing that the Boschhof stalls still had the highest milk production of any farm in the surrounding counties.

The new manager had ideas that pleased the owner. On a trip through the area, for example, Mauk had come across a herd of sheep leading a miserable existence on a plot of poor, dry, stony meadow. He suggested to the owner that he should board them at the Boschhof; it would not cost him any money, he merely had to give them every fifth ewe, which he could scarcely bring through anyway in the conditions under which they lived. The man was glad to accept; he had a second herd, and in this way the Boschhof became involved in raising sheep, without any of the worries normally associated with acclimatization. Bosch found this initiative sufficiently important to report to his friend Fritz Egnell about it in detail in 1936. "Since we must attempt to achieve the greatest possible degree of autarky . . . we are asking for payment in ewes and calculate that by the year 1940 we will have a herd of 1,000 to 1,200 head."

Bosch's decision to begin breeding horses had a more significant impact. Many years before, in 1913, one of the tycoons of Upper Swabia had tried to elicit Bosch's support for this activity. (This occurred during the period when people had become accustomed to depending on Bosch's support for all sorts of things.) "The whole business is quite alien to me. Though I am the son of a peasant I have never really had anything to do with horses . . ." Naturally this was an exaggeration; he had only to think of the great stalls for the unhitching of teams that had played such a large role in his father's business. He probably suspected, however, that the blue-blooded proponent of this idea was thinking of race horses and the like, which were not at all his kind of endeavor. Walter Mauk's suggestion was of a very different nature. The transformation of military technology with the decrease in cavalry that it entailed would not entirely spell the end of horses in the military. The artillery needed tough, easily cared for horses; horses were also required for the transport of supplies through the mountains. It would therefore be necessary to locate some remounting areas in the mountains. If a suitable type of horse could be developed, it would undoubtedly be useful for the farmers in these areas as well. Bosch found this notion to be very persuasive. Haflinger horses from Tyrol were available. Small, powerful, and indestructible, they could not fail to interest Bosch as a possibility for breeding.

Herds of horses and donkeys appeared at the Boschhof, which had sufficient fodder to support the new line of business as long as the sheep-raising plan remained limited and modest reductions were made in the number of cattle. The first result was that they were able to do with fewer employees; horses and donkeys require only one fourth of a person each for their care. The leases they had acquired for land in Hohenburg and other high mountain areas now showed their value in a twofold sense;

these pastures not only encouraged bovine health and bone structure and improved the quality of the milk, but their firm surface and stony slopes were also well adapted for horses and donkeys.

For a long time Bosch also considered expanding the whole agricultural undertaking and diversifying the risk by acquiring grain and sugar beet fields in northern Germany. He occupied himself extensively with this notion during his last years. He wanted to buy a farm that was "on the sunny side," as he wrote in August 1936, by which he meant better land, better climate, and a type of property that could rely on a more favorable attitude on the part of the government than farming and the improvement of agricultural land. "I poor dolt am sitting here on the shady side . . ." The plan was never carried out, however.

Although Robert Bosch was the son of a peasant and reclaimed fields and pastures from swamps and moors, one would not want to call him a farmer although he himself might not have resisted the appellation during the last two decades of his life. Naturally there was a bit of self-reflexive irony involved when he wrote about meetings with his "colleagues" among the farmers, but when he sat down with them he wanted to be seen as their equal, as someone who was ready to learn from the experiences they had to report but also expected that he would be listened to. Where this equality was denied him and he was regarded as the industrialist who could "afford" to be a part-time farmer, he became angry. Not that he would have expected thanks or recognition for the fact that he continued to invest such substantial means in agriculture; he was no friend of sentimentality. But he was of the opinion that people could, indeed must, learn from the things he had introduced—not because of his fame, but for the sake of improving German agriculture and the diet of the German people. The fact that he was draining swamps was not necessarily something that should be taken for granted; he was taking on tasks that were actually the responsibility of society and the state. And he liked to make it clear to those who implied that it was merely a question of money that *his* improvements were made considerably more cheaply than those of the official agricultural bureaus.

The attempt to bring industrial methods to bear on agricultural production was a systematic effort for Bosch. It was not as if he equated industry with superiority or industrialist with someone whose views were purely progressive. From time to time he was forced to distance himself quite sternly and consciously from his industrial colleagues, too; but industry, with its competitive environment, was compelled to save and to make technological progress. To Bosch's way of thinking, the fact that agriculture used parliamentary power politics to secure its favorable position through high tariffs was one of the original sins. He stubbornly rejected the objection that was frequently raised by Paul Reusch, namely, that a certain degree of capital savings and reserves would be created behind the tariff walls and would open up possibilities for a technological development that would lead to higher yields. When it came to bringing an "industrial element" to agriculture, Bosch naturally interpreted this concept from his own vantage point of concern about the workforce; it meant developing plants in the countryside, having the best possible technical apparatus, and achieving mass production as rapidly and simply as possible. The stalls and silos were produced in volume, with an imaginative force of implementation that lacked the patience to gather experience gradually. As a result, a number of failed attempts were unavoidable; Bosch had some things to learn in this regard. With all his unconstrained daring and rebellious will to exploit the capitalist techniques he had learned for manufacturing and distributing goods, he lacked a sense of the limits of economic usefulness when it came to the basics of agriculture. And occasionally he did not even have a sense of what was economically and technically useful. This was not something he could learn from studying, but insight gradually led to changes in the program, which became more flexible and finally reached the goal Bosch had presumably sought from the beginning but had not succeeded in reaching for a long time—bringing his more general sense of purpose into harmony with the economic power and profitability of this business sector. For only when this had become possible would he have created a complete and convincing example.

36

———◆———

HEALTH CARE

In the fall of 1941, when Paul Reusch was endeavoring to purchase an important painting by an old Swabian master for the Stuttgart art museum, he asked his friend Bosch to help him raise the necessary funds. Bosch replied that "strangely enough," he had "never had much tolerance" for such efforts. He did not help raise the money; he donated it out of his own pocket. This was done to please Reusch, for Bosch had no connection to medieval painting; we know that when he spent money on works of art it was for the benefit of artists who were still creating. The letter to Reusch, written during Bosch's last year, said, among other things, "My dear friend, our thoughts on such matters, where they touch on our homeland, are identical, except that you have more interest in art and history; in my desire to be supportive I am more inclined toward medicine."

At the time, political developments within Germany had put a stop to Bosch's involvement in popular education and his personal attempts to influence foreign policy. The associations and working groups that had been the beneficiaries of Bosch's participation—whether warmly supportive or more critical in tone—had vanished. Faced with the dearth of opportunities to become involved in educational and political affairs, Bosch found an outlet for his energies in measures related to health policy. Such measures therefore played the most prominent role among the charitable activities of his old age, and they crowned it in a way that was wholly fulfilling to him. At the same time, these were only the final echoes of a desire to help that went back decades, especially when it came to this particular realm of human and social life.

Bosch's position on medical matters was an expression of the power of his rational thought and of the concern for justice and fairness that stamped his character; it also reflected aspects of his own individual constitution. His letters often discussed his well-being, mentioning symptoms of illness, regained energy, good or poor sleep, or heart ailments in a tone that was not exactly complaining but was often worried. Uncertainty about the reliability of his capacities seemed to constantly hold him back; sometimes it may also have served as a protection against the unwanted demands made on him. He was incessantly concerned about his health, and this might sometimes have given the impression that he was complaining or even that he had a tendency to hypochondria, but then his remarks would take the form of purely objective reports. He was capable of reporting on his illnesses in a completely detached way once he had acquired a more or less convincing understanding of their causes and biological characteristics. He was constantly observing himself; he would be anxious when some discomfort was beginning to affect him but would become relaxed and confident as soon as he knew where he stood. Bosch's nature was fundamentally healthy. His body, trained in gymnastics and hiking, retained its tense, almost elegant elasticity of movement through his old age. He was tall and slim, with a fine-boned build. His uncompromising manner might sometimes create the impression of robustness, but this was a product of his nervous energy. His physique was sensitive, even overly sensitive in its responsiveness to changes in temperature and to odors. There are anecdotes about his lifestyle that are not without a certain grotesque element. For example, there was the matter of leather and shoes. Bosch often suffered from the effects of the alternation of heat and cold on his feet. This was especially uncomfortable on his hunting trips and exposed him to the danger of catching cold. He suspected that the cause might have to do with the use of chrome for tanning! But the information he was able to glean from Gustav Jäger in 1914 was not conclusive. All kinds of tanning experiments were undertaken in the firm, and a village shoemaker was finally found who knew how to locate leather that had been tanned with bark in small country tanneries; Bosch remained faithful to this supplier for decades and assured people that he no longer felt the same degree of discomfort.

Back in Bosch's student days Gustav Jäger had won him over to his theory of health and had made him into a grateful apostle. The early photographs of Bosch, with his double-breasted jacket buttoned up to the chin, show that he remained faithful in his dress to the pattern that Jäger had prescribed as correct for health. In this way, Bosch appeared as an avowed propagandist of Jäger's group, although he had no calling or talent for gaining converts to the religion of wool. Later, when Bosch was confronted with official duties, with meetings in Berlin and the inevitable invitations, he made peace with fashionable tailoring—not happily, but submitting to the dictates of the fashion world in order to avoid causing curiosity or annoyance by his outward appearance. His way of life remained as it had been. At home with his parents, he had already been accustomed to a refined, although by no means luxurious, household. With his extreme sensitivity, Bosch remained very restrained in his use of stimulants; he did not smoke and he drank very little.

The war had had a serious effect on his otherwise generally unbroken health. In the year 1917 he had suffered a serious dilation of the heart that put him out of work for months and was accompanied by pain, constriction, fatigue, and sleep disorders. This was more or less corrected by visits to spas in Wiesbaden and by his efforts to adopt a work pace that was adjusted to this state of affairs; the change took years, however. According to a note from 1931, Bosch's affliction continued to worsen during the first years after the war, causing indecisiveness and apathy; he considered this to have been the cause of a number of decisions he later regretted. It is certain that the memories of this illness made Bosch even more distrustful of himself and the ability of his constitution to withstand excitement. In really critical moments, however, he remained coldblooded and clearheaded, for example in 1920, when he was spending the night in his hunting lodge and was threatened by an attacker. Shots were fired through his window; it was never clear whether it was a political fanatic or a poacher. The incident passed without physical damage to Bosch, as did a serious railroad accident in January 1920 that could easily have cost him his life, as he woke up with the impression recounted in a letter of January 15, 1920, that "I was in the midst of an earthquake and could see that the walls were pushing in on me and was just waiting for the ceiling to come down, which probably would have meant the end. But at least I did not have such a severe shock that it resulted in any suffering on my part." The psychological pressures, from which he was unable to escape, caused the development and recurrence of his heart disease. Bosch mentioned it in a letter written on March 13, 1933, to his nephew Carl Bosch. "Just as in 1917 during the war, dilation of the heart due to the stress and worries over the political situation. Lying around and fantasizing about our current circumstances makes me utterly sick and empty."

Despite Bosch's susceptibility to nervous disturbances, his physical capacity remained remarkable through his old age. It was moderated somewhat; he chose shorter hikes, more in tune with the old-age complaints that were causing him difficulties. As soon as the hunting season opened, he would somehow become filled with the desire and capacity for adventure, even in times when his health was uncertain. He could still be found on the golf course when he was almost eighty. He remarked in a letter that he was "not an excellent golfer"; he had started too late, at sixty-seven, but the relaxing training was a good way to retain his flexibility. The freshness of his visual observation and memory was not impeded by aging. He was proud of his memory. In his later years, for those occasions when he complained that he had forgotten some detail, or that his wits were not as sharp as they had once been, he had invented the somewhat coquettishly ironic phrase, "My memory has gotten just about as bad as that of young people."

Bosch's own constitution, its health and response to illness, formed the background of his involvement in questions of public hygiene and medicine. Where the latter was concerned, his commitment, at first, was to what he had been taught at home. Like many well-to-do households in Ulm, his had been under the influence of a very active and successful doctor named Widemann who was a believer in homeopathy. Using this method was almost an article of faith for Bosch. The fact that Gustav

Jäger published a modest essay that affirmed the justification of Samuel Hahnemann's basic ideas and developed their experimental basis was something that he viewed as a welcome confirmation. Still, this was not yet a reason to regard homeopathy as something deserving of his special support; at the time, in Württemberg, there was no need for such involvement. The medical opinions of Queen Olga of Württemberg, a Russian princess, had made homeopathy, which in other places might have been discriminated against or looked down upon, seem quite acceptable. Many members of the Württemberg aristocracy were adherents of its philosophy, and the rural classes were well disposed to it; only the provincial university had closed its doors to it despite various attempts to make inroads there. For the "revolution" in medicine that had been unleashed by Karl Reinhold Wunderlich and Greisinger had caused a backlash even after its ringleaders were no longer active in Tübingen or had died.

At the beginning, Bosch followed more closely in the footsteps of Gustav Jäger and his general tendency toward a "natural way of life." The conspicuous concern for lighting and ventilation that accompanied Bosch's construction of innumerable workshops, beginning with the first independent factory he built in 1900, can be seen as an outgrowth of impulses he first received from Jäger. When Bosch began to think more broadly about hygiene, he supported hiking and gymnastics clubs; he liked to recall his own youthful experience as a gymnast and remained quite fond of this activity in his philanthropy even after its popularity began to decline in favor of competitive sports. He regarded sports, or at least the value attached to them, with skepticism despite the fact that he was naturally aware of the objective, technical, and psychological stimulus that had been given to his particular field of endeavor by the various motor sports. The fact that Bosch declined the invitation to join the Society of Friends of German Sport in October 1931 was characteristic, "since one can no longer speak of an underestimation of sports, but rather, I should think, of an overestimation."

The large monetary contributions Bosch made during the war benefited health both directly and indirectly. The construction of a homeopathic hospital, which had been planned for some time, could not be carried out, but the contribution of 13 million marks for the Neckar Canal contained hygienic specifications; indeed, the final provision stated that if the contribution was rejected by the state or its goal was not reached, the entire amount was to be given to the Ministry of the Interior as a fund for the struggle against diseases affecting masses of people. In this he may have been thinking primarily about the struggle against tuberculosis. The city of Stuttgart, which received the unrestricted interest on the gift, was able to purchase and furnish several homes for mothers and children. The most important venture in this context was the purchase and renovation of the charming old saltwater spa Rappenau as a children's home; it became a lasting monument to Bosch's charity during the war years. Its achievements no longer occurred in Bosch's name, and they were removed from his immediate decision-making power, but they were founded on his supporting initiative.

In the fall of 1890, after Bosch had met him at the Gustav Jäger Club, Dr. Heinrich Göhrum had joined Bosch's circle as his family doctor and adviser in his medical ventures, finally becoming his close confidant. After nearly a half century of friendship, Bosch wrote to Göhrum, who was only a few months older, on June 9, 1936, sending him best wishes from the "old friend, whom you have always stood by in times of need, and who will be grateful to you until the end!" As a young doctor, Göhrum had also fallen under Jäger's spell and had participated in some of his projects. In Göhrum, Bosch had found a man whose ideas reached beyond homeopathic therapy to the will to reform life in the broadest sense—for example, through the improvement of residential hygiene and land reform. In these areas, Göhrum's disinterested advice and organizational enthusiasm assumed fundamental importance, particularly since they were in harmony with Bosch's own inclinations. This applied mainly to the support of homeopathy; however, Göhrum's involvement was not limited to this area. He was constantly on the lookout for new medical approaches and hypotheses, which he presented to Bosch; if other people approached Bosch with suggestions or offered opinions, Göhrum was willing to acquaint himself sufficiently with the opinions and procedures that were suggested to be able to make an independent determination about them. The two men's medical relationship expanded to become a trusteeship in medical science that played a significant role whenever it came to supporting research or determining the line that should be taken in the medical publishing firm that Bosch later founded. For cancer research, in particular, Bosch gave away hundreds of thousands of marks, irrespective of the direction the research took. The results, it is true, were not unambiguous. Sometimes Göhrum, who had a certain friendly inclination toward scientific outsiders, would allow himself to be more intrigued by the problems that were suggested than was justified by the management style of the venturesome individuals whom he had recommended for Bosch's support. As a result, Bosch more than once felt that he had been taken advantage of financially and withdrew his generosity. Naturally he had always given the contributions unconditionally, for he knew that scientific experiments, especially along new lines, were expensive, and he did not demand any accounting; however, if he had gone so far as to provide funding for clinical facilities so that the experiment's practical effectiveness could be tested, this was a different matter. In such cases, he expected that the funds would be spent in a clearly accountable fashion so that it would be possible to prove the effectiveness of the procedure in daily practice. But there were some people who had the impression that he did not care about the money! In fact, he was glad to contribute it, but he did care that it be used sensibly and that his "good-naturedness" did not become the object of myth or speculation. More than once there was conflict between Bosch and his grantees, and a door was slammed shut. It is difficult to measure the result of this voluntary medical philanthropy, whose beneficiaries were located on the Rhine and in Berlin, in terms of solid gains for medicine.

As a patient, Bosch had always had his own opinions about rules for living, diseases, and the requirements of the healing process, and he presented these opinions verbally or in writing to his doctors. However willful he may have been, however, he always submitted to their orders, even if he seemed to himself like the subject of an experiment that he regarded with rather pained curiosity. Ultimately, Bosch felt that he had gained from the experience during the years of his illness in 1937 and 1938, of knowing after every experiment "that was not the right thing for me." He had tried to rid himself of the embarrassing effects of aging through special diets, ozone treatments, massage, and other means; he gradually established a tolerable relationship with the symptoms.

This struggle to regain his health was no longer carried out within the framework of homeopathy. Göhrum himself had supported Bosch in consulting various specialists. This change was not tantamount to a rejection of the familiar methods of treatment, but it was a significant enlargement of his approach. In the fall of 1937, he wrote to a doctor who had temporarily treated him, "I am, however, almost what I would call happy that as a result of my serious illness I have had so many experiences, and that with respect to my illness I am of the opinion that in this hospital people should not only be healed according to the principles of homeopathy, but rather that all disciplines should be applied that have proven themselves. As for me personally, I am of the opinion that especially in acute cases one will occasionally have to resort to shots and even to surgery, at the same time as I prefer homeopathy for the treatment of chronic problems. This is the view of a layman, and indeed as such I cannot have any other."

When this letter was written, the skeleton of the mighty building that would represent the crowning achievement of Bosch's medical policy was already standing. The path to its completion would still have many pitfalls to avoid, but the fact that there had been obstacles ultimately served the venture well in terms of both its design and its mission. It is possible to speak of an almost forty-year path to achieving this goal. Bosch had come to homeopathy through family tradition, not as a result of any negative experience with "school medicine." In his younger years, he had probably not been especially interested in the competing claims of various medical theories or in the contradiction between "contraria contrariis curentur" and "similia similibus curentur," as Samuel Hahnemann had expressed it. If he had made a study of the history of homeopathic theory, he would doubtless have been deeply moved by the open-mindedness, independence, and instinctual correctness of the exact observations made by the young Hahnemann, as well as his willingness to take on recognized authorities and his search for natural laws. The ideological generalities of the older man might have contradicted Bosch's more realistic sense. Speaking for homeopathy were the personal experiences Bosch had had with homeopathic treatment; for a constitution as fine and sensitive as his, the minute dosages or "nothings" used in homeopathic medicine seemed to have been just the right thing to awaken and encourage the forces of healing by their slight sensations.

In 1901 he joined the homeopathic movement, if one can call it that, with an active commitment. Until 1900, one of the large hospitals in

Stuttgart, the Paulinen Hospital, had treated its patients homeopathically. The director died, his successor refused to use homeopathy, and the followers of this doctrine suddenly found themselves orphaned in their clinical practice. The Stuttgart Homeopathic Hospital Association was founded at that time, and Bosch immediately joined. His membership, which at first was only an expression of agreement, soon became the project's principal source of support. For here, with the growth of his financial means, his plan to help in a decisive way took form early. Bosch only restrained himself at first, in keeping with longtime experience, so that other people's enthusiasm and willingness to make sacrifices would not be paralyzed by his own generosity. He even made his support contingent on the fact that the organizers first secure a seed fund of 100,000 marks. The first plans were drawn up in 1914. In 1916, the year of his great philanthropic contributions, Bosch set aside 3 million marks for this project; part of the sum, 1.25 million, was used in such a way that Bosch, "based on his estimate of his own worth," became a life member of the two homeopathic associations that were legally responsible for the project. In the meantime, these associations, in expectation of Bosch's contribution, had purchased the property and begun construction on Trauberg Mountain in the hilly area south of the city.

The optimistic forecast that a stately hospital would soon rise on the spot was disappointed; they had not reckoned with the war and its needs for people and materials. The building's foundations had barely emerged from the ground when the sponsors were forbidden to continue. Could they hope that after the war they would be able to continue? That was what they thought at first, but the way this war ended completely overturned their plans. In December 1919, they decided to do without the new building for the time being, and instead to purchase and renovate a new housing complex in the inner city, in the Marienstrasse. In this way the idea of the homeopathic hospital had been saved for the moment, even if its realization, with sixty-six and later seventy-three beds, seemed to be only a stopgap measure. Dr. Alfons Stiegele was appointed as its director. Objections from the project's neighbors prevented them from accepting those patients with communicable diseases that were subject to reporting requirements; this seemed to them to restrict their research and clinical practice. Even before agreeing to this restriction, the foundation had created two small sanatoriums for lung diseases in the Allgäu, Riedackerhof and Riedhof.

In his letters Bosch repeatedly discussed his motives for founding a homeopathic hospital. As a boy, he had already heard that "traditional medicine put every conceivable difficulty in the way of homeopathy." Württemberg was in a special situation; there, open resistance to homeopathy did not seem advisable due to the position of the royal family. "To all intents and purposes, traditional medicine, which was completely materialistic in its orientation, had gradually become so accepted that no doctor could use means that had not been sanctified and thus rendered permissible by a priest of pure science . . . Homeopathy was superstition." This point of view made Bosch indignant; he was "irritated by the unjust way homeopathy was treated." This was the origin of his decision "to build a homeopathic hospital, together with others who share these convictions." As late as June 1941, he recalled his original motives in a letter that stated: "Originally the hospital was supposed to be an element in the struggle . . ." Bosch's intense involvement was essentially part of a moral tension, his need to come to the assistance of a group of people whom he sensed were being unfairly attacked, and to help them get over the "unjustified feelings of inferiority" among homeopaths that he remarked upon in a letter written in July 1938.

If Bosch's remarks became less heated in later years, this did not mean that he rejected the teachings he had followed ever since he had been a child. "Naturally, homeopathy is preferable for internal illnesses," he wrote in June 1941. Gradually, however, as a result of the experiences gained at the interim hospital as well as the general development of Bosch's medical and scientific attitudes, he allowed the borders between the two medical fronts to become blurred. The reform-oriented publications of Lieck and the expert opinion of the Berlin surgeon August Bier, which was issued in 1929 and was favorable to homeopathy, had their effect. In Stuttgart they flattered themselves that Bier's position was due in no small part to the experiences and successes that had resulted from their own systematic work. They had not been satisfied with merely caring for the patients seeking healing who came to the stopgap hospital in the Marienstrasse. At the suggestion of Dr. Heinrich Meng, the head physician, from 1925 to 1929, they had introduced regular courses on homeopathic treatments, with the aim of making it possible for doctors to familiarize themselves with homeopathy theoretically and practically, regardless of their scientific background or particular point of view. But this was not all. In 1925, Meng's flexible organizational will also led them to found a medical publishing business, Hippocrates Publishers. In 1928 they added the magazine *Hippocrates.* Bosch contributed the funds for this venture, which required substantial subsidies before it became relatively well established. The purpose of the publishing house was to produce both scientific and popular literature; it would publish inexpensive and easy to understand enlightenment for the average citizen, as well as works for medical experts. The most important undertaking was an anthology entitled *Book of Popular Medicine;* the publishing company had gotten into trouble with it because of a number of the authors involved. The company was able to dispose of it without a severe crisis thanks only to the fact that Bosch provided the financial backing. Objections were raised on this point by the suspicious National Medical Board, which thought it had identified "mercantile interests" behind the propaganda for popular medicine. The publisher was able to respond that "Bosch never asked us for any interest, but let us keep whatever profits there were." All in all, he had sacrificed 500,000 marks. It goes without saying that once a number of personnel crises had been surmounted and the management was working well together, Bosch ceased being concerned about the details of this publishing venture. The internal friction was removed by making Göhrum the sole scientific adviser in place of the previous advisory board. The general line for the magazine was set down in 1936 as follows: "*Hippocrates* is not meant to slip over the line into popular medicine, but should serve the unified efforts of medicine."

By naming themselves after the great Greek doctor who remained aloof from all contemporary factions, they gave this venture a certain historicizing accent; it was an attempt to search out a common tradition of healing. Bosch himself had now turned his thoughts more toward history, and was particularly interested in the development of knowledge about nature. He did not resist when it was suggested that he become involved with the collection and preservation of documents of medical history. Dr. Richard Hähl, a doctor from Stuttgart and the author of the great biography of Samuel Hahnemann, had labored tirelessly for many years to collect his master's memorabilia, particularly his manuscripts and letters, but also furniture, paintings, and the like. In order to prevent this collection from being broken up, Bosch purchased it in 1926 in exchange for a pension agreement; Hähl was also provided with the means to continue his collecting activity. Bosch's later willingness to participate in the historical investigation, scientific research, and description of a medical phenomenon like Paracelsus derived from a similar willingness to support research and preservation in the field of medicine. Bosch had read Erwing Kolbenheyer's novel about Paracelsus and found it gripping; he remarked in 1926 that the book was "very much worth reading," and he liked to give it as a gift. His local interest in this great man of Swabian lineage was an additional factor; Bosch eagerly seized upon the notion of founding a museum in Stuttgart that would bear Paracelsus's name and be dedicated to the history of medicine. He was grateful that the city supported his plan by providing a building in which to house it. Bosch's contribution was sufficient to ensure that its future development would be significant.

All these undertakings were only precursors, accompaniments, or successors of the big plan that remained at the center—the founding of a great hospital. In keeping with the evolution of Bosch's personal opinion, it was now "converted to biological medicine." Homeopathy had become so widely accepted following the First World War that a separate and exclusive effort was no longer called for. Nonetheless, homeopathy would remain central, particularly for research, and it would have the opportunity to prove its equality by comparison with allopathy. The fifty-year anniversary of the Robert Bosch firm provided the stimulus for realizing this plan, which had been discussed and postponed for such a long time. Shortly before this, the project's organizers had decided to give up the old Trauberg construction site and purchased a wonderful location on the southern slope of Cold Mountain, near Cannstadt, in a location easily accessible for traffic. Here in the old vineyards there were no neighbors with objections or claims, and a large building could be built with terraces that offered a beautiful view of the hills and valley surrounding Stuttgart. The gift amounted to 5.5 million marks; it was doubled when the original mission of medical treatment was expanded to include research. Bosch's generosity continued to increase during the development of the project, not just because problems arose as a result of the generally difficult economic and political situation, but also because their ambition grew as they attempted to provide the most diverse and up-to-date examples of hospital technology. This was true of the bathing facilities in particular. The process of construction, which began in May 1937, ran into unexpected difficulties when the geological structure of the land forced the organizers to build a much more extensive foundation than they had planned. The political situation, with its dark threats, was even worse. The construction market in western and southwestern Germany was affected by the construction of the Siegfried Line and the resultant shortages of raw materials and workers, as well as restrictions on the use of iron. It almost seemed as if the same fate that had earlier prevented the construction of the building in Trauberg was now threatening to engulf the second attempt as well. It proved necessary to abandon the plan to have the hospital ready to open by July 1, 1939. But the danger of approaching war also had the effect of spurring them on to complete the building. To manage the construction process, Bosch hired former police chief Paul Hahn, whose acquaintance he had made during the troubled years of 1919 and 1920, and whom he knew to be a man of action who was not easily fazed and was a skillful manager of men to boot. Hahn's skill and persistence carried the day, and the Robert Bosch Hospital opened in April 1940. The completion of this project brought pride and joy to the founder, who had set his heart on it after so many of the other efforts in which he had been involved had been removed from the private sphere.

Naturally, Bosch followed the development of the hospital with lively interest; he had proposed some guidelines for its management in a brief speech at its dedication. In a letter to Dr. Eugen Bircher, the doctor in Zurich on whose help he had relied a few years earlier, he reported in a characteristically sober and objective tone: "Patients come from the Rhineland and from central Germany, as well, and outpatients alone sometimes total fifty people a day seeking help. The upper floors could be completely filled with people who would stay on permanently, as a kind of sanatorium. Sometimes I thought to myself that I should never have gotten involved in this, but now it gives me pleasure after all, and indeed a certain satisfaction. I also hear good things about the food, which is something I had not expected, frankly, in such a short time. The business side is also better than I had dared to hope. Perhaps it will be possible to reach the point some day where necessary new investments will be able to be borne by the hospital itself. Naturally I do not charge interest or depreciation."

The Robert Bosch Hospital, along with the Bosch Aid Foundation, is the most visible monument to Robert Bosch's many efforts and successes in the city of Stuttgart. Beyond the care it provided to patients, the hospital developed into a scientific research center; indeed, it may have achieved more useful results in this area than other institutions whose programmatic intentions were explicit in this regard.

The medical faculty of the University of Tübingen gave an honorary doctorate of medicine to Bosch on the occasion of his eightieth birthday. When the plan became known, Bosch waited with some curiosity to see whether it would become reality. This time, there were no arguments of the sort he had had three decades earlier with the Technical University in Stuttgart. The honor was awarded, and it pleased him; he interpreted it as a gesture of reconciliation among the various medical theorists.

37

———•———

SUPPORT OF
CULTURAL POLICY

In donating 1 million marks to the Technical University of Stuttgart in 1910, Robert Bosch had made his first, widely heralded foray into the realm of scientific research and education. His interest in various specialized questions had played a role, and he had also been influenced by the advice of Carl Bach. Bosch's attachment to the Stuttgart institute, which he himself had attended and which had produced a number of his most outstanding colleagues, lasted until the end of his life. It was not always free of irritation; from time to time he was annoyed by one decision or another, and then the old friends of his youth, Paul Reusch or Richard Stribeck, had to calm him down. There was never any doubt, however, that he would participate in the Carl Bach Foundation or that he would be a substantial contributor to the Friends of the University. The university owed him a particular debt of gratitude when it came to the expansion of the curriculum. Bosch did not think much of guest professors giving lectures in general education courses, and when the university representatives asked him for his vote, his response was dismissive: "nostrums like this" were no way to get anything done. Instead, they should "bring in men of action and character" who would raise the level of the institute.

Bosch's personal interest remained essentially focused on technical and scientific education. Naturally, once his willingness to give had been established, he was approached for innumerable ventures and by individuals of various kinds. Bosch never gave indiscriminately, and seldom because he was good natured. He saw purely charitable gifts in emergency situations as being fundamentally different from operating grants for particular projects. His refusals were also characteristic; certainly the study of history might be good and necessary, but the establishment of a national war museum, or the collection of nineteenth-century documents—something for which the historian and Bismarck admirer Erich Marcks tried to enlist his support—could be left to others. Prehistory evoked a similar response. Was there still that much left to study about the "prehistory of our homeland, our Germanic culture?" First the universities should popularize what they already knew! Bosch's position on prehistory was not inflexible; in fact, he always had a certain weakness for paleontology. On occasion, he also supported geographic expeditions, almost by accident, as it were—for example, a 1927 expedition to Abyssinia whose results he regarded with skepticism.

Among Bosch's contributions in support of technical education, a large amount was set aside for the Ministry of Culture in 1917. Teacher seminars and public schools should be provided with better tools for the teaching of science. Gottlob Honold, through his own philanthropy, had introduced a similar measure for the middle and high schools. Naturally, Bosch participated in the creation of the Deutsches Museum and its collections in Munich, although not to the extent that Oskar von Miller had imagined. One of the anecdotes Bosch liked to tell concerned the way in which this genius among fund-raisers thought he could put one over on Bosch when he was in his cups and get him to commit to the construction of the museum library. Von Miller got caught in his own trap. Bosch respected the man's achievements, but von Miller was making a mistake if he thought he could dispose of Bosch's wealth lightly.

In 1917, the year of his great philanthropic contributions, Bosch also turned his attention to the German Association of Craftsmen. Bosch's agreement with its guiding principles was underscored by a series of personal connections. Hugo Borst's association with the Stuttgart study group had been the source of his interest in the young artists' movement;

his consciousness had had an impact on the firm's advertising, which was in its beginning phase. Gottlob Honold, with his innate sense of form, gave his inventions sleek and compelling outlines. Among the most active leaders of the association were the Heilbronn industrialist Peter Bruckmann, who had just revived the issue of the Neckar Canal, and Borst's brother-in-law Ernst Jäckh, who kept Bosch informed about many public and nonpublic political events and positions and had helped win Bosch's support for his various efforts and undertakings. The fundamental goals of the German Association of Craftsmen, to educate both producers and consumers in keeping with the very best quality, good work, and clean form, corresponded to Bosch's basic human instincts as well as to his practical experience. Friedrich Naumann had pointed out how significant this goal was in terms of the international economy, and ultimately Bosch, too, recognized it as necessary, based on the insight that after the war it would be necessary to cut back on workers and production models in order to maintain and expand Germany's position in the world. Bosch pledged to make a very substantial annual contribution designed to enable the association to intensify its work, as indeed it did at first.

Bosch's relationship to the organization, as a patron, quickly turned into an angry love. Supporters of the nice-sounding theses about the formal law of function and of the call for "genuine" materials that carried their own unalloyed expressive values were in a crisis that was not entirely novel. The tension among various opinions had persisted for some time; it was exacerbated when individual creativity, rightly or wrongly, felt itself threatened intellectually by collective organizations and the kind of calculation that is inherent in all technology. Was it not confusing and misleading to speak of machines or technological phenomena as if they were expressions of creative artistic ability, of a new—even *the* new—"style"? Wasn't this a kind of phony Romanticism that no longer fled into the past to borrow its signs and symbols in rather indiscriminate historicism, but instead paraded its young contemporary consciousness while confidently trumpeting its prophecy about the future? These questions and their consequences for the establishment of aesthetic values were undoubtedly of only marginal significance for Bosch in his involvement with the organization; but when Bosch reacted with sensitivity to Hans Pölzig's lecture at

the association in 1919, in which Pölzig pointed to the automobile industry to illustrate his theses that art and rational industrial technology had
nothing to do with each other, the incident was of more than passing anecdotal interest. Pölzig explained that art, in its genuine creations, was the
work of great personalities or skilled craftsmen and had eternal validity,
while technology was subject to the law of the continuous devaluation of
forms by new inventions, new materials, and improvements and savings
based on pragmatic considerations. After a few years, Pölzig claimed, the
novelties we now admire will have become historical curiosities or will
have been tossed on the scrap heap for lack of anything better to do with
them. At the time, Bosch responded to these comments as if they were an
attack on his achievements. He could be pacified only with difficulty, and
years later he often mentioned the incident with aggravation. This was
where his rational good sense reached its limit—when it came to
empathizing with the elemental nature of artistic creativity; but he did not
draw any immediate conclusions from his aggravation. He may have
grumbled from time to time about the "playground of the immature" when
he came across tentative experiments or noisy self-promotion, and his
response to many attempts was an "inner head-shaking," as he wrote in a
letter in June 1930. Overall, it is possible to say that the organizational
power of the German Association of Craftsmen, through which it remained
faithful after 1918 to the notion of beautifully formed and skillfully made
work—despite all the confusion and all the self-indulgent discussion of
abstract problems—would not really have been conceivable without the
background of Bosch's financial support.

Bosch turned his attention to the support of popular general education
after he came across a man whose knowledge and character he trusted.
This had been true in other cases, as well. Bosch had supported the
Teaching Workshop because he had a high opinion of August Utzinger's
pedagogical abilities; he postponed the founding of the factory newspaper,
which had been discussed on several occasions, until the appearance of
someone to whom he could confidently entrust the task, namely Otto
Debatin. As a forerunner of his interest in public education, one might
cite the fact that in 1912 Bosch was already supporting the very down-to-

earth attempt of Theodor Etzel and Georg Muschner to make the weekly publication *The Selection,* which had been founded in 1910 and was struggling to survive, into a popularly conceived but essentially high-level publication for the educationally inclined masses. In the beginning, Bosch had taken a lively interest in the paper, writing to industrialist friends to ask them to help him with the launching of *The Selection.* He found it disappointing when he did not find the echo he had anticipated, and he was not very happy to be made a partisan in literary disagreements. As far as Bosch was concerned, this undertaking was only partially successful, however remarkable its individual achievements may have been. At least it should reach the point where it could sustain itself, if not necessarily make a profit, and thus show whether it was possible for an organ of this kind that was not linked to any party or religious group to create an audience for its collection of old gems and good new pieces. Six years later, Bosch finally abandoned the attempt; it was evident that a publication of this kind either needed greater personal and literary charm or would have to be more modest in its expectations. The stratum of potential readers in Germany was already too thin for an undertaking of this thoughtful quality; the territory was occupied by newspapers belonging to political groups, and soon the burgeoning growth of illustrated magazines would begin to choke off less hardy shoots.

Bosch's participation in the founding of the Universum Film AG was also a passing phenomenon. This was a product of the war, created out of the awareness of the propagandistic possibilities inherent in the new technology and the insight that in this field Germany lagged behind the allied powers. The goal was to establish an effective business. The German government encouraged it with friendly pressure, and the authority of Erich Ludendorff, which at that time was required for almost everything, was called in to speed up its founding. Bosch himself felt little need to become a participant in the new film industry, but it was considered a patriotic duty not to refuse. The capitalist possibilities that might be concealed here (and that were naturally painted in bright colors at first, although they would have disastrous consequences later) did not interest Bosch at all. The profit, if there was one, was to be diverted entirely to efforts in public education, as Hans Walz wrote to his contact person in Berlin on August 2, 1918. Did not film, in addition to its effectiveness as propaganda and its entertainment value, have an intrinsic usefulness for popular education? To encourage the latter was the objective, although at the time rather ineffective concern that was repeatedly voiced by the people in Stuttgart. Bosch, in his initial optimism, believed that "soon it would be possible to begin with the real work of popular reform and education." As the film industry evolved in the direction of large-scale capitalist deals and individual moguls, and struggles broke out over its leadership among people whom he regarded with mistrust and alienation, Bosch withdrew from this stage after a brief and not very satisfying guest performance.

The man who, after 1916, gave rich and varied shape to Bosch's latent popular pedagogical will was Theodor Bäuerle. Before the war, Bäuerle had been a seminary teacher in Backnang. He had begun to concern himself rather early on with questions of continuing popular education, and his experiences in the field had deepened his appreciation of the urgency of finding answers to them, particularly in light of recent events. The war proved to be a selection process of the least desirable kind, removing the most capable, energetic, and determined men from both the officer corps and the troops. At the same time, the army at war also provided the most vivid proof of the essence and necessity of hierarchical leadership.

At this moment in time, Bosch was particularly open to questions like this. He had gathered enough experiences in his own business to know that ability is not demonstrated by examination and that the capacity to fill responsible positions is not the monopoly of any particular class; Bosch, after all, took particular pleasure in those colleagues who grew into their responsibilities from a grade-school or middle-school background and discharged them capably.

The nonprofit association Support for the Gifted, which was created in 1916 with a starting capital of 2 million marks, was the fruit of these considerations. Earlier in his life, Bosch had already supported or made possible the training of talented individuals; his files are filled with reports and evaluations demonstrating the progress of this or that artist. Personal philanthropy of this sort obviously had a rather accidental character; it was a friendly gesture related more to the person who recommended the artist than to the latter's vocal or literary talent. Now this task became systematized and focused on the main task of identifying outstanding talents for business, although not in a narrow or exclusive sense. The process involved studying human nature, advising, providing guidance for educational progress, giving support to deserving individuals. At first the new venture depended entirely on Bäuerle's dedication; only gradually did Bosch and Bäuerle develop a certain methodology. They were armed against disappointments, for human nature, even with all the refinements of psychological evaluation, is not predictable. The ability to learn is not the same as the ability to succeed in life, and there is no "psychometer" capable of predicting character! The most fundamental thing was that they were aware from the very beginning of the danger that hangs over projects of this kind (and that would be quite evident in later, broader undertakings of a similar nature, including those sponsored by the government): Does support of the gifted necessarily lead to a change in their social position? As self-evident as it is (this is something that the postwar years showed quite clearly) that the upper classes, especially given their relatively low birth rate, need new blood to expand their numbers and to acquire more younger members, at the same time it would necessarily be quite disastrous to rob the crafts, the peasantry, and the middle classes in business of their most talented members. Nothing could have been farther from Bosch's mind than that his endeavors should merely serve to identify government functionaries or academic officials! Naturally, individual talent did not preclude a career as a bureaucrat—the state needs outstanding talents, too—but this must not be the norm. The support of the gifted was fundamentally intended to make them more capable in their professions, not to tempt them to leave them. This philanthropic initiative was eaten up by inflation. As a way of continuing to support the idea, Bosch decided to give regular support to the Markel Foundation, which had been founded in 1920 along the same lines by an Anglo-German gentleman named Dr. Markel. Its management was also controlled by Theodor Bäuerle.

On May 1, 1918, after extensive preparations and with the active support of the Ministry of Culture, notably the assistant secretary Dr. V. Marquard, the Association for the Support of Popular Education was founded. Here, again, one may want to compare Bosch with Ernst Abbe, who diverted statutory sums from the Carl Zeiss Foundation for purposes related to voluntary public education. Abbe, who occasionally appeared as a speaker at events sponsored by independent educational organizations, was interested in all kind of projects like this; he also understood their financial limitations.

Abbe was open to the possibility of an organizational link, but in Stuttgart they created their own venture, limiting its scope to their home region of Württemberg. Bosch himself, in a departure from his usual custom, took over the chairmanship, not out of any particular need for pedagogical or organizational activity, but in order to publicly support the new venture from the outset with the authority of his name; it would be especially useful in their dealings with government offices. Marquard, an unconstrained, far-sighted man with strong creative will, became his deputy.

Through Bäuerle, Bosch had been made aware of the work of Nikolai Grundtvig, whose expansion of the rural popular universities had been so effective in Denmark after 1864. At first Bosch found it difficult to accept the term, but eventually he took it as a given. Grundtvig's objective success, which Bosch saw as reflected in the high level of Danish agriculture, had direct appeal for him. A memorandum from the year 1923 on this whole complex of questions expressed Bosch's conviction that the extension of efforts that had previously been primarily urban to the countryside, and the improvement of the general and specialized training of the peasants, was the only way to achieve independence in the area of food production. But this argument, based primarily on pragmatic considerations, was not the decisive one. In the heartland of German industry, it was easy to pay more attention to the masses of workers, among whom one could also sense a stronger and more pressing desire for education. Bosch probably sensed that the many popular universities being founded following the change in government policy were the result of a boom that would be temporary. But where sufficient substance existed, the new creation outlasted any fashion.

In Stuttgart, they sometimes emphasized the fact that their plans for the project they launched in May 1918 went back to 1916, to a time when such thoughts were not yet in the air. It is noteworthy that for Bosch the essential achievement of education was not factual knowledge, but rather the insight of an honest man into his *lack of knowledge*. This, at least in Bosch's imagination, would strengthen the individual's own character, giving him respect for the greater achievements of others. The aim was not enforced intellectualization, but rather voluntary engagement with realities and with the traditional cultural values of one's native land, free of class prejudice or arrogance.

The key sentences in Bosch's essay were: "The goal of the popular university must be to give every human being the awareness that as a human being he possesses certain inalienable rights, which he has an immediate right and duty to acquire and struggle for. The education that he possesses must create the awareness for him, as well, that it is not permissible to demand things that are not achievable, and it is a particular necessity and the most desirable goal of education that human beings should acquire a cultivation of the heart, an acknowledgment of the rights and the value of other human beings. In order not to be misunderstood, I will say that I would regard the cultivation of the heart, in this sense, as a particularly desirable goal for the universities, as well. The goal of the popular university should not be to fill people full of all kinds of things that are learned mechanically in order to pass an examination. The person who has passed such an examination has a tendency to look down on the person who has not done so. But when a mature human being, led by a proper teacher, attends a course on some subject, he gradually becomes clear about the connections between historical, economic, and purely human issues. He will develop his own standpoint and firm views about events of all kinds. Such people also know the extent of what is possible. They acquire the capacity to see reality and to act appropriately." Bosch's conclusion reflects his characteristic optimism. "Education liberates." It "raises the level" of the populace and gives it the power "to stand up for itself economically . . . to act in the right way politically," and "to recognize false theories for what they are."

The association had only a few members, but little value was attached to this. They put together a board consisting of a few men who were interested in education and were experts in various subject areas. After the project was in place and had generated various initiatives and achievements, the government expressed its appreciation by providing an annual subvention that matched Bosch's contribution of 40,000 marks, and the Ministry of Culture named a representative to the management. Bäuerle was and remained the moving force behind the association. No one emphasized this more strongly than Bosch, who refused to accept any recognition for the project's achievements, passing this on to his representative instead.

A rich program of educational offerings was developed, at first at the popular university in Stuttgart and then in the towns of Denkendorf and

Comburg, which also had popular universities. There were courses of various lengths and concentrations. Comburg, a splendid site near Schwäbisch-Hall, soon became a popular inn and focal point for leisure-time activities, choral weeks, club seminars, and conferences for educators. It was natural to develop a program to promote libraries and to influence the press by means of special inserts. They founded their own publishing house, and directly and indirectly encouraged amateur theater. There was a flourishing "local culture" division led by the poet and teacher Hans Reyling, a native of Ulm. A calendar with pictures of their Swabian homeland helped create an emotional bond; it was imitated all over the country. A number of the association's initiatives, such as the music conservatory, the popular theater, and the art gallery, later developed into independent institutions.

Beyond the "support of education and culture," which was never narrowly interpreted but extended to all questions of general human interest, Bäuerle's own lively involvement prompted the association to lend its intellectual and then organizational support to the founding of the Volunteer Labor Service. The idea of the labor service had evolved immediately following the military and political collapse in 1918, and had been conceived at the time, among other things, as a replacement for military service, except that from its inception it was also meant to include women. A proposal by the democratic representative Walter Schücking in 1920 failed to elicit any response in parliament, although it was eloquently reasoned; the unions feared it might pose a threat to their collective bargaining. It is well known that it took a very long time before a positive assessment of this idea and its ramifications could be heard from the ranks of the unions. In its early phases, out of very realistic considerations, Bosch had rejected the idea himself. Nothing useful would be achieved in the sense of an increase in knowledge or skills, and unpaid, conscripted labor would usually prove to be more expensive, in the end, than voluntary, paid labor. The economic crisis and its result, unemployment, made it necessary to set aside considerations of this kind; the psychological fate of a generation of young people without the pedagogical discipline of orderly work was something that could no longer be judged according to economic profitability or the level of technical training that would be involved. Bosch's sense of social and pedagogical duty was for him a burning matter of conscience. The government, given its financial troubles, seemed ill-suited and unprepared to take on such a task; it would therefore have to be undertaken by people who had both a pioneering spirit and a sense of responsibility. It was a question of providing models for a possibility that would gain its powers of ethical conviction from the voluntary nature of the commitment and collaboration involved. In various locations throughout Germany, people were attempting to realize this idea, and in the voluntary encounters of students and workers, and of urban and peasant youth, they were creating living examples of popular community working rationally and objectively for the public good. As early as May 1921, Bäuerle had demanded in a speech before the Provincial Committee for the Support of Youth that national service should be promoted as a way of strengthening the popular will. Economic, not pedagogical, considerations must predominate. At the time, this had been music of the future. But now, in the recession, Bäuerle, with Bosch's enthusiastic support, created the organizational framework, the Heimatwerk, a regional organization whose excellent achievements gained it recognition as an exemplary program.

This venture was replaced by the legislative creation of a national labor service. The Association for the Support of Popular Education, in the form in which it had been operating, had become problematic as a result of Germany's domestic changes. Certain personnel changes made among the members of the board after 1933 did not alter anything. When Bäuerle became seriously ill in 1936 and was forced to ask to be relieved of his responsibilities, Bosch decided to give up the association. It was a step that did not come easily to Bosch, for under Bäuerle's guidance he had felt personal joy and professional satisfaction as he watched its various undertakings develop over the years. But Bosch did not want to see his tie to the organization, which had been based on trust, replaced by some external official relationship that was alien to him. There was no successor in sight of the type he would have wished to have, and he did not want a manager of the kind the National Socialists urgently wanted to present him with; hence he had the association disbanded in June 1936 in order to avoid a psychological break in its history. This conscious destruction of a creation that he had undertaken with so much hope almost two decades earlier, and which had borne such splendid fruit, was not without tragedy for Bosch.

PART VI

THE THIRD REICH

38

———◆———

THE POLITICAL CHANGE OF 1933

At the beginning of 1932, Chancellor Heinrich Brüning made the statement that Germany would not be in a position to continue to make its reparations payments. The road, full of tribulations, had led from the outlandish stipulations of the Treaty of Versailles to the Dawes Plan and then to the Young Plan, which was intended to assign definite amounts to the victorious allies' claims and to organize the payments around firm deadlines, and which in fact did this in a formal sense. The setting of limits could be regarded as progress in the direction of an objective standard, however terrifyingly high the numbers remained and however far into the future the payment deadlines stretched. As far as Germany's expectations were concerned, this transitional phase also conjured up bitter memories, particularly in the matter of the credits that were awarded for German property that had been confiscated abroad. Within Germany, the struggle over the petition for a referendum against the Young Plan was an emotional test of strength that created deep divisions and sharp confrontations among its people. Every argument that drew a line distinguishing the new situation from the old was met with unthinking accusations of treason.

The fact that the transitional character of the Young Plan was quite clear, and that the president of the Reich, Paul von Hindenburg, stood behind it, did not stop its opponents. The consequences of privatizing part of the political obligations could be viewed in different ways. While the commercialization of Germany's obligations did create a nonpolitical, purely business interest, it could also be interpreted as a form of bondage for Germany that would continue independent of possible shifts in international alliances and their subsequent consequences. It was impossible to anticipate the effects of linking the German annuities to the debts that had been incurred during the war by Britain, France, and other countries to the United States, particularly since Germany was not to be a participant in their final settlement.

The Young Plan, which formally set Germany's financial and economic sovereignty free from the control of the reparations agents, only remained in effect, practically speaking, for two years. However cleverly the mechanism was constructed, however self-sacrificing the efforts of the German central government were to secure the public treasury by a policy of ruthless savings and deflation to the degree that this was possible within the existing framework—the world economic disorder that had been created as a result of the reparations policy of previous years had grown too large. America's own economic crisis, with its broad impact, was an additional factor; in the summer of 1931, the acute money shortage in Vienna set off the great German banking crisis. President Herbert Hoover's suggestion, in June 1931, that a year of general debt forgiveness be agreed upon among all the nations concerned did not receive an immediate response, but it was followed by a standstill agreement with a renewed consideration of the possibility of financial rehabilitation. The withdrawal of capital was accompanied by a reduction of tax revenues, declining exports, and growing unemployment. The threat to the very foundations of the lives of masses of people became an international problem; it was felt most severely in Germany, where inflation had eaten up people's savings, and least severely in France, with its economic structure based on small peasants and midsized businesses. The world economic crisis, as a cruel teacher of economic rationality, found its least eager student in Germany, the very country whose psychological stance had always been, and continued to be, the most crucial.

Brüning opened the year 1932, which would decide his political fate, with the announcement that it would soon be necessary to put an end to the payments of tribute if the world economy were to be halfway normalized in keeping with the stabilization about which the statesmen had been making such discerning observations at their innumerable meetings. His political plans were constructed along these lines, and it was for this reason that he supported Hindenburg's candidacy for re-election as president of the Reich. He had completely deceived himself about the degree of Hindenburg's loyalty to him and his policy, in which until now he had always been supported by the president. Hindenburg's opposition to Wilhelm Gröner, the minister of the army and interior, along with his cold refusal to go along with the chancellor in his plans concerning the indebtedness of east German landowners, forced the resignation of the Brüning-Dietrich cabinet. Foreign affairs played no role in the new turn of events. In this area, the newly appointed Papen Cabinet inherited a legacy that was generally well tended. At the Lausanne Conference, the nonprivatized German tribute payments were nullified after France received assurances of a special payment.

These developments, during the first half of 1932, had been profoundly disturbing to Bosch. On the question of the presidency, he had even abandoned his customary reticence. What he had valued in Brüning was his courage in initiating utterly unpopular measures. Even if these measures might be debatable individually, Bosch considered the general direction—particularly in the area of social insurance—necessary, and thought that even the use of emergency decrees was appropriate since the parliament, which basically had no majority, lacked the strength to generate rapid response and express a decisive will. Whether Brüning's actions might result in severe psychological stress was something the party leaders could decide. Bosch's main concern was with the leadership of foreign policy. He was somewhat relieved when Baron Constantin von Neurath, the former ambassador in London, who was at least known to be a serious-minded fellow, now moved into the Foreign Office in the Wilhelmstrasse, and that the intelligent Secretary Bernhard von Bülow continued to serve as an influential adviser. For Bosch regarded the new chancellor with uncertainty and discomfort. Brüning's clumsiness in America during the First World War did not exactly recommend him.

The Lausanne Agreement of July 9, 1932, did not bring a turnaround in the world economic crisis. The crisis had torn the fabric of the international trade and credit network too deeply. The question of the Allied debts to the United States was still unresolved, and it remained to be seen whether and when the disarmament negotiations taking place at the League of Nations in Geneva would sow new confusion in the desired process of equalization among the nations. Brüning had stated Germany's claim to equal rights. This much was certain, at any rate: The cancellation of the reparation debts would have done away with the most dangerous threat to a possible economic recovery. When would such a recovery make itself felt? Careful statistical observations of the labor market, the orders for durable goods, and the movement of prices showed signs of stabilization and recovery in the second half of the year, particularly its last months. "The decline in business that had begun in the year 1930 continued until the end of July 1932," is how Bosch's business report of March 9, 1933, assessed the situation. "In the following three months, the downward trend came to a halt, and in the two final months of the fiscal year it was possible to observe a slight improvement over the previous year."

This was written with a caution born of the limited experiences of the Bosch firm's own ventures. But these ventures stretched throughout the world and now also extended into the most varied branches of industry. One could view their boundaries as the lines on a sensitive political-economic seismograph. The firm's management had responded to the economic crisis with the greatest flexibility and adaptability, and had brought its people through it. These were the fruits of a considered financial policy and of the forward-looking way in which they had operated during the various intermittent booms of the previous decade and a half. Naturally, the psychological atmosphere of the region in which they were located had not failed to have a certain impact, for Württemberg, although it was certainly not spared all suffering, had proven that it had a stubborn ability to hold out. The varied mixture of industries, their geographical dispersion throughout almost the entire province, the small peasant economy that supported a large part of the workforce residing in the villages, all proved to be fortuitous, both socially and politically. The despairing mood, which swung left or right in rebellious radicalism, could not establish itself there to the same extent as in other parts of the Reich that were fully industrial-ized or burdened with agricultural debt. Through all the bad years, unem-ployment remained well below the national average. It was during this time that the saying became current that Württemberg was "crisis proof," and the legend arose that it represented the model of an economic struc-ture that had only to be adopted elsewhere in order to achieve appropriate goals in population and economic policy. The result was National Social-ism's attempt to remake East Prussia à la Württemberg, which was pro-moted by years of propaganda and was as illusory as it was economically and psychologically foolish.

In the spring of 1932, Robert Bosch had put down on paper his memo-randum on solving economic crises. He waited in vain for a response. Domestic political passions and the uncertainty of foreign relations had cast a pall on all rational arguments. Bosch's belief that Hindenburg's re-election would have a politically soothing effect gave way to disappoint-ment. But it appeared, however annoying the actions of the Papen Cabinet might be to him in their motives and style, and however distant he found the half-Romantic notions that the new chancellor was being served up by young conservative literati, that the line in foreign policy was not being abandoned. This encouraged Bosch to become active him-self. Evidently, the government was not making good enough progress through diplomatic contacts alone, either in the almost ghostly behind-the-scenes maneuvering in Geneva, or in the complicated and noisy meetings arranged by Coudenhove-Kalergi. Bosch, with the encourage-ment of some younger friends from among his Rotary Club associates, decided to take a personal step. In December 1932, he traveled to Paris for a confidential exchange of views with industrialists who were friendly to Germany, and with members of the so-called Mayrisch Committee, which had been formed to smooth the path of economic cooperation between France and Germany. The plan and the task had moved him pro-foundly. It is true that among his French conversation partners there was no one of comparable industrial stature, but the overall impression of the exchanges, which were carried on without any official fuss and bother and which reached the circles of *anciens combattants* whose participation had been arranged by Bosch's earlier collaborator Paul Distelbarth, was satisfying. Bosch promised himself good results from the continuation and cultivation of this kind of loosely knit experiment. "I have become convinced, in France," he wrote on January 3, 1933, to Georg Escherich, "that there exists in that country an extraordinarily strong trend that is in favor of rapprochement with Germany." A corresponding movement was to be organized in Germany as well; all the more since the French, thanks to the position of their veterans' organization, were "way ahead of us . . . At the meeting I had in Paris, there was a representative of the *Information,* and Count d'Ormesson, who writes in the *Temps,* also wants to support our movement. The movement, in other words, runs smack through the people and even through the large industrialists. In the last six to eight weeks, the latter, in fact, have not only been inclined to be in favor of a rapprochement of this kind; they want to participate . . . This issue is a matter of great concern to me right now, and I hope that we will be able to prevail."

As a result of the hoped-for "true confederation" of the two nations, Bosch saw the possibility "of making Europe into one big economic block." In his optimistic willingness to serve this goal, he published a somewhat lengthy essay in late 1931 in the *Stuttgart New Daily Paper,* which, to his joy, was also reprinted elsewhere, for example in the *Cologne Newspaper.* This essay pleads for mutual understanding. "In France there are haters, but the people as a whole do not hate Germany." The number of those individuals "who promote hatred, for political or material reasons, is declining." The fact that the French, after they had succeeded in forcing the Treaty of Versailles on Germany, had turned themselves into a gigantic fortress and were arming their allies, as well, was understandable; they "had no other choice . . . But it has become clear in the course of a decade: it is impossible to dishonor sixty-five million members of a people and forever burden them with the stigma of shame. A people like the Germans, which during the winter of revolution built bridges, not for strategic, but for peaceful purposes; a people that following its defeat drained fields, built waterlines and long-distance gas lines and hospitals; a people that can count one half of the Nobel Prize winners among its members; such a people is unconquerable." The French, too, sensed that "this people will rise again—and then what? No one wants more war." This was the way to interpret the declarations of the veterans' organizations, the belated insights of the business representatives, the various statements by French politicians during the previous year. "If we draw up a balance sheet for the year that has just come to a close, we see three great assets: the disappearance of reparations, which are gone forever . . . ; the willingness of France to concede to us the right to a new defense organization, in the form of a militia; and the recognition of our equal status." Bosch saw, in all of this, not merely a "silver lining on the horizon," but "a new dawn." The overall situation for rapprochement was more favorable than it had almost ever been. "For months, we have unmistakably had a gradually rising improvement of our economic situation. If Germany and France unite, it will increase trust, in general, and the whole world can and will breathe easier." A few days later, he wrote to Friedrich Mück in Heilbronn that he was "somewhat surprised" that so far no "chauvinist attacks" had been leveled at him.

The optimistic tenor of Bosch's mood was in for a rude shock when only a few weeks later Adolf Hitler was named chancellor of the Reich. "What is going on in domestic politics here interests me less," he had written in a New Year's letter to Escherich on January 3, 1933. "Perhaps the reason is that I see I cannot do anything to help." The behind-the-scenes maneuvering in Berlin during these weeks was pregnant with weighty decisions that saw the tactical union of the new chancellor, Kurt von Schleicher, with the National Socialist leader Gregor Strasser, the new alliance between Papen and Hitler, and the services of Hindenburg's adaptable secretary Otto Meissner as the go-between; these were concealed from the angle of view in Stuttgart, or were, at any rate, veiled by a cloud of unverifiable rumors. Now this cloud dispersed. The reality was not one that Bosch had anticipated.

Bosch's previous relations with the National Socialist German Workers' Party (NSDAP) had been very one-sided. Once, several years earlier, he had received a letter from the Stuttgart headquarters in which he was informed that "we must be prepared, sooner or later, for violence from the left," that "the outbreak of riots is not far off." The NSDAP had "adopted as part of its program, among other things, the protection of legally

acquired property." It alone, "thanks to the enthusiasm of its supporters," et cetera, was in a position to respond to the terror. "Unfortunately,
this cannot be accomplished without significant sums of money." There
was, therefore, no alternative, especially since "rich Jewish circles are
closed to us . . . but to turn to the German and *volkisch*-German circles in
industry and commerce with the request for support," and so on. "We
hope that you will not be unmoved by our urgent plea." With the title "A
Letter That Went Unanswered," the letter was published in *The Bosch
Spark Plug* of March 31, 1927. Earlier, Bosch's silence had already
aroused displeasure; a few sentences of commentary added to the com-
munication mentioned that the party newspaper had been upset about
Herr Bosch's "stone-cold heart among his moneybags." Bosch and his
colleagues laughed about it, as they did about the internal fight that the
solicitation letter caused in the party—its members were accusing each
other of being responsible. A few years later, in 1930, when a Berlin
monthly named Robert Bosch as one of the financial supporters of the
National Socialists, he considered whether to send in a correction. But,
as he remarked in his letter to his nephew Carl (September 26, 1930),
"ultimately, one can take the position: Let them talk—it must be sufficiently well-known that I am not a National Socialist."

Naturally, he had an interest in the task of combining the power of
nationalist and socialist feelings, but the forms in which this was being
undertaken frightened him. When Walter Rathenau was murdered,
Bosch had passionately refused all attempts to gloss it over or explain it
away; that, to him, would simply be abandoning the ethical standard that
applied to public acts. The fact that part of the educated youth in the universities was susceptible to this kind of nationalist ideology filled him
with serious alarm. He adamantly refused to be utilized in any way by
groups like the University Circle of the German Type—the very name
made him mistrustful, and he rejected their militant meetings, which
went beyond mere physical training. In general, this man who took such
an interest in pedagogical tasks found the propagandistic treatment of
youth quite ridiculous. In 1930, when he was asked to give a talk to
young people over the radio, he shook his head. "All they do there is tell
the young people what they want to hear . . . They encourage them in the
belief that nowadays it is possible to run before one has learned to walk."

He did not want to appear, in this framework, as a "prophet in the desert," where he would finally be "laughed at." But hadn't there been a kind of psychological shift, at the very time when the young people were being flattered by their elders? "Today, one can hear it said everywhere," he wrote to the *Frankfurt News* in a thoughtful letter dated December 8, 1931, "that the young people want to come under strict leadership. One can hear that young people are saying: With the National Socialists we are finding what we want and need; we want to follow someone. If so, it would seem that the period in which the younger people felt called upon to re-create the whole world, as they did right after the overthrow of the old state, is passing."

This socio-psychological observation, made in passing, was not accidental. It identified a turning point in German sentiment. If, after 1918, there had been a breakdown of relationships as a result of the forces of individualism that had broken through and cast off the war-induced restrictions in military and civil life—even if this breakdown had been cast in socialist rhetoric—now, under various names, a growing need for structure and hierarchy was emerging in leagues and groups and formations. Military tradition gained renewed authority over a people who had been subjected to general military service for more than a century. Once a certain distance had been gained from the suffering caused by the First World War, the country's youth had once again fed its imagination on Germany's military achievements during the four years of conflict. Bosch himself was immune to the appeal of this kind of sentiment, but its appearance troubled him.

He had never concerned himself analytically with the National Socialists' publications. His political judgment was based on the phenomena as he observed them, and on the individuals he saw in action. He had, it is true, grown critical of the capacity of German parliamentarism and its multitude of factions to accomplish anything, but he remained confident that through experience and education orderly rules might be established in a world that was gradually moving away from war and its consequences, and that these rules would give the political leaders more significant opportunities than they had previously enjoyed. With Paul Reusch, who during the disturbances of 1919 had raised the call for a "second Bismarck" in the expectation that he would bring about the recovery from Germany's misery, Bosch had been involved in many exchanges on the subject of politics and authority. It was to Reusch that he had addressed the sober comment, on February 10, 1932, that "It may be possible for a dictator to rule a people, but not the world economy. One could imagine a dictator who would last as long as one human life. But after the death of the first, how would it be possible for a second dictator to impose his rule?"

Only a year after these lines were written, the hypothetical idea had become a tangible reality. The new reality consistently decried this notion of dictatorship, and at first it remained within the traditional forms and constitutional requirements in order to hollow them out until they collapsed without resistance. A great deal of uncertainty clouded the first weeks. The burning of the Reichstag on February 28, 1933, and the way it was used to attack basic civic freedoms, the regulation concerning the flag of the Reich, the actions against provincial governments, et cetera, all gave clues to what was to come. At the Bosch firm, they were not immediately clear about the impact of events, and they were by no means inclined to capitulate. The swastika flag was not raised, and Bosch was once more able to enjoy the pleasures of anonymous denunciations. A wave of systematic and arbitrary persecution began, as people were relieved of their positions or were arrested. It reached as far as Bosch's inner circle of personal acquaintances and friends, and this disturbed him profoundly, since for the most part these were men whose human integrity he valued. "I am very depressed by our situation," he wrote on April 12, 1933, from Mooseurach to a young Swabian acquaintance in Paris, Frank Rübelin, who had had a hand in the earlier conference on Franco-German rapprochement. "I have a dilation of the heart, as I did in 1917, which is why I am here. Every day I see the suffering among us. Personally, I receive letters every day with pleas for help, money, or work. It is not impossible that one of my friends will succeed in getting me sent to a concentration camp, even if only for a short time. That kind of excitement would naturally not be the right thing for my heart problem. But in times like these, some people succeed in satisfying their lust for personal revenge. As for myself, I am not leaving the country, at any rate, even if I am faced with the danger of being interned. For the internment could not last long . . . My old heart would just have to survive another stress test; this will not fail to happen in any case, given the political situation."

In this letter he saw his personal situation in dark hues. Among the people who had been persecuted that week were Bosch's ally in his Franco-German projects, Paul Distelbarth. At the time, people were quick to make accusations of treason, and Bosch had to reckon with the possibility that he, too, would be drawn in. Things settled down again, however, and Distelbarth, whose actions in the confusion of this period were not exactly well-considered, was fully rehabilitated. For Bosch, one consequence was that now the very interest in foreign affairs that had filled his life so completely at the end of 1932 led to his first personal contacts with National Socialists. For although in *Mein Kampf* Hitler's programmatic statements had referred angrily to the decadence of the French people and the destruction of French sovereignty as one precondition for an aggressive German *Ostpolitik*, there had since been a change in tone toward Germany's neighbor to the west. One might argue over whether it was a tactical ploy or a more profound change of heart; if Bosch had had to fear, until now, that the Nazis would disturb his efforts aimed at Paris, he now found that in this very area he was, if not exactly encouraged to continue his private efforts—for these were incompatible with the abrupt totalitarian demand for *Gleichschaltung*, or coordination, of all public activities—at least he met with some agreement. Through acquaintances in Munich a personal relationship was forged with the industrialist Wilhelm Keppler, from Baden, who at the time was one of Hitler's economic advisers. Bosch engaged in an exchange of letters with Keppler beginning as early as February 1933. Bosch had refused to take part in the meeting of industrialists organized by Hermann Göring on February 20, 1933, at which Hitler was to speak. "If I am not able to participate in an open discussion, with an exchange of views in which I can present the Chancellor with my profound concerns and the reasons for them; in a conversation at which many people are present I will certainly not accomplish anything," he wrote on February 20, 1933. And a few days later, on February 23, 1933: "I will be very pleased, if you are able to make this possible, to speak with Herr Hitler about our foreign policy. I see in it the actual solution of the difficulties in which we find ourselves." And he explained to the recipient that a *rapid* rapprochement with France would bear valuable fruit, even if the people in the Foreign Office were of the opinion that this would mean achieving only 50 percent of their goals; to count on any help from Britain, America, or "perhaps even Italy" was a delusion. "They have their own worries right now."

Before it came to the conversation between Bosch and Hitler that Keppler described, more than half a year had passed. In the meantime, Baron von Lersner had turned to Bosch with a request for funds for the Papen group within the administration. He received a rejection. Papen might be willing to come to an agreement, but what about Hitler? Or Hugenberg? "What will the future course be? I would like to have certainty on this point," Bosch wrote on March 8, 1933. The letter that declined this request is full of mistrust, above all of Alfred Hugenberg, whom Bosch was not at all happy to see at the head of the Ministry of the Economy and Nutrition. "But I must refuse to place myself on the side of those who are in favor of a land monopoly—by which I mean both those who work on the surface of the earth and those who work inside our earth's outer crust—and impoverish the working population . . . A policy of quotas helps neither agriculture nor industry." The recipient of this letter must have had a difficult time in figuring out what to do with it.

Bosch's foreign policy worries were assuaged, at first, by the chancellor's declaration on May 17 about Germany's desire for peace. "In the matter of our rapprochement with France," he wrote to Georg Escherich on May 26, "Hitler has now found the right words. Who will find them in the matter of the Jews?" But the crisis in relations with Vienna, which occurred right at the end of May and led to the prohibition of travel to Austria, as Chancellor Engelbert Dollfuss attempted to solidify his authoritarian regime against radicalism from left and right, put Bosch in a bad mood. They should keep their hands off Austria, he wrote to Hans Walz on June 9. To carry out the *Anschluss* abruptly would only make it harder to come to an equitable solution with France; *after* the understanding with the West it would be a simple matter to put together an agreement. "Do we have to let our Nazis into Austria, and then in uniform? Why don't we wait? Austria will do what we do anyway." He also had a thought based on principle: "One must not always think one has to show one's power. Precisely the opposite is right. If England wants something, then the English don't say, 'We are in a position to do thus and so, therefore let's do it.' Rather, they wait until they can say, 'Things don't want to settle down there, they require your assistance,' or, 'It is God's wish that we create order,' and things of this kind."

Bosch was also uncomfortable about the prospects for experiments with economic organization; perhaps he was reminded of the fruitless debates and memorandums that had occurred on the former National Economic Council. At that time, as in the current debates, there had been much discussion of "organization by profession . . . There is no more a 'just solution' of this question than there is a 'just price' for grain. One person's owl is another's nightingale," he commented on June 9, 1933. Bosch was more profoundly concerned about the uncertainty in how economic policy was to be guided. One could sense that things would not last long with Hugenberg. Bosch, who didn't like him, would be glad to see him go. "Keppler might possibly be good, but I have doubts about whether he will prevail. He would probably be too accommodating toward Hitler. Whether he is the same way toward others?" Bosch, who failed to recognize that the dynamic that was developing was oriented toward Hitler alone, thought that something might be gained by action on these questions by Hindenburg, although he found it "profoundly sad" that "the bourgeoisie has so little courage . . . Always considerate, always diplomatic." This was in the early summer of 1933.

The conversation with Hitler took place on September 22, 1933. Bosch had evidently been told that the chancellor was informed about him. For in a letter to Hermann Bücher dated September 9, he wrote, "Perhaps I will succeed in making a certain impression. He is said to know me very well by my actions, and in Bavaria they are supposedly of the opinion—this is what I heard—that I have always been national and socialist, and basically they are right. Earlier on, I was laughed at on account of my position on the social question, made fun of and hated. Today I seem to be recognized for it. If I could be of some use in that way, you have no idea how happy it would make me." There are no notes about the conversation, which was brief. Bosch's impression was that it did not have any result objectively. Bosch was immediately annoyed when Hitler asked him what wishes he had to present. None; the request for a meeting had come from the chancellor, after all. The chancellor talked on, had flattering things to say about Swabia; they were democrats, but of a different sort than the Berliners—all of which Bosch knew full well, but now felt was beside the point. With his particular interest in recommending a policy of rapprochement with France, he seemed to find no opposition. Hitler, in his typical style, gave Bosch a rundown on the policy that he would pursue, with the seductive self-confidence that so impressed some people in conversation while fatiguing or boring others. When the chancellor paused for a moment, Bosch, who wanted to get a word in edgewise, remarked: "You must feel quite odd sitting on Bismarck's chair." This was surely not meant to be malicious; it was just an example of his social awkwardness. Hitler, in a rage, walked to the window and rapped with his fingers on the panes. To no one's surprise, there was no warmth at all between the two men. A few weeks later, when he was asked for his impression, Bosch told an acquaintance: "This individual wants to be a statesman and doesn't know what justice is." The sentence is full of his profound sense of alienation from the man. There is a comment in one of Bosch's letters to Wilhelm Keppler, shortly after the meeting, that has a certain historical and documentary charm, and also reveals the kind of argumentation with which Hitler sought to gain the support of visitors like Bosch. "The conditions that we have right now are again quite depressing to me, so that at night I have a good deal of time to spend thinking and also reading biographies, memoirs, etc. The Führer, in the conversation that I had with him, expressed the opinion that for Germany the monarchy would probably be the right form of government. I myself also think that a constitutional monarchy is probably the best, but it must be set up the way the English one is. The Constitution must prevent things from happening like what we experienced under Wilhelm II." This was followed by a recommendation to the recipient to read the book *Edward VI and His Times.*

Bosch met Hitler personally on a few other occasions at automobile exhibitions or state receptions in Stuttgart without their contact ever going beyond the bounds of the merely conventional. He never accepted the invitations to party congresses or the like. In the meantime, the firm itself had had to learn, by trial and error, not only how to deal with the new circumstances that had been created by National Socialism, but how to adjust to them as a historical phenomenon that would last for some time. The great worry about an abrupt change in economic policy that would have favored the sectors of large-scale agriculture and heavy industry, which was something Bosch and his colleagues had feared under Alfred Hugenberg, had already faded by June 1933 with Hugenberg's unhappy resignation. If the administration of his successor, the insurance executive Kurt Schmitt, was colorless at first, Bosch had more confidence in Hjalmar Schacht, whom he knew from earlier days and who was reinstalled as president of the Reichsbank on March 16, 1933, and in late January 1935 took charge of the economic ministry as well. Bosch had already come into contact with Schacht through Ernst Jäckh during the First World War, and had occasionally sought his advice on questions having to do with publications that might be deserving of his support.

Bosch might shake his head over the political career of this ambitious man, which had led the cofounder of the Democratic Party to become a comrade-in-arms of Hugenberg and Hitler, but he valued his cool cleverness, technical knowledge of his business, and strong will, which was tough and, when necessary, willing to go on the offensive. What he undertook would probably not always be entirely clear, but this much seemed certain: Schacht would not permit himself to be pushed to the wall by dilettantes or romantics or private interests. Schacht himself, to the degree that his character allowed, responded to Bosch with feelings of respectful warmth.

39

———

EFFECTS OF THE
STATE-GENERATED BOOM

If Bosch had regarded the domestic political developments with the eyes of a businessman, he would have followed the example of a number of industrialists from the Rhineland and would have participated strongly in the financing of National Socialism. For the very first legislative initiatives of the new regime resulted in a significant stimulus to precisely that sector in which Bosch himself was involved and for which he was a supplier—motor vehicles and motorcycles. For the German Automobile Exhibition of February 1933, Bosch had written down a couple of guidelines in which he had complained about the lack of understanding, indeed, often amounting to dislike, in which the automobile had been held by German administrations and parliaments. In addition to the earlier legal harassment, there had again and again been an attitude of dislike and restrictiveness on the part of the finance ministers. Despite this unfavorable situation, the automobile industry had achieved excellent results in the last few years. With a rational trade policy, great exports could once more be achieved.

The initiative came from a different quarter. At that very automobile exhibition, Hitler announced his policy of support for motorization, including, above all, "gradual tax relief" and the "initiation and completion of a generous plan of highway construction." This was followed, in the revision of the tax law for motor vehicles that was implemented on April 11, 1933, by the stipulation that after March 31, 1933, all newly registered passenger cars and motorcycles were to be exempted from the tax. This was good tidings for the industry, which had forfeited almost half of its production during the last two years of crisis. Even before this announcement, the industry had been able to sense the lessening of the great economic crisis and had hired new workers, thanks to increasing orders. But precisely the exemption of *new* cars from the tax, even if the tax itself were not so onerous as the continuing burden of the tax on fuels that was linked to the government's price policy, had an extremely productive psychological effect. Daimler-Benz, Auto-Union, and Opel could announce at the beginning of April that they had full employment. The same was naturally true at Bosch. The short hours with which they had managed to retain their core employees through the difficult period vanished, and the workforce began to grow once more. The year 1933, which had begun with 8,332 employees working an average of 45 hours a week, ended with 11,235 employees and a 48-hour work week. By April 1934, they had reached 13,000; they had been at this level once before, in August 1925. (The numbers refer to Stuttgart and Feuerbach, not the recently acquired factories in Berlin and Dessau.) The primarily domestic focus of this boom is clear from a remark in the business report of March 6, 1934, which stated that the increase in sales to the domestic market amounted to almost 80 percent. Exports had declined. In 1932, exports had still accounted for more than 60 percent of the entire income from sales; now they made up only about 40 percent. In the summer of 1933, the firm decided to build a large new facility for local sales and manufacturing purposes, on land that had been acquired for this purpose some years earlier. The building on the corner of Rosenbergstrasse and the Seidenstrasse had been planned for some time and funds for this purpose were available and waiting to be called on, but until now the firm had been making do. Now, since construction activity had been dormant for several years, the project's commencement also had a propagandistic effect; the Bosch leadership made it part of the slogan of the day, as the new jobs and confidence that this great investment bespoke were communicated to the general consciousness. When the facility was completed, it was clear how necessary the expansion had been, for the number of workplaces was growing. In Feuerbach, too, renovation, expansion, and new construction continued during the next few years. There, above all, the Bosch firm solved the interesting problem of a central heating plant. Later developments, after the existing orders from the civilian sector began to be complemented by the demands of the military, particularly the air force, influenced the character of the expansion in a way that Bosch himself had never anticipated when he created the great facilities in Feuerbach. In order to provide alternative locations in case of war, when decentralization would offer at least some possibility of responding to the danger of air strikes, the new factories that were constructed in the next few years were located, in part, outside the Stuttgart region in the vicinity of Berlin (Dreilinden), in Hildesheim, or in country towns in Württemberg.

At Bosch they were characteristically cautious about how the powerful upswing that had begun in 1933 was reflected in their balance sheets. Depreciation always reckoned with the potential need for new investments. Hence the entire huge machine shop, together with the licenses, patents, and the like, were shown with a book value of only one mark each. The net income had increased from 832,000 marks in 1932—which had been preceded by a loss of 553 marks in 1931—to about a million marks in 1933. Bosch did not pay a dividend, but contributed a million marks to the Bosch Aid Foundation. Not until 1934, after a hiatus of nine years, and after the net profit, as a result of the full utilization of factory capacity, had surpassed 3.5 million marks—to which were added more than 700,000 marks in the profit balance carried forward—did the firm specify a dividend of 6 percent on the base capital of 30 million marks. This was repeated in 1935. During the four following years, with rising net profits, the dividend remained at 8 percent; in 1940 the firm went back to 5 percent. In all these years, significant regular and special reserves were set aside out of the profits, in order to be armed in case there were unexpected taxes or new acquisitions—particularly in view of the possibility, which was anticipated in every year following 1940, of a changeover to peacetime production.

If the years around 1933, in particular, had been characterized by the agitated search for fresh tasks and by bold forays into new manufacturing territories, Bosch now consciously hung back and continued, as the business report for 1936 stated, to steer clear of "fundamentally new areas of production." This naturally did not mean that things remained stationary. The period was characterized by the intensification of scientific research and the practical testing of the most varied replacement materials. The number of innovations that people expected to encounter at the big fairs declined, although quite a few new tasks resulted from the expansion of the customers' needs, particularly when it came to spotlights. In the period before 1933, Bosch had already begun to develop a sideline that would enable the firm to make use of its experiences with headlights, gathered over the course of decades, outside the motor vehicle sector. This occurred in the form of portable spotlights, which were designed for firemen, police, emergency services, railroads, and the like, and could be used for night work. They were relatively handy (despite the fact that a dry-cell battery was used as the power source) and generated a strong light. Now, in 1933, out of the combination of job creation and motorization policies, the construction of the autobahn had begun. In the short or long term, this could only mean that traffic would move from the existing network of roads to the autobahn; it also offered drivers the possibility of much higher average speeds than had been the rule up until then. This resulted in new elements of danger, especially during the hours of evening and night when visibility was decreasing or absent, and when cars were following each other at differing speeds and it became necessary to brake suddenly. The braking distance was twice as long as the reach of the normal low beams. Here, in a clever combination, they came up with the Bosch long-distance headlight (1936), which bundled the high beams of the two front headlights tightly together over 800 to 1,000 meters. In this way drivers knew what was going on in front of them; if the headlights of an oncoming vehicle appeared and the main headlights had to be shifted to the low beam, the long-distance headlight moved down and to the right, with the help of a clever tilting mechanism, so that it kept control of the right lane without blinding the oncoming driver—something that was important enough when, for example, a passenger car doing 80 to 100 kilometers per hour was following an inadequately lighted, slower truck. At almost the same time these tasks were being taken on, the factory developed a wide-beam searchlight for winding roads. When the approaching threat of war required the blackout of motor vehicles, Bosch created camouflage inserts for the market. Without making it necessary to remove the normal electrical headlights, the firm replaced the dispersion lens and polished silver ring of the existing devices with an external hood and matte plate.

The chronicle of the production of accessories mentions a motor vehicle part that essentially lay outside Bosch's traditional area of manufacturing—the steering wheel. The varnished wood or metal tube, in the form of a ring, had been out of favor for some time. The varnish wore out; when accidents occurred, there was the danger of splinters; the proportions had to be quite awkward in order to make the steering wheel stable. As a result, people had begun to use new, nonsplintering materials. At Bosch, this suggestion was taken up eagerly; after all, at the Bakelite factory in Feuerbach they had gathered a wealth of experience in the fabrication of synthetic resins. A steel frame in various sizes was fitted with hard rubber equipped with grips for the fingers and a push button; a lever for the lights or for the gas was mounted on the steering column. The whole thing was utterly elegant in its slender form, and it was also practical, since it left the view of the dashboard less cluttered. It was manufactured in volume right from the start and conquered the market with extraordinary rapidity. In 1935, the Bosch steering lock, mounted on the steering column—something that was still a novelty at the time—was shown at the automobile exhibition. It was an antitheft device outfitted with all possible refinements in its connection to the ignition.

In the second half of the 1930s, two tasks in the government sector acquired particular significance for the designers and manufacturing workers: the creation of the German air force and of the so-called *Volkswagen*—the "people's car." Bosch had been working on ignition devices for airplanes for a long time; this had been the detour by which the firm arrived at the study of radio technology. The triumphal flights of the Zeppelin airships had also served as a proving ground for the Stuttgart factory's work in this area. The achievements had been associated with a rather limited number of orders; these now rose sharply. In the case of the airplane, the magneto ignition device had remained in use for reasons of reliability, weight, and space utilization. Bosch had already marketed a special type designed for commuter and sport airplanes. Next had come the starter motor. Since there was no battery, it had been developed as a flywheel device with a separate electrical motor. Its development, including the ability to achieve a high level of performance in a short time, and to start the motor even in cold weather, proved to be as difficult as it was successful. When military airplanes began to be mass produced, their assembly also helped create a market for Bosch's electric tools; without their assistance, the tempo with which the factories were expected to and, in fact, had to achieve full productivity was unthinkable.

That the challenge of creating integrated electrical equipment for the Volkswagen was given to Bosch was almost self-evident. The Bosch firm had the most experience; they also had the equipment for mass production and hence the necessary elasticity when it came to calculations of cost and price. Still, the preparations and tests dragged on after 1936, and it was years before the planning was completed. The chief designer from Daimler-Benz, Dr. Ferdinand Porsche, also lived in Stuttgart; this made it easier to work together. The greatest difficulty was caused by the necessity of keeping the products within a very limited range of costs; the models available for generators and starter motors, either combined or as separate units, were well tested but too expensive. At the same time, they had to attempt to keep the service requirements as simple as possible. So the starter motor and generator were both completely redesigned with the smallest possible size and weight and a capacity of 130 watts. The distributor for battery ignition was also designed so that its lubrication was automatically taken care of by the motor. The whole thing had to be arranged in such a way that an absolute minimum of expert training was required, and the car needed to be able to withstand tough use even with only moderate care.

During these years, *The Bosch Spark Plug* was able to mark several milestones in the firm's production statistics. In August 1936, the five-millionth magneto ignition device was manufactured; in March, the five-millionth headlight. Bosch spark plugs reached a total of 100 million in March 1937, and in December 1935, the workshop shipped out the one-millionth injection nozzle for diesel motors.

The effect of the government-subsidized boom was most vividly expressed in the growing number of employees at Bosch in the period leading up to the Second World War. In 1933, there had been 11,235 workers and staff members at the Stuttgart and Feuerbach plants; in 1934, there were 14,980; in 1935, 16,117; in 1936, 18,282; in 1938, 23,233. The big jump in the last number revealed the powerful impact of motorized weaponry. For 1935, the firm reported that including the subsidiaries the number amounted to approximately 19,000; for the following years the corresponding statistics were 22,276, 24,315, and 30,443. The growth in the subsidiary firms occurred mainly at the Blaupunkt radio factory, which was naturally benefiting from government propaganda in support of radio. The development of Junkers & Company did not keep pace as far as numbers were concerned. The business report for 1938 saw the reasons for this "in the recession in private housing construction" and in the growing preference for small apartments that lacked their own sanitary facilities.

The note in the business report for 1934 to the effect that given the stormy tempo of development "suitable employees were not easy to find" refers to a predicament that could be solved only with difficulty. As at the beginning of the first decade after 1900, the Bosch firm often had to make do without skilled workers. But how things had changed in the interim! The work process was articulated in a very conscious manner; the observations and conclusions regarding vocational education had been refined; "training" had become a highly rationalized and systematic exercise, and by this time the existing workforce could provide plenty of trainees. Hence the process of assimilating a new stratum of workers into the rhythm of the work could be carried out without the social and labor tensions that had contributed to the critical situation in 1913. And the "Bosch spirit" had been tested and had established itself precisely in the periods of restriction when employees were forced to work part-time and the firm had gone to great lengths to avoid layoffs. Now they were reaping the harvest not only of their solid financial policy and determined rationalization, but also of one and a half decades of pedagogical efforts, which had been carried out, not least, by *The Bosch Spark Plug*.

At Bosch they had never been concerned about the political activities or opinions of their employees, but naturally the latter had been made to feel, at times, that the German Metal Workers' Union was the favored location for a contest in which the Social Democratic and Communist parties carried out their struggle, either noisily or quietly. The at times ironic, at times benevolent, at other times polemical and critical voice of *The Bosch Spark Plug* was now compelled to fall silent. The totalitarian claim to power interrupted even this tradition, which was so unique. Objectively there was little to criticize, either positively or negatively, for the theses that were now being promoted as "socialist" had, for the most part, long been part of Bosch's practice on questions relating to the workers, and had had their chance to prove themselves. The transition, as a result of which the firm no longer consulted with the unions and the labor arbitrator about sociopolitical questions, but instead consulted with the German Labor Front and the Labor Trustee, occurred without any fundamental break. There were some personnel replacements among the representatives of the staff and workers, a change in title for this or that institution, a different tone. At first, Bosch himself was treated by the new political overlords with suspicious caution, while his sociopolitical stance was more or less praised from afar as exemplary. The leader of the German Labor Front, Dr. Robert Ley, visited the factory in Feuerbach in October 1933. To what extent the much-described and vehemently discussed sociopolitical program was just so much wasted paper or words, how profoundly it really affected, won over, perhaps changed people, was difficult to say, for they stood at the beginning of that segment of German history when due to the reigning monopoly of opinion only the ruling elite expressed itself in public.

This was also true of the world around Bosch. It is possible, as was typical of the period, to follow this development by taking the development of *The Bosch Spark Plug* as a model. The paper tried hard not to lose its lively individual physiognomy, but the period in which one thesis confronted another, when an uninhibited publishing policy kept an eye on many areas of knowledge, was over. A national regulation concerning plant newspapers restricted the paper to events that took place inside the factory. It seems inevitable that the paper would be infiltrated with the new trend in terminology; the quotes that had formerly been taken from Ford, Rathenau, Naumann, and others were replaced by citations from the speeches and writings of leading figures of the period. This was the case everywhere in Germany. It did have its amusing side—the same papers that only a short time before had criticized the excessive and showy construction plans for the office buildings of the health insurance agencies and trade unions were now filled with naive National Socialist boastfulness of the sort that surrounded the planned National House of German Labor, which was to be as boring as it was gigantic, and which Robert Ley intended to build on the right bank of the Rhine. The emotional tenor of the commentary could be read with admiration, irony, or anger and bitterness.

40

———•———

THE DEVELOPMENT OF
MATERIALS

When Robert Bosch brought in his brother-in-law Eugen Kayser to found
the Metal Works in Feuerbach, it was a step that would have very significant consequences for the treatment of raw materials and semifinished
products. The factory's own needs were large enough to serve as a secure
basis for the transition to in-house production. The new production site
was not to be a mere appendage of the Stuttgart factory, however, but was
to be an independent supplier for outside customers as well. Hence the
facility, with its great metal presses, rolling machines, and foundries,
grew rapidly. Stuttgart required not only magnets but other metal parts as
well; their uniform mass production, with many interchangeable parts,
could be carried out most advantageously under the Bosch firm's own
auspices. The basic materials were steel, iron, and copper, both pure and
in various alloys.

But the factory did not only need metals. Nonconductive insulation
material that would resist the increasing tension created by the production of sparks was of the greatest importance for the more highly developed engines, and especially for spark plugs. The materials for this
included soapstone, isinglass, and porcelain. At first, the factory's needs

could be satisfied in the marketplace. But as Bosch's technical development expanded, the needs did, too. Would it be possible to satisfy these needs by doing their own research, testing, and production? Gustav Klein supported the addition of a Ceramics Department to the Metal Works, but the First World War delayed its development; the first oven did not come on line until 1918. The new venture brought its share of difficulties; since the factory had primarily worked in metal, it lacked technological and scientific expertise in ceramics, as well as skilled, experienced staff. This was only a temporary phenomenon, however, and the new initiative would soon demonstrate its usefulness; as a sideline, the Ceramics Department produced fireclay vessels for use in their own foundry. Soon it also began to make progress on its central mission, and in a few years it was no longer merely a "department" that had moved from the generator department to the Metal Works, but declared its independence as the Insulation Works. In 1922, Bosch decided to build a new facility; it was completed in the following year, which was the most difficult year of inflation, and was built on a scale large enough to encompass the processing of synthetic resins. This was the period during which the imperfections of various synthetic materials that had been used as stopgap measures during the war began to be corrected by more penetrating scientific analysis and technical refinements. It was an international process of particular urgency for Germany, which was being pressed for reparations payments. The challenge was not only to overcome the embarrassing word "synthetic" when speaking of the use of new manufacturing materials whose suitability was superlative, but also to locate raw materials in areas under their hegemony and thus avoid payments to foreign countries. In Germany, the new technological impulse that had galvanized chemistry labs and inspired physics researchers to test for stability, caloric reaction, and so forth, coincided with the requirements of foreign exchange policy.

Even before the First World War, the extraction of nitrogen from atmospheric air, in which Carl Bosch had played a key role, had assumed an international political importance that was not confined to the war. Now this achievement was matched by the extraction of synthetic fuel from black and brown coal and by Buna as an alternative to rubber. Both of these inventions, as is well known, were German. Artificial silk (rayon) and spun rayon also had particular significance for Germany, which had neither cotton nor silk and was poor in wool. With Bakelite and other similar artificial resins, a whole new industry emerged—one that did not have to engage in the struggle against the notion of "synthetics."

Manufacturing at Bosch was not immediately affected by these innovations, although they had a strong impact on motorization (through changes affecting fuel and tires). Still, they carried out tests and gathered astonishing experiences in these areas as well. For example, until then cotton had been considered *the* appropriate material for insulating the copper armature; now a paper strip woven through with hemp threads proved to be equally effective. The use of cotton could be reduced in other ways as well. These were actually only preludes or accompaniments to a second process of rationalization that began in the 1920s but only started to reach its full impact in the 1930s, and that was directed not so much at the methods of manufacturing as at the quality and cost-effectiveness of raw materials and semifinished goods as well as their sources. This took place, above all, in the so-called "Four-Year Plan." One cannot claim that the ideological overtures to this development harmonized very well with the economic background music that characterized Robert Bosch's frequent statements and the reports of the business management. For everything that looked like economic self-sufficiency, protective tariffs, or attempts at autarky was opposed and rejected at Bosch. The firm took the division of labor among nations, according to the rules of the international marketplace with its exchange of finished products and raw materials, more or less as a given, or at any rate they said to themselves, "Whoever wants to sell to the 'world' must also be willing to buy from the world the things that are offered and that he himself needs." Bosch's international position was completely unique proof of the vanquishing power of good, reliable work. But the talk about his monopoly, which had always been an exaggeration, was deceptive. The world demonstrated plenty of desire and ability to compete, particularly when it came to prices. At Bosch, they watched with concern and anger as the forces of national economic separation gathered strength, and they defended themselves against those voices that saw Germany as having a particular role in this regard.

But the confusion brought about by the retreat from gold-based currencies and the confusion in trade policies, through which the tradition of most-favored-nation status was being replaced by bilateral and partially contingent agreements, proved stronger than Bosch's fundamentally rational assumptions about the best ways in which to achieve maximum economies. It was a strange consequence of the Treaty of Versailles, and particularly of the reparations payments, which were demanded in gold, that they forced the German economy away from its exports and back within the domestic limits that formed its base. The public trade in foreign exchange, with allotments and delivery orders, was a reflection of this state of affairs.

A peculiar historical coincidence was responsible for the fact that this restriction of the international movement of gold coincided with an extremely intense period of technical and scientific activity. Although hasty and superficial public relations claims had just declared that the era of new inventions was now over, and the "end of capitalism," which had been driven essentially (it was thought) by the giddy excitement over technical innovation, was at hand, the facts were actually quite the opposite. Technology was making revolutionary incursions into the traditional economic system, and its need for new investments was giving a very strong incentive to capitalist expansion. This process was taking place internationally, in varying degrees, although its character was not uniform. Along with more or less voluntary decisions, there were a variety of approaches that involved government regulation and intervention, from the English model, to the new policy of intervention in the United States, to the practice of government control in Germany, and finally to the state enterprises in Russia.

The evolution of the raw materials that they were working on at Bosch, with the tough dedication that the new tasks required, must be viewed within the general framework of the situation as it existed at that time. Bosch had approached the replacement of copper with aluminum with some trepidation, for copper was the classic material, so to speak, for all electricians. But the theoretically recognized suitability of aluminum to serve as a conductor of electricity was proven in practice to be valid. The new metal, which could now, for the first time, be produced with essentially domestic materials, could be used quite satisfactorily in appropriate alloys for the most varied work processes of precision engineering. The greater space requirements that played such a big role in the early period of aluminum use were compensated for by its lighter weight. With the development of anodyzation appeared yet another new material, along with aluminum; the era of "light metals" seemed to herald a new age in which many technological solutions would have to be reconsidered. This occurred at a time when the airplane, like the motor vehicle only a few decades earlier, was becoming the center of a new international industry. Here every savings in weight would translate into a technical and economic savings.

At Bosch they never undertook to produce aluminum and other light metals, but the suitability of these materials for the firm's manufacturing processes were tested very carefully, from an economic as well as a technical point of view. A separate scientific staff was created for materials development, as well as a highly evolved system of ongoing chemical and physical testing of the various alloys. They wanted to know how the alloys themselves reacted, how the lubricating oils responded at various temperatures, and so on. Cold and hot caloric chambers were created with dry or humid, dusty or pure air. A wonderful and strange wealth of testing methods appeared, from the primitive-mechanical to the use of spectral analysis for chemicals, or of X-ray techniques for physical examinations. Robert Bosch himself may have been astonished when he looked at these things, which after all were not peculiar to his company but represented a necessary accompaniment to the penetration of production by science in the new large-scale industries. Bosch's own natural proclivities favored the innovative and reliable craftsman who had a feeling for the material and knew almost instinctually what was required and what could be expected from it. But materials were in the midst of a huge transformation, and instinct or feeling alone was not enough. When the Metal Works and the Stamping Works were created, Bosch had not had such a far-reaching development in mind, but a signal had been given, and Bosch's belief in the progress of rational knowledge, his consciousness of a need to lead in this area as well, assigned the greatest potential to the whole area of scientific research.

The most important development for the firm as a whole may have come from the Insulation Works, where they had the task of finding the most suitable material for the spark plugs, which were being subjected to ever-greater stress. Soapstone was the subject of repeated experiments; here Richard Stribeck played an active role in analysis, clarification, and development; one of the solutions was named for him: Stribit. Pyranit 2 was, like aluminum, derived from bauxite; it was an odd fact that an electrical conductor and an insulator could be made from the same aluminum oxide. In a vivid description of the insulation of spark plugs (*The Bosch Spark Plug*, no. 7/8, 1940), the director of the spark plug department, Gustav Werner, made the comment: "We believe in the sentence: 'Something that remains in one piece during a test has not been tested, because we don't know its limits!' "

All these achievements came from the firm's own laboratories, but Bosch never followed the dictum that one had to have invented everything oneself; where motor vehicle accessories were concerned, the factory manufactured items (starter motor, brakes, et cetera) whose basic idea had been purchased and then had been developed for production at the Bosch factory. As they observed the progress of metallurgy, they had come across the work of a Japanese scholar, Professor Mishima, who had achieved an extraordinary increase in magnetic power with a new steel alloy involving a mixture of aluminum and nickel. It was more than 550 percent more effective than chromium steel; if cobalt was added, Alni-steel (the name derived from aluminum and nickel) produced 680 percent more magnetic energy (taking 3 percent chromium steel as 100 percent)—a most astonishing fact. The investigations, in which Stribeck, once again, was deeply involved, also satisfied the requirements of technical machining; even at temperatures of up to 500 degrees centigrade, the new steel, in contrast to other steels, lost none of its magnetism. As a result, it was particularly well suited to the needs of the variety of forms required for electrical appliances. In addition, it was affected very little by aging. The relative difficulty of working it mechanically, a result of its brittleness and hardness, was something they were glad to put up with in exchange for such lasting advantages. In 1935, Bosch purchased the patent for Alni-steel for all the European countries. As far as their own production was concerned, the new material meant that little by little they could move to smaller sizes with less weight, something that was quite essential in the case of the increasingly dense design of airplane equipment. In addition, with this decision Bosch had entered a sector of the steel industry that would take on great importance for specialty products despite the limited quantities involved. The fact that Bosch had taken an interest in it lent the matter a corresponding importance. Within a brief period, the Bosch firm was able to sell licenses for the production of Alni-steel in all of the European countries. The Japanese invention developed into a significant source of foreign exchange for the German national economy.

The efforts to make the most extensive possible use of the metallic raw materials that were available within Germany led Bosch, in 1937, to become a miner himself, so to speak. Within the framework of the Four-Year Plan, German metal reserves, both old and new, were to be explored. On the Mosel and in the Hunsrück area scattered deposits of lead and zinc had been found long before. Bosch bought the rights to various minefields from the German Montan G.m.b.H. in Wiesbaden, and created the metal mining company Westmark G.m.b.H. in Traben-Trarbach with a starting capital of 200,000 marks. It was more a nod to official policy, a way of participating in the overall direction of economic policy, than a rational business decision. These metals did not play such an essential role in Bosch's own production that the firm, from the standpoint of company policy, would have needed to become self-sufficient in this particular area. The venture—as the start-up sum indicates—remained a marginal affair; but the firm brought up everything from the minefields that could be extracted.

The researchers and technicians in the experimental laboratories were completely engrossed in their new tasks and were proud of what they were accomplishing in these areas. The internal business organization, the management of production, and so on, developed according to the constraints of the raw materials situation. Achieving savings in raw materials and carefully collecting, sorting, and making use of scraps developed into an elaborate system; they could cite astonishing rows of figures to show how much of their own (or others') raw material had been saved as a consequence of this policy. Where the sale of the finished goods was concerned, however, things were not so simple. The lively propaganda and occasionally excessive self-congratulation with which the accomplishments of the German raw materials industry were announced to the world did not fail to have an effect on their foreign competitors—and on their customers—as well. It was said that German manufacturing was only working with "substitutes," that it was losing its earlier reliability. An artificially exaggerated as well as a spontaneous natural mistrust could be observed, and this was quite awkward for those concerns that had learned to take the whole world as their market. At Bosch, too, they encountered these criticisms and had to take the prejudices into account; in other words, they had to use the traditional raw materials for their export products. But this was only a transitional phase, for their experiences provided sufficient assurance that the changeover to the new and more developed raw materials would not mean any loss of durability or reliability in their products, particularly since precisely these new materials and other alterations had been tested in "truly barbaric fashion," as *The Bosch Spark Plug* noted (no. 9/10, 1940). Gradually, the firm became more confident in its dealings with foreign customers.

The first hints of this development at Bosch stretched back to the end of the 1920s and could even be seen as going all the way back to Gottlob Honold's material analyses in 1901, which had been as significant as his early design ventures. The foreign exchange question and the Four-Year Plan had exerted a powerful influence on its tempo and the uses to which it was put, however. Bosch gained a preeminent position when it came to factory materials, which would stand the firm in good stead during the increasing material shortages at the beginning of the Second World War. This also meant preparing for peacetime work, which at some point would return; no one at Bosch had any illusions about the difficulties that this would entail, and they wanted to be as well prepared as possible, both scientifically and technologically. For this reason, the whole area of materials research and treatment was consistently supplied with large sums of money, without regard to any evident profitability, as an investment in future possibilities for effective action.

41

———•———

POLITICAL WORRIES AND
BUSINESS DECISIONS

On October 11, 1933, Bosch addressed an urgent letter to Foreign Minister
Constantin von Neurath. The letter began with a sentence that was unusually emotional for Bosch: "I am writing with my heart's blood." He did not
want to force his advice about the impending cabinet discussions on the
recipient; the minister himself knew perfectly well how things stood. "But
it could be that it is not unwanted if an old man confirms what you yourself
already know, but what is doubtless seen by quite a few others as false,
even treasonous." The letter went on to say that the chancellor probably
saw a Franco-German understanding as necessary at this time, "but at
least in his entourage there are men who are of the opinion that this is the
moment when one must remain strong; the French fear us, this is the time
to hold out, and then everything we want will lie at our feet!"

Bosch's concerns had to do with the difficulties that had arisen in
connection with the "equal rights" accorded to Germany in December
1932—in principle, in matters of rearmament. Bosch had not been concerned with the details of the military-political formulations or the more
artificial than sensible interplay of concealed approval and disapproval
and of half-concessions and distorted interpretations. This whole concep-

tual world was not something he felt comfortable with. At the time, in November 1932, he had written to an acquaintance: "At the moment I have only one pressing wish, namely that our government will accept Herriot's suggestion and realize the dream of my old democratic father, namely a militia." This notion had led nowhere; it seemed to the military experts too much like outdated Romanticism and did not seem to fit in with their ideas about war technology, which were based on modern weaponry. Consequently there had been a hardening of the positions, which Bosch regretted. He could understand, as he wrote to Neurath, "a position of this kind . . . to wait even longer" out of a desire to gain time to become stronger oneself, "but it is not in our interest . . . We must not attempt to achieve a new peace by means of violence, but must do as Bismarck did in 1866." The letter went on to give a variation on this theme: "Michel must marry Marianne, and if the marriage is to go well, the marriage contract must be signed in an amicable fashion. No good German will be in favor of giving anything away. But the important thing now is not to make as many gains as can be made. The future belongs to us if Germany and France make common cause, for Germany's economic superiority is powerful. In the future, we will need to be very clever if the marriage is to go well. Marianne will have to fetch the money from her mattress, so that Michel can sow and reap. The result: moderation in our demands now; to the extent that we can be moderate and must restrain ourselves, the marriage should take place."

The letter overestimated the influence of the foreign minister on the most serious decisions, for it still failed to recognize the dramatic style of Hitler's policy making. Bosch's exhortations and explanations had probably barely reached their addressee when Germany's withdrawal from the League of Nations occurred on October 14, 1933. Bosch, who with his enormous donation almost a decade and a half earlier had made it possible for the German League for the League of Nations to begin work, was alarmed. As little as he may have liked the style of work in Geneva, he feared Germany's isolation more. The assurances of the government's representatives in their speeches and press interviews were at first somewhat reassuring. Bosch had met the chancellor's special envoy, Joachim von Ribbentrop, in the spring at Wilhelm Keppler's home; Ribbentrop had asked Bosch (on December 7, 1933) whether he had "liked" his interview in a Paris newspaper, and added: "We will keep fighting until the goal has been achieved." Bosch answered that he was "naturally extremely pleased," and that he "only wished that Hitler would succeed in bringing about an understanding soon." But with Ribbentrop, in particular, Bosch had an uncomfortable feeling, for Ribbentrop had supported the very thesis that Bosch mistrusted so intensely: "We must be strong before there can be an understanding" (cited in a letter from Bosch to Frank Rümelin, April 12, 1933). The notion of "strength" was too open to interpretation. The optimism that Bosch had brought back from his earlier trip to Paris had been based on the expectation that no psychological mistakes would be made in Germany and that based on a willingness to be helpful, they would reach halfway serviceable agreements soon. The fruits of these agreements, if they were given time to ripen, could be harvested at a later date.

At a minimum, Bosch could count on the fact that the continuation of his own efforts would not be disturbed, and would not be interpreted as a disturbance either. It was a semiprivate politics for which he was quite willing to make sacrifices. He saw it as his contribution to serving the need of the world's peoples for peace. The form this took was personal, although it occasionally involved public appearances. Discussions of principle, as they had been conducted in the congresses and publications of the Pan-Europe movement, played only a minor role; the peoples of the two nations, the *Volk*, were to be brought closer together. Meanwhile, Bosch's relationship with Coudenhove-Kalergi had been broken off. The latter had written an essay in the Basel newspaper *The Swiss Observer* stating that National Socialism, in calling for the unification of all German-speaking territories, was attempting to divide and separate Switzerland. Bosch had read these thoughts, as he wrote to their author on October 23, 1933, "not merely shaking my head, but with horror." He felt that they represented a threat to the possible conversation between Berlin and Paris. Everyone who had previously supported Coudenhove-Kalergi would be delighted "if Hitler, working together with Daladier, creates this [Pan-Europe] for us." People are asking: "How can Coudenhove-Kalergi, through his actions, expose all the people who have supported him up to now?" He was literally giving his opponents the weapons to use against himself and his previous supporters. "I emphasize *previous*, for the relations between the supporters of rapprochement between Germany and France and you, Count, have been broken off." This spelled the end of a relationship that had never been without its personally problematic aspects for Bosch.

Now he sought a way "from below." Paul Distelbarth had pointed it out and had begun to pursue it. The participants in the war from 1914–18 were to lead the way in reconciling the two peoples. This should take place not so much within the framework of contacts between clubs and formal associations, which had become somewhat stilted with their more or less standard speeches, as through personal encounters. The culmination of these efforts was the visit by forty-five French war veterans in the early summer of 1935. Bosch had invited them. It was the first such attempt to create a friendly link, and it was only possible because Bosch took the risk of promoting the voluntary initiative. There were a couple of preparatory experiments. In September 1933, the soccer players from Stuttgart had played a friendship match in Strasbourg with their sporting colleagues from the Bosch firm in Paris; the following year the latter paid a visit to Stuttgart. In 1934, twenty-five children of Bosch employees spent two weeks at the French war veterans' settlement in Clairvivre, and French children were guests in Stuttgart. Everything had occurred in the most pleasing harmony; as a result they decided to undertake a larger project, whose brilliant and touching reality was profoundly gratifying to Bosch. At this point, official noises were made. There was an exchange of telegrams with Hitler and a reception with the chief mayor of Stuttgart, Karl Strölin (as there was with Edouard Herriot during the subsequent return visit to Lyon); the war victims' organizations participated. This, they hoped, would be repeated, and the far-reaching emotional resonance of this kind of person-to-person understanding would create a good foundation for a political leadership that sought honest conciliation. This would, however, remain the only such journey for peace. For by the following year, the political constellation had changed so significantly that it no longer seemed very favorable to a repetition. The initiative that Bosch had increasingly displayed in foreign affairs over the last few years also faded. One would not want to say that he gave in to resignation; his inner involvement continued to be quite strong, but he could not help feeling that, as far as the leading individuals were concerned, his counsel or expressions of opinion were spoken into the wind.

Bosch had always thought primarily about the *European* situation. It was the clarification of *this* situation that was necessary to secure the peace—something that could only be achieved bilaterally by Berlin and Paris. The issues that arose with the awakening of an aggressive Italian colonial imperialism, the reaction of the British and French worlds, and the tensions that followed the expansion of Japan's Manchukuo in East Asia appealed less to Bosch's imagination. One thing, however, was unmistakably clear: the ability to "localize" potential conflicts was becoming more and more questionable, and this was something worth thinking about. In Germany's case there was no point in looking to the League of Nations. Was it possible that the chains of its procedures could be loosened through a broader overview that did not confine itself to the paragraphs expressing specifically anti-German sentiments? Bosch began to lend his support to the German section of the New Commonwealth, which was headed by Admiral von Freyberg; through Jäckh he had also become personally acquainted with the organization's founder, Lord Davies. In this context, he wrote a letter to Henry Ford in June 1935 asking him to work with them to help make the world safe from another war. "I think you and I are two of the world's oldest industrialists, who have been involved in bringing together science and industry and introducing new ideas into the industrial sphere in our countries and elsewhere in the world." The plan was to create an impartial court of arbitration in Europe for all questions arising from the Treaty of Versailles that threatened to become dangerous, and to build an air force that would be at the disposal of this court. If Ford ever came to Europe, Bosch would like to introduce him to the leading men in the movement; or perhaps he might decide to send a representative. Bosch's attempt to draw Ford into the arena of international security policy was a failure. The American, who was skeptical about the policy of his own country, did not demonstrate any need to give helpful opinions about the skirmishes that threatened to break out between the world's peoples, or about plans for a better world organization.

The domestic political situation continued to be a source of emotional and spiritual unease for Bosch. On July 6, 1933, a statement by Hitler had declared that the National Socialist revolution had "ended." This was not much more than a newspaper announcement. Bosch would have been grateful for it had there not been men whom he respected still sitting in concentration camps, still subject to professional persecution and public ostracism. Here or there, Bosch was able to give advice or assistance. Just as, years before, he had offered jobs to Russian revolutionaries who were fleeing Russia, now he made apprenticeships available to young people who had been dismissed from their schools. This led to a fight with the German Labor Front; Debatin had to lead it. Later, when the Community of Christians, which had been founded by Friedrich Rittelmeyer in Stuttgart, was destroyed and its leaders sent to a camp, Bosch offered them work and a bourgeois existence following their release. In those years, Bosch learned to cherish the upright stance of religious leaders, which made a profound impression on him. He was deeply moved by the fate of the private preparatory school Castle Salem. In 1925, the Swabian poet Ludwig Finckh had successfully sought Bosch's involvement on behalf of the pedagogical goals and programs of the school's director, Kurt Hahn. Bosch communicated with Hahn frequently, by letter and in person, made places in his firm available to students from Salem, and also asked Hahn's political advice in affairs having to do with Britain. Bosch himself appeared to the younger man as the ideal type of the unwaveringly serious yet high-minded German, and he sent his English friends to him after 1933 to convince them of the continuing existence of another Germany. Because Hahn was a Jew, his institute, which had been created under the protection of Prince Max of Baden, was ripped from his hands; he subsequently opened a new school in the mountains of Scotland. "The Labor Trustee told me that the school in Salem had provided the model for the new types of party schools," Bosch wrote to a mutual acquaintance on February 22, 1934. "I hope this is correct and is the case, and I would like to say that Hahn is more likely to view this as a case of compensatory justice, or at least could see it that way, than the fact that he must now realize his plans in Scotland, instead of having the possibility of doing it here." To see Hahn's very significant if somewhat controversial pedagogical venture as the model for the new types of party schools was probably an overly optimistic interpretation; Bosch experienced Hahn's departure as both a professional and a personal loss. When Bosch went to Britain in 1936, he visited Hahn in order to take a look at his school in Scotland, oblivious of the German agents spying on him. He was moved and excited when he was asked to speak to the young students about his life and about Germany.

For Bosch, as an unregenerate individualist, it was particularly galling that schematic thinking was now becoming widespread as an aspect of everyday vocabulary. Finckh, to whom Bosch was quite well disposed, was roundly criticized on this point when he tried to gain Bosch's support of an appeal on behalf of the preservation of the environment in Hegau. "I must unfortunately decline to sign your appeal on behalf of Hohenstoffeln," Bosch wrote on February 28, 1934. "In the appeal the statement is made that under the former state, in a liberalistic economy, everything was permitted. Quite apart from the fact that this is an enormous exaggeration, I see in the word 'liberalistic,' which nowadays has become an everyday slogan, a debasement of the economy of which I was a member—I think honorably—for five decades as a businessman . . . I might also remind you," he continued with rather grim humor, "that the principal destruction in Hohenstoffeln was permitted not during the 'liberalistic' era, but in December 1933." This episode was a minor matter; however, it characterizes not only the two men but the tenor of the times as well.

This letter was one of the last to contain political references, and this, too, was typical of the times. The later historians of Germany's National Socialist years will encounter great difficulty when it comes to extracting intimate facts or personal judgments from the letters of contemporaries, for those Germans who were intellectually opposed to the regime had gotten out of the habit of writing candid letters, and with good reason. For all practical purposes, the privacy of the mails had been suspended for those personalities who were involved in public life; both the writers and their recipients were in constant danger. How much suffering and anxiety resulted from this! The complicated circumlocutions that many people adopted were never Bosch's style. Hence, from now on, his letters lacked all reference to current affairs, except for theoretical excursions or historical reflections, for example, in the letters to Eugen Diesel or Johannes Haller. Georg Escherich was surrounded by suspicion, Paul Reusch even more so; his leading position in the Ruhr Valley had been undermined and would ultimately be destroyed by the party. Bosch learned to remain silent about political matters in his letters; it cannot have been easy for him. How reduced, for instance, his comment on the alarming flight of Rudolf Hess to Scotland sounds in a letter to Escherich: "The Hess case causes a good deal of concern" (May 15, 1941).

In Bosch's surroundings, the opinions and the mood were not unanimous. Along with angry haters, there were also individuals with a well-meaning willingness to ascribe the excesses and tactless actions to the lower party organs. Others preferred to maintain a cool detachment, not to let anything touch them personally; they also wished to see the evil tales and uncertain rumors kept from Bosch to the degree that this was possible, in order not to upset him. The factory itself had to reach some kind of accommodation with the new powers if it was not to be threatened with interference. Among the various shades of wounded inner resistance and merely tactical decisions, a number of the leading figures joined the party or became supporting members of the SS. This was seen, as it was throughout Germany, as a kind of protective or preventive measure against the danger of being saddled with an official party commissar. This was something they constantly had to reckon with; it would have meant the end of the employment of oppositional officials and teachers.

Bosch was deeply angered when the National Socialist laws forced him to give up his ownership interest in the German Publishing Institute, and hence simultaneously in the Württemberg Newspaper Publishers. He had been motivated to take action in order to protect the press in Württemberg from the influence of north German capital. Now he was being put under intense pressure to divest himself of his property; alternatively, as he was told somewhat sarcastically, he could resign from his firm and become a newspaper publisher! He resisted stubbornly; the party even called on Göring to help carry out their extortion and reach an agreement—what good was it to invoke the principle of the inviolability of private property if the law was written in such a way as to bring the majority of the German press under the control of the party or its associated organizations! The struggle was upsetting. Its effect was supposed to be smoothed over by an invitation to Göring to visit Bosch for a hunt in Urach. But this did not make things better, for when Göring arrived, his host was no longer there. The hunting master of the Reich had stopped so often to be celebrated along the way that he was two hours late, and to wait so long for the much younger man seemed to Bosch to be beneath his dignity.

Bosch avoided contact with the local party leaders. He had nothing in common with *Gauleiter* Wilhelm Murr, although the latter was a passionate hunter, or with the ill-tempered prime minister, Othmar Mergenthaler. Only with the new chief mayor, Karl Ströhlin, whose attitude was one of respect and warmth, did a more intimate relationship develop. Ströhlin did not forget what the city had owed Bosch earlier, or indeed what it owed him at present. He occasionally asked his advice and gave little tokens of his attentiveness; Bosch appreciated Ströhlin's desire to get things done, which became less politically biased as the years went by. Once, when Bosch was photographed in a conversation with Hitler at an automobile exhibition, and the picture appeared in *The Bosch Spark Plug*, Ströhlin wrote to tell Bosch how "especially" pleased he was to see it, because it was a way of "doing away with all the earlier misinterpretation." (Ströhlin did not comment on how annoyed Bosch appeared in the photograph.) There had been no lack of such "misinterpretations." It was a bit comical when Heinrich Göhrum, "as his personal doctor and friend," wrote to a National Socialist acquaintance of his, almost solemnly, that it was impossible, as people were saying in party circles, that Bosch had spoken of the Führer as a madman—that must have been "one of the many other people with the name Bosch, or an individual with a similar or different name" (1933). Things were not without their difficulties! These difficulties went beyond the grotesque in 1936 when the firm celebrated the fiftieth anniversary of its founding with an impressive ceremony. The ministers of Württemberg stayed away, and the party offices returned their invitations demonstratively the day before, because the commemorative book only mentioned Bosch, not Hitler!

Of course there could not fail to be an attempt to persuade Bosch to join the NSDAP. It was delivered by the provincial hunting master, and it went awry. Bosch's financial contribution would not have been unwelcome; in the party's central office they were not shy about applying the tried-and-true assessment method even to Bosch. He found this unpleasant; he had contributed millions for the common good, and he knew that the true sense of sacrifice was not dependent on any political constellation, but he was offended that they should think it within their power to tax him some definite amount. The correspondence reveals that he contributed 100,000 marks for the Haus der Kunst in Munich, and 50,000 marks for the Haus der Technik in Berlin—both only reluctantly, because he was extremely unhappy with Fritz Todt's methods. But at least these were tangible projects. When Kurt von Schröder, who was one of the most eager fund-raisers for Hitler's special projects, came to him with his wishes for a disproportionately high assessment, Bosch turned a cold shoulder. In view of the special requirements that had been imposed on him in the way of emergency factory sites and other burdens, he found it "let us say incomprehensible that Schröder should make demands on us"—this from a note to Walz dated April 24, 1936. The construction of a hospital and the preservation of the Bosch family seat were tasks that were awaiting him; in the meantime he was expected to entrust his money to a stranger. "But I cannot see my way clear to doing that, for my responsibilities, which are both moral and essential to my life, simply must take precedence over those of the Führer, which I do not even know; and at the same time the continuing existence of the firm is also of the greatest importance for Germany."

The development of foreign policy in the first years after 1933, if one can even speak of such a thing, was in a state of uneasy suspension. Mussolini attempted to counter the psychological uncertainties that had led to the power shift in Germany by proposing a basic agreement of the western states with Italy and Germany. The so-called "Four-Power Pact" of July 15, 1933, which Germany also joined, could serve this purpose quite well. It also had the ancillary purpose of elevating the prestige of the Italian head of state. Up to that point, Italy's policies had not been very accommodating toward Germany, but Mussolini could count on the fact that his domestic policies enjoyed the unmistakable support of the new policy makers in Germany, and that this would facilitate his efforts. The closer ties sought by both sides had long since been proposed by Hitler in his writings in the form of the thesis that an alliance between Britain, Germany, and Italy should begin by weakening France so that Germany could have its back free for the task of gaining new territory in the east. (This thesis was made less acute, momentarily, by the Ten-Year

Pact with Poland that was signed in January 1934.) Mussolini, for his part, had to want to see the German position strengthened, since the launching of his imperial plans in Africa would undoubtedly lead to a crisis in relations with London and Paris. The meeting between Hitler and Mussolini in Venice, in June 1934, confirmed this development even if their opinions were quite far apart on the question of Austria. Meanwhile, the German chancellor was tireless in expressing his peaceful intentions where France was concerned; except for the Saar region (whose vote in case of a plebiscite was never in doubt), the Reich, he maintained, had no territorial claims toward the west.

With its resignation from the League of Nations, Germany had regained its freedom of action in a formal legal sense and was determined to interpret its "equal rights," which had been recognized in Geneva but were embedded in tricky paragraphs, at its own risk. March 15 saw the announcement that the Reich would now create a military air force along with its civilian air fleet; a few days later, on March 16, 1935, came the announcement of the reintroduction of universal compulsory military service. At first this essentially looked like a willingness to prepare for territorial disputes in Europe. The visits of the British ministers John Simon and Anthony Eden, which occurred shortly thereafter, were intended as a way to reach clarity on this point; they succeeded only imperfectly. At any rate, Hitler believed that he could win Britain over to his new policy by proposing and concluding a pact with London—irrespective of his public statements on military sovereignty—that foresaw the reestablishment of a war flotilla, complete with firm agreements on the types and pace of construction of the German navy.

Germany's policy toward Geneva had had the effect of intensifying the French efforts to reach an accommodation with Russia. The Soviets joined the League of Nations in 1934, and the visits of Jean-Louis Barthou and Pierre Laval to Moscow were followed by a military-political agreement between Russia and France despite the lack of clarity over financial issues that had hung over the two nations since the prewar period. The German government responded, on March 7, 1936, by invading the "demilitarized" zone of the Rhineland, declaring the Locarno Pact null and void. The effect was unmistakable. Whether one recognized or questioned Germany's "right," whether one thought Hitler's arguments and offers during the negotiations carried any objective weight or were merely tactical ploys, the conditions under which Bosch had been carrying out his private foreign policy (if one may call it that), and the people-to-people understanding between France and Germany had suffered a heavy blow, if not become psychologically impossible. Huge military parades in Germany revived the spirit of soldiery; in France, anti-German feeling once again became a significant factor and was accompanied by sentiments that were sometimes fearful and sometimes aggressive. The resentment aroused, especially in the Anglo-Saxon countries, by the domestic political measures imposed by the German government were an additional factor. In the official world of Germany, people believed they could make light of these phenomena or could discount them as mere anti-party feelings.

At Bosch they definitely experienced what it meant for the country to rearm. The new air force and the equipment required by a modern, motorized army made the workshops in Stuttgart and Feuerbach, and the decentralized factories being created elsewhere in the Reich, indispensable. This time they were not caught unawares by the war production boom as they had been in 1914; they were very deeply involved in it. This was a source of great concern for Bosch, who feared the consequences of mutually accelerating weapons production. Was it possible to influence it in any way? As far as the political authorities were concerned, it must have seemed hopeless. Perhaps a conversation with the military experts might make sense. Albrecht Fischer, the knowledgeable former head of the Union of Metal Industrialists of Württemberg, who for some years had represented the interests of the Bosch firm in sociopolitical matters, had some contacts with the army high command. After some initial reflection, Bosch and Fischer paid a visit to the minister of the army, Lieutenant General Werner von Blomberg, on September 16, 1936. The purpose of the visit was to use economic and political arguments to gain an ally against the one-sidedness and rapidity of the arms race, and to remind him of the danger and likely course of a war considering the political tensions and the international situation that governed the supplies of raw materials. Bosch had the sense that he had simply been sent packing by von Blomberg. The general flatly refused to engage in any discussion of the actual issues; his task was to carry out the Führer's orders. Bosch returned from the visit with a bad taste in his mouth and was angry at himself for even having taken the step, to which he had been driven by his concern about what lay ahead.

It was naturally not merely the results of this unsatisfying conversation but rather the seriousness of the international tensions that caused the Bosch firm to lay the groundwork for radical changes in its sales and manufacturing organization outside Germany. The firm's leaders were not exactly counting on the outbreak of a new power struggle; they hoped that the memory of the barely healed wounds and an insight into the enormous risk a war entailed would have an inhibiting effect on the heads of state. But the world smelled of war. Since October 1935, the "border incidents" in northwest Africa had mushroomed into the Italian campaign against Ethiopia. Two months after Italy swallowed up the Kingdom of Ethiopia, the crisis situation in Spain, which was festering amid peasant unrest, separatist actions, and never-ending cabinet changes, turned into a civil war as a result of General Francisco Franco's actions, thus turning the country into an exercise ground for all the other powers. Now volunteer units were testing the technical and tactical features of the new weapons. Diplomatic policy and votes about sanctions or "noninterference," whether carried out in Geneva or in London, proved to be practically impotent when confronted with the dynamics of a will that was backed up by sheer power. Experiences of this kind, which could be regarded as opening skirmishes, had to make people skeptical about the seriousness and import of the verbal assurances of political goodwill and cultural responsibility with which these developments were naturally surrounded.

The year 1935 had seen yet another organizational expansion of Bosch's business. Italy's efforts at colonizing the wide reaches of North Africa had created a new market there. For this reason, since the political risks had at first seemed less serious there, Bosch reached an understanding with the leading Italian firm Fabbrica Italiana Magneti Marelli whereby the two firms would undertake joint distribution of their products in Italy and its colonies by using a newly created company, Mabo, which was headquartered in Milan. Bosch's withdrawal from the French and English partnerships had more far-reaching consequences, for there Bosch had been involved in production as well. A Dutch subsidiary of Mendelssohn & Company, in Amsterdam, the N. V. Administratiekantoor voor Internationale Belegging (Nakib), purchased Bosch's shares in the Lavalette firm in 1937. Several years earlier, they had begun to replace the name Bosch by the exclusive use of the name Lavalette in order to avoid exacerbating national sensitivities. At the same time, the Germans who were active in the firm's top management departed so that their presence would not be a hindrance to the firm's participation in the weapons boom, which was also gaining in importance for France. The Nakib also purchased several other smaller foreign subsidiaries from Bosch; the firm's experiences after the last war had been too bitter, and the scale of their involvement had grown enormously since then. The ownership share of C.A.V.-Bosch Limited, London-Acton, was sold directly to its English partner. The business report for 1937 made note of this transaction. It also affirmed that the exchange of experiences and patents with this firm and with the firm of Joseph Lucas Limited, Birmingham, continued to be guaranteed by multiyear agreements, and that the change would not act as a hindrance to continuing exports. In a gentlemen's agreement, the continuation and possible reintensification of the relationship, which had been both useful and gratifying on a personal level, was spelled out.

These restructurings, which were carried out by Hans Walz with Bosch's approval, should be understood essentially as outgrowths of the international situation, which was becoming less and less clear. The restructuring of the Robert Bosch Company from a joint stock company to a corporation with limited liability, which occurred on December 10, 1927, was basically formal in its significance. For even as a joint stock company, the business—particularly since the systematic repurchase of the shares that had been given to directors at the firm's founding—retained the distinct character of an individually and family-owned undertaking. This character was now affirmed and solidified. Robert Bosch, who had served as the chairman of the supervisory board, was installed as the sole business proprietor and authorized signatory for top management. This changed nothing as far as the daily operations were concerned. Bosch also took advantage of this opportunity to dissolve the Eisemann Works, which belonged to him; this operation, including its outlets, which had also gone by the name of Eisemann, were now merged completely into the parent company. A newly founded Eisemann

G.m.b.H. was supposed to continue to produce and distribute a few Eisemann specialties such as Forfex haircutters, hand lanterns, and marine lighting. The existing management of the Bosch AG remained in place. Walz, the manager, and Wild and Fellmeth were joined by Dr. Rassbach, who was promoted from assistant managing director to managing director. Durst, the director of technical operations, was appointed an assistant managing director, as were Gutmann and Rall.

A new employee, Dr. Karl Goerdeler, joined the firm. He had resigned from his position as mayor of Leipzig in the spring of 1937 since he no longer wanted to expose himself to interference and attacks by the National Socialist party. On two occasions, Goerdeler, who was flexible, intellectually quick, and worked with great intensity, had been entrusted by the administration of the Reich with the task of heading up a special commission for price review and control. The first appointment, which was made by Brüning in December 1931, lasted until December 1932. The Hitler regime also had recourse to Goerdeler from November 1934 until the summer of 1935. These assignments, under very different economic conditions, had sharpened Goerdeler's economic overview and had brought him into contact with innumerable offices and types of economic ventures. When the Friedrich Krupp AG wanted to name him to its board of directors, the party leadership objected and Krupp withdrew his offer. The connection between Goerdeler and Bosch was made by Theodor Bäuerle. At first, it was a loose association involving some consulting in financial matters and representation in dealings with government bureaus, something that was rather important in a period during which growing demands were being imposed on Bosch's production. The fact that the party looked askance on this was taken less seriously in Stuttgart than in Essen. Goerdeler, like Jäckh during the First World War and the postwar years, was a source of political information and was able to talk about the tendencies and power groupings in the top bureaucracy or in leading military circles. Quite early on he began to see the developments in Germany in very dark hues. Bosch responded to his judgments with friendly affection, if not without ambivalence, for the rational realism that he shared with Goerdeler on issues of foreign affairs and the financial situation, with their gloomy consequences, contrasted with the naive hope that made him conclude: That must not, it simply cannot be.

42

———◆———

CULMINATION AND
CONCLUSION

If someone had asked Bosch, he might have admitted that he lacked a sense of formality, but he would not have meant this in the sense in which the novelist Theodor Fontane would have used the expression, with ironic superiority. Bosch felt constrained by anything that was self-consciously formal, indeed even by the claims of anything that had been established by convention. He did not feel that it suited him. Naturally, he had had to learn to make certain compromises. Over the years he had had occasional meetings with advisers, ministers, and excellencies of all kinds, and he no longer avoided them; his curiosity and need for social intercourse led him to take pleasure in these encounters. Late in life he entered into a carefully tended relationship with Württemberg's longtime representative to the Bundesrat, the skeptical and cosmopolitan Baron Axel von Varnbüler. This was not a stiff or dignified relationship; it extended as far as questions of personal hygiene.

But then formality caught up with Bosch after all. His seventieth birthday seems to have been the first occasion for this, although his colleagues actually managed to make the ceremony rather simple. Since the recessionary situation in which they found themselves in 1931 forbade any extensive special arrangements, the day had a rather intimate character. The president of the Reich awarded Bosch the Eagle Shield. Bosch went along with this; at least it was not something that could be pinned on one's chest!

The firm was already looking ahead to 1936, and although there had repeatedly been serious uncertainties about Bosch's health, they could confidently prepare for a real celebration. It would be a twofold celebration, for only a few weeks separated September 23, Bosch's seventy-fifth birthday, from November 11, the day fifty years earlier on which Bosch had opened the Workshop for Precision and Electrical Engineering in the now legendary rear building at Rotebühlstrasse 75B. The celebration, which had been prepared carefully and with style, came off brilliantly. A week before the event, on September 17, 1936, Bosch had written a bit skeptically to his friend Fritz Egnell in Stockholm, "I believe the event will not be exactly pleasant for me. I am curious as to how I will survive it." Then, as he wrote to Paul Reusch on October 17, he had "gotten through the strenuous event pretty well . . . and it was lovely and uplifting."

Among the honors bestowed on him that day, he may have been especially happy about the fact that the Institute of British Automobile Engineers had elected him as an honorary member, and that the French war veterans' organizations had sent a special delegation. Thousands of people had gathered in the great municipal hall. Hans Walz, the manager of the firm, gave an impressive summary of the essential elements of the factory's rise, mentioning how much it owed to the character of its founder. Economics Minister Hjalmar Schacht spoke some intelligent words about Bosch's unique role in German industry and finance. When the long series of official congratulations had finally come to an end, Bosch himself spoke only a few sentences. He had to say that what had been said was "quite exaggerated." He asked for a moment of silence in honor of those whose deaths had preceded them, and whose achievements had helped the factory to be successful. He had begun with apparently unaffected freshness, holding down his excitement, but when he saw the masses of people silent before him, his voice filled with emotion.

The celebration provided the occasion for the founding of the great hospital for the benefit of medical research and suffering humanity; in the years ahead Bosch would be much occupied with its completion. The history of technology was enriched by a comprehensive, richly illustrated and dignified edition of the history of the factory, *Fifty Years of Bosch 1886–1936*. Experts from the various areas of production had contributed to the collection of the data; the director of the new museum and archives department, Dr. Fritz Schildberger, organized the diverse materials and gave them coherent form, primarily concentrating on the various phases of technological expansion and refinement. Bosch seems to have been pleased with this monumental gift, but his criticism was characteristic. In a letter to the writer Walter Ostwald dated November 21, 1940, he remarked that "various things were not expressed that I would have liked to see . . . firstly with regard to the effects a great firm has on its surroundings, near and far. My efforts in sociopolitical matters are not mentioned at all, either."

The last comment is not actually correct in its acerbic "not . . . at all," but what was said seemed to take up too little space when looked at with the eyes of the seventy-five-year-old Bosch as he considered this summary of his life's accomplishments. Bosch's colleagues had played decisive and occasionally dominant roles in the technical issues of design and production; like Bosch, other companies also had scientific research; but when he himself looked back on his life and accomplishments and attempted to identify what it was that distinguished him, he saw his unique sociopolitical role.

Only a few weeks after the celebration, Bosch resigned from the leadership of the National Union of Automobile Industrialists. It had been some time since they had seen much of him there. "More and more, I withdraw from public life, and have no need to be active in this direction," he wrote to the president of the organization, Allmers, on October 17, 1936. He remained on the board as an honorary director, but in a conversation with Ernst Sachs, who came from Schweinfurt in Upper Swabia, he once remarked that he would be missed less at the meeting of the National Union than at his grade school reunion, which he then promptly attended. In the committees of the National Union there had been many battles between the builders of engines and cars and the people working in parts and accessories. Bosch had not always felt comfortable there, since he had never held back with his criticism of the complexity and high price of the automobile in its early days. Sachs himself had been Bosch's spirited partner in this effort. Originally a locksmith's apprentice, he had become a creative industrialist via a career as a racing driver, and his factory in Schweinfurt had given the decisive impetus to the German ball-bearings industry. He was a good-humored and active man with a great, unspoiled practical intelligence, and he and Bosch were always boon companions. Sachs died in 1932. The time had come for Bosch to say good-bye to many a trusted friend. In 1934, Otto Mezger died in Stuttgart; after 1933 he had been forced to suffer attacks and persecution, a circumstance that had also deeply hurt Bosch. For many years Mezger had continued to be Bosch's favorite companion for the observation of nature or for the hunting he so enjoyed. Georg Escherich seems to have taken Mezger's place in some ways; Bosch also lost this friend, who was deeply mourned, in the summer of 1941. Julius Faber, who had been involved with the firm for almost a quarter of a century and was a member of the supervisory board, had died in April 1940; the personal intimacy between Bosch and this rough good-humored man had lessened, but Bosch had continued to respect the expectations and habits of their old comradeship. The death of his nephew Carl Bosch in 1940 also touched him deeply, particularly since their relationship had become closer due to the visits they had exchanged in the past few years. Without making much ado about it, Bosch was secretly proud of the fact that his brother's son stood at the helm of the largest chemical factory in the world. The Boschs never engaged in a cult of family, and questions of chemistry were far removed from Robert Bosch's interest, but he admired the fact that his nephew was an entomologist of some repute and also practiced astronomy. He only regretted that Carl had not come along on his hunts.

As his age and infirmities increased, Bosch made a wise pact; he adjusted to them, dealt rather well with embarrassing and painful illnesses, and planned to live on into his advanced years while he gradually accustomed himself to the inevitability of death according to the order of all things. His worries about the factory now played a relatively minor role. He knew it was in the hands of men who enjoyed his full and complete trust. But it was his hope that he would experience his son's growth to adulthood and that he would be able to personally guide his first steps into professional life. His daughter Paula's marriage to Friedrich Zundel, in 1927, had resulted in the birth of a male heir, Georg. Bosch's thoughts about the future, which had been overshadowed in his adult years by the many depressing months he had spent standing by his son's sickbed, could now look ahead with joyful and observant confidence. How would the boy's individuality develop? The worldwide scope of his planning had found its way back home to his small circle.

But the outside world was seething with turbulence, even after the Spanish Civil War had come to its military conclusion. Could it not serve as a tempting or warning example that the hand that dares to wield weapons, that sets tanks in motion and orders airplanes to take off, is more powerful historically than the hand that shapes legal and political formulas or turns the pages of the weighty volumes of international law and commentaries on the treaties between countries? In early March 1938, Hitler ordered the German divisions to march into Austria. The internal situation of that country had assumed an absurd level of susceptibility to crisis as a consequence of the innate problems of the state and of subversion by Germans loyal to the Reich. The appearance of the troops, which was greeted with an enthusiasm that was partly genuine and partly artificially incited, seemed in a few days or even hours to have blotted out the efforts of many years of diplomacy, conferences, organizational work, and publications simply by presenting the real facts of power.

Bosch was appalled when he heard the news. His relationship to the *Anschluss* was complicated. From his anti-Bismarckian and democratic upbringing, for which the notion of an encompassing German nation (*Grossdeutschland*) was an article of faith, he was familiar with the emotional view that saw Austria as a central territory of the German national character, and therefore part of the territory of the German state. But at the same time he saw things realistically. One cannot say that as a businessman or hunter he had come away with any particular affection for the Austrian authorities; he spoke of them with humorous displeasure. But naturally this was not decisive. As far as his conception of foreign affairs was concerned, he saw the efforts to bring about the *Anschluss* as a strain on relations with Paris, both psychologically and in real terms. His firm conviction was that a thoroughgoing political and economic understanding with France would ultimately lead to the satisfying resolution of a close relationship with Austria.

The fact that the great powers appeared to be acquiescing to Hitler's action drove his worries away, and Bosch felt a certain admiration for the boldness of German policy. When Hitler visited Stuttgart in April 1938, and even Bosch was invited to the reception, Bosch hesitated in his decision as to whether he would congratulate Hitler for his success. He did not do so, and he evidently did not regret it later, for with the completion of the *Anschluss* the dynamic of a new German policy toward the southeast had been unleashed. Whether this policy was seen in terms of Germany's concerns about securing its national character, or of geopolitics, it had to raise questions about the national structure of Czechoslovakia in the form in which it existed at the time. The entire problem of the Versailles system, in which the "right of self-determination of peoples" was proclaimed but was then displaced by past practice in border questions, was reopened. In the previous war, Bosch had been an adherent of Naumann's *Mitteleuropa* hypothesis, according to which a unified, strong, and durable economic region could emerge if based on voluntary but firm treaties that would secure the governmental and national structures. Within such a region, the historical tensions and national contradictions might be reduced or perhaps even dissolved. It quite soon became obvious that Hitler was prepared to use quite different methods—a return to the use of military force. Late summer 1938 brought the struggle for peace, with the efforts of British Prime Minister Neville Chamberlain to forge a new agreement that would set aside the errors of Versailles, even if it meant bypassing the apparatus that had been developed in Geneva. Britain called on the authority of the former prime minister Lord Walter Runciman; the expert opinion he called for recommended that those border territories of Bohemia that had been settled by Germany be surrendered to the Reich.

For several weeks the European catastrophe seemed unavoidable; its imminence was the subject of the Munich meeting of the heads of state of Germany, Britain, France, and Italy. When reasonable men accept responsibility, it seems that things can be settled without weapons! A strange optimism befell the world, as *all* the participants saw themselves celebrated as friends and saviors of peace. Without firing a shot, Germany had gained new territory for its settlements; Czechoslovakia's system of border defenses had been surrendered without struggle because of the Englishman's expert opinion.

The Bosch Spark Plug of October 1, 1938, published a document that was typical of these crucial weeks. On September 28, forty employees of Joseph Lucas Limited in Birmingham had written a moving letter "to all our friends in the Bosch organization," in which they wished "passionately and with all our heart" that the black clouds would disappear, and that people at Bosch would help to assure that "an atmosphere is created among us that is above all suspicion and doubt . . . In any case, we would like to assure you that our personal friendship for you will always remain and that we will never forget the many acts of friendship that you have shown us." When this letter arrived in Stuttgart, the Munich Treaty had already been concluded; Chamberlain had even brought home a gentlemen's agreement between Hitler and himself that the two governments would consult before undertaking any further political actions. The warmhearted answer, signed by fifty-four of the "people from Bosch-Co." (members of the group of engineers and workers who had participated in the exchange of people and patents that had continued over the years), expressed their gratification that peace had been preserved—something they had never ceased to believe in "even in the most urgent hours of the crisis."

When Hitler, shortly thereafter, gave his threatening and disgruntled speech in Saarbrücken, with an undertone of disappointment about Munich, this kind of faith was severely tested. After March 1939, any notion of international understanding was reduced to a mere phantom of the imagination, a complete fantasy of wish fulfillment. After the invasion of Prague by German troops had taken the world by surprise, it was impossible to think seriously about a peaceful solution to the existing problems. It is naturally difficult to say to what extent a peaceful solution might have been possible, in the atmosphere that had been created in Munich, and whether if that atmosphere had not first been destroyed by speeches, a German-British and then a German-French conversation might have taken place about the 1919 resolution of the Danzig problem or the Polish Corridor. At the time, Warsaw's policies were not held in high regard in either London or Paris, and objectively, Germany held many trump cards in its hand. But the attack on Czechoslovakia's central territory, its timing and its effect as blackmail, seemed in London to be a mockery of Britain's prime minister and the agreement he had reached with such happiness and had taken so seriously. Britain's policy, which had been flexible until this point, became rigid. Hitler, poorly advised by Foreign Minister Joachim von Ribbentrop, with his fateful combination of ambitious Philistinism and ignorant incompetence, was deceived by his past successes. Even the amazing tactical move of the Nazi-Russian Nonaggression Pact in August 1939 could not alter the fundamental forces that were moving toward war. Only stupidity or propagandistic self-delusion could possibly believe in the containment of a German-Polish conflict. The world had also not failed to notice that Hitler's number one military adviser, Lieutenant General Ludwig Beck, considered the most capable thinker in the German army, had resigned from the leadership of the general staff *before* the invasion of Prague because he saw in it the germ of a new world war that would end in inconceivable catastrophe for the German fatherland.

The large-scale concentrated attack on Poland set the war in motion. It was obvious that it would assume a worldwide character unless political restraint and wisdom imposed their limits on actions that were purely military and strategic in nature. The technology of war would make it into a confrontation that would involve *everyone*. Bosch, with profound resignation, sensed this too. Some years earlier, he had read Eugen Diesel's intelligent essay "On the Fate of the Peoples"; its orderly overview had made a strong impression on him. "If I were to find anything lacking," he remarked on July 27, 1934, in a cordially appreciative letter to his friend, "it would perhaps be reference to the fact that *in earlier times* it was never peoples who went to war, with the exception of the Crusades. Dynasties went to war, after dynasties existed. This could be more strongly emphasized." This type of historical interpretation, already oversimplified, was now completely out of date. Ideological motives were now being injected into the struggle for power to an even greater extent than a quarter of a century before, but it was not clear to what degree they represented a living expression of elementary forces or were merely propaganda aimed at numbing others or oneself.

It is not possible to find evidence for Bosch's personal position or his judgment about the various phases of the war in his documents or letters. Like his friends, he had learned to be silent. When Paul Reusch, in a long letter dated August 26, 1940, wrote: "Of the war I will say nothing," the short sentence speaks volumes. People buried their fears and hopes inside themselves. Occasionally the greetings would contain a wish for an early peace; this deeply felt although utterly insubstantial formula could be found in millions of German and non-German letters. "Finally, the terrible battle, bringing breakthrough and destruction, has been fought . . . It is terrible," wrote Bosch on August 6, 1941, to his daughter Margarete as the first summer campaign against Russia was nearing its high point. His mood showed through in intimate conversations. "I am happy that the war is here," he said in the fall of 1939 to Johannes Hieber. "This is the only way we will get rid of the criminals." After a later visit from Bosch, Gottfried Traub made note of his guest's angry hope that a soldier would be found who would get rid of Hitler, for with him there would never be peace.

Among the people close to Bosch, there was no unified assessment of the war situation. Even in his circle, the brilliant course of the first campaigns, carefully worked out and carried through with united forces, created excited expectations; people were not fully clear about the aims and long-term consequences but believed in the German fighting man and the vision of Germany's economic and technical plans. Among the foreign sales representatives there were some who wrote back about the decadence of English society and its lack of patriotism, which contrasted strangely with the recognized quality of the official British representatives—Bosch remarked on this once in a letter. During these years, he himself read quite a bit of English political literature, including the openhearted self-criticism of the British, from which Germany's official war propaganda, not fully cognizant of the self-critical nature of such writing, drew its principal nourishment. Conversations with Bosch quite often turned on this very question: Is there still sufficient vitality in the English people for them to be able to stand up to America? "If only the English would convince themselves that they are only being forced out of their world empire by America" (to his daughter Margarete, August 6, 1941).

This was written before Hitler had declared war on the United States, an act that—even more than Germany's previous delivery of war supplies to England—had mobilized the huge military potential of America's army against Germany at the same time as it silenced the internal political opposition to Roosevelt. Now one thing was completely clear: Whatever course relations between the two Anglo-Saxon world powers might take, however their joint or separate relationships to the Soviet Union (which had been attacked by the German armies in June 1941) might evolve, as a military operation the war would initially follow the rhythm that had been forced upon it by the policies of Germany, no matter how many speeches and essays railed about the union of plutocracy and Bolshevism.

The full power of America's rich supplies of material and manpower was naturally appreciated by Bosch. At Bosch, they were much too familiar with the capabilities of industry for mass production in that country, and they knew that the Americans knew how to produce much more than mere "bluff," as the German people were asked to believe by an official pronouncement. Here, above all, they had an opponent who was practically invulnerable, and one could count the days until its air force would be sent in to attack German industry and the German hinterland. This gave Bosch and his colleagues plenty of cause to be concerned about the fate of the factory facilities in Stuttgart and Feuerbach; with the motorization of the armies and the recent creation of tank divisions and air fleets, the factory had become a central component of the nation's armaments, as important as it was vulnerable. When their thoughts turned to the last war, there was a humorous anecdote that Bosch occasionally liked to tell, amid all the more serious concerns, when things were slow. At one time, several bombing attacks had been aimed at Bosch. They did not hit their target but did some damage to a bakery that had opened nearby. The hard-working baker filed several depositions to the effect that Bosch was at fault for the damage that had been inflicted on him, and demanded compensation. Whereupon Bosch sent him the rather witty but impolite rejoinder that the baker would have to assume the damages, since he had chosen to locate in such a dangerous neighborhood, in order to increase his sales. Such thoughts, as they considered the dangers that lay in store for them now, must have seemed like excerpts from a rather bizarre and harmless petit bourgeois idyll. Bosch's dark imagination foresaw terror and destruction. He prepared to defend himself to the degree that this would be possible, but he could not quite believe that this would be effective. His worries about Germany, about his homeland in the narrower sense—the city, the factory—tortured him. Some people were able to brush these worries aside; they might try to shield Bosch by urging him to spend some time in the mountains, in Pfronten or Mooseurach. But the worries always returned.

In the workshops, the National Socialists were applying force. The struggle for workers had to be fought. "We are and remain fanatical adherents of freedom of movement," the chief of personnel assured them at an assembly (*The Bosch Spark Plug*, no. 1, 1941), but they were forced to stop the practice of releasing trained workers, something that had never been discussed in the past. In his factory regulations of 1934, Bosch had expressly failed to include any fines to be levied against workers or staff members. This had been possible because of the reliable attitude of the old core group of employees. Now they could no longer manage without a weapon of this kind, and they decided, very reluctantly, to introduce fines. This did not fit in with the factory's tradition; when would they be able to be free of such things? The adjustments were much more severe than during the previous war, when Bosch had succeeded in defending the eight-hour day against the claims of the military administration. All that was now a thing of the past. Totalitarian regulation and its demands forced their way into this factory with its unique historical character, and the Bosch firm had to be satisfied to await the day when it would once more be free of such compulsions and could return to its old mission in its technical, business, and sociopolitical plans and decisions. The experiences that had been gained during the war would not be entirely in vain, but as long as the war continued, the people in the laboratories and testing stations were thinking about their peacetime goals. Their financial policy was also aimed in this direction, and from the first they set aside the greatest possible reserves, precisely because of the war.

On September 23, 1941, Robert Bosch celebrated his eightieth birthday. He did not want to go to the trouble of attending the great factory celebration again; it went on without him while he gathered his family, colleagues, and close friends around himself in Baden-Baden. German officialdom tried to make up for the displeasure it had expressed five years earlier; the head of the National Labor Front, Robert Ley, appeared with the certificate that named Bosch a "Pioneer of Labor." At the same time, he also became an "Honorary Master of German Craft." Tübingen awarded him an honorary doctorate in medicine, and the City of Stuttgart gave him a piece of property for the planned Paracelsus Museum, in which historical documents relating to the science of biological healing were to be collected. This pleased him very much, for it meant that the problems related to the history of medicine that had occupied him so intensely in the last few years would be certain to receive lasting attention in his home city. This time, the National Socialist administration of Württemberg had not refrained from sending its personal congratulations. It was a rather peculiar atmosphere, for in the celebratory gathering with its two different vocabularies one could find speakers for the party along with such robust opponents as Reusch, Goerdeler, and now Schacht.

Among the gifts presented to the eighty-year-old was a portfolio with portraits of great, or at any rate important, men who had come from the province of Württemberg. This was a gift from Hermann Bücher. Conrad Matschoss, who had written the technological history, advised Bücher on the selection of subjects, and Eugen Diesel wrote a thoughtful introductory essay about the elemental aspects of personal appearance, individuality and types of individuals, and the possibility of identifying a "Swabian physiognomy" as a distinct phenomenon. The idea for this collection was fortuitous indeed, for it touched Bosch's pride in his place of origin, which had to be especially vivid on these anniversary occasions with their reference to the relationship of his life's accomplishments to his surroundings and the people of the region. In thanking Bücher, Bosch remarked on how regrettable it would be if this work, and Diesel's essay in particular, were not to find a larger audience; if it were to do so, however, a few things would have to be changed. Bosch had spoken with Reusch, and the two Swabians had agreed that the selection made by Bücher and Matschoss would have to be expanded, "that there were more men who belonged in the book, and others they could just as well do without." This was followed by a couple of characteristic sentences.

"First of all, this would include Mauser, who has not accomplished anything and is completely lacking in greatness. Daimler was such a small man too"—here the old grudge flared up—"but no one can question his accomplishments, and so he can stay in. But one might think of including Schubart, the poet, or of David Strauss and others . . ." It was no accident that Bosch remarked on the absence of these two militant individuals. He wanted to talk further with Reusch and Bäuerle; the collection could become an attractive and informative tribute to his fatherland, an unexpected consequence of a wonderful day.

Pride and emotion can be heard in the missive that proclaimed his thanks to the firm's employees on October 27, 1941: "My dear comrades, old and young . . ." Once more, he could feel the awareness "that a profound community of consciousness and deed has united us in this well-rounded factory family . . . Take care of the spirit of devotion to this great mutual task during my lifetime and after, for the continuing benefit of all the members of the firm and for the benefit of the firm itself, which is dear to me, since it is my life's work!"

This became a parting greeting, although no one suspected it, least of all Bosch himself. Every so often he would joke that he would live to be a hundred. A few weeks before his eightieth birthday, he noted in a letter to his daughter, written on August 6, 1941, "My suffering is a considerable burden now, and it takes a good deal of humor to walk in spite of it." The letter was sent from the mountains, where in the weeks leading up to the party he managed to have sufficient "humor" for an avid and successful hunt; once more this offered him refreshment and distraction from the worries that leapt from the pages of the newspapers. Dying could hold little terror for a man of Bosch's convictions; it was a part of the growth and becoming of all living beings. Yet he clung to life, for it still seemed to have more responsibilities in store for him. Once this frightful war had come to an end, he wanted to remain at his post, giving advice, making decisions, and guiding the steps of his young son as he took over the heavy responsibilities.

A painful inflammation of the ear in November 1941 may have been a warning sign about a danger that had gone unsuspected. It went away, treated with the usual remedies, and apparently left no traces. But this was an illusion. On March 9, 1942, as Bosch was working on his correspondence in his workroom as usual, he began to feel unwell. He completed his day's work, disposing of a number of important matters in progress, then suddenly felt a terrible pain that was difficult to assuage. Surgical intervention seemed unavoidable. They found an infection of the middle ear that was already very far advanced, rendering the surgeon's skills powerless. It was possible to relieve the suffering but not to delay death's progress. During the early morning hours of March 12, 1942, Robert Bosch passed away.

The funeral was held on March 18. On the afternoon before, the factory employees had taken their leave of him in one of the factory halls, which had been specially prepared for the occasion. The government of the Reich had ordered a state funeral; Minister of the Economy Funk spoke on its behalf in the hall of the Württemberg Museum of Industry. At the cremation, which was held at the Prague Cemetery, Hans Walz, who in speaking to the employees had focused on the man of the factory, and at the official funeral had spoken about the lasting significance of the deceased, gave an appreciation of Bosch's human strengths that was gripping in its intimacy and candor. He spoke of his sense of the lawfulness and the enhancement of life, of his original drive for freedom as an element that was essential to the growth of all creativity. Hermann Bücher spoke the words of parting on behalf of Bosch's closest friends. Across the valley, as it lay in the pale March sun, came the sound of bells ringing in the garrison church located next to the factory; it was a grateful greeting to the man who had contributed these bells to the church.

In a letter to Fritz Egnell almost a decade and a half earlier, Bosch had once written the sentence, "The dead are fortunate." Fate brought him peace before the storms of destruction sought out his factory and destroyed his fatherland. This was an act of mercy.

POSTSCRIPT

It was completely in character for Robert Bosch to leave detailed instructions for the event of his demise. These were repeatedly altered, expanded, and reworked as circumstances dictated. The final version dated from May 31, 1938, and invoked the "descendants according to the rules of the law of inheritance." This is not deserving of further mention, nor are the individual dispositions of the will important.

Its central concern was for the Robert Bosch G.m.b.H., in order "not only to keep it alive over a long period, but to secure for it a powerful and rich development that will help it surmount the inevitable difficulties and crises of the future. No sacrifice should be avoided that could help to achieve this." A task of this magnitude should be assumed either by a capable heir, or by individuals whom he trusted, in case a suitable heir was not available.

A very characteristic feature was the detailed way in which, in repeated and varied formulations, Bosch stressed the duty of his seven executors (five of whom were drawn from the board of managers and supervisory board of the Robert Bosch G.m.b.H.) "as far as possible to effectively continue, through their actions, to carry on my spirit and will in the administration of the assets that are present at my death and that will be created in the future." In guidelines dated September 8, 1938, he had mentioned this "spirit and will," but had also remarked that it was not important "to hold to the letter of these guidelines." Even beyond the individuals whom he had appointed, he wanted to see personalities who, in addition to having their own opinions in business matters, would "play a creative role in helping to solve difficult questions." He always wanted to have a "body of people who will work together with as little friction as possible," people who act "according to purely objective observation, with justice and fairness."

His wish, in other words, was that it should be possible for a member of his family to rise to leadership. The executors of his will should help to assure that if several applicants should appear (son, possible stepson), the most qualified individual should be elected to leadership; if they were equally well suited, the bearer of the name Bosch, following the order of succession, should be given preference. A special provision opened the path to leadership to children from second marriages and grandchildren; this provision was to be implemented no more than thirty years after his death. "It is important to me that a family director should receive special preference, in comparison to the other descendants, because in his awareness of the heavy responsibility that weighs on him he must dedicate all his strength unreservedly to the service of the Robert Bosch G.m.b.H., and not only work toward the achievement of the goals that have been set, but also devote himself to it with professional energy, without sparing himself, whereas this is not the case with other descendants." These were very characteristic statements. Somewhat later his fear of the dangerous effect of inherited wealth was expressed: "Absolutely no drones should be raised . . ." The conclusion of the will stated: "It is a matter of honor for the heirs, if they receive shares in the Robert Bosch G.m.b.H., to exercise their rights to them in accordance with my spirit and will and to remain at one with each other for the benefit of the whole."

Occasionally the guidelines referred back to earlier essays, whose purpose was to remind the heirs of the traditions of social policy, cultural policy, and health policy that had been connected with his activities.

In his observations of May 31, 1938, Bosch had mentioned "the inevitable difficulties and crises of the future." He could have no idea of their extent. The present description of his life, which was completed during the weeks of military and political collapse, could not aim to fill in the history of the factory itself in the years following Bosch's death. When I completed the book, I wrote that his departure at this point in time was a blessing. He was spared personal and professional events filled with tragedy.

Among his circle of acquaintances, in the summer of 1942 Theodor Bäuerle was arrested and held by the Gestapo for several weeks; the Bosch firm had long been viewed with suspicion. Governor Wilhelm Murr had said threateningly that he would "no longer tolerate the parallel government of Bosch." Bäuerle had protected someone who was being persecuted and had been mistreated. The accents became even harsher after the assassination attempt against Hitler on July 20, 1944. With Walz's permission, Karl Goerdeler had taken advantage of the many trips he had made over the years on company business to widen his anti-Hitler activities; more than one important meeting was held in the administration building in Militärstrasse 4. Bosch and his closest colleagues were informed about this. The terrible failure of the action of July 20 put the firm in the greatest danger. Numerous hearings and arrests were carried out. Proceedings were held before the People's Court; they led to penitentiary sentences and concentration camps. The degree to which Bosch himself felt attached to Goerdeler, with a trust that was both personal and professional, is evidenced by the fact that he had put him on the list of alternates for the first group of executors of his will.

And the factory? The heavy air attacks of the year 1944 were also directed at the facilities of the Robert Bosch firm. At the end of February 1944, the factory was badly hit; in the nights of terror of July 24–26, the administration building and the core of the old facilities were destroyed by bombs. The last concentrated attack was on September 12–13. Only the recent addition on the corner of the Seidenstrasse and Rosenbergstrasse, which had received a few hits earlier, remained relatively stable; it became the new home of the administration.

The last months of the war brought with them an extremely difficult emotional burden for the leading men of the company. Their disappointment over the failure of the assassination attempt was combined with their worries about new actions of the Gestapo against individuals. The destruction of factory facilities not only made it difficult to take care of technical and business matters, but also cast its shadow on the perspectives that might make it possible to find a way out in the years that lay just ahead. The uncertainties and the pressure of responsibilities were utterly unbearable. The fate that was bearing inexorably down on them was one they had seen coming for a long time; they had not had any illusions about its seriousness. When the foreign troops marched in, at least a clear situation was created. They could breathe again, but they also knew that they would not breathe easy from now on.

Others will have to describe what the end of the war brought, and the occupation, first French, then American. The writer will find many things, in the atmosphere of sociopolitical struggle, that could be compared to the situation after 1918—the individual tragic fates and the inconceivable difficulties that were encountered in salvaging the technical and economic heritage of Robert Bosch for a changed future. The misunderstandings, the hopes and disappointments, the endless back and forth among many and changing conversation partners are impossible to describe, much less comprehend, from the vantage point of today. This biographer would have to conclude this postscript in complete resignation if he did not believe that spiritual and moral achievements hold within themselves a value that can never be lost, and that the people of Swabia, in their indestructible substance, will be the first to find their way again.

Perhaps the description of the life and achievements of Robert Bosch is a contribution to communicating this kind of faith to others; in this case it would not only be a piece of history but could also provide something resembling living strength.

Theodor Heuss
Stuttgart, June 1946

INDEX